Beginning
C++
The Complete Language

Ivor Horton

Wrox Press Ltd.

Beginning C++: The Complete Language

© 1998 Wrox Press

First Published   April 1998

Published by Wrox Press Ltd, 30 Lincoln Road, Olton, Birmingham B27 6PA , UK.
Printed in Canada
1 2 3 4 5 TRI 99 98

ISBN 1-861000-12-X

Trademark Acknowledgements

Wrox has endeavoured to provide trademark information about all the companies and products mentioned in this book by the appropriate use of capitals. However, Wrox cannot guarantee the accuracy of this information.

Credits

Author
Ivor Horton

Contributing Author
Allan Stokes

Managing Editor
John Franklin

Editors
Ian Nutt
Jon Hill
Victoria Hudgson
Alex Stockton
Timothy Briggs

Technical Reviewers
Robert Goodwin
Kevlin Henney
Mungo Henning
Giovanni Lamonica
Claus Loud
David Marleau
Julian Templeman

Cover/Design/Layout
Andrew Guillaume

Copy Edit
Wrox Team

Index
Simon Gilks
Nancy Humphreys
Seth Maislin

About the Author

Ivor Horton, the best-selling author of *Beginning Visual C++ 5, Beginning C* & *Beginning Java* has brought computer programming to a wide and varied audience. Ivor is a firm believer that programming is often easier than it looks for novices and he enjoys trying to make the subject more approachable for beginners. Ivor spent many years working for IBM, both programming and training others to program.

Foreword

My approach to teaching programming in C++ has three basic threads.

The first is to demystify the language by getting past the jargon — jargon is convenient shorthand for the professional, but it can effectively lock out the beginner. The second is to explain what the elements of the language are for, as much as how they work. The third is to demonstrate them in working examples, which explain why the elements of a programming language work the way they do. I believe you remember better what you understand fully, so, to learn a language like C++, you need plenty of hands-on experience and an appreciation of what's happening when things go right — and when they go wrong.

Learning C++ is hard work — not because it's particularly difficult — but simply because there's so much of it. To succeed, you need to maintain a steady pace that suits your lifestyle and the time you have available. You also need continuity. You can't leave it for a month and expect to pick up right where you left off. Don't overreach yourself — you won't get through it all in a week or two. Just digesting and understanding close to a thousand pages is going to take longer than that. Make sure that you not only understand the contents of a chapter, but you actually apply it for real with fully working examples of your own.

Don't be afraid to experiment. You will learn as much if not more by your mistakes as you learn from doing it right. If you don't know how to do something, don't look it up right away — see if you can figure it out. And above all, have fun. Programming is interesting, entertaining, definitely frustrating, but, above all, it should be enjoyable.

Ivor Horton

Beginning
C++
The Complete Language

Table Of Contents

Beginning

C++
The Complete Language

Introduction

Welcome to *Beginning C++: The Complete Language*. This is a tutorial guide to standard C++. During the course of the book we'll cover all the fundamentals of syntax, grammar, object-oriented capability and the standard library. You'll soon gain enough programming know-how to write your own C++ applications.

Why C++?

C++ is arguably the most widely used programming language in existence, and its popularity is growing. It's used in professional application development because of its immense flexibility and power. It is also more accessible than many people give it credit. With the right guidance, getting to grips with C++ is easier than you might imagine. By developing your C++ skills, you will learn a language already spoken by millions, and you will acquire a powerful new tool in your programming toolbox.

Why the ANSI/ISO Standard?

Since 1989, C++ has been the subject of an ongoing standards process. This is the work of a joint ANSI/ISO group, whose motivation is to develop a worldwide standard for the C++ language. On November 14, 1997, the group announced the completion of its Final Draft International Standard (ISO/IEC FDIS 14882)*. This leaves a last (formal) vote by the steering committee, the dotting of 'i's, crossing of 't's, and the final inking of the document — all of which should be completed in 1998.

*For more details see the press release at **http://www.research.att.com/~bs/iso_release.html**.

For the current draft standard, check one of the following sites:
http://www.maths.warwick.ac.uk/cpp/pub/

For more information, refer to the **comp.std.c++** FAQ at:
http://reality.sgi.com/employees/austern_mti/std-c++/faq.html

The development of the standard has been a difficult process — the first vote on the draft in March 1995 resulted in some major changes to the language. Consequently, as well as representing the maturation of one of the most important and widely-used programming languages currently available, the Final Draft International Standard renders many books on C++ incomplete. This is one of the motivations for writing this book.

That's the theory, but how does this standard square up in practice? There are C++ compilers everywhere, for every conceivable platform, but do they fully support the standard? Some compilers are more compliant than others, and many use the 1995 draft, so expect to see a flurry of updates over the next year. In time-honoured fashion, YMMV — your mileage may vary.

Obviously, though, you want to be able to compile and experiment with the source code presented in the following chapters. In this book, therefore, we'll present the standard as it is, but wherever a feature of the standard is not widely implemented, we'll point that out. The code thereafter will follow the standard. Fortunately, this is relatively rare.

Conventions

We'll use a number of different styles of text and layout in the book to help differentiate between the various types of information. Here are examples of the styles I use along with explanations of what they mean:

> *These boxes hold important, not-to-be-forgotten information which is directly relevant to the surrounding text. For example, they are used to summarize major points of C++ programming style.*

Background information, asides on programming code and the like, are shown like this.

FYI   **For Your Information (FYI) boxes contain stuff which adds to the discussion.**

Bulleted information is shown like this:

- **Important Words** are in a bold font.
- Keys that you press on the keyboard, like *Ctrl* and *Enter*, are in italics.
- All file, function names and other code snippets are in this style: **Video.cpp**.

Code shown for the first time, or other relevant code, is in the following format:

```cpp
#include <iostream>

int main()
{
   return 0;
}
```

while less important code, or code that has been seen before, looks like this:

```
Box* pBox = pCarton;
```

The output from programs is shown as:

```
Your time is up...
```

Exercises

At the end of each chapter you'll find a selection of exercises, that are designed to test you further on the content of the chapter and of earlier chapters. Model solutions to all of the exercises are available on our web sites (see below). If you find a particularly neat solution, send it to us, and we may include it on the site!

Tell Us What You Think

We have tried to make this book as accurate and enjoyable for you as possible, but what really matters is what the book actually does for you. Please let us know your views, whether positive or negative, either by returning the reply card in the back of the book or by contacting us at Wrox Press at **feedback@wrox.com**

Source Code and Keeping Up-to-Date

We aim to keep the prices of our books reasonable, and so to replace an accompanying disc we make the source code, model answers and project example for the book available on both our web sites:

http://www.wrox.com/
http://www.wrox.co.uk/

The code is also available via FTP:

ftp://ftp.wrox.com
ftp://ftp.wrox.co.uk

If you don't have access to the Internet, then we can provide a disk for a nominal fee to cover postage and packing.

Errata and Updates

We've made every effort to make sure there are no errors in the text or the code. However, to err is human and as such we recognize the need to keep you, the reader, informed of any mistakes as they're spotted and corrected.

While you're visiting our web site, please make use of our *Errata* page, which is dedicated to fixing any small errors in the book, or offering new ways around a problem and its solution. Errata sheets are available for all our books — please download them, or take part in the continuous improvement of our tutorials and upload a 'fix' or pointer to the solution.

For those without access to the Net, call us on **1-800 USE WROX** and we'll gladly send errata sheets to you. Alternatively, send a letter to:

Wrox Press Inc.,
1512 N Fremont, Suite 103
Chicago,
IL 60622-2567
USA

Wrox Press Ltd,
30, Lincoln Road,
Olton,
Birmingham,
B27 6PA
UK

`http://www.wrox.com`

`http://www.wrox.co.uk`

Basic Ideas

In this first chapter, I will introduce the general characteristics of C++. All the concepts presented here will be covered in more detail in later chapters — this is just to set the scene before we get into the specifics of writing C++ programs. We will see what a simple C++ program looks like and how it all hangs together. We'll also be looking at the broad concepts of programming in C++, and how you create an executable program from the source code files you'll be writing.

Don't try to memorize all the information in this chapter. Concentrate on getting a feel for the ideas involved. Everything that is mentioned will come up again in later chapters, and you will learn best by using it, not just reading about it. In this chapter you will find out about:

▶ What the features of C++ are that make it so popular

▶ What the elements of a basic C++ program are

▶ How to document your program source code

▶ How your source code becomes an executable program

▶ How object-oriented programming differs from procedural programming

Programming Languages

You are probably familiar with the basic ideas of programming and programming languages, but to make sure we're on common ground, let's do a quick survey of some of the terms we'll be using as we progress through the book. We can also put C++ into perspective in relation to some of the other programming languages you'll have heard of.

Whatever the programming language, the programs you write are made up of separate **instructions**; these are referred to collectively as **source code**, and are stored on disk in a **source file**. There are lots of programming languages, each with their advantages and disadvantages, and their protagonists and detractors. Along with C++, other languages that you're likely to have come across include BASIC, COBOL, FORTRAN, Pascal and C.

FORTRAN, for example, is a language that's been around for nearly 40 years and is still used extensively for scientific and engineering calculations, although C++ and other languages have eroded much of its usage. COBOL is a language exclusively for business data processing applications, and is almost as old as FORTRAN. While little new code is written in COBOL, there is an immense amount of code that was written years ago and is still in use. Again, C++ has become the language of choice for many business data processing programs.

C is the forerunner of C++, and because of this the two languages share a common set of syntax and functionality. In fact, the C programming language forms a subset of C++. However, the extensions and improvements that C++ provides have matured as the language has developed, and C++ is a richer and more versatile language than its ancestor, as we shall see.

Interpreted vs Compiled Program Execution

Programming languages are designed to make it relatively easy for you to describe the actions you want a computer to carry out, compared with the form of program that a computer can actually execute. Your computer can only execute programs that consist of **machine instructions** (also called **machine code**), so it can't execute your program directly. There are basically two ways in which a program written in one of the languages I mentioned above can get executed, and for the most part, a particular language will choose one or the other. Programs written in BASIC, for example, are usually **interpreted** — that is, another program called an **interpreter** inspects the BASIC source code, figures out what it is supposed to do, and then causes that to be done.

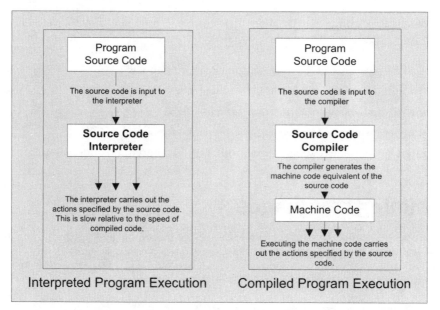

C++, on the other hand, is a **compiled** language. Before you can execute your C++ program, it must be converted to machine language by another program, called a **compiler**. The compiler inspects the C++ program and generates the machine instructions that will produce the actions specified by the source code. Of course, in reality neither interpreting nor compiling are quite as simple as I have described them here, but in principle that's how they work.

With an interpreted language, execution is 'indirect', by which I mean the intent of the source code needs to be determined each time a program is executed. For this reason, it is much slower — sometimes of the order of a 100 times slower — than the equivalent program in a compiled language. A given language is usually *either* compiled *or* interpreted, and it's typically the design and intended use of the language that determines which.

Something of an exception to this rule is Java, a relatively new language that has many of the characteristics of C++. Because it is intended to be portable across different computers and used on the Internet, Java is essentially an interpreted language. Having said that, there are also **just-in-time compilers** that will produce the machine code equivalent portions of the original Java source as machine code programs at execution time, and thereby greatly enhance the execution speed.

Libraries

If you had to create everything from scratch every time you wrote a program, it would be tedious indeed. The same kind of functionality is often required in many programs — reading data from the keyboard, for example, or displaying information on the screen. To address this, programming languages tend to come supplied with considerable quantities of pre-written code that provides standard facilities such as these, so you don't have to write the code for them yourself.

Standard code intended for use in any program is kept in a **library**. The library that comes with a particular programming language is as important as the language itself, as the quality and scope of the library can have a significant effect on how long it will take you to complete a given programming task.

Why is C++ Such a Great Language?

C++ enjoys remarkable popularity across virtually all computing environments: personal computers, Unix workstations and mainframe computers. This is all the more remarkable when you consider the degree to which history weighs against a new programming language, no matter how good it is. The inertia implicit in the number of programs written in previous languages inevitably slows the acceptance of a new language. Added to this, there is always a tendency among most professional programmers to stick with what they know and in which they are expert and productive, rather than jump in at the deep end with something new and unfamiliar, in which it will take time to develop fluency. Of course, the fact that C++ was built on C (which itself was the language of choice in many environments before the advent of C++) helped tremendously, but there's a great deal more to it than that. C++ provides you with a unique combination of advantages:

> ▶ C++ is effective across an incredible range of applications. You can apply C++ to just about anything, from word processing to scientific applications, from operating system components to computer games.

> ▶ C++ combines the facility for efficient procedural programming that it inherits from C, with a powerful object-oriented programming capability.

> ▶ C++ provides extensive facilities in its **standard library**.

> ▶ There are many commercial C++ libraries supporting a wide range of operating system environments and specialized applications.

You will also find that just about any computer can be programmed in C++, so the language is pervasive across almost all computer platforms. This means that it should be possible to transfer a program written in C++ from one machine to another with relatively limited effort. Of course, if this is truly going to be a straightforward process, you need to have had in mind when you wrote the program that you intended to run it on a different machine.

The ANSI Standard for C++

Standardization is fundamental to transferring a program written for one type of computer to another. The establishment of a standard makes a consistent implementation of the language possible across a variety of machines. A full set of standard facilities across all conforming compilers means that you will always know exactly what you are going to get. Using ANSI standard C++ makes the migration of applications between different machines easier, and eases the problems of maintaining applications that run in more than one environment.

Of course, there are other things to consider. If your program is to be portable, you must not introduce facilities from non-standard libraries into your code, and you must take care to minimize the amount of dependency on the development machine that you build into the way the program works. To do otherwise may make migrating the code an uphill task.

Another benefit of ANSI standard C++ is that it standardizes what you need to learn in order to program in C++. The existence of the standard will itself force conformance over time, since it provides the only definitive reference for what a C++ compiler and library should provide. It removes the license to be 'flexible' that compiler writers have had in the absence of an agreed standard, so if you haven't already done so, insist on ANSI standard conformance when you buy your next C++ compiler.

A Simple C++ Program

Let's take a look at a very simple C++ program, and find out what its constituents are. You don't need to enter this code right now; it's just here so that you can get a feel for what goes to make up a program. We won't go into all the detail at the moment either, as everything that appears here will be explored at length in later chapters.

This is a comment and it is ignored by the compiler.

This includes the contents of the header file **iostream** in the program.

This says that from this point on in this source file, we may be using names that belong to the namespace **std**.

```
// Example 1.1 A simple C++ program

#include <iostream>

using namespace std;

int main()
{
    cout << "The best place to start is at the beginning";
    return 0;
}
```

This identifies the function as **main()**, and the type of value returned from it as **int**.

This is a statement that outputs a message to the screen. Statements end with a semi-colon.

This statement ends the function **main()** and returns control to the operating system.

The braces delimit a **block**, which in this case is the function body.

This is the **body** of the function **main()**. This contains the executable code for the function.

The program shown above will display the message:

The best place to start is at the beginning

The program consists of a single function, **main()**. The first line of the function is:

```
int main()
```

A **function** is a self-contained block of code that is referenced by a name, **main** in this case. There may be a lot of other code in a program, but *every* C++ program consists of at least the function **main()**, and there can be only one function called **main()** within a program. Execution of a C++ program always starts with the first statement in **main()**.

Our function **main()** contains two executable statements:

```
cout << "The best place to start is at the beginning";
return 0;
```

These are executed in sequence, starting at the beginning. In general, the statements in a function are always executed sequentially, unless there is a statement that specifically alters the sequence of execution. We'll see what sort of statements can do that in Chapter 4.

In C++, input and output are performed using **streams**. If you want to output something, you put it into an output stream, and when you want something to be input, you get it from an input stream. The standard output and input streams in C++ are called **cout** and **cin**, and they use your computer's screen and keyboard respectively.

The code above outputs the character string "The best place to start is at the beginning" to your screen by placing it in the output stream with the **insertion operator**, **<<**. When we come to write programs that involve input, we'll see its partner, **the extraction operator**, **>>**.

The name **cout** is defined in the **header file iostream**. This is a standard header file that provides the definitions necessary for you to use the standard input and output facilities in C++. If our program did not include the line:

```
#include <iostream>
```

then it would not compile, because the **iostream** header file contains the definition of **cout**, and without it the compiler does not know what **cout** is.

> *Note that there are no spaces between the angled brackets and the standard header file name. With many compilers, spaces are significant between the two angled brackets, < and >; if you insert any spaces here, the program may not compile.*

The second and final statement in the body of the function is:

```
return 0;
```

This ends the program and returns control to your operating system. It also returns the value zero to the operating system. Other values can be returned to indicate different end conditions for the program, and can be used by the operating system to determine if the program executed successfully. However, whether or not they can be acted upon will depend on the operating system concerned.

Names

Lots of things in a C++ program have **names** (also referred to as **identifiers**) that are used to refer to them. There are five kinds of things that you will give names to in your C++ programs:

▶ **functions** are self-contained, named blocks of executable code. We will go into the detail of how we define these in Chapter 8.

▶ **variables** are named areas in memory that you use to store items of data. We start with these in Chapter 2.

▶ **types** are names for the *kinds* of data that you can store. The type **int**, for example, is used for integers (whole numbers). We will see something on these in Chapter 2 and more in subsequent chapters — particularly Chapters 11 and 12.

▶ **labels** provide a means of referring to a particular statement. These are rarely used, but we will look at them in action in Chapter 4.

▶ **namespaces** are a way of identifying a set of named items in your program under a single collective name. If that sounds confusing, don't worry: I'll say more about them shortly, and we'll look at them again in Chapter 10.

In most modern C++ compilers, a name can only contain upper and lower case letters, the underscore character, and the digits 0 to 9. The ANSI standard also permits characters from the Universal Character Set (which we will come to in a moment) to be included in a name, but you are unlikely to find that you need this capability.

Since names must be made up only of the permitted characters, you must not put whitespace characters (spaces, tabs, etc.) in the middle of a name. If you do, the single name will not be seen by the compiler as such — it will be seen as two names, and therefore will not be processed correctly. Another restriction is that names may not begin with a digit. Here are some examples of legal names:

```
value2      Mephistopheles        BettyMay       Earth_Weight      PI
```

and here are some names that are not legal:

```
8Ball      Mary-Ann        Betty  May       Earth-Weight      2PI
```

> *Note that names containing a double underscore (__) or starting with an underscore followed by an upper-case letter are reserved for use by the C++ standard library, so you should not choose such names for use in your programs. Your compiler is unlikely to check for this kind of thing, so you will only find out that you have a conflicting name when things go wrong!*

We will discuss names further in the contexts in which they are used, starting in the next chapter when we talk about variables.

Namespaces

I'm sure you noticed there was a line in the simple C++ program that I didn't explain in the discussion above. To understand it, you need to know what a namespace is, and for *those* to make any sense, I had first to tell you about names. As a reminder, the line in question was:

```
using namespace std;
```

A namespace name is a bit like a family name or a surname. Each individual within a family will have their own name, and within most families each family member has a unique name. In the Smith family there may be Jack, Jill, Jean and Jonah, and between family members they will refer to each other using these names. However, members of other families may have the same names as members of the Smith family. Within the Jones family, for instance, there might be John, Jean, Jeremiah and Jonah. When Jeremiah Jones refers to Jean, it is clear that he means Jean Jones. If he wants to refer to Jean in the Smith family, he will use the fully qualified name: Jean Smith. If you're not a member of either family, you can only be sure that people know whom you are talking about if you use the full names of individuals, like Jack Smith or Jonah Jones.

This is pretty much how namespaces work — a namespace name is analogous to a surname. Inside a namespace, you can use the individual names of things within the namespace. From outside the namespace, you can only refer to something within the namespace by a combination of the name of the particular entity and the namespace name. The purpose of a namespace is to provide a mechanism that minimizes the possibility of accidentally duplicating names in various parts of a large program and thereby creating confusion. In general, there may be several different namespaces within a program.

The entities in the C++ standard library are all defined within a namespace called **std**, so the names of all the entities within the standard libraries are qualified with **std**. The full name of **cout**, therefore, is actually **std::cout**. Those two colons together have a very fancy title: it's called the **scope resolution operator**, and there will be more to say about it later on. In this example, it serves to separate the namespace name, **std**, from the name of the stream, **cout**.

That **using** directive at the beginning of the simple C++ program indicates that we want to refer to things within the namespace called **std** without specifying the namespace name each time. Continuing our analogy, it makes our program file a sort of honorary member of the **std** family, so we can refer to everyone by their first name alone. One effect of this is to obviate the need to refer to **cout** as **std::cout**, making the program code little simpler. If we omitted the **using** directive, we would have had to write the output statement as:

```
std::cout << "The best place to start is at the beginning";
```

Keywords

There are reserved words in C++, called **keywords**, which have special significance within the language. The words **return** and **namespace** that we saw and discussed earlier are examples of keywords.

You will see many more keywords as we progress through the book. You *must* ensure that the names that you choose for entities in your program are not the same as any of the keywords in C++. You will find a list of all the keywords that are used in C++ in Appendix B.

> *Keywords, like the rest of the C++ language, are case sensitive.*

C++ Statements and Statement Blocks

Statements are the basic units for specifying both what your program is to do, and the data elements it acts upon. Most C++ statements end with a semicolon. There are a quite a few different sorts of statements, but perhaps the most basic is a statement that introduces a name into your program source file.

A statement that introduces a name into a source file is called a **declaration**. A declaration just introduces the name and specifies what kind of thing the name refers to, as opposed to a **definition**, which results in the creation of whatever the name refers to. As it happens, most declarations are also definitions.

Here's an example of a statement that declares a variable name, and defines and initializes a variable:

```
double result = 0.0;
```

This declares the name **result** to be a variable of type **double** (declaration), causes memory to be allocated to accommodate the variable (definition), and sets its initial value to 0.0 (initialization).

Here is an example of another kind of statement, called a **selection statement**:

```
if (length > 25)
   boxLength = size + 2;
```

This statement tests a condition, "Is the value of **length** greater than 25?" and then does something if that condition is true. In this case, it executes the statement on the second line, which adds 2 to the value stored in the variable **size**, and stores the result in the variable **boxLength**.

We can enclose several statements between a pair of curly braces, in which case they are referred to as a **statement block**. The body of a function is an example of a block, as we saw in our first example program. A statement block is also referred to as a **compound statement**, since in many circumstances it can be considered as a single statement, as we'll see when we look at C++'s decision-making capabilities in Chapter 4. In fact, wherever you can put a single statement in C++, you could equally well put a block of statements between braces. As a consequence, blocks can be placed inside other blocks — this concept is called **nesting**. In fact, blocks can be nested, one within another, to any depth you need.

A statement block also has important effects on the variables that you use to store data items, but we will defer discussion of this until we discuss something called **variable scope** in the next chapter.

Program Structure

Each of your C++ programs will consist of one or more files. By convention, there are two kinds of file that you can use to hold your source code: **header files** and **source files**. You use header files to contain code that *describes* the data types that your program needs, as well as some other sorts of declarations. These files are referred to as header files because you usually include them at the beginning (the 'head') of your other source files. Header files are usually distinguished by having the filename extension **.h**, although this is not mandatory and other extensions, such as **.hxx**, are used to identify header files in some systems.

Source files, which have the filename extension **.cpp**, contain function definitions — the executable code for your program. Any declarations or definitions for data types you have created yourself that are required for the code in a **.cpp** file are added by including the contents of one or more **.h** files at the beginning of the **.cpp** file.

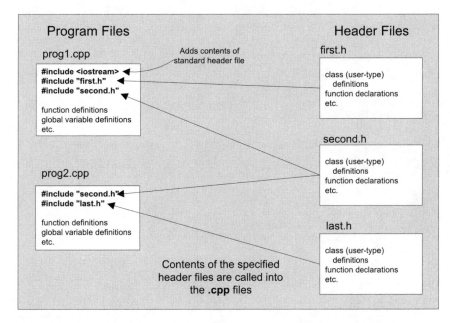

The diagram shows a program where the source code is contained in two **.cpp** files and three header files. The first **.cpp** file uses the information from the first two header files, and the second **.cpp** file requires the contents of the last two header files. You will learn more about the **#include** directives that do this in Chapter 10.

A number of **standard header files** are supplied with your compiler and contain declarations that you need in order to use the standard library facilities. They include, for example, declarations for the available standard library functions. The first **.cpp** file in the figure above includes the **iostream** header file, which we met in our example C++ program. As you will have noticed, in this instance the filename has no extension. In fact, to distinguish them from other header files, none of the ANSI standard header filenames has an extension.

> *At the time of writing, this is a relatively new addition to the ANSI standard, and you may find compilers that still use the* **.h** *extension for standard library header files. Details of the ANSI standard library headers are in Appendix C.*

Your compiler system may have a whole range of other header files, providing the definitions necessary to use operating system functions, or other goodies to save you programming effort. Our example shows just a few header files in use, but in most serious C++ applications many more will be involved.

Creating an Executable from your Source Files

Creating a program module that you can execute from your C++ source code is essentially a two-step process. In the first step, your **compiler** converts each **.cpp** file to an **object file** that contains the machine code equivalent of the source file contents. In the second step, the **linker** combines the object files produced by the compiler into a file containing the complete executable program.

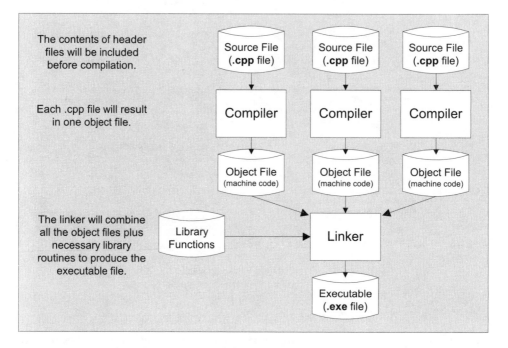

The illustration shows three source files being compiled to produce three corresponding object files. The filename extension used to identify object files varies between different machine environments, so it is not shown here. The source files that make up your program may be compiled independently in separate compiler runs, or most compilers will allow you to compile them in a single run. Either way, the compiler treats each source file as a separate entity, and produces one object file for each **.cpp** file. The link step then combines the object files for a program, along with any library functions that are necessary, into a single executable file.

In practice, compilation is an iterative process, since you're almost certain to have made typographical and other errors in the source code. Once you've eliminated these from each source file, you can progress to the link step, where you may find that yet more errors surface! Even when the link step produces an executable module, your program may still contain logical errors; that is, it doesn't produce the results you expect. To fix these, you must go back and modify the source code and start trying to get it to compile once more...

Let's take a closer look at what happens during the two basic steps that we have identified, compiling and linking, since there are some interesting things going on under the covers.

Compiling

The compilation process for a source file has two main stages, but the transition between them is automatic. The first stage is the **preprocessor phase**, which is carried out before the compilation phase proper. The preprocessor phase modifies the contents of the source file according to the preprocessor directives that you have placed in the file. The **#include** directive, which adds the contents of a header file to a **.cpp** file, is an example of a preprocessor directive, but there are many others (as we will see in Chapter 10).

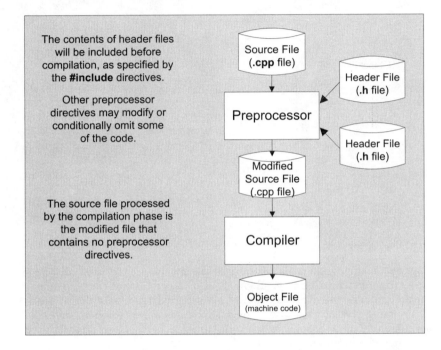

The contents of header files will be included before compilation, as specified by the **#include** directives.

Other preprocessor directives may modify or conditionally omit some of the code.

The source file processed by the compilation phase is the modified file that contains no preprocessor directives.

Source File
(**.cpp** file)

Header File
(**.h** file)

Preprocessor

Header File
(**.h** file)

Modified
Source File
(.cpp file)

Compiler

Object File
(machine code)

This facility for modifying the source file before it is compiled provides you with a lot of flexibility in accommodating the constraints of different computers and operating system environments. The code you need in one environment may be different from that required for another, because of variations in the available hardware or the operating system. In many situations, you can put the code for several environments in the same file, and arrange for the code to be tailored to the current environment during the preprocessor phase.

Although the preprocessor is shown in the illustration as a distinct operation, you do not normally execute it independently of the compiler. Invoking the compiler will execute the preprocessor automatically, before compiling your code.

Linking

While the output from the compiler for a given source file is machine code, it is quite a long way from being executable. For one thing, there will be no connection established between one object file and another. The object file corresponding to a particular source file will contain references to functions or other named items that are defined in other source files, and these will still be unresolved. Similarly, links to library functions will not yet be established; indeed, the code for these functions will not yet be part of the file. Dealing with all these things is the job of the **linker** (sometimes called the **linkage editor**).

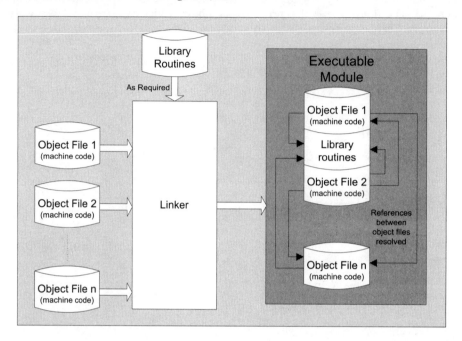

As the diagram illustrates, the linker combines the machine code from all of the object files and resolves any cross-references between them. It also integrates the code for any library functions that the object modules use. This is actually a simplified representation of what the linker does, as we are assuming that all the links between modules are established *statically* within the executable module. It is also possible for some links to be *dynamic*; that is, they are only established when the program executes.

The linker establishes links to functions statically — that is, before the program executes — for functions included in the source files that make up the program. Functions that are linked to dynamically — that is, during program execution — are compiled and linked to create a different kind of executable module called a **dynamic link library** or **shared library**. Links to functions in a dynamic link library are established when the program calls the functions, and not before.

Dynamic link libraries present several important advantages. A primary one is that the functions in the dynamic link library can be shared between several programs that are executing concurrently. This saves occupying memory with duplicates of the same function. Another advantage is that the dynamic link library will not be loaded into memory *until* one of the functions it contains is called. This implies that if you don't use a function from a given dynamic link library, it won't occupy space in memory. Dynamic link libraries are a system capability that ties in closely with your operating system, so we won't be discussing them further in this book.

Characters and Character Sets

The characters that you can use in your C++ programs are the upper and lower case letters, **A** to **Z** and **a** to **z**, the digits **0** to **9**, the space character, the control characters for new line, horizontal and vertical tabs, form feed and bell, plus the following special characters:

_	{	}	[	]	#	(	)	<	>	%
:	;	.	?	*	+	−	/	^	&	|
~	!	=	,	\	"	'				

These are also referred to as **symbols** (as opposed to digits and alphabetic characters, and control characters that are not really 'displayed').

Character Encoding

Take note that this definition of the characters that are used in C++ does *not* say how the characters are encoded. Your particular compiler will determine how the characters that you use to write your C++ source code are represented in the computer. On a PC, these characters will typically be represented in the machine by 8-bit extended ASCII codes (such as ISO Latin-1), but other ways of encoding characters can be used, and there are various extended ASCII codes to support different national languages. Additionally, on mainframe computers the Extended Binary Coded Decimal Interchange Code (EBCDIC) is often used. This is an 8-bit code that differs significantly from the extended ASCII codes.

> *By the term 'extended ASCII code', I mean an 8-bit code in which the first 128 characters are the same as the normal 7-bit ASCII code. These are listed in Appendix A.*

Escape Sequences

When you want to use character constants in a program, certain characters can be problematic. A **character constant** is a data item that your program will use in some way, and it can be either a single character or a character string like the one we had in our simple example. Obviously, you can't enter characters such as 'newline' or 'tab' directly as character constants, since they will just do what they are supposed to do: go to a new line, or tab to the next tab position in your source code file. What you want in a character constant is the appropriate code for the character.

You can enter control characters as constants by means of an **escape sequence**. An escape sequence is an indirect way of specifying a character, and always begins with a backslash, ****. The escape sequences that represent control characters are:

Escape Sequence	Control Character
\n	newline
\t	horizontal tab
\v	vertical tab

Escape Sequence	Control Character
\b	backspace
\r	carriage return
\f	form feed
\a	alert — bell

There are some other characters that are a problem to represent directly. Clearly, the backslash character itself is difficult, because it signals the start of an escape sequence, and there are others with special significance too. The 'problem' characters you can specify with an escape sequence are:

Escape Sequence	Character
\\	backslash
\'	single quote
\"	double quote
\?	question mark

> *Since the backslash signals the start of an escape sequence, the only way to enter a backslash as a character constant is by using two successive backslashes.*

Escape sequences also provide a general way of representing characters such as those in languages other than the one your keyboard supports, since you can use a hexadecimal (base 16) or octal (base 8) number after the backslash to specify the code for a character. Since you're using a numeric code, you can specify any character in this way. In C++, hexadecimal numbers start with **x** or **X**, so **\x99A** and **\XE3** are examples of escape sequences in this format.

You can also specify a character by using up to three octal digits after the backslash, like **\165** for example. The absence of **x** or **X** determines that the code will be interpreted as an octal number.

Try It Out — Using Escape Sequences

We can produce an example of a program that uses escape sequences in specifying a message to be displayed on the screen. To see the results yourself, you'll need to enter, compile, link and execute the program that appears below.

As I explained in the Introduction, exactly how you perform these steps will depend on your compiler, and you'll need to consult your compiler's documentation for more information. If you look up 'edit', 'compile' and 'link' (and, with some compilers, 'build'), you should be able to find out what you need to do with little difficulty.

```
// Program 1.2 Using escape sequences
#include <iostream>
using namespace std;
```

```
int main()
{
  cout << "\n\"Least said\n\t\tsoonest mended.\"\n\a";
  return 0;
}
```

When you do compile, link, and run this program, you should see the following output displayed:

```
"Least said
        soonest mended."
```

You should also hear a 'beep' or some equivalent noise from whatever sound output facility your computer has.

How It Works

The output we get is determined by what's between the outer double quotes in the statement:

```
cout << "\n\"Least said\n\t\tsoonest mended.\"\n\a";
```

Everything between the outer double quotes gets sent to **cout**. A string of characters between a pair of double quotes is called a **string literal**. The double quote characters just identify the beginning and end of the string literal; they are not part of the string themselves. A backslash in a string literal *always* indicates the start of an escape sequence, so the first character that's sent to **cout** is **\n** — the newline character — which positions the screen cursor at the beginning of the next line.

The next character sent to **cout** is another escape sequence, **\"**, so a double quote will be displayed on the screen, followed by the characters that follow: **Least said**. Next, we have another newline character, **\n**, so the cursor will move to the beginning of the next line. We then send two tab characters to **cout** with **\t\t**, so the cursor will be moved two tab positions to the right. The characters **soonest mended.** will then be displayed from that point on, followed by another double quote from the escape sequence **\"**. Lastly, we have another newline character, which will move the cursor to the start of the next line, followed by the **\a** escape sequence that will cause the 'beep' to sound.

The interior double quote characters are not interpreted as the end of the string literal because each of them is preceded by a backslash, and is therefore denoted as an escape sequence. If we did not have the escape sequence, **\"**, we would have no way of outputting a double quote, since it would be interpreted as marking the end of the string.

In C++, the name **endl** ('end line') is also used to represent a single newline character in an output statement. Using **endl**, the statement in the code above to output the string could be written:

```
cout << endl
     << "\"Least said"
```

```
        << endl
        << "\t\tsoonest mended.\"\a"
        << endl;
```

This statement sends five separate string literals — **endl**, **"\"Least said"**, **endl**, **"\t\tsoonest mended.\"\a"**, and **endl** — in sequence to **cout**. This will produce exactly the same output as the original statement.

> *Be aware that the final character of **endl** is the letter '1', not the number '1'. It can sometimes be difficult to tell the two apart.*

You don't have to choose between using either **endl** or the escape sequence for newline. They are not mutually exclusive, so you can mix them to suit yourself. For example, we could produce the same result as the original again with this statement:

```
cout << endl
     << "\"Least said\n\t\tsoonest mended.\"\a"
     << endl;
```

Here we have just used **endl** for the first and last newline characters. The one in the middle is still produced by an escape sequence.

Characters in the Universal Character Set

The **Universal Character Set** (UCS) is an ISO (International Standards Organization) standard for representing characters with a 32-bit code, which translates to 8 hexadecimal digits. UCS is defined by the standards document ISO/IEC 10646. The idea of UCS is to be able to represent all national language characters (French, Chinese, English, Russian or whatever), *plus* all the symbols you are likely to need, with unique codes.

You won't need to use UCS codes very often, but just in case you do, C++ provides a way to do it. To represent a UCS character, you simply write the character as **\uNNNNNNNN**, where **NNNNNNNN** is the hexadecimal representation of the UCS character code. The Latin character set in UCS has character codes in which the first four hexadecimal digits are zero, **\u0000NNNN**. You can write these UCS characters in an abbreviated form by omitting the leading zeros, like this: **\uNNNN**.

Whitespace

Whitespace is the term used in C++ to describe spaces, horizontal and vertical tabs, and newline characters. In many instances, whitespace separates one part of a statement from another, and enables the compiler to identify where one element in a statement ends and the next element begins. For example, look at the following line of code:

```
int fruit;
```

This statement involves **int**, which is a type name, and **fruit**, which is the name of a variable. There must be at least one whitespace character (usually a space) between **int** and **fruit** for the compiler to be able to distinguish them. This is because **intfruit** would be a perfectly acceptable name for a variable or indeed anything else, and the compiler would interpret it as such.

On the other hand, consider this statement:

```
fruit = apples + oranges;
```

No whitespace characters are necessary between **fruit** and **=**, or between **=** and **apples**, although you are free to include some if you wish. This is because the **=** is not alphabetic or numeric, so the compiler can separate it from its surroundings. Similarly, no whitespace characters are necessary on either side of the **+** sign. In fact, you could write the previous statement as:

```
fruit
  =
apples
  +
oranges;
```

If you were to do this, you are unlikely to be congratulated for good programming style, but the compiler won't mind.

Apart from its use as a separator between elements in a statement, or in a string between quotes, the compiler ignores whitespace. You can, therefore, include as much whitespace as you like to make your program more readable. In some programming languages, the end of a statement is at the end of the line, but in C++ the end of a statement is wherever the semicolon occurs. This enables you to spread a statement over several lines if you wish, so you can write a statement like this:

```
cout << endl << "\"Least said" << endl << "\t\tsoonest mended.\"\a" << endl;
```

Or like this:

```
cout << endl
     << "\"Least said"
     << endl
     << "\t\tsoonest mended.\"\a"
     << endl;
```

Documenting your Programs

Documenting your programs is extremely important. Code that seems crystal clear when you write it can look extraordinarily obscure when you've been away from it for a month. You can document your code using **comments**, of which there are two sorts in C++: single-line comments, and comments that can span several lines.

You begin a single-line comment with a double slash. For example:

```
// Program to forecast stock market prices
```

The compiler will ignore everything on the line following the double slash, but that doesn't mean the comment has to fill the whole line. You can use this style of comment to explain a statement:

```
length = shrink(length, temp);        // Compensate for wash shrinkage
```

You can also temporarily remove a line of code from your program just by adding a double slash to the beginning of the line:

```
// length = shrink(length, temp);        // Compensate for wash shrinkage
```

This converts the statement to a comment, which is something you might want to do during testing of a program, for example. Everything from the first **//** in a line to the end of the line is ignored, including any further occurrences of **//**.

The multi-line comment is sometimes used for writing more verbose, general descriptive material — explaining the algorithm used within a function, for example. Such a comment begins with **/***, ends with ***/**, and everything between these two is ignored. This enables you to embellish multi-line comments to highlight them; for example:

```
/***************************************************
 * This function predicts future stock prices     *
 * using advanced tealeaf simulation techniques.  *
 ***************************************************/
```

You can also use this style of comment for temporarily disabling a *block* of code. Just put **/*** at the beginning of the block, and ***/** at the end. However, you must take particular care not to nest **/* ... */** comments, because you will cause error messages from your compiler if you do. This is because the closing ***/** of the *inner* nested comment will match with the opening **/*** of the *outer* comment:

```
// You must not nest multi-line comments
/* This starts an outer comment
/* This is an inner comment, but the start will not be recognized
   because of the outer comment.
   Instead, the end of the inner comment will be interpreted as the end
   of the outer comment. */
   This will cause the compiler to try to compile this part of the
   outer comment as C++ code. */
```

The last part of the outer comment is left 'dangling' and the compiler will try to compile it, which will inevitably result in failure. For this reason, the **//** form of comment is the most widely used in C++ programs.

FYI You may also hear multi-line comments being described as 'C-style' comments. This is because the **/* ... */** syntax is the only one available for creating comments in the C language.

The Standard Library

The standard library contains a substantial number of functions and other things that support, augment and extend the basic language capabilities of C++. The contents of the standard library are just as much a part of C++ as the syntax and semantics of the language itself. The standard for C++ defines both, and so *every* compiler that conforms to the standard will supply the complete standard library.

Bearing this in mind, the scope of the standard library is extraordinary. You get a vast range of capability, ranging from essential elements such as basic language support, input and output functions and exception handling (an exception is an unusual occurrence during program execution — often an error of some kind), to utility functions, mathematical routines and a wide range of prewritten and tested facilities that you can use to store and manage data during execution of your program.

To use C++ most effectively, you should make sure that you have a good familiarity with the contents of the standard library. You will be introduced to many of the capabilities of the standard library as you learn the C++ language in this book, but the degree of coverage within the book will inevitably be incomplete. It would take another book comparable with the size of this one to cover the capability and use of the standard library comprehensively.

The definitions and declarations necessary to use standard library facilities appear in the standard header files we touched upon earlier. There are a few cases when the standard header files will be included into your program files by default, but in most instances you must add a **#include** directive for the appropriate header for the library facilities that you want to use. You will find a comprehensive list of the header files in Appendix C, with a brief description of what sort of functionality each one supports.

Almost everything in the C++ standard library is defined within the namespace **std**. This means that all the names you will use from the library are prefixed with **std**. As you saw earlier in the chapter, when you reference something from the standard library, you need to prefix the name with **std**, as in the statement:

```
std::cout << "The best place to start is at the beginning";
```

Alternatively, you can put a **using** directive at the beginning of your source file:

```
using namespace std;
```

This allows you to omit the **std** prefix for standard library names, since all the names in **std** will be automatically available in your program file, so you can just write:

```
cout << "The best place to start is at the beginning";
```

Programming in C++

Because C++ inherits and enhances the power and flexibility of the original C language, you have a comprehensive capability for handling time-critical, low-level programming tasks, and for dealing with problems where a traditional procedural approach may be preferable. The major strengths of C++, though, are its powerful and extensive object-oriented features. These provide the potential for writing programs that are less error-prone, less time-consuming to maintain, simpler to extend and easier to understand than their equivalent procedural solutions.

There are fundamental differences between these two programming methodologies, so let's contrast them to highlight just *how* they are different, and see some of the reasons why an object-oriented approach can be so attractive.

Procedural and Object-Oriented Programming

Historically, procedural programming is the way almost all programs have been written. To create a procedural programming solution to a problem, you focus on the process that your program must implement to solve the problem. A rough outline of what you do, once the requirements have been defined precisely, is as follows:

▶ You create a clear, high-level definition of the overall process that your program will implement.

▶ You segment the overall process into workable units of computation that are, as far as possible, self-contained. These will usually correspond to functions.

▶ You break down the logic and the work that each unit of computation is to do into a detailed sequence of actions. This is likely to be down to a level corresponding to programming language statements.

▶ You code the functions in terms of processing basic types of data: numerical data, single characters and character strings.

Apart from the common requirement of starting out with a clear specification of what the problem is, the object-oriented approach to solving the same problem is quite different:

▶ From the problem specification, you determine what types of **objects** the problem is concerned with. For example, if your program deals with baseball players, you are likely to identify **BaseballPlayer** as one of the types of data your program will work with. If your program is an accounting package, you may well want to define objects of type **Account** and type **Transaction**. You also identify the set of **operations** that the program will need to carry out on each type of object. This will result in a set of application-specific data types that you will use in writing your program.

▶ You produce a detailed design for each of the new data types that your problem requires, including the operations that can be carried out with each object type.

▶ You express the logic of the program in terms of the new data types you have defined and the kinds of operations they allow.

The program code for an object-oriented solution to a problem will be completely unlike that for a procedural solution, and almost certainly easier to understand.

Suppose that you are implementing a program that deals with boxes of various kinds. A feasible requirement of such a program would be to package several smaller boxes inside another, larger box. In a procedural program, you would need to store the length, breadth and height of each box in a separate group of variables. The dimensions of a new box that could contain several other boxes would need to be calculated explicitly in terms of the dimensions of each of the contained boxes, according to whatever rules you had defined for packaging a set of boxes.

An object-oriented solution might involve first defining a **Box** data type. You could then define an operation to add two **Box** objects directly, producing a third **Box** object that could contain the first two. Using this operation, you could write statements like:

```
bigBox = box1 + box2 + 3 * box3;
```

Here, each of the variables is of type **Box** — you'll remember that earlier in the chapter we had variables of type **double** and **int**. This statement would create a **Box** object big enough to contain 3 **Box** objects the size of **box3**, as well as one each the sizes of **box1** and **box2**.

Being able to write statements like this is clearly much easier than having to deal with all the dimensions separately, and the more complex the calculations you take on, the greater the advantage is going to be. This is a trivial illustration, though, and there is a great deal more to the power of objects than that you can see here. The purpose of this discussion is just to give you an idea of how readily problems solved using an object-oriented approach can be understood. We will be exploring object-oriented programming in C++ fully, starting in Chapter 11.

Summary

This chapter has been broad-brush stuff, to give you a feel for some of the general concepts of C++. You will be meeting everything we have discussed in this chapter again, and in much more detail, in subsequent chapters. However, some of the basics that we've looked at are:

- A program in C++ consists of at least one function, which is called **main()**

- The executable part of a function is made up of statements contained between a pair of braces

- A pair of braces defines a statement block

- In C++, a statement is terminated by a semicolon

- Keywords are a set of reserved words that have specific meanings in C++. No entity in your program can have a name that coincides with any of the keywords in the language

- A C++ program will be contained in one or more files

- The code defining functions is usually stored in files with the extension **.cpp**

- The code that defines your own data types is usually kept in header files with the extension **.h**

- The standard library provides an extensive range of capabilities that support and extend the C++ language

- Input and output in C++ are performed using streams, and involve the use of the insertion and extraction operators, **<<** and **>>**

- Object-oriented programming involves defining new data types specific to your problem. Once you have defined the data types that you need, a program can be written in terms of the new data types.

Exercises

Ex 1.1 Create a program that will print out the text **"Hello World"** to your screen.

Ex 1.2 Change your program so that it uses the hexadecimal values of the characters to spell out the phrase. If you're working on a computer that uses ASCII to encode its characters, you'll find a table of the values you need in Appendix A. (Hint: using hexadecimal ASCII values, **"He"** can be displayed using **cout << "\x48\x65";**)

Ex 1.3 The following program will produce three compiler errors. Find these errors and correct them so the program can compile cleanly and run.

```
#include <iostream>
using namespace std;

int main()
{
  cout << endl
       << "Hello World"
       << endl

  return0;
)
```

Ex 1.4 What will happen if your program does not contain the line **using namespace std;** but *does* contain the line **cout << "Hello world";**? Apart from replacing the **using** directive, how else could you fix the problem?

FYI

You'll find model answers to all exercises in this book on our websites, at http://www/wrox/com/ **and** http://www/wrox/co/uk/

You can also download the code via ftp, from ftp://www/wrox/com/ **or** ftp://www/wrox/co/uk/

Basic Data Types and Calculations

In this chapter we'll look at some of the basic data types that are built into C++, and that you're likely to use in all your programs. We'll also be investigating how you perform some simple numerical computation. All of C++'s object-oriented capability is founded on the basic data types built into the language, because all the data types you'll create are ultimately defined in terms of the basic types. It's therefore important to get a good grasp of using them. By the end of the chapter, you will be able to write a simple C++ program of the traditional form: input...process...output.

In this chapter, you will learn about:

- Data types in C++
- What literals are, and how you define them in a program
- Binary and hexadecimal representation for integers
- How you declare and initialize variables in your program
- How calculations using integers work
- Programming with values that are not integers — floating point calculations
- How you can prevent the value stored in a variable from being modified
- How to create variables that can store characters

Data and Data Types

C++ is a **strongly typed language** — in other words, every data item in your program has a **type** associated with it that defines what it is. Your C++ compiler will make extensive checks to ensure that, as far as possible, you use the right data type in any given context, and that when you combine different types they are made to be compatible. Because of this type checking, the compiler is able to detect and report most errors that would arise from the accidental interpretation of one type of data as another, or from attempts to combine data items of types that are mutually incompatible.

The numerical values that you can work with in C++ fall into two broad categories: integers (in other words, whole numbers), and floating point values (which can be fractional). You can't conclude from this that there are just two numerical data types, however. There are actually several data types in each of these categories, where each type has a permitted range of values that it can store. By way of explanation, let's look at how you carry out arithmetic calculations in C++, starting with how you can calculate using integers.

Performing Simple Calculations

To begin with, we can get some bits of terminology out of the way. An operation (such as a mathematical calculation) is defined by an **operator** — **+** for addition, for example, or ***** for multiplication. The values that an operator acts upon are called **operands**, so in an expression such as **2 * 3**, the operands are **2** and **3**.

Because the multiply operator requires *two* operands, it is called a **binary operator**. Some other operators only require *one* operand, and these are called **unary operators**. An example of a unary operator is the minus sign in **-2**. The minus sign acts on one operand — the value **2** — and changes its sign. This contrasts with the binary subtraction operator in expressions such as **4 - 2**, which acts on two operands, the **4** and the **2**.

Calculations involve operations on numbers, so a good starting point is to get a general idea of how you specify numeric values. In C++, fixed values of any kind, such as **42**, or **2.71828**, or **"Mark Twain"**, are referred to as **literals**. In Chapter 1, when we were outputting text strings to the screen, we used a **string literal** — a constant defined by a series of characters between a pair of double quotes, of which **"Mark Twain"** is an example. Now we will investigate the types of literals that are numeric constants. These are the ordinary numbers you meet every day: your shoe size, the boiling point of lead, the number of angels that can sit on a pin — in fact, any defined number.

There are two broad classifications of numeric constants that you can use in C++:

Integer literals, which are whole numbers, written without a decimal point.
Floating point literals (commonly referred to as floating point numbers) are decimal numbers that include a decimal point, or an exponent, or both. (We will look into exponents a little later on.)

You use an integer when what you are dealing with is evidently a whole number: the number of players in a team, or the number of pages in a book. You use floating point literals when the values are not integral: the circumference of a circle divided by its diameter, or the exchange rate of the UK£ against the US$. You also use floating point values when you are dealing with very small or very large quantities: the weight of an electron, the diameter of the galaxy, or the velocity of a bat out of hell perhaps. The term 'floating point number' is used because while these values are represented by a fixed number of digits, the decimal point 'floats' and can be moved in either direction in relation to the fixed set of digits.

Letting the Point Float

0.00000000000000000001234567
12345670000000000000000000.0

Both the numbers in the illustration have the same number of digits of precision, but they are very different numbers. This flexibility in positioning the decimal point allows a huge range of numbers to be represented and stored, from the very small to the very large, in a modest amount of memory.

We'll look at how to use integers first, as they are the simpler of the two. We will come back to working with floating point values as soon as we are done with integers.

Integer Literals

You can write integer literals in a very straightforward way. Here are some examples:

-123   **+123**   **123**   **22333**

Here, the '**+**' and '**-**' signs in the first two examples are examples of the unary operators I mentioned earlier. You could omit the '**+**' in the second example, as it is implied by default, but if you think putting it in makes things clearer, that's not a problem. The literal **+123** is the same as **123**. The fourth example is the number that you would normally write as 22,333, but you must not use commas within an integer literal. If you include a comma, the compiler is likely to treat your number as two numbers, separated by the comma.

You can't write just any old integer value that you want, either. To take an extreme example, an integer with a hundred digits will not be accepted. There are upper and lower limits on integer literals, and these are determined by the amount of memory that is devoted to storing each type of integer value. We will come back to this point a little later in the chapter, when we discuss integer variables.

Of course, although we've written the examples of integer literals as decimal values, inside your computer they are stored as binary numbers. Understanding binary is quite important in programming, so in case you're a little rusty on how binary numbers work, let's have a quick overview.

Binary Numbers

First, let's consider exactly what we intend when we write a common, everyday decimal number, such as 324, or 911. Obviously, what we mean is 'three hundred and twenty-four', or 'nine hundred and eleven'. Put more precisely, we mean:

$$\textbf{324} \text{ is: } \mathbf{3 \times 10^2 + 2 \times 10^1 + 4 \times 10^0}, \text{ which is } \mathbf{3 \times 10 \times 10 + 2 \times 10 + 4}$$
$$\textbf{911} \text{ is: } \mathbf{9 \times 10^2 + 1 \times 10^1 + 1 \times 10^0}, \text{ which is } \mathbf{9 \times 10 \times 10 + 1 \times 10 + 1}$$

We call it decimal notation because it is built around powers of ten (derived from the Latin *decimalis* meaning 'of tithes', which was a tax of 10% — ah, those were the days...).

Representing numbers in this way is very handy for people with ten fingers and/or ten toes, or indeed ten of any kind of appendage. However, your PC is rather less handy, being built mainly of switches that are either on or off. It's OK for counting up to two, but not spectacular at counting to ten. I'm sure you're aware that this is the primary reason why your computer represents numbers using base 2, rather than base 10. Representing numbers using base 2 is called the **binary** system of counting. Digits can only be 0 or 1, which is ideal when you only have on/off switches to represent them. In an exact analogy to our system of counting in base 10, the binary number 1101, for example, breaks down like this:

$$1 \times 2^3 + 1 \times 2^2 + 0 \times 2^1 + 1 \times 2^0, \text{ which is } 1 \times 2 \times 2 \times 2 + 1 \times 2 \times 2 + 0 \times 2 + 1$$

This amounts to 13 in the decimal system. In the following figure, you can see the decimal equivalents of all the possible numbers you can represent using 8 binary digits (a **binary** digit is more commonly known as a **bit**).

Binary	Decimal	Binary	Decimal
0000 0000	0	1000 0000	128
0000 0001	1	1000 0001	129
0000 0010	2	1000 0010	130
...	...	...	...
0001 0000	16	1001 0000	144
0001 0001	17	1001 0001	145
...	...	...	...
0111 1100	124	1111 1100	252
0111 1101	125	1111 1101	253
0111 1110	126	1111 1110	254
0111 1111	127	1111 1111	255

Notice that using the first 7 bits we can represent numbers from 0 to 127, which is a total of 2^7 numbers, and that using all 8 bits we get 256, or 2^8 numbers. In general, if we have n bits, we can represent 2^n integers, with values from 0 to 2^n-1.

Adding binary numbers inside your computer is a piece of cake, since the 'carry' from adding corresponding digits can only be 0 or 1, and very simple circuitry can handle the process. The illustration shows how the addition of two 8-bit binary values would work.

Binary	Decimal
0001 1101	29
+ 0010 1011	+ 43
0100 1000	72

carries

Hexadecimal Numbers

When we start dealing with larger binary numbers, like this one:

1111 0101 1011 1001 1110 0001

The limitations of binary notation can soon be found when put into practical use. Consider the number 16,103,905 — a measly 8 digit decimal number. In binary, this converts to 1111 0101 10011 1001 1110 0001, a huge 24 digits in length. You can sit more angels on a pinhead than that! Clearly, we need a more economical way of writing this, but decimal is not always appropriate. Sometimes (as we will see in the next chapter), we might need to be able to specify that the tenth and twenty-fourth bits from the right are set to 1, without the overhead of binary notation. To figure out the decimal integer required to do this sort of thing is hard work, and there's a good chance you'll miscalculate. A much easier solution is to use hexadecimal notation, where the numbers are represented using base 16.

Arithmetic to base 16 is a much more convenient option, and it fits rather well with binary. Each hexadecimal digit can have values from 0 to 15 (the digits from 10 to 15 being represented by letters A to F, as shown in the table below), and values from 0 to 15 correspond nicely with the range of values that four binary digits can represent.

Hexadecimal	Decimal	Binary
0	0	0000
1	1	0001
2	2	0010
...	...	...
9	9	1001
A	10	1010
B	11	1011
C	12	1100
D	13	1101
E	14	1110
F	15	1111

Because a hexadecimal digit corresponds to 4 binary digits, we can represent our large binary number as a hexadecimal number simply by taking groups of four binary digits, starting from the right, and writing the equivalent hexadecimal digit for each group. The binary number:

$$1111\ 0101\ 1011\ 1001\ 1110\ 0001$$

will therefore come out as:

$$F\quad 5\quad B\quad 9\quad E\quad 1$$

We have six hexadecimal digits corresponding to the six groups of four binary digits. Just to prove that it all works out with no cheating, we can convert this number directly from hexadecimal to decimal by again using the analogy with the meaning of a decimal number, as follows:

F5B9E1 as a decimal value is given by:

$$15 \times 16^5 + 5 \times 16^4 + 11 \times 16^3 + 9 \times 16^2 + 14 \times 16^1 + 1 \times 16^0$$

This turns out to be:

$$15{,}728{,}640 + 327{,}680 + 45{,}056 + 2{,}304 + 224 + 1$$

Thankfully, this adds up to the same number we got when converting the equivalent binary number to a decimal value: 16,103,905.

Negative Binary Numbers

There is another aspect to binary arithmetic that you need to understand: negative numbers. So far, we have assumed that everything is positive — the optimist's view, if you will — and so our glass is still half full. But we can't avoid the negative side of life — the pessimist's perspective that our glass is already half empty. How can a negative number be represented inside a computer? Well, we only have binary digits at our disposal, so the solution has to be to use one of those.

For numbers that we want to allow to have negative values (referred to as **signed numbers**), we must first decide on a fixed length (in other words, the number of binary digits) and then designate the leftmost binary digit as a **sign bit**. We have to fix the length in order to avoid any confusion about which bit is the sign bit.

Since your computer's memory consists of 8-bit bytes, our binary numbers are going to be stored in some multiple (usually a power of two) of 8 bits. Thus we can have some numbers with 8 bits, and some with 16 bits (or whatever), and as long as we know what the length is in each case, we can find the sign bit — it's just the leftmost bit. If the sign bit is 0, the number is positive, and if it is 1, the number is negative.

This seems to solve our problem, but actually we're not quite there yet. When two integers are added, we don't want the computer to be messing about checking whether either or both of the numbers are negative. We just want to use the regular 'add' circuitry to produce the appropriate result. If we add -8 in binary to +12, we would really like to get the answer +4.

If we try this with our simplistic solution, which is just to set the sign bit of the positive value to 1 to make it negative, and then perform the arithmetic with conventional carries, it doesn't quite work:

12 in binary is	0000 1100
-8 in binary, we suppose, is	1000 1000

If we now add these together, we get:	1001 0100

This seems to be -20, which is not what we wanted at all. It's definitely not +4, which we know is 0000 0100. "Ah," I hear you say, "you can't treat a sign just like another digit." But that is just what we *do* have to do when dealing with computers because, dumb things that they are, they have trouble coping with anything else. We really need a different representation for negative numbers.

Let's see how the computer would like us to represent -8, by trying to subtract +12 from +4, since that should give us the right answer:

+4 in binary is	0000 0100
+12 in binary is	0000 1100

Subtract the latter from the former, and we get	1111 1000

For each digit from the fourth from the right onwards, we had to 'borrow' 1 to do the subtraction, just as we would when performing ordinary decimal arithmetic. This result is supposed to be -8, and even though it doesn't look like it, that's exactly what it is. Just try adding it to +12 or +15 in binary, and you will see that it works!

What *exactly* did we get when we subtracted 12 from 4? It turns out that what we have here is called the **two's complement** representation of negative binary numbers. At this point, I need to ask a little faith on your part and avoid getting into explanations of *why* it works. I will just show you how the 2's complement form of a negative number can be constructed from a positive value, and you can prove to yourself that it does work. Let's return to our previous example, where we need the 2's complement representation of -8. We start with +8 in binary:

0000 1000

We now 'flip' each binary digit, changing zeros to ones, and vice versa:

1111 0111

This is called the 1's complement form, and if we now add 1 to this, we will get the 2's complement form:

1111 1000

This is exactly the same as the representation of -8 we got by subtracting +12 from +4. Just to make absolutely sure, let's try the original sum of adding -8 to +12:

+12 in binary is   0000 1100
Our version of -8 is   1111 1000

If we add *these* together, we get: 0000 0100

The answer is 4 — magic. It works! The 'carry' propagates through all the leftmost 1's, setting them back to zero. One fell off the end, but we shouldn't worry about that — it's probably the one we borrowed from off the end in the subtraction sum we did to get -8! In fact, what's happening is that we're making an assumption that the sign bit, 1 or 0, repeats forever to the left. Try a few examples of your own; you'll find it always works, automatically. The really great thing is that it makes arithmetic very easy (and fast) for your computer.

Now that we have got binary and hexadecimal numbers straight, let's get back to integer literals in C++.

Hexadecimal Integer Literals

The previous examples of integer literals were decimal integers, but you can also write integers as hexadecimal values. To indicate that you are writing a hexadecimal value, you prefix the number with **0x** or **0X**, so if you write **0x999**, you are writing a hexadecimal number. Plain old **999**, on the other hand, is a decimal value. Here are some more examples of integer literals written as hexadecimal values:

Hexadecimal values	Corresponding decimal expression	Decimal value
0x1AF	$1*16^2+10*16^1+15*16^0$	431
0x123	$1*16^2+2*16^1+3*16^0$	291
0xA	$10*16^0$	10
0xCAD	$12*16^2+10*16^1+13*16^0$	3245
0xFF	$15*16^1+15*16^0$	255

You will remember that in Chapter 1 we saw hexadecimal notation being used in escape sequences that defined characters. What we're discussing here is different — we are defining integers. We'll come back to defining character literals later in this chapter.

Octal Integer Literals

You can also write integers as **octal** values, that is, using base 8. You identify a number as octal by writing it with a leading zero. The following table shows some examples of octal values:

Octal values	Corresponding decimal integers
0123	83
077	63
010101	4161

Of course, octal numbers can only have digit values from 0 to 7. Octal is used very infrequently these days, and it survives in C++ largely for historical reasons. However, it is important to be aware of its existence, because if you accidentally write a decimal number with a leading zero, the compiler will try to interpret it as octal.

> *Do not write decimal integer values with a leading zero. The compiler will interpret such values as octal (base 8), so a value written as 065 will be equivalent to 53 in decimal notation.*

As far as your compiler is concerned, it doesn't matter which number base you choose when you write an integer value — ultimately, it will be stored in your computer as a binary number. The different ways available to you for writing an integer are there just for your convenience. You could write the integer value fifteen as **15**, as **0xF**, or as **017**. These will all result in the same internal binary representation of the value, so you should choose one or another of the possible representations to suit the context in which you are using it.

Integer Arithmetic

The basic arithmetic operations that you can carry out on integers are:

Operator	Operation
+	Addition
–	Subtraction
*	Multiplication
/	Division
%	Modulus (the remainder after division)

These operators work largely in the way you would expect, and notice that they are all *binary* operators. However, the divide operation is slightly idiosyncratic, so let's examine that in a little more detail. Since integer operations always produce an integer result, an expression such as **11/4** does not result in a value of 2.75. Instead, it produces 2. 'Integer division' returns the number of times that the denominator divides into the numerator. Any remainder is simply discarded.

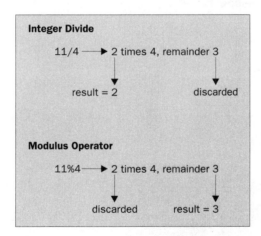

The modulus operator, **%**, complements the divide operator in that it provides a means for you to obtain the remainder after integer division if you need it. The expression **11%4** results in the value 3, which is the remainder after dividing 11 by 4. Let's see the arithmetic operators in action in an example.

Try It Out – Integer Arithmetic in Action

We can write a program to output the result of a miscellaneous collection of expressions involving integers to illustrate how the arithmetic operators work.

```
// Program 2.1 - Calculating with integer constants
#include <iostream>                      // For output to the screen
using namespace std;                     // Import the names from std

int main()
{
    cout << 10 + 20              << endl;  // Output is  30
    cout << 10 - 5               << endl;  // Output is   5
    cout << 10 - 20              << endl;  // Output is -10

    cout << 10 * 20              << endl;  // Output is 200
    cout << 10 / 3               << endl;  // Output is   3, remainder is lost
    cout << 10 % 3               << endl;  // Output is   1, the remainder

    cout << 10 + 20 / 10 - 5     << endl;  // Output is   7
    cout << (10 + 20) / (10 - 5) << endl;  // Output is   6
    cout << 10 + 20 / (10 - 5)   << endl;  // Output is  14
    cout << (10 + 20) / 10 - 5   << endl;  // Output is  -2

    cout << 4 * 5 / 3 % 4 + 7 / 3 << endl; // Output is   4
    return 0;                              // End the program
}
```

The output from this example is:

```
30
5
-10
200
3
1
7
6
14
-2
4
```

It doesn't look particularly elegant with that 'ragged right' arrangement, does it? This is a consequence of the way that integers are output by default. Very shortly, we will come back to find out how we can make it look prettier. First though, let's look at the interesting parts of this example.

How It Works

Each statement evaluates an arithmetic expression and outputs the result to the screen, followed by a newline character that moves the cursor to the beginning of the next line. All the arithmetic expressions here are **constant expressions**, since their values can be completely determined by the compiler before the program executes.

The first six statements are straightforward, and the reasons why they produce the results they do should be obvious to you:

```
cout << 10 + 20      << endl;  // Output is  30
cout << 10 - 5       << endl;  // Output is   5
cout << 10 - 20      << endl;  // Output is -10

cout << 10 * 20      << endl;  // Output is 200
cout << 10 / 3       << endl;  // Output is   3, remainder is lost
cout << 10 % 3       << endl;  // Output is   1, the remainder
```

Only the last two lines deserve further comment. Since integer operations produce integer results, the expression **10/3** results in 3, as 3 divides into 10 three times. The remainder, 1, that is left after dividing by 3 is discarded. The last line demonstrates that the **%** operator gives us the remainder after division, so we can always find out what it is when we need to.

The next four statements show the effects of using parentheses:

```
cout << 10 + 20 / 10 - 5    << endl;  // Output is   7
cout << (10 + 20) / (10 - 5) << endl;  // Output is   6
cout << 10 + 20 / (10 - 5)  << endl;  // Output is  14
cout << (10 + 20) / 10 - 5  << endl;  // Output is  -2
```

The parentheses override the 'natural order' of execution of the operators in the expressions. The expressions within parentheses are always evaluated first, starting with the innermost pair if they are nested, and working through to the outermost.

In an expression involving several different operators, the order in which the operators are executed is determined by giving some operators priority over others. The priority assigned to an operator is called its **precedence**. With the operators for integer arithmetic that we have seen, the operators *****, **/**, and **%** form a group that takes priority over the operators **+** and **-**, which form another group. You would say that each of the operators *****, **/**, and **%** has a **higher precedence** than **+** and **-**. Operators within a given group — **+** and **-**, for example — have equal precedence. The last output statement in the example illustrates how precedence determines the order in which the operators are executed:

```
cout << 4 * 5 / 3 % 4 + 7 / 3 << endl;  // Output is   4
```

The **+** operator is of lower precedence than any of the others, so the addition will be performed last. This means that values for the two sub-expressions, **4*5/3%4** and **7/3**, will be calculated first. The operators in the sub-expression **4*5/3%4** are all of equal precedence, so the sequence in which these will be executed is determined by their **associativity**. The associativity of a group of operators can be either **left** or **right**. An operator that is *left* associative binds first to the operand on the left of the operator, so a sequence of such operators in an expression will be executed from left to right. Let's illustrate this using our example.

In the expression **4*5/3%4**, each of the operators is left associative, which means that the left operand of each operator is whatever is to its left. Thus, the left operand for the multiply is **4**, the left operand for the divide is **4*5**, and the left operand for the modulus operation is **4*5/3**. The expression is therefore evaluated as **((4*5)/3)%4** — which, as we said, is left to right.

The associativity of the operators in an expression determines the sequence of execution of operators from the same group. It does not say anything about the operands. For example, in our expression **4*5/3%4+7/3**, it is not defined whether the sub-expression **4*5/3%4** is evaluated before **7/3**, or vice versa. It could be either, depending on what your compiler decides. Your reaction to this might be, "Who cares?" since it makes no difference to the result. Here, that's true: which of the operands for the addition is evaluated first is not important, but there are circumstances where it *can* make a difference, and we'll be seeing some of them as we progress.

Nearly all operator groups are left associative in C++, so most expressions involving operators of equal precedence are evaluated from left to right. The only right associative operators are the unary operators, which we have already touched upon, and assignment operators, which you will meet later on.

We can put the precedence and associativity of the integer arithmetic operators into a little table that will indicate the order of execution in an arithmetic expression:

Operators	Associativity
unary **+ −**	right
* / %	left
+ −	left

Each line in the table is a group of operators of equal precedence. The groups are in sequence, with the highest precedence operators in the top line and the lowest precedence at the bottom. As it only contains three lines, this table is rather simplistic, but we will accumulate many more operators and add further lines to this table as we learn more about C++. If you want to see the precedence table for all the operators in C++, you will find it in Appendix D.

Fixing the Appearance of the Output

Although it may not appear so, the output from our example is right justified. The 'ragged right' appearance is due to the fact that the output for each integer is in a **field width** that's exactly the correct number of characters to accommodate the value. We can set the field width for each data item to a value of our choice, as follows:

```
// Program 2.1A - Producing neat output
#include <iostream>                               // For output to the screen
#include <iomanip>                                // For manipulators
using namespace std;                              // Import the names from std

int main()
{
  cout << setw(10) << 10 + 20           << endl;  // Output is   30
  cout << setw(10) << 10 - 5            << endl;  // Output is    5
  cout << setw(10) << 10 - 20           << endl;  // Output is  -10

  cout << setw(10) << 10 * 20           << endl;  // Output is  200
  cout << setw(10) << 10 / 3            << endl;  // Output is    3
  cout << setw(10) << 10 % 3            << endl;  // Output is    1
  cout << setw(10) << 10 + 20 / 10 - 5  << endl;  // Output is    7
  cout << setw(10) << (10 + 20) / (10 - 5) << endl;  // Output is    6
```

```
    cout << setw(10) << 10 + 20 / (10 - 5)    << endl;  // Output is   14
    cout << setw(10) << (10 + 20) / 10 - 5    << endl;  // Output is - 2
    cout << setw(10) << 4 * 5 / 3 % 4 + 7 / 3 << endl;  // Output is    4
    return 0;                                           // End the program
}
```

Now the output looks like this:

```
        30
         5
       -10
       200
         3
         1
         7
         6
        14
        -2
         4
```

How It Works

That's much nicer, isn't it? The tidy formatting is accomplished by the changes to the output statements. Each value to be displayed is preceded in the output by **setw(10)**, as in the first statement:

```
    cout << setw(10) << 10 + 20              << endl;  // Output is   30
```

setw() is called a **manipulator** because it enables you to manipulate, or control, the appearance of the output. A manipulator doesn't output anything; it just modifies the output process. Its effect is to **set** the field width for the next value to be output to the number of characters that you specify between the parentheses, which is 10 in this case. The additional **#include** statement for the standard header file **iomanip** is necessary to make the **setw()** manipulator available in your program. There are other manipulators that we will try out in other examples as we go along. Meanwhile, you can try out this example with different field widths to see their effect.

Using Variables

Calculating with integer constants is all very well, but you were undoubtedly expecting a bit more sophistication in your C++ programs than that. To do more, we need to be able to store data items in a program, and this facility is provided by variables. A **variable** is an area in memory that's identified by a name that you supply, and which you can use to store an item of data of a particular type. Specifying a variable therefore requires two things: you must give it a name, and you must identify what kind of data you propose to store. First of all, let's consider what options we have for defining variable names.

Variable Names

The name you give to a variable can consist of any combination of upper or lower case letters, underscores, and the digits 0 to 9, but it must *begin* with a letter or an underscore. As I said in Chapter 1, the ANSI standard says that a variable name can also include UCS characters, but I recommend that you don't do this unless it is absolutely necessary, as most compilers do not support this capability. We saw some examples of valid variable names in Chapter 1, but here are a few more:

value   monthlySalary   Eight_Ball   FIXED_VALUE   JimBob

A variable name cannot begin with a digit, so names such as **8ball** and **7UP** are not valid. Also, C++ is a **case sensitive** language, which means that **republican** and **Republican** are different names. You should not use variable names that begin with an underscore followed by a capital letter, or which contain two successive underscores, as names of this form are reserved for use within the libraries.

Generally, your variables' names should be indicative of the kind of data that they hold. For instance, a name like **shoe_size** is going to mean a whole lot more than **ss** — always assuming you are dealing with shoe sizes, of course. You will find that you often want to use names that combine two or more words to make your program more understandable. One common approach for doing this uses the underscore character between words, for example:

line_count   pay_rise   current_debt

A convention that is frequently adopted in C++ is to reserve names that begin with a capital letter for naming **classes**, which are user-defined types. We will see how to define our own data types in Chapter 11. With this approach, **Point**, **Person**, and **Program** are all immediately recognizable as user-defined types. Of course, you are free to assign any names that you want (as long as they are not keywords), but if you choose names that are meaningful and name your variables in a consistent manner, it will make your programs more readable and less error prone. A list of all the C++ keywords can be found in Appendix B.

Integer Variables

Suppose we want to use a variable to record how many apples we have. We can create a variable, **apples**, with a **declaration statement** for the variable.

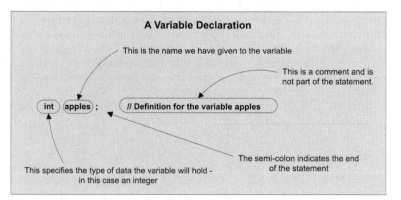

A Variable Declaration

This is the name we have given to the variable

This is a comment and is not part of the statement.

int apples ;   // Definition for the variable apples

The semi-colon indicates the end of the statement

This specifies the type of data the variable will hold - in this case an integer

This statement is called a **declaration** because it declares the name **apples**. *Any* statement that introduces a name into your program is a declaration for that name. The statement in the illustration is also called a **definition**, because it causes memory to be allocated for the variable **apples**. Later, we will meet statements that *are* declarations, but are *not* definitions. A variable is created by its definition, so you can only refer to it after the definition statement. If you attempt to refer to a variable prior to its definition, you will get an error message from the compiler.

When we define a variable, we can also specify an initial value. For example:

```
int apples = 10;                    // Definition for the variable apples
```

This defines the variable called **apples** and sets its initial value as 10. The definition in the diagram had no initial value specified, so the memory assigned to the variable would contain whatever junk value was left over from previous use of the memory. Having junk values floating around in your program is a bad idea, so we can identify our first golden rule:

> *Always initialize your variables when you define them. If you don't know what value a variable should have when you define it, initialize it to zero.*

Let's try out some integer variables in a little program.

Try It Out – Using Integer Variables

Here's a program that figures out how our apples can be divided equally amongst a group of children:

```cpp
// Program 2.2 - Working with integer variables

#include <iostream>              // For output to the screen
using namespace std;

int main()
{
  int apples = 10;              // Definition for the variable apples
  int children = 3;            // Definition for the variable children

  // Calculate fruit per child
  cout << endl                 // Start on a new line
      << "Each child gets "    // Output some text
      << apples / children     // Output number of apples per child
      << " fruit.";            // Output some more text

  // Calculate number left over
  cout << endl                 // Start on a new line
      << "We have "            // Output some text
      << apples % children     // Output apples left over
      << " left over.";        // Output some more text

  cout << endl;
  return 0;                     // End the program
}
```

45

I have been very verbose with the comments here, just to make it clear what is going on. You would not normally put such self-evident information in the comments. This program produces the output:

```
Each child gets 3 fruit.
We have 1 left over.
```

How It Works

This example is unlikely to overtax your brain cells. The first two statements in **main()** define the variables **apples** and **children**:

```
int apples = 10;              // Definition for the variable apples
int children = 3;             // Definition for the variable children
```

The variable **apples** is initialized to 10, and **children** is initialized to 3. Had we wanted, we could have defined both variables in a single statement. For example:

```
int apples = 10, children = 3;
```

This statement declares both **apples** and **children** to be of type **int**, and initializes them as before. A comma is used to separate the variables that we are declaring, and the whole thing ends with a semicolon. Of course, it is not so easy to add explanatory comments here as there is less space, but we could split the statement over two lines:

```
int apples = 10,              // Definition for the variable apples
    children = 3;             // Definition for the variable children
```

A comma still separates the two variables, and now we have space for the comments at the end of each line. You can declare as many variables as you want in a single statement, and you can spread the statement over as many lines as you see fit. However, it's considered good style to stick to one declaration per statement.

The next statement calculates how many apples each child gets when they are divided up:

```
cout << endl                  // Start on a new line
    << "Each child gets "     // Output some text
    << apples / children      // Output number of apples per child
    << " fruit.";             // Output some more text
```

Notice that the four lines here make up a single statement, and that we have put comments on each line that are therefore effectively in the middle of the statement. The arithmetic expression uses the divide operator to obtain the number of apples that each child gets. This expression just involves the two variables that we have defined, but in general you can mix variables and literals in an expression in any way that you want.

The next statement outputs the number of apples left over:

```
cout << endl                  // Start on a new line
    << "We have "             // Output some text
    << apples % children      // Output apples left over
    << " left over.";         // Output some more text
```

Here, we use the modulus operator to calculate the remainder, and the result is output between the text strings in a single output statement. If we wanted, we could have generated all of the output with a single statement. Alternatively, we could equally well have output each string and data value in a separate statement.

In this example, we used the **int** type for our variables, but there are other kinds of integer variables.

Integer Variable Types

The type of an integer variable will determine how much memory is allocated for it, and consequently the maximum and minimum value that you can store in it. There are four basic types of integer variables:

Type Name	Typical Memory per Variable
char	1 byte
short	2 bytes
int	4 bytes
long	4 or 8 bytes

char might seem an odd name for an integer type, but as we will see later, its primary use is to store a character. The types **short** and **long** can also be written as **short int** and **long int** respectively, but these forms are not used very often.

You have already seen how to declare a variable of type **int**, and you declare variables of type **short** and type **long** in exactly the same way. For example, you could define and initialize a variable called **bean_count**, of type **short**, with the statement:

```
short bean_count = 5;
```

As I said, you could also write this as:

```
short int bean_count = 5;
```

Similarly, you can declare a variable of type **long** with the statement:

```
long earth_diameter = 12756000L;    // Equatorial diameter of the earth in meters
```

Notice that I have appended an **L** to the initializing value, which indicates that it's of type **long**. If you don't put the **L** here, it won't cause a problem, but it's a good idea to make the types of your initializing values consistent with the types of your variables.

Variables of type **short**, type **int**, and type **long**, can store negative as well as positive values, so you can *also* write them as **signed short**, **signed int** and **signed long**. You can even use just the keyword **signed** by itself as a type — it means **signed int**. However, I don't recommend that you do this, as it does not help the readability of your program; and anyway, **int** is fewer characters to type!

An integer variable that's **signed** can store both negative and positive integers. An **unsigned** integer variable can only store positive values, and you'll doubtless be astonished to learn that three such types are **unsigned short**, **unsigned int**, and **unsigned long**. These types are typically used to store values that are viewed as bit patterns rather than numbers. We will see more about this in Chapter 3, when we look at the bitwise operators that you use to manipulate individual bits in a variable.

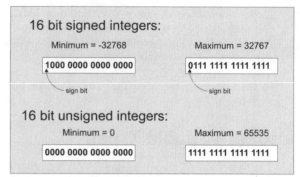

The diagram illustrates the difference between 16-bit signed and unsigned integers. As we've seen, with signed integers, the leftmost bit indicates the sign of the number. It will be 0 for a positive value and 1 for a negative value. For unsigned integers, *all* the bits can be treated as data bits. Since an unsigned number is always regarded as positive, there is no sign bit — the leftmost bit is just part of the number.

If you think that the binary value for -32768 looks strange, remember that negative values are normally represented in 2's complement form. As we saw earlier, to convert a positive binary value to a negative binary value (or vice versa) in 2's complement form, you just flip all the bits, and then add 1. Of course, you cannot represent +32768 as a 16-bit signed integer, as the available range only runs from -32768 to +32767.

Type **char** may actually be signed or unsigned, depending on how your compiler chooses to implement it. If you want a single byte to store integer values, you should explicitly declare the variable either as type **signed char** or **unsigned char**. Note that although type **char** will be equivalent to either **signed char** or **unsigned char**, all three are considered to be different types. Of course, the words **char**, **short**, **int**, **long**, **signed**, and **unsigned** are all keywords.

Integers in Memory

The basic unit of memory in C++ is a byte. As far as C++ is concerned, a byte has sufficient bits to contain any character in the basic character set used by your C++ compiler, but is otherwise undefined. This provides for the possibility that a C++ compiler could use something other than 8-bit ASCII to represent its basic character set, but you will almost always be safe in assuming that a character is 8 bits.

The memory allocated for each type of integer variable is not stipulated exactly within the ANSI C++ standard. What *is* said on the topic is the following:

> A variable of type **char** occupies one byte.

> A value of type **int** will occupy the number of bytes that is natural for the hardware environment in which the program is being compiled.

> The **signed** and **unsigned** versions of a type will occupy the same amount of memory.

> A value of type **short** will occupy at least as many bytes as type **char**; a value of type **int** will occupy at least as many bytes as type **short**; and a value of type **long** will occupy at least as many bytes as type **int**.

In a sentence, type **char** is the smallest with one byte, and type **long** is the largest. Type **int** is somewhere between the two, but occupies the number of bytes best suited to your computer's integer arithmetic capability. The reason for this vagueness is that the number of bytes used for type **int** on any given computer should correspond to that which results in the most efficient integer arithmetic. The actual number of bytes allocated to each integer type by your compiler will determine the range of values that can be stored. Here are the ranges for some typical sizes of integer variables:

Type	Size (bytes)	Range of Values
char	1	**-128** to **127**
unsigned char	1	**0U** to **255U**
short	2	**-32768** to **32767**
unsigned short	2	**0U** to **65535U**
int	4	**-2147483648** to **2147483647**
unsigned int	4	**0U** to **4294967295U**
long	8	**-9223372036854775808L** to **9223372036854775807L**
unsigned long	8	**0** to **18446744073609551615UL**

The **U** at the end of the integers for the unsigned types designates that these literals are unsigned. Without the **U**, the literals define signed integers. You can also use a lower case **u** to designate that your integer is unsigned, if you prefer.

In the same vein, notice that I've again placed an **L** at the end of the values for the ranges of the 8-byte integers. This indicates an integer of type **long**. Any integer with an upper or lower case letter **L** appended will be stored as type **long**. If you specify a decimal integer without a letter **L** appended, it will be stored as type **int** — unless it falls outside the range of type **int**, in which case it will be stored as type **long**. If it is outside the range of type **long**, you should get an error message from the compiler.

Remember that the range of values applicable for each integer type is dependent on your compiler. The table shows 'typical' values, but your compiler may well allocate different amounts of memory.

The Assignment Operator

We can store the result of a calculation in a variable using the **assignment operator =**. Let's look at an example. Suppose we declare three variables with the statements:

```
int total_fruit = 0;
int apples = 10;
int oranges = 6;
```

We can calculate the total number of fruit with the statement:

```
total_fruit = apples + oranges;
```

This statement will first calculate the value on the right hand side of the **=**, the sum of **apples** and **oranges**, and then store the result in the **total_fruit** variable that appears on the left hand side of the **=**.

It goes almost without saying that the expression on the right hand side of an assignment can be as complicated as you need. If we have defined variables called **boys** and **girls**, we can calculate how many of the fruit each child will receive if we divide the total equally between them with the statement:

```
int fruit_per_child = 0;
fruit_per_child = (apples + oranges) / (boys + girls);
```

Note that we could equally well have declared the variable **fruit_per_child** and initialized it with the result of the expression directly:

```
int fruit_per_child = (apples + oranges) / (boys + girls);
```

You can initialize a variable with *any* expression, as long as all the variables involved are defined.

Try It Out – Using the Assignment Operator

We can package some of the code fragments above into an executable program, just to see them in action:

```
// Program 2.3 - Using the assignment operator

#include <iostream>                      // For output to the screen
using namespace std;

int main()
{
  int apples = 10;
  int oranges = 6;
  int boys = 3;
  int girls = 4;

  int fruit_per_child = (apples + oranges) / (boys + girls);

  cout << endl
      << "Each child gets "
      << fruit_per_child << " fruit.";

  cout << endl;
  return 0;
}
```

This produces the output:

```
Each child gets 2 fruit.
```

This is exactly what we would expect from the preceding discussion.

Multiple Assignments

You can also perform multiple assignments in a single statement. For example, the following code sets the contents of **apples** and **oranges** to the same value:

```
apples = oranges = 10;
```

The assignment operator is right associative, so this statement executes by first storing the value 10 in **oranges**, and then storing the value in **oranges** in **apples**, so it is effectively:

```
apples = (oranges = 10);
```

This implies that the expression **(oranges = 10)** has a value — namely, the value stored in **oranges**, which is 10. This is not merely a curiosity. Occasions will arise where it is convenient to assign a value to a variable within an expression, and then to use that value for some other purpose. You can write statements such as:

```
fruit = (oranges = 10) + (apples = 11);
```

This will store 10 in **oranges**, 11 in **apples**, then add the two together and store the result in **fruit**. It illustrates that an assignment expression has a value. However, although you *can* write statements like this, I don't recommend it. As a rule, you should limit the number of operations per statement. Assume that another programmer will want one day to develop your code; as such, it's your job to promote clarity and avoid ambiguity.

Modifying the Value of a Variable

Because the assignment operation first evaluates the right hand side and then stores the result in the variable on the left, we can write a statement like this one:

```
apples = apples * 2;
```

This calculates the value of the right hand side, **apples * 2**, and then stores the result back in the **apples** variable. The effect of the statement is therefore to double the value contained in **apples**.

The need to operate on the existing value of a variable comes up very frequently. So much so, in fact, that C++ has a special form of the assignment operator to provide a shorthand way of expressing this.

The op= Assignment Operators

The **op**= assignment operators are so called because they are composed of an operator and an 'equals' sign. Using one such operator, the statement above for doubling the value of **apples** could be written as:

```
apples *= 2;
```

This is exactly the same operation as the statement in the last section. The **apples** variable is multiplied by the value of the expression on the right hand side, and the result is stored back in **apples**. The right hand side can be any expression you like. For instance, you could write:

```
    apples *= oranges + 2;
```

This is equivalent to:

```
    apples = apples * (oranges + 2);
```

Here, the value stored in **apples** is multiplied by the number of **oranges** plus 2, and the result stored back in **apples** (though quite why you would want to multiply apples and oranges together is beyond me!).

The **op=** form of assignment also works with the addition operator, so to increase the number of **oranges** by 2, you could write:

```
    oranges += 2;
```

This is the same as the statement:

```
    oranges = oranges + 2;
```

You should be able to see a pattern emerging by now. You could write the general form of an assignment statement using the **op=** operator as:

lhs op= rhs;

Here, **lhs** is a variable and **rhs** is an expression. This is equivalent to the statement:

lhs = lhs op (rhs);

> *lhs is an lvalue, which is an entity to which you can assign a value. Lvalues are so called because of their ability to appear on the left hand side of an assignment.*

You can use a whole range of operators in the **op=** form of assignment. Here is the complete set, including some operators you will meet in the next chapter:

add	+	bitwise AND	&
subtract	–	bitwise OR	|
multiply	*	bitwise exclusive OR	^
divide	/	shift left	<<
modulus	%	shift right	>>

Note that there can be no spaces between the operator and the **=**. If you include a space, it will be flagged as an error.

Incrementing and Decrementing Integers

You have seen how we can modify a variable using the assignment operator, and how we can increment one with the **+=** operator. I'm sure you've also deduced that we could decrement a variable with **-=** as well. However, there are two other rather unusual arithmetic operators that can perform the same tasks. They are called the **increment** and **decrement operators**, **++** and **--** respectively.

These operators are more than just another option, and we will find them to be quite an asset once we get further into applying C++ in earnest. The increment and decrement operators are unary operators that can be applied to an integer variable. For example, assuming the variables are of type **int**, the following three statements all have exactly the same effect:

```
count = count + 1;
count += 1;
++count;
```

They each increment the variable **count** by 1. The last form, using the increment operator, is clearly the most concise. The action of this operator is different from the other operators that we have seen, in that it *directly* modifies the value of its operand. The effect in an expression is to increment the value of the variable, and then to use that incremented value in the expression. For example, if **count** has the value 5, this statement

```
total = ++count + 6;
```

results in **count** having the value 6, and the variable **total** being assigned the value 12. You use the decrement operator in the same way:

```
total = --count + 6;
```

Assuming **count** is 6 before executing this statement, the decrement operator will reduce it to 5, and this value will be used to calculate the value to be stored in **total**, which will be 11.

So far, we have written the operators in front of the variables to which they apply. This is called the **prefix** form. The operators can also be written *after* the variables to which they apply; this is the **postfix** form, and the effect is slightly different. When you use the postfix form of **++**, the variable to which it applies is incremented *after* its value is used in context. For example, we can rewrite our earlier example as:

```
total = count++ + 6;
```

With the same initial value of 5 for **count**, **total** is assigned the value 11, since the *initial* value of **count** is used to evaluate the expression, before the increment by 1 is applied. The variable **count** will then be incremented to 6. The statement above is equivalent to the two statements:

```
total = count + 6;
++count;
```

Generally, it isn't a good idea to use the increment operator in the way that we have done here. In an expression like **a++ + b**, or even **a+++b**, it is less than obvious what is meant, or indeed what the compiler will do. These two expressions are actually the same, but in the second case you might really have meant **a + ++b**, which has a different meaning — it evaluates to one more than the other two expressions. It would be clearer to write:

```
total = 6 + count++;
```

Alternatively, you can use parentheses:

```
total = (count++) + 6;
```

The rules that we have discussed in relation to the increment operator also apply to the decrement operator. For example, if **count** has the initial value 5, the statement

```
total = --count + 6;
```

results in **total** having the value 10 assigned, whereas if we write the statement:

```
total = 6 + count-- ;
```

the value of **total** is set to 11.

One situation you must avoid is applying the prefix form of these operators more than once in the same expression. Suppose the variable **count** has the value 5, and you write:

```
total = ++count * 3 + ++count * 5;
```

First of all, it looks rather untidy. But second, and crucially, the order of evaluation of the operands to the **+** operator is *undefined* in C++. This means that the result, which depends on which of the operands for the addition is evaluated first, may vary from one compiler to the next. If the left operand is evaluated first, we get **6*3 + 7*5**, so **total** will be 53. However, if the right operand is evaluated first, we get **7*3 + 6*5**, and **total** will have the value 51. This is not a desirable feature in a program, to say the least, so don't modify a variable more than once in a statement.

The increment and decrement operators are usually applied to integers, particularly in the context of **loops**, as we shall see in Chapter 5. We will see in later chapters that they can be applied to certain other data types in C++ as well, with rather specialized (but very useful) effects.

The const Keyword

You will often feel the need to use literals of one kind or another in your programs: the number of days in January, perhaps, or π, the ratio of the circumference of a circle to its diameter. However, you should avoid using numeric literals explicitly within calculations; it is much better to use a variable that you have initialized to the appropriate value instead. For example, multiplying a value by 3 does not necessarily communicate that you are converting from yards to feet, but multiplying by a variable with the name **feet_per_yard** that you have initialized to the value 3 makes it absolutely clear what you're doing. Explicit numeric literals in a program are sometimes referred to as **magic numbers**, particularly when their purpose and origin is less than obvious.

Another good reason for using a variable instead of a magic number is that you reduce the number of maintenance points in your code. Imagine that your magic number represents something that changes from time to time — an interest rate, for instance — and that it crops up on several occasions in your code. When the rate changes, you could be faced with a sizable task to correct your program. If you've defined a variable for the purpose, you only need to change the value once, at the point of initialization.

Of course, if you use a variable to hold a constant of this kind, you really want to nail the value down and prevent any accidental modifications. You can use the keyword **const** to do this. For example:

```
    const int feet_per_yard = 3;          // Conversion factor yards to feet
```

You can define any kind of 'variable' as **const**, and the compiler will check that you do not attempt to alter the value of such a variable. For example, if you put something **const** on the left of an assignment operator, it will be flagged as an error. The obvious consequence of this is that you must always supply an initial value for a variable that you declare as **const**.

Be aware that declaring a variable as **const** alters its type. A variable of type **const int** is quite different from a variable of type **int**.

Try It Out – Using const

We could implement a little program to convert into inches a length expressed as yards, feet, and inches.

```
// Program 2.4 - Using const

#include <iostream>                       // For output to the screen
using namespace std;

int main()
{
  const int inches_per_foot = 12;
  const int feet_per_yard = 3;
  int yards = 0;
  int feet = 0;
  int inches = 0;

  // Read the length from the keyboard
  cout << "Enter a length as yards, feet, and inches: ";
  cin >> yards >> feet >> inches;

  // Output the length in inches
  cout << endl
       << "Length in inches is "
       << inches + inches_per_foot * (feet + feet_per_yard * yards)
       << endl;
  return 0;
}
```

A typical result is:

```
Enter a length as yards, feet, and inches: 2 2 11

Length in inches is 107
```

How It Works

We have two conversion constants defined by the statements:

```
const int inches_per_foot = 12;
const int feet_per_yard = 3;
```

Declaring them with the keyword **const** will prevent direct modification of these variables. You could test this by adding a statement such as:

```
inches_per_foot = 15;
```

With a statement like this after the declaration of the constant, the program would no longer compile.

We prompt for input and read the values for **yards**, **feet**, and **inches** with these statements:

```
cout << "Enter a length as yards, feet, and inches: ";
cin >> yards >> feet >> inches;
```

Notice how the second line specifies several successive input operations using **cin**, using the extraction operator I mentioned briefly in the last chapter. It's analogous to using **cout**, the stream output operation, for multiple values. The first value entered will be stored in **yards**, the second in **feet**, and the third in **inches**. The input handling here is very flexible: you can enter all three values on one line, separated by spaces (in fact, by any whitespace characters), or you can enter them on several lines.

We perform the conversion to inches within the output statement itself:

```
cout << endl
     << "Length in inches is "
     << inches + inches_per_foot * (feet + feet_per_yard * yards)
     << endl;
```

As you can see, the fact that our conversion factors were declared as **const** in no way affects their use in expressions, just as long as we don't try to modify them.

Floating Point Values

Numerical values that are not integers are stored as **floating point** numbers. Internally, floating point numbers have three parts: a sign (positive or negative), a mantissa (which is a value greater than or equal to 1 and less than 2 that has a fixed number of digits), and an exponent. Inside your computer, of course, both the mantissa and the exponent are binary values, but for the purposes of explaining how floating point numbers work, we will talk about them as decimal values.

The value of a floating point number is the signed value of the mantissa, multiplied by 10 to the power of the exponent.

Mantissa	Exponent	Value
1.2345	3	1.2345×10^3 (which is 1234.5)

You can write a floating point literal in three basic forms:

▶ As a decimal value including a decimal point, for example 110.0.

▶ With an exponent, for example 11E1, where the decimal part is multiplied by the power of 10 specified after the E (for exponent). You have the option of using either an upper or a lower case letter E to precede the exponent.

▶ Using both a decimal point and an exponent, for example 1.1E2.

All three examples above correspond to the same value — 110.0 — and will be stored internally as the equivalent of 0.11E3. Note that spaces are not allowed within floating point literals, so you must not write 1.1 E2, for example. The latter would be interpreted as two separate values, 1.1 and E2 (which is 100.0).

> *A floating point literal must contain a decimal point, or an exponent, or both. If you write a numeric literal with neither, then you have an integer.*

Floating Point Data Types

There are three floating point data types that you can use. They are:

float	Single precision floating point values
double	Double precision floating point values
long double	Extended precision floating point values

The term **precision** here refers to the number of significant digits in the mantissa. The data types are in order of increasing precision, with **float** providing the lowest number of digits in the mantissa, and **long double** the highest. Note that the precision only determines the number of digits in the *mantissa*. The range of numbers that can be represented by a particular type is determined primarily by the range of possible exponents.

The precision and range of values are not prescribed by the ANSI standard for C++, so what you get with each of these types depends on your compiler, which will usually make the best of the floating point facilities provided by your computer. Generally, type **long double** will provide a precision that is greater than or equal to that of type **double**, which in turn will provide a precision that is greater than or equal to that of type **float**.

Typically, you will find that type **float** will provide 7 digits precision, type **double** will provide 15 digits precision, and type **long double** may provide 19 digits precision, although

double and **long double** turn out to be the same on several compilers. As well as increased precision, you will usually get an increased range of values with types **double** and **long double**.

Typical ranges of values that you can represent with the floating point types on a PC are:

Type	Precision(Decimal digits)	Range(+ or -)
float	7	1.2×10^{-38} to 3.4×10^{38}
double	15	2.2×10^{-308} to 1.8×10^{308}

Clearly, zero can be represented exactly for each of these types, but values between zero and the lower limit in the positive or negative range cannot be represented, so these lower limits for the ranges are the smallest *non-zero* values that you can have.

By default, floating point literals are of type **double**, so let's look at how we define variables of that type first. You can specify a floating point variable using the keyword **double**, as in this statement:

```
double inches_to_mm = 25.4;
```

This declares the variable **inches_to_mm** to be of type **double**, and initializes it with the value 25.4. You can also use **const** when declaring floating point variables, and this is a case where you could sensibly do so. If you want to fix the value of the variable, the declaration statement might be:

```
const double inches_to_mm = 25.4;   // Define a constant conversion factor
```

If you don't need the precision and range of values provided by **double** variables, you can opt to use the keyword **float** to declare your floating point variable. For example:

```
float pi = 3.14159f;
```

This statement defines a variable **pi** with the initial value 3.14159. The **f** at the end of the literal specifies it to be a **float** type. Without the **f**, the literal would have been of type **double**, which would not cause a problem in this case, although you may get a warning message from your compiler. You can also use an upper case letter **F** to indicate that a floating point literal is of type **float**.

To specify a literal of type **long double**, you append an upper or lower case **L** to the number. You could therefore declare and initialize a variable of this type with the statement

```
long double root2 = 1.41421356237309504ƒ0488L;   // Square root of 2
```

Using floating point variables is quite straightforward, but there's no substitute for experience, so let's try an example.

Try It Out – Floating Point Arithmetic

Let's suppose that we want to construct a circular pond in which we want to keep 20 fish with an average length of 9 inches. Having looked into the matter, we know that we must allow two square feet of surface area on the pond for every 6 inches of fish. We need to figure out the diameter of the pond that will keep the fish happy. Here's how we can do it.

```
// Program 2.5 - Figuring for fish in floating point
#include <iostream>                   // For output to the screen
#include <cmath>                      // For square root calculation
using namespace std;

int main()
{
  double fish_count = 20.0;
  double ave_length = 9.0 / 12.0;          // Average length of fish in feet
  double pond_area = 0.0;
  double pond_diameter = 0.0;
  const double fish_factor = 2.0 / 0.5;  // Area per unit length of fish
  const double pi = 3.14159265;

  // Calculate the required surface area
  pond_area = fish_count * ave_length * fish_factor;

  // Calculate the pond diameter from the area
  pond_diameter = 2.0 * sqrt(pond_area / pi);

  cout << endl
       << "Pond diameter required is "
       << pond_diameter
       << " feet.";

  cout << endl;
  return 0;
}
```

This example produces the output:

```
Pond diameter required is 8.74039 feet
```

How It Works

We first declare six variables that we will use in the calculation:

```
double fish_count = 20.0;
double ave_length = 9.0 / 12.0;          // Average length of fish in feet
double pond_area = 0.0;
double pond_diameter = 0.0;
const double fish_factor = 2.0 / 0.5;  // Area per unit length of fish
const double pi = 3.14159265;
```

Notice the use of a constant expression to specify the value for **fish_factor**. You can use any expression that produces a result of the appropriate type to define an initializing value for a variable. We have declared **fish_factor** and **pi** as **const** because we do not want to allow them to be altered.

We get the required area for the pond with the following statement:

```
pond_area = fish_count * ave_length * fish_factor;
```

The product of **fish_count** and **ave_length** gives the total length of all the fish, and multiplying this by **fish_factor** gives the required area.

The area of any circle is given by the formula πr^2, where r is the radius. We can therefore calculate the radius of our pond as the square root of the area divided by π. The diameter is then twice the radius, and the whole calculation is carried out by this statement:

```
pond_diameter = 2.0 * sqrt(pond_area / pi);
```

We obtain the square root using a function that is declared in the standard header file **cmath**. The **sqrt()** function returns the square root of the value of the expression placed between the parentheses after the function name. In this case, the value returned is of type **double** because the value of the expression is of type **double**, but there is also a version that returns the square root of a **float** value as type **float**. The **cmath** header file contains declarations for many other standard library numerical functions, including trigonometric and hyperbolic functions, logarithms, exponentiation and power functions, and many others. We will look into functions in detail, including how we can define our own functions, in Chapter 8.

Working with Floating Point Values

For most computations using floating point values, you will find that type **double** is adequate. However, you need to be aware of the limitations and pitfalls of working with floating point variables. If you're not careful, your results may be inaccurate, or even incorrect. The following are common sources of errors when using floating point values:

▶ Some decimal values do not convert exactly to binary floating point values. The small errors that occur can easily be amplified in your calculations to produce large errors.

▶ Taking the difference between two nearly identical values can lose precision. If you take the difference between two values of type **float** that differ in the sixth significant digit, you will produce a result that may have only one or two digits of accuracy. The other significant digits that are stored may represent errors.

▶ Dealing with a wide range of possible values can lead to errors. You can create an elementary illustration of this by adding two values stored as type **float** with 7 digits of precision, but where one value is 10^8 times larger than the other. You can add the smaller value to the larger as many times as you like, and the larger value will be unchanged.

Let's see how these errors can manifest themselves in practice, albeit in a somewhat artificial situation.

Try It Out – Errors in Floating Point Calculations

Here's an example contrived to illustrate how the first two points can combine to produce errors:

```cpp
// Program 2.6 Floating point errors
#include <iostream>
using namespace std;

int main()
{
  float value1 = 0.1f;
  float value2 = 2.1f;
  value1 -= 0.09f;                 // Should be 0.01
  value2 -= 2.09f;                 // Should be 0.01
  cout << value1 - value2 << endl; // Should output zero
  return 0;
}
```

The value displayed should be zero, but on my computer this program produces:

```
7.45058e-009
```

How It Works

The reason for the error is that none of the numerical values is stored exactly. If you add code to output the values of **value1** and **value2** after they have been modified, you should see a discrepancy between them.

Of course, the final difference between the values of **value1** and **value2** is a very small number, but we could be using this totally spurious value in other calculations where the error could be amplified. If we multiply this result by 10^{10}, say, we'll get an answer around 7.45, when the result should really be zero.

> *Do not rely on an exact floating point representation of a decimal value.*

Tweaking the Output

This program output our floating point value in a very sensible fashion. It gave us 5 decimal places, and it used scientific notation (that is, a mantissa and an exponent). However, if we'd wanted, we could have chosen to have the output displayed using 'normal' decimal notation by employing some more output manipulators:

```cpp
// Program 2.6A Experimenting with floating point output
#include <iostream>
#include <iomanip>
using namespace std;

int main()
{
  float value1 = 0.1f;
  float value2 = 2.1f;
  value1 -= 0.09f;                 // Should be 0.01
  value2 -= 2.09f;                 // Should be 0.01
```

```
    cout << setprecision(14) << fixed;      // Change to fixed notation
    cout << value1 - value2 << endl;        // Should output zero

    cout << setprecision(5) << scientific;  // Return to scientific notation
    cout << value1 - value2 << endl;        // Should output zero

    return 0;
}
```

When I run the modified program, this is the output I get:

```
0.00000000745058
7.45058e-009
```

How It Works

This code uses three new modifiers: **setprecision()**, which specifies how many decimal places a floating point number should be output with, and **fixed** and **scientific**, which complement one another and choose the format in which a floating point number should be displayed.

By default, your C++ compiler will select either **scientific** or **fixed**, depending on the particular value you're outputting, and we saw in the first version of this program that it performed that task admirably. The default number of decimal places is not defined in the standard, but 5 is common.

Let's look at the changes we've made. Apart from the **#include** for **iomanip**, just as we needed when we were using **setw()** earlier in the chapter, the interest is in these four lines of code:

```
    cout << setprecision(14) << fixed;      // Change to fixed notation
    cout << value1 - value2 << endl;        // Should output zero

    cout << setprecision(5) << scientific;  // Return to scientific notation
    cout << value1 - value2 << endl;        // Should output zero
```

The first line is easy: we use the manipulators like we used **setw()**, by sending them to the output stream with the insertion operator. Their effects can then clearly be seen in the first line of output: we get a floating point value with 14 decimal places and no exponent.

However, these manipulators differ from **setw()** in that they're **modal**. In other words, they remain in effect until the end of the program, unless you say otherwise. That's the reason for the third line above — we now have to set scientific mode and a precision of 5 *explicitly* in order to return to 'default' behavior. You can see that we've succeeded, though, because the second line of output is the same as the one produced by the original program.

> *Actually, the* **iomanip** *header is only required here for the* **setprecision()** *manipulator.* **fixed** *and* **scientific** *both come from* **iostream***. There are more manipulators to discuss, but the rule is that the ones requiring values (like* **setw()** *and* **setprecision()***) are defined in* **iomanip***, while the others are defined in* **iostream***.*

Working with Characters

I mentioned in the context of the integer types that although variables of type **char** *can* store an integer value, they are not often used for this purpose. Their primary use is in storing single characters. You write a character literal as the character that you require, placed between single quotes. For example, **'z'**, **'3'**, and **'?'** are all character literals. We can define a variable of type **char** with the statement:

```
char letter = 'A';        // Stores a single letter - initial value 'A'
```

This defines the variable **letter** of type **char**, with an initial value **'A'**. If your compiler represents characters using ASCII codes, this will have the decimal value 65. Because you can treat variables of type **char** as integers, you could equally well declare and initialize **letter** with this statement:

```
char letter = 65;         // Stores a single letter - initial value 'A'
```

Of course, you can operate on **letter** as an integer, so you can write:

```
letter += 2;
```

This will result in the value stored in **letter** being incremented to 67, which is **'C'** in ASCII. You can find all the ASCII codes in Appendix A, at the back of this book.

FYI
Although we have assumed ASCII coding in our examples, you should know that it does not have to be so. On many mainframe computers in particular, characters are represented using EBCDIC (Extended Binary Coded Decimal Interchange Code), where the codes are different. The standard for C++ does not require that characters are stored as 8-bit bytes, although generally this will be the case.

You can specify a variable of type **char** using the modifiers **signed** or **unsigned**, which will affect the range of integers that can be represented. For example, we can declare a variable as:

```
unsigned char ch = 0U;
```

In this case, with a compiler implementing 8-bit characters, the numerical values can range from 0 to 255.

When you read from a stream into a variable of type **char**, the first non-whitespace character will be stored. This means that you cannot read whitespace characters in this way — they are simply ignored. Further, you cannot read a numerical value into a variable of type **char** — if you try, you'll find that the character code for the number will be stored. When you output a variable of type **char** to the screen, it will be as a character, not a numerical value. We can see this with an example.

Try It Out – Handling Character Values

This example will read a character from the keyboard, output the character and its numerical code, increment the value of the character, and output the result as a character and as an integer.

```
// Program 2.7 - Handling character values

#include <iostream>                    // For output to the screen
using namespace std;

int main()
{
  char ch = 0;
  int ch_value = 0;

  // Read a character from the keyboard
  cout << "Enter a character: ";
  cin >> ch;
  ch_value = ch;                   // Get integer value of character

  cout << endl
       << ch << " is " << ch_value;

  ch_value = ++ch;                      // Increment ch and store as integer
  cout << endl
       << ch << " is " << ch_value
       << endl;

  return 0;
}
```

Typical output from this example is:

```
Enter a character: w

w is 119
x is 120
```

How It Works

After prompting for input, the program reads a character from the keyboard with the statement:

```
cin >> ch;
```

Only non-whitespace characters are accepted, so you can press *Enter* or enter spaces and tabs and they will all be ignored.

Stream output will output the variable **ch** as a character. To get the numerical code, we need a way to convert it to an integer type. The next statement does this:

```
ch_value = ch;                     // Get integer value of character
```

The compiler will arrange to convert the value stored in **ch** from type **char** to type **int** so that it can be stored in the variable **ch_value**. We will see more about automatic conversions in the next chapter, when we discuss expressions involving values of different types.

Now we can output the character and its integer code with the statement:

```
cout << endl
    << ch << " is " << ch_value;
```

Next, we demonstrate that we can operate with variables of type **char** as integers:

```
ch_value = ++ch;                    // Increment ch and store as integer
```

This statement increments the contents of **ch** and stores the result in the variable **ch_value**, so we have both the next character and its numerical representation. This is output to the display with exactly the same statement as was used previously. Although we just incremented **ch** here, variables of type **char** can be used with all of the arithmetic operators, just like any of the integer types.

Extended Character Sets

Single byte character codes such as ASCII or EBCDIC are generally adequate for national language character sets using Latin characters. Of course, these character sets are mutually exclusive, so if you want to handle Greek, Cyrillic and Latin characters simultaneously, you need to work with a multibyte character set. The same applies if you want to handle character sets for Asian languages, such as Hiragana, Katakana and Kanji, which are used for Japanese.

To work with multibyte characters, you can use type **wchar_t**. The type name derives from **wide char**acters, because the character is 'wider' than the usual single byte character. The size of variables of type **wchar_t** is not stipulated by the C++ standard, and will be determined by your compiler. It is often two bytes, but it can also be 4 bytes in some compilers. Unicode is an example of a two byte character set, so it allows for the definition of up to 65,536 different character codes. There are Unicode characters defined for most of the world's national languages.

The Double Byte Character Set (DBCS) is another 2-byte set used for Asian character sets, notably Katakana. Another set still is the 4-byte Universal Character Set that we mentioned in Chapter 1. UCS will accommodate over four billion different characters, and is intended to accommodate all the symbols sets you might conceivably need, as well as all the national characters sets in use worldwide.

You can define wide-character literals by prefixing the literal with the letter L. For example:

```
wchar_t wide_letter = L'Z';
```

This defines the variable **wide_letter** to be of type **wchar_t**, and initializes it to the wide-character representation for Z. Your keyboard may not have keys for representing other national language characters, but you can still create them using hexadecimal notation. For example:

```
wchar_t wide_letter = L'\x0402';
```

The value between the single quotes is an **escape sequence** that allows us to specify a character by an octal or hexadecimal representation of the character code. The backslash indicates the start of the escape sequence, and the **x** after the backslash signifies that the code is hexadecimal. The absence of **x** or **X** would indicate that the characters that follow are to be interpreted as octal digits. If your compiler supports UCS characters, which are 4 byte characters, you could also initialize a variable of type **wchar_t** with a UCS character specified as **\uNNNNNNNN**, where **N** is a hexadecimal digit, or as **\uNNNN**, which is equivalent to **\u0000NNNN**.

Functional Notation for Initial Values

There is an alternative notation for specifying the initial value for a variable when you declare it, called **functional notation**. The term stems from the fact that you put the initial value between parentheses after the variable name, so it looks like a function call, as you'll discover later on.

Let's look at an example. Instead of writing a declaration as:

```
int unlucky = 13;
```

you have the option to write the statement as:

```
int unlucky(13);
```

Both statements achieve exactly the same result: they declare the variable **unlucky** as type **int**, and give it an initial value of 13.

You can initialize other types of variables using functional notation. For instance, you could declare and initialize a variable to store a character with this statement:

```
char letter('A');
```

However, functional notation for initializing variables is primarily used for the initialization of variables of a data type that you have defined. In this case, it really does involve calling a function. The initialization of variables of the fundamental types in C++ normally uses the approach we have taken up to now. You'll have to wait until Chapter 11 to find out about creating your own types and how those kinds of variables get initialized!

Summary

In this chapter, we have covered the basics of computation in C++. We have learnt about most of the elementary types of data that are provided for in the language, although we will learn about logical variables that can have the values **true** or **false** in the next chapter. The essentials of what we have discussed up to now are as follows:

> Numeric and character constants are called literals.

> You can define integer literals as decimal, hexadecimal or octal values.

> A floating point literal must contain a decimal point or an exponent or both.

> Named objects in C++, such as variables, can have names that consist of a sequence of letters and digits, the first of which is a letter, and where an underscore is considered to be a letter. Upper and lower case letters are distinct; hence variable names are case-sensitive.

> Names that begin with an underscore followed by a capital letter, and names that contain two successive underscores are reserved for use within the standard library, so they should not be used for names of your own variables.

> All literals and variables in C++ are of a given type.

> The basic types that can store integers are **short**, **int**, and **long**. They store signed integers by default, but you can also use the type modifier **unsigned** with any of these types.

> A variable of type **char** can store a single character. The type **char** may be signed or unsigned by default, depending on your compiler. You can also use variables of the types **signed char** and **unsigned char** to store integers.

> The floating point data types are **float**, **double**, and **long double**.

> The name and type of a variable appear in a declaration statement, ending with a semicolon. A declaration for a variable that results in memory being allocated is also a definition of the variable.

> Variables may be given initial values when they are declared, and it is good programming practice to do so.

> You can protect the value of a 'variable' of a basic type by using the modifier **const**. The compiler will check for any attempts within the program source file to modify a variable declared as **const**.

> An lvalue is an object or expression that can appear on the left-hand side of an assignment. Non-**const** variables are examples of lvalues.

Although we have discussed quite a few basic types in this chapter, don't be misled into thinking that's all there are. There are some other basic types, as well as more complex types based on the basic set, as we shall see, and eventually you will be creating original types of your own.

Exercises

Ex 2.1 Write a program that will compute the area of a circle. The program should prompt for the radius of the circle, calculate the area using the formula **area = pi * radius * radius**, and then display the result.

Ex 2.2 Using your solution for Exercise 2.1, improve the code so that the user can control the precision of the output. (Hint: use the **setprecision()** manipulator.)

Ex 2.3 Create a program that asks the user for three **double** floating point values. Using a single statement, square each value and add them together. Then, display the result. Try the calculation first using parentheses — this is good practice and makes code clearer for others to read. Then remove them — it should still work thanks to the relative precedence of the operators involved.

Ex 2.4 Create a program that converts inches to feet-and-inches — for example, an input of 77 inches should produce an output of 6 feet and 5 inches. Prompt the user to enter an integer value corresponding to the number of inches, and then make the conversion and output the result. (Hint: use a **const** to store the inches-to-feet conversion rate, and employ the modulus operator.)

More on Handling Basic Data Types

In this chapter, we will expand on the types that we discussed in the previous chapter and look at how variables of the basic types interact in more complicated situations. We will also introduce some new features of C++, and look at some of the ways that these are used.

In this chapter you will learn:

- How expressions involving mixed types of data are evaluated
- How you can convert a value from one basic type to another
- What the bitwise operators are, and how you can use them
- How you can define a new type that limits variables to a fixed range of possible values
- How you can define alternative names for existing data types
- What the storage duration of a variable is, and what determines it
- What variable scope is, and what its effects are

Mixed Expressions

You may be aware that your computer can only perform arithmetic operations on pairs of values of the same type. It can add two integers, and it can add two floating point values, but it cannot directly add an integer to a floating point value. The expression **2 + 7.5**, for example, cannot be evaluated as it stands.

The only way this calculation can be done is to convert one of the values into the same type as the other — typically, the integer value will be converted to its floating point equivalent, so the expression will be calculated as **2.0 + 7.5**. The same applies to mixed expressions in C++. Each binary operation requires both operands to be of the same type; if they are different, one of them must be converted to the type of the other. Consider the following sequence of statements:

```
int value1 = 10;
long value2 = 25L;
```

```
float value3 = 30.0f;
double result = value1 + value2 + value3;    // Mixed calculation
```

The value of **result** is calculated as the sum of three different types of variables. For each add operation, one of the operands will be converted to the type of the other before the addition can be carried out. The conversion to be applied, and which operand it applies to, is determined by a set of rules that are checked in sequence until one is found that applies to the operation to be carried out. The statement above is actually executed with the steps:

▶ **value1 + value2** is calculated by converting **value1** to type **long** before the addition. The result is also of type **long**, so the calculation is **10L + 25L = 35L**.

▶ The next operation is **35L + value3**. The previous result, **35L**, is converted to type **float** before it is added to **value3**. The result is of type **float**, so the operation will be **35.0f + 30.0f = 65.0f**.

▶ Finally, the previous result is converted to type **double** and stored in **result**.

The rules for dealing with mixed expressions only come into play when the types of the operands for a binary operator are different. These rules, in the sequence in which they are applied, are as follows:

1. If either operand is of type **long double**, the other is converted to **long double**.
2. If either operand is of type **double**, the other is converted to **double**.
3. If either operand is of type **float**, the other is converted to **float**.
4. Any operand of type **char**, **signed char**, **unsigned char**, **short**, or **unsigned short** is converted to type **int**, as long as type **int** can represent all the values of the original operand type. Otherwise, the operand is converted to type **unsigned int**.
5. An enumeration type is converted to the first of **int**, **unsigned int**, **long**, or **unsigned long** that accommodates the range of the enumerators.
6. If either operand is of type **unsigned long**, the other is converted to **unsigned long**.
7. If one operand is of type **long** and the other is of type **unsigned int**, then provided type **long** can represent all the values of an **unsigned int**, the **unsigned int** is converted to type **long**. Otherwise, both operands are converted to type **unsigned long**.
8. If either operand is of type **long**, the other is converted to type **long**.

You haven't seen enumeration types yet, but we will be looking at them little later in this chapter. They appear here so you have the complete set of rules. This all looks rather complicated, but it really isn't. Some of the apparent complexity arises because the range of values for integer types can be implementation dependent, so the rules need to accommodate that. The compiler checks the rules in sequence until it finds one that applies. If the operands are the same type after applying that rule, then the operation is carried out. If not, another rule is sought.

The basic idea is very simple. With two operands of different types, the type with the lesser range of values is converted to the other. The formal rules roughly boil down to:

1. If the operation involves two different floating point types, the one with the lesser precision will be promoted to the other.
2. If the operation involves an integer and a floating point value, the integer will be promoted to the floating point type.

3. If the operation involves mixed integer types, the type with the more limited range will be promoted to the other.
4. If the operation involves enumeration types, they will be converted to a suitable integer type.

The term **conversion** means an automatic conversion of one type to another. The term **promotion** generally means a conversion of a data value from a type with a lesser range to a type with a greater range. We will see shortly that you can convert explicitly from one data type to another. Such a conversion is referred to as a **cast**, and the action of explicitly converting a value to a different type is called **casting**.

Assignments and Different Types

If the type of an expression on the right of an assignment operator is different from that of the variable on the left, the result of evaluating the expression on the right hand side will automatically be converted to the type of the variable on the left before it is stored. In many cases, you can lose information in this way. For example, suppose we have a floating point value defined as:

```
double root = 1.732;
```

If we now write the statement:

```
int value = root;
```

The conversion of the value of **root** to **int** will result in **1** being stored in **value**. A variable of type **int** can only store a whole number, so the fractional part of the value stored in **root** is discarded in the conversion to type **int**. You can even lose information with an assignment between different types of integers:

```
long count = 60000;
short value = count;
```

If **short** is two bytes and **long** is four bytes, the former does not have the range to store the value of **count**, and an incorrect value will result.

Many compilers will detect these kinds of conversions and provide you with a warning message when they occur, but don't rely on this. To prevent these kinds of problems you should, as far as possible, avoid assigning a value of one type to a variable of a type with a lesser range of values. Where such an assignment is unavoidable, you can specify the conversion explicitly to demonstrate that it is no accident and that you really meant to do it. Let's see how that works.

Explicit Casts

With mixed expressions involving the basic types, your compiler automatically arranges casting where necessary, but you can also force a conversion from one type to another by using an **explicit cast**. To cast the value of an expression to a given type, you write the cast in the form:

static_cast<*the type to convert to*>(*expression*)

The keyword **static_cast** reflects the fact that the cast is checked statically — that is, when your program is compiled. Later, when we get to deal with classes, we will meet *dynamic* casts, where the conversion is checked dynamically — that is, when the program is executing. The effect of the cast is to convert the value that results from evaluating **expression** to the type that you specify between the angled brackets. The **expression** can be anything from a single variable to a complex expression involving lots of nested parentheses.

Here's a specific example of the use of **static_cast<>()**:

```
double value1 = 10.5;
double value2 = 15.5;
int whole_number = static_cast<int>(value1) + static_cast<int>(value2);
```

The initializing value for the variable **whole_number** is the sum of the integral parts of **value1** and **value2**, so they are each explicitly cast to type **int**. The variable **whole_number** will therefore have the initial value 25. The casts do *not* affect the values stored in **value1** and **value2**, which will remain as 10.5 and 15.5 respectively. The values 10 and 15 produced by the casts are just stored temporarily for use in the calculation, and then discarded. Although both casts cause a loss of information in the calculation, the compiler will always assume that you know what you are doing when you explicitly specify a cast.

In the situation we referred to earlier, relating to assignments with different types, you can always make it clear that you know the cast is necessary by making it explicit:

```
int value = static_cast<int>(root);
```

Generally, the need for explicit casts should be rare, particularly with basic types of data. If you have to include a lot of explicit casts in your code, it's often a sign that you could choose more suitable types for your variables. Still, there are circumstances when casting is necessary, so let's look at a simple example of this situation.

Try It Out – Explicit Casting

Suppose we need to be able to convert a length in yards (as a decimal value) to yards, feet and inches (as integer values). We can put together a program to do this:

```
// Program 3.1 Using Explicit Casts

#include <iostream>
using namespace std;

int main()
{
  const long feet_per_yard = 3;
  const long inches_per_foot = 12;

  double yards = 0.0;                     // Length as decimal yards
  long yds = 0;                           // Whole yards
  long ft = 0;                            // Whole feet
  long ins = 0;                           // Whole inches
```

```
        cout << "Enter a length in yards as a decimal: ";
        cin >> yards;

        // Get the length as yards, feet and inches
        yds = static_cast<long>(yards);
        ft = static_cast<long>((yards - yds) * feet_per_yard);
        ins = static_cast<long>(yards * feet_per_yard * inches_per_foot) %
                                                      inches_per_foot;


        cout << endl
             << yards << " yards converts to "
             << yds    << " yards "
             << ft     << " feet "
             << ins    << " inches.";

        cout << endl;
        return 0;
    }
```

Typical output from this program will be:

Enter a length in yards as a decimal: 2.75

2.75 yards converts to 2 yards 2 feet 3 inches.

How It Works

The first two statements in **main()** declare a couple of conversion constants that we will use:

```
    const long feet_per_yard = 3;
    const long inches_per_foot = 12;
```

We declare these variables as **const** to prevent them from being modified accidentally in the program, and use the type **long** to be consistent with the other values. Although the type **short** would have been adequate to store these values, using it may actually increase (rather than decrease) the size of your program in the long run. This is because of additional, implicit conversions that may be necessary when using them in expressions with other integer types.

The next four declarations define the variables we will use in the calculation:

```
    double yards = 0.0;                     // Length as decimal yards
    long yds = 0;                           // Whole yards
    long ft = 0;                            // Whole feet
    long ins = 0;                           // Whole inches
```

We prompt for the required input, and then read a value from the keyboard with these statements:

```
    cout << "Enter a length in yards as a decimal: ";
    cin >> yards;
```

The next statement computes the whole number of yards from the input value with an explicit cast:

```
yds = static_cast<long>(yards);
```

The cast to type **long** discards the fractional part and stores the integral result in **yds**. If you omit the explicit cast here, some compilers will compile the program without warning you that they have inserted the required cast. However, there is clearly a potential loss of data in this conversion, and you should always write an explicit cast in such cases to indicate that you intend this to happen. If you leave it out, it's not clear that you realized the need for the conversion and the potential data loss.

We obtain the number of whole feet in the length with the statement:

```
ft = static_cast<long>((yards - yds) * feet_per_yard);
```

We want the number of whole feet that are not contained in the whole yards, so we subtract the value in **yds** from **yards**. The compiler will arrange for the value in **yds** to be converted automatically to type **double** for the subtraction, and the result will be of type **double** as well. The value of **feet_per_yard** will then be converted automatically to **double** to allow the multiplication to take place, and finally our explicit cast will be applied to the result, to convert it from type **double** to type **long**.

The final part of the calculation is to obtain the residual number of whole inches:

```
ins = static_cast<long>(yards * feet_per_yard * inches_per_foot) %
                                              inches_per_foot;
```

This is done by calculating the total number of inches in the original length, converting this to type **long** with an explicit cast, and then getting the remainder after dividing by the number of inches in a foot. Lastly, we output the results with the statement:

```
cout << endl
     << yards << " yards converts to "
     << yds   << " yards "
     << ft    << " feet "
     << ins   << " inches.";
```

Old-Style Casts

Prior to the introduction of **static_cast<>()** (and the other casts: **const_cast<>()**, **dynamic_cast<>()** and **reinterpret_cast<>()**, which we'll discuss later in the book) into C++, an explicit cast of the result of an expression to another type was written as:

(*the type to convert to*)*expression*

The result of **expression** is cast to the type between the parentheses. For example, the statement to calculate **ins** in our previous example could be written:

```
ins = (long)(yards * feet_per_yard * inches_per_foot) % inches_per_foot;
```

Essentially, there are four different kinds of casts, and the old-style casting syntax covers them all. Because of this, code using the old-style casts is more prone to error — it is not always clear what you intended, and you may not get the result you expected. Although you will still see the old style of casting used extensively (it's still part of the language), I strongly recommend that you stick to using only the new casts in your code.

Finding Out About Types

I've mentioned several times that the number of bytes used for some types is not specified in the C++ standard, and that this is therefore set by your compiler. It's quite possible that you would want to know how many bytes particular types of variables will occupy with your compiler. You could hunt for this information in your compiler's documentation, but you can also get the information programmatically by using the **sizeof**() operator.

sizeof() is a unary operator, so it takes a single operand. It will return an integer value that is a measure of the amount of memory occupied by a particular variable, or by a type. The value returned by **sizeof()** is actually defined as a multiple of the size of type **char**, but since variables of type **char** occupy 1 byte, the value returned will be a measure of the number of bytes that the operand occupies.

To obtain the number of bytes occupied by variables of type **type**, you use the expression **sizeof(type)**. You could therefore output the size of variables of type **int** with this statement:

```
cout << endl
     << "Size of type int is "
     << sizeof(int);            // Output the size of type int
```

The expression **sizeof(int)** returns the size of anything declared as type **int**, and you can find out the size of any data type in this way. To get the size of **long double** values, you could write:

```
cout << endl
     << "Size of type long double is "
     << sizeof(long double);    // Output the size of type long double
```

You can also apply the **sizeof()** operator to a particular variable, or even to an expression. In this case the expression does not have to be between parentheses, although you can include them if you wish. Here's an example that will output the number of bytes occupied by the variable **number**:

```
long number = 999999999;
cout << endl
     << "Size of the variable number is "
     << sizeof number;          // Output the size of a variable
```

You can treat the value returned by the **sizeof()** operator as an integer, but in fact it's of type **size_t**. This type is defined in the standard header file called **cstddef**, usually as **unsigned int**, and I can hear your next question already: "What's the point of having a different type name here? Why not just make it **unsigned int**?"

The reason for doing this is that it builds in flexibility. The **sizeof()** operator always returns a value of type **size_t**, which your compiler may well define to be **unsigned int**, but it doesn't have to be so. It might be convenient for the developers of a C++ compiler to define **size_t** to be equivalent to some other integral type, and they are free to do so. It won't affect your code, since your assumption is that its type is **size_t**. You'll see how to define a synonym for an existing type for yourself later in this chapter.

Try It Out – Finding the Sizes of Data Types

We can easily put together a program to list the sizes of all the data types we have seen:

```cpp
// Program 3.2 Finding the sizes of data types

#include <iostream>
using namespace std;

int main()
{
  // Output the sizes for integer types
  cout << endl
       << "Size of type char is "
       << sizeof(char);
  cout << endl
       << "Size of type short is "
       << sizeof(short);
  cout << endl
       << "Size of type int is "
       << sizeof(int);
  cout << endl
       << "Size of type long is "
       << sizeof(long);

  // Output the sizes for floating point types
  cout << endl
       << "Size of type float is "
       << sizeof(float);
  cout << endl
       << "Size of type double is "
       << sizeof(double);
  cout << endl
       << "Size of type long double is "
       << sizeof(long double);
  cout << endl;
  return 0;
}
```

On my computer, this program produces the output:

```
Size of type char is 1
Size of type short is 2
Size of type int is 4
Size of type long is 4
```

```
Size of type float is 4
Size of type double is 8
Size of type long double is 8
```

You could modify this example to use the **sizeof()** operator to obtain the sizes of sample variables and expressions, too.

Finding the Limits

There are occasions when you may want to know more about a particular type than just its size. You might want to know what the upper and lower limits on the values it can hold are, for instance. The standard header file called **limits** contains this kind of information about all the standard data types. The information is provided through a class for each type, and since we haven't discussed classes yet, the way this works will not be obvious to you at this point. However, we'll look at how you get the information here, and leave the explanations of the detail until we deal with classes specifically in Chapter 12.

Let's take an example. To display the maximum value you can store in a variable of type **double**, you could write:

```
cout << endl
     << "Maximum value of type double is "
     << numeric_limits<double>::max();
```

The expression **numeric_limits<double>::max()** produces the value we want. By putting different type names between the angled brackets, you can obtain the maximum values for other data types. You can also replace **max()** by **min()** to get the minimum value.

You can retrieve many other items of information about various types. The number of binary digits, for example, is returned by this expression:

```
numeric_limits<type_name>::digits
```

You just insert the **type_name** in which you are interested between the angled brackets. For floating point types, you will get the number of binary digits in the mantissa. For signed integer types, you will get the number of binary digits *excluding* the sign bit.

To see this sort of thing in action, we can put together a little example to display the maximums and minimums for the numerical data types.

Try It Out – Finding Maximum and Minimum Values

Here's the program code:

```
// Program 3.3 Finding maximum and minimum values for data types

#include <limits>
#include <iostream>
using namespace std;
```

```cpp
int main()
{
  cout << endl
       << "The range for type short is from "
       << numeric_limits<short>::min()
       << " to "
       << numeric_limits<short>::max();
  cout << endl
       << "The range for type int is from "
       << numeric_limits<int>::min()
       << " to "
       << numeric_limits<int>::max();
  cout << endl
       << "The range for type long is from "
       << numeric_limits<long>::min()
       << " to "
       << numeric_limits<long>::max();
  cout << endl
       << "The range for type float is from "
       << numeric_limits<float>::min()
       << " to "
       << numeric_limits<float>::max();
  cout << endl
       << "The range for type double is from "
       << numeric_limits<double>::min()
       << " to "
       << numeric_limits<double>::max();
  cout << endl
       << "The range for type long double is from "
       << numeric_limits<long double>::min()
       << " to "
       << numeric_limits<long double>::max();
  cout << endl;
  return 0;
}
```

On my computer, this program produces:

```
The range for type short is from -32768 to 32767
The range for type int is from -2147483648 to 2147483647
The range for type long is from -2147483648 to 2147483647
The range for type float is from 1.17549e-038 to 3.40282e+038
The range for type double is from 2.22507e-308 to 1.79769e+308
The range for type long double is from 2.22507e-308 to 1.79769e+308
```

The **limits** header file also defines symbols for limit values. For example, the constant **INT_MAX** represents the maximum value of a value of type **int**, whereas **SCHAR_MIN** represents the minimum value of a **signed char**. However, these are just symbols that will be replaced in your code by the equivalent number. The values retrieved in the manner used in the example have a type, and are therefore type-checked by the compiler when you use them. The symbols exist for historical reasons, and the mechanism shown in the example is now the preferred way of getting at this information.

Bitwise Operators

As their name suggests, the **bitwise operators** enable you to operate on an integer variable at the bit level. You can apply the bitwise operators to any type of integer, both `signed` and `unsigned`, including the type `char`. However, they are usually applied to `unsigned` integer types.

A typical application for these operators is when you want to use individual bits in an integer variable. An example of this would be **flags**, which is the term used to describe binary state indicators. You can use a bit for any value that has two states: on or off, male or female, true or false. You can also use bitwise operators to work with several items of information stored in a single variable.

For example, suppose that you need to record information about fonts. You might want to store information about the style and the size of each font, plus whether it is bold or italic. You could pack all this into a two-byte integer variable:

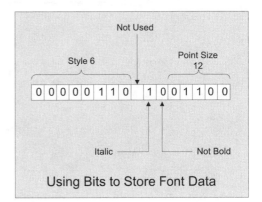

Using Bits to Store Font Data

You could use one bit to record whether the font was italic, and another bit to specify whether it was bold. You could use a byte to select one of up to 256 different styles. With another five bits, you could record the point size up to 32. The bitwise operators provide you with the means of accessing and modifying the individual bits and groups of bits from an integer very easily.

The Bitwise Shift Operators

The bitwise **shift operators** shift the contents of an integer variable by a specified number of bits to the left or right. The `>>` operator shifts bits to the right, while `<<` is the operator for shifts to the left. Bits that fall off either end of the variable are lost.

Let's take an example where we assume type `int` to be two bytes, just to keep our illustrative diagrams simple. We can declare and initialize a variable called **number** with the statement:

```
unsigned int number = 16387U;
```

As we saw in the last chapter, we should write unsigned literals with a letter `U` or `u` appended to the number. We can shift the contents of this variable and store the result with the statement:

```
unsigned int result = number << 2;    // Shift left two bit positions
```

The left operand of the shift operator is the value to be shifted, while the number of bit positions that the value is to be shifted is specified by the right operand. This illustration shows the effect of the operation:

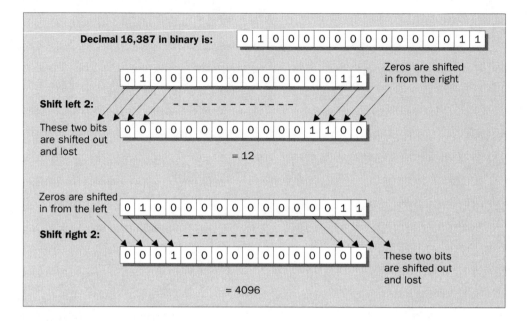

As you can see, shifting the value 16,387 two positions to the left produces the value 12. The rather drastic change in the value is the result of losing the high order bit.

To shift the value to the right, we can write:

```
result = number >> 2;                // Shift right two bit positions
```

This shifts the value 16,387 two positions to the right, and produces the result 4,096. Shifting right two bits is effectively dividing the value by 4.

As long as bits are not lost, shifting n bits to the left is equivalent to multiplying the value by 2, n times. In other words, it is equivalent to multiplying by 2^n. Similarly, shifting right n bits is equivalent to dividing by 2^n. But beware: as we saw with the left shift of the variable **number**, if significant bits are lost, the result is nothing like what you would expect. However, this is no different from the 'real' multiply operation. If you multiplied the two-byte number by four you would get the same result, so shifting left and multiplying are still equivalent. The problem of accuracy arises because the value of the result of the multiplication is outside the range of a two-byte integer.

If you need to modify the original value, you can do so by using an **op=** assignment operator. In this case, we would use the **>>=** or the **<<=** operator. For example:

```
number >>= 2;          // Shift the contents of number two positions to the right
```

This is equivalent to:

```
number = number >> 2;    // Shift the contents of number two positions to the right
```

You might imagine that confusion could arise between these shift operators and the insertion and extraction operators that we have been using for input and output. As far as the compiler is concerned, the meaning will generally be clear from the context. If it isn't, the compiler will generate a message, but you do need to be careful. For example, if you want to output the result of shifting a variable **number** left by two bits, you could write:

```
cout << (number << 2);
```

Here, the parentheses are essential. Without them, the compiler will interpret the shift operator as a stream operator, so you will not get the result that you intended.

Shifting Signed Integers

You can apply the bitwise shift operators to both signed and unsigned integers. However, the effect of the right shift operator on **signed** integer types can vary between different systems, and it depends on your compiler's implementation. In some cases, the right shift will introduce '0' bits at the left to fill the vacated bit positions. In other cases the sign bit is propagated to the right, so '1' bits fill the vacated bit positions to the left.

The reason for propagating the sign bit, where this occurs, is to maintain consistency between a right shift and a divide operation. We can illustrate this with a variable of type **char**, just to show how it works. Suppose we define **value** to be of type **char** with the value -104 in decimal:

```
signed char value = -104;
```

Its binary value is 10011000. We can shift it 2 bits to the right with this operation:

```
value >>= 2;            // Result 11100110
```

The binary result is shown in the comment. Two zeros are shifted out at the right hand end, and because the sign bit is 1, further 1s are inserted on the left. The decimal value of the result is -26, which is the same as if we had divided by 4, as we would expect. With operations on **unsigned** integer types, of course, the sign bit is not propagated and zeros are inserted on the left.

As I said, what *actually* happens when you right-shift negative integers is implementation defined, so you must not rely on it working one way or the other. Since for the most part you will be using these operators for operating at the bit level — where maintaining the integrity of the bit pattern is important — you should always use **unsigned** integers to ensure that you avoid the high order bit being propagated.

Logical Operations on Bit Patterns

There are four bitwise operators that you can use to modify bits in an integer value. These are:

Operator	Description
~	This is the **bitwise complement operator**. This is a unary operator that will invert the bits in its operand, so 1 becomes 0 and 0 becomes 1.
&	This is the **bitwise AND operator**, which will AND the corresponding bits in its operands. If the corresponding bits are both 1, then the resulting bit is 1. Otherwise, it is 0.
^	This is the **bitwise exclusive OR operator**, which will exclusive-OR the corresponding bits in its operands. If the corresponding bits are different, i.e. one is 1 and the other is 0, then the resulting bit is 1. If the corresponding bits are the same, the resulting bit is 0.
|	This is the **bitwise OR operator**, which will OR the corresponding bits in its operands. If either of the two corresponding bits is 1, then the result is 1. If both bits are 0, then the result is 0.

The operators appear here in order of precedence, so the bitwise complement operator has the highest precedence in this set, and the bitwise OR operator the lowest. As you can see in the complete operator precedence table in Appendix D, the shift operators **<<** and **>>** are of equal precedence, and they're below the **~** operator but above the **&** operator.

If you haven't come across operators like these before, you are likely to be saying, "Very interesting, but what are they *for*?" Let's see if we can put them into some kind of context.

Using the Bitwise AND

You would typically use the bitwise AND operator to select particular bits or groups of bits in an integer value. To see what this means, we can reuse the example we had at the beginning of this section, which used an integer to store the characteristics of a font.

Let's suppose we declare and initialize a variable to specify a 12 point, italic, style 6 font — in fact, the very same one that we illustrated in the diagram. In binary, the style will be 00000110, the italic bit will be 1, the bold bit will be 0, and the size will be 01100. Remembering that there is an unused bit as well, we need to initialize the value of the **font** variable to the binary number 0000 0110 0100 1100. Since groups of 4 bits correspond to a hexadecimal digit, the easiest way to do this is to specify the initial value in hexadecimal notation:

```
unsigned int font = 0x064C;          // Style 6, italic, 12 point
```

 When setting up bit patterns like this, hexadecimal notation is invariably more appropriate than using decimal values.

To use the size, we need to be able to extract it from the **font** variable; the bitwise AND operator will enable us to do this. Because bitwise AND only produces a 1 bit when both bits are 1, we can define a value that will 'select' the bits defining the size when we AND it with **font**. All we need to do is define a value that contains 1s in the bit positions that we are interested in, and 0s in all the others. This kind of value is called a **mask**, and we can define such a mask with the statement:

```
unsigned int size_mask = 0x1F;          // Mask is 0000 0000 0001 1111
                                        // to select size
```

The five low order bits of **font** represent its size, so we set these bits to 1. The remaining bits are 0, so they will be discarded. (Binary 0000 0000 0001 1111 translates to hexadecimal 1F.) We can now extract the point size from **font** with the statement:

```
unsigned int size = font & size_mask;
```

Where both corresponding bits are 1, the resultant bit is 1. Any other combination results in a 0. The values therefore combine like this:

font	0000	0110	0100	1100
size_mask	0000	0000	0001	1111
font & size_mask	0000	0000	0000	1100

Separating the binary values into groups of 4 bits has no real significance; it just makes it easier to see how many bits there are. As you can see, the effect of the mask is to separate out the five rightmost bits, which represent the point size.

We could use the same mechanism to select out the style for the font, but we will also need to use a shift operator to move the style value to the right. We can define a mask to select the left 8 bits as:

```
unsigned int style_mask = 0XFF00;       // Mask is 1111 1111 0000 0000
                                        // for style
```

We can then obtain the style value with the statement:

```
unsigned int style = (font & style_mask) >> 8;     // Extract the style
```

The effect of this statement is:

font	0000	0110	0100	1100
style_mask	1111	1111	0000	0000
font & style_mask	0000	0110	0000	0000
(font & style_mask) >> 8	0000	0000	0000	0110

You should be able to see that you could just as easily isolate the bits indicating italic and bold by defining a mask for each, with the appropriate bit set to 1. Of course, you still need a way to test the resulting bit, and we will see how to do that in the next chapter.

Another use for the bitwise AND is to turn bits off. Part of the effect we saw above is that any bit that is 0 in a mask will produce 0 in the result. To turn the italic bit off, for example, you just bitwise-AND the **font** variable with a mask that has the italic bit as 0 and all the other bits as 1. We will look at the code to do this in the context of the bitwise OR operator, for reasons that I will explain there.

Using the Bitwise OR

You can use the bitwise OR operator for *setting* single or multiple bits. Continuing with our manipulations of the **font** variable, it is conceivable that we would want to set the italic and bold bits on demand. We can define masks to select these bits with the statements:

```
unsigned int italic = 0X40U;          // Seventh bit from the right
unsigned int bold = 0X20U;            // Sixth bit from the right
```

Now we can set the bold bit with the statement:

```
font |= bold;                         // Set bold
```

The bits combine here as follows:

```
font                    0000   0110   0100   1100
bold                    0000   0000   0010   0000
font | bold             0000   0110   0110   1100
```

Now, the **font** variable specifies that the font it represents is bold as well as italic. Note that this operation will result in the bit being set, regardless of its previous state. If it was on before, it remains on.

You can also set multiple bits by ORing the masks together, so the following statement will set both the bold and the italic bit:

```
font |= bold | italic;                // Set bold and italic
```

It's easy to fall into the trap of allowing language to make you select the wrong operator. Because you say, "Set italic *and* bold," there is a temptation to use the **&** operator, but this would be wrong. ANDing the two masks together would result in a value with all bits zero, so you would not change anything.

As I said at the end of the last section, you can use the **&** operator to turn bits off — you just need a mask that contains a 0 at the position of the bit you want to turn off, and 1 everywhere else. However, this raises the issue of *how* you specify such a mask. If you want to specify it explicitly, you'll need to know how many bytes there are in your variable — not exactly convenient if you want your program to be in any way portable. However, you can obtain the mask that you want by using the bitwise complement operator on the mask that you would normally use to turn the bit on. We can obtain the mask to turn bold off from the **bold** mask itself:

```
bold                    0000   0000   0010   0000
~bold                   1111   1111   1101   1111
```

The effect of the complement operator is that each bit in the original is flipped, 0 to 1 or 1 to 0. You should be able to see that this will produce the result we are looking for, regardless of whether type **unsigned int** is two bytes or four bytes.

> *The bitwise complement operator is sometimes called the NOT operator, because for every bit it operates on, what you get is* not *what you started with.*

Thus, all we need to do when we want to turn bold off is to bitwise-AND the complement of the mask, **bold**, with the variable, **font**. The following statement will do it:

```
font &= ~bold;                              // Turn bold off
```

You can also set multiple bits to zero by combining several masks using the **&** operator, and then bitwise-ANDing the result with the variable you want to modify. For example:

```
font &= ~bold & ~italic;                    // Turn bold and italic off
```

This sets both the italic and bold bits to zero in the **font** variable. Note that no parentheses are necessary here, because **~** has a higher precedence than **&**.

Using the Bitwise Exclusive OR

The bitwise exclusive OR operator is used much less frequently than the **&** and **|** operators, and there are few common examples of its use. An important application, though, arises in the context of graphics programming. One way of creating the illusion of motion on the screen is to draw an object, erase it, and then redraw it in a new position. This process needs to be repeated very rapidly if you are to get smooth animation, and the erasing is a critical part of it. You don't want to erase and redraw the whole screen, as this is time consuming and the screen will flash. Ideally, you want to erase only the object or objects on screen that you are moving. You can do this and get reasonably smooth animation by using what is called **exclusive OR mode**.

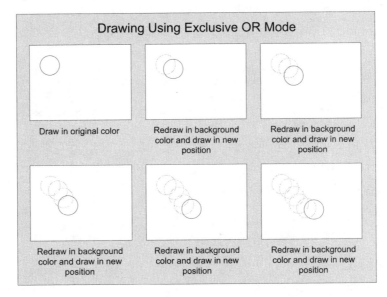

Exclusive OR mode is based on the idea that once you have drawn an object on the screen in a given color, it will then disappear if you redraw it in the background color. When you draw an object on the screen in exclusive OR mode, the color automatically alternates between the color you have selected for the object and the background color each time you draw the object. The key to achieving this is the use of the bitwise exclusive OR operator to alternate the colors rapidly and automatically. It uses a characteristic of the exclusive OR operation, which is that if you exclusive-OR two values together, and then exclusive-OR one of the original values with the result, you will obtain the other value. That sounds complicated, so let's see how it works by taking a specific example.

Suppose we want to alternate between a foreground color (we'll use red), and a background color (white). A color is often represented by three 8-bit values, corresponding to the intensities for each of red, blue, and green, stored in a single four-byte integer. By altering the proportions of red, blue and green in a color, you can get around 16 million different colors in the range from white to black, and everything in between. A bright red would be **0xFF0000**, where the red component is set to its maximum and the intensities of the other two components for green and blue are zero. In the same scheme, green would be **0xFF00**, and blue would be **0xFF**. White has equal, maximum components of red, blue and green, so it would be **0xFFFFFF**.

We can therefore define variables representing red and white with the statements:

```
unsigned long red = 0XFF0000UL;       // Color red
unsigned long white = 0XFFFFFFUL;     // Color white - RGB all maximum
```

Next, we create a mask that we'll use to switch the color back and forth between red and white, and initialize to red a variable containing the drawing color:

```
unsigned long mask = red ^ white;     // Mask for switching colors
unsigned long draw_color = red;       // Drawing color
```

The variable **mask** is initialized to the bitwise exclusive OR of the colors that we want to alternate, so it will be:

red	1111	1111	0000	0000	0000	0000
white	1111	1111	1111	1111	1111	1111
mask (which is **red ^ white**)	0000	0000	1111	1111	1111	1111

If we exclusive-OR **mask** with **red** we will get **white**, and vice versa. Therefore, having drawn an object using the color in **draw_color**, we can switch the color with the statement:

```
draw_color ^= mask;                   // Switch the drawing color
```

The effect of this is as follows:

draw_color	1111	1111	0000	0000	0000	0000
mask	0000	0000	1111	1111	1111	1111
draw_color ^ mask	1111	1111	1111	1111	1111	1111

Clearly, we have changed the value of **draw_color** from red to white. Executing the same statement again will flip the color back to red:

```
draw_color ^= mask;                   // Switch the drawing color
```

This works as follows:

draw_color	1111	1111	1111	1111	1111	1111
mask	0000	0000	1111	1111	1111	1111
draw_color ^ mask	1111	1111	0000	0000	0000	0000

As you can see, **draw_color** is back to the value of red again. This technique will work with any two colors, although of course it has nothing to do with colors in particular at all: you can use it to alternate between any pair of integer values.

Try It Out – Using the Bitwise Operators

We can put together an example that exercises the bitwise operators, so that you can see them working together. We can also illustrate the use of the exclusive OR for switching between two values, and how you use masks to select and set individual bits. Here's the code:

```cpp
// Program 3.4 Using the bitwise operators
#include <iostream>
#include <iomanip>
using namespace std;

int main()
{
  unsigned long red = 0XFF0000UL;        // Color red
  unsigned long white = 0XFFFFFFUL;      // Color white - RGB all maximum

  cout << hex;                           // Set hexadecimal output format
  cout.fill('0');                        // Set fill character for output

  cout << "\nTry out bitwise AND and OR operators.";
  cout << "\nInitial value   red         = " << setw(8) << red;
  cout << "\nComplement      ~red        = " << setw(8) << ~red;

  cout << "\nInitial value   white       = " << setw(8) << white;
  cout << "\nComplement      ~white      = " << setw(8) << ~white;

  cout << "\n Bitwise AND    red & white = " << setw(8) << (red & white);
  cout << "\n Bitwise OR     red | white = " << setw(8) << (red | white);

  cout << "\n\nNow we can try out successive exclusive OR operations.";

  unsigned long mask = red ^ white;

  cout << "\n            mask = red ^ white = " << setw(8) << mask;
  cout << "\n                  mask ^ red = " << setw(8) << (mask ^ red);
  cout << "\n                  mask ^ white = " << setw(8) << (mask ^ white);

  unsigned long flags = 0xFF;            // Flags variable
  unsigned long bit1mask = 0x1;          // Selects bit 1
  unsigned long bit6mask = 0x20;         // Selects bit 6
  unsigned long bit20mask = 0x80000;     // Selects bit 20

  cout << "\n\nNow use masks to select or set a particular flag bit.";
  cout << "\nSelect bit 1 from flags    : " << setw(8) << (flags & bit1mask);
  cout << "\nSelect bit 6 from flags    : " << setw(8) << (flags & bit6mask);
  cout << "\nSwitch off bit 6 in flags  : " << setw(8) << (flags &= ~bit6mask);
  cout << "\nSwitch on bit 20 in flags  : " << setw(8) << (flags |= bit20mask);
  cout << endl;

  return 0;
}
```

This example will produce the output:

```
Try out bitwise AND and OR operators.
Initial value   red           = 00ff0000
Complement      ~red          = ff00ffff
Initial value   white         = 00ffffff
Complement      ~white        = ff000000
 Bitwise AND    red & white   = 00ff0000
 Bitwise OR     red | white   = 00ffffff

Now we can try out successive exclusive OR operations.
        mask = red ^ white = 0000ffff
                mask ^ red = 00ffffff
              mask ^ white = 00ff0000

Now use masks to select or set a particular flag bit.
Select bit 1 from flags      : 00000001
Select bit 6 from flags      : 00000020
Switch off bit 6 in flags    : 000000df
Switch on bit 20 in flags    : 000800df
```

How It Works

There is a **#include** directive for the **iomanip** standard header file, which we saw in the last chapter, because the code uses manipulators to control the formatting of the output. To start with, we define two integer variables containing values representing the colors that we will use in subsequent bitwise operations:

```
unsigned long red = 0XFF0000UL;      // Color red
unsigned long white = 0XFFFFFFFUL;   // Color white - RGB all maximum
```

We'll want to display our data as hexadecimal values, so we specify this with the statement:

```
cout << hex;                         // Set hexadecimal output format
```

Here, **hex** is a manipulator that sets the output representation for integer values as hexadecimal. Note that this is modal — all subsequent integer output to the standard output stream in the program will now be in hexadecimal format. We don't need to keep sending **hex** to the output stream, **cout**. If necessary, you could change back to decimal output with the statement:

```
cout << dec;                         // Set decimal output format
```

This uses the **dec** manipulator to reset integer output to the default decimal representation. Note that setting the output format to hexadecimal *only* affects integer values. Floating point values will continue to be displayed in normal decimal form.

It would also make things clearer if we output our integers with leading zeros, and we set this mode with the statement:

```
cout.fill('0');                      // Set fill character for output
```

Here, **fill()** is a function that sets the fill character to whatever character you put between the parentheses. This is also modal, so any subsequent integer output will use this fill character when necessary. Both decimal and hexadecimal output is affected. If you wanted asterisks instead, you would use:

```
cout.fill('*');                          // Set fill character for output
```

To set the fill character back to the default, you just use a space between the parentheses:

```
cout.fill(' ');                          // Set fill character for output
```

You should not put the call to **fill()** in an output statement. If you do, the previous fill character will be sent to the output stream, because that's what gets returned by **fill()**. The way this works will be clearer after we have discussed functions in Chapter 8.

The value of **red** and its complement are displayed by the statements:

```
cout << "\nInitial value  red        = " << setw(8) << red;
cout << "\nComplement     ~red       = " << setw(8) << ~red;
```

We use the **setw()** manipulator that we saw in the last chapter to set the output field width to 8. If we make sure all our output values will be in a field of the same width, it will be easier to compare them. Setting the width is *not* modal; it only applies to the output from the next statement that comes after the point where the width is set. From the output for **red** and **white**, you can see that the **~** operator is doing what we expect: flipping the bits of its operand.

We combine **red** and **white** using the bitwise AND and OR operators with these statements:

```
cout << "\n Bitwise AND   red & white = " << setw(8) << (red & white);
cout << "\n Bitwise OR    red | white = " << setw(8) << (red | white);
```

Notice the parentheses around the expressions in the output. These are necessary because the precedence of **<<** is higher than **&** and **|**. Without the parentheses, the statements would not compile. If you check the output, you will see that it is precisely as we discussed. The result of ANDing two bits is 1 if both bits are 1; otherwise the result is 0. When we bitwise-OR two bits, the result is 1 unless both bits are 0.

Next, we create a mask to use to flip between the values **red** and **white** by combining the two values with the exclusive OR operator:

```
unsigned long mask = red ^ white;
```

If you inspect the output for the value of **mask**, you will see that the exclusive OR of two bits is 1 when the bits are different, and 0 when they are the same. By combining **mask** with either of the two color values using exclusive OR, we can obtain the other. This is demonstrated by these statements:

```
cout << "\n          mask ^ red = " << setw(8) << (mask ^ red);
cout << "\n          mask ^ white = " << setw(8) << (mask ^ white);
```

The last group of statements demonstrates how to use a mask to select a single bit from a group of flag bits. The mask to select a particular bit must have that bit as 1 and all other bits as zero. Thus, the masks to select bits 1, 6, and 20 from a 32-bit **long** variable are defined as:

```
unsigned long bit1mask = 0x1;            // Selects bit 1
unsigned long bit6mask = 0x20;           // Selects bit 6
unsigned long bit20mask = 0x80000;       // Selects bit 20
```

To select a bit from **flags**, we just need to bitwise-AND the appropriate mask with the value of **flags**. For example:

```
cout << "\nSelect bit 6 from flags    : " << setw(8) << (flags & bit6mask);
```

You can see from the output that the result of the expression **(flags & bit6mask)** is an integer with just bit 6 set. Of course, if bit 6 in **flags** was zero, the result of the expression would be zero.

To switch a bit off, you need to bitwise-AND the **flags** variable with a mask containing 0 for the bit you want to switch off, and 1 everywhere else. You can easily produce this by applying the complement operator to a mask with the appropriate bit set, and **bit6mask** is just such a mask. The statement to switch off bit 6 in **flags** and display the result is:

```
cout << "\nSwitch off bit 6 in flags  : " << setw(8) << (flags &= ~bit6mask);
```

Of course, if bit 6 were already 0, it would remain as such. To switch a bit on, you just OR **flags** with a mask having the bit you want to switch on as 1:

```
cout << "\nSwitch on bit 20 in flags  : " << setw(8) << (flags |= bit20mask);
```

This sets bit 20 of **flags** to 1 and displays the result. Again, if the bit were already 1, it would remain as 1.

More on Output Manipulators

Taking the last chapter into account, we've now seen five of the modal output manipulators that the **iostream** header defines: **scientific**, **fixed**, **dec**, **hex** and **oct**. The time seems right, therefore, to list these and all the other similar manipulators in one place. Don't worry for now about the **bool** values mentioned in the last two entries — they're coming up in the next chapter.

Manipulator	Action performed
dec	Format integer values as base 10 (decimal). This is the default representation.
hex	Format integer values as base 16 (hexadecimal).
oct	Format integer values as base 8 (octal).
left	Left-align values in the output field, and pad them on the right with the fill character. The default fill character is a space, as we've seen.

Manipulator	Action performed
`right`	Right-align values in the output field, and pad them on the left with the fill character. This is the default alignment.
`fixed`	Output floating point values in fixed point notation — that is, without an exponent.
`scientific`	Output floating point values in scientific notation — that is, as the mantissa plus an exponent. The default mode selects `fixed` or `scientific` notation, depending on the value to be displayed.
`showpoint`	Show the decimal point and trailing zeros for floating-point values.
`noshowpoint`	The opposite of the above manipulator. This is the default.
`showbase`	Prefix octal output with `0` and hexadecimal output with `0x` or `0X`.
`noshowbase`	Show octal and hexadecimal output without the prefix. This is the default.
`showpos`	Show plus signs (**+**) for positive values.
`noshowpos`	Don't show plus signs for positive values. This is the default.
`uppercase`	Display upper case **A** through **F** for hexadecimal digits when outputting integers in hexadecimal format, and `0X` if `showbase` is set. Display **E** for the exponent when outputting values in scientific notation, rather than using lower case **e**.
`nouppercase`	Use lower case for the above items. This is the default.
`boolalpha`	Display **bool** values as **true** and **false**.
`noboolalpha`	Display **bool** values as **1** and **0**.

You may want to set more than one of these modes at a time, and one way to do this is to insert multiple manipulators into the stream. For example, if you wanted to output your integer data as hexadecimal values that were left aligned in the output field, you could write:

```
cout << hex << left << value;
```

This will output **value** (and all subsequent integers in the program, unless the settings are changed) as a left-justified hexadecimal number.

Enumerated Data Types

You will sometimes be faced with the need for variables that have a limited set of possible values that can be usefully referred to by name: the days of the week, for example, or the months of the year. There is a specific facility in C++ to handle this situation, called an **enumeration**. When you define an enumeration, you are really creating a new type, so it is also referred to as an **enumerated data type**. Let's create an example using one of the ideas I just mentioned — a variable that can assume values corresponding to days of the week. We can define this as follows:

```
enum Weekday { Monday, Tuesday, Wednesday, Thursday, Friday, Saturday, Sunday };
```

This declares an enumerated data type called **Weekday**, and variables of this type can only have values from the set that appears between the braces. If you try to set a variable of type **Weekday** to a value that is not one of the values specified, it will cause an error. The symbolic names listed between the braces are called **enumerators**.

In fact, each of the names of the days will be automatically defined as representing a fixed integer value. The first name in the list, **Monday**, will have the value 0, **Tuesday** will be 1, and so on through to **Sunday** with the value 6. We can declare **today** as an instance of the enumeration type **Weekday** with the statement:

```
Weekday today = Tuesday;
```

TYPE

You use the **Weekday** type just like any of the basic types we have seen. This declaration for **today** also initializes the variable with the value **Tuesday**. If you output the value of **today**, 1 will be displayed.

By default, the value of each successive enumerator in the declaration of an enumeration is one larger than the value of the previous one, and the values begin at 0. If you would prefer the implicit numbering to start at a different value, a declaration like this one will make the enumerators equivalent to 1 through 7:

```
enum Weekday { Monday = 1, Tuesday, Wednesday, Thursday, Friday,
               Saturday, Sunday };
```

The enumerators don't need to have unique values. You could define **Monday** and **Mon** as both having the value 1, for example, with this statement:

```
enum Weekday { Monday = 1, Mon = 1, Tuesday, Wednesday,
               Thursday, Friday, Saturday, Sunday };
```

This allows the possibility of using either **Mon** or **Monday** as the value for the first day of the week. A variable, **yesterday**, that you have declared as type **Weekday** could then be set with the statement:

```
yesterday = Mon;
```

You can also define an enumerator in terms of a previous enumerator in the list. Throwing everything we've seen so far into a single example, you could declare the type **Weekday** as:

```
enum Weekday { Monday,                       Mon   = Monday,
               Tuesday   = Monday + 2,        Tues  = Tuesday,
               Wednesday = Tuesday + 2,       Wed   = Wednesday,
               Thursday  = Wednesday + 2,     Thurs = Thursday,
               Friday    = Thursday + 2,      Fri   = Friday,
               Saturday  = Friday + 2,        Sat   = Saturday,
               Sunday    = Saturday + 2,      Sun   = Sunday };
```

Now, variables of type **Weekday** can have values from **Monday** to **Sunday**, and from **Mon** to **Sun**, and the pairs correspond to the integer values 0, 2, 4, 6, 8, 10, and 12.

If you wish, you can assign explicit values to all the enumerators. For example, we could define this enumeration:

```
enum Punctuation { Comma = ',', Exclamation = '!', Question='?' };
```

Here, we've defined the possible values for variables of type **Punctuation** as the numerical equivalents of the appropriate symbols. If you look in the ASCII table in Appendix A, you'll see that the symbols are 44, 33 and 63 respectively in decimal, which demonstrates that the values you assign don't have to be in ascending order. If you don't specify all them explicitly, values will continue to be assigned by incrementing by 1 from the last specified value, as in our second **Weekday** example.

The values you specify for enumerators must be **compile time constants**—that is, constant expressions that the *compiler* can evaluate. Such expressions can only include literals, enumerators that have been defined previously, and variables that you have declared as **const**. You cannot use non-**const** variables, even if you have initialized them.

Anonymous Enumerations

By declaring variables at the same time as you define the enumeration, you can omit the enumeration type provided that you don't need to declare other variables of this type later on. For example:

VARIABLES

```
enum { Monday, Tuesday, Wednesday, Thursday,
                Friday, Saturday, Sunday } yesterday, today, tomorrow;
```

Here, we have declared three variables that can assume values from **Monday** to **Sunday**. Since the enumeration type is not specified, we cannot refer to it. You cannot declare other variables for this enumeration *at all*, since doing so would require you to repeat the definition, which is simply not permitted. Doing so would imply that you were redefining values for **Monday** to **Sunday**, and that isn't allowed.

A common use of anonymous enumeration types is as an alternative way of defining integer constants. For example:

```
enum { feetPerYard = 3, inchesPerFoot = 12, yardsPerMile = 1760 };
```

This enumeration contains three enumerators with explicit values assigned. Although we have declared no variables of this enumerated data type, we can still use the enumerators in arithmetic expressions. We could write the statement:

```
cout << endl << "Feet in 5 miles = " << 5 * feetPerYard * yardsPerMile;
```

The enumerators are converted to type **int** automatically. It may look as if little (if anything) is to be gained by using an enumeration to define integer constants, but we will see when we come to discuss classes that it provides a very useful way of including a constant within a class. For now, let's look a little more closely at the conversion of enumerated data types.

Casting Between Integer and Enumeration Types

As well as the enumerators themselves, you can use a variable of an enumeration type in a mixed arithmetic expression. An enumerated data type will be cast automatically to the appropriate type, but the reverse is not true: there is no automatic conversion from an integer type to an enumeration type. If we have declared the variable **today** to be of type **Weekday** that we defined above, we can write:

```
today = Tuesday;                    // Assign an enumerator value
int day_value = today + 1;          // Calculate with an enumerator type
```

The value of **today** is **Tuesday**, which corresponds to **1**, so **day_value** will be set to **2**. Although the enumerator **Wednesday** corresponds to the value **2**, the following statement will *not* compile:

```
today = day_value;                  // Error - no conversion!
```

However, we can achieve the objective of this statement by putting in an explicit cast:

```
today = static_cast<Weekday>(day_value);    // OK
```

With an explicit cast, the integer value you are casting must be within the range of the enumerators, or the result is undefined. This does not mean that it must correspond to the value of an enumerator, just that it must be equal to or greater than the lowest enumerator, and less than or equal to the highest enumerator. For example, we could define an enumeration, **Height**, and declare a variable of that type with the statement:

```
enum Height { Bottom, Top = 20 } position;
```

The enumerator **Bottom** corresponds to the value 0, while **Top** corresponds to the value 20. The range is therefore from 0 to 20, so we could assign a value to the variable **position** with the statement:

```
position = static_cast<Height>(10);
```

The value assigned to **position** doesn't correspond to either of the enumerators, but it is nonetheless a legal value because it falls within the range of the minimum and maximum values of the enumerators. For a variable of the **Punctuation** type that we saw earlier, you could legally cast any integer from 33 to 63 to that type and store it, although in this instance it is difficult to see what purpose it would serve.

Try It Out – Enumerated Data Types

Enumerations become more obviously useful when you can make decisions by comparing the value of a variable of an enumerated data type against possible enumerators. We'll be looking at that in the next chapter, so here we can just have a simple example to demonstrate some of the operations on enumerated data types we've seen so far:

```cpp
// Program 3.5 - Exercising an enumeration
#include <iostream>
using namespace std;

int main()
{
  enum Language { English, French, German, Italian, Spanish };

  // Display range of enumerators
  cout << "\nPossible languages are:\n"
       << English << ". English\n"
       << French  << ". French\n"
       << German  << ". German\n"
       << Italian << ". Italian\n"
       << Spanish << ". Spanish\n";

  Language tongue = German;
  cout << "\n Current language is " << tongue;

  tongue = static_cast<Language>(tongue + 1);
  cout << "\n Current language is now " << tongue;
  return 0;
}
```

This will display the output:

```
Possible languages are:
0. English
1. French
2. German
3. Italian
4. Spanish

 Current language is 2
 Current language is now 3
```

How It Works

We first define an enumeration, **Language**, with the statement:

```cpp
enum Language { English, French, German, Italian, Spanish };
```

Variables of type **Language** can have any of the enumerators between the braces as a value. We list all the possible values with the next statement:

```cpp
cout << "\nPossible languages are:\n"
     << English << ". English\n"
     << French  << ". French\n"
     << German  << ". German\n"
     << Italian << ". Italian\n"
     << Spanish << ". Spanish\n";
```

An enumerator is displayed as its numeric value, so we output a text string alongside each one to show what language it corresponds to.

We declare and initialize a variable of type **Language** with the statement:

```
Language tongue = German;
```

The value of this variable displays as **2**, and then we give it a new value in the next statement:

```
tongue = static_cast<Language>(tongue + 1);
```

In the expression **tongue + 1**, the value of **tongue** is converted to type **int**, and then 1 is added to produce the value 3 as type **int**. This is then converted back to type **Language** by the explicit cast, before it gets stored back in **tongue**. Without the explicit cast, the statement would not compile because there is no automatic conversion from an integer type to an enumeration type. Of course, the value of **tongue** then displays as **3**.

Synonyms for Data Types

We've seen how enumerations provide a way to define our own data types. The **typedef** keyword enables you to specify your own data type *name* as an alternative to another type. Using **typedef**, you could declare the type name **BigOnes** as being equivalent to the standard type **long** with the declaration:

```
typedef long BigOnes;         // Defining BigOnes as a type name
```

This defines **BigOnes** as an alternative type specifier for **long**, so you could declare a variable **mynum** as type **long** with the statement:

```
BigOnes mynum = 0;            // Declare & initialize a long int variable
```

There is no difference between this declaration and one using the standard built-in type name. You could equally well use:

```
long int mynum = 0;           // Declare & initialize a long int variable
```

This has exactly the same result. In fact, if you declare your own type name (such as **BigOnes**), you can use both type specifiers within the same program to declare different variables that will end up having the same type. However, it's hard to come up with a reason that would justify doing this.

Since **typedef** simply creates a synonym for a type that already exists, it may appear to be a bit superfluous. This is not at all the case. One important use for **typedef** is to provide flexibility in the data types used by a program that may need to be run on a variety of computers. We can consider a particular instance to make it clear how this works.

Let's suppose we are writing a program that uses several variables to record values that count events of some kind — we could be recording the number of chocolate bars produced per hour on high speed manufacturing machinery, for instance. We know that the typical values for these counts require four-byte integers to be used.

On some computers, type **int** will be two bytes, which is insufficient for the range of integers in our program. On other computers, type **int** will be four bytes, which is just what we want. We could resolve this by using type **long**, which will generally be at least four bytes, but on some machines it may be eight bytes, which is wasteful — particularly if our program stores a lot of integers. We can provide the flexibility to deal with this situation by declaring our own type for use throughout the program. For example:

```
typedef int EventCount;      // Define the integer type for the program
```

Now we can write our program in terms of the type **EventCount**, rather than the standard type, **int**. This gives us the advantage that should we want to compile our program on a machine where the range for type **int** is insufficient, we can redefine **EventCount** as:

```
typedef long EventCount;      // Define the integer type for the program
```

Now, all the integers that are declared as **EventCount** within the program will be of type **long**.

We will see later that **typedef** can also fulfill a very useful role in enabling us to simplify more complex type declarations than we have met so far. We will also see later that classes provide us with a means of defining completely new data types, where we have complete control over the properties and operations that apply to the new type.

The Lifetime of a Variable

All variables have a finite lifetime when your program executes. They come into existence from the point at which you declare them and then, at some point, they disappear — at the latest, when your program terminates. How long a particular variable lasts is determined by a property called its **storage duration**. There are three different kinds of storage duration that a variable can have:

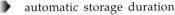 automatic storage duration

▶ static storage duration

▶ dynamic storage duration

Which of these a variable will have depends on how you create it. We will defer discussion of variables with dynamic storage duration until Chapter 7, but we can look into the characteristics of the other two in this chapter.

Another property that variables have is **scope**. The scope of a variable is simply that part of your program in which the variable name is valid. Within a variable's scope, you can legally refer to it, to set its value or use it in an expression. Outside of the scope of a variable, you cannot refer to its name — any attempt to do so will cause a compiler error. Note that a variable may still *exist* outside of its scope, even though you cannot refer to it by name. We will see examples of this situation a little later in this discussion.

All of the variables that we have declared up to now have had automatic storage duration, and are therefore called **automatic variables**. Let's take a closer look at these first.

Automatic Variables

The variables that we have declared so far have been declared within a block — that is, between a pair of curly braces. These are called automatic variables and are said to have **local scope** or **block scope**. An automatic variable is 'in scope' from the point at which it is declared until the end of the block containing its declaration.

An automatic variable is 'born' when it is declared and automatically ceases to exist at the end of the block containing the declaration. This will be at the closing brace matching the first opening brace that precedes the declaration of the variable. Every time the block of statements containing a declaration for an automatic variable is executed, the variable is created anew, and if you specified an initial value for the automatic variable, it will be reinitialized each time it is created.

There is a keyword, **auto**, which you can use to specify automatic variables, but it is rarely used since it is implied by default. Let's put together an example of what we've discussed so far.

Try It Out – Automatic Variables

We can demonstrate the lifetime of automatic variables with the following example:

```cpp
// Program 3.6 Demonstrating variable scope
#include <iostream>
using namespace std;

int main()
{                                  // Function scope starts here
  int count1 = 10;
  int count3 = 50;
  cout << endl << "Value of outer count1 = " << count1;

  {                                // New block scope starts here...
    int count1 = 20;              // This hides the outer count1
    int count2 = 30;
    cout << endl << "Value of inner count1 = " << count1;
    count1 += 3;                  // This changes the inner count1
    count3 += count2;
  }                                // ...and ends here.

  cout << endl
       << "Value of outer count1 = " << count1
       << endl
       << "Value of outer count3 = " << count3;

  // cout << endl << count2;   // Uncomment to get an error
  cout << endl;
  return 0;
}                                  // Function scope ends here
```

The output from this example will be:

```
Value of outer count1 = 10
Value of inner count1 = 20
Value of outer count1 = 10
Value of outer count3 = 80
```

How It Works

The first two statements declare and define two integer variables, **count1** and **count3**, with initial values of 10 and 50 respectively:

```
int count1 = 10;
int count3 = 50;
```

Both of these variables exist from this point in the code to the closing brace at the end of the program. The scope of these variables also extends to the closing brace at the end of **main()**.

> *Remember that the lifetime and scope of a variable are two different things. It's important not to get these two ideas confused.*

Following the variable definitions, the value of **count1** is output to produce the first of the lines shown above:

```
cout << endl << "Value of outer count1 = " << count1;
```

There is then a second opening brace that starts a new block. Two variables, **count1** and **count2**, are defined within this block, with values 20 and 30 respectively. The **count1** declared here is *different* from the first **count1**. Although the first **count1** still exists, its name is masked by the second **count1**. Any use of the name **count1** following the declaration within the inner block refers to the **count1** declared within that block.

I should say that I've duplicated names in this way only to illustrate what happens: it's not a good approach to programming in general. Doing this kind of thing in a real program would be confusing and unnecessary, and produce code that was extremely prone to error.

The output statement shows by the value in the second line that we are using the **count1** in the inner scope — that is, inside the innermost braces:

```
{                                    // New block scope starts here...
  int count1 = 20;                   // This hides the outer count1
  int count2 = 30;
  cout << endl << "Value of inner count1 = " << count1;
```

Had we still been using the outer **count1**, this statement would have output the value 10. The variable **count1** is then incremented by the statement:

```
count1 += 3;                         // This changes the inner count1
```

The increment applies to the variable in the inner scope, since the outer one is still hidden.

However, **count3**, which was defined in the outer scope, is incremented without any problem by the next statement:

```
count3 += count2;
```

This shows that the variables that were defined at the beginning of the outer scope are still accessible in the inner scope. They could be defined *after* the second of the inner pair of braces and still be within the outer scope, but in that case they would not exist at the point that we are using them.

After the brace ending the inner scope, **count2** and the inner **count1** cease to exist. The variables **count1** and **count3** are still there in the outer scope, and their values are displayed by this statement, demonstrating that **count3** was indeed incremented in the inner scope:

```
cout << endl
     << "Value of outer count1 = " << count1
     << endl
     << "Value of outer count3 = " << count3;
```

If you uncomment the next line:

```
// cout << endl << count2;    // uncomment to get an error
```

The program will no longer compile correctly, because it attempts to output a non-existent variable.

Positioning Variable Declarations

You have great flexibility over where you place the declarations for your variables. The most important issue to consider is what scope the variables need to have. Beyond that, you should generally place a declaration close to where the variable is first to be used in a program. You should always write your programs with a view to making them as easy as possible for another programmer to understand, and declaring a variable close to its first point of use can be helpful in achieving that.

It is possible to place variable declarations outside of all of the functions that make up a program. Let's look what effect that has on the variables concerned.

Global Variables

Variables declared outside of all blocks and classes are called **globals**, and have **global scope** (which is also called **global namespace scope**). This means that they are accessible in all the functions in the source file, following the point at which they are declared. If you declare them at the very top, they will be accessible from anywhere in the file.

Globals also have **static storage duration** by default. Global variables with static storage duration will exist from the start of execution of the program, until execution of the program ends. If you do not specify an initial value for a global variable, it will be initialized with 0 by default. Initialization of global variables takes place before the execution of **main()** begins, so they are always ready to be used within any code that is within the variable's scope.

The illustration below shows the contents of a source file, **Example.cpp**, and the arrows indicate the scope of each of the variables.

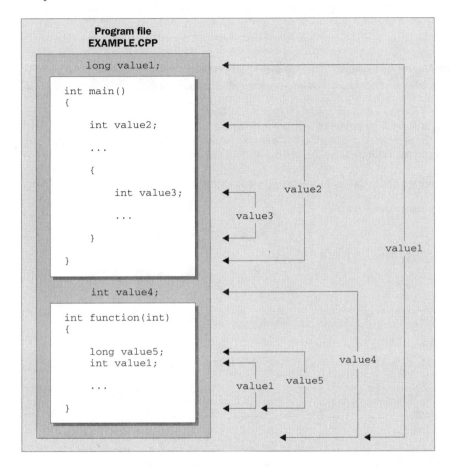

The variable **value1** that appears at the beginning of the file is declared at global scope, as is **value4**, which appears after the function **main()**. The global variables have a scope that extends from the point at which they are declared to the end of the file. Even though **value4** exists when execution starts, it cannot be referred to in **main()** because **main()** is not within the variable's scope. For **main()** to use **value4**, you would need to move its declaration to the beginning of the file. Both **value1** and **value4** will be initialized with 0 by default, which is not the case for the automatic variables. Remember that the local variable called **value1** in **function()** will hide the global variable of the same name.

Since global variables continue to exist for as long as the program is running, this might raise the question in your mind, "Why not make all variables global and avoid this messing about with local variables that disappear?" This sounds very attractive at first, but there are serious disadvantages that completely outweigh any advantages that you might gain.

Real programs are generally composed of a large number of statements, a significant number of functions, and a great many variables. Declaring all of these at the global scope greatly magnifies the possibility of accidental, erroneous modification of a variable, as well as making the job of naming them sensibly quite intractable. They will also occupy memory for the duration of program execution. By keeping variables local to a function or a block, you can be sure they have almost complete protection from external effects. They will only exist and occupy memory from the point at which they are defined to the end of the enclosing block, and the whole development process becomes much easier to manage.

Try It Out – The Scope Resolution Operator

As we have seen, a global variable can be hidden by a local variable with the same name. However, it is still possible to 'get at' the global variable by using the **scope resolution operator** (**::**), which you saw in Chapter 1 when we were discussing namespaces. We can demonstrate how this works with a revised version of the last example:

```cpp
// Program 3.7 Using the scope resolution operator
#include <iostream>
using namespace std;

int count1 = 100;                  // Global version of count1

int main()
{                                  // Function scope starts here
  int count1 = 10;
  int count3 = 50;
  cout << endl << "Value of outer count1 = " << count1;
  cout << endl << "Value of global count1 = " << ::count1;

  {                                // New block scope starts here...
    int count1 = 20;              // This hides the outer count1
    int count2 = 30;
    cout << endl << "Value of inner count1 = " << count1;
    cout << endl << "Value of global count1 = " << ::count1;
    count1 += 3;                  // This changes the inner count1
    count3 += count2;
  }                              // ...and ends here.

  cout << endl
       << "Value of outer count1 = " << count1
       << endl
       << "Value of outer count3 = " << count3;

  // cout << endl << count2;   // Uncomment to get an error
  cout << endl;
  return 0;
}                                  // Function scope ends here
```

If you compile and run this example, you will get the following output:

```
Value of outer count1 = 10
Value of global count1 = 100
Value of inner count1 = 20
Value of global count1 = 100
Value of outer count1 = 10
Value of outer count3 = 80
```

How It Works

The shaded lines indicate the changes that we have made to the previous example, and they are the only ones whose effects we need to discuss. The declaration of **count1** prior to the definition of the function **main()** is global, so in principle it is available anywhere through the function **main()**. This global variable is initialized with the value of 100 in its declaration:

```
int count1 = 100;               // Global version of count1
```

However, we have two other variables called **count1**, which are defined within **main()**, so the global **count1** is hidden by the local **count1** variables throughout the program. In fact, in the inner block it is hidden behind *two* variables called **count1**: the inner **count1** and the outer **count1**. The first new output statement is:

```
int count1 = 10;
int count3 = 50;
cout << endl << "Value of outer count1 = " << count1;
cout << endl << "Value of global count1 = " << ::count1;
```

This uses the scope resolution operator to make it clear to the compiler that we want to reference the global **count1**, *not* the local one. You can see that this works by the value displayed in the output. The global scope resolution operator also does its stuff within the inner block, as you can see from the output generated by this statement:

```
int count1 = 20;                    // This hides the outer count1
int count2 = 30;
cout << endl << "Value of inner count1 = " << count1;
cout << endl << "Value of global count1 = " << ::count1;
```

This outputs the value 100, as before — the long arm of the scope resolution operator used in this fashion always reaches a global variable. You should be able to see that the task the operator is performing here is very similar to the one it performed in Chapter 1. By not specifying a namespace in front of the operator, we are requesting that it search the global namespace for the name that follows it.

We'll be seeing a lot more of this operator when we get to talking about object-oriented programming, in which context it is used extensively. We'll also talk further about namespaces, including how to create your own, in Chapter 10.

Static Variables

It is conceivable that you might want to have a variable that's defined and accessible locally, within a block, but which also continues to exist after exiting the block in which it is declared. In other words, you need to declare a variable within a block scope, but to give it static storage duration. The **static** specifier provides you with the means of doing just this, and the need for it will become more apparent when we come to deal with functions in Chapter 8.

A variable that you declare as **static** will continue to exist for the life of a program, even though it is declared within a block and is only available from within that block (or its sub-blocks). It still has block scope, but it has static storage duration. To declare a static variable called **count**, you would write:

```
static int count;
```

Variables with static storage duration are always initialized for you if you don't provide an initial value yourself. The variable **count** declared here will be initialized with 0. If you don't specify an initial value when you declare a static variable, it will always be initialized with 0, converted to the type applicable to the variable. Remember that this is *not* the case with automatic variables. If you don't initialize your automatic variables, they will contain junk values left over from the program that last used the memory they occupy.

Specialized Type Modifiers

There are two type modifiers that deal with specialized situations and can be applied to a variable when you declare it: **register** and **volatile**. The **register** modifier is used to indicate that a variable is critical to the speed of execution, and should therefore be placed in a machine register. (A register is a special, high-speed storage facility located separate from main memory, usually on the processor chip.) An example of how you use this modifier is:

```
register int index = 0;
```

Here, we are requesting that the variable **index** use a register. The compiler is under no obligation to accede to this request, and in many compilers it will not result in a register being allocated for this purpose. In general, you should not use **register** unless you are absolutely sure of what you are doing. Most compilers will do a better job of deciding how registers should be used without any prompting.

The **volatile** modifier is used to indicate that the value of a variable can be modified asynchronously by an external process, such as an interrupt routine. The effect is to inhibit optimization that the compiler might otherwise carry out. For example, when a program references a non-**volatile** variable, the compiler might be able to reuse an existing value for that variable that was previously loaded into a register, to avoid the overhead of retrieving the same value from memory. If the variable was declared as **volatile**, its value will be retrieved every time it is used.

Declaring External Variables

We saw in Chapter 1 that programs can consist of several source files, and that most programs of any size will generally do so. If you have a program that consists of more than one source file, you may need to access a global variable from one source file that is declared in another. The **extern** keyword allows you to do this. Suppose you have one program file that contains the following:

```
// File1.cpp
int shared_value = 100;
```

```
    // Other program code
```

If you have code in another file that needs to access the **shared_value** variable, you can arrange for this as follows:

```
// File2.cpp
extern int shared_value;        // Declare variable to be external

int main()
{
  int local_value = shared_value + 10;
..// Plus other code...
}
```

The first statement here declares **shared_value** to be external, so this is *only* a declaration, not a definition. The reference to **shared_value** in **main()** is then to the variable defined in the first file, **File1.cpp**.

You must not use an initializing value when declaring an external variable. If in the second file you wrote:

```
extern int shared_value = 0;     // Wrong! Not an external declaration.
```

The variable would be defined locally, and the **extern** declaration would be ignored.

Precedence and Associativity

We have accumulated quite a number of new operators in this chapter, so let's summarize the precedence and associativity of the operators we have seen so far:

Operator	Associativity	Operator	Associativity
static_cast<>() postfix **++** postfix **--**	right	binary **+** binary **-**	left
~ unary **+** unary **-** prefix **++** prefix **--**	right	**<<** **>>**	left
		&	left
		^	left
		|	left
* **/** **%**	left	**=** **op=**	right

These are in sequence from highest precedence to lowest, and each line in the table contains operators that have the same precedence. The sequence of execution of operators with the same precedence in an expression is determined from their associativity. As I mentioned previously, a table showing the precedence of all the C++ operators appears in Appendix D.

Summary

In this chapter, we have covered some more complicated aspects of computation in C++. We have also talked a little about how you can define data types of your own, although what we have seen here has nothing to do with the capability to define completely general types of your own. That will be discussed in Chapter 11. The essentials of what we have looked at are:

▶ You can mix different types of variables and constants in an expression. The compiler will arrange for variables to be automatically converted to an appropriate type where necessary.

▶ Automatic conversion of the type of the right hand side of an assignment to that of the left hand side will also be made where these are different. This can cause loss of information when the left hand side type is not able to contain the same information as the right hand side: **double** converted to **int**, for example, or **long** converted to **short**.

▶ You can explicitly convert a value of one basic type to another by using **static_cast<>()**.

▶ By default, a variable declared within a block is automatic, which means that it only exists from the point at which it is declared to the end of the block in which its declaration appears, indicated by the closing brace of the block that encloses its declaration.

▶ A variable may be declared as **static**, in which case it continues to exist for the life of the program. However, it can only be *accessed* within the scope in which it was defined. If you don't initialize a static variable explicitly, it will be initialized to 0 by default.

▶ Variables can be declared outside of all the blocks within a program, in which case they have global namespace scope, and static storage duration by default. Variables with global scope are accessible from anywhere within the program file that contains them, following the point at which they are declared, except where a local variable exists with the same name as the global variable. Even then, they can still be reached by using the scope resolution operator (**::**).

▶ The keyword **typedef** allows you to define synonyms for other types.

▶ The **extern** keyword allows you to reference a global variable defined in another file.

Exercises

Ex 3.1 Write a program that calculates the reciprocal of a non-zero integer entered by the user. (The reciprocal of an integer, **n**, is 1/**n**.) The program should store the result of the calculation in a variable of type **double**, and then output it.

Ex 3.2 Create a program that prompts the user to input an integer in decimal form. Then, invert the last bit of its binary representation. That is, if the last bit is 1, then change it to 0, and vice versa. The result should then be displayed as a decimal number. How does the adjustment affect the resulting integer value? (Hint: use a bitwise operator.)

Ex 3.3 Write a program to calculate how many square boxes can be contained in a single layer on a rectangular shelf, with no overhang. Use variables of type **double** for the length and depth of the shelf (in feet) and for the length of one side of a single box (in inches). You'll need to declare and initialize a constant to convert from feet to inches. In a single statement, calculate the number of boxes that the shelf can hold in a single layer, assigning the answer to a variable of type **long**.

Ex 3.4 Without running it, can you work out what the following code snippet will produce?

```
unsigned int k = 430U;

unsigned int j = (k >> 4) & ~(~0 << 3);
cout << j;
```

Choices and Decisions

Decision-making is fundamental to any kind of computer programming. Without the ability to alter the sequence of instructions in a program based on the result of comparing data values, it would not be possible to solve most problems with computer programs.

In this chapter, we will explore how you make choices and decisions in your C++ programs. This will enable you to check the validity of program input, and to write programs that can adapt their actions depending on the input data. Your programs will be able to handle problems where logic is fundamental to the solution. By the end of this chapter, you will have learned:

- How to compare data values
- How to alter the sequence of program execution based on the result
- What logical operators and expressions are, and how you can apply them
- How to deal with multiple choice situations

Comparing Data Values

To make decisions, we need a mechanism for comparing things, and there are several kinds of comparisons we can make. A decision such as, "If the traffic signal is red, stop the car," involves a comparison for equality. We compare the color of the signal with a reference color, red, and if they are equal we stop the car. On the other hand, a decision like, "If the speed of the car exceeds the limit, slow down," involves a different relationship: we are checking whether the speed of the car is greater than the current speed limit. Both of these comparisons are similar in that they result in one of two values: they are either **true** or **false**. This is precisely how comparisons work in C++.

We can compare data values using some operators called **relational operators**. We have six fundamental operators for comparing two values:

`<`	less than	`<=`	less than or equal to
`>`	greater than	`>=`	greater than or equal to
`==`	equal to	`!=`	not equal to

FYI Here, the 'equal to' comparison operator has two successive equals signs. This is *not* the same as the assignment operator (=), which consists of only a single equals sign. It's a very common mistake to use one equals sign instead of two when you intended to compare for equality. This will not generally result in an error message from the compiler, so you need to take particular care to avoid this kind of error.

Each of these binary operators compares two values and results in a **true** value if the comparison is true, or **false** if it is not. The values **true** and **false** are keywords in C++, and are also a new type of literal. We call them **Boolean literals** (after George Boole, who was the father of Boolean algebra), and they are of type **bool**.

If you cast the value **true** to an integer type, the result will be 1, and if you cast **false** to an integer, the result will be 0. You can also cast numerical values to type **bool**. Zero will cast to **false**, and any non-zero value will cast to **true**.

As with the other standard types, you can create a variable of type **bool** for the purpose of storing Boolean values. You declare these just like you would any other variable, for example:

```
bool decision = true;       // Declare, define and initialize a logical variable
```

This declares and defines the variable **decision** as Boolean, and assigns it an initial value of **true**.

Applying the Comparison Operators

We can see how comparisons work by having a look at a few simple examples of applying the operators. Suppose we have two integer variables called **i** and **j**, with the values 10 and -5 respectively. We can use these in the following logical expressions:

```
i > j           i != j          j > -8          i <= j + 15
```

All of these expressions evaluate to **true**. Note that in the last expression, **i <= j + 15**, the addition operation **j + 15** is executed first because **+** has a higher precedence than **<=**. You could store the result of any of these expressions in a variable of type **bool**. For example:

```
decision = i > j;            // true if i is greater than j, false otherwise
```

We can compare variables of type **char**, too. Let's assume that we have the following variables defined:

```
char first = 'A';
char last = 'Z';
```

We can now write some examples of comparisons using these variables. Take a look at the following:

```
first < last           'E' <= first           first != last
```

The first expression checks whether the value of **first**, which is **'A'**, is less than the value of **last**, which is **'Z'**. This is always true. You can check this is the case for ASCII by looking at the codes for these characters in Appendix A — the upper case letters are represented by an ascending sequence of numerical values from 65 to 90, 65 representing **'A'** and 90 representing **'Z'**. The result of the second expression is **false**, since **'E'** is greater than the value of **first**. The last expression is **true**, since **'A'** is definitely not equal to **'Z'**.

We can output **bool** values just as easily as any other type of value, so let's see how they look with an example.

Try It Out – Comparing Data Values

This example reads two **char** values from the keyboard, and outputs the result of their comparison:

```
// Program 4.1 Comparing data values
#include <iostream>
using namespace std;

int main()
{
  char first = 0;                       // Stores the first character
  char second = 0;                      // Stores the second character

  // Prompt for and read in the first character
  cout << "Enter a character: ";
  cin >> first;

  // Prompt for and read in the second character
  cout << "Enter a second character: ";
  cin >> second;

  cout << "The value of the expression first < second is: "
       << (first < second)
       << endl
       << "The value of the expression first == second is: "
       << (first == second)
       << endl;

  return 0;
}
```

An example of the output from this program is:

```
Enter a character: p
Enter a second character: t
The value of the expression first < second is: 1
The value of the expression first == second is: 0
```

How It Works

The prompting for input and reading the characters from the keyboard is standard stuff that you have seen before. We output the results of applying the **<** and **==** operators in the statement:

```
cout << "The value of the expression first < second is: "
     << (first < second)
     << endl
     << "The value of the expression first == second is: "
     << (first == second)
     << endl;
```

Note that the parentheses around the comparison expressions *are* necessary here, otherwise the compiler will not be able to interpret the statement correctly and will output an error message. The expressions compare the first and second characters that were entered. You can see from the output above that the value **true** is displayed as **1**, and the value **false** is displayed as **0**.

If we wanted the Boolean values actually to display as **true** and **false** on the screen, we could use the output manipulator **boolalpha** to do this. Just add this statement at the beginning of **main()**:

```
cout << boolalpha;
```

If you compile and run the example again, you will get **bool** values displayed as **true** or **false**. To return output of Boolean values to the default setting within your program, you can use the **noboolalpha** manipulator.

Comparing Floating Point Values

Of course, you can also compare floating-point values. Let's consider some slightly more complicated numerical comparisons. First, we'll define some variables with the following statements:

```
int i = -10;
int j = 20;
double x = 1.5;
double y = -0.25E-10;
```

Now take a look at the following logical expressions:

```
-1 < y              j < (10 - i)              2.0 * x >= (3 + y)
```

As you can see, we can use expressions that result in a numerical value as operands in comparisons. Since the comparison operators are all of lower precedence than the arithmetic operators (see Appendix D), none of the parentheses is strictly necessary, but they do help to make the expressions clearer.

The first comparison produces the value **true**, because the variable **y** has a very small negative value (–0.000000000025), which is greater than –1. The second comparison results in the value **false**, because the expression **10 - i** has the value 20, which is the same as **j**. The third expression is **true**, since **3 + y** is slightly less than 3.

We can use relational operators to compare values of any of the basic types, so all we need now is a practical way of using the results of a comparison to modify the behavior of a program. Let's look into that immediately.

The if Statement

The basic **if** statement allows your program to execute a single statement, or a block of statements enclosed between braces, if a given condition is **true**. This is illustrated in the figure opposite:

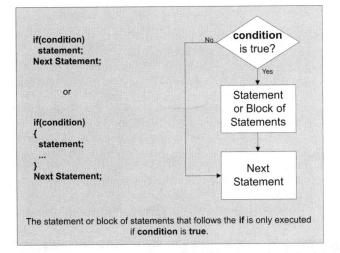

The statement or block of statements that follows the **if** is only executed if **condition** is **true**.

A simple example of an **if** statement to test the value of a variable called **letter**, of type **char**, is as follows:

```
if(letter == 'A')
   cout << "The first capital, alphabetically speaking." << endl;

cout << "This statement always executes." << endl;
```

If **letter** has the value **'A'**, the condition is true and these statements will produce the output:

```
The first capital, alphabetically speaking.
This statement always executes.
```

If the value of **letter** is not equal to **'A'**, only the second line will be output. The condition to be tested appears in parentheses immediately following the keyword **if**. Notice the position of the semicolon here. It goes after the statement following the **if** and the condition between the parentheses. There must not be a semicolon after the condition in parentheses, as the **if** and the condition are bound with the statement or block that follows. They should not exist by themselves.

You can also see how the statement following the **if** is indented to indicate it that is only executed as a result of the condition being **true**. The indentation is not necessary for the program to compile, but it does help you to recognize the relationship between the **if** condition and the statement that depends on it. Sometimes, you will see simple **if** statements like this one written on a single line:

```
if(letter == 'A') cout << "The first capital, alphabetically speaking." << endl;
```

Generally, I prefer to write the statement (or block) bound to the **if** condition on a separate line; I think it is much clearer that way.

We could extend this example to change the value of **letter** if it contains the value **'A'**:

```
if(letter == 'A')
{
  cout << "The first capital, alphabetically speaking." << endl;
  letter = 'a';
}

cout << "This statement always executes." << endl;
```

Now we execute the statements in the block only if the condition is **true**. Without the braces, only the first statement would be the subject of the **if**, and the statement assigning the value **'a'** to **letter** would always be executed. Note that there is a semicolon after each of the statements in the block, and not after the closing brace at the end of the block. There can be as many statements as you like within the block, or even nested blocks. As a result of **letter** having the value **'A'**, we now change its value to **'a'**, after outputting the same message as before. Neither of these statements will be executed if the condition is **false**. Of course, the statement following the block is always executed.

Try It Out – Making a Decision

Let's try out an **if** statement for real. We can create a program to range check the value of an integer entered from the keyboard:

```
// Program 4.2 Using an if statement
#include <iostream>
using namespace std;

int main()
{
  cout << "Enter an integer between 50 and 100: ";

  int value = 0;
  cin >> value;

  if(value < 50)
    cout << "The value is invalid - it is less than 50." << endl;

  if(value > 100)
    cout << "The value is invalid - it is greater than 100." << endl;

  cout << "You entered " << value << endl;
  return 0;
}
```

The output will depend on the value that you enter. For a value between 50 and 100, the output will be something like:

```
Enter an integer between 50 and 100: 77
You entered 77
```

Outside of the range 50 to 100, a message indicating that the value is invalid will precede the output showing the value entered. If it is below 50, the output will be:

```
Enter an integer between 50 and 100: 27
The value is invalid - it is less than 50.
You entered 27
```

If the value is greater than 100, the output will be similar to:

```
Enter an integer between 50 and 100: 270
The value is invalid - it is greater than 100.
You entered 270
```

How It Works

After prompting for, and reading a value, the first **if** statement checks whether the value entered is below the lower limit of 50:

```
if(value < 50)
   cout << "The value is invalid - it is less than 50." << endl;
```

The output statement will only be executed if the **if** condition is **true**, which is when **value** is less than 50. The next **if** statement checks the upper limit:

```
if(value > 100)
   cout << "The value is invalid - it is greater than 100." << endl;
```

The output statement will be executed if **value** is greater than 100. The last output statement is:

```
cout << "You entered " << value << endl;
```

This statement is always executed.

Nested if Statements

The statement that is to be executed when the condition in an **if** statement is **true** can itself be an **if** statement. This arrangement is called a **nested if**. The condition of the inner **if** is only tested if the condition for the outer **if** is **true**. An **if** that is nested inside another can *also* contain a nested **if**. You can generally continue nesting **if**s like this, one inside the other, to whatever level you require.

Try It Out – Using Nested ifs

We can demonstrate the nested **if** with a working example that will test a character entered from the keyboard to see if it is alphabetic. While this example is a perfectly reasonable use of a nested **if**, it has some built-in assumptions that it would be best to avoid; see if you can spot the problem. Here's the code:

```cpp
// Program 4.3 Using a nested if
#include <iostream>
using namespace std;

int main()
{
  char letter = 0;                              // Store input in here
```

117

```
    cout << endl
        << "Enter a letter: ";          // Prompt for the input
    cin >> letter;                       // then read a character
    cout << endl;

    if(letter >= 'A')                    // Test for 'A' or larger
    {
      if(letter <= 'Z')                  // Test for 'Z' or smaller
      {
        cout << "You entered an upper case letter."
             << endl;
        return 0;
      }
    }

    if(letter >= 'a')                    // Test for 'a' or larger
      if(letter <= 'z')                  // Test for 'z' or smaller
      {
        cout << "You entered a lower case letter."
             << endl ;
        return 0;
      }

    cout << "You did not enter a letter." << endl;
    return 0;
}
```

A typical output from this example is:

```
Enter a letter: H

You entered an upper case letter.
```

How It Works

This program starts with the usual comment lines and the **#include** statement for the header file supporting input/output, **iostream**. After allocating memory for the **char** variable **letter** and initializing it to zero, the function **main()** prompts for a letter to be entered.

The **if** statement that follows the input checks whether the character entered is **'A'** or larger:

```
    if(letter >= 'A')                    // Test for 'A' or larger
    {
      if(letter <= 'Z')                  // Test for 'Z' or smaller
      {
        cout << "You entered an upper case letter."
             << endl;
        return 0;
      }
    }
```

If **letter** is greater than or equal to **'A'**, the nested **if** that checks for the input being **'Z'** or less is executed. If it *is* **'Z'** or less, we conclude that we have an upper case letter, display a message and we are done, so we execute a **return** statement to end the program. Both statements are enclosed between braces, so they are both executed when the nested **if** condition is **true**.

This pair of nested **if**s is built on two assumptions about the codes used to represent alphabetic characters. The first assumption is that the letters A to Z are represented by a set of codes where the code for **'A'** is the minimum and the code for **'Z'** is the maximum. The second assumption is that the codes for the upper case letters are contiguous, so no non-alphabetic characters lie between the codes for **'A'** and **'Z'**. It is not a good idea to build these kinds of assumptions into your code, because it limits the portability of your program. In EBCDIC coding, for instance, the alphabetic character codes are not contiguous. We will see how we can avoid this constraint in a moment.

The next **if**, using essentially the same mechanism as the first **if**, checks whether the character entered is lower case, displays a message and **return**s. If you were watching closely, though, you'll have noticed that the test for a lower case character contains only one pair of braces, while the upper case test has two. In fact, both methods are fine: remember that in C++, **if(condition){...}** is effectively a single statement, and does not need to be enclosed within more braces. By the same token, if you feel the extra braces make the code clearer, it's your prerogative to use them. Finally, like the upper case test, this code contains implicit assumptions about the codes for lower case letters.

The output statement following the last **if** block will only be executed if the character entered was not a letter, and it displays a message to that effect. The **return** statement is then executed. You can see that the relationship between the nested **if**s and the output statement is much easier to follow because of the indentation applied to each. Indentation is generally used in C++ to provide visual cues to the logic of a program.

As I said at the start of the example, the program illustrates how a nested **if** works, but it is not a good way to test for characters. By using the standard library, we could write the program so that it would work independently of the character coding. Let's see how we could do that.

Code-neutral Character Handling

The standard library provides a wide range of functions that you can use in your programs to perform a similarly wide range of tasks. We won't look at how to create our own functions until Chapter 8, but that shouldn't stop us from using ones that have already been created. Before we continue, however, you'll find it helpful to have an idea of what's going on when you use a function, and some of the terminology they introduce.

A function is a named, self-contained block of code that carries out a specific task. Often, this will involve it performing some operation on data that you supply, and then returning the result of that operation to your program. In those circumstances, a function behaves rather like the **sizeof()** operator we saw in the last chapter: we supplied it with some data (a variable), and it returned a result (the size of that variable). In general, a call to a function looks like this:

```
FunctionName(argument1, argument2, ... )
```

Depending on the function in question, you can supply zero, one or more values for it to work with by placing them in parentheses after its name when you **call** it from your program. The values you pass to the function in this way are called **arguments**. Like all values in C++, the arguments you pass to a function, and the value it returns to your program, have types that you must take care to conform with in order to use the function.

By including the header file **cctype** in your program, you can get access to an extremely useful set of functions for testing characters. In each case, you pass the function a variable or a literal of type **int**. If you pass a **char** type, it will automatically be converted to **int**.

Function	Action carried out
`isupper()`	Tests for an upper case letter, `'A'` to `'Z'`.
`islower()`	Tests for a lower case letter, `'a'` to `'z'`.
`isalpha()`	Tests for an upper or lower case letter.
`isdigit()`	Tests for a digit, `0` to `9`.
`isxdigit()`	Tests for a hexadecimal digit, `0` to `9`, `'a'` to `'f'` or `'A'` to `'F'`.
`isalnum()`	Tests for a letter or a digit (i.e. an alphanumeric character).
`isspace()`	Tests for whitespace, which can be a space, a newline, a carriage return, a form feed or a horizontal or vertical tab.
`iscntrl()`	Tests for a control character.
`isprint()`	Tests for a printable character, which can be an upper or lower case letter, a digit, a punctuation character or a space.
`isgraph()`	Tests for a graphic character, which is any printable character other than a space.
`ispunct()`	Tests for a punctuation character, which is any printable character that's not a letter or a digit. This will be either a space or one of the following: `_ { } [ ] # ( ) < > % : ; . ? * + - / ^ &	~` `! = , \ " '`

Each of these functions returns a value of type **int**. The value will be positive (**true**) if the character is of the type being tested for, and **0** (**false**) if it isn't. You may be wondering why these functions don't return a value of type **bool**, which would seem to make much more sense. The reason is that these functions were part of the standard library before type **bool** was introduced into C++.

The **cctype** header file also provides two functions for converting between upper and lower case characters, which should be passed the character to be converted as type **int**:

▶ **tolower()** If you pass an upper case letter, the lower case equivalent is returned, otherwise the letter you pass is returned unchanged.

▶ **toupper()** If you pass a lower case letter, the upper case equivalent is returned, otherwise the letter you pass is returned unchanged.

Both of these functions also return a value of type **int**.

We can use these functions to implement the previous example without any assumptions about the character coding. Different character codes in different environments will always be taken care of by the standard library functions, so we don't need to worry about it. Using the standard library functions here will also eliminate the need to use nested **if**s, so the code will be simpler than before.

Try It Out – Using Standard Library Character Conversions

While we modify the last example to use standard library functions, we might as well extend the capability of the program to try out the conversion functions too:

```
// Program 4.4 Using standard library character testing and conversion
#include <iostream>
#include <cctype>                       // Character testing and conversion
using namespace std;

int main()
{
  char letter = 0;                      // Store input in here

  cout << endl
       << "Enter a letter: ";           // Prompt for the input
  cin >> letter;                        // then read a character
  cout << endl;

  if(isupper(letter))                   // Test for upper case letter
  {
    cout << "You entered a capital letter."
         << endl;
    cout << "Converting to lower case we get "
         << static_cast<char>(tolower(letter)) << endl;
    return 0;
  }

  if(islower(letter))                   // Test for lower case letter
  {
    cout << "You entered a small letter."
         << endl;
    cout << "Converting to upper case we get "
         << static_cast<char>(toupper(letter)) << endl;
    return 0;
  }

  cout << "You did not enter a letter." << endl;
  return 0;
}
```

Typical example of the output is:

```
Enter a letter: t

You entered a small letter.
Converting to upper case we get T
```

How It Works

The **if** expressions have been changed to use the standard library functions. We no longer need the nested **if**s, because the two conditions we tested for before are now covered in one go by either the **isupper()** or the **islower()** function.

We really don't care how these functions work. In order to use them, we just need to know what job they do, how many and what types of arguments to pass them, and what type of value they return. Armed with that information, we've been able to use standard library functions to make our code much simpler and more generic. This version of the program will work with whatever character coding is used for type **char**.

Notice how we use the result returned from a conversion function directly in the output statements — for example:

```
cout << "Converting to upper case we get "
     << static_cast<char>(toupper(letter)) << endl;
```

The value returned by the **toupper()** function is of type **int**, so we cast it to **char** and send it to the output stream, **cout**. If we wanted to store the returned character and remove the need for the explicit cast, we could save it back in the original variable, **letter**, with a statement such as:

```
letter = toupper(letter);
```

We could then output the converted character by using the variable **letter** in the output statement:

```
cout << "Converting to upper case we get " << letter << endl;
```

If you need to use wide characters (of type **wchar_t**), you can include the header file **<cwctype>**. This includes wide character equivalents of all the functions declared in **<cctype>**. Each of the testing function names has a 'w' after the 'is', so they are called:

```
iswupper()      iswdigit()      iswspace()      iswgraph()
iswlower()      iswxdigit()     iswcntrl()      iswpunct()
iswalpha()      iswalnum()      iswprint()
```

They each should be passed a wide character, and all return an **int** value, just as the functions handling characters of type **char** do. In similar vein, the wide character conversion functions are called **towlower()** and **towupper()**.

The if-else Statement

The **if** statement that we have been using so far executes a statement *if* the condition specified is **true**. Program execution then continues with the next statement in sequence. Of course, it might be that we want to execute a particular statement or block of statements only when the condition is **false**. To cater for this, we have an extension of the **if** that allows one course of action to be followed if the condition is **true**, and another to be executed if the condition is **false**. Execution then continues with the next statement in sequence.

Still using variables of type **char**, we could write an **if-else** statement that would report whether the character stored in the variable **letter** was alphanumeric:

```
if(isalnum(letter))
   cout << "It is a letter or a digit."
        << endl;
else
   cout << "It is neither a letter nor a digit."
        << endl;
```

This uses the function **isalnum()** from the header **cctype** that we saw earlier. If the variable **letter** contains a letter or a digit, the function **isalnum()** will return a positive integer. The

if statement interprets this as **true**, so the first message will be displayed. If **letter** contains something other than a letter or a digit, **isalnum()** will return 0. For the purposes of the **if**, this is automatically converted to **false**, and the output statement after **else** will be executed.

Try It Out – Extending the if

We can see the **if-else** statement in action in an example. Let's try it with a numerical value this time:

```
// Program 4.5 Using the if-else
#include <iostream>
using namespace std;

int main()
{
  long number = 0;                    // Store input here
  cout << "Enter an integer less than 2 billion: ";
  cin >> number;
  cout << endl;

  if(number % 2L == 0)                // Test remainder after division by 2
    cout << "Your number is even."    // Here if remainder is 0
         << endl;
  else
    cout << "Your number is odd."     // Here if remainder is 1
         << endl;
  return 0;
}
```

A typical example of output from this program is:

```
Enter an integer less than 2 billion: 123456

Your number is even.
```

How It Works

After reading the input value into **number**, the value is tested in the **if** condition by taking the remainder after division by 2 (using the remainder operator, **%**, that we saw in Chapter 2) and checking whether it is 0. The remainder of a division of an integer by 2 can only be 1 or 0, and the code is commented to indicate this fact. If the remainder is equal to zero, then the **if** condition is **true** and the statement immediately following the **if** is executed. If the remainder is 1, then the **if** condition is **false**, and the statement following the **else** keyword is executed. After either outcome, the **return** statement is executed to end the program.

Note that the **else** keyword is written without a semicolon, just like the **if** part of the statement. Again, indentation is used as a visible indicator of the relationship between various statements. You can clearly see which statement is executed for a **true** result, and which for a **false** result. You should always indent the statements in your programs to show their logical structure.

Here's an alternative way of coding the **if** condition in this example. Recall that any non-zero value produces **true** when converted to type **bool**, and a value of 0 converts to **false**. We could therefore use the result of the modulus operation as the condition, and not bother with comparing it to 0. If we do that, the **if-else** statement could look like this:

```
if(number % 2L)                          // Test remainder after division by 2
   cout << "Your number is odd."         // Here if remainder is 1
         << endl;
else
   cout << "Your number is even."        // Here if remainder is 0
         << endl;
```

The **if** and the **else** clauses just need to be reversed; this is because if the value of **number** is even, then **(number % 2L == 0)** returns **true**, while **(number % 2L)** will be converted to **false**. This may seem a little confusing at first, but remember that the first version of the condition was equivalent to:

"Is it true that the remainder is 0?"

While, since 1 will be converted to **true**, the second version is equivalent to:

"Is the remainder 1?"

The **if-else** combination provides a choice between two options. The general logic of the **if-else** is shown in the illustration below:

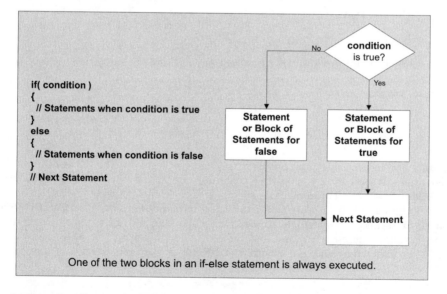

One of the two blocks in an if-else statement is always executed.

The flowchart in the diagram indicates the sequence in which statements are executed, depending on whether the **if** condition is **true** or **false**. As the illustration implies, and as we have seen before, a block can always be used wherever a statement can appear.

Nested if-else Statements

We have already seen that you can nest **if** statements within **if** statements. As you have no doubt anticipated, you can also nest **if-else** statements within **if**s, **if**s within **if-else** statements, and indeed **if-else** statements within other **if-else** statements. This provides us with plenty of versatility (and considerable room for confusion), so let's look at a few examples. Taking the first case first, an example of an **if-else** nested within an **if** might be:

```
if(coffee == 'y')
  if(donuts == 'y')
    cout << "We have coffee and donuts."
         << endl;
  else
    cout << "We have coffee, but not donuts"
         << endl;
```

Here, **coffee** and **donuts** are variables of type **char** that can have the value **'y'** or **'n'**. The test for **donuts** is only executed if the result of the test for **coffee** is **true**, so the messages reflect the correct situation in each case. The **else** belongs to the **if** that tests for **donuts**. However, it is easy to get this confused.

If we write much the same thing, but with incorrect indentation, we can be trapped into the wrong conclusion about what happens here:

```
if(coffee == 'y')
  if(donuts == 'y')
    cout << endl
         << "We have coffee and donuts.";
  else                              // This else is indented incorrectly
    cout << "We have no coffee..."       // Wrong!
         << endl;
```

The indentation of the code now misleadingly suggests that we're looking at an **if** nested within an **if-else**, which is simply not the case. The first message is correct, but the output as a consequence of the **else** being executed is quite wrong. This statement can only be executed if the test for coffee is **true**, since the **else** belongs to the test for donuts, not the test for coffee. This mistake is easy to see, but with larger and more complicated **if** structures, we need to keep in mind the rule about which **if** owns which **else**.

> An **else** *always belongs to the nearest preceding* **if** *that's not already spoken for by another* **else***. The potential for confusion here is known as the* dangling else *problem.*

Whenever a bunch of **if-else** statements looks a bit complicated in a program, you can apply this rule to sort things out. When you're writing your own programs, you can always use braces to make the situation clearer. It isn't really necessary in such a simple case, but we could write the last example as follows:

```
if(coffee == 'y')
{
  if(donuts == 'y')
    cout << "We have coffee and donuts."
         << endl;
```

```
      else
        cout << "We have coffee, but not donuts"
                << endl;
  }
```

Now it should be absolutely clear. The **else** definitely belongs to the **if** that is checking for donuts.

Understanding Nested ifs

Now that we know the rules, understanding the case of an **if** nested within an **if-else** becomes easy:

```
  if(coffee == 'y')
  {
    if(donuts == 'y')
      cout << "We have coffee and donuts."
            << endl;
  }
  else if(tea == 'y')
    cout << "We have no coffee, but we have tea"
          << endl;
```

> *Notice the formatting of the code here. When an **if** is nested beneath an **else**, writing '**else if**' on one line is the accepted convention, and I will be following it in this book.*

This time, the braces are essential. If we left them out, the **else** would belong to the **if** that's looking out for **donuts**. In this kind of situation, it is easy to forget to include them and create an error that may be hard to find. A program with this kind of error will compile without a problem, as the code is perfectly correct. It may even produce the right results some of the time, but it doesn't express what was intended.

If we removed the braces in this example, we'd get the right results only as long as **coffee** and **donuts** were both equal to **'y'**, so that the **if(tea == 'y')** check wouldn't be executed.

Finally, we'll look at **if-else** statements nested in other **if-else** statements. This can get very messy, even with just one level of nesting. Let's beat the coffee and donuts analysis to death by using it again:

```
  if(coffee == 'y')
    if(donuts == 'y')
      cout << "We have coffee and donuts."
            << endl;
    else
      cout << "We have coffee, but not donuts"
            << endl;
  else if(tea == 'y')
    cout << "We have no coffee, but we have tea, and maybe donuts...";
          << endl
  else
    cout << "No tea or coffee, but maybe donuts..."
          << endl;
```

The logic here doesn't look quite so obvious, even with the correct indentation. No braces are necessary, as the rule you saw earlier will verify, but it would look a bit clearer if we included them:

```
if(coffee == 'y')
{
  if(donuts == 'y')
    cout << "We have coffee and donuts."
          << endl;
  else
    cout << "We have coffee, but not donuts"
          << endl;
}
else
{
  if(tea == 'y')
    cout << " We have no coffee, but we have tea, and maybe donuts..."
          << endl;
  else
    cout << "No tea or coffee, but maybe donuts..."
          << endl;
}
```

There are much better ways of dealing with this kind of logic in a program. If you put enough nested **if**s together, you can almost guarantee a mistake somewhere. The following section will help to simplify things.

Logical Operators

As we have just seen, using **if**s where we have two or more related conditions can be a bit cumbersome. We have tried our **if**fy talents on looking for coffee and donuts, but in practice you may want to check much more complex conditions. You could be searching a personnel file for someone who is over 21 but under 35, female with a college degree, unmarried and who speaks Hindi or Urdu. Defining a test for this could involve the mother of all **if**s.

C++'s **logical operators** provide a neat and simple solution. Using logical operators, we can combine a series of comparisons into a single expression, so we end up needing just one **if**, almost regardless of the complexity of the set of conditions. What's more, there are just three of them:

&&	Logical AND
||	Logical OR
!	Logical negation (NOT)

The first two, **&&** and **||**, are binary operators that combine two operands of type **bool** and produce a result of type **bool**. The third operator, **!**, is unary, so it applies to a single operand of type **bool** and produces a **bool** result. We'll first consider what each of these is used for in general terms, then we'll look at an example. It's important that you separate in your mind the bitwise operators we saw earlier, which operate on the bits within integer operands, and these logical operators that apply to operands of type **bool**.

Logical AND

You would use the AND operator, **&&**, where you have two conditions that must both be **true** for a **true** result. You want to be rich *and* healthy. When we were using a nested **if** earlier to determine whether a character was an upper case letter, the value being tested had to be both greater than or equal to **'A'**, *and* less than or equal to **'Z'**. Both conditions must be **true** for the character to be an upper case letter. The **&&** operator *only* produces a **true** result if both operands are **true**. In all other cases the result is **false**. We can show this in a little table, where the top row and left column show the operands:

Operands	true	false
true	true	false
false	false	false

Taking the example of a value stored in a **char** variable called **letter**, we could replace the test using two **if**s with one that uses only a single **if** and the **&&** operator:

```
if(letter >= 'A' && letter <= 'Z')
   cout << "This is an upper case letter."
        << endl;
```

The output statement will be executed only if both of the conditions combined by the operator **&&** are **true**. No parentheses are necessary in the expression because the precedence of the comparison operators is higher than that of **&&**. As usual, you're free to put parentheses in if you want. You could write the statement as:

```
if((letter >= 'A') && (letter <= 'Z'))
   cout << "This is an upper case letter."
        << endl;
```

Now there can be no doubt that the comparisons between parentheses will be executed first.

Logical OR

The OR operator, **||**, applies when you have two conditions and you want a **true** result when either or both of them are **true**. The **||** operator only produces a **false** result when both of its operands are false. All other combinations produce a **true** result. This is shown in the table:

Operands	true	false
true	true	true
false	true	false

For example, you might be considered creditworthy for a loan from the bank if your income was at least $100,000 a year, or if you had $1,000,000 in cash. This could be tested using the following **if**:

```
    if(income >= 100000.00 || capital >= 1000000.00)
      cout << "Of course, how much do you want to borrow?"
            << endl;
```

The response emerges when either or both of the conditions are **true**. (A better response might be, "*Why* do you want to borrow?" It's strange how banks will only lend you money when you don't need it.)

Logical Negation

The third logical operator, **!**, takes one operand with a logical value — **true** or **false** — and inverts its value. So, if the value of a Boolean variable **test** is **true**, then **!test** is **false**; if **test** is **false**, then **!test** is **true**. For example, if **x** has the value 10, then this expression:

$$!(x > 5)$$

is **false**, since **x > 5** is **true**. We could also apply the **!** operator in an expression that was a favorite of Charles Dickens:

$$!(income > expenditure)$$

If this expression is **true**, the result is misery — at least, as soon as the bank starts bouncing your checks.

All the logical operators can be applied to expressions that evaluate to **true** or **false**. Operands can be anything from a simple variable of type **bool** to a complex combination of comparisons and logical variables.

Try It Out - Combining Logical Operators

You can combine conditional expressions and logical operators to any degree that you feel comfortable with. For example, we could construct a questionnaire to decide whether a person was a good loan risk. Let's write it as a working example:

```
// Program 4.6 Combining logical operators
#include <iostream>
using namespace std;

int main()
{
  int age = 0;                    // Age of the prospective borrower
  int income = 0;                 // Income of the prospective borrower
  int balance = 0;                // Current bank balance

  // Get the basic data
  cout << endl << "Please enter your age in years: ";
  cin >> age;

  cout << "Please enter your annual income in dollars: ";
  cin >> income;
```

```
         cout << "What is your current account balance in dollars: ";
         cin >> balance;
         cout << endl;

         // We only lend to people over 21, who make
         // over $25,000 per year, or have over
         // $100,000 in their account, or both.

         if(age >= 21 && (income > 25000 || balance > 100000))
         {
            // OK, you are good for the loan - but how much?
            // This will be the lesser of twice income and half balance

            int loan = 0;                       // Stores maximum loan amount
            if(2 * income < balance / 2)
              loan = 2 * income;
            else
              loan = balance / 2;

            cout << "You can borrow up to $"
                 << loan
                 << endl;
         }
         else
            cout << "Sorry, we are out of cash today."
                 << endl;
         return 0;
      }
```

An example of the output from this program is:

```
Please enter your age in years: 25
Please enter your annual income in dollars: 28000
What is your current account balance in dollars: 185000

You can borrow up to $56000
```

How It Works

We first declare three integer variables that we will use to store values entered via the keyboard:

```
int age = 0;                 // Age of the prospective borrower
int income = 0;              // Income of the prospective borrower
int balance = 0;             // Current bank balance
```

We then read in three values that will determine eligibility for a loan:

```
cout << endl << "Please enter your age in years: ";
cin >> age;

cout << "Please enter your annual income in dollars: ";
cin >> income;

cout << "What is your current account balance in dollars: ";
cin >> balance;
```

The **if** statement that follows determines whether or not a loan will be granted:

```
if(age >= 21 && (income > 25000 || balance > 100000))
```

The condition requires that the applicant's age is at least 21, and that either their income is greater than $25,000 or their balance is greater than $100,000. The parentheses around the expression **(income > 25000 || balance > 100000)** are necessary so that the result of ORing these income and balance conditions together is ANDed with the age test. Without the parentheses, the age test would be ANDed with the income test, and the result would be ORed with the balance test. This is because the **&&** operator has a higher precedence than the **||** operator, as you can see from the table in Appendix D. Without the parentheses, the condition would have allowed anyone with a balance over $100,000 to get a loan, even if they were only 8 years old! That's not what was intended.

If the **if** condition is **true**, the following statement block is executed:

```
{
    // OK, you are good for the loan - but how much?
    // This will be the lesser of twice income and half balance

    int loan = 0;                        // Stores maximum loan amount
    if(2 * income < balance / 2)
      loan = 2 * income;
    else
      loan = balance / 2;

    cout << "You can borrow up to $"
         << loan
         << endl;
}
```

In this block, we determine the maximum loan amount with another **if** statement. This determines that the maximum loan is the lesser of twice the salary, and half the current bank balance.

Of course, if the first **if** condition is **false**, the **else** is executed:

```
else
    cout << "Sorry, we are out of cash today."
         << endl;
```

As you can see, this outputs a message indicating that the cash will not be forthcoming.

The Conditional Operator

The **conditional operator** is sometimes called the **ternary operator** because it involves three operands, and is the only operator to do so. It has similarities to the **if-else** statement, in that it selects one of two choices, depending on the value of a condition. However, where the **if-else** statement provides a way of select one of two statements to be executed, the conditional operator is a way to choose between two *values*. It is best understood by looking at an example.

Suppose we have two variables, **a** and **b**, and we want to assign the value of the higher of the two to a third variable, **c**. We can do this with the statement:

```
c = a > b ? a : b;          // Set c to the higher of a and b
```

The conditional operator has a logical expression as its first operand, in this case **a > b**. If this expression is **true**, the second operand — in this case **a** — is selected as the value resulting from the operation. If the first operand is **false**, the third operand — in this case **b** — is selected as the value. Thus, the result of the conditional expression is **a** if **a** is greater than **b**, and **b** otherwise. In the statement above, this value is stored in **c**. This use of the conditional operator in this assignment statement is equivalent to the **if** statement:

```
if(a > b)
  c = a;
else
  c = b;
```

The conditional operator can also be used to select the lower of two values. In the previous program, we used an **if-else** to decide the value of the loan, but we could have used this statement instead:

```
loan = 2 * income < balance / 2 ? 2 * income : balance / 2;
```

This would produce exactly the same result, and no parentheses are necessary because the precedence of the conditional operator is lower than that of the other operators in this statement. Of course, if you think parentheses would make things clearer, you can include them:

```
loan = (2 * income < balance / 2) ? (2 * income) : (balance / 2);
```

The conditional operator, which is often represented simply by **?:**, can be written generally as:

condition ? *expression1* : *expression2*

If the **condition** evaluates as **true**, the result is the value of **expression1**; if it evaluates to **false**, the result is the value of **expression2**. If **condition** evaluates to a numerical value, then it will be automatically converted to type **bool**, with a non-zero value resulting in **true** and 0 resulting in **false**, as we've seen before.

Note that only one of **expression1** or **expression2** will be evaluated, which has implications for expressions such as:

```
a < b ? ++i : --i;
```

If **a** is less than **b**, **i** will be incremented. The variable **i** will only be decremented if **a < b** is **false**.

Try It Out – Using the Conditional Operator with Output

A common use of the conditional operator is to control output, depending on the result of an expression or the value of a variable. You can vary a message by selecting one text string or another depending on the condition specified.

```
// Program 4.7 Using the conditional operator to select output.
#include <iostream>
using namespace std;

int main()
{
  int mice = 0;                   // Count of all mice
  int brown = 0;                  // Count of brown mice
  int white = 0;                  // Count of white mice

  cout << "How many brown mice do you have? ";
  cin >> brown;

  cout << "How many white mice do you have? ";
  cin >> white;

  mice = brown + white;

  cout << "You have "
       << mice
       << (mice == 1 ? " mouse " : " mice ")
       << "in total."
       << endl;
  return 0;
}
```

The output from this program might be:

```
How many brown mice do you have? 2
How many white mice do you have? 3
You have 5 mice in total.
```

How It Works

You've seen most of the operations in this program before. The only bit of interest is in the output statement that is executed after the numbers of mice have been entered:

```
cout << "You have "
     << mice
     << (mice == 1 ? " mouse " : " mice ")
     << "in total."
     << endl;
```

The expression using the conditional operator evaluates to **" mouse "** if the value of the variable **mice** is 1, or **" mice "** otherwise. This allows us to use the same output statement for any number of mice, and select singular or plural as appropriate.

There are many other situations where you can apply this sort of mechanism — selecting between **"is"** and **"are"**, for example, or **"he"** and **"she"**, or indeed any situation where you have a binary choice. You can even combine two conditional operators to choose between three options on occasion. For example:

```
cout << (a < b ? "a is less than b." :
                  (a == b ? "a is equal to b." : "a is greater than b."));
```

This statement will output one of three messages, depending on the relative values of the variables **a** and **b**. The second choice for the first conditional operator is the result of another conditional operator.

The switch Statement

Often, you're faced with a multiple-choice situation, in which you need to execute a particular set of statements from a number of choices (that is, more than two), depending on the value of an integer variable or expression. An example of the sort of thing I'm talking about would be a lottery: you buy a numbered ticket, and if you're lucky, you win a prize. For instance, if your ticket number is 147, you have won first prize; if it's 387 you can claim second prize; ticket number 29 gets you third prize; any other ticket number wins nothing at all. The statement that will handle precisely this sort of situation is called the **switch** statement.

The **switch** statement enables you to select from multiple choices based on a set of fixed values for a given expression. The choices are called **cases**. In the lottery example, there would be four cases: one for each of the winning numbers, plus the 'default' case for all losing numbers. Here's how you could write a **switch** statement to select a message for a given ticket number:

```
switch(ticket_number)
{
  case 147:
    cout << "You win first prize!";
    break;
  case 387:
    cout << "You win second prize!";
    break;
  case 29:
    cout << "You win third prize!";
    break;
  default:
    cout << "Sorry, you lose.";
}
```

The **switch** statement is harder to describe than to use. The selection between a number of cases is determined by the value of an integer expression that you specify between parentheses following the keyword **switch**. The result of the selection expression can also be of an enumerated data type, because values of such types can be automatically converted to integers. In this example it is simply the variable **ticket_number**, which must be an integer type — what else could it be?

You define the possible choices in a **switch** statement by using as many **case values** as you need. The case values appear in a **case label**, which is of the form:

case *case_value*:

It's called a case *label* because it labels the statements it precedes. The statements following a particular case label will be executed if the value of the selection expression is the same as that of the case value. Each case value must be unique, but they don't need to be in any particular order, as you can see in the example.

The case value must be an **integer constant expression**, which is an expression that the *compiler* can evaluate, so it can only involve literals, **const** variables or enumerators. Furthermore, any literals that you do include must either be of an integer type or be cast to an integer type.

The **default** label in the example identifies the **default case**, which is a catch-all; the statements that follow are executed if the selection expression does not correspond to any of the case values. You don't have to specify a default case, though — if you don't, and none of the case values is selected, the **switch** will do nothing.

The **break** statement that appears after each set of case statements is absolutely necessary for the logic here. It breaks out of the **switch** after the case statements execute, and causes execution to continue with the statement following the closing brace for the **switch**. If you omit the **break** statement for a case, the statements for the all the following cases will also be executed. Notice that we *don't* need **break** after the final case (usually the default case) because execution leaves the **switch** at this point anyway, but it doesn't hurt to include it either.

Note that **switch**, **case**, **default** and **break** *are all keywords.*

Try It Out – The switch Statement

We can examine how the **switch** statement works with the following example:

```
// Example 4.8 Using the switch statement
#include <iostream>
using namespace std;

int main()
{
  int choice = 0;                         // Store selection value here

  cout << endl
       << "Your electronic recipe book is at your service." << endl
       << "You can choose from the following delicious dishes: "
       << endl
       << "1 Boiled eggs" << endl
       << "2 Fried eggs" << endl
       << "3 Scrambled eggs" << endl
       << "4 Coddled eggs" << endl
       << endl << "Enter your selection number: ";
  cin >> choice;

  switch(choice)
  {
    case 1:
      cout << endl << "Boil some eggs." << endl;
      break;
    case 2:
      cout << endl << "Fry some eggs." << endl;
      break;
    case 3:
      cout << endl << "Scramble some eggs." << endl;
      break;
```

```
      case 4:
        cout << endl << "Coddle some eggs." << endl;
        break;
      default:
        cout << endl << "You entered a wrong number, try raw eggs." << endl;
  }
  return 0;
}
```

How It Works

After defining your options in the output statement, and reading a selection number into the variable **choice**, the **switch** statement is executed with the selection expression specified simply as **choice** in parentheses, immediately following the keyword **switch**. The possible choices in the **switch** are enclosed between braces, and are each identified by a case label. If the value of **choice** corresponds with any of the case values, then the statements following that case label are executed. We only have one statement plus a **break** statement for each case in this example, but in general there can be as many statements as you need following a case label, and you don't need to enclose them between braces.

The **break** statement at the end of each group of **case** statements transfers execution to the statement after the **switch**. The **break** isn't mandatory, but if you don't include it, all the statements for the cases following the one selected will be executed, which isn't usually what you want. You can demonstrate this for yourself by removing the **break** statements from this example and seeing what happens.

If the value of **choice** doesn't correspond with any of the case values specified, the statements preceded by the **default** label are executed. If we had not included a **default** case here and the value of **choice** was different from all of the case values, then the **switch** would have done nothing and the program would continue with the next statement after the **switch**, which is the **return** statement.

Try It Out – Sharing a case

As I said earlier, each of the case values must be a compile-time constant and must be unique. The reason that no two case values can be the same is that the compiler would have no way of knowing which statements should be executed if that particular value came up. However, different case values don't need to have unique actions. Several case values can share the same action, as shown in the following example:

```
// Example 4.9 Multiple case actions
#include <iostream>
#include <cctype>
using namespace std;

int main()
{
  char letter = 0;
  cout << endl
       << "Enter a letter: ";
  cin >> letter;
```

```
   if(isalpha(letter))
     switch(tolower(letter))
     {
        case 'a':
        case 'e':
        case 'i':
        case 'o':
        case 'u':
          cout << endl << "You entered a vowel." << endl;
          break;
        default:
          cout << endl << "You entered a consonant." << endl;
     }
   else
     cout << endl << "You did not enter a letter." << endl;

   return 0;
}
```

An example of the output from this program is:

```
Enter a letter: E

You entered a vowel.
```

How It Works

In this example, we are using one of the standard library's character conversion routines in combination with a **switch** to determine whether a character entered was a vowel or a consonant. The **if** condition first checks that we really do have a letter and not some other character:

```
   if(isalpha(letter))
```

If the value returned by **isalpha()** is non-zero, then the **switch** will be executed:

```
      switch(tolower(letter))
      {
         case 'a':
         case 'e':
         case 'i':
         case 'o':
         case 'u':
           cout << endl << "You entered a vowel." << endl;
           break;
         default:
           cout << endl << "You entered a consonant." << endl;
      }
```

The **switch** is controlled by the value returned from the function **tolower()** We could just have used the variable **letter**, but then we would have needed to specify all the upper case vowels as case values, as well as the lower case vowels. If **tolower()** returns a value corresponding to a vowel, the message confirming that will be displayed. Otherwise the **default** case will be executed, displaying the message that the character entered was a consonant.

If **isalpha()** returns 0, the switch will not be executed, and the **else** is executed to output the message that the character entered was not a letter.

It's possible to dispense with the **if** statement by combining the test for a letter with the conversion to lower case, but it requires some trickery and it does make the code more complicated. For example, you could write the **switch** as:

```
switch(tolower(letter) * (isalpha(letter) != 0))          // Convert to lower
                                                          // case and test
{
  case 'a':
  case 'e':
  case 'i':
  case 'o':
  case 'u':
    cout << endl << "You entered a vowel." << endl;
    break;
  case 0:
    cout << endl << "You did not enter a letter." << endl;
    break;
  default:
    cout << endl << "You entered a consonant." << endl;
}
```

The reason for the complicated selection expression is that the **isalpha()** function does not produce a **bool** value. If it did, we could simply use **tolower(letter) * isalpha(letter)**, since this would evaluate to 0 when **isalpha()** returns **false**, and to the lower case letter returned by **tolower()** otherwise, as **true** will convert to 1.

As we have seen, though, **isalpha()** returns an **int** that's zero if you pass it a letter, and a positive integer *that is not necessarily 1* if what you pass it isn't a letter. Another alternative would be to cast the value returned by **isalpha()** to type **bool**. Then, we could write the switch as:

```
switch(tolower(letter) * static_cast<bool>(isalpha(letter)))
{
  case 'a':
  case 'e':
  case 'i':
  case 'o':
  case 'u':
    cout << endl << "You entered a vowel." << endl;
    break;
  case 0:
    cout << endl << "You did not enter a letter." << endl;
    break;
  default:
    cout << endl << "You entered a consonant." << endl;
}
```

This will work because the integer returned by **isalpha()** will be cast to **bool**, and the compiler will arrange for this value to be converted to **int** for the multiply operation, so it will end up as 0 or 1. On balance, however, these **switch** statements are beginning to get rather confusing. The original version using the **if** is certainly the clearest code, and is therefore preferable despite our clever logic.

Unconditional Branching

The **if** statement provides you with the flexibility to choose to execute one set of statements or another, depending on a specified condition, so that the sequence of statement execution varies depending on the values of the data in the program. We have just seen that **switch** provides a way to choose from a fixed range of options depending on the value of an integer expression. The **goto** statement, in contrast, is a blunt instrument. It enables you to branch to a specified program statement unconditionally. The statement to be branched to must be identified by a **statement label**, which is an identifier defined according to the same rules as a variable name. This is followed by a colon and placed before the statement that you want to reference using the label. Here is an example of a labeled statement:

```
MyLabel: x = 1;
```

This statement has the label **MyLabel**, and an unconditional branch to this statement would be written as follows:

```
goto MyLabel;
```

Whenever possible, you should avoid using **goto**s in your program. They tend to encourage convoluted code that can be extremely difficult to follow. Note that a **goto** that branches into the scope of a variable but bypasses its declaration will cause an error message from the compiler.

FYI

As goto is theoretically unnecessary — there is always an alternative approach to using goto – a significant cadre of programmers says you should never use it. I don't subscribe to such an extreme view. It is a legal statement, after all, and there are occasions when it can be convenient. However, I *do* recommend that you only use it where you can see an obvious advantage over the other options that are available.

Decision Statement Blocks and Variable Scope

A **switch** statement generally has its own block between braces that encloses the case statements. An **if** statement will also often have braces enclosing the statements to be executed if the condition is **true**, and the **else** part may have braces too. You need to be conscious of the fact that these statement blocks are no different to any other blocks when it comes to defining variable scope. Any variable declared within a block ceases to exist at the end of the block, so you cannot reference it outside the block.

For example, consider the following rather arbitrary calculation:

```
if(value > 0)
{
  int savit = value - 1;    // This only exists in this block
  value += 10;
}
else
{
```

```
      int savit = value + 1;    // This only exists in this block
      value -= 10;
   }

   cout << savit;               // This will not compile! savit does not exist
```

The output statement at the end will cause an error message because the variable **savit** is undefined at this point. Any variable defined within a block can only be used within that block, so if you want to access data that originates inside a block from outside it, you must put the declaration for the variable storing that information in an outer block.

Note that declarations within a **switch** statement block must be reachable in the course of execution, and it must not be possible to bypass them. The following code illustrates how illegal declarations in a **switch** can arise:

```
   int test = 3;

   switch(test)
   {
     int i = 1;                 // ILLEGAL - cannot be reached

     case 1:
     {
       int j = 2;               // OK - can be reached and is not bypassed
       cout << endl << test + j;
       break;
     }

     int k = 3;                 // ILLEGAL - cannot be reached

     case 3:
       cout << endl << test;
       int m = 4;               // ILLEGAL - can be reached but can be bypassed
       break;

     default:
       cout << endl << "Default reached.";
       break;

     int n = 5;                 // ILLEGAL - cannot be reached
   }
```

In this **switch** statement, only one of the declarations — the one for **j** — is legal. For a declaration to be legal, it must first be possible for the declaration to be reached in the normal course of execution. This is not the case for variables **i**, **k** and **n**. Secondly, it must not be possible to enter the scope of a variable while bypassing its declaration, which is the case for the variable **m**. Variable **j**, however, is only 'in scope' from its declaration to the end of the enclosing block, so this declaration cannot be bypassed.

Summary

In this chapter, we have added the capability for decision-making to our programs. In fact, you now know how all the decision-making statements in C++ work. The essential elements of decision-making that you have learned are:

▶ You can compare two values using one of the comparison operators. This will result in a value of type **bool**, which can be **true** or **false**.

▶ You can cast a **bool** value to an integer type — **true** will cast to 1 and **false** will cast to 0.

▶ Numerical values can be cast to type **bool** — a 0 value casts to **false**, and a non-zero value casts to **true**.

▶ The **if** statement can execute a statement or block of statements depending on the value of a condition expression. If the condition is **true**, or non-zero, the statement or statement block will be executed. If the condition if **false**, or 0, it won't be.

▶ The **if-else** statement provides an additional option over the simple **if**. The **else** statement is executed if the condition is **false**, or 0.

▶ **if** and **if-else** statements can be nested.

▶ The **cctype** header file provides declarations for standard library functions for classifying characters and for converting letters to upper or lower case. The **cwctype** header file provides declarations for the wide character equivalents of these.

▶ The **switch** statement provides a means of selecting between a fixed set of options, depending on the value of an integer expression.

▶ The conditional operator selects between two values depending on the value of an expression.

▶ Using a **goto** statement, you can branch unconditionally to a statement with a specified label.

Exercises

Ex 4.1 Write a program that prompts the user to enter two positive integers, and then tests whether the larger integer is exactly divisible by the smaller one. In the process, you'll need to check that the input values are both valid (greater than zero), and then establish which of them is the larger.

Ex 4.2 Create a program that asks the user to input an integer between 1 and 100. Using a nested **if**, check that the integer is within this range. If so, determine whether the integer is greater than, less than, or equal to 50.

Ex 4.3 Write a program that accepts input of a single character from the user. Use a standard library function to check whether it's a letter — if it isn't, output a message and end the program. Once you're sure you've got a letter, use the bitwise operators to output its binary code. Remember that you can use a mask to determine the value of a single bit in an integer value, and you'll need to need to check each bit in turn.

Ex 4.4 Write a program that will prompt the user to enter an amount of money between $0 and $10 (decimal places allowed). Determine how many quarters (25c), dimes (10c), nickels (5c) and cents are needed to make up that amount and this information to the screen. Additionally, ensure that the output makes grammatical sense. (For example, if you need only 1 dime, then the output should not write the plural '1 dimes'.)

Loops

A **loop** is another fundamental idea in programming. It provides a way for you to repeat one or more statements as many times as your application requires. You can employ a loop to handle any repetitive task, and for most programs of any consequence, loops are essential. Using a computer to calculate the company payroll, for example, would not be practicable without a loop.

C++ provides a number of ways to implement a loop, all of which have their own particular area of application. In this chapter we'll begin by looking at the theory behind loops, and then get down to their practical uses — including, of course, how to write them. Along the way, you will learn:

- How loops work, and the principles behind the different kinds of loop
- How the **while** loop works
- What the merits of the **do-while** loop are
- How to use a **for** loop
- What the **break** statement does in a loop
- What the **continue** statement is used for in a loop
- How to construct nested loops

Understanding Loops

A loop is a mechanism that enables you to execute the same sequence of statements repeatedly until a particular condition is met. The statements inside a loop are sometimes called **iteration statements**.

There are two essential elements to a loop: the **statement** or block of statements that forms the body of the loop that is to be executed repeatedly, and a **loop condition** of some kind that determines when to stop repeating the loop.

A loop condition can take a number of different forms, to provide different ways of controlling the loop. For example, you might want to:

▶ Execute the loop a given number of times

▶ Execute the loop until a given value exceeds another value

▶ Execute the loop until a particular character is entered from the keyboard

You can set the loop condition to suit the circumstances. In the final analysis, however, loops come in two basic flavors, and these are illustrated in the diagram.

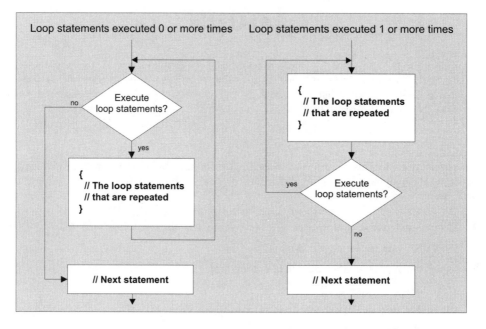

The difference between these two structures is evident at the point where we enter them. On the left, the loop condition is tested *before* the loop statements are executed; consequently, the loop statements will not be executed at all if the test condition fails at the outset.

On the right, the test comes *after* the loop statements. The effect of this arrangement is that the loop statements are executed before the condition is tested for the first time, so this kind of loop always executes at least once.

There are three different kinds of loop in C++. These are:

▶ The **while** loop

▶ The **do-while** loop

▶ The **for** loop

The **while** loop and the **for** loop have the same structure as the loop on the left hand side of the illustration, so statements in the body of either of these loops may not be executed at all. The **do-while** loop, on the other hand, has the structure shown on the right hand side of the diagram, so the body of this type of loop is executed at least once. Let's start by looking at the detail of how the **while** loop works, since that's the simplest of the three.

The while loop

The **while** loop uses a logical expression to control execution of the loop body. The general form of the **while** loop is:

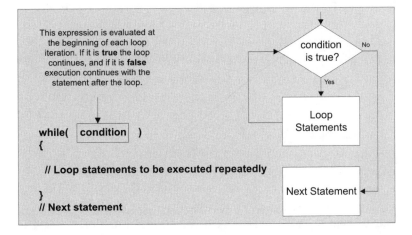

The flowchart shows the logic of this loop. As long as the value of **condition** is **true**, the loop statement or block of loop statements is executed. When **condition** is **false**, execution continues with the statement following the loop. You can use any expression to control the loop, as long as it evaluates to a value of type **bool**, or to a value of an integer type.

> *If the condition controlling the loop produces an integer, the loop will continue as long as the value is non-zero. As we have seen, any non-zero integer is converted to type **bool** as **true**, and only 0 converts to **bool** as **false**.*

Of course, **while** is a keyword, so you can't use it to name anything in your programs.

Try It Out – Using a while Loop

As a first example, we could use a **while** loop to calculate the sum of the integers from 1 to 10:

```
// Program 5.1 Using a while loop to sum integers
#include <iostream>
using namespace std;

int main()
{
    int i = 1;                    // Stores the integers to be added
    int sum = 0;                  // Stores the sum of integers
```

```
   while(i <= 10)
   {
     cout << i << endl;              // Output current value of i
     sum += i++;
   }

   cout << "Sum is " << sum << endl;  // Output final sum
   return 0;
}
```

When you execute this program, the output will be:

```
1
2
3
4
5
6
7
8
9
10
Sum is 55
```

How It Works

The first two statements in **main()** define two integers that we'll use in our calculation. A running total will be held in **sum**, while **i** will contain the value of the next integer to be added to **sum**.

```
int i = 1;                        // Stores the integers to be added
int sum = 0;                      // Stores the sum of integers
```

The first time that execution of the program reaches the loop, therefore, **i** will be 1. The loop condition, which is the expression **i <= 10**, will therefore be **true**, and execution will pass to the loop statements:

```
cout << i << endl;                // Output current value of i
sum += i++;
```

What happens now? First of all, we output the current value of **i** — that's nothing new. Then, since we're using the postfix form of the increment operator, the value of **i** is added to **sum**, and after that **i** is incremented. This completes the loop block, so execution passes back to the **while**, and the loop condition is tested again with the new value of **i**.

I'm sure you can see that this pattern will now repeat itself. **i** is increased to 2, 3, 4 and so on, with its value getting added to **sum** on each iteration of the loop. However, after the value 10 has been added, **i** gets incremented to 11, and the loop condition will be **false**. When that happens, the loop is 'broken', and execution continues with the next statement after the loop, which outputs the sum:

```
cout << "Sum is " << sum << endl;  // Output final sum
```

The net effect has been to go round the loop 10 times, and therefore to add the integers from 1 to 10.

The do-while Loop

The **do-while** loop is similar to the **while** loop in that the loop continues for as long as the specified loop condition remains **true**. However, the difference is that the loop condition is checked at the *end* of the **do-while** loop, rather than at the beginning, so the loop statement is always executed at least once.

The logic and general form of the **do-while** loop are shown in the following illustration. Notice particularly the semicolon that comes after the **while** statement, which is absolutely necessary. If you leave it out, the program won't compile.

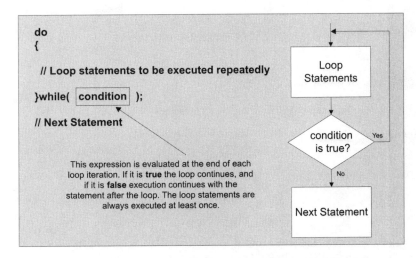

This kind of logic is ideal for situations where you have a block of code that you *always* want to execute once, and may want to execute more than once. I can tell you're not convinced that's something you'd ever need to do, so let's have another example.

Try It Out – Using a do-while Loop to Control Input

Suppose we want to calculate the average of an arbitrary number of input values — they could be temperatures, for example, collected over a period of time. We have no way of knowing in advance how many values will be entered, but it's a safe assumption that there's always going to be at least one, and that makes it an ideal candidate for a **do-while** loop. Here's the program:

```
// Program 5.2 Using a do-while loop to control input
#include <iostream>
using namespace std;

int main()
{
  char ch = 0;                                // Stores response to prompt for
input
  int count = 0;                              // Counts the number of input values
  double temperature = 0.0;                   // Stores an input value
  double average = 0.0;                       // Stores the total and average

  cout << endl;

  do
  {
    cout << "Enter a temperature reading: ";  // Prompt for input
    cin >> temperature;                       // Read input value

    average += temperature;                   // Accumulate total of values
    count++;                                  // Increment value count

    cout << "Do you want to enter another? (y/n): ";
    cin >> ch;                                // Get response
    cout << endl;
  } while(ch == 'y');

  average /= count;                           // Calculate the average
  cout << "Average temperature is " << average
       << endl;
  return 0;
}
```

A sample session with this program is:

```
Enter a temperature reading: 53
Do you want to enter another? (y/n): y

Enter a temperature reading: 65.5
Do you want to enter another? (y/n): y

Enter a temperature reading: 74
Do you want to enter another? (y/n): y

Enter a temperature reading: 69.5
Do you want to enter another? (y/n): n

Average temperature is 65.5
```

How It Works

First, the program declares and initializes the variables required for the loop and the calculation:

```
char ch = 0;                    // Stores response to prompt for input
int count = 0;                  // Counts the number of input values
double temperature = 0.0;       // Stores an input value
double average = 0.0;           // Stores the total and average
```

The variable **ch** will be used to store a response to a prompt for further input, which will be tested at the end of the loop. As long as **'y'** is entered, the program will continue to read input values. (Ideally, the program would also accept **'Y'**; we'll fix that shortly.) The purposes of the other three variables are clear from the comments.

The loop that reads the input values is:

```
do
{
  cout << "Enter a temperature reading: ";  // Prompt for input
  cin >> temperature;                        // Read input value

  average += temperature;                    // Accumulate total of values
  count++;                                    // Increment value count

  cout << "Do you want to enter another? (y/n): ";
  cin >> ch;                                  // Get response
  cout << endl;
} while(ch == 'y');
```

Because we're using a **do-while** loop, we'll always read at least one value. After prompting for input, the loop block reads a value from the keyboard and stores it in the **temperature** variable. This value is then added to **average**, so when the loop ends, **average** will contain the sum of all the input values. We also increment **count**, because we will need to know how many values there are in order to calculate the average. Finally in the loop, we prompt for a *y* or an *n* to be entered to indicate whether there are more values or not. When **'n'** (in fact, any character other than **'y'**) is entered, the loop condition **ch == 'y'** will be **false**, and the loop will end. Execution then continues with the statement:

```
average /= count;                            // Calculate the average
```

This calculates the average by dividing the total that we accumulated in **average** by **count**, the number of values. The value stored in **count** will be automatically converted to **double**, the same type as **average**, before the division operation is carried out. Finally, we output the result and the program ends.

More Complex while Loop Conditions

Of course, we are not limited to a simple comparison for controlling a **while** (or a **do-while**) loop. *Any* expression that results in a **true** or **false** value can be used. A problem with the previous example is that if you enter *Y* at the keyboard (instead of *y*), with the intention of entering another value, the program will end. This is not exactly foolproof programming. It would be better to allow input of either *Y* or *y* to continue the loop. You could do this quite easily by modifying the loop condition to:

```
} while(ch == 'y' || ch == 'Y');
```

Now either upper case **'Y'** or lower case **'y'** is acceptable as input to continue the loop. Alternatively, you could use one of the standard library's character conversion functions, which we introduced in the last chapter. First, include the header file at the top of your code:

```
// Program 5.2 Using a do-while loop to control input
#include <iostream>
#include <cctype>
```

Now you can substitute the following loop condition into the program above, which will make sure it's always the lower case version of **ch** that gets compared with **'y'**:

```
} while(tolower(ch) == 'y');
```

As I explained earlier, you can also use an expression that evaluates to a numeric value as the loop condition. In this case, the compiler will arrange that the result is converted to type **bool**. Remember that 0 converts to **false**, and *any* non-zero value, positive or negative, converts to **true**. Thus, a **while** loop controlled by a numerical value will only end when the condition is 0.

The for Loop

The **for** loop is primarily used for executing a statement or block of statements a predetermined number of times, but it can be used in other ways, as we shall see.

You control a **for** loop using three expressions separated by semicolons, which are placed between parentheses following the keyword **for**. These are shown in the diagram:

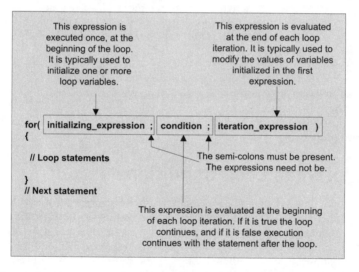

This expression is executed once, at the beginning of the loop. It is typically used to initialize one or more loop variables.

This expression is evaluated at the end of each loop iteration. It is typically used to modify the values of variables initialized in the first expression.

```
for( initializing_expression ; condition ; iteration_expression )
{
    // Loop statements

}
// Next statement
```

The semi-colons must be present. The expressions need not be.

This expression is evaluated at the beginning of each loop iteration. If it is true the loop continues, and if it is false execution continues with the statement after the loop.

Any or all of the expressions controlling the **for** loop can be omitted, but you must always insert the semicolons. The reasons you might want to do this are not obvious, but it can be useful, and we'll explore some of the circumstances under which this is the case later in this chapter.

The next diagram shows the logic of the **for** loop as a flowchart:

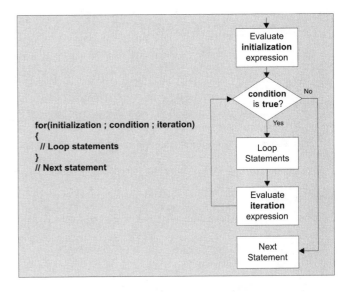

```
for(initialization ; condition ; iteration)
{
  // Loop statements
}
// Next statement
```

The **initialization expression** is evaluated only once, at the beginning of the loop. The loop condition is checked next, and if it is **true**, the loop statement or statement block is executed. If the condition is **false**, on the other hand, the loop statement is skipped and execution continues with the next statement after the loop. In this respect, the **for** loop is closer in operation to the **while** loop than to the **do-while** loop.

Presuming the condition was **true** and that the loop statement was therefore executed, the **iteration expression** is evaluated next, and then the condition is checked once more to see if the loop should continue.

Try It Out – Using the for Loop

In the typical use of the **for** loop, the first expression is used to initialize a counter, the second expression is used to check whether the counter has reach a given limit, and the third expression is used to increment the counter. We can demonstrate this in action by using a **for** loop to re-implement our program for summing integers.

```cpp
// Program 5.3 Using a for loop
#include <iostream>
using namespace std;

int main()
{
  int sum = 0;                          // Accumulates the sum of integers
  int count = 0;                        // The number to sum

  cout << "How many integers do you want to sum? ";
  cin >> count;

  for(int i = 1 ; i <= count ; i++)
    sum += i;
```

```
    cout << endl
        << "The sum of the integers from 1 to " << count << " is " << sum
        << endl;

    return 0;
}
```

This program will produce output something like this:

```
How many integers do you want to sum? 1000

The sum of the integers from 1 to 1000 is 500500
```

How It Works

We read the upper limit for the integers to sum from the keyboard with the statements:

```
cout << "How many integers do you want to sum? ";
cin >> count;
```

The loop statement that accumulates the sum is indented, to show that it is part of the **for** loop:

```
for(int i = 1 ; i <= count ; i++)
  sum += i;
```

Because there's only one loop statement, no braces are necessary. The effect of this loop is to accumulate the sum of the integers from 1 to **count** in the variable **sum**. The sequence of actions in the loop is as follows:

1. Execute the first expression. This declares the integer variable, **i**, and initializes it to 1.

2. Evaluate the second expression. This checks that **i** is less than or equal to **count**. If **i <= count** evaluates to **true**, go to step 3. If it evaluates to **false**, go to step 6.

3. Execute the loop statement. This adds the current value of **i** to **sum**.

4. Execute the third expression. This increments the value of **i**.

5. Go back to step 2.

6. Leave the loop.

Thus, successive values of **i** will be added to **sum**, starting with 1 and finishing with the value of **count**. Eventually, when **i** is incremented to **count + 1**, the **for** loop ends. Execution of the program then continues with the next statement after the loop, which outputs the total accumulated in **sum**.

Not only is it *legal* to declare variables within a **for** loop initialization expression, it is actually very common. This has some significant implications that we need to explore further.

Loops and Variable Scope

The **for** loop, like the **while** and **do-while** loops, defines a scope. The loop statement or block, as well as any expressions that control the loop, *all* fall within the scope of a loop. This also includes all three expressions used to control a **for** loop. In ANSI C++, any automatic variables declared within the scope of a loop do not exist outside the loop. Thus, the variable **i** that we declared in the loop initialization expression of the previous example is destroyed when the loop ends. If you try to reference the variable **i** after the loop, with a statement such as

```
cout << endl
     << "The loop counter has the value " << i << endl;
```

the program will no longer compile, and you will get an error message from an ANSI-compliant compiler to the effect that **i** does not exist.

But suppose that you really *needed* the value of **i** after the loop. How could you get hold of it? You simply declare the variable **i** before the loop is executed. For example:

```
int i = 1;                          // Declare and initialize loop counter

for( ; i <= count ; i++ )           // First expression is omitted
    sum += i;

cout << endl
     << "The sum of the integers from 1 to " << count << " is " << sum
     << endl;

cout << endl
     << "The loop counter has the value " << i << endl;
```

Now we can get at the value of **i** after the loop, because it's declared outside the loop's scope. Since **i** is also initialized prior to the execution of the loop, we don't need to include the loop initialization expression in this program. In general, however, it's a good idea to initialize the counter in the **for** statement — that way, you can always be confident of its value, no matter what changes you make to the rest of your program.

> *Notice that despite the initialization expression being omitted, the semicolon that separates the initialization expression from the loop condition must still be included.*

for Loops in non ANSI-compliant Compilers

The limitation on the scope of a variable declared within the **for** loop's initialization expression is a late addition to the ANSI standard for C++. There are many compilers that do not support this behavior by default, and some can't handle it at all. You need to be aware of this when you're using more than one **for** loop in a single block, because your code may not compile with one of these non-compliant compilers. Let's see how such a problem might arise.

In ANSI C++, you can write the following code:

```
int count = 10;

// Calculate the sum of integers 1 to count
long sum = 0;
for(int i = 1 ; i <= count ; i++)
  sum += i;

// Calculate the product of integers 1 to count
long product = 1;
for(int i = 1 ; i <= count ; i++)
  product *= i;
```

With a compiler that does not support ANSI standard behavior, this will not compile. You will get an error message to the effect that you are redeclaring the variable **i**. The reason for this is that the compiler is allowing the scope of **i** to extend to the end of the block that encloses the **for** loops. Thus, **i** declared within the first loop still exists when you attempt to declare the variable **i** in the second loop.

This problem typically arises with two **for** loops that declare the same variable, but *any* declaration of **i** subsequent to the first loop and within the same block will produce an error. In order to ensure your code is consistent with the ANSI standard, but still compiles with compilers that support the old behavior, you have a number of options. However, the best of them is probably to do this:

```
// Calculate the sum of integers 1 to count
long sum = 0;
{
  for(int i = 1 ; i <= count ; i++)
    sum += i;
}

// Calculate the product of integers 1 to count
long product = 1;
{
  for(int i = 1 ; i <= count ; i++)
    product *= i;
}
```

By enclosing each **for** statement in its own block, you're making absolutely sure that any automatic variables declared within the loop are destroyed when the loop ends. In effect, you're limiting the scope of the variables in exactly the way the ANSI standard specifies.

Controlling a for Loop with Floating Point Values

Our examples with the **for** loop so far have used an integer variable to control the loop, but in general you can use anything you like. The following example uses floating point values:

```
const double pi = 3.14159265;
for(double radius = 2.5 ; radius <= 20.0 ; radius += 2.5)
  cout << "radius = " << setw(12) << radius
       << "  area = " << setw(12) << pi * radius * radius
       << endl;
```

This loop is controlled by the **radius** variable, which is of type **double**. It has an initial value of 2.5, and is incremented on each loop iteration until it exceeds 20.0, whereupon the loop will end. The loop statement calculates the area of a circle for the current value of **radius**, using the standard formula πr^2, where r is the radius of the circle. We use the manipulator **setw()** in the loop statement to give each output value the same field width; this will ensure the output values line up nicely. Of course, to use the manipulators in a program, we would need to include the header file **iomanip**.

You need to take care when you use floating point variables to control **for** loops. As I explained in Chapter 2, fractional values may not be represented exactly as a binary floating point number. This can lead to some unwanted side effects, as we shall see.

Try It Out – Problem With Floating Point Variables In Loop Controls

This program demonstrates the problem with floating point values by using a slight variation of the above loop:

```cpp
// Program 5.4 Floating point control in a for loop
#include <iostream>
#include <iomanip>
using namespace std;

int main()
{
  const double pi = 3.14159265;
  cout << endl;

  for(double radius = .2 ; radius <= 3.0 ; radius += .2)
    cout << "radius = " << setw(12) << radius
         << "  area = " << setw(12) << pi * radius * radius
         << endl;
  return 0;
}
```

On my computer, this produces the output:

```
radius =          0.2  area =      0.125664
radius =          0.4  area =      0.502655
radius =          0.6  area =       1.13097
radius =          0.8  area =       2.01062
radius =            1  area =       3.14159
radius =          1.2  area =       4.52389
radius =          1.4  area =       6.15752
radius =          1.6  area =       8.04248
radius =          1.8  area =       10.1788
radius =            2  area =       12.5664
radius =          2.2  area =       15.2053
radius =          2.4  area =       18.0956
radius =          2.6  area =       21.2372
radius =          2.8  area =       24.6301
```

How It Works

On this occasion, it's more a case of why it doesn't! By inspection of the code, you might have expected that you would get the area of the circle with radius 3.0 at the end of this list. After all, the loop is specified to continue as long as **radius** is less than or equal to 3.0. But last value that is displayed is with **radius** at 2.8; what's going wrong?

The loop ends earlier than we anticipate because when 0.2 is added to 2.8, the result is greater than 3.0. (This is an astounding piece of arithmetic at face value, but read on!) The reason for this is a very small error in the representation of 0.2 as a binary floating point number; you cannot represent 0.2 exactly in binary floating point. The error will be in the last digit of precision, so if your compiler supports 15 digits precision for type **double**, the error will be of the order of 10^{-15}. Usually, this is of no consequence, but here we depend on adding 0.2 successively to get exactly 3.0 — which doesn't happen. You can see what the difference is by adding a statement in the loop to display the difference between 3.0 and the next value of **radius**:

```
for(double radius = .2 ; radius <= 3.0 ; radius += .2)
  cout << "radius = " << setw(12) << radius
       << "   area = " << setw(12) << pi * radius * radius
       << "  delta to 3 = "        << ((radius + .2) - 3.0)
       << endl;
```

On my machine, the last line of output is now:

```
radius =          2.8   area =       24.6301   delta to 3 = 4.44089e-016
```

As you can see, **radius + .2** is greater than 3.0 by around 4×10^{-16}, and so the loop terminates before the next iteration.

You might be wondering why the values of **radius** are output as nice, neat values, in spite of the inaccuracy we have just discussed. This is a result of the process that generates the displayed values. If you want a precise representation of the values of **radius**, you can output them in scientific notation — that is, in the form of the mantissa plus an exponent.

Try It Out – Displaying Numbers in Scientific Notation

To find out exactly what's going on in the loop, you can display the values in the previous example by modifying the program to use some of the floating point output manipulators we saw in Chapter 2:

```
// Program 5.5 Displaying numbers in scientific notation
#include <iostream>
#include <iomanip>
#include <limits>
using namespace std;

int main()
{
  const double pi = 3.14159265;
  cout << endl;
```

```
      for(double radius = .2 ; radius <= 3.0 ; radius += .2)
        cout << "radius = "
             << setprecision(numeric_limits<double>::digits10 + 1)
             << scientific << radius
             << "  area = "
             << setw(10) << setprecision(6)
             << fixed << pi * radius * radius
             << endl;
      return 0;
    }
```

With the changes made above, I get the output:

```
radius = 2.0000000000000001e-001   area =    0.125664
radius = 4.0000000000000002e-001   area =    0.502655
radius = 6.0000000000000009e-001   area =    1.130973
radius = 8.0000000000000004e-001   area =    2.010619
radius = 1.0000000000000000e+000   area =    3.141593
radius = 1.2000000000000000e+000   area =    4.523893
radius = 1.3999999999999999e+000   area =    6.157522
radius = 1.5999999999999999e+000   area =    8.042477
radius = 1.7999999999999998e+000   area =   10.178760
radius = 1.9999999999999998e+000   area =   12.566371
radius = 2.1999999999999997e+000   area =   15.205308
radius = 2.3999999999999999e+000   area =   18.095574
radius = 2.6000000000000001e+000   area =   21.237166
radius = 2.8000000000000003e+000   area =   24.630086
```

The number of digits displayed for the mantissa here is typical for an IBM-compatible PC; it could be different on other machines. As you can see, the **radius** values are not quite as exact as they appeared to be earlier.

How It Works

We include the **limits** header because we need to access information about the number of (base 10) digits that a floating-point value of type **double** has in the mantissa. The output statement in the loop modifies the way in which the floating point values are presented:

```
      cout << "radius = "
           << setprecision(numeric_limits<double>::digits10 + 1)
           << scientific << radius
           << "  area = "
           << setw(10) << setprecision(6)
           << fixed << pi * radius * radius
           << endl;
```

By judicious use of the **scientific** and **setprecision()** manipulators, we arrange to display the radius values in scientific notation. In order to guarantee that *all* the digits are shown, we have to use some of the information defined in the **limits** header file, which we saw in Chapter 3. The integer value specified by **numeric_limits<double>::digits10** is the number of decimal digits in the mantissa of a value of type **double**. This value typically reflects the number of *whole* decimal digits in the mantissa. Since the mantissa is really binary, and does not necessarily correspond to a whole number of decimal digits, there can still be a couple of extra binary digits that will cause the output to be rounded. We therefore add 1 to the number of digits, to ensure that no rounding occurs.

Since we don't need the value for the area in scientific notation, we use the **fixed** manipulator to reset the output mode for floating point values to present subsequent values without an exponent. We also set the field width for the area to 10 characters with the manipulator **setw(10)**. Of course, the number of digits of precision is still going to be the maximum plus one, and we don't need that either, so reset the number of digits to a more sensible value with the manipulator **setprecision(6)**.

Using More Complex Loop Control Expressions

You're not limited to simple control expressions in the **for** loop. Let's look at a slightly more complex example. Returning to the first code we saw in this chapter — calculating the sum of the first 10 integers — it is possible to perform the calculation in the **for** loop's iteration expression, and dispense with the loop statement altogether:

```
int count = 10;
int sum = 0;
for(int i = 1 ; i <= count ; sum += i++)
  ;
```

Notice the semicolon on a line by itself after the loop control expressions. This is effectively an empty loop statement. The calculation is done in the iteration expression, **sum += i++**. This adds the current value of **i** to **sum**, and then the postfix increment operator adds 1 to **i**, ready for the next iteration. Using the third control expression in this way is quite convenient for simple loop operations, but you should not overuse this technique. The measure of when it is *in*appropriate is the degree to which it reduces the readability of your code.

You can also initialize multiple variables in the first **for** loop control expression. All you have to do is separate the initialization expressions with commas. Let's take an example.

Try It Out – Initializing Multiple Variables

In this program, three variables are initialized inside the loop control expression:

```
// Program 5.6 Multiple initializations in a loop expression
#include <iostream>
#include <iomanip>

using namespace std;

int main()
{
  int count = 0;
  cout << endl << "What upper limit would you like? ";
  cin >> count;

  cout << endl
       << "integer"                      // Output column headings
       << "       sum"
       << "        factorial"
       << endl;

  for(long n = 1, sum = 0, factorial = 1 ; n <= count ; n++)
  {
```

```
        sum += n;                            // Accumulate sum to current n
        factorial *= n;                      // Calculate n!
        cout << setw(4) << n    << "       "
             << setw(7) << sum << " "
             << setw(15) << factorial
             << endl;
   }
   return 0;
}
```

The program calculates the sum of the integers for each integer from 1 to **count**, where **count** is a value that you enter. It also calculates the factorial of each integer. (The factorial of an integer n, written $n!$, is simply the product of all the integers from 1 to n; for example, $5! = 1 \times 2 \times 3 \times 4 \times 5 = 120$.) Don't enter large values for **count**, as factorials grow very rapidly and easily exceed the capacity of even a **long** integer variable. Typical output from this program is:

```
What upper limit would you like? 10

integer      sum        factorial
   1          1                1
   2          3                2
   3          6                6
   4         10               24
   5         15              120
   6         21              720
   7         28             5040
   8         36            40320
   9         45           362880
  10         55          3628800
```

How It Works

First, we read the value for **count** from the keyboard, after displaying a prompt:

```
int count = 0;
cout << endl << "What upper limit would you like? ";
cin >> count;
```

For four-byte **long** values, anything over 13 will produce a factorial outside the maximum value you can store, so you will get incorrect results.

The variables **n**, **sum**, and **factorial** are declared and initialized within the loop expression:

```
for(long n = 1, sum = 0, factorial = 1 ; n <= 10 ; n++)
```

Commas separate each variable from the next, just as in a declaration statement. In the loop itself, after the mathematical operations, different values are passed to the **setw()** manipulator for each variable to be output in the loop statement:

```
cout << setw(4) << n    << "       "
     << setw(7) << sum << " "
     << setw(15) << factorial
     << endl;
```

This is just to align the values in columns under the headings that are displayed before the loop executes.

The Comma Operator

Although the comma looks as if it's just a separator, it is actually a binary operator. It combines two expressions into a single expression, where the result of the combined expression is the result of its right operand. This means that anywhere you can put an expression, you can also put a series of expressions separated by commas. For example, consider the following statements:

```
int i = 1;
int value1 = 1;
int value2 = 1;
int value3 = 1;
value1 += ++i, value2 += ++i, value3 += ++i;
```

The first four statements initialize each of four variables to 1. The last statement consists of three assignment expressions, separated by the comma operator. Because the comma operator is left associative and has the lowest precedence of all the operators (see Appendix D), the statement will be executed as:

```
(((value1 += ++i), (value2 += ++i)), (value3 += ++i));
```

The result will be that **value1** will be set to 3, **value2** will be set to 4, and **value3** will be set to 5. The value of the composite expression is the value of the rightmost expression in the series, so the overall value (which is discarded here, because we don't assign it to anything) is 5. We can demonstrate the effect of the comma operator by modifying the loop in the previous example to incorporate the calculations into the second loop control expression.

Try It Out – The Comma Operator

Here's the modified version of the last program:

```
// Program 5.7 Demonstrating the comma operator
#include <iostream>
#include <iomanip>

using namespace std;

int main()
{
  int count = 0;
  cout << endl << "What upper limit would you like? ";
  cin >> count;

  cout << endl
       << "integer"                   // Output column headings
       << "      sum"
       << "        factorial"
       << endl;

  for(long n = 1, sum = 0, factorial = 1 ; sum += n, factorial *= n, n <= count ;
                                                                          n++)
    cout << setw(4) << n   << "    "
         << setw(7) << sum << " "
```

```
        << setw(15) << factorial
        << endl;
   return 0;
}
```

For the same input, this program will produce exactly the same output as the last example.

How It Works

To illustrate the comma operator, we have put the calculations for the sum and factorial into the second loop expression:

```
for(long n = 1, sum = 0, factorial = 1 ; sum += n, factorial *= n, n <= count ;
                                                                            n++)
   cout << setw(4) << n   << "     "
        << setw(7) << sum << " "
        << setw(15) << factorial
        << endl;
```

Despite the identical output, the code and the computation that is carried out are different from our earlier example. The second loop control expression will be evaluated at the *beginning* of each iteration, so **sum** will be incremented and **factorial** will be calculated each time. The value of the composite expression will be the value of the expression **n <= count**, so this still determines when the loop ends. When this condition fails, we will *already have calculated* **sum** and **factorial** with the current value of **n**, but these will not be displayed because the loop statement will not be executed. In our case this isn't important — it's just a spurious calculation — but in many cases it could cause problems.

You could put the calculation in the third control expression, but this would not produce the correct output. Since the loop statement is executed before the iteration expression for the loop is evaluated, the values in **sum** and **factorial** would not correspond with the current value of **n** at the time of output.

To be honest, there is no merit in coding this in this way here, and you should consider the example as a demonstration of syntax rather than good style. However, just occasionally there are situations where the comma operator can be useful, when you need to evaluate several expressions in one.

Nested Loops

You can place a loop inside another loop. In fact, you can 'nest' loops within loops to whatever depth you require for the solution of your problem. Furthermore, nested loops can be of any kind: you can nest a **for** loop inside a **while** loop inside a **do-while** loop, if you need to. They can be mixed in any way that you want.

The most common application of nested loops is in the context of arrays, which you will meet in the next chapter, but they do have other uses too. We can illustrate how nesting works with an example that will provide lots of opportunity for nesting loops.

Try It Out – Using a Nested Loop

Multiplication tables are the bane of many children's lives at school, but we can use a nested loop to generate one. Here's the program:

```
// Program 5.8 Using a nested loop to generate multiplication tables
#include <iostream>
#include <iomanip>
#include <cctype>

using namespace std;

int main()
{
  int table = 0;                                   // Table size
  const int table_min = 2;                         // Minimum table size
  const int table_max = 12;                        // Maximum table size
  char ch = 0;                                     // Response to prompt

  do
  {
    cout << endl
         << "What size table would you like ("
         << table_min << " to " << table_max << ")? ";
    cin >> table;                                  // Get the table size
    cout << endl;

    // Make sure table size is within the limits
    if(table < table_min || table > table_max)
    {
      cout << "Invalid table size entered. Program terminated." << endl;
      exit(1);
    }

    // Create the top line of the table
    cout << "      |";
    for(int i = 1 ; i <= table ; i++)
      cout << " " << setw(3) << i << " |";
    cout << endl;

    // Create the separator row
    for(int i = 0 ; i <= table ; i++)
      cout << "------";
    cout << endl;

    for(int i = 1 ; i <= table ; i++)              // Iterate over the rows
    {
      cout << " " << setw(3) << i << " |";         // Start the row

      // Output the values in a row
      for(int j = 1 ; j <= table ; j++)
        cout << " " << setw(3) << i*j << " |";     // One for each column
      cout << endl;                                // End the row
    }

    // Check if another table is required
    cout << endl << "Do you want another table (y or n)? ";
```

```
      cin >> ch;
      cout << endl;
   } while(tolower(ch) == 'y');

   return 0;
}
```

An example of the output produced by this program is:

```
What size table would you like (2 to 12)? 10

      |  1 |  2 |  3 |  4 |  5 |  6 |  7 |  8 |  9 | 10 |
---------------------------------------------------------------
  1 |  1 |  2 |  3 |  4 |  5 |  6 |  7 |  8 |  9 | 10 |
  2 |  2 |  4 |  6 |  8 | 10 | 12 | 14 | 16 | 18 | 20 |
  3 |  3 |  6 |  9 | 12 | 15 | 18 | 21 | 24 | 27 | 30 |
  4 |  4 |  8 | 12 | 16 | 20 | 24 | 28 | 32 | 36 | 40 |
  5 |  5 | 10 | 15 | 20 | 25 | 30 | 35 | 40 | 45 | 50 |
  6 |  6 | 12 | 18 | 24 | 30 | 36 | 42 | 48 | 54 | 60 |
  7 |  7 | 14 | 21 | 28 | 35 | 42 | 49 | 56 | 63 | 70 |
  8 |  8 | 16 | 24 | 32 | 40 | 48 | 56 | 64 | 72 | 80 |
  9 |  9 | 18 | 27 | 36 | 45 | 54 | 63 | 72 | 81 | 90 |
 10 | 10 | 20 | 30 | 40 | 50 | 60 | 70 | 80 | 90 |100 |

Do you want another table (y or n)? n
```

How It Works

We have included three standard header files:

```
#include <iostream>
#include <iomanip>
#include <cctype>
```

Just as a refresher, the first is for stream input/output, the second is to get access to stream manipulators, and the third is because we'll be using the **tolower()** character conversion function.

We start the program proper by declaring some variables that we need:

```
int table = 0;                    // Table size
const int table_min = 2;          // Minimum table size
const int table_max = 12;         // Maximum table size
char ch = 0;                      // Response to prompt
```

The second and third declarations define the limits on the size of the tables we want to support. These should not be altered anywhere, so we declare them as **const** to make sure. This also brings the advantages we discussed in Chapter 2, removing magic numbers, and reducing maintenance points.

The program generates a table in the **do-while** loop, which allows additional tables to be generated if required. The loop performs four tasks, which are described by the comments here:

```
do
{
  // Read the table size from the keyboard...
```

```
      // Make sure the table size is within limits...

      // Create and output the table...

      // Get an indication whether another table is required...

  } while(tolower(ch) == 'y');
```

Clearly, the variable **ch** will store the response entered when the prompt for another table is displayed. The code to read the table size is:

```
cout << endl
     << "What size table would you like ("
     << table_min << " to " << table_max << ")? ";
cin >> table;                               // Get the table size
cout << endl;
```

This uses the **const** values **table_min** and **table_max** to output the limits on the permitted size of tables. To deal with the situation of an invalid size for the table being entered, we just compare the value with the permitted limits:

```
if(table < table_min || table > table_max)
{
  cout << "Invalid table size entered. Program terminated." << endl;
  exit(1);
}
```

If the value of **table** is less than the minimum or greater than the maximum allowed, we just display a message and end the program using the standard library **exit()** function. We will see later in the chapter how we can handle this in a less brutal, more user-friendly fashion.

Next, the table is generated. The first **for** loop nested inside the **do-while** loop generates the top line of the table, containing the multipliers:

```
cout << "     |";
for(int i = 1 ; i <= table ; i++)
  cout << " " << setw(3) << i << " |";
cout << endl;
```

The loop statement outputs multiplier values separated by spaces and vertical bars, from 1 to the size of the table. Each output column is six characters wide, so all the table entries will need to be the same width to ensure everything lines up.

The next nested **for** loop generates a row of dashes to separate the top line from the rest of the table:

```
for(int i = 0 ; i <= table ; i++)
  cout << "------";
cout << endl;
```

Each iteration of this loop adds six dashes to the row. By starting the count at zero instead of one, we output a total of **table + 1** sets in all: one for the left hand column of multipliers, and one for each of the columns of table entries.

The final loop, which itself contains a nested loop, outputs the left hand column of multipliers and the products that are the table entries:

```
for(int i = 1 ; i <= table ; i++)            // Iterate over the rows
{
  cout << " " << setw(3) << i << " |";        // Start the row

  // Output the values in a row
  for(int j = 1 ; j <= table ; j++)
    cout << " " << setw(3) << i * j << " |";  // One for each column
  cout << endl;                               // End the row
}
```

Including the outer **do-while** loop, we have three levels of nesting here. Each iteration of the 'middle' **for** loop creates one row of the table. On each iteration, the output statement to start a new line and display the left-hand multiplier is executed. Then the inner loop is executed, which generates the table entries for the current row. Each iteration of the inner **for** loop generates one entry, so the variable **j** is essentially a column number in the table. Since **j** varies from 1 to **table**, there will be **table** entries in each row. The value to be displayed at each position is the product of the row number, **i**, and the column number, **j**.

When the complete table has been displayed, there is a prompt for whether another table is required:

```
cout << endl << "Do you want another table (y or n)? ";
cin >> ch;
cout << endl;
```

The character entered is stored in **ch**, and this is used in the **do-while** loop condition. If **ch** is **'y'** or **'Y'**, another iteration of the **do-while** loop will be executed to produce another table. Otherwise, the loop ends and so too does the program.

Skipping Loop Iterations

Sometimes, situations arise where you want to skip one loop iteration, and press on with the next one. The **continue** statement will do this for you, and you write it simply as:

```
continue;
```

When this is executed within a loop, execution transfers immediately to the end of the current iteration, and provided the loop control expression allows it, execution continues with the next iteration. This is best understood by using it in an example.

Try It Out – Using the continue Statement

Let's suppose you want to output a table of characters, along with their corresponding character codes in hexadecimal and decimal. Of course, you don't want to output the characters that don't have a symbolic representation — some of these, such as tabs and newline, will mess up the output. So, we want a program that will output just the 'printable' characters.

Here's how we can do that:

```cpp
// Program 5.9 Using the continue statement
#include <iostream>
#include <iomanip>
#include <cctype>
#include <limits>

using namespace std;

int main()
{
  // Output the column headings
  cout << endl
       << setw(13) << "Character  "
       << setw(13) << "Hexadecimal "
       << setw(13) << "Decimal   "
       << endl;

  cout << uppercase;                             // Uppercase hex digits

  unsigned char ch = 0;                          // Character code

  // Output characters and corresponding codes
  do
  {
    if(!isprint(ch))                             // If it does not print
      continue;                                  // skip this iteration

    cout << setw(7)  << ch
         << hex                                  // Hexadecimal mode
         << setw(13) << static_cast<int>(ch)
         << dec                                  // Decimal mode
         << setw(13) << static_cast<int>(ch)
         << endl;
  } while(ch++ < numeric_limits<unsigned char>::max());
  return 0;
}
```

This will output all the printable characters with code values from 0 to the maximum **unsigned char** value. On my computer, this displays the printable ASCII characters.

How It Works

We output headings for the columns of output with the statement:

```cpp
cout << endl
     << setw(13) << "Character  "
     << setw(13) << "Hexadecimal "
     << setw(13) << "Decimal   "
     << endl;
```

Since we've used a field width of 13 for each heading, we'll need to take care to position the output values in the middle of each column.

To get the hexadecimal values displayed using upper case digits, we have the statement:

```
cout << uppercase;                          // Uppercase hex digits
```

This uses **uppercase** output modifier to make all subsequent hexadecimal output use **A** to **F** rather than **a** to **f**.

Once we've set up a variable to hold the character codes, the really interesting bit is the **do-while** loop:

```
do
{
  if(!isprint(ch))                          // If it does not print
    continue;                               // skip this iteration

  cout << setw(7)  << ch
       << hex                               // Hexadecimal mode
       << setw(13) << static_cast<int>(ch)
       << dec                               // Decimal mode
       << setw(13) << static_cast<int>(ch)
       << endl;
} while(ch++ < numeric_limits<unsigned char>::max());
```

This iterates through character codes from 0 to the value produced by **numeric_limits<unsigned char>::max()**, which is the maximum value of type **unsigned char**.

Within the loop, we first check that the current value of **ch** represents a printable character using the function **isprint()**, which we saw in the last chapter. If **isprint(ch)** returns 0, the expression **!isprint(ch)** will be **true**, and the **continue** statement will be executed. This will skip the rest of the loop statements and go straight to the next iteration. Thus, we only execute the output statement in the loop for printable characters.

In the output statements, we use the manipulators **hex** and **dec** to set the output mode for integers to what we require. In order to get the value of **ch** to display as a numeric value, we must cast it to **int** in the output statement. Left as it is, it always displays as a character.

Note that to keep the code simple, we have to use **unsigned char** rather than just **char** as the type for **ch**. Type **char** can be equivalent to (but not the same as) **signed char** or **unsigned char**, depending on the implementation, and you would need to program to allow for the possibility of type **char** turning out to be equivalent to **signed char**. One complication of signed values is that you cannot cover the whole range by counting up from 0, as adding 1 to the maximum value for **signed char** produces the minimum value.

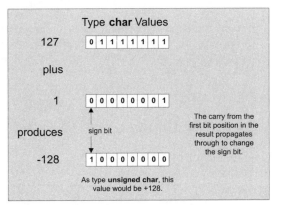

169

You could deal with this by setting the initial value of **ch** to the minimum for the type using **numeric_limits<char>::min()**, but when you cast the negative code values to **int**, of course you would get a negative result, so the hexadecimal codes would show the leading digits as **F**.

Note also that a **for** loop would not be suitable here. Because the condition is checked before the loop block is executed, you might be tempted to write the loop as:

```
for(unsigned char ch = 0 ; ch <= numeric_limits<unsigned char>::max() ; ch++)
{
  // Output character and code
}
```

This loop will never end, because after executing the loop block with **ch** at the maximum value, the next increment of **ch** will give it a value of 0, and the second loop control expression will never be **false**.

Breaking Out of a Loop

Sometimes, you need to end a loop prematurely; something might arise within the loop statement that indicates there is no point in continuing. In this case, you can use the **break** statement. Its effect here is much the same as it was in the **switch** statement that we saw in the previous chapter: if you execute a **break** statement within a loop, the loop ends immediately and execution continues with the statement following the loop.

The **break** statement is used most frequently with an indefinite loop, so let's look next at what one of those looks like.

Indefinite Loops

An **indefinite loop** can potentially run forever. If you leave out the test condition in a **for** loop, for example, the loop is left with no mechanism for stopping. Unless there is some means of exiting the loop from within the loop block itself, the loop will run indefinitely — that's how it gets its name.

There are several practical uses for indefinite loops: programs that monitor some kind of alarm indicator, for example, or that collect data from sensors in an industrial plant, are sometimes written using an indefinite loop. You will find that an indefinite loop is useful when you don't know in advance how many iterations are required, such as when you are reading a variable quantity of input data. You arrange for the exit from the loop to be coded within the loop block, not within the loop control expression.

In the most common form of the indefinite **for** loop, all the control expressions are omitted:

```
for( ; ; )
{
  // Statements that do something
  // There needs to be some way of ending the loop in here
}
```

Note that we still need the semicolons, even though there are no loop control expressions. The only way this loop can end is if there is some code within the loop to terminate it.

You can have an indefinite **while** loop, too:

```
while(true)
{
  // Statements that do something
  // There needs to be some way of ending the loop in here
}
```

Since the condition for continuing the loop is always **true**, we have an indefinite loop. Of course, you can also have a version of the **do-while** loop that is indefinite, but it has no advantages over the other two types of loop and it is not normally used.

An obvious way to end an indefinite loop is to use the **break** statement, as I suggested at the start of this section. Executing **break** within a loop terminates the loop immediately, and execution continues with the statement following the loop. This is often used to handle invalid input and provide an opportunity for a correct value to be entered, or to repeat an operation such as playing a game until the user elects not to continue. We could illustrate this with a new version of Program 5.8, which generated a multiplication table.

Try It Out – Using break

In Program 5.8, we terminated the program if an unacceptable table size was entered. We can now modify the program to allow the user three attempts to enter a correct value. Here's the new version of the program:

```
// Program 5.10 Controlling input with an infinite loop
#include <iostream>
#include <iomanip>
#include <cctype>

using namespace std;

int main()
{
  int table = 0;                          // Table size
  const int table_min = 2;                // Minimum table size
  const int table_max = 12;               // Maximum table size
  const int input_tries = 3;
  char ch = 0;                            // Response to prompt

  do
  {
    for(int count = 1 ; ; count++)        // Indefinite loop
    {
      cout << endl
           << "What size table would you like ("
           << table_min << " to " << table_max << ")? ";
      cin >> table;                       // Get the table size
      cout << endl;
```

```
      // Make sure table size is within the limits
      if(table >= table_min && table <= table_max)
        break;                                    // Exit the input loop
      else if(count < input_tries)
        cout << "Invalid input - Try again.";
      else
      {
        cout << "Invalid table size entered - for the third time."
             << "\nSorry, only three goes - program terminated."
             << endl;
        exit(1);
      }
    }

    // Create the top line of the table
    cout << "     |";
    for(int i = 1 ; i <= table ; i++)
      cout << " " << setw(3) << i << " |";
    cout << endl;

    // Create the separator row
    for(int i = 0 ; i <= table ; i++)
      cout << "------";
    cout << endl;

    for(int i = 1 ; i <= table ; i++)            // Iterate over the rows
    {
      cout << " " << setw(3) << i << " |";       // Start the row

      // Output the values in a row
      for(int j = 1 ; j <= table ; j++)
        cout << " " << setw(3) << i*j << " |";   // One for each column
      cout << endl;                              // End the row
    }

    // Check if another table is required
    cout << endl << "Do you want another table (y or n)? ";
    cin >> ch;
    cout << endl;
  } while(tolower(ch) == 'y');

  return 0;
}
```

The normal output from this example is the same as the previous version of the program, but if you enter three successive invalid table sizes, you will get:

```
What size table would you like (2 to 12)? 1

Invalid input - Try again.
What size table would you like (2 to 12)? 14

Invalid input - Try again.
What size table would you like (2 to 12)? 46

Invalid table size entered - for the third time.
Sorry, only three goes - program terminated.
```

How It Works

The maximum number of attempts at correct input is defined by the variable **input_tries** that we declare in this line:

```
const int input_tries = 3;
```

This is used in the only new feature in the program, which is the **for** loop that manages the input:

```
for(int count = 1 ; ; count++)                  // Indefinite loop
{
  cout << endl
       << "What size table would you like ("
       << table_min << " to " << table_max << ")? ";
  cin >> table;                                  // Get the table size
  cout << endl;

  // Make sure table size is within the limits
  if(table >= table_min && table <= table_max)
    break;                                        // Exit the input loop
  else if(count < input_tries)
    cout << "Invalid input - Try again.";
  else
  {
    cout << "Invalid table size entered - for the third time."
         << "\nSorry, only three goes - program terminated."
         << endl;
    exit(1);
  }
}
```

The **for** loop has no control expression to stop it, so it will run for an indefinite number of iterations. The variable **count** records the number of input attempts, so this determines when we give up on input. The first **if** statement within the loop will cause **break** to be executed if valid input is entered in response to the prompt. This will end the **for** loop and allow the rest of the program to execute.

If invalid input is entered, the second **if**, which checks the value of **count**, is executed. As long as **count** is less than 3, a message is displayed and the loop goes to its next iteration to allow another try. Once three failed attempts have been made, the program terminates.

If we had declared and initialized **count** outside the input loop, we could have used an indefinite **while** loop:

```
int count = 1;
while(true)
{
  // Read input as before...

  // Make sure table size is within the limits
  if(table >= table_min && table <= table_max)
    break;                                        // Exit the input loop
  else if(count++ < input_tries)
    cout << "Invalid input - Try again.";
  else
```

```
        {
            // Prompt and end the program as before...
        }
    }
```

Let's try another example that uses a **for** loop with no control expressions at all.

Try It Out – Using a for Loop With No Control Expressions

We can write another version of our program that calculated the average of several temperature samples. This time we'll use an indefinite **for** loop and a **break** statement to manage the input.

```cpp
// Program 5.11 Calculating an average in an indefinite loop
#include <iostream>
#include <cctype>

using namespace std;

int main()
{
  char ch = 0;                          // Stores response to prompt for input
  int count = 0;                        // Counts the number of input values
  double temperature = 0.0;             // Stores an input value
  double average = 0.0;                 // Stores the total and average

  for( ; ; )                            // Indefinite loop
  {
    cout << "Enter a value: ";          // Prompt for input
    cin >> temperature;                 // Read input value
    average += temperature;             // Accumulate total of values
    count++;                            // Increment value count

    cout << "Do you want to enter another? (y/n): ";
    cin >> ch;                          // Get response
    cout << endl;
    if(tolower(ch) == 'n')              // Check for no
      break;                            // if so end the loop
  }
  cout << endl
       << "The average temperature is " << average / count;
  return 0;
}
```

Typical output from this example will be:

```
Enter a value: 65.5
Do you want to enter another? (y/n): y

Enter a value: 67.9
Do you want to enter another? (y/n): y

Enter a value: 72.3
Do you want to enter another? (y/n): n

The average temperature is 68.5667
```

How It Works

The only new aspect here is the means of exiting the loop:

```
for( ; ; )                          // Infinite loop
{
    cout << "Enter a value: ";      // Prompt for input
    cin >> temperature;             // Read input value
    average += temperature;         // Accumulate total of values
    count++;                        // Increment value count

    cout << "Do you want to enter another? (y/n): ";
    cin >> ch;                      // Get response
    cout << endl
    if(tolower(ch) == 'n')          // Check for no
        break;                      // if so end the loop
}
```

Our **for** loop has no control expressions, so it will run for an indefinite number of iterations. The **if** statement within the loop will cause **break** to be executed when **n** or **N** is entered in response to the prompt. This will end the loop and allow the average temperature to be calculated and displayed. Once again, we could equally well have used a **while** loop here:

```
while(true)                         // Infinite loop
{
    cout << "Enter a value: ";      // Prompt for input
    cin >> temperature;             // Read input value
    average += temperature;         // Accumulate total of values
    count++;                        // Increment value count

    cout << "Do you want to enter another? (y/n): ";
    cin >> ch;                      // Get response
    cout << endl;
    if(tolower(ch) == 'n')          // Check for no
        break;                      // if so end the loop
}
```

In this situation, there is no practical difference between the **while** loop and the **for** loop. Which you choose is just a question of which you prefer or find easier to read.

Summary

We will be seeing further applications of loops in the next chapter, and almost any program of consequence will involve a loop of some kind. Because they are so fundamental to programming, you need to be sure you have a good grasp of the ideas covered in this chapter. The essential points we have unearthed about loops are:

▶ A loop is a mechanism for repeating a block of statements.

▶ There are three kinds of loop that you can use: the **while** loop, the **do-while** loop, and the **for** loop.

▶ The **while** loop repeats for as long as a specified condition is **true**.

▶ The **do-while** loop always performs at least one iteration, and continues for as long as a specified condition is **true**.

▶ The **for** loop is typically used to repeat a given number of times, and has three control expressions. The first is an initialization expression, executed once at the beginning of the loop. The second is a loop condition, executed before each iteration, which must evaluate to **true** for the loop to continue. The third is executed at the end of each iteration and is usually used to increment a loop counter.

▶ Any kind of loop may be nested within any other kind of loop to any depth.

▶ Executing a **continue** statement within a loop will skip the remainder of the current iteration and go straight to the next iteration, providing the loop control condition allows it.

▶ Executing a **break** statement within a loop will cause an immediate exit from the loop.

▶ A loop defines a scope, so that variables declared within a loop are not accessible outside the loop. In particular, variables declared in the initialization expression of a **for** loop are not accessible outside the loop.

Exercises

Ex 5.1 Write a program that iterates through the odd numbers less than 30, and outputs the square of each number.

Ex 5.2 Create a program that loops 30 times, but only outputs numbers that are not divisible by 3 or 5. Decide on the most appropriate form of loop, and use an **if** statement inside it.

Ex 5.3 Create a program that uses a **do-while** loop to count the number of characters (not including whitespace) entered by the user. The count should end when it first encounters a **#** character in the input.

Ex 5.4 Write a program that uses a **do-while** loop to add integers entered by the user. In the loop condition, use a variable of type **char**, in which you can store the user's answer to the question, "Do you want to enter another?" When the loop is terminated, the program should output the total of all the inputs. To extend the program, add a nested **while** loop to ensure the user answers the "...another?" question sensibly (with a 'y' or an 'n').

Ex 5.5 Create a program that asks the user a series of questions that begin, "Is your number bigger than..." in order to deduce what integer between 1 and 100 they are thinking of. The user should only be able to answer 'y' or 'n' to each question. (Hint: each time round the loop, you should be seeking to halve the range in which the number could lie, so store an upper bound and a lower bound, and change one or the other according to the user's answers.)

Arrays and Strings

So far, we've covered all the basic data types of consequence, and have accumulated a basic knowledge of how to perform calculations and make decisions in a program. This chapter is about broadening the application of the basic programming techniques that we have covered so far, from using single data elements to working with whole collections of data items. We will also look at string handling. In this chapter, you will learn:

▶ What an array is and how you can use it

▶ How to declare and initialize arrays of different types

▶ What a null-terminated string is

▶ How to use an array of type **char** to store a character string

▶ How to declare and use multi-dimensional arrays

▶ How to create and use arrays of type **char** as arrays of null-terminated strings

▶ How to create variables of type **string**

▶ What operations are available with objects of type **string**, and how you can use them

Data Arrays

We already know how to declare and initialize variables of the basic types. Each variable can store a *single* data item of the specified type — we can have a variable that stores an integer, or a variable that stores a character, and so on. An **array** can store *several* data items of the same type. You can have an array of integers, or an array of characters — in fact, an array of any type of data.

Let's think about an example of when you might need such a thing. We have already written a program to calculate an average temperature. But suppose that you also wanted to calculate how many samples were above the average and how many were below it. You would need to retain the original sample data in order to do this, but storing each data item in a separate variable would be tortuous to code, and utterly impractical for anything more than a very few items. An array provides you with the means of performing this task easily, and many other things besides.

Using an Array

An array is simply a number of memory locations, each of which can store an item of data of the same data type, and all of which are referenced through the same variable name. For example, you could store 366 temperature samples in an array declared as:

```
double temperatures[366];      // An array of temperatures
```

This declares an array of type **double** with the name **temperatures**, and with 366 **elements**. That means this array has 366 memory locations, each of which can be used to hold a value of type **double**. The number of elements specified between the brackets is called the **size** of the array.

You refer to the individual items in an array by using an integer that's usually referred to as an **index**. The index of a particular element is simply the offset from the first element in the array. The first element has an offset of zero and therefore an index of **0**, while an index value of **3** will refer to the fourth element of an array — three elements from the first. To reference an element, you put its index between square brackets after the array name, so to set the fourth element of the **temperatures** array to 99.0, you would write:

```
temperatures[3] = 99.0;        // Set the fourth array element to 99
```

Let's look at another array. The basic structure of an array called **height** is illustrated below:

height[0]	height[1]	height[2]	height[3]	height[4]	height[5]
26	37	47	55	62	75

The array is of type **int**, and it has six elements. Each box represents the memory location holding the value of an array element. Each array element can be referenced using the expression above it. This array is declared with the statement:

```
int height[6];                 // Declare an array of six heights
```

The compiler will allocate six contiguous storage locations for values of type **int** as a result of this declaration (which is therefore also a definition). If a value of type **int** on your computer requires 4 bytes, then this array will occupy 24 bytes.

> *The type of the array will determine the amount of memory required for storing each element. All the elements of an array are stored in one, continuous block of memory.*

As shown, each element in the **height** array contains a different value. These might be the heights of the members of a family, for instance, recorded to the nearest inch. As there are six elements, the index values run from **0** through to **5**. If you wanted to, you could sum the first three elements of **height** with the statement:

```
int sum3 = height[0] + height[1] + height[2];      // The sum of three elements
```

Here, the individual elements of the array are behaving just like ordinary integer variables. However, you cannot assign the *whole* of one array to another array in an assignment — you can only operate on the individual elements of an array.

Try It Out – Using an Array

Let's jump straight in and see an array in action. We can use an integer array in a program to calculate the average height of a group of people, and then work out how many are above average.

```cpp
// Program 6.1 Using an array
#include <iostream>
#include <cctype>

using namespace std;

int main()
{
  int height[10];                        // Array of heights
  int count = 0;                         // Number of heights
  char reply = 0;                        // Reply to prompt

  // Input loop for heights. Read heights until we are done, or the array is full
  do
  {
    cout << endl
         << "Enter a height as an integral number of inches: ";
    cin >> height[count++];

    // Check if another input is required
    cout << "Do you want to enter another (y or n)? ";
    cin >> reply;
  } while(count < 10 && tolower(reply) == 'y');

  // Indicate when array is full
  if(count == 10)
    cout << endl  << "Maximum height count reached." << endl;

  // Calculate the average and display it
  double average = 0.0;                  // Stores average height
  for(int i = 0; i < count ; i++)
    average += height[i];                // Add a height
  average /= count;                      // Divide by the number of heights
  cout << endl
       << "Average height is " << average << " inches."
       << endl;

  // Calculate how many are above average height
  int above_average = 0;                 // Count of above average heights
  for(int i = 0 ; i < count ; i++)
    if(height[i] > average)              // Greater than average?
      above_average++;                   // then increment the count
```

```
      cout << "There "
           << (above_average == 1 ? "is " : "are ")
           << above_average << " height"
           << (above_average == 1 ? " " : "s ")
           << "above average."
           << endl;
    return 0;
  }
```

Typical output from this program is:

```
Enter a height as an integral number of inches: 75
Do you want to enter another (y or n)? y

Enter a height as an integral number of inches: 56
Do you want to enter another (y or n)? y

Enter a height as an integral number of inches: 63
Do you want to enter another (y or n)? y

Enter a height as an integral number of inches: 42
Do you want to enter another (y or n)? y

Enter a height as an integral number of inches: 70
Do you want to enter another (y or n)? n

Average height is 61.2 inches.
There are 3 heights above average.
```

How It Works

We start by declaring the array and two other variables that we will need:

```
int height[10];                        // Array of heights
int count = 0;                         // Number of heights
char reply = 0;                        // Reply to prompt
```

The **height** array has a size of 10, so we can store a maximum of 10 integer values. We'll use the variable **count** to refer to the next free element in the array, and because the first array index is zero, this will also reflect the number of values stored in the array. Initially, the first element is free and there are no values stored, so **count** is 0.

We read the height values in a **do-while** loop:

```
do
{
  cout << endl
       << "Enter a height as an integral number of inches: ";
  cin >> height[count++];

  // Check if another input is required
  cout << "Do you want to enter another (y or n)? ";
  cin >> reply;
} while(count < 10 && tolower(reply) == 'y');
```

After a prompt, we read a height value from the keyboard and store it in the element referenced by the current value of **count**. The variable **count** is then incremented to refer to the next free element. Next, we display a prompt to determine whether further heights are to be entered. The response is recorded in **reply**. The **do-while** loop condition checks both the number of values stored against the size of the array, and the reply to the prompt for more elements. If either the value of **count** has reached 10, which is the number of elements in the array, or the character in **reply** is not **'y'** or **'Y'**, the loop ends.

Note that C++ does not check index values to ensure they are valid. It is up to you to make sure that you don't reference elements outside the bounds of the array. If you store data using an index value that's outside the valid range for an array, you will overwrite something in memory, or cause a storage protection violation. Either way, your program will almost certainly come to a sticky end.

After the loop ends, we check whether the value in **count** indicates that we filled the array, and, if so, we display a message. This will take care of the case when someone attempts to enter more than the maximum number of values we can accommodate. We then calculate the average height:

```
double average = 0.0;                    // Stores average height
for(int i = 0; i < count ; i++)
  average += height[i];                  // Add a height
average /= count;                        // Divide by the number of heights
cout << endl
     << "Average height is " << average << " inches."
     << endl;
```

We accumulate the sum of the heights in the variable **average** using a **for** loop. The loop will execute with values for **i** from **0** to **count - 1**, which are precisely the index values for the elements containing values. When **i** is incremented to **count**, the loop ends. To calculate the average height, we simply divide the accumulated sum in **average** by the count of the number of heights (given by **count**).

The last calculation is to count how many height values are above average:

```
int above_average = 0;                   // Count of above average heights
for(int i = 0 ; i < count ; i++)
  if(height[i] > average)                // Greater than average?
    above_average++;                     // then increment the count
```

This uses another **for** loop to compare each height with the value in **average**. If a value is greater than **average**, the count in **above_average** is incremented. Finally, we output the count of above average heights with this statement:

```
cout << "There "
     << (above_average == 1 ? "is " : "are ")
     << above_average << " height"
     << (above_average == 1 ? " " : "s ")
     << "above average."
     << endl;
```

The conditional operators just adjust the output to deal with the difference between singular and plural heights. They choose between **"is "** and **"are "**, and whether **"s "** is appended to the word **" height"**.

Avoiding Magic Numbers

We discussed the undesirability of using magic numbers in your programs back in Chapter 2, but we let one slip through the net in the last example: the size of the **height** array. We could avoid this by declaring and initializing a constant with the array size that we want:

```
const int max_heights = 10;                       // Array size
```

Now we can define the array with the size specified by **max_heights**:

```
int height[max_heights];                          // Array of heights
```

There are two other places in the code that need to be updated to use this new constant: the loop condition of our **do-while** loop, and the **if** statement loop that follows it:

```
do
{
  cout << endl
       << "Enter a height as an integral number of inches: ";
  cin >> height[count++];

  // Check if another input is required
  cout << "Do you want to enter another (y or n)? ";
  cin >> reply;
} while(count < max_heights && tolower(reply) == 'y');

// Indicate when array is full
if(count == max_heights)
  cout << endl  << "Maximum height count reached." << endl;
```

Now the program has no magic numbers, and if we want to adjust the size of the array, we just need to modify the initial value of **max_heights**. Be aware that you *must* declare **max_heights** as **const** here. If you don't, the compiler will not accept it as a size for the array.

The size of an array can be a constant integral expression, but the *compiler* must be able to evaluate it to an integer constant in order to arrange for the appropriate amount of memory to be allocated. This implies that the expression can only contain literals, **const**s and enumerators.

Initializing Arrays

To initialize an array, the initializing values for the elements are enclosed within braces and placed following an 'equals' sign after the declaration of the array name. An example of a declaration and initialization of an array is:

```
int samples[5] = {2, 3, 5, 7, 11};
```

The values in the list correspond to successive index values of the array, so in this case **samples[0]** has the value 2, **samples[1]** has the value 3, **samples[2]** has the value 5, and so on. A list of initial values between braces is called an **aggregate initializer list**, or simply an **initializer list**. An array is one example of an **aggregate** in C++; there are others.

You mustn't specify more initializing values than there are elements in the array, but you *can* specify fewer. If there *are* fewer, the values are assigned to successive elements, starting with the first element, which has the index **0**. The array elements for which you don't provide an initial value will be initialized with 0. This is not the same as supplying no initializer list. Without an initializer list, the array elements will contain junk values.

> *The syntax of C++ allows for an empty initializer list, in which case all elements will be initialized to zero. However, I recommend that you always put at least one initializing value in a list.*

Try It Out - Initializing an Array

We can illustrate the above discussion with the following, rather limited example that outputs the values contained in two arrays.

```
// Program 6.2 Initializing an array
#include <iostream>
#include <iomanip>

using namespace std;

int main()
{
  const int size = 5;
  int values[size] = {1, 2, 3};
  double junk[size];

  cout << endl;

  for(int i = 0 ; i < size ; i++)
    cout << " " << setw(12) << values[i];
  cout << endl;

  for(int i = 0 ; i < size ; i++)
    cout << " " << setw(12) << junk[i];
  cout << endl;

  return 0;
}
```

In this example we declare two arrays, the first of which, **values**, is initialized in part, and the second, **junk**, is not initialized at all. The program generates two lines of output that look like this on my computer:

```
           1            2            3            0            0
4.24399e-314  2.2069e-312  1.11216e-306  1.81969e-307  1.99808e-307
```

The second line of output (corresponding to values of **junk[0]** to **junk[4]**) may well be different on your computer.

How It Works

As you can see from the output, the first three elements of the **values** array contain the initializing values, and the last two have the default value of 0. In the case of the **junk** array, all the values are spurious because we didn't provide any initial values. The array elements will contain whatever values the program that last used these memory locations left there.

Setting Array Elements to Zero

Rather than having arrays sitting around containing junk values, it's easy to initialize a whole array to zero, using a technique we've already discussed. In the above example, we could have arranged for all the elements of the **junk** array to be 0 with either this statement:

```
double junk[size] = {0};     // Initialize all elements to zero
```

Or this one:

```
double junk[size] = {};      // Initialize all elements to zero
```

An initialization value of 0 will always be converted to the appropriate type for the array. The explicit value in the first of these statements is used to initialize the first element, and the remainder will be set to 0 too, as they have no initializing values. I prefer the first form because I think it makes your intention more obvious.

Defining Array Size with the Initializer List

Another thing you're allowed to omit in an array declaration is the *size* of the array, provided that you supply initializing values. The number of elements in the array will then be the same as the number of initializing values. For example, consider the array declaration:

```
int values[] = {2, 3, 4};
```

This defines an array with three elements, which will have the initial values 2, 3 and 4. It is equivalent to writing:

```
int values[3] = {2, 3, 4};
```

The advantage of the first form here is that you can't get the array size wrong, because the compiler determines it for you! It's important to realize, though, that you cannot have zero size arrays in C++, so the initializer list must always contain at least one initializing value if you omit the array size.

Finding the Number of Array Elements

We saw earlier how we could avoid magic numbers for the number of elements in an array by defining a constant initialized with the size of the array. Of course, you can't do that if you let the compiler decide the number of elements from the initializer list.

In Chapter 3, we saw that the **sizeof()** operator can supply the number of bytes that a variable occupies. The **sizeof()** operator can also help you to figure out the number of elements in an array. Suppose we've declared an array as:

```
int values[] = {2, 3, 5, 7, 11, 13, 17, 19};
```

The expression **sizeof values** will evaluate to the number of bytes occupied by the entire array. The expression **sizeof values[0]**, on the other hand, will evaluate to the number of bytes occupied by a single element — the first element in this case, but any one would do since they are all the same. Thus, the expression **sizeof values / sizeof values[0]** will evaluate to the number of elements in the array. Let's try it out.

Try It Out – Getting the Number of Array Elements

Here's a very simple program that uses the above technique:

```
// Program 6.3 Obtaining the number of array elements
#include <iostream>

using namespace std;

int main()
{
  int values[] = {2, 3, 5, 7, 11, 13, 17, 19, 23, 29};

  cout << endl
       << "There are "
       << sizeof values / sizeof values[0]
       << " elements in the array."
       << endl;

  int sum = 0;
  for(int i = 0 ; i < sizeof values / sizeof values[0] ; sum += values[i++])
    ;

  cout << "The sum of the array elements is " << sum
       << endl;

  return 0;
}
```

This example produces the output:

```
There are 10 elements in the array.
The sum of the array elements is 129
```

How It Works

The number of array elements is determined by the compiler from the number of initializing values in the declaration:

```
int values[] = {2, 3, 5, 7, 11, 13, 17, 19, 23, 29};
```

After the array declaration, we immediately output the number of elements with this statement:

```
cout << endl
     << "There are "
     << sizeof values / sizeof values[0]
     << " elements in the array."
     << endl;
```

As we discussed, we use the **sizeof()** operator to calculate the number of elements. The array is type **int** here (so we could have used **sizeof(int)** in place of **sizeof values[0]**), but this expression will produce the correct number of elements regardless of the type of the array.

Just to prove that we can do it, we use the same expression again in the **for** loop condition:

```
int sum = 0;
for(int i = 0 ; i < sizeof values / sizeof values[0] ; sum += values[i++])
    ;
```

This loop sums the elements of the array in the third control expression, **sum += values[i++]**. This also increments the counter, **i**, after the current element has been added to **sum**. The loop statement itself is empty, a fact indicated by the semicolon that appears on its own on the next line.

Finally, we output the value of **sum** with the statement:

```
cout << "The sum of the array elements is " << sum
     << endl;
```

Arrays of Characters

An array of type **char** can have a dual personality. It can simply be an array of characters, where each element stores one character, *or* it can represent a string. In the latter case, each character in the string is stored in a separate array element, and the end of the string is indicated by a special string termination character, **'\0'**, which is called the **null character**.

This representation for a character string is called a **C-style string**, as opposed to the **string** type that is defined in the standard library. Entities of type **string** do not need a string termination character.

> *For the moment, we'll just consider C-style strings in the context of arrays in general, and come back to type **string** towards the end of this chapter. You'll find that using type **string** is more powerful and convenient for string manipulation than arrays of type **char**.*

We can declare and initialize an array of characters with a statement like this:

```
char vowels[5] = {'a', 'e', 'i', 'o', 'u'};
```

Each element of the array is initialized with the corresponding character from the initializer list. As with numeric arrays, if you provide fewer initializing values than there are array elements, the elements that do not have explicit initializing values will be initialized with zero — that is, the null character whose bits are all 0, not the character **'0'**. You could also leave it to the compiler to set the size of the array to the number of initializing values:

```
char vowels[] = {'a', 'e', 'i', 'o', 'u'};   // An array with five elements
```

We can also declare an array of type **char** and initialize it with a string literal. For example:

```
char name[10] = "Mae West";
```

Since we are initializing the array with a string literal, the null character will be appended to the characters in the string, so the contents of the array will be:

'M'	'a'	'e'	' '	'W'	'e'	's'	't'	'\0'	'\0'

The last element will also be set to the null character, because there is no initializing value for it. Once again, you can leave the compiler to set the size of the array when you initialize it with a string:

```
char name[] = "Mae West";
```

This time, the array will have nine elements: eight elements to store the characters in the string, plus one extra element to store the string termination character. Of course, we could have used this approach when we declared the **vowels** array:

```
char vowels[] = "aeiou";                    // An array with six elements
```

The difference between this and the previous declaration for **vowels** is that here we are initializing the array with a string literal. This has **'\0'** appended to it to mark the end of the string, so the **vowels** array will contain six elements.

You can display a string stored in an array just by using the array name. The string in our **name** array, for example, could be displayed with this statement:

```
cout << name << endl;
```

This will display the entire string of characters, up to the **'\0'**. There *must* be a **'\0'** at the end. If there isn't, you will continue to output characters from successive memory locations until a string termination character turns up or an illegal memory reference occurs.

> *You can't output the contents of an array of a numeric type by just using the array name. This method only works for **char** arrays.*

Try It Out – Analyzing a String

Let's see how we could use an array of type **char** in an example. This program will read a line of text, and work out how many vowels and consonants are used in it.

```
// Program 6.4 Analyzing the letters in a string
#include <iostream>
#include <cctype>

using namespace std;

int main()
{
  const int maxlength = 100;                // Array dimension
  char text[maxlength] = {0};               // Array to hold input string
```

```
    cout << endl << "Enter a line of text:" << endl;

    // Read a line of characters including spaces
    cin.getline(text, maxlength);

    cout << "You entered:" << endl << text << endl;

    int vowels = 0;                          // Count of vowels
    int consonants = 0;                      // Count of consonants
    for(int i = 0 ; text[i] != '\0' ; i++)
      if(isalpha(text[i]))                   // If it is a letter
        switch(tolower(text[i]))             // Test lower case version
        {
          case 'a':
          case 'e':
          case 'i':
          case 'o':
          case 'u':
            vowels++;                        // It is a vowel
            break;
          default:
            consonants++;                    // It is a consonant
        }

    cout << "Your input contained "
         << vowels      << " vowels and "
         << consonants << " consonants."
         << endl;

    return 0;
}
```

Here is an example of the output from this program:

```
Enter a line of text:
A rich man is nothing but a poor man with money.
You entered:
A rich man is nothing but a poor man with money.
Your input contained 14 vowels and 23 consonants.
```

How It Works

We declare an array of type **char** that has the number of elements defined by a **const** variable:

```
const int maxlength = 100;                // Array dimension
char text[maxlength] = {0};               // Array to hold input string
```

We will store the input in the **text** array. However, we can't use our usual method for getting input, using the extraction operator (**>>**), because it won't do what we want in these circumstances. Consider this statement:

```
cin >> text;
```

This would certainly read characters into the **text** array, but only up to the first space. The extraction operator regards a space as a delimiter between input values, so it won't read an entire string containing spaces. We can't even use the extraction operator to read the input a character at a time, as *any* whitespace character, including **'\n'**, is regarded as a delimiter. This means we cannot store a newline character, and therefore cannot use it to indicate the end of the string. To read a whole line of text, including spaces, we need to use a different capability that is available with the standard input stream.

So, after prompting for input, we read from the standard input stream with this statement:

```
cin.getline(text, maxlength);
```

The **getline()** function for the **cin** stream reads in and stores a whole line of characters, including spaces. The input ends when a newline character, **'\n'**, is read, which will be when you press the *Return* key.

You can see that unlike the other functions we've used so far, **getline()** is being passed *two* arguments. The input is stored in the location specified by the first of these; in this case, it's the **text** array. The second is the maximum number of characters that you want to store. This count includes the string termination character, **'\0'**, which will be automatically appended to the end of the input string.

Although we haven't done so here, it's possible to pass a *third* argument to the **getline()** function. This enables you to specify an alternative character to **'\n'** to indicate the end of the input. For example, if you wanted to indicate the end of a string by entering an exclamation mark, you could use this statement:

```
cin.getline(text, maxlength, '!');
```

Why would you want to do this? A primary reason would be to allow multiple lines of text to be entered. With **'!'** indicating the end of the input instead of **'\n'**, you could enter as many lines of text as you wanted, including **'\n'** characters. You just enter **'!'** when you are done. Of course, the total number of characters you enter is still limited by **maxlength**.

Returning to the example, and simply to show that we can, we output the string that was entered using just the array name:

```
cout << "You entered:" << endl << text << endl;
```

Now that we have read and redisplayed the input line, we analyze the text string in quite a straightforward manner:

```
int vowels = 0;                        // Count of vowels
int consonants = 0;                    // Count of consonants
for(int i = 0 ; text[i] != '\0' ; i++)
  if(isalpha(text[i]))                 // If it is a letter
    switch(tolower(text[i]))           // Test lower case version
    {
      case 'a':
      case 'e':
      case 'i':
      case 'o':
      case 'u':
        vowels++;                      // It is a vowel
        break;
      default:
        consonants++;                  // It is a consonant
    }
```

We accumulate the counts of vowels and consonants in the two variables that we declare here. The **for** loop condition tests for finding the string termination character, rather than the more typical test for a counter limit being reached. Within the loop, we use the **isalpha()** library function to check for a letter. If we find one, we use the lower case version of the letter as the selection expression in a **switch** statement. This avoids having to write **case**s for upper as well as lower case letters. Since we only get to the **switch** if **text[i]** is a letter, and since any letter that is not a vowel must be a consonant, we can increment **consonants** as the default action.

Finally, we output the counts we have accumulated with the statement:

```
cout << "Your input contained "
     << vowels     << " vowels and "
     << consonants << " consonants."
     << endl;
```

Multidimensional Arrays

The arrays we have declared so far have required a single index value to select an element. Such an array is called a **one-dimensional array**, because varying one index can reference all the elements. However, you can also declare arrays that require two or more separate index values to access an element. These are referred to generically as **multidimensional arrays**. An array that requires two index values to reference an element is called a two-dimensional array. An array needing three index values is a three-dimensional array, and so on for as many dimensions as you think you can handle.

Suppose, as an avid gardener, that you wish to record the individual weights of the carrots that you grow in your small vegetable garden. To store the weight of each of your carrots, which you planted in three rows of four, you could declare a two-dimensional array:

```
double carrots[3][4];
```

To reference a particular element of the **carrots** array, you need two index values: the first index value specifies the row, from 0 to 2, and the second index value specifies a particular carrot in that row, from 0 to 3. To store the weight of the third carrot in the second row, you could write:

```
carrots[1][2] = 1.5;
```

The arrangement of this array in memory is shown in the diagram.

The rows are stored contiguously in memory. As you can see, the two-dimensional array is effectively a *one*-dimensional array of three elements, each of which is a one-dimensional array with four elements. We've got an array of three arrays of size four.

When referring to an element, you use two index values. The right-hand index value selects the element within a row, and varies more rapidly. If you read the array from left to right, the right-hand index corresponds to the column number. The left-hand index selects the row, and therefore represents a row number. With arrays of more than two dimensions, the rightmost index value is always the one that varies most rapidly, and the leftmost index the least rapidly.

As indicated in the illustration, you can use the array name plus a *single* index value between square brackets to refer to an entire row in the array. You will see this approach at its most useful when we discuss functions in Chapter 8.

The array name by itself references the entire array. Note that with this array, you cannot display the contents of either of a row or the whole array using this notation. For example, the line:

```
cout << carrots;                    // Not what you may expect!
```

will output a single hexadecimal value, which happens to be the address in memory of the first element of the array. We will see why this is the case when we discuss pointers in the next chapter. Arrays of type **char** are a little different, as we saw earlier.

To display the entire array, one row to a line, you must write something like:

```
for(int i = 0 ; i < 3 ; i++)
{
  for(int j = 0 ; j < 4 ; j++)
    cout << setw(12) << carrots[i][j];
  cout << endl;
}
```

This uses magic numbers, 3 and 4, which we can avoid by using the **sizeof()** operator:

```
for(int i = 0 ; i < sizeof carrots / sizeof carrots[0] ; i++)
{
  for(int j = 0 ; j < sizeof carrots[0] / sizeof(double) ; j++)
    cout << setw(12) << carrots[i][j];
  cout << endl;
}
```

Of course, it would be better still not to use magic numbers for the array dimension sizes in the first place, so we *should* code this as the altogether tidier:

```
const int nrows = 3;
const int ncols = 4;
double carrots[nrows, ncols];

// Code to set up the values for array elements...

for(int i = 0 ; i < nrows ; i++)
{
  for(int j = 0 ; j < ncols ; j++)
    cout << setw(12) << carrots[i][j];
  cout << endl;
}
```

Declaring an array of three dimensions just adds another set of square brackets. You might want to record three temperatures each day, seven days a week, for 52 weeks of the year. You could declare the following array to store such data as type **long**:

```
long temperatures[52][7][3];
```

The array stores three values in each row. There are seven such rows for a whole week's data, and 52 sets of these for all the weeks in the year. This array will have a total of 1092 elements of type **long**. To display the middle temperature for day 3 of week 26, you could write:

```
cout << temperatures[25][2][1];
```

Remember that all the index values start at 0, so the weeks run from 0 to 51, the days run from 0 to 6, and the samples in a day run from 0 to 2.

Initializing Multidimensional Arrays

The way in which you specify initial values for a multidimensional array derives from the notion that a two-dimensional array is an array of one-dimensional arrays. The initializing values for a one-dimensional array are written between braces and separated by commas. Following on from that, we could declare and initialize our **carrots** array, for example, with this statement:

```
double carrots[3][4] = {
                         {2.5, 3.2, 3.7, 4.1},     // First row
                         {4.1, 3.9, 1.6, 3.5},     // Second row
                         {2.8, 2.3, 0.9, 1.1}      // Third row
                       };
```

Each row is a one-dimensional array, so the initializing values for each row are contained within their own set of braces. These three initializer lists are themselves contained within a set of braces, because the two-dimensional array is a one-dimensional array of one-dimensional arrays. You can extend this principle to any number of dimensions — each extra dimension requires another level of braces enclosing the initial values.

A question that should immediately spring to mind is, "What happens when you omit some of the initializing values?" The answer is more or less what you might have expected from past experience. Each of the innermost pairs of braces contains the values for the elements in the rows. The first list corresponds to **carrots[0]**, the second to **carrots[1]** and the third to **carrots[2]**. The values between each pair of braces are assigned to the elements of the corresponding row. If there are not enough to initialize all the elements in the row, then the elements without values will be initialized to 0. Let's look at an example:

```
double carrots[3][4] = {
                    {2.5, 3.2        },    // First row
                    {4.1             },    // Second row
                    {2.8, 2.3, 0.9   }     // Third row
              };
```

The first two elements in the first row have values, while only one element in the second row has a value, and three elements in the third row have values. The elements will therefore be initialized as follows:

carrots[0][0]	carrots[0][1]	carrots[0][2]	carrots[0][3]
2.5	3.2	0.0	0.0
carrots[1][0]	carrots[1][1]	carrots[1][2]	carrots[1][3]
4.1	0.0	0.0	0.0
carrots[2][0]	carrots[2][1]	carrots[2][2]	carrots[2][3]
2.8	2.3	0.9	0.0

As you can see, the elements which have no explicit initializing values have all been set to 0. If you don't include sufficient sets of braces to initialize all of the rows in the array, the elements in the rows without initializing values will all be set to 0. Logically, then, you can zero *all* the elements in the array with the statement:

```
double carrots[3][4] = {0};
```

If you include several initial values in the initializer list, but omit the nested braces enclosing values for the rows, values are assigned sequentially to the elements, as they are stored in memory — with the rightmost index varying more rapidly. For example, suppose we declare the array like this:

```
double carrots[3][4] = {1.1, 1.2, 1.3, 1.4, 1.5, 1.6, 1.7};
```
                                    4

The array will be set up with the values shown below:

carrots[0][0]	carrots[0][1]	carrots[0][2]	carrots[0][3]
1.1	1.2	1.3	1.4
carrots[1][0]	carrots[1][1]	carrots[1][2]	carrots[1][3]
1.5	1.6	1.7	0.0
carrots[2][0]	carrots[2][1]	carrots[2][2]	carrots[2][3]
0.0	0.0	0.0	0.0

The initializing values are just allocated to successive elements along the rows. When there are no more values, the remaining elements are initialized to 0.

Setting Dimensions by Default

You can let the compiler determine the size of the first (leftmost) dimension of any array from the set of initializing values. We could have declared our two-dimensional **carrots** array with the statement:

```
double carrots[][4] = {
                    {2.5, 3.2         },      // First row
                    {4.1              },      // Second row
                    {2.8, 2.3, 0.9    }       // Third row
                 };
```

This will have three rows, as before, because there are three sets of braces within the outer pair. If there were only two sets, the array would have two rows, so the statement:

```
double carrots[][4] = {
                    {2.5, 3.2         },      // First row
                    {4.1              }       // Second row
                 };
```

will create an array as though it were declared as:

```
double carrots[2][4] = {
                    {2.5, 3.2         },      // First row
                    {4.1              }       // Second row
                 };
```

Arrays of three or more dimensions can be declared such that the compiler sets the size of the first dimension from the set of initializing values. Here is an example of a three-dimensional array declaration:

```
int numbers[][3][4] = {
                     {
                       { 2,  4,  6,  8},
                       { 3,  5,  7,  9},
                       { 5,  8, 11, 14}
                     },
                     {
```

```
                        {12, 14, 16, 18},
                        {13, 15, 17, 19},
                        {15, 18, 21, 24}
                      }
                };
```

This array has three dimensions, of sizes 2, 3 and 4. The outer braces enclose two further sets of braces, and each of these in turn contains three sets, each of which contains the four initial values for the corresponding row. As this simple example demonstrates, handling arrays of dimension three or more gets increasingly complicated, and you need to take great care when placing the braces enclosing the initial values. The braces are nested to as many levels as there are dimensions in the array.

Multidimensional Character Arrays

You can declare arrays of two or more dimensions to hold any type of data. A two-dimensional array of type **char** is particularly interesting, because it can be an array of strings. When you initialize a two-dimensional array of type **char** with character strings between double quotes, you don't need the braces around the string for a row — the double quotes do the job of the braces in this case. For example:

```
char stars[6][80] = {
                      "Robert Redford",
                      "Hopalong Cassidy",
                      "Lassie",
                      "Slim Pickens",
                      "Boris Karloff",
                      "Oliver Hardy"
                    };
```

Each row in the array stores a string containing the name of a movie star. A terminating null character, **'\0'**, will be appended to each string.

Try It Out – Using a Two-dimensional Character Array

We can demonstrate an array like this in an example. This program will select your lucky star, based on an integer that you enter:

```
// Program 6.5 Storing strings in an array
#include <iostream>
using namespace std;

int main()
{
  char stars[][80] = {
                      "Robert Redford",
                      "Hopalong Cassidy",
                      "Lassie",
                      "Slim Pickens",
                      "Boris Karloff",
                      "Mae West",
                      "Oliver Hardy",
                      "Sharon Stone"
```

```
                                    };
        int choice = 0;

        cout << endl
             << "Pick a lucky star!"
             << " Enter a number between 1 and "
             << sizeof stars / sizeof stars[0] << ": ";
        cin >> choice;

        if(choice >= 1 && choice <= sizeof stars / sizeof stars[0])
          cout << endl
               << "Your lucky star is " << stars[choice - 1];
        else
          cout << endl                               // Invalid input
               << "Sorry, you haven't got a lucky star.";

        cout << endl;
        return 0;
    }
```

A typical example of the output from this program is:

```
Pick a lucky star! Enter a number between 1 and 8: 6

Your lucky star is Mae West
```

How It Works

Apart from its incredible inherent entertainment value, the main point of interest in this example is the declaration of the array **stars**. It is a two-dimensional **char** array, which can hold multiple strings, each of which can contain up to 80 characters, including the terminating null character that's automatically added by the compiler. The initializing strings for the array are enclosed between braces and separated by commas:

```
char stars[][80] = {
                     "Robert Redford",
                     "Hopalong Cassidy",
                     "Lassie",
                     "Slim Pickens",
                     "Boris Karloff",
                     "Mae West",
                     "Oliver Hardy",
                     "Sharon Stone"
                   };
```

Because we have omitted the size of the first array dimension, the compiler creates the array with the number of rows necessary to accommodate all the initializing strings. As we saw earlier, you can only omit the size of the first dimension. The sizes of any other dimensions that are required must be specified.

We prompt for an integer to be entered with this statement:

```
cout << endl
     << "Pick a lucky star!"
     << " Enter a number between 1 and "
     << sizeof stars / sizeof stars[0] << ": ";
```

The upper limit on the integer to be entered is given by the expression **sizeof stars /
sizeof stars[0]**. This gives the number of rows in the array, so the statement automatically
adapts to any changes you may make to the number of names in the array. We use the same
technique in the **if** statement that arranges for the output to be displayed:

```
if(choice >= 1 && choice <= sizeof stars / sizeof stars[0])
  cout << endl
       << "Your lucky star is " << stars[choice - 1];
else
   cout << endl                              // Invalid input
       << "Sorry, you haven't got a lucky star.";
```

The **if** condition checks that the integer entered is within range before attempting to display a
name. When we need to reference a string for output in the statement, we only need to specify
the first index value. A single index value selects a particular 80-element sub-array, and because
this contains a string, the output operation will display the contents up to the terminating null
character. The index is specified as **choice – 1** because the **choice** values start from **1**,
whereas the index values used to select a name from the array clearly need to start from **0**.
This is quite a common idiom when you're programming with arrays.

FYI   One disadvantage of using arrays as we have in this example is the memory that is
almost invariably left unused. All of our strings are less than 80 characters, and the
surplus elements in each row of the array are wasted. We will see a better way of dealing
with situations that involve null-terminated strings in the next chapter.

A Better Class of String

We have seen how an array of type **char** can be used to store a null-terminated (C-style) string,
which is an artifact from the origins of C++. There is a better alternative. The **string** header
file defines the **string** type, which has facilities that make it easier to use than a null-
terminated string. The **string** type is defined by a **class** (or to be more precise, a **class
template**). The fact that we haven't yet discussed classes won't present any difficulty here,
because, essentially, a class simply introduces a new type into the language. In practice, using a
class-defined type is no different from using one of the basic data types — all you need to
understand is what class-defined types are capable of.

An entity of a class type is usually referred to as an **object** (rather than a variable), so we will
use this terminology in our discussion of the **string** type. There are one or two things in this
section that we won't be able to explain fully yet, but the discussion *will* allow you to compare
the **string** type with null-terminated strings, and to see why it is generally better to use the
former.

Although the **string** type is not one of the basic data types, it is part of the ANSI standard, so
you can regard it as just another data type that you have at your disposal. You can work with
objects of type **string** in very much the same way that you work with variables of the basic
data types. To begin, let's look at how we create a **string** object.

Declaring string Objects

An object of type **string** contains a string of characters of type **char**, which can be an empty string if you choose. You can declare an object of type **string** with the statement:

```
string myString;                // Declares an empty string
```

This statement declares a **string** object called **myString**. In this case, **myString** is an *empty* **string** object — that is, it represents a string that contains no characters, and has zero length.

You can declare and initialize a **string** object with a string literal:

```
string proverb = "Many a mickle makes a muckle.";
```

Here, **proverb** is a **string** object that represents the string shown in the string literal. You could also use functional notation to initialize the object if you wanted, by writing the previous statement as:

```
string proverb("Many a mickle makes a muckle.");
```

The string that is stored does not need a string termination character. A **string** object keeps track of the length of the string it represents. You can obtain the length of the string for a **string** object by using its **length()** function, which takes no arguments. For example:

```
cout << proverb.length();
```

This statement calls the **length()** function for the **proverb** object, and outputs the value returned using the insertion operator for the **cout** stream. This will display the length of the string stored in **proverb**, which in this case will be 29, the number of characters in the string. The period in the expression **proverb.length()** is called the **member access operator**, or just the **dot operator**. It identifies the function **length()** as a **member** of the **proverb** object. You will learn more about what this means when we investigate how we can define our own data types in Chapter 11.

There are some other possibilities for initializing a **string** object. You can't initialize a **string** object with a single character, but you *can* initialize one with a number of instances of the same character (including one instance!). Let me remove the confusion I have undoubtedly created by illustrating what I mean. You can declare and initialize a sleepy time **string** object with the statement:

```
string sleeping(6, 'z');
```

The **string** object, **sleeping**, will contain the string **"zzzzzz"**. If you wanted a **string** to suit a light sleeper with just one **'z'**, you could write:

```
string light_sleep(1, 'z');
```

This would initialize **light_sleep** with the string literal **"z"**. However, you *can't* write:

```
string light_sleep = 'z';       // Wrong! Won't compile!
```

A further option for initializing a **string** object is to use an existing **string** object. Given that **proverb** has been declared as above, you can write the following to declare another object:

```
string sentence = proverb;
```

The **sentence** object will be initialized with the same literal string as **proverb**, so it too will contain **"Many a mickle makes a muckle."**. You could also use functional notation in this case if you wished, so you could just as well have written the previous declaration as:

```
string sentence(proverb);
```

Characters within a **string** object are indexed starting from 0, just like an array. We can use this fact to select part of an existing **string** and use that to initialize a **string** object. For example, this line

```
string phrase(proverb, 0, 13);
```

reproduces part of the **proverb** object in a new **string** object, **phrase**.

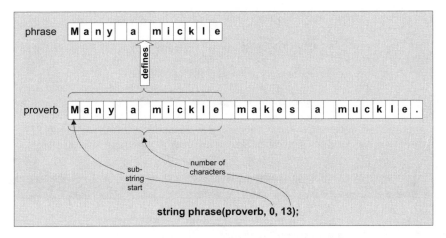

The first argument between the parentheses is the name of the **string** object we are using as the source of the initialization. The second argument is the starting index within that **string** object. The third argument is the number of characters to be selected as the initial value. So here we are selecting the first 13 characters of **proverb**, starting at the first character (with the index position 0), as the initial value for the **phrase** object. It will therefore contain **"Many a mickle"**.

Operations with string Objects

Perhaps the simplest operation you can perform on a **string** object is assignment. You can assign the value of a string literal or another **string** object to a **string** object. For example:

```
string adjective = "hornswoggling";    // Declares a string
string word = "rubbish";               // Declares another string

word = adjective;                      // Modifies word
adjective = "twotiming";               // Modifies adjective
```

The third statement here assigns the value of **adjective**, which is **"hornswoggling"**, to **word**, so **"rubbish"** is replaced. The last statement assigns the new string literal, **"twotiming"** to **adjective**, so the original value **"hornswoggling"** is replaced. Thus, after this, **word** contains **"hornswoggling"** and **adjective** contains **"twotiming"**.

Concatenating Strings

You can join strings together using the addition operator — the technical term for this is **concatenation**. We can demonstrate concatenation using the objects that we just defined:

```
string description = adjective + " " + word + " whippersnapper";
```

After executing this statement, the **description** object will contain the string **"twotiming hornswoggling whippersnapper"**. You can see that we can happily concatenate string literals with **string** objects using the **+** operator.

Note that you *can't* concatenate string literals alone with **+**. One of the operands must always be an object of type **string**. The following statement, for example, will not compile:

```
string description = " whippersnapper" + " " + word;
```

The problem here is that the compiler will try to evaluate the right hand side of the assignment as **((" whippersnapper" + " ") + word)**, and the **+** does not work with two string literals. However, judicious use of parentheses can make the statement legal:

```
string description = " whippersnapper" + (" " + word);
```

Here, the **+** operation between the parentheses *is* legal, and produces a value of type **string** as a result, which can be concatenated with the string literal **" whippersnapper"**.

Try It Out – Concatenating Strings

That's quite enough theory for the moment; it's time for a bit of practice. This program will read your first and second name from the keyboard.

```
// Program 6.6 Concatenating strings
#include <iostream>
#include <string>

using namespace std;

int main()
{
  string first;                          // Stores the first name
  string second;                         // Stores the second name

  cout << endl << "Enter your first name: ";
  cin >> first;                          // Read first name

  cout << endl << "Enter your second name: ";
  cin >> second;                         // Read second name
```

```
    string sentence = "Your full name is ";      // Create basic sentence
    sentence += first + " " + second + ".";      // Augment with names

    cout << endl
         << sentence                              // Output the sentence
         << endl;
    cout << "The string contains "                // Output its length
         << sentence.length()
         << " characters."
         << endl;

    return 0;
}
```

Here's some sample output from this program:

```
Enter your first name: Phil

Enter your second name: McCavity

Your full name is Phil McCavity.
The string contains 32 characters.
```

How It Works

We first declare two **string** objects with the statements:

```
string first;                          // Stores the first name
string second;                         // Stores the second name
```

Since we have not specified any initial values here, both of these will be initialized with empty strings. Next, we prompt for names to be entered, and read the names from the keyboard:

```
cout << endl << "Enter your first name: ";
cin >> first;                          // Read first name

cout << endl << "Enter your second name: ";
cin >> second;                         // Read second name
```

The stream extraction operator, **>>**, works with **string** objects in the same way that it does with arrays of type **char**. Characters are read until the first whitespace character is found, so you cannot read a string containing spaces in this way. You'll meet a solution to this problem shortly.

After getting the names, we create another **string** object, but this time we initialize it explicitly with a string literal:

```
string sentence = "Your full name is ";          // Create basic sentence
```

The object **sentence** will be initialized with the string specified. We then use this object to assemble a string that contains a message that we want to display:

```
sentence += first + " " + second + ".";          // Augment with names
```

203

The right hand side concatenates **first** with the literal **" "**, then **second** is appended to that, and finally the literal **"."** is appended to the result. With the sample input shown above, the right hand side will evaluate to a **string** object containing **"Phil McCavity."**

As this statement demonstrates, the **+=** operator also works with objects of type **string** in the same way as we have seen with the basic types, so the value of the right hand side is appended to the **sentence** object on the left. Thus, after executing this statement, **sentence** will contain **"Your full name is Phil McCavity."**.

When you use the **+=** operator to append a value to a **string** object, the right hand side can be an expression resulting in a null-terminated string, or a single character of type **char**, or an expression producing an object of type **string**.

Lastly in the program, we use the stream insertion operator to output the contents of **sentence**, and the length of the string:

```
cout << endl
     << sentence                    // Output the sentence
     << endl;
cout << "The string contains "      // Output its length
     << sentence.length()
     << " characters."
     << endl;
```

As this statement shows, we can output the value of a **string** object just as we can output the values of variables of any of the other types we have seen.

Accessing Characters in a String

You can refer to a particular character in a **string** by using an index value between square brackets, just as you do with an array. The first character in a **string** object has the index value **0**. You could refer to the third character in **sentence**, for example, as **sentence[2]**. It's also possible to use such an expression on the left of the assignment operator, so you can *modify* individual characters as well as access them. The following statement would change all the characters in **sentence** to upper case:

```
for(int i = 0 ; i < sentence.length() ; i++)
   sentence[i] = toupper(sentence[i]);
```

We can exercise this array-style access method in a version of the program we saw earlier that determined the number of vowels and consonants in a string. The new version will use a **string** object.

Try It Out – Accessing Characters

This program does much the same as Program 6.4, but using a **string** object rather than an array of type **char**.

```
// Program 6.7 Accessing characters in a string
#include <iostream>
#include <string>
#include <cctype>
```

```
using namespace std;

int main()
{
    string text;                                   // Stores the input

    cout << endl << "Enter a line of text:" << endl;

    // Read a line of characters including spaces
    getline(cin, text);

    int vowels = 0;                                // Count of vowels
    int consonants = 0;                            // Count of consonants
    for(int i = 0 ; i < text.length() ; i++)
      if(isalpha(text[i]))                         // Check for a letter
        switch(tolower(text[i]))                   // Test lower case
        {
          case 'a':
          case 'e':
          case 'i':
          case 'o':
          case 'u':
            vowels++;
            break;
          default:
            consonants++;
        }

    cout << "Your input contained "
         << vowels    << " vowels and "
         << consonants << " consonants."
         << endl;

    return 0;
}
```

An example of the output from this program is:

```
Enter a line of text:
A nod is as good as a wink to a blind horse.

Your input contained 14 vowels and 18 consonants.
```

How It Works

There's no point going over the code that hasn't changed, so we can confine this explanation to the new features of the program. First, we declare our object of type **string**:

```
string text;                                   // Stores the input
```

The **text** object, of type **string**, contains an empty string initially, but we will read a line from the keyboard and store it here. After displaying a prompt, the input is obtained using the **getline()** function:

```
// Read a line of characters including spaces
getline(cin, text);
```

This version of **getline()** is declared in the **string** header file; it reads a line of input from **cin** up to the point when a newline character is read, and stores the line in **text**. Note that this time, we don't need to worry about how many characters are in the input. The **string** object will automatically accommodate whatever is entered. If you wanted to change the delimiter indicating the end of the input line to a character other than **'\n'**, you could use a version of **getline()** with a third argument:

```
getline(cin, text, '#');
```

This will now look for **'#'** as the character indicating the end of the input. As with the **getline()** function that we used to read into a **char** array, this will allow multiple lines of text to be entered if necessary.

Having read the text, we count the vowels and consonants in much the same way as we did before, with just a small change to the loop condition in the **for** loop:

```
for(int i = 0 ; i < text.length() ; i++)
```

We use the **length()** function of the **text** object to get the number of characters in the string, and this number controls the **for** loop. We can access each character by means of the index value, **i**, just as we could with our **char** array.

The major advantage of using a **string** object in this example is that we don't need to worry about the length of the string it contains.

Accessing Substrings

It's possible to obtain a substring of a **string** object by using the **substr()** function. You specify the index position where the substring starts, and a length — the number of characters in the substring. The function returns a **string** object containing the substring. For example:

```
string phrase = "The higher the fewer";
string word = phrase.substr(4, 6);
```

This will extract the six-character substring from **phrase** that starts at index position 4, so **word** will contain **"higher"** after the second statement executes. If the length you specify overruns the end of the **string** object, then the function just returns all the characters up to the end of the string. The following statement would demonstrate this behavior:

```
string word = phrase.substr(4, 100);
```

Of course, there aren't 100 characters in the whole of **phrase**, let alone in a substring. In this case, the result will be that **word** will contain the substring from index position 4 to the end, which is **"higher the fewer"**.

You could obtain the same result by omitting the length altogether:

```
string word = phrase.substr(4);
```

This will also return the substring from index position 4 to the end. If you omit both arguments to the **substr()** function, the whole of **phrase** will be selected as the substring.

If you specify a starting index position for the substring that falls outside the valid range for the **string** object you're dealing with, an **exception** will be thrown and your program will terminate abnormally — unless, that is, you've implemented some code to handle the exception. We will be discussing exceptions in Chapter 17.

Comparing Strings

We saw in our last example how you can use an index to access individual characters in a **string** object for comparison purposes. When you access an individual character using an index value, the result is of type **char**, so you can use the comparison operators to compare individual characters.

When you need to compare entire strings, you can *also* use any of the comparison operators, with **string** objects as operands. Just to remind you, the comparison operators we are talking about here are:

```
>            >=            <            <=            ==            !=
```

You can use these operators in several ways. They can be used for comparing two objects of type **string**, or for comparing an object of type **string** with a string literal or a C-style string stored in an array of type **char**. The operands are compared character by character, until either the characters are different, or the end of either or both operands is reached. When differing characters are found, numerical comparison of the character codes determines which of the strings has the lesser value. If no differing characters are found and the strings are of different lengths, then the shorter string is 'less than' the longer string. Two strings are equal if they contain the same number of characters and all corresponding characters are equal. Since we are comparing character codes, the comparisons are obviously going to be case sensitive.

We could compare two **string** objects using an **if** statement, as follows:

```
string word1 = "age";
string word2 = "beauty";
if(word1 < word2)
  cout << word1 << " comes before " << word2;
else
  cout << word1 << " does not come before " << word2;
```

The code above looks a good candidate for using the conditional operator. We could produce the same result with the statement:

```
cout << word1
     << (word1 < word2 ? " comes " : " does not come ")
     << "before " << word2;
```

Try It Out - Comparing Strings

This program reads a number of names and finds the maximum and minimum of those entered.

```
// Program 6.8 Comparing strings
#include <iostream>
#include <string>
```

```
#include <cctype>

using namespace std;

int main()
{
  const int max_names = 6;                              // Maximum number of names
  string names[max_names];                              // Array of names
  int count = 0;                                        // Number of names
  char answer = 0;                                      // Response to a prompt

  do
  {
    cout << endl << "Enter a name: ";
    cin >> names[count++];                              // Read a name

    cout << endl << "Do you want to enter another name? (y/n): ";
    cin >> answer;                                      // Read response
  } while(count < max_names && tolower(answer) == 'y');

  // Indicate when array is full
  if(count == max_names)
    cout << endl << "Maximum name count reached." << endl;

  // Find the minimum and maximum names
  int index_of_max = 0;
  int index_of_min = 0;

  for(int i = 1 ; i < count ; i++)
    if(names[i] > names[index_of_max])                  // Current name greater?
      index_of_max = i ;                                // then it is new maximum
    else if(names[i] < names[index_of_min])             // Current name less?
      index_of_min = i;                                 // then it is new minimum

  // Output the minimum and maximum names
  cout << endl
       << "The minimum name is " << names[index_of_min]
       << endl;
  cout << "the maximum name is " << names[index_of_max]
       << endl;
  return 0;
}
```

Here's some sample output from this example:

```
Enter a name: Meshak

Do you want to enter another name? (y/n): y

Enter a name: Eshak

Do you want to enter another name? (y/n): y

Enter a name: Abednego

Do you want to enter another name? (y/n): n
```

```
The minimum name is Abednego
The maximum name is Meshak
```

How It Works

The names are stored in an array of type **string** that we declare using a constant to define the array size:

```
const int max_names = 6;                          // Maximum number of names
string names[max_names];                          // Array of names
```

Declaring an array of type **string** is just the same as declaring any other kind of array. This declaration will create an array of **max_names** elements, where each element is a **string** object containing an empty string. You could initialize the array in the same way that you did with two-dimensional arrays of type **char**. For example:

```
string names[max_names] = {"Zeus", "Venus"};      // Array of names
```

This statement would initialize the first two elements of the **names** array with the string literals between the braces. The remaining elements would be empty strings.

We read the names in a **do-while** loop that limits the number of names read to the size of the array:

```
do
{
  cout << endl << "Enter a name: ";
  cin >> names[count++];                          // Read a name

  cout << endl << "Do you want to enter another name? (y/n): ";
  cin >> answer;                                  // Read response
} while(count < max_names && tolower(answer) == 'y');
```

You have seen this sort of thing before — it's a straightforward mechanism for reading a number of data items. A name is read from the keyboard into the current element of the **names** array. The extraction operator will read characters up to the first whitespace character.

When we have read all the input, we find the index values corresponding to the array elements containing the maximum and minimum strings in a **for** loop:

```
for(int i = 1 ; i < count ; i++)
  if(names[i] > names[index_of_max])             // Current name greater?
    index_of_max = i ;                           // then it is new maximum
  else if(names[i] < names[index_of_min])        // Current name less?
    index_of_min = i;                            // then it is new minimum
```

Within the loop, the nested **if** statement uses the **>** and **<** comparison operators for **string** objects to check whether the current array element is greater than the current maximum or less than the current minimum. If we find a new maximum, we avoid checking for a new minimum by placing the test for a new minimum in the **else** clause. Clearly, a new maximum cannot also be a new minimum. Note that the loop counter starts at 1, since we assume initially that the value at index position 0 is both the minimum and the maximum.

Finally, we output the maximum and minimum names that we have found with the statements:

```
cout << endl
     << "The minimum name is " << names[index_of_min]
     << endl;
cout << "The maximum name is " << names[index_of_max]
     << endl;
```

The compare() Function

Given an object of type **string**, we can call the **compare()** function to compare the object with another object of type **string**, or a string literal, or a null-terminated string stored in an array of type **char**. To call the **compare()** function for a **string** object, you write:

object_name.compare(*other_object*)

The period following the object name is the dot operator, which we met earlier in conjunction with the **length()** function. The object your **string** is to be compared with, **other_object**, goes between the parentheses. Here's an example of an expression that calls the **compare()** function for an object called **word** and compares it with a string literal:

word.compare("and")

Here, the function will compare the contents of **word** with the string **"and"**, and will return a value of type **int**. The function will return a positive integer if **word** is greater than **"and"**; zero if **word** is equal to **"and"**; and a negative integer if **word** is less than **"and"**. In the last example, we could have used the **compare()** function in place of the comparison operators, but the code would have been less clear. The **for** loop would be:

```
for(int i = 1 ; i < count ; i++)
    if(names[i].compare(names[index_of_max]) > 0)      // Current name greater?
        index_of_max = i;                               // then it is new maximum
    else if(names[i].compare(names[index_of_min]) < 0)  // Current name less?
        index_of_min = i;                               // then it is new minimum
```

Sometimes, as you can see above, using the **compare()** function makes it more difficult to follow what's going on than when you use the comparison operators. However, there are situations where the **compare()** function *does* have an advantage. You can **compare()** substrings by passing two extra arguments to the function: the start index of the substring, and the number of characters in it. Look at the following statements:

```
string word1 = "A jackhammer";
string word2 = "jack";
if(word1.compare(2, 4, word2) == 0)
    cout << "Equal" << endl;
```

The **if** statement compares a substring of **word1** with the whole of **word2**:

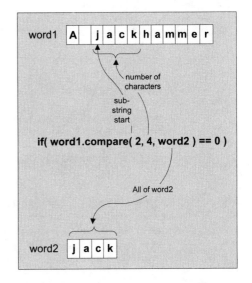

The first argument to **compare()** is the starting index position of the substring in **word1** that is to be compared with **word2**. The second argument is the number of characters in the substring. Since, in this case, **word2** and the substring of **word1** that we have specified are equal, the output statement will be executed. Obviously, if **word2** is a different length from the substring you specify, they are unequal by definition.

You might want to **compare()** a substring of one **string** with a substring of another, and there's a way of doing that as well — it involves passing *five* arguments! For example:

```
string word1 = "A jackhammer";
string word2 = "It is a jack-in-the-box";
if(word1.compare(2, 4, word2, 8, 4) == 0)
  cout << "Equal" << endl;
```

The first three arguments to **compare()** are the same as before. The last two arguments are the index position of the substring in **word2**, and its length:

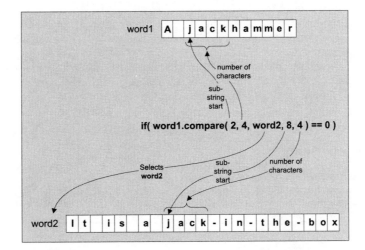

211

The substring of **word1** is compared with the substring of **word2**. Once again, the substrings in this case are identical, and the output statement will be executed.

We're not done yet! **compare()** can also compare a substring of a **string** object with a null-terminated string. The next example compares the same substring of **word1** that we have been using with the string literal that appears as an argument:

```
if(word1.compare(2, 4, "jack") == 0)
  cout << "Equal" << endl;
```

Since the substring of **word1** is again equal to **"jack"**, the **if** expression is **true** and the output will be output.

Still another option is to select the first *n* characters from the null-terminated string by specifying the number of characters you want to use. This next statement compares the same substring from **word1** with the first four characters from **"jacket"**:

```
if(word1.compare(2, 4, "jacket", 4) == 0)
  cout << "Equal" << endl;
```

Naturally, in all of these examples, the **if** statements could have tested for *in*equality by checking for the return value from **compare()** being non-zero. As I said earlier, the return value can be zero, negative or positive. Just to remind you how it works, if we declare **word** as,

```
string word = "banana";
```

The expression **word.compare("apple")** will return a positive integer, and **word.compare("orange")** will return a negative integer.

In this section, you've seen the **compare()** function work quite happily with different numbers of arguments of various kinds. In fact, what we have here are lots of different functions with the same name; these are called **overloaded functions**, and we'll be looking at them further, and at how you can create your own, in Chapter 9.

Searching a String

There are many different methods available to you for searching a **string** object, and they all involve functions that return the index position of what you are looking for.

Let's start with the simplest sort of search. A **string** object has a function called **find()** that you can use to discover the index position of a substring or a single character within the string. The substring you choose to search for can be another **string** object or a null-terminated string. For example:

```
string sentence = "Manners maketh man";
string word = "man";
cout << sentence.find(word) << endl;      // Outputs 15
cout << sentence.find("Man") << endl;     // Outputs  0
cout << sentence.find('k') << endl;       // Outputs 10
cout << sentence.find('x') << endl;       // Outputs string::npos
```

In each statement using **find()**, the **sentence** object is searched from the beginning. The function returns the index position of the first character of the first occurrence of whatever is being sought.

In the last statement, **'x'** does not occur in the string being searched, so the value **string::npos**, which is a built-in constant that represents an illegal character position, is returned. With my compiler this happens to be 4,294,967,295, but it may well be different on your system. Of course, you could check for this eventuality with a statement such as:

```
if(sentence.find('x') == string::npos)
   cout << "Character not found" << endl;
```

Another variation on the **find()** function allows you to search *part* of the string, starting from a specified position. For example, with **sentence** defined as before, you could write:

```
cout << sentence.find("an", 1) << endl;          // Outputs  1
cout << sentence.find("an", 3) << endl;          // Outputs 16
```

Each of these statements searches **sentence** from the index position given by the second argument, to the end of the string. The first statement finds the first occurrence of **"an"**, while the second statement finds the second occurrence, because the search starts from index position 3 in **sentence**. You could use a **string** object as the first argument to specify the string you are searching for here, too.

You can also search for a substring of a null-terminated, C-style string corresponding to a given number of characters in it. In this case, the first argument to **find()** is the null-terminated string, the second argument is the index position at which you wish to start searching and the third argument is the number of characters of the null-terminated string that you want to take as the string you are looking for. For example:

```
cout << sentence.find("akat", 1, 2) << endl;        // Outputs 9
```

This statement searches for the first two characters of **"akat"** (that is, **"ak"**) in **sentence**, starting from position 1. The following searches would both fail and return **string::npos**:

```
cout << sentence.find("akat", 1, 3) << endl;     // Outputs string::npos
cout << sentence.find("akat", 10, 2) << endl;    // Outputs string::npos
```

The first search fails because the string **"aka"** is not in **sentence**. The second search is looking for **"ak"**, which *is* in **sentence**, but fails because it does not occur after position 10 in **sentence**.

Try It Out - Searching a String

We can write a program that will search a **string** object for a given substring, and work out how many times the substring occurs.

```
// Program 6.9 Searching a string
#include <iostream>
#include <string>
```

```
using namespace std;

int main()
{
  // The string to be searched
  string text = "Smith, where Jones had had \"had had\", had had \"had\"."
                " \"Had had\" had had the examiners' approval.";

  string word = "had";                   // Substring to be found

  cout << endl  << "The string is: " << endl << text << endl;

  // Count the number of occurrences of word in text
  int count = 0;                         // Count of substring occurrences

  for(int index = 0 ; (index = text.find(word, index)) != string::npos ;
                                      index += word.length(), count++)
    ;

  cout << "Your text contained "
       << count << " occurrences of \""
       << word  << "\"."
       << endl;

  return 0;
}
```

This program produces the output:

```
The string is:
Smith, where Jones had had "had had", had had "had". "Had had" had had the
examiners' approval.
Your input contained 10 occurrences of "had".
```

Of course, **"Had"** is not found because it starts with an upper case letter.

How It Works

We declare the **string** object to be searched like this:

```
string text = "Smith, where Jones had had \"had had\", had had \"had\"."
              " \"Had had\" had had the examiners' approval.";
```

String literals are automatically concatenated in statements like this one, so we are able to spread the initializing string literal over two lines. Note that we have to use the escape sequence **\"** to put double quotes in the string, as a double quote by itself would be interpreted by the compiler as a delimiter.

We define the substring we are looking for as:

```
string word = "had";                   // Substring to be found
```

This declares another **string** object, **word**, which contains the character string **"had"**. All the searching and counting is then done in the expressions controlling the **for** loop:

```
int count = 0;                          // Count of substring occurrences
for(int index = 0 ; (index = text.find(word, index)) != string::npos ;
                                      index += word.length(), count++)
    ;
```

There is quite a lot happening in this loop, so the basic elements are shown in the illustration below.

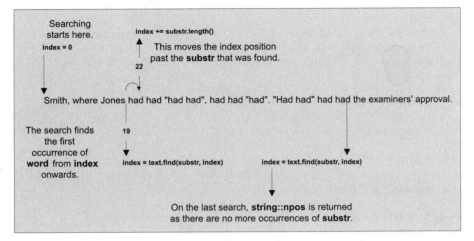

The first expression initializes the variable **index**, which is used to specify the position in **text** where each search operation is to begin. The expression that determines whether the loop continues or not is **(index = text.find(word, index)) != string::npos**. This will search **text**, starting at position **index**, to find the first occurrence of **word**, and store the index position where **word** is found back into **index**. If the value stored in **index** is **string::npos**, then **word** was not found and the loop ends. If **word** *was* found, the third **for** loop control expression is executed. This does two things: it increments the value in **index** with the expression **index += word.length()**, and since **word** was found, it increments the count of the number of occurrences of **word** by 1. The value **word.length()** is added to **index** to move the position in **text** past the copy of **word** that was just found, ready to start the next search.

When the loop is done, we output the number of occurrences of **word** in **text** with the statement:

```
cout << "Your text contained "
    << count << " occurrences of \""
    << word << "\"."
    << endl;
```

Searching a String for Characters from a Set

Suppose you had a string — a paragraph of prose, perhaps — and you wanted to break it up into individual words. You would need to find where the separators were, and those could be any of a number of different characters; there could be spaces, commas, periods, colons and so on. You need a function that can find where any one of a given set of characters occurs in a string — this could tell you where the delimiters for the words are. The good news is that this is exactly what the **find_first_of()** function does:

```
string text = "Smith, where Jones had had \"had had\", had had \"had\"."
               " \"Had had\" had had the examiners' approval.";
string separators = " ,.\"";
cout << text.find_first_of(separators)          // Outputs 5
     << endl;
```

Because the first character in **text** that's in the set defined by **separators** is a comma, the last statement will output 5. You can define the argument here as a null-terminated string if you need to. If you wanted to find the first vowel in **text**, for example, you could write:

```
cout << text.find_first_of("AaEeIiOoUu")        // Outputs 2
     << endl;
```

The given output results because the first vowel is **'i'**, in position 2.

You can also search backwards from the end of the **string** object to find the *last* occurrence of a character from a given set by using the **find_last_of()** function. For example, to find the last vowel in **text**, you could write:

```
cout << text.find_last_of("AaEeIiOoUu")         // Outputs 92
     << endl;
```

The last vowel in **text** is the second **'a'** in **approval**, at index position 92.

With the **find_first_of()** and **find_last_of()** functions, you can specify an extra argument that defines where, in the string being searched, to begin the search process. If you use a null-terminated string as the first argument, you can also have a third argument specifying how many characters from the set are to be included.

A further option available to you is to find a character that's *not* in a given set. The **find_first_not_of()** and **find_last_not_of()** functions are your tools for this job. To find the position of the first character in **text** that is not a vowel, you could write:

```
cout << text.find_first_not_of("AaEeIiOoUu")  // Outputs 0
     << endl;
```

The first character that is not a vowel is clearly the first, at index position 0. Let's try some of these functions in a working example.

Try It Out – Finding Characters from a Given Set

We can program the example we used to illustrate what **find_first_of()** is used for, sorting out the words from a string containing prose. This will involve combining the use of **find_first_of()** and **find_first_not_of()**.

```
// Program 6.10 Searching a string for characters from a set
#include <iostream>
#include <string>
```

```cpp
using namespace std;

int main()
{
  // The string to be searched
  string text = "Smith, where Jones had had \"had had\", had had \"had\"."
                " \"Had had\" had had the examiners' approval.";

  string separators = " ,.\"";                    // Word delimiters

  // Find the start of the first word
  int start = text.find_first_not_of(separators);
  int end = 0;                                     // Index for the end of a word

  // Now find and output the words
  int word_count = 0;                             // Number of words
  cout << endl;
  while(start != string::npos)
  {
    end = text.find_first_of(separators, start + 1);
    if(end == string::npos)                       // Found a separator?
      end = text.length();                        // No, so set to last + 1

    cout << text.substr(start, end - start)       // Output the word
         << endl;
    word_count++;                                 // Increase the count

    // Find the first character of the next word
    start = text.find_first_not_of(separators, end + 1);
  }

  cout << "Your string contained "
       << word_count << " words."
       << endl;

  return 0;
}
```

The output from this program is:

```
Smith
where
Jones
had
had
had
had
had
had
had
Had
had
had
had
the
examiners'
approval
Your string contained 17 words.
```

How It Works

We will take the initial declarations of the **string** objects as read, and go straight to how the analysis of the string works. We need to find the first character of the first word, so we read past any separator characters at the beginning of **text** with the statement:

```
int start = text.find_first_not_of(separators);
```

As long as this returns a valid value — that is, a value other than **string::npos** — we know that **start** will contain the index position of the first character of the first word. In a moment, we'll find out where it ends.

We'll accumulate a count of the number of words in the variable **word_count**, which we declare as:

```
int word_count = 0;                                        // Number of words
```

The **while** loop finds the end of the current word, displays it, and then finds the beginning of the next word:

```
while(start != string::npos)
{
  end = text.find_first_of(separators, start + 1);
  if(end == string::npos)                        // Found a separator?
    end = text.length();                         // No, so set to last + 1

  cout << text.substr(start, end - start)        // Output the word
       << endl;
  word_count++;                                  // Increase the count

  // Find the first character of the next word
  start = text.find_first_not_of(separators, end + 1);
}
```

The **while** condition will check the initial index position recorded in **start**. If **text** happens to be empty, or to contain only characters defined in **separators**, then the loop will end immediately. If not, then we have at least word on our hands and the loop is executed. We find the first position after **start** at which a character from the **separators** set occurs. This is done with a search starting at position **start + 1**, using the **find_first_of()** function. The index position returned is stored in **end**.

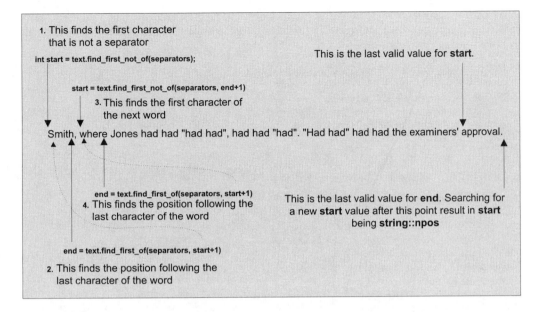

1. This finds the first character that is not a separator

`int start = text.find_first_not_of(separators);`

This is the last valid value for **start**.

`start = text.find_first_not_of(separators, end+1)`

3. This finds the first character of the next word

Smith, where Jones had had "had had", had had "had". "Had had" had had the examiners' approval.

`end = text.find_first_of(separators, start+1)`
4. This finds the position following the last character of the word

This is the last valid value for **end**. Searching for a new **start** value after this point result in **start** being **string::npos**

`end = text.find_first_of(separators, start+1)`

2. This finds the position following the last character of the word

Of course, it is possible that this last search will fail, leaving **end** with the value **string::npos**. This can occur if the string **text** ends with a letter, or indeed anything other than one of our specified **separators**. To deal with this, we check the value of **end** in the **if** statement, and if the search did fail, we set **end** to the length of **text**. This will be one character beyond the end of the string (because indexes start at 0, not 1), as we want **end** to correspond to the position *after* the last character in a word.

We then extract the word using the **substr()** function. The variable **start** contains the index position of the first letter in a word, and the expression **end - start** will be the number of characters in the word. When we have displayed the word, we increment **word_count** and look for the start of the next word with this statement:

```
start = text.find_first_not_of(separators, end + 1);
```

This searches again for the first character that is not one of the **separators**, and the search starts *after* the character position recorded in **end**. If **start** contains a valid index, then there is another word and this will be displayed on the next iteration. If there are no more words, **start** will be set to **string::npos** and the loop will end.

Finally, we output the count of the number of words found with the statement:

```
cout << "Your string contained "
     << word_count << " words."
     << endl;
```

Searching a String Backwards

The **find()** function searches forwards through a string, either from the beginning or from a position that you specify. If you want to search backwards, from the end of the string, you can use the **rfind()** function, its name perhaps derived from reverse **find**.

The `rfind()` function comes in the same varieties as the `find()` function. You can search a whole `string` object for a substring defined as either another `string` object, or as a null-terminated string; or you can search for a character. For example:

```
string sentence = "Manners maketh man";
string word = "an";
cout << sentence.rfind(word)   << endl;        // Outputs 16
cout << sentence.rfind("man")  << endl;        // Outputs 15
cout << sentence.rfind('e')    << endl;        // Outputs 11
```

Each of these searches finds the last incidence of the argument to the `rfind()` function, and returns the position of the first character where it was found.

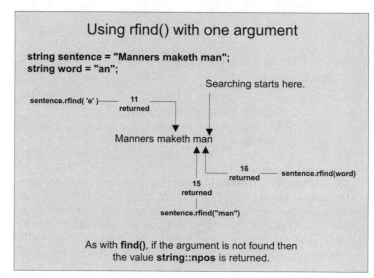

Searching with **word** as the argument finds the last occurrence of **"an"** in the string. The `rfind()` function returns the index position of the first character in the substring sought. If the substring is not present, the value `string::npos` will be returned. For example:

```
cout << sentence.rfind("miners") << endl;      // Outputs string::npos
```

Since **sentence** does not contain the substring **miners**, the value of `string::npos` will be returned and displayed by this statement. The other two searches are similar to the first, searching backwards from the end of the string for the first occurrence of the argument.

Just as with the `find()` function, you can add an extra argument to `rfind()` to specify the starting position for the backwards search, and you can add a third argument when the first argument is a C-style string. The third argument specifies the number of characters from the C-style string that are to be taken as the substring for which you are searching.

Modifying a String

Naturally, when you have searched a string and found what you are looking for, you may well want to change it in some way. We have already seen how we can use an index value within square brackets to modify a single character in a string object, but we can also insert a substring into a `string` object, or replace an existing substring. Unsurprisingly, you insert a substring by means of a function called `insert()`, and you replace a substring using a function called `replace()`. Let's look at inserting a substring first.

Inserting a String

Perhaps the simplest sort of insertion is to insert an object of type **string** before a given position in another **string** object. Here's an example of how this works:

```
string phrase = "We can insert a string.";
string words = "a string into ";
phrase.insert(14, words);
```

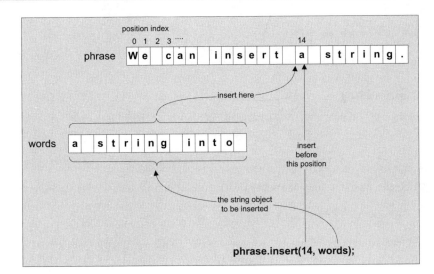

As shown in the diagram, the **words** string is inserted immediately before the character at index position 14 in **phrase**. After this operation, **phrase** will contain the string **"We can insert a string into a string."**.

You can also insert a null-terminated string into a **string** object. For example, we could achieve the same result as the previous operation with this statement:

```
phrase.insert(14, "a string into ");
```

Of course, the **'\0'** character is discarded from a null-terminated string before insertion, since it is a delimiter and not part of the string proper.

The next level of sophistication is the insertion of a substring into an object of type **string**. You just need to supply two extra arguments in the **insert()** function call: one to specify the start position of the substring, and the other to specify the number of characters. For example:

```
phrase.insert(13, words, 8, 5);
```

This inserts the five-character substring that starts at position 8 in **words**, into **phrase**. Given that they represent our original strings, this will insert **" into"** into **"We can insert a string."**, so that **phrase** becomes **"We can insert into a string."**.

There is a similar facility for inserting a given number of characters from a null-terminated string into a **string** object. The following statement produces the same result as the last one:

```
phrase.insert(13, " into something", 5);
```

This will insert the substring consisting of first five characters of **" into something"** into **phrase** before the character at index position 13.

If you ever need to insert a string of several identical characters into a **string** object, you can do that too:

```
phrase.insert(16, 7, '*');
```

This statement will cause seven asterisks to be inserted in **phrase** immediately before the character at position 16. This will result in **phrase** containing the uninformative sentence, **"We can insert a *******string."**.

Replacing a Substring

You can replace any substring of a **string** object with a different substring — even if the two substrings have different lengths. If we go back to one of our old favorites and define **text** as:

```
string text = "Smith, where Jones had had \"had had\", had had \"had\".";
```

We can replace the name **"Jones"** with a less common name with the statement:

```
text.replace(13, 5, "Gruntfuttock");
```

This replaces five characters of **text**, starting from position 13, with the string **"Gruntfuttock"**. If you now output **text**, it would display as:

```
Smith, where Gruntfuttock had had "had had" had had "had".
```

A more realistic approach to doing this would be to search for the substring to be replaced first. For example:

```
string separators = " ,.\"";                      // Word delimiters
int start = text.find("Jones");                   // Find the substring
int end = text.find_first_of(separators, start + 1); // Find the end
text.replace(start, end - start, "Gruntfuttock");
```

Here, we're finding the position of the first letter of **"Jones"** in **text**, and storing the index value in **start**. We find the character following the last character of **"Jones"** by searching for one of the delimiters in **separators** with the **find_first_of()** function. We then use these index positions in the **replace()** operation.

The replacement string can be a **string** object or a null-terminated string. In the former case, you can specify a start index and a length to select a substring from the **string** object to use as the replacement string. For example, the replace operation above could have been:

```
string name = "Amos Gruntfuttock";
text.replace(start, end - start, name, 5, 12);
```

These two statements would have the same effect as the previous use of **replace()**, since the replacement string starts at position 5 of **name** (which is the **'G'**), and contains 12 characters.

If the first argument is a null-terminated string, you can specify a number of characters to be selected from it to be the replacement string. For example:

```
text.replace(start, end - start, "Gruntfuttock, Amos", 12);
```

This time, the string to be substituted is the first 12 characters of **"Gruntfuttock, Amos"**, so the effect is again exactly the same as the previous replace operation.

A further possibility, rather like the **insert()** function, is to specify the replacement string as consisting of a given character repeated a given number of times. For example, we could replace **"Jones"** by three asterisks with the statement:

```
text.replace(start, end - start, 3, '*');
```

This statement assumes that **start** and **end** are determined as before, and the result of it is that **text** will contain:

```
Smith, where *** had had "had had" had had "had".
```

Try It Out – Replacing Substrings

We can try the replace operation in an example. Here's a program that will replace a given word in a string with another word.

```cpp
// Program 6.11 Replacing words in a string
#include <iostream>
#include <string>

using namespace std;

int main()
{
  // Read the string to be searched from the keyboard
  string text;
  cout << endl << "Enter a string terminated by #:" << endl;
  getline(cin, text, '#');

  // Get the word to be replaced
  string word;
  cout << endl << "Enter the word to be replaced: ";
  cin >> word;

  // Get the replacement
  string replacement;
  cout << endl << "Enter the replacement word: ";
  cin >> replacement;

  if(word == replacement)
  {
    cout << endl
         << "The word and its replacement are the same." << cout
         << "Operation aborted." << cout;
    exit(1);
  }
```

```
    // Find the start of the first occurrence of word
    int start = text.find(word);

    // Now find and replace all occurrences of word
    while(start != string::npos)
    {
      text.replace(start, word.length(), replacement);        // Replace word
      start = text.find(word, start + replacement.length());
    }

    cout << endl
         << "Your string is now:" << endl
         << text << endl;

    return 0;
}
```

Here is a sample of output from this program:

```
Enter a string terminated by #:
A rose is a rose
is a rose.#

Enter the word to be replaced: rose

Enter the replacement word: dandelion

Your string is now:
A dandelion is a dandelion
is a dandelion.
```

How It Works

We declare an object called **text**, of type **string**, that we will use to hold a character string in which we will replace every instance of a given word. After prompting for the input, we read the string from the keyboard with the statement:

```
getline(cin, text, '#');
```

We've seen this function before. It reads from the stream specified by the first argument into the **string** object specified by the second argument. The third argument defines the character that signifies the end of the string. Specifying **'#'** as the string terminator allows multiple lines of text to be entered, so in this case all the newline characters that precede the terminating **'#'** will be stored in the string.

After prompting for the word to be replaced, we read it into the **string** object, **word**:

```
cin >> word;
```

This time, the first whitespace character will terminate the input, so we will just store a single word. The word to be substituted is read into the **replacement** object in the same way.

The subsequent **if** statement just deals with the situation where the word to be replaced and its replacement are the same:

224

```
if(word == replacement)
{
  cout << endl
       << "The word and its replacement are the same." << cout
       << "Operation aborted." << cout;
  exit(1);
}
```

You could handle this in any way you wanted — you could even choose not to check, and just go through the motions of replacing identical words — but I chose to abort the program, to remind the user who's in charge! It should also remind you that the comparison operators work with **string** objects.

Now we're ready to make the substitutions. First, we find the index position of the first occurrence of **word** with the statement:

```
int start = text.find(word);
```

If **word** doesn't happen to be in **text**, then **start** will contain the value **string::npos**. This will be dealt with in the **while** loop that performs the replacement:

```
while(start != string::npos)
{
  text.replace(start, word.length(), replacement);          // Replace word
  start = text.find(word, start + replacement.length());
}
```

If **start** contains **string::npos** at the outset, then the loop will terminate immediately. Assuming **word** *does* exist in **text**, then the **replace()** function will be executed. Starting at the index position given by **start**, it replaces **word.length()** characters by the string **replacement**. Since **replacement** may well be a different length from **word**, we must take care in defining where to begin looking for the next occurrence of **word**. In the call to the **find()** function that does this, we specify the starting index position by adding the length of **replacement** to **start**. The loop will continue until **word** is no longer found in **text**.

Lastly, this statement displays the updated string:

```
cout << endl
     << "Your string is now:" << endl
     << text << endl;
```

Removing Characters from a String

You could remove a substring from a **string** object by using the **replace()** function. All you need to do is specify the replacement string as an empty string. However, there is also a specific function for this purpose: **erase()**. You can specify the substring to be erased by its starting index position and length. For example, to erase the first 6 characters from **text**, you could write:

```
text.erase(0, 6);                          // Remove the first 6 characters
```

Again, you would usually use this function to remove a specific substring that you had previously searched for. A more typical example of the usage of **erase()** might be:

```
string word = "rose";
int index = text.find(word);
if(index != string::npos)
  text.erase(index, word.length());
```

Here, we attempt to find the position of **word** in **text**, and after confirming that it does indeed exist, we remove it using the **erase()** function. The number of characters in the substring to be removed is obtained by calling the **length()** function for **word**.

Arrays of Type string

We used an array of **string**s in one of our earlier examples, but they bear a little closer examination. You can have arrays of objects of type **string** in the same way that you can have arrays of any other type. For example, we can create an array of type **string** with the statement:

```
string words[] = {"this", "that", "the other"};
```

The array **words** will have three elements, as determined from the three initializing string literals that appear between the braces. Of course, we could also have explicitly specified the array dimension, as in this statement:

```
string words[10] = {"this", "that", "the other"};
```

Now we have an array of 10 elements of type **string**, where the first three are initialized with the string literals between the braces, and the remaining seven are empty strings.

There is no problem referencing individual characters in a **string** array element. In the **words** array, we can change the seventh character of the third element to **'t'** with the statement:

```
words[2][6] = 't';
```

We could now display this particular string with the statement:

```
cout << words[2];
```

After the change, the string will display as:

```
the otter
```

Using arrays of type **string** is very much like using any other kind of array. All the operations on a **string** array element are exactly the same as we have discussed for single **string** variables.

Summary

In this chapter, we have seen how to create arrays of values, and explored the special properties of arrays of type **char**, but we have not yet finished with arrays. We will see more of them, especially in the next chapter where we'll explore the relationship between pointers and arrays.

We have also seen how we can use the **string** type that's defined in the standard library. In general, the **string** type is easier to use for string-handling applications than arrays of type **char**, so this should be your first choice when you need to process character strings.

The important points we have discussed in this chapter are:

▶ An array is a named collection of values of the same type that are stored contiguously in memory, where an individual value is accessed by means of one or more index values.

▶ A one-dimensional array requires one index value to reference its elements, a two dimensional array requires two index values, and an *n*-dimensional array requires *n* index values.

▶ Elements of an array can be used on the left of an assignment and in expressions in the same way that an ordinary variable of the same type can.

▶ A one-dimensional array of type **char** can be used to store a null-terminated character string.

▶ You can allow the compiler to determine the size of the leftmost dimension of an array from the number of initializing values in the declaration statement.

▶ You can use a two-dimensional array of type **char** as a one-dimensional array of null-terminated character strings.

▶ The type **string** stores a character string that does not need a termination character.

▶ Individual characters in a **string** object can be accessed and modified by using an index value between square brackets after the **string** variable name. Index values start at 0.

▶ Objects of type **string** have functions to search, modify and extract substrings from them.

▶ You can declare arrays of type **string** in the same way that you declare arrays of any other type.

Exercises

Ex 6.1 Create an array to store the first names of up to 10 students. Create another array that stores the grade (0–100) of each student. Use a loop to prompt the user to enter names and grades into these arrays. Calculate the average grade (use a loop counter), display it and then display the names and grades of all the students in a table.

Ex 6.2 A meteorologist friend of yours has to take three readings of air humidity a day (morning, midday and evening), Monday to Friday. Write a short program that allows the user to enter these readings, in chronological order, into a 5 by 3 **float** array. It should then calculate and display the weekly average for each of the three times of day.

Ex 6.3 Extend Program 6.9, so that the search for the search for the substring **"had"** finds all instances of the word 'had', regardless of case. (Hint: make a copy of the original string, with all the upper case letters converted to lower case.)

Ex 6.4 Create a string object and initialize it with, "Now is the winter of our discontent". Write a program that will display the string, then prompt the user to enter a word. If this word appears in the string above, replace the word with "FOUND" and re-display the string. For example, if the user enters the word "winter", then the pre-initialized string should be displayed as: "Now is the FOUND of our discontent".

Ex 6.5 Write a program that prompts for input of two strings, and then tests them to find whether one is an anagram of the other. One method you could use for this is to compare each character of the first string with *every* character of the second. If you get a match, you delete the character from the second string, and move on to the next character in the first string. After you've checked all the characters in the first string, the second string will be *empty* if the two were anagrams of one another.

7

Pointers

It's time for us to begin looking at **pointers**, which are a vital element of C++ programming. Pointers are important because they form the foundation that enables you to allocate and use memory *dynamically*, and make your programs more effective and efficient in many other ways.

In this chapter you will learn:

- What a pointer is, and how you declare one
- How to obtain the address of a variable
- How pointers relate to arrays
- How arithmetic with pointers works, and what it is used for
- What standard library functions are available for processing null-terminated strings
- How to create memory for new variables while your program is executing
- How to release memory that you have allocated dynamically
- How you can convert from one type of pointer to another

What is a Pointer?

Every variable and literal in your program has an **address** in memory — this is the location in the memory of your computer where the data is stored. Similarly, in order to execute, the functions your program uses must be located somewhere in memory; so a function has an address, too. These addresses will depend on where your program is loaded into memory when you choose to run it, and they can therefore vary from one execution to the next.

A **pointer** is a variable that you can use to store a memory address. The address stored in a pointer usually corresponds to the position in memory where a variable is located, but it can also be the address of a function, as we will see in the next chapter.

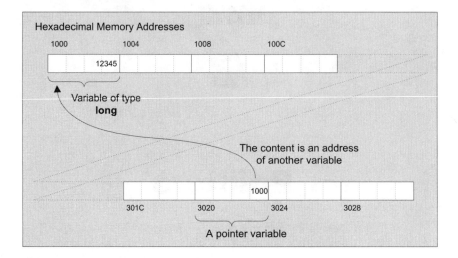

You can see from the diagram how a pointer gets its name: it 'points to' the location in memory where something is stored — a variable or a function. However, it's no use if your pointer just stores a memory address. In order to make use of the entity stored at that particular address, you need to know exactly *what* it is, not just *where* it is. As you know, an integer has a very different representation from a floating point value, and in general you need fewer bytes to store an integer, too. Thus, to use a data item stored at the address contained in a pointer, you also need to know the type of the data.

As a consequence of this simple logic, a pointer is not just 'a pointer'; it is a pointer *to a particular type of data item*. This will become clearer when we get down to specifics, so let's look at how to declare a pointer.

Declaring a Pointer

The declaration of a pointer is similar to that of an ordinary variable, except that the type name has an asterisk following it, to indicate that you're declaring a variable that's a pointer to that type. For example, to declare a pointer called **pnumber** that will 'point to' values of type **long**, you could use the following statement:

```
long* pnumber;
```

This declares a pointer variable, **pnumber**, which can store the address of a variable of type **long**. The type of this variable is 'pointer to **long**', and when the type is written alone (in a cast statement, for instance), it is usually written as **long***.

The declaration above has been written with the asterisk next to the type name, but this is not the only way of writing it. You can also write the declaration of a pointer with the asterisk adjacent to the variable name, as in this statement:

```
long *pnumber;
```

This declares precisely the same variable as before. The compiler will accept either notation, but the former is perhaps the more common, since it expresses the type, 'pointer to **long**', more clearly. However, there is opportunity for confusion when you mix declarations of ordinary variables and pointers in the same statement. Try to work out what this statement does:

```
long* pnumber, number;
```

In fact, it declares a variable **pnumber** of type 'pointer to **long**', and a variable **number** that's just of type **long**, although the notation that juxtaposes the asterisk and the type name makes this less than clear. If you declared the same two variables in the alternative form:

```
long *pnumber, number;
```

This is rather less confusing, as the asterisk is now clearly associated with the variable **pnumber**. However, the real solution to this problem is simply not to do it in the first place. It's always better to declare all your variables on separate lines, which avoids any possibility of confusion:

```
long number;            // Declaration of long variable
long* pnumber;          // Declaration of variable of type 'pointer to long'
```

This has the added advantage that we can easily append comments to the declarations to explain their uses when necessary.

In our example, we used **pnumber** as the pointer variable name. It is not obligatory, but it is a common convention in C++ to use variable names beginning with **p** to denote pointers. This makes it easier to see which variables in a program are pointers, which in turn can make your source code easier to follow.

Pointers to types other than **long** are declared in exactly the same way. To illustrate this, we can declare variables that are pointers to **double** and **string** respectively with the statements:

```
double* pvalue;         // Pointer to a double value
string* psentence;      // Pointer to a string value
```

Using Pointers

To use a pointer, we just need to store the address of another variable of the appropriate type in it, so let's see how we obtain the address of a variable in the first place.

The Address-Of Operator

The **address-of** operator, **&**, is a unary operator that obtains the address in memory where a variable is stored. We could declare a pointer, **pnumber**, and a variable, **number**, with the statements:

```
long number = 12345;
long* pnumber;
```

Since the types of the variable **number** and the pointer **pnumber** are compatible, we can write the following assignment:

```
pnumber = &number;      // Store address of number in pnumber
```

233

This means that **pnumber** is assigned the address of **number**. The result of this operation is illustrated below:

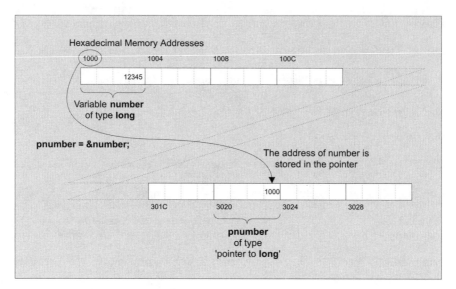

You can use the **&** operator to obtain the address of any type of variable, but you have to store the address in a pointer of the appropriate type. If you want to store the address of a **double** variable, for example, the pointer must have been declared as type **double***, which is 'pointer to **double**'. If you try to store an address in a pointer of the wrong type, then your program will not compile.

Taking the address of a variable and storing it in a pointer is all very well, but the really interesting aspect is how you can use it. Fundamental to using a pointer is accessing the data in the memory location to which the pointer points. This is done using the indirection operator.

The Indirection Operator

The **indirection operator**, *****, is used with a pointer variable to access the contents of the memory location pointed to. The name 'indirection operator' stems from the fact that the data is accessed 'indirectly'. The same operator is sometimes also called the **dereference operator**, and the process of accessing the data in the memory location pointed to by a pointer is termed **dereferencing** the pointer. Let's see how this works in practice.

Try It Out – Using the Indirection Operator

This example just demonstrates using the indirection operator, *****, to display the value of the variable a pointer points to:

```
// Program 7.1 The indirection operator in action
#include <iostream>
using namespace std;

int main()
{
```

```
long number = 50L;
long* pnumber;                          // Pointer declaration
pnumber = &number;                      // Store the address of number
cout << endl
     << "The value stored in the variable number is "
     << *pnumber
     << endl;
return 0;
}
```

When you compile and run the program, it will produce the output:

```
The value stored in the variable number is 50
```

How It Works

We first declare a regular variable of type **long**, which is initialized to 50.

```
long number = 50L;
```

Next, we declare a pointer variable:

```
long* pnumber;                          // Pointer declaration
```

Since its type is **long***, this variable can store addresses of variables of type **long**. We store the address of **number** in **pnumber** with the statement:

```
pnumber = &number;                      // Store the address of number
```

The address-of operator, **&**, produces the address in memory of **number**, and this is stored as the value of **pnumber**. We can now display the value stored in **number** by dereferencing **pnumber**:

```
cout << endl
     << "The value stored in the variable number is "
     << *pnumber
     << endl;
```

The indirection operator applied to a pointer refers to the contents of the address stored in the pointer. Since **pnumber** contains the address of **number**, ***pnumber** refers to the value of **number**.

An aspect of the indirection operator that can seem confusing is the fact that we now have several different uses for the same symbol, *****. It is the multiply operator, the indirection operator, and it is also used in the declaration of a pointer. Each time you use *****, the compiler is able to distinguish its meaning by the context. When you multiply two variables — **price * quantity**, for instance — there is no meaningful interpretation of this expression for anything other than a multiply operation. You will see an example of this contextual interpretation of ***** in the next program in this chapter, Program 7.2.

Why Use Pointers?

A question that usually springs to mind at this point is, "Why use pointers at all?" After all, taking the address of a variable you already know about and sticking it in a pointer so that you can come along and dereference it later on seems like an overhead you can do without. Don't be too hasty: there are several reasons why pointers are important.

235

First of all, as you will see shortly, you can use pointer notation to operate on data stored in an array, which often executes faster than if you use array notation. Second, when we get to define our own functions later in the book, you will see that pointers are used extensively for enabling access within a function to large blocks of data, such as arrays, that are defined outside the function.

Third, and most important, you will also see later that you can allocate space for new variables dynamically — that is, during program execution. This sort of capability allows your program to adjust its use of memory depending on the input. You can create new variables while your program is executing, as and when you need them. Since you don't know in advance how many variables you are going to create dynamically, the only way you can do it is by using pointers — so make sure you get the hang of this bit!

To get more of a feel for how pointers work, let's try another very simple example that just exercises the mechanics of using a pointer.

Try It Out – Using Pointers

We can try out the various aspects of pointer operation we have seen up to now with the following example:

```cpp
// Program 7.2 Exercising pointers
#include <iostream>
using namespace std;

int main()
{
  long* pnumber;                      // Pointer declaration
  long number1 = 55L;
  long number2 = 99L;                 // A couple of variables

  pnumber = &number1;                 // Store address in pointer
  *pnumber += 11;                     // Increment number1 by 11
  cout << endl
       << "number1 = "      << number1
       << "   &number1 = " << pnumber
       << endl;

  pnumber = &number2;                 // Change pointer to address of number2
  number1 = *pnumber * 10;            // 10 times number2

  cout << "number1 = "      << number1
       << "   pnumber = "  << pnumber
       << "   *pnumber = " << *pnumber
       << endl;

  return 0;
}
```

On my computer, this program produces the following output:

```
number1 = 66    &number1 = 0068FDF4
number1 = 990   pnumber = 0068FDF0    *pnumber = 99
```

It is likely that the values for the addresses displayed will be different on your machine.

How It Works

There is no input to this example; all operations are carried out with the values set in the program. After storing the address of **number1** in the pointer **pnumber**, the value of **number1** is incremented indirectly, through the pointer, in this statement:

```
*pnumber += 11;                        // Increment number1 by 11
```

The indirection operator determines that we are adding 11 to the contents of the variable pointed to, which is **number1**. This demonstrates that we can use a dereferenced pointer on the left of an assignment operation. If we forgot the *****, the program would attempt to change the address stored in the pointer. (We'll discuss pointer arithmetic in detail a little later on.)

This statement displays the value of **number1**, and the address of **number1** stored in **pnumber**:

```
cout << endl
    << "number1 = "     << number1
    << "    &number1 = " << pnumber
    << endl;
```

For a pointer to a numeric type, sending the pointer name by itself (in this case, **pnumber**) to the output stream produces the address value. Because it's a pointer type, the stored value is displayed in hexadecimal. Memory addresses are generally represented in hexadecimal notation — and that's not just in C++. Because **number** is an ordinary integer variable, its value is displayed in decimal.

After the first line of output, the contents of **pnumber** are set to the address of **number2** with the statement:

```
pnumber = &number2;                    // Change pointer to address of number2
```

Now **pnumber** points to the variable **number2**. The address of **number1**, which was previously contained in **pnumber**, has been overwritten. We can now change the variable **number1** to the value of 10 times **number2** through the pointer **pnumber**:

```
number1 = *pnumber * 10;               // 10 times number2
```

The expression on the right of the assignment accesses the value of **number2** indirectly through the pointer and multiplies it by 10. The compiler knows how to interpret the occurrences of ***** in this line, because it considers the context of each one. The next output statement displays the results of these calculations:

```
cout << "number1 = "     << number1
    << "    pnumber = " << pnumber
    << "    *pnumber = " << *pnumber
    << endl;
```

This displays the value of **number1**, the address stored in **pnumber**, and the value stored at the address contained in **pnumber**. Again, the value of **pnumber** displays as hexadecimal because it is an address. The expression ***pnumber** resolves to an ordinary integer value — the value stored in **number2** — so this displays as decimal.

Initializing Pointers

If anything, using pointers that aren't initialized is even more hazardous than using ordinary variables and arrays that aren't initialized. With a pointer variable containing a junk value, you can overwrite random areas of memory. The resulting damage just depends on how unlucky you are, so it's more than just a good idea always to initialize your pointers.

It's very easy to initialize a pointer to the address of a variable that has already been defined. You can initialize the pointer **pnumber** with the address of the variable **number** simply by using the address-of operator with the variable name as the initial value for the pointer:

```
int number = 0;            // Initialized integer variable
int* pnumber = &number;    // Initialized pointer
```

When you're initializing a pointer with another variable like this, remember that the variable must already have been declared prior to the pointer declaration. If this is not so, your compiler will complain.

Of course, you may not want to initialize a pointer with the address of a specific variable when you declare it. In this case, you can initialize it with the pointer equivalent of zero:

```
int* pnumber = 0;          // Pointer not pointing to anything
```

This declaration ensures that **pnumber** does not point to anything. Consequently, if you try to dereference it before it has had a proper value assigned, your program will fail in a manner that clearly indicates the fact. A pointer initialized in this way is called a **null pointer**. However, you *can* test the pointer to see whether it's null before you try to dereference it:

```
if(pnumber == 0)
   cout << endl << "pnumber is null.";
```

Remember to use the double equals sign **==** in the comparison! You could equally well use the equivalent statement:

```
if(!pnumber)
   cout << endl << "pnumber is null.";
```

Of course, you can also use this form:

```
if(pnumber != 0)
{
   // Pointer is not null, so do something useful
}
```

The symbol **NULL** is also defined in the standard library as 0, and you will often see this used to initialize null pointers. However, **NULL** is really there only for compatibility with C, and it's good practice in C++ to use 0, as I have done here.

Initializing Pointers to Type char

A variable of type 'pointer to **char**' has the interesting property that it can be initialized with a string literal. For example, we can declare and initialize such a pointer with the statement:

```
char* pproverb = "A miss is as good as a mile.";
```

This looks very similar to initializing a **char** array, but you shouldn't judge on appearances: it is rather different. The statement will create a null-terminated string literal (actually an array of type **const char**) from the character string appearing between the quotes, and store the address of the first character of the string literal in the pointer **pproverb**. This is shown in the figure:

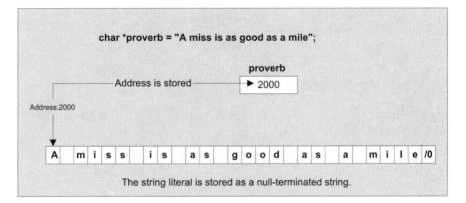

The string literal is stored as a null-terminated string.

Unfortunately, all is not quite as it seems. The type of the string literal is **const**, but the type of the pointer is not. The statement doesn't create a modifiable copy of the string literal; it merely stores the address of the first character. This means that if you write some code that attempts to modify the string, like this statement, which tries to change the first character to **'X'**:

```
*pproverb = 'X';
```

the compiler won't complain, because it can see nothing wrong. However, when you try to *run* the program, you'll get an error: the string literal in memory is still a constant, and you're not allowed to change it.

You might wonder, with good reason, why the compiler allowed you to assign a **const** value to a non-**const** type in the first place, when it causes these problems. The reason is that string literals only became constants with the release of the C++ standard, and there's a great deal of legacy code that relies on the 'incorrect' assignment. Its use is deprecated, however, and the correct resolution of the problem is to declare the pointer like this:

```
const char* pproverb = "A miss is as good as a mile.";
```

This declares that what **pproverb** points to is **const**, so the type is consistent with that of the string literal. There's plenty more to say about using **const** with pointers, so we will come back to this subject later in this chapter. For now, let's see how using variables of type **char*** operates in another example.

Try It Out – Lucky Stars With Pointers

We could write a new version of our 'lucky stars' example (Program 6.5) that uses pointers instead of an array, to see how that would work:

```cpp
// Program 7.3 Initializing pointers with strings
#include <iostream>
using namespace std;

int main()
{
  // The lucky stars referenced through pointers
  const char* pstar1 = "Mae West";
  const char* pstar2 = "Arnold Schwarzenegger";
  const char* pstar3 = "Lassie";
  const char* pstar4 = "Slim Pickens";
  const char* pstar5 = "Greta Garbo";
  const char* pstar6 = "Oliver Hardy";
  const char* pstr   = "Your lucky star is ";

  int choice = 0;                         // Star selector

  cout << endl
       << "Pick a lucky star!"
       << " Enter a number between 1 and 6: ";
  cin >> choice;

  cout << endl;

  switch(choice)
  {
    case 1:
      cout << pstr << pstar1;
      break;
    case 2:
      cout << pstr << pstar2;
      break;
    case 3:
      cout << pstr << pstar3;
      break;
    case 4:
      cout << pstr << pstar4;
      break;
    case 5:
      cout << pstr << pstar5;
      break;
    case 6:
      cout << pstr << pstar6;
      break;
    default:
      cout << "Sorry, you haven't got a lucky star.";
  }

  cout << endl;
  return 0;
}
```

An example of output from this program is:

```
Pick a lucky star! Enter a number between 1 and 6: 5

Your lucky star is Greta Garbo
```

How It Works

The array of our original example has been replaced by six pointers, **pstar1** to **pstar6**, each initialized with a name. We have also declared an additional pointer, **pstr**, initialized with the phrase that we want to use at the start of a normal output line. Because all these pointers are used to point to string literals, we have declared them as **const**.

Since we have discrete pointers, it is easier to use a **switch** statement to select the appropriate output message than the **if** that was employed in the original version. Any incorrect values that are entered are all taken care of by the **default** option of the **switch**.

Outputting the string pointed to by a pointer couldn't be easier. As you can see, you simply write the pointer name. Now, you may have noticed that the standard output stream **cout** treats pointer names differently, depending on what type the pointer points to. In Program 7.2, this code:

```
cout << pnumber;
```

would have output the address contained in the pointer **pnumber**. In this example, on the other hand, the code:

```
cout << pstar1;
```

would output a string literal — not an address. The difference lies in the fact that **pnumber** is a pointer to a numeric type, while **pstar1** is a 'pointer to **char**'. The output stream, **cout**, treats a variable that's a 'pointer to **char**' as a null-terminated string, and displays it as such.

So, what have we gained? Well, using pointers has eliminated the waste of memory that occurred with the array version of this program, since each string now occupies just the number of bytes necessary to accommodate it. However, the program does seem a little long-winded now. If you were thinking, "There must be a better way," then you'd be right — we could use an array of pointers.

Try It Out – Arrays of Pointers

With an array of pointers to type **char**, each element can point to an independent string, and the lengths of each of the strings can be different. We can declare an array of pointers in the same way that we declare any other array. Here's an alternative version of the previous example that uses a pointer array:

```
// Program 7.4 Using an array of pointers to char
#include <iostream>
using namespace std;

int main()
{
```

```
      const char* pstars[] = {
                              "Mae West",                    // Initializing a pointer array
                              "Arnold Schwarzenegger",
                              "Lassie",
                              "Slim Pickens",
                              "Greta Garbo",
                              "Oliver Hardy"
                            };
      const char* pstr = "Your lucky star is ";
      int choice = 0;

      const int starCount = sizeof pstars / sizeof pstars[0];    // Get array size

      cout << endl
          << "Pick a lucky star!"
          << " Enter a number between 1 and "
          << starCount
          << ": ";
      cin >> choice;

      cout << endl;
      if(choice >= 1 && choice <= starCount)                 // Check for valid input
        cout << pstr << pstars[choice - 1];                  // Output star name
      else
        cout << "Sorry, you haven't got a lucky star.";      // Invalid input

      cout << endl;
      return 0;
    }
```

How It Works

In this case, we are nearly getting the best of all possible worlds. We have a one-dimensional array of **char** pointers declared such that the compiler works out what the array size should be from the number of initializing strings:

```
      const char* pstars[] = {
                              "Mae West",                    // Initializing a pointer array
                              "Arnold Schwarzenegger",
                              "Lassie",
                              "Slim Pickens",
                              "Greta Garbo",
                              "Oliver Hardy"
                            };
```

The memory usage that results from this statement is illustrated below:

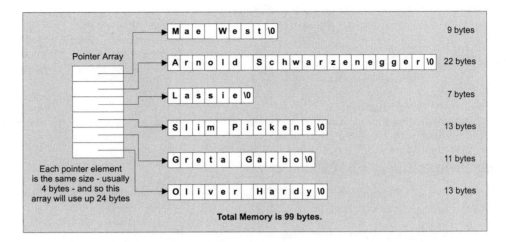

As you see, memory is required for each null-terminated string, and also for the elements in the array, each of which is a pointer. That's a total of 99 bytes. Compared to using an array of type **char**, the pointer array requires less memory. With the old static array, each row must have at least the length of the longest string; six rows of 22 bytes each is 132 bytes, so by using a pointer array we have saved 33 bytes. Of course, the exact saving is dependent on how many strings you have and the diversity in their lengths. Sometimes there will not be any saving at all, but generally the pointer array is the more efficient.

Saving space is not the only advantage that you get by using pointers. In many circumstances you can save time too. For example, think of what happens if you want to swap **"Greta Garbo"** in fifth position with **"Mae West"** at the beginning. This is typical of the sort of operation you'd need to sort the strings into alphabetical order. With the pointer array as above, you just need to swap the pointers around — the strings themselves can stay right where they are.

If the strings were stored in an array of type **char**, then a great deal of copying would be necessary. We would need to copy the whole string **"Greta Garbo"** to a temporary location while we copied **"Mae West"** in its place, and then we would need to copy **"Greta Garbo"** to its new position, which would require significantly more computer time to execute. This logic applies equally to using objects of type **string**.

Getting back to the example, we store the address of the basic message for a star selection in another pointer:

```
const char* pstr = "Your lucky star is ";
```

We then calculate the number of elements in the pointer array, **pstars**, with this statement:

```
const int starCount = sizeof pstars / sizeof pstars[0];   // Get array size
```

Having the array size calculated in this way will enable us to make the rest of the program adapt automatically to accommodate however many stars there are. We do this in the prompt for the input value for **choice**:

```
cout << endl
    << "Pick a lucky star!"
    << " Enter a number between 1 and "
    << starCount
    << ": ";
```

After reading the **choice** value as in the previous version of the program, we select the string that we want to output by means of a very simple **if** statement. We either display a selection from the **pstars** array, or a suitable message if the user enters an invalid value. The **if** condition uses the **starCount** variable as the upper limit for **choice**, so again, any number of star choices will be accommodated automatically. If you want more choices in the program, you can just add them to the list of initializing strings.

Sorting Strings Using Pointers

As I suggested in our discussion of the previous example, you can sort strings without having to move the strings around, if you use pointers to refer to them.

We could produce a new version of Program 6.10, where we extracted words from a text string. This will give us some useful experience in applying **string** objects, and using arrays of pointers to **string** objects. At the same time, we'll get some practical experience of sorting using pointers.

Try It Out – Sorting Strings Using Pointers

We will read a string of words from the keyboard, and sort them into a well-defined order. Here's the code:

```
// Program 7.5 Sorting strings using pointers
#include <iostream>
#include <string>

using namespace std;

int main()
{
  string text;                               // The string to be sorted
  const string separators = " ,.\"\n";       // Word delimiters
  const int max_words = 1000;                // Maximum number of words
  string words[max_words];                   // Array to store the words
  string* pwords[max_words];                 // Array of pointers to the words

  // Read the string to be searched from the keyboard
  cout << endl << "Enter a string terminated by #:" << endl;
  getline(cin, text, '#');

  // Extract all the words from the text
  int start = text.find_first_not_of(separators);   // Word start index
  int end = 0;                                       // End delimiter index
  int word_count = 0;                               // Count of words stored
  while(start != string::npos && word_count < max_words)
  {
    end = text.find_first_of(separators, start + 1);
    if(end == string::npos)                  // Found a separator?
      end = text.length();                   // No, so set to last + 1
```

```
        words[word_count] = text.substr(start, end - start);  // Store the word
        pwords[word_count] = &words[word_count];              // Store the pointer
        word_count++;                                          // Increment count

        // Find the first character of the next word
        start = text.find_first_not_of(separators, end + 1);
    }

    // Sort the words in ascending sequence by direct insertion
    int lowest = 0;                                            // Index of lowest word

    for(int j = 0; j < word_count - 1; j++)
    {
        lowest = j;                                            // Set lowest

        // Check current against all the following words
        for(int i = j + 1 ; i < word_count ; i++)
            if(*pwords[i] < *pwords[lowest])                   // Current is lower?
                lowest = i;

        if(lowest != j)
        {                                                      // Then swap pointers
            string* ptemp = pwords[j];                         // Save current
            pwords[j] = pwords[lowest];                        // Store lower in current
            pwords[lowest] = ptemp;                            // Restore current
        }
    }

    // Output the words in ascending sequence
    for(int i = 0 ; i < word_count ; i++)
        cout << endl << *pwords[i];

    cout << endl;
    return 0;
}
```

An example of the output that this program can produce is:

```
Enter a string terminated by #:
In this world nothing can be said to be certain, except death and taxes.#

In
and
be
be
can
certain
death
except
nothing
said
taxes
this
to
world
```

How It Works

The text string containing the words to be sorted will be read into the variable declared as:

```
string text;                              // The string to be sorted
const string separators = " ,.\"\n";      // Word delimiters
```

The constant **separators** contains all the characters that act as word delimiters; these are space, comma, period, double quote, and newline. You could add tab to this list if necessary. Alternatively, you could construct the string containing the separators by searching **text** for all the characters that are not letters, digits, or single quotes.

We'll store the words we extract from **text** in an array that will have a capacity for up to 1000 words:

```
const int max_words = 1000;               // Maximum number of words
string words[max_words];                  // Array to store the words
string* pwords[max_words];                // Array of pointers to the words
```

The **words** array will store the words, while the array of pointers, **pwords**, will store the addresses of each of the elements in **words**. This is a little cumbersome, but we need the pointers if we are to avoid repeatedly copying the **string** objects when we are sorting them. We also have to allocate space for **max_words string** objects and pointers, even though we will not generally need them all. Later in this chapter we'll see a much better way to do this, using **dynamic memory allocation**.

We read multiple lines of text into **text** in the manner you have seen previously; input is terminated by entering **#**, so you can enter as many lines as you wish:

```
cout << endl << "Enter a string terminated by #:" << endl;
getline(cin, text, '#');
```

Extracting individual words from **text** and storing them in the **words** array is done in the **while** loop:

```
// Extract all the words from the text
int start = text.find_first_not_of(separators);    // Word start index
int end = 0;                                        // End delimiter index
int word_count = 0;                                 // Count of words stored
while(start != string::npos && word_count < max_words)
{
  end = text.find_first_of(separators, start + 1);
  if(end == string::npos)                           // Found a separator?
    end = text.length();                            // No, so set to last + 1

  words[word_count] = text.substr(start, end - start);  // Store the word
  pwords[word_count] = &words[word_count];              // Store the pointer
  word_count++;                                         // Increment count

  // Find the first character of the next word
  start = text.find_first_not_of(separators, end + 1);
}
```

This also works by using the approach you saw the last time that we did something of this kind. We find the index position of the first letter of a word and save it in **start**. We find the first separator following the word and store its index position in **end**. We then use the **substr()** function to extract the word as a **string** object, which we store in the next available element of the **words** array. We also store the *address* of that element of **words** in the corresponding element of the **pwords** array. The loop condition ensures that we stop searching for words if we reach the end of **text**, or we fill the **words** array.

In preparation for the sort operation, we declare a variable called **lowest** to record the index position of the 'lowest' word found during the sort:

```
int lowest = 0;                               // Index of lowest word
```

The sorting of the words is done in the nested **for** loop:

```
for(int j = 0; j < word_count - 1; j++)
{
  lowest = j;                                 // Set lowest

  // Check current against all the following words
  for(int i = j + 1 ; i < word_count ; i++)
    if(*pwords[i] < *pwords[lowest])          // Current is lower?
      lowest = i;

  if(lowest != j)
  {                                           // Then swap pointers
    string* ptemp = pwords[j];                // Save current
    pwords[j] = pwords[lowest];               // Store lower in current
    pwords[lowest] = ptemp;                   // Restore current
  }
}
```

The operation will rearrange the pointers in the **pwords** array so that they point to words in the **words** array in ascending sequence. The process is very simple. The outer loop steps through the **pwords** array from the first element to the last. In the inner loop, we compare the word each pointer points to with all the words pointed to by the following pointers, to find the index position of the 'lowest'. If we find that the lowest pointer is not the one we are considering, we swap the pointers, using **ptemp** as a temporary store. This process is repeated for each element in the **pwords** array.

By this method, the first element will contain the pointer to 'lowest' word of all. The second element will point to the lowest bar the first, and so on for all the pointers that we have stored in the array. Note that in the output, **"In"** comes before **"and"** because my machine uses ASCII, in which the character code for **'I'** is lower than that for **'a'**.

Finally, we output the words in ascending sequence in the **for** loop:

```
for(int i = 0 ; i < word_count ; i++)
  cout << endl << *pwords[i];
```

The elements of the **pwords** array point to the words in ascending sequence. To output them in order, we just display the dereferenced pointers of the array.

Tidying the Output

Outputting one word to a line is fine for a short piece of text, but with a lot of text it would be rather inconvenient. It would be nice to have all the words that begin with the same letter output as a group. If you're ready for a slightly more complicated output mechanism, you could replace the **for** loop above with the following code:

```
// Output up to six words to a line in groups starting with the same letter
char ch = (*pwords[0])[0];                      // First letter of first word
int words_in_line = 0;                          // Words in a line count
for(int i = 0; i < word_count ; i++)
{
  if(ch != (*pwords[i])[0])                      // New first letter?
  {
    cout << endl;                               // Start a new line
    ch = (*pwords[i])[0];                       // Save the new first letter
    words_in_line = 0;                          // Reset words in line count
  }
  cout << *pwords[i] << "  ";
  if(++words_in_line == 6)                       // Every sixth word
  {
    cout << endl;                               // Start a new line
    words_in_line = 0;
  }
}
```

This will again output all the words in ascending sequence, but this time words that begin with the same letter will be grouped together. Each group will start on a new line, with up to six words to a line.

The first letter for a group is stored in the variable **ch**. Notice how we refer to the first character of the first **string** object. The expression ***pwords[0]** dereferences the pointer in the first element of the **pwords** array to give the word that it points to. The expression **(*pwords[0])[0]** then gives the first letter of the word, since the additional set of square brackets outside the parentheses encloses the index of the letter in the word. The precedence of square brackets is higher than that of the indirection operator, *****, so the parentheses are necessary here. The variable **words_in_line** keeps track of the number of words on the current line; when it reaches 6, a newline character is output. Of course, whenever the first letter of a word to be displayed is different from the character in **ch**, we are starting a new group, so that also causes a newline to be output and **words_in_line** to be reset to 0.

Constant Pointers and Pointers to Constants

When we were dealing with pointers to type **char** earlier in this chapter, we saw that using **pointers to constants** for handling string literals is the technique enforced by the C++ standard. In our Lucky Stars program, for example, we made sure that the compiler would pick up any attempts to modify the strings pointed to by elements of the **pstars** array by declaring the array using **const**:

```
const char* pstars[] = {
                        "Mae West",
                        "Arnold Schwarzenegger",
                        "Lassie",
                        "Slim Pickens",
```

```
                              "Greta Garbo",
                              "Oliver Hardy"
                         };
```

In this declaration, we are declaring the objects pointed to by elements of the pointer array as constant. The compiler will inhibit any direct attempt to change these, so an assignment statement such as this one would be flagged as an error *by the compiler*, preventing a nasty problem at runtime:

```
    *pstars[0] = 'X';
```

However, we could still legally write the next statement, which would copy the *address* stored in the element on the right of the assignment operator to the element on the left:

```
    pstars[0] = pstars[5];
```

Now, those lucky individuals due to be awarded Ms West would get Mr Hardy instead, since both pointers now point to the same name. Note that this *hasn't* changed the values of the objects pointed to by the pointer array element — it has only changed the address stored in **pstars[0]**, so our **const** specification has not been disobeyed.

We really ought to be able to inhibit this kind of change as well, since some people may reckon that good old Olly may not have quite the same sex appeal as Mae West, and of course we can. Have a look at the following statement:

```
    const char* const pstars[] = {
                              "Mae West",
                              "Arnold Schwarzenegger",
                              "Lassie",
                              "Slim Pickens",
                              "Greta Garbo",
                              "Oliver Hardy"
                         };
```

The extra **const** declares a **constant pointer**, and now the pointers *and* the strings they point to are being declared as constant. Nothing about this array can be changed.

To summarize, we can distinguish three situations arising from using **const** with pointers and the things to which they point:

> **A pointer to a constant.** Here, what's pointed to cannot be modified, but we can set the pointer to point to something else:
> ```
>     const char* pstring = "Some text that cannot be changed";
> ```
> Of course, this also applies to pointers to other types. For example:
> ```
>     const int value = 20;
>     const int* pvalue = &value;
> ```
> **value** is a constant and cannot be changed. **pvalue** is a pointer to a constant, so you can use it to store the address of **value**. You couldn't store the address of **value** in a non-**const** pointer (because that would imply that you can modify a constant through a pointer), but you *could* assign the address of a non-**const** variable to **pvalue**. In the latter case, you would be making it illegal to modify the variable through the pointer. In general, it's always possible to strengthen **const**-ness in this fashion, but weakening it is not permitted.

249

> A **constant pointer.** Here, the address stored in the pointer can't be changed, so a pointer like this can only ever point to the address it's initialized with. However, the *contents* of that address are not constant and can be changed.

We could take a numeric example to illustrate a constant pointer. Suppose we declare an integer variable **value** and a constant pointer **pvalue** as:

```
int value = 20;
int* const pvalue = &value;
```

This declares that the pointer **pvalue** is **const**, so it can only ever point to **value**. Any attempt to make it point to another **int** variable will result in an error message from the compiler. The contents of **value** are not **const**, though, and you can change them whenever you want. Again, if **value** was declared as **const**, you couldn't initialize **pvalue** with **&value**. The pointer **pvalue** can only point to a non-**const** variable of type **int**.

> A **constant pointer to a constant.** Here, both the address stored in the pointer and the thing pointed to have been declared as constant, so neither can be changed.

Taking a numerical example, we can declare **value** as:

```
const int value = 20;
```

value is now a constant: you can't change it. We can still initialize a pointer with the address of **value**, though:

```
const int* const pvalue = &value;
```

pvalue is a constant pointer to a constant. You can't change what **pvalue** points to, and you can't change the value at the address it contains.

> *Naturally, this behavior isn't confined to the **char**s and **int**s we've been dealing with so far. This discussion applies to pointers of any type.*

Pointers and Arrays

There is a close connection between pointers and array names. Indeed, there are many situations where you can use an array name as though it were a pointer. Looking back at Chapter 6, and applying what we now know, we can see that an array name by itself can behave like a pointer when used in an output statement. If you try to output an array by just using its name (and as long as it is not an array of type **char**), what you will get is the hexadecimal address of the array in memory. Because an array name behaves like a pointer in this way, you can use one to initialize a pointer. For example:

```
double values[10];
double* pvalue = values;
```

This will store the address of the array **values** in the pointer **pvalue**.

Having noted the similarity between an array name and a pointer, I should emphasize that they are quite different entities, and you should remain conscious of this. The most significant difference between a pointer and an array name is that you can modify the address stored in a pointer, while the address that an array name refers to is fixed.

Pointer Arithmetic

You can perform operations on a pointer to alter the address it contains. In terms of arithmetic operators, you're limited to addition and subtraction, but you can also compare pointers to produce a logical result.

As far as addition goes, you can add an integer value (or an expression that evaluates to an integer) to a pointer. The result of the addition is an address. You can subtract an integer from a pointer, and that also results in an address. Finally, you can take the difference between two pointers, and in this case the result is an integer, not an address. No other arithmetic operations on pointers are legal.

Arithmetic with pointers works in a special way. Suppose you add 1 to a pointer with a statement such as:

```
pvalue++;
```

This increments the pointer by 1. Exactly *how* you increment the pointer by 1 here doesn't matter — you could use an assignment or the **+=** operator if you wanted, so the effect would be just the same with this statement:

```
pvalue += 1;
```

The interesting point here is that the address stored in the pointer will not be incremented by 1 in the normal arithmetic sense. Pointer arithmetic implicitly assumes that the pointer points to an array, and that the arithmetic operation is on the address contained in the pointer. The compiler knows the number of bytes required to store one element of the array, and adding 1 to the pointer increments the address in the pointer by that number of bytes. In other words, adding 1 to the pointer moves the pointer to the next element in the array.

For example, if **pvalue** is 'pointer to **double**', as in our previous declaration, and the compiler allocates 8 bytes for a variable of type **double**, then the address in **pvalue** will be incremented by 8. This is illustrated in the diagram below.

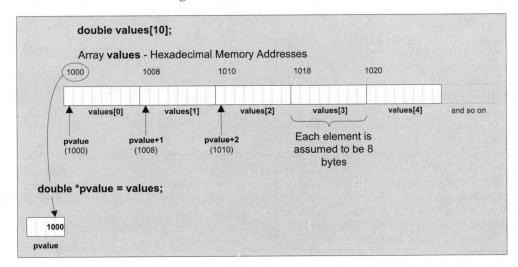

As the diagram shows, **pvalue** starts out with the address corresponding to the beginning of the array. Adding 1 to **pvalue** increments the address it contains by 8, so the result is the address of the next array element. It follows that incrementing the pointer by 2 moves the pointer two elements along. Of course, the pointer **pvalue** need not necessarily point to the beginning of the **values** array. We could assign the address of the third element of the array to the pointer with this statement:

```
pvalue = &values[2];
```

Following this, the expression **pvalue + 1** would evaluate to the address of **values[3]**, the fourth element of the **values** array, and we could make the pointer point to this element directly by writing this statement:

```
pvalue += 1;
```

This statement has incremented the address contained in **pvalue** by the number of bytes occupied by one element of the **values** array. In general, the expression **pvalues + n**, where **n** can be any expression resulting in an integer, will produce a result by adding **n * sizeof(double)** to the address contained in the pointer **pvalue**, since **pvalue** was declared to be of type 'pointer to **double**'.

The same logic applies to subtracting an integer from a pointer. If **pvalue** contains the address of **values[2]**, the expression **pvalue - 2** evaluates to the address of the first element of the array, **values[0]**. In other words, incrementing or decrementing a pointer works in terms of the type of the object pointed to. Increasing a pointer to **long** by one changes its contents to the next **long** address, and so increments the address by **sizeof(long)** bytes. Decrementing the pointer by 1 decrements the address it contains by **sizeof(long)**.

> *The address resulting from an arithmetic operation on a pointer can be in a range from the address of the first element of the array to which it points, to the address that is one beyond the last element. Outside of these limits, the behavior of the pointer is undefined.*

You can, of course, dereference a pointer on which you have performed arithmetic. (There wouldn't be much point to it, otherwise!) For example, assuming that **pvalue** is still pointing to **values[2]**, the statement:

```
*(pvalue + 1) = *(pvalue + 2);
```

is equivalent to this:

```
values[3] = values[4];
```

When you want to dereference a pointer after incrementing the address it contains, the parentheses are necessary because the precedence of the indirection operator is higher than that of the arithmetic operators, **+** and **-**. If you wrote the expression ***pvalue + 1**, instead of ***(pvalue + 1)**, this would add one to the value stored at the address contained in **pvalue**, which is equivalent to executing **values[2] + 1**. Furthermore, since the result is a numerical value that's not an address (and therefore not an lvalue), its use in the assignment statement above would cause the compiler to generate an error message.

Remember that an expression such as **pvalue + 1** does not change the address in **pvalue**. It is simply an expression that evaluates to a result which is of the same type as **pvalue**. In this case, it is the address of the element following that pointed to by **pvalue**.

Of course, if a pointer contains an invalid address (such an address outside the limits of the array it relates to), and you store a value using the pointer, you will attempt to overwrite the memory located at that address. This generally leads to disaster, with your program failing one way or another. It may not be obvious that the cause of the problem is the misuse of a pointer.

Taking the Difference between Two Pointers

You can subtract one pointer from another, but this is only meaningful when they are of the same type and point to elements in the same array. Suppose we have a one-dimensional array, **numbers**, of type **long**, declared as:

```
long numbers[] = {10L, 20, 30, 40, 50, 60, 70, 80};
```

We can declare and initialize two pointer variables:

```
long *pnum1 = &numbers[6];          // Points to seventh array element
long *pnum2 = &numbers[1];          // Points to second array element
```

Now we can calculate the difference between these two pointers as:

```
int difference = pnum1 - pnum2;          // Result is 5
```

The variable **difference** will be set to 5 because the calculation of the difference between the addresses is in terms of elements, not in terms of bytes.

Using Pointer Notation with an Array Name

We can use an array name as though it was a pointer for addressing the elements of an array. If we have a one-dimensional array declared as:

```
long data[5];
```

then using pointer notation, we can refer to the element **data[3]**, for example, as ***(data + 3)**. This kind of notation can be applied generally, so that corresponding to the elements **data[0], data[1], data[2], ...**, we can write ***data, *(data + 1), *(data + 2)**, and so on. The array name **data** by itself refers to the address of the beginning of the array, so an expression such as **data + 2** produces the address of the element two elements along from the first.

You can use pointer notation with an array name in just the same way as you use the notation with an index value — in expressions, or on the left of an assignment. You could set the values of the **data** array to even integers with this loop:

```
for(int i = 0 ; i < 5 ; i++)
   *(data + i) = 2 * (i + 1);
```

*(data + i) will refer to successive elements of the array. ***(data + 0)** corresponds to **data[0]**, ***(data + 1)** refers to **data[1]**, and so on. The loop will set the values of the array elements to 2, 4, 6, 8, and 10.

If you now wanted to sum the elements of the array, you could write:

```
long sum = 0;
for(int i = 0 ; i < 5 ; i++)
  sum += *(data + i);
```

Let's try some of this in a practical context with a little more meat to it.

Try It Out – Array Names as Pointers

Since we have tried out pointers with strings, let's exercise this aspect of array addressing with a numerically-oriented program that calculates prime numbers (a prime number is an integer that is divisible only by 1 and itself).

```
// Program 7.6 Calculating primes
#include <iostream>
#include <iomanip>
using namespace std;

int main()
{
  const int max = 100;                    // Number of primes required
  long primes[max] = {2, 3, 5};           // First three primes defined
  int count = 3;                          // Count of primes found
  long trial = 5;                         // Candidate prime
  bool isprime = true;                    // Indicates when a prime is found

  do
  {
    trial += 2;                           // Next value for checking
    int i = 0;                            // Index to primes array

    // Try dividing the candidate by all the primes we have
    do
    {
      isprime = trial % *(primes + i) > 0;  // False for exact division
    } while(++i < count && isprime);

    if(isprime)                           // We got one...
      *(primes + count++) = trial;        // ...so save it in primes array
  } while(count < max);

  // Output primes 5 to a line
  for(int i = 0 ; i < max ; i++)
  {
    if(i % 5 == 0)                        // Newline on 1st line and after every 5th prime
      cout << endl;
    cout << setw(10) << *(primes + i);
  }
  cout << endl;
  return 0;
}
```

The output from this program is:

2	3	5	7	11
13	17	19	23	29
31	37	41	43	47
53	59	61	67	71
73	79	83	89	97
101	103	107	109	113
127	131	137	139	149
151	157	163	167	173
179	181	191	193	197
199	211	223	227	229
233	239	241	251	257
263	269	271	277	281
283	293	307	311	313
317	331	337	347	349
353	359	367	373	379
383	389	397	401	409
419	421	431	433	439
443	449	457	461	463
467	479	487	491	499
503	509	521	523	541

How It Works

We have the usual **#include** statements for **iostream** for input and output, and for **iomanip**, since we will be using a stream manipulator to set the field width for output. We use the constant **max** to define the number of primes that we want the program to produce:

```
const int max = 100;                    // Number of primes required
long primes[max] = {2, 3, 5};           // First three primes defined
int count = 3;                          // Count of primes found
```

The **primes** array that stores the results has the first three primes already defined to start the process off. The variable **count** will record how many primes we have, so it is initialized to 3.

The test for primes uses the variables declared in the following statements:

```
long trial = 5;                         // Candidate prime
bool isprime = true;                    // Indicates when a prime is found
```

The variable **trial** will hold the next candidate to be tested, so we start it off at 5. The Boolean variable **isprime** is a flag that we will use to indicate when the value in **trial** is prime.

All the work is done in two loops: the outer **do-while** loop picks the next candidate to be checked and adds the candidate to the **primes** array if it is prime, and the inner loop actually checks the candidate to see whether it is prime or not. The outer loop will continue until we have filled the **primes** array.

Before the inner loop is executed, the **trial** variable is set to the next candidate to be tested with the statement:

```
trial += 2;                             // Next value for checking
```

The algorithm in the loop is very simple, and is based on the fact that any number that is not a prime must be divisible by a smaller number that *is* prime. We find the primes in ascending sequence, so at any point the **primes** array will contain all of the prime numbers lower than our current candidate. If none of the primes we have is a divisor of the candidate, then the candidate must be prime.

FYI

> In fact, only division by primes less than or equal to the *square root* of the number in question needs to be checked, so this example isn't as efficient as it might be.

Checking for whether the variable **trial** is prime is done in the inner loop:

```
do
{
  isprime = trial % *(primes + i) > 0;  // False for exact division
} while(++i < count && isprime);
```

Within the loop, **isprime** is set to the value of the expression **trial % *(primes + i) > 0**. This finds the remainder after dividing **trial** by the prime number stored at the address **primes + i**. If the remainder is positive, it results in **true**.

The loop will end if **i** reaches **count**, or whenever **isprime** is set to **false**. If any of the primes we have in the **primes** array divides into **trial** exactly, we know that **trial** is not prime, so this will end the loop. If we try dividing all the primes into **trial** and none of them divides into it exactly, **isprime** will always be **true** and the loop will be ended by **i** reaching **count**.

After the inner loop ends, either because **isprime** was set to **false** or we exhausted the set of divisors in the **primes** array, we must decide whether or not the value in **trial** was prime. This is indicated by the value in **isprime**, which we test in the **if** statement:

```
if(isprime)                           // We got one...
   *(primes + count++) = trial;       // ...so save it in primes array
```

If **isprime** contains **false**, then one of the divisions was exact and so **trial** is not prime. If **isprime** is **true**, the assignment statement stores the value from **trial** in **primes[count]** and then increments **count** with the postfix increment operator.

Once **max** primes have been found, we display them five to a line with a field width of 10 characters as a result of these statements:

```
if(i % 5 == 0)                   // Newline on 1st line and after every 5th prime
   cout << endl;
cout << setw(10) << *(primes + i);
```

This starts a new line when **i** has the values 0, 5, 10, and so on.

Using Pointers with Multidimensional Arrays

Using a pointer to store the address of a one-dimensional array is relatively straightforward, but with multidimensional arrays, things can get complicated. I should say that this subject is a little tricky, and you may want to skip over it on a first reading. However, if your previous experience is with C, this section is well worth a glance.

You can usually do everything you need to do with multidimensional arrays using array notation, and I recommend that you stick to it whenever you can. If you have to use a pointer with multidimensional arrays, you need to keep clear in your mind what is happening. By way of illustration, we can use an array called **beans**, declared as follows:

```
double beans[3][4];
```

We can declare and initialize the variable **pbeans**, of type pointer to **double**, as follows:

```
double* pbeans = &beans[0][0];
```

Here, we are setting the pointer to the address of the first element of the array, which is of type **double**. We could also set the pointer to the address of the first *row* in the array with this statement:

```
double* pbeans = beans[0];
```

This is equivalent to using the name of a one-dimensional array, which is replaced by its address — we've seen this in an earlier discussion. However, because **beans** is a two-dimensional array, the following attempt to put an address in the pointer is illegal:

```
double* pbeans = beans;          // Will cause an error!!
```

The problem is one of type. The type of the pointer we have defined is **double***, but the array is of type **double[3][4]**. A pointer to store the address of this array must be of type **double*[4]**. C++ associates the size of an array with its type, and the statement above is only legal if the pointer has been declared with the size required. This is done with a slightly more complicated notation than we have seen so far:

```
double (*pbeans)[4] = beans;
```

The parentheses here are essential — otherwise, you would be declaring an array of pointers. Now the initialization of the pointer to point to **beans** is legal, but note that this pointer can *only* be used to store addresses of an array with the dimensions shown.

Pointer Notation with Multidimensional Array Names

You can use pointer notation with an array name to reference elements of the array. You can reference each element of the array **beans** declared above, which had three rows of four elements, in three ways:

▶ **Using the array name in the usual fashion, with two index values.**
For example, **beans[i][j]**. This uses conventional array indexing to refer to the element with offset **j** in row **i** of the array.

> **Using the array name in pointer notation.**
> For example, ***(*(beans + i) + j)**. We can determine the meaning of the expression by working from the inside outwards. **beans** refers to the address of the first row of the array, so **beans + i** refers to row **i** of the array. The expression ***(beans + i)** is the address of the first element of row **i**, so ***(beans+i) + j** is the address of the element in row **i** with offset **j**. The whole expression ***(*(beans+i) + j)**, therefore, refers to the value of that element. Unless you have a good reason for referencing the elements of an array in this way, it is best avoided. It is not obvious what you mean, and your code will be that much harder to understand.

> **Using a mixture of pointer notation and an index value.**
> This is legal, but not recommended. The following are legal references to the same element of the array:
>
>   *(beans[i] + j)
>   (*(beans + i))[j]

where we have mixed array and pointer notation.

Try It Out – Using Pointer Notation with Multidimensional Arrays

In Program 5.8, we generated a multiplication table. We could produce another version of this program that stores the table as an array. To avoid duplicating all the code that is no longer of interest, we will simplify it to calculate a table of fixed size:

```
// Program 7.7 Using pointer notation with a multidimensional array
#include <iostream>
#include <iomanip>
#include <cctype>

using namespace std;

int main()
{
  const int table = 12;                          // Table size
  long values[table][table] = {0};               // Stores the table values

  // Calculate the table entries
  for(int i = 0; i < table ; i++)
    for(int j = 0; j < table ; j++)
      *(*(values + i) + j) = (i + 1) * (j + 1);  // Full use of pointer notation

  // Create the top line of the table
  cout << "    |";
  for(int i = 1 ; i <= table ; i++)
    cout << " " << setw(3) << i << " |";
  cout << endl;

  // Create the separator row
  for(int i = 0 ; i <= table ; i++)
    cout << "------";
  cout << endl;

  for(int i = 0 ; i < table ; i++)               // Iterate over the rows
  {
```

```
        cout << " " << setw(3) << i + 1 << " |";              // Start the row

    // Output the values in a row
    for(int j = 0 ; j < table ; j++)
      cout << " " << setw(3) << values[i][j] << " |";  // Array notation
    cout << endl;                                      // End the row
  }

  return 0;
}
```

This example produces the output:

```
     |   1 |   2 |   3 |   4 |   5 |   6 |   7 |   8 |   9 |  10 |  11 |  12 |
------------------------------------------------------------------------------
   1 |   1 |   2 |   3 |   4 |   5 |   6 |   7 |   8 |   9 |  10 |  11 |  12 |
   2 |   2 |   4 |   6 |   8 |  10 |  12 |  14 |  16 |  18 |  20 |  22 |  24 |
   3 |   3 |   6 |   9 |  12 |  15 |  18 |  21 |  24 |  27 |  30 |  33 |  36 |
   4 |   4 |   8 |  12 |  16 |  20 |  24 |  28 |  32 |  36 |  40 |  44 |  48 |
   5 |   5 |  10 |  15 |  20 |  25 |  30 |  35 |  40 |  45 |  50 |  55 |  60 |
   6 |   6 |  12 |  18 |  24 |  30 |  36 |  42 |  48 |  54 |  60 |  66 |  72 |
   7 |   7 |  14 |  21 |  28 |  35 |  42 |  49 |  56 |  63 |  70 |  77 |  84 |
   8 |   8 |  16 |  24 |  32 |  40 |  48 |  56 |  64 |  72 |  80 |  88 |  96 |
   9 |   9 |  18 |  27 |  36 |  45 |  54 |  63 |  72 |  81 |  90 |  99 | 108 |
  10 |  10 |  20 |  30 |  40 |  50 |  60 |  70 |  80 |  90 | 100 | 110 | 120 |
  11 |  11 |  22 |  33 |  44 |  55 |  66 |  77 |  88 |  99 | 110 | 121 | 132 |
  12 |  12 |  24 |  36 |  48 |  60 |  72 |  84 |  96 | 108 | 120 | 132 | 144 |
```

How It Works

We first declare the size of the array and the array itself:

```
const int table = 12;                          // Table size
long values[table][table] = {0};               // Stores the table values
```

We must declare **table** as **const** because we use it to specify the size of table. An array size must be a constant expression, so non-**const** variables are not allowed. The array will have 12 rows of 12 elements.

We use pointer notation to store the table entries in a nested **for** loop:

```
for(int i = 0; i < table ; i++)
  for(int j = 0; j < table ; j++)
    *(*(values + i) + j) = (i + 1) * (j + 1);   // Full use of pointer notation
```

The expression **values + i** refers to row **i** of the array, and ***(values + i)** refers to the address of the first element of row **i**. By adding **j** to that with the expression ***(values + i) + j**, we get the address of the **j**th element in row **i**. We dereference that with the expression ***(*(values + i) + j)** to refer to the *contents* of the **j**th element in row **i** of the array.

To output the entries in the table, we have another nested loop:

```
for(int i = 0 ; i < table ; i++)               // Iterate over the rows
{
  cout << " " << setw(3) << i + 1 << " |";      // Start the row
```

```
    // Output the values in a row
    for(int j = 0 ; j < table ; j++)
      cout << " " << setw(3) << values[i][j] << " |"; // Array notation
    cout << endl;                                      // End the row
  }
```

We use normal array notation to output the values stored in the array. The expression in pointer notation ***(*(values + i) + j)** is equivalent to **values[i][j]** in array notation. I'm sure you'll agree that array notation is a lot easier to understand in this situation!

Operations on C-Style Strings

In Chapter 4, we saw briefly the functions that are declared in the **cctype** header file, which analyze and convert single characters. The standard library also contains some functions that you can use to analyze and transform null-terminated strings. The bulk of these are declared in the header file **cstring**, which you must include in order to use them.

> *Don't confuse the* **cstring** *header that we will use here with the* **string** *header file that we've already seen, which defines the* **string** *type.*

The functions in the **cstring** header make extensive use of pointers both as arguments and return values, and that's why we've deferred discussion of them to this point. They supply functionality for null-terminated strings similar to that we saw provided for **string** objects in the last chapter. In that sense, these functions are something of an anachronism, but they're still in the language, and you'll certainly see them used.

Operations on C-style strings are interesting to us here because they provide some exercise for pointer operations. There are a total of 22 functions in the **cstring** header file, but we'll just take a look at the ones involved with concatenating null-terminated strings.

Concatenating Strings

In the last chapter, we saw that we could combine **string** objects simply by using the **+** operator. With null-terminated strings, it's not quite so easy. The **cstring** header file declares two functions for concatenating null-terminated strings: **strcat()** and **strncat()**.

The **strcat()** function takes two strings as arguments, of types **char*** and **const char*** respectively, and appends the latter of these to the former, modifying the first argument in the process. It takes care of overwriting the **'\0'** at the end of the first string, and adding **'\0'** to the end of the composite string, but you're responsible for making sure that the string pointed to by the first argument has enough space to hold the result. The first argument is also the return value of the function.

strncat() takes three arguments, the first two of which are the same as those for **strcat()**. The third argument is an integer that specifies how many characters from the second string should be added to the first; if you ask for more characters than there are in the string, the whole string will be appended. Apart from that, the conditions of use and the return value are the same as for **strcat()**.

These functions are quite easy to use. Suppose we declare two arrays of type **char** as follows:

```
char name[50] = "Bing";
char surname[] = "Crosby";
```

We could append a space to the string in **name** with the statement:

```
strcat(name, " ");
```

Then we could append the **surname** with this statement:

```
strcat(name, surname);
```

The result will be that **name** contains the string **"Bing Crosby"**. Because the functions always return the first argument, we could have done the whole thing in a single statement:

```
strcat(strcat(name, " "), surname);
```

This has the disadvantage that it is less easy to figure out what is going on. In this statement, the first **strcat()** function call appends a space to **name**. The result of this is then used as the first argument to the outer **strcat()** function call, which appends the surname.

To help you verify that there is space in the first argument to hold the composite string, you can use the **strlen()** function, which returns the length of the string you pass as its only argument. You might use something like:

```
if(sizeof name / sizeof name[0] > (strlen(name) + strlen(surname) + 1))
   cout << strcat(strcat(name, " "), surname);
```

The **if** condition works out how many characters **name** can hold, and makes sure that this is greater than the length of the string we're going to construct (the extra **+ 1** in the **if** condition is for the space character).

The other functions defined in **cstring** perform operations like copying (**strcpy()**), comparing (**strcmp()**) and searching (**strchr()**) null-terminated strings, and they are broadly similar in operation to the ones we've seen here. By taking pointers to **char** as arguments, the functions avoid the overhead of having to move and copy whole strings in memory; this is something we'll be seeing a lot more of in the next chapter and indeed the rest of the book.

Remember that I've introduced these functions so that you'll recognize them if you see them, and because they're a small demonstration of how pointers can be useful. When you're writing your own code, I strongly recommend that you use **string** objects in preference to variables of type **char*** for your string-handling needs.

Dynamic Memory Allocation

All of the code we have written up to now allocates space for data at compile time. We specify the variables and the array sizes that we need in the source code, and that's what will be allocated when the program executes, whether we need it or not. Working with a fixed set of variables in a program can be very restrictive, and it is often wasteful.

When we were extracting words from a text string in Program 7.5, we allocated space for 1000 words. A lot of the time we would not need to store 1000 words, and in those cases the excess space was allocated needlessly. It prevented some other program from using the space, even though it was completely unused by our program. On the other hand, if we tried to analyze a text string of 1001 words, the program would be unable to handle it — even though, in all probability, there would be memory lying idle in the computer.

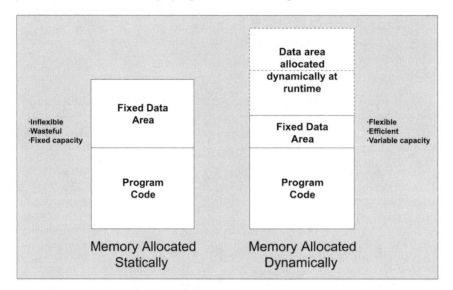

In another context, you might find that it would be appropriate to use a large integer array with one set of data, whereas a large floating point array would be required for a different set of input data. If the arrays required were very large, you might not have enough memory in your machine to accommodate both at the same time. The solution to all these difficulties and disadvantages is to use **dynamic memory allocation**, which means that you allocate the memory you need to store the data you are working with when your program executes (runtime), rather than when you compile it (compile time).

By definition, dynamically allocated variables can't be declared at compile time, and so they can't be named in your source program. When you allocate memory dynamically, the space that is made available by your request is identified by its address. The obvious (and only) place to store this address is in a pointer. With the power of pointers and the dynamic memory management tools in C++, writing this kind of flexibility into your programs is quick and easy.

Back in Chapter 3, I introduced the three kinds of storage duration that variables can have — automatic, static, and dynamic — and discussed how variables of the first two varieties are created. Variables allocated in the free store will always have *dynamic* storage duration.

The Free Store, Alias the Heap

In most instances, there is unused memory in your computer when your program is executed. In C++, this unused memory is called the **free store**, or sometimes the **heap**. You can allocate space within the free store for a new variable of a given type by using a special C++ operator that returns the address of the space allocated. This operator is **new**, and it is complemented by the operator **delete**, which de-allocates memory that you have previously allocated with **new**.

You can allocate space in the free store for some variables in one part of a program, and then release the allocated space and return it to the free store once you have finished with the variables concerned. The memory then becomes available for reuse by other dynamically allocated variables later in the same program. This enables you to use memory very efficiently, and in many cases it results in programs that can handle much larger problems, involving considerably more data than might otherwise be possible.

> *When you allocate space for a variable using **new**, you are creating the variable in the free store. The variable continues to exist until the memory it occupies is released by the operator **delete**.*

The Operators new and delete

Suppose that we need space for a variable of type **double**. We can define a pointer to type **double**, and then request that the memory is allocated at execution time. We can do this using the operator **new** with the following statements:

```
double* pvalue = 0;                    // Pointer initialized with null
pvalue = new double;                   // Request memory for a double variable
```

This is a good moment to recall that *all pointers should be initialized*. Using memory dynamically typically involves having a lot of pointers floating around, so it is particularly important that they should not contain spurious values. You should always try to arrange that if a pointer doesn't contain a legal address, it should contain 0.

The **new** operator in the second line of code above will return the address of the memory in the free store allocated to a **double** variable, and this address will be stored in the pointer **pvalue**. We can then use this pointer to reference the variable by using the indirection operator, as we have seen. For example:

```
*pvalue = 999.0;
```

Of course, under extreme circumstances the memory allocation may not be possible, because the free store is used up at the time of allocation. Alternatively, it could be that the free store is fragmented by previous usage, meaning that there is no area of the free store with a sufficient number of contiguous bytes to accommodate the variable for which you want to obtain space. This is not likely with the space required to hold a **double** value, but might just happen when you're dealing with entities that can be large, such as arrays or complex class objects. This is clearly something that we need to consider, but just for the moment we'll assume that we always get the memory we request. We will come back to this topic in Chapter 17, though, when we discuss **exceptions**.

You can initialize a variable created with **new**. Let's reconsider the example above: the **double** variable allocated by **new**, with its address stored in **pvalue**. We could have initialized its value to **999.0** as it was created, by using this statement:

```
pvalue = new double(999.0);            // Allocate a double and initialize it
```

When you no longer need a dynamically allocated variable, you can free up the memory that it occupied in the free store with the **delete** operator:

```
delete pvalue;                          // Release memory pointed to by pvalue
```

This ensures that the memory can be used subsequently by another variable. If you don't use **delete**, and you subsequently store a different address in the pointer **pvalue**, it will be impossible to free up the original memory location or to use the variable that it contains, since access to the address will have been lost.

It's important to realize that the **delete** operator frees the memory but does *not* change the pointer. Following the above statement, **pvalue** still contains the address of the memory that was allocated, but the memory is now free and may immediately be allocated to something else — possibly by another program. To avoid the risk of attempting to use the pointer containing the now spurious address, and unless you are going to reassign it or it goes out of scope, you should always reset the pointer when you release the memory. To do this, you would write:

```
delete pvalue;                          // Release memory pointed to by pvalue
pvalue = 0;                             // Reset the pointer to 0
```

Dynamic Memory Allocation for Arrays

Allocating memory for an array dynamically is straightforward. Assuming that we have already declared **pstring**, of type 'pointer to **char**', we could allocate an array of type **char** in the free store by writing:

```
pstring = new char[20];                 // Allocate a string of twenty characters
```

This allocates space for a **char** array of 20 characters and stores its address in **pstring**. To remove the array that we have just created in the free store, we must use the **delete** operator. The statement to do that would look like this:

```
delete [] pstring;                      // Delete array pointed to by pstring
```

> *The square brackets here are important: they indicate that what we are deleting is an array. When removing arrays from the free store, you should always include the square brackets, or the results will be unpredictable. Note also that you do not specify any dimensions here, simply [ ].*

Of course, we should also reset the pointer, now that it no longer points to memory that we own:

```
pstring = 0;                            // Reset the pointer
```

Let's see how dynamic memory allocation works, using numeric data first of all.

Try It Out – Using the Free Store

We can see how these operations work in practice by rewriting our earlier program that calculated 100 primes to calculate an arbitrary number of primes. We will use memory in the free store to store however many are required.

```
// Program 7.8 Calculating primes using dynamic memory allocation
#include <iostream>
#include <iomanip>
using namespace std;

int main()
{
  int max = 0;                            // Number of primes required
  int count = 3;                          // Count of primes found
  long trial = 5;                         // Candidate prime
  bool isprime = true;                    // Indicates when a prime is found

  cout << endl
       << "Enter the number of primes you would like: ";
  cin >> max;                             // Number of primes required

  long* primes = new long[max];           // Allocate memory for them
  *primes = 2;                            // Insert three seed primes...
  *(primes + 1) = 3;
  *(primes + 2) = 5;

  do
  {
    trial += 2;                           // Next value for checking
    int i = 0;                            // Index to primes array

    // Try dividing the candidate by all the primes we have
    do
    {
      isprime = trial % *(primes + i) > 0;  // False for exact division
    } while(++i < count && isprime);

    if(isprime)                           // We got one...
      *(primes + count++) = trial;        // ...so save it in primes array
  } while(count < max);

  // Output primes 5 to a line
  for(int i = 0 ; i < max ; i++)
  {
    if(i % 5 == 0)                 // Newline on 1st line and after every 5th prime
      cout << endl;
    cout << setw(10) << *(primes + i);
  }
  cout << endl;
  delete [] primes;                       // Free up memory
  return 0;
}
```

The output is essentially the same as the previous version of the program, except of course that you choose how many primes are calculated, so we won't reproduce it again here.

How It Works

Overall, the program is very similar to the previous version. After reading the number of primes required from the keyboard and storing it in the `int` variable, `max`, we allocate an array of that size in the free store using the operator `new`. We specify the size of the array required by putting the variable `max` between the square brackets following the array type specification:

```
long* primes = new long[max];              // Allocate memory for them
```

The address that's returned by `new` is stored in the pointer, `primes`. This will be the address of the first element of an array of `max` elements of type `long`.

Next, we set the first three array elements to the values of the first three primes:

```
*primes = 2;                               // Insert three seed primes...
*(primes + 1) = 3;
*(primes + 2) = 5;
```

We have used pointer notation here, but we could equally well use array notation. If you prefer, you could write these statements as:

```
primes[0] = 2;                             // Insert three seed primes...
primes[1] = 3;
primes[2] = 5;
```

> *You can't specify initial values for elements of an array allocated dynamically. You have to use explicit assignment statements to set values for elements of the array.*

The calculation of the prime numbers is exactly as before. No changes are necessary, even though the memory that the primes will occupy has been allocated at runtime. Equally, the output process is the same. Acquiring space dynamically is really not a problem at all. Once the space has been allocated it in no way affects how the computation is written.

Once we have finished with the array, we remove it from the free store using the `delete` operator, not forgetting to include the square brackets to indicate that it's an array we are deleting:

```
delete [] primes;                          // Free up memory
```

Since this is the end of the program, there is no possibility of misusing the pointer, so there is no need to reset it to 0. If the program continued, then naturally it would be a different matter.

Hazards of Dynamic Memory Allocation

There are two kinds of problem that can arise when you allocate memory dynamically. The first is called a **memory leak**, and is caused by errors in your code. Unfortunately, memory leaks are quite common. The second is called **memory fragmentation**, and is usually due to poor use of dynamic allocation. Memory fragmentation problems are relatively rare.

Memory Leaks

A memory leak occurs when you allocate memory using **new**, and fail to release it when you are done with it. In this situation, it's common to lose the address of the memory block by overwriting the address in the pointer you were using to access it. This typically occurs in a loop, and it is easier to create this kind of problem than you might think. The effect is that your program gradually consumes more and more of the free store, with the program potentially failing at the point when all of the free store has been allocated, and yet another request for memory is made.

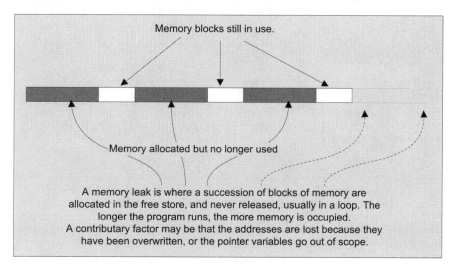

Memory blocks still in use.

Memory allocated but no longer used

A memory leak is where a succession of blocks of memory are
allocated in the free store, and never released, usually in a loop. The
longer the program runs, the more memory is occupied.
A contributary factor may be that the addresses are lost because they
have been overwritten, or the pointer variables go out of scope.

It's relatively easy to see where you've simply forgotten to use **delete** to free memory, as long as use of the memory ceases at a point in your code that is close to where you allocated it. It becomes more difficult to spot the omission in complex programs, where memory may be allocated in one part of a program but should be released in a quite separate part. The best strategy for dealing with this is to add the **delete** operation at an appropriate place in your program immediately after you've used the **new** operator.

Pointers and Variable Scope

When it comes to scope, pointers are just like any other variable. A pointer variable exists from the point at which you declare it in a block, to the closing brace of the block. After that it no longer exists, and so the address it contained is no longer accessible.

This relates to the discussion of memory leaks. If a pointer contains the address of a block of memory in the free store, and the pointer goes out of scope, then it's no longer possible to **delete** the memory. It is most important to keep in mind the scope of your pointers, particularly when you are using dynamically allocated memory.

Fragmentation of the Free Store

Memory fragmentation can arise in programs that allocate and release memory blocks frequently. Each time the **new** operator is used, it allocates a contiguous block of bytes in the free store. If you create and destroy many variables of different sizes, it is possible to arrive at a situation in which the allocated memory is interspersed with small blocks of free memory, none of which is large enough to accommodate a new dynamic variable that your program (or some other program that is executing concurrently) needs to allocate. The aggregate of the free memory can be quite large, but all the individual blocks may be quite small — too small for the current requirements.

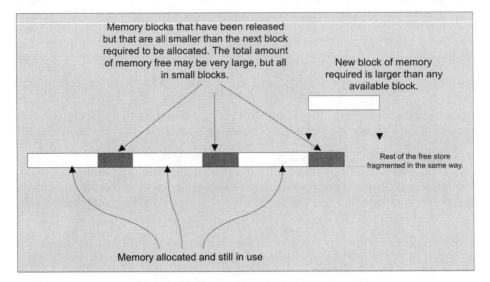

Memory blocks that have been released but that are all smaller than the next block required to be allocated. The total amount of memory free may be very large, but all in small blocks.

New block of memory required is larger than any available block.

Rest of the free store fragmented in the same way.

Memory allocated and still in use

This problem arises relatively infrequently these days, with virtual memory providing very large amounts of memory even on quite modest computers. When it does occur, the solution is to avoid allocating small blocks of memory. Instead, allocate larger blocks and manage the use of the memory yourself.

Try It Out – Sorting Strings Again

I began this discussion of dynamic memory allocation by criticizing our program for extracting and sorting words from a text string, and we're now in a position to be able to do something about it. The version we'll construct here won't impose that arbitrary, 1000-word limit on your text, and won't waste memory if you enter fewer than 1000 words.

As we put this example together, you'll see once again that using dynamically allocated memory doesn't require many alterations to the mechanics of a program. I can explain the changes from Program 7.5, which in large measure are to do with the *management* of dynamic memory, by breaking the code into sections and highlighting the new lines and amendments.

Reading and Counting the Words in a Multi-line String

In fact, we can read the string from the keyboard in *exactly* the same way as in Program 7.5. The difference here is in when and how pointers are assigned to the words in the string. Last time, we created a fixed array of pointers before the string was entered, and assigned the pointers to the words as we counted them. This time, we can defer creation of the pointers until after the text has been input, but in order to do that, we still need to find out how many words there are:

```
// Program 7.9 Sorting strings using dynamic memory allocation
#include <iostream>
#include <string>

using namespace std;

int main()
{
  string text;                                  // The string to be sorted
  const string separators = " ,.\"\n";          // Word delimiters
```

```
// Three lines deleted
```

```
  // Read the string to be searched from the keyboard
  cout << endl << "Enter a string terminated by #:" << endl;
  getline(cin, text, '#');
```

```
// Count the words in the text
  int start = text.find_first_not_of(separators);     // Word start index
  int end = 0;                                         // End delimiter index
  int word_count = 0;                                 // Count of words stored
```

```
while(start != string::npos)
  {
    end = text.find_first_of(separators, start + 1);
    if(end == string::npos)                      // Found a separator?
      end = text.length();                       // No, so set to last + 1
```

```
// Two lines deleted
```

```
    word_count++;                                // Increment count

    // Find the first character of the next word
    start = text.find_first_not_of(separators, end + 1);
  }
```

All the changes here are deletions. The five lines that we've removed were to do with the creation and assignment of fixed-size arrays of words and pointers to words, which we no longer require at this stage of the program. We've also been able to get rid of the condition on the **while** loop that restricted the number of words our program can handle. At the end of this code, we've got a string in **text** and a count of the number of words in it in **word_count**, so we know exactly how much memory we need to allocate.

Creating the Array of Pointers to the Words

Now it's time to write some new code. We need an array of **word_count** pointers to refer to the words in **text**. There's only one line of code necessary to create this array:

```
// Allocate an array of pointers to strings in the free store
  string** pwords = new string*[word_count];
```

The operator **new** creates an array of **word_count** elements of type **string***, which is type 'pointer to **string**'. We need to store the address returned by **new** in **pwords**, so **pwords** must also be a pointer. Since what it points to is an array of elements of type **string***, the type of **pwords** has to be **string****, which is type 'pointer to pointer to **string**'.

Creating Objects for the Words

With the array of pointers to the words available, we are ready to create the **string** objects that will represent the words. We will create a **string** object for a word from the substring containing all the characters of a word, so we need to find the index position of the start of a word, and the count of the number of characters in the word. In the interests of code reuse, we can perform this task with a loop that's almost identical to the one we used for counting the words in **text** in the first place:

```
// Create words in the free store and store the addresses in the array
start = text.find_first_not_of(separators);        // Start of first word
end = 0;                                            // Index for the end of a word
int index = 0;                                      // Pointer array index

while(start != string::npos)
{
  end = text.find_first_of(separators, start + 1);
  if(end == string::npos)                           // Found a separator?
    end = text.length();                            // No, so set to last + 1

  pwords[index++] = new string(text.substr(start, end - start));

  start = text.find_first_not_of(separators, end+1);  // Find start of next word
}
```

The variable **start** holds the index position of the first character of each word in turn, while **end** contains the position of the first separator after the word that begins at **start**. The length of the word is therefore given by the expression **end - start**, and we can use that fact to create the **string** object for a word in the free store, in the line that's the only one to change from our word-counting loop.

We initialize the string object with a word that we extract from **text** by using the **substr()** function. The operator **new** returns the address of the memory for the object, which we store in **pwords[index]**. We also increment **index** to the position of the next free array element, using the postfix increment operator.

Sorting and Outputting the Words

Apart from the fact that it was created dynamically, **pwords** is an array of pointers like any other. That means we can use exactly the same code for sorting and outputting the words that we had in Program 7.5. So that you've got it all in one place, here it is again:

```
// Sort the words in ascending sequence by direct insertion
int lowest = 0;                                         // Index of lowest word

for(int j = 0 ; j < word_count - 1 ; j++)
{
  lowest = j;                                           // Set lowest

  // Check current against all the following words
  for(int i = j + 1 ; i < word_count ; i++)
    if(*pwords[i] < *pwords[lowest])                    // Current is lower?
      lowest = i;

  if(lowest != j)
  {                                                     // Then swap pointers
```

```
        string* ptemp = pwords[j];                      // Save current
        pwords[j] = pwords[lowest];                     // Store lower in current
        pwords[lowest] = ptemp;                         // Restore current
    }
}

// Output up to six words to a line in groups starting with the same letter
char ch = (*pwords[0])[0];                              // First letter of first word
int words_in_line = 0;                                 // Words in a line count
for(int i = 0 ; i < word_count ; i++)
{
    if(ch != (*pwords[i])[0])                           // New first letter?
    {
        cout << endl;                                  // Start a new line
        ch = (*pwords[i])[0];                           // Save the new first letter
        words_in_line = 0;                             // Reset words in line count
    }
    cout << *pwords[i] << "  ";
    if(++words_in_line == 6)                            // Every sixth word
    {
        cout << endl;                                  // Start a new line
        words_in_line = 0;
    }
}
```

Freeing Free Store Memory

This time round, the output doesn't mark the end of the program. We must use the **delete** operator to release the memory for the words, and for the pointer array:

```
// Delete words from free store
for(int i = 0 ; i < word_count ; i++)
    delete pwords[i];

// Now delete the array of pointers
delete[] pwords;

    return 0;
}
```

We delete the **string** objects containing the words in the **for** loop. We then delete the pointer array, **pWords**. Note that because we are deleting an array here, we must put square brackets after the keyword **delete**.

If you piece together all the sections of code above, you should be able to get the resulting program to produce the following output:

```
Enter a string terminated by #:
Little Willie from his mirror
Licked the mercury right off,
Thinking, in his childish error
It would cure the whooping cough.
At the funeral Willie's mother
Brightly said to Mrs Brown,
"Twas a chilly day for Willie
When the mercury went down."#
```

```
At
Brightly  Brown
It
Licked  Little
Mrs
Thinking  Twas
When  Willie  Willie  Willie's
a
childish  chilly  cough  cure
day  down
error
for  from  funeral
his  his
in
mercury  mercury  mirror  mother
off
right
said
the  the  the  the  to
went  whooping  would
```

Isn't that nice?

Converting Pointers

The **reinterpret_cast<>()** operator will allow you to cast between any pointer types, with the constraint that if the pointer type you are casting was declared as **const**, you cannot cast it to a type that is not **const**. You can also convert any integer numeric value to a pointer type, and vice versa. This does not change the values involved; it only changes the way the value is interpreted. Consequently, this is a very risky operator, so you should only use it when absolutely necessary.

The general form of the **reinterpret_cast<>()** operator is:

reinterpret_cast<*pointer_type*>(*expression*)

The **expression** between the parentheses is interpreted as the **pointer_type** between the angled brackets. To illustrate the general conversion potential, we could suppose that, for some strange reason, we wanted to interpret a **float** value as a **long**. We could do this with the following statements:

```
float value = 2.5f;
float* pvalue = &value;
long* pnumber = reinterpret_cast<long*>(pvalue);
```

After these have been executed, the pointer **pnumber** points to the value in **value** (which is 2.5), but will *interpret* it as type **long**. The value itself is unchanged — it has exactly the same bit pattern as before. You could output the value interpreted as type **long** with the statement:

```
cout << endl << *pnumber;
```

On my computer, this demonstrates that the floating point value 2.5 looks like 1,075,838,976 as type **long**. The reverse process — storing a **long** value and then interpreting it as type **float** — will almost certainly produce a floating point value that is not properly formed.

At the risk of laboring the point, I want to repeat that the **reinterpet_cast<>()** operator is very hazardous, since it provides the means of arbitrarily interpreting a value of one type as another. You should avoid using this operator unless it is absolutely essential to the solution of your problem, and you know precisely what you are doing.

Summary

We have explored some very important concepts in this chapter. You will be making extensive use of pointers in your C++ programs, so make sure that you have a good grasp of them — you'll see a lot more of them throughout the rest of the book.

The vital points that we have covered in this chapter are:

▶ A pointer is a variable that contains an address.

▶ You obtain the address of a variable using the address-of operator, **&**.

▶ To refer to the value pointed to by a pointer you use the indirection operator, *****. This is also called the dereference operator.

▶ You can add or subtract integer values to or from the address stored in a pointer. The effect is as though the pointer refers to an array, and the pointer is altered by the number of array elements specified by the integer value.

▶ The operator **new** allocates a block of memory in the free store, and makes it available for use in your program by returning the address of the memory allocated.

▶ You use the operator **delete** to release a block of memory that you have allocated previously using the operator **new**.

▶ The **reinterpret_cast<>()** operator converts from one type of pointer to another.

Exercises

Ex 7.1 Write a program that declares and initializes an array containing the first five even numbers. Then, implement a **for** loop to output the numbers, using array notation. Once that's working as it should be, change the loop to use pointer notation instead.

Ex 7.2 Create a program that dynamically allocates memory for an array of ten integers. Get the user to input ten integers, display them, and then return the allocated memory to the free store before terminating the program.

Ex 7.3 Amend your answer to Exercise 6.1 to use dynamic memory to store the students' details. This will remove the ten-student limit of the earlier exercise, and won't waste memory when there are fewer than ten students.

Ex 7.4 You know that a two-dimensional array is an 'array of arrays'. You also know that it's possible to create an array dynamically through a pointer. Put these two facts together, and you can begin to see that it's possible to create a 2-D array dynamically by using a 'pointer to a pointer'. Your task in this exercise is to construct a 4x4, two-dimensional array of integers by this method. To get you started, here are the first two lines:

```
int** ppint;
ppint = new int*[4];
```

This gives you an array of four pointers that you can access using **ppint[0]**, **ppint[1]**, and so on. Assign each of these to an array of four integers, and you're home — but watch out how you **delete** them at the end!

8

Programming with Functions

Dividing your program into manageable chunks of code is an idea that's fundamental to programming in every language. A **function** is a basic building block in all C++ programs. So far, we've made use of some of the functions from the standard library, but the only functions you've written yourself are the ones called **main()**. This chapter is all about defining your own functions.

In this chapter you will learn:

▶ What a function is, and why you should segment your programs into functions

▶ How to declare and define functions

▶ How arguments are passed to a function, and how a value is returned

▶ What pass-by-value means

▶ How specifying a parameter as a pointer affects the pass-by-value mechanism

▶ How using **const** as a qualifier for a parameter type affects the operation of a function

▶ What pass-by-reference means, and how you can declare a reference in your program

▶ How to return a value from a function

▶ What an inline function is

▶ The effect of declaring a variable as **static** within a function

Program Partitioning

All the programs we have written so far have consisted of just one function, **main()**. As you know, all C++ programs must have a function called **main()** — it's where program execution starts. However, C++ allows you to include as many other functions in your programs as you need, and we've already used quite a few functions from the standard library in our examples. Defining and using your own functions is just as easy. An illustration of the overall structure of an arbitrary program divided into several functions is shown below.

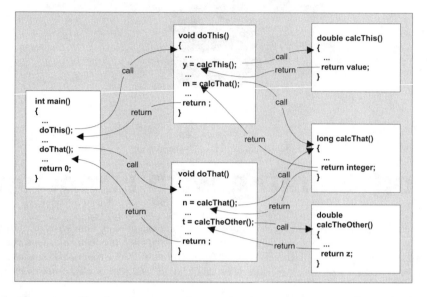

Generally, when you call a function at a given point in your program, the code that the function contains is executed; when it is finished, execution of the program continues immediately after the point where the function was called. Any function can call other functions (that's what **main()** does, after all) that may in turn call other functions so, a single function call could result in several functions being executed.

When one function calls another, which calls another, and so on, you have a situation where several functions are still in action, and each function is waiting for the function that it called to return. In the diagram above, **main()** calls **doThat()**, which calls **calcThat()**, so all three functions are in progress simultaneously. While the **calcThat()** function is executing, the **doThat()** function is waiting for it to return, and **main()** is waiting for **doThat()** to return.

For a function to be executing, the code for it must be resident somewhere in memory. Now, it's all very well saying that one function 'waits for another to return', but in order for that to happen, something must keep track of where in memory calls were made from, and where functions must return to. This information is all recorded and maintained automatically in the **call stack**. The call stack will contain information on all the outstanding function calls at any given time, as well as details of the arguments passed to each function. The debugging facilities that come with most C++ development systems usually provide ways for you to view the call stack during execution of your program.

Why you should Partition your Programs

There are several reasons for partitioning your programs. First, it makes programs much easier to read and to manage. It is easy to envisage how **main()** could become an unmanageable size, by taking an extreme example. Many applications these days run to hundreds of thousands of lines of code, and some into millions of lines. Just imagine trying to deal with **main()** if it contained 100,000 lines of code! Grasping the logic of the program would be just about impossible, as would be tracking down anything but the simplest bug. Partitioning a program of this sort of size is absolutely essential.

Second, functions can be reused. For example, suppose that you wrote a function to sort strings for use in one particular program. There is nothing to prevent you from using that same function in another context. The standard library is a powerful example of the benefits of reusing functions. Thousands of hours of programming and testing effort have been invested developing the standard library, but you have immediate access to the functionality that it provides.

Third, breaking your program down into several functions can reduce the amount of memory required to run it. Most applications involve some calculation that is used repeatedly. If the code for such a calculation is contained in a function that you call when needed, then the code for that calculation is written just once. Without such a function, it would be necessary to repeat the code each time it was needed, and so the compiled program would be larger.

Understanding Functions

You've written a quite few **main()** functions by now, so you should have a pretty good idea of what a function looks like, but we'll go over the basic ideas just to be sure everything is clear. Let's look first at the broad principles of how a function works:

A function is a self-contained block of code with a specific purpose. The immediate implication of this is that you need a reasonably clear idea of how the solution to your programming problem breaks down into functional units. With C++, there's actually rather more to it than that, but we can defer detailed discussion until we begin to talk about defining data types in Chapter 11. You'll find that this will have a profound effect on the approach that you take to designing a program.

For the moment, let's look at how to put a function together. During the discussion, it will be helpful to have the following example in mind:

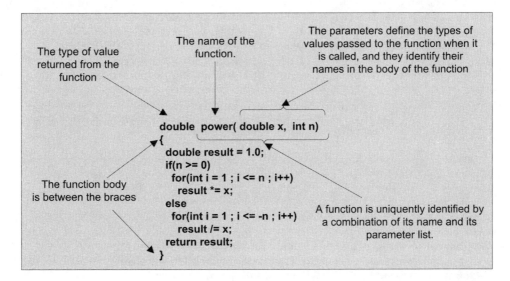

Defining a Function

You specify what a function does in a **function definition**, completely shown in the illustration. There are two parts to the definition: the **function header**, which is the first line of the definition, before the opening brace, and the **function body**, which lies between the braces. As you know from your experience with **main()**, the function body contains the code that is executed when you call the function.

The Function Header

Let's first examine the function header of the example. This is the first line of the function:

```
double power(double x, int n)
```

It consists of three parts: the data type of the **return value** (which is **double** in this case); the name of the function, **power**; and the function's **parameter list**, enclosed between parentheses. The names of the parameters here are **x** and **n**, and these are the names that will be used in the statements that specify what the function does. They will correspond to the arguments passed when the function is called. The parameter **x** is of type **double**, and the parameter **n** is of type **int**, so when the function is called, values of these types should be passed to it.

> *Note that no semicolon is required at the end of the function header.*

The General Form of a Function Header

The general form of a function header can be written as follows:

return_type FunctionName(parameter_list)

The *FunctionName* is the name that you use to call the function for execution in a program. It is usually good practice to give each of your functions a different name, but as you saw with some of the standard library functions in Chapter 6, it is possible for several different functions to have the same name, as long as each function has a different parameter list.

Function names are governed by the same rules as variable names. Therefore, a function name is a sequence of letters and digits, the first of which is a letter, and where an underscore counts as a letter. The name of your function should generally reflect what it does, so a function that counts beans might be called **CountBeans()**, while a function that calculates the result of raising a value to a given power could be called **power()**.

The *return_type* sets the data type of the value that is to be returned by the function, and can be any legal data type — including any data types that you've created yourself. If the function does not return a value, the return type is specified by the keyword **void**.

The *parameter_list* identifies what can be passed to our function from the calling function, and specifies the type and name of each parameter. A parameter name is used within the body of the function to access the item of data that was passed by the calling function. It may be the case that a function doesn't have any parameters, which is indicated by an empty parameter list, or by the keyword void. A function that has no parameters and does not return a value would therefore have the header:

```
void MyFunction()
```

Or alternatively:

```
void MyFunction(void)
```

Note that the type of a parameter cannot be **void**.

> *Since a function with a return type specified as* **void** *doesn't return a value, it can't be used in an expression in the calling program. The function doesn't evaluate to anything, so trying to test its value or assign it to something wouldn't make sense. Attempting to use such a function in this way will cause the compiler to generate an error message.*

The Function Body

A function performs its computations by executing the statements in its body. In our example , the first line of the function body declares a **double** variable called **result**, which is initialized with the value 1.0. **result** is an automatic variable: it's defined locally in the function, and it exists within the body of the function. This means that the variable **result** ceases to exist after the function has completed its execution.

Calculation is performed in one of the two **for** loops, depending on the value of **n**. If **n** is greater than or equal to zero, the first **for** loop will be executed. If the value of **n** happens to *be* zero, the body of the loop will not be executed at all, since the loop condition will immediately be **false**. In this event, **result** will be left at 1.0. Otherwise, the loop control variable **i** will assume successive values from **1** to **n**, and the variable **result** will be multiplied by **x** once for each loop iteration, which will generate the required value. If **n** is negative, the second **for** loop will be executed, which divides **result** by **x** for each loop iteration.

Always remember that the variables declared within the body of a function, and all the function parameters, are local to the function. The names of the variables and parameters used in this function can legally be used in other functions for quite different purposes, if you so desire. The scope of variables declared within a function is determined in the way that we have already seen: a variable is created at the point at which it is defined, and ceases to exist at the end of the block containing it. The only exceptions to this rule are variables declared as **static**, and we shall discuss these a little later in the chapter.

Before we discuss arguments, parameters, and return values in more depth, let's give our function **power()** a whirl in a complete program.

Try It Out – Using a Function

We can exercise the function **power()** with the following example:

```
// Program 8.1 Calculating powers
#include <iostream>
#include <iomanip>
using namespace std;
```

```
// Function to calculate x to the power n
double power(double x, int n)
{
  double result = 1.0;
  if(n >= 0)
    for(int i = 0 ; i < n ; i++)
      result *= x;
  else
    for(int i = 0 ; i < -n ; i++)
      result /= x;
  return result;
}

int main()
{
  cout << endl;

  // Calculate powers of 8 from -3 to +3
  for(int i = -3 ; i <= 3 ; i++)
    cout << setw(10) << power(8.0, i);

  cout << endl;
  return 0;
}
```

This program produces the output:

```
0.00195313   0.015625       0.125          1           8          64         512
```

How It Works

All the action occurs in the **for** loop in **main()**:

```
for(int i = -3 ; i <= 3 ; i++)
  cout << setw(10) << power(8.0, i);
```

The **power()** function is called seven times. The first argument is 8.0 on each occasion, but the second argument has successive values of **i**, from –3 to +3. Thus, seven values are output, corresponding to 8^{-3}, 8^{-2}, 8^{-1}, 8^0, 8^1, 8^2, and 8^3.

Parameters and Arguments

You pass information to a function by means of the **arguments** that you specify when you invoke it. The arguments are placed between parentheses following the function name in the call, as in this line from the example above:

```
cout << setw(10) << power(8.0, i);
```

The arguments that you specify when you call a function replace the parameters that you used in its definition. The code in the function then executes as though it was written using your argument values assigned to the corresponding parameters. The relationship between the arguments in a call to a function and the parameters in its definition is illustrated below:

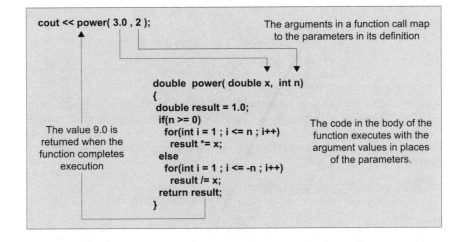

The difference between arguments and parameters is quite subtle. A parameter appears in a function definition and specifies the data type expected by the function. An argument is the actual value passed to the function when you call it.

The sequence of the arguments in the function call must correspond to the sequence of the parameters in the parameter list in the function definition. It's also a good idea to make sure that the data types of your arguments correspond to those demanded by the parameter list: the compiler will not necessarily warn you if it needs to make implicit type conversions, and so you run the risk of losing information.

Within a program, C++ will allow you to define a number of functions with the same name. Functions that share a common name must have parameter lists. The combination of the function's name and parameter list is called the **function signature**. When there are multiple functions with the same name within a program, the compiler uses the function signature to establish which of the functions has been called. This is another good reason for ensuring that your argument and parameter types correspond.

Return Values

In general, when a function with a return type other than **void** is called, it must return a single value of the type specified in the function header. The return value is calculated within the body of the function, and is returned when execution of the function is complete.

Thus, in any expression in which the function **power()** is called, **power()** will act as a value of type **double**. However, you don't *have* to call a function that returns a value from within an expression. You can just call the function by itself, with a statement such as:

```
power(10.5, 2);
```

Here, the function will be executed and the value returned from it will be discarded. Executing **power()** in this way is rather inefficient, but this is not necessarily the case with all functions. For example, we might have a function that copies a file, and for which the return value just provides additional information about the operation (success or failure, perhaps) that you may choose to discard on occasions. Of course, this is also the way that functions with a return type of **void** are called.

The fact that a function can return only a single value might appear to constrain us, but this really isn't the case. The single value returned could be a *pointer* to anything you like: an array of data, or even an array of pointers. A *particular* function always returns a value of a given type.

The return Statement

The **return** statement in our example returns the value of **result** to the point where the function was called. What might immediately strike you is that I just claimed that **result** ceases to exist on completion of the function, so how is it returned? The answer is that a *copy* of the value being returned is made automatically, and this copy is made available to the calling point of the function.

The general form of the return statement is as follows:

return   *expression*;

Here, *expression* must evaluate to a value of the type specified in the function header for the return value. The expression can be anything you want, as long as you end up with a value of the required type. It can include function calls, and it can even include a call of the same function in which it appears, as we shall see in the next chapter.

If the return type has been specified as **void**, there can be no expression appearing in the **return** statement. It must be written simply as:

```
    return;
```

If the closing brace of a function body is reached during execution, this is equivalent to executing a **return** statement with no expression. In fact, when the return type of the function is **void**, this is the preferred way to operate. Of course, in a function with a return type other than **void**, this would be an error and the function would not compile.

Function Declarations

Our previous example, Program 8.1, worked perfectly well, but let's try rearranging the code so that the function **main()** *precedes* the definition of the function **power()**. The code in the program file will look like this:

```
// Program 8.2 Calculating powers - rearranged
#include <iostream>
#include <iomanip>
using namespace std;

int main()
{
  cout << endl;

  // Calculate powers of 8 from -3 to +3
  for(int i = -3 ; i <= 3 ; i++)
    cout << setw(10) << power(8.0, i);

  cout << endl;
  return 0;
}
```

```
// Function to calculate x to the power n
double power(double x, int n)
{
  double result = 1.0;
  if(n >= 0)
    for(int i = 0 ; i < n ; i++)
      result *= x;
  else
    for(int i = 0 ; i < -n ; i++)
      result /= x;
  return result;
}
```

If you attempt to compile this version of the program, you won't succeed. The compiler has a problem because the function **power()** is not defined when it is processing the function **main()**. Of course, we could simply abandon this version in favor of Program 8.1, but this will not solve the problem generally. There are two relevant issues here.

First, as we shall see later, a program can consist of several source files. In this situation, the definition of the function called may not precede the function doing the calling — for that matter, it may be contained in a completely separate file.

Second, suppose that we have a function **A()** that calls a function **B()**, which in turn calls the function **A()** again. Then, if we put the definition of **A()** first, it will not compile because it calls **B()**; the same problem will arise if we define **B()** first, since it calls **A()**.

Naturally, there is a solution to these problems. We can declare a function before we use or define it by means of something called a **function prototype**.

Function Prototypes

A function prototype is a statement that describes a function sufficiently for the compiler to be able to compile calls to it. It declares the name of the function, its return type, and the types of its parameters. A function prototype is often referred to as a **function declaration**, and is similar to a variable declaration in that a function cannot be called within a program file unless the call is preceded in the file by a declaration. A definition of a function is also a declaration, which is why we didn't need a function prototype for **power()** in Program 8.1.

We could write the function prototype for our **power()** function as:

```
double power(double x, int n);
```

If you place the function prototype at the beginning of a program file that contains calls to the function, the compiler will be able to compile the code regardless of where the definition of the function is. To get Program 8.2 to compile, we can just insert the prototype for the function **power()** before the definition of **main()**:

```
// Program 8.2 Calculating powers - rearranged
#include <iostream>
#include <iomanip>
using namespace std;

double power(double x, int n);          // Prototype for power function
```

```
int main()
{
  // main() function as before
}

double power(double x, int n)
{
  // power() function as before
}
```

The function prototype here is identical to the function header, with a semicolon appended. A function prototype is always terminated by a semicolon, but in general it doesn't have to be *identical* to the function header. You can use different names (but not different types) for the parameters from those used in the definition. For instance:

```
double power(double value, int exponent);
```

This will work just as well. The benefit of the names we have chosen here is marginal, but it does illustrate how it can often be helpful to use more explanatory names in the function prototype, when such names would be too cumbersome for use in the function definition itself.

Since the compiler only needs to know what *type* each parameter is, you can even omit the parameter names from the prototype altogether, like this:

```
double power(double, int);
```

There is no particular merit in writing your function prototypes like this, and it is much less informative than the version with parameter names. If both function parameters were of the same type, then a prototype, like this one, would not give you any clue as to which parameter was which. I recommend that you always include parameter names in your function prototypes.

Using Function Prototypes

You should get into the habit of writing at the beginning of your program file a prototype for each function that you use in the program — with the exception of **main()**, of course, which never requires a prototype. This removes the possibility of compiler errors arising from the functions not being sequenced appropriately; also, it allows other programmers to get an overview of the functionality of your code.

We have been using library functions quite frequently, so where are the prototypes for these functions? In fact, they are in the standard header files that we have been including. One of the primary uses for header files is to collect together the function prototypes for a related group of functions. We will discuss this further in Chapter 10.

Passing Arguments to a Function

It is very important to understand precisely *how* arguments are passed to a function, because it will affect how you write your functions, and ultimately how they will operate. There are also a number of pitfalls to be avoided, so we will look at the mechanism for this quite closely.

As we have discussed, the arguments specified when a function is called should usually correspond in type and sequence to the parameters appearing in the definition of the function, but this does not have to be the case. If the type of an argument specified in a function call doesn't correspond with the parameter type in the function definition, then the compiler will (where possible) convert the argument type to the parameter type. The rules for automatic conversions of this kind are the same rules that control automatic conversions in an assignment statement, as we discussed in Chapter 3. If an automatic conversion turns out not to be possible, you will get an error message from the compiler.

There are two mechanisms used generally in C++ to pass arguments to functions. One is called the **pass-by-value** method, and the other is called the **pass-by-reference** method. We will look into the pass-by-value mechanism first, and then come back to the pass-by-reference method afterwards.

The Pass-by-Value Mechanism

With this mechanism for transferring data to a function, the variables or constants that you specify as arguments are not actually passed to a function at all. Instead, just as with the return value, copies of the arguments are created, and these copies are used as the values to be transferred. We can illustrate this in a diagram, using the example of our **power()** function:

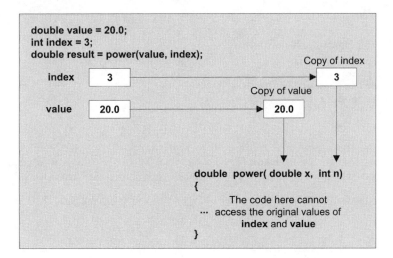

Each time you call the **power()** function, the compiler arranges for copies of the arguments that you specify to be stored in a temporary location in memory, which is the call stack I mentioned earlier in this chapter. During execution, all references to the function parameters in the code making up the body of the function will be mapped to these temporary copies of the arguments. Once the execution of the function is complete, the copies of the arguments are discarded.

We can demonstrate the effects of this with a simple example.

Try It Out – Passing Arguments to a Function

We can write a function that attempts to modify one of its arguments, and of course fails miserably.

```cpp
// Program 8.3 Failing to modify the original value of a function argument
#include <iostream>
#include <iomanip>
using namespace std;

double changeIt(double it);                  // Function prototype

int main()
{
  double it = 5.0;
  double result = changeIt(it);

  cout << "After function execution, it = " << it      << endl
       << "Result returned is "                        << result << endl;

  return 0;
}

// Function to attempt to modify an argument and return it
double changeIt(double it)
{
  it += 10.0;                                // This modifies the copy of the original
  cout << endl
       << "Within function, it = " << it << endl;
  return it;
}
```

This example will produce the output:

```
Within function, it = 15
After function execution, it = 5
Result returned is 15
```

How It Works

You can see from the output that adding 10 to the variable **it** in the function **changeIt()** has no effect on the variable **it** in **main()**. The variable **it** in the function **changeIt()** is local to the function, and will refer to a copy of whatever argument value was passed when the function was called.

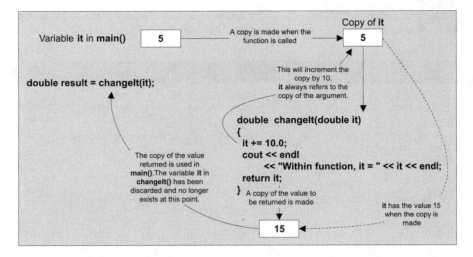

Of course, when the value of **it** that is local to **changeIt()** is returned, a copy of *its* current value is made, and therefore that copy is returned to the calling program.

This pass-by-value mechanism provides quite a lot of security to the calling program. But suppose that we *do* want to modify values in the calling function. Can we find a way to do it when we need to? Sure we can — one way of doing it is to use a pointer.

Passing a Pointer to a Function

When you use a pointer as an argument, the pass-by-value mechanism operates just as it did before. However, a pointer contains the address of another variable, and a copy of the pointer will point to exactly the same place in memory as the original.

We could change the definition of our **changeIt()** function to accept an argument of type **double***. In **main()**, we can then pass the *address* of the variable **it** when we call the function. Of course, we must also change the code in the body of **changeIt()** to dereference the pointer that is passed. The way that this works is illustrated below:

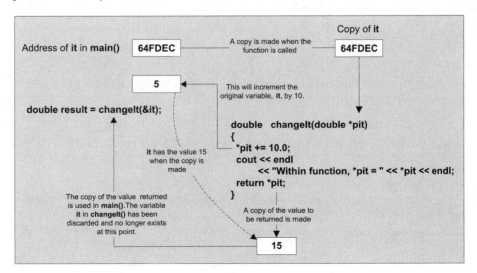

Since the function **changeIt()** now has the address of the original location in **main()** where **it** is stored, it can modify the variable directly. Let's see this in operation.

Try It Out – Passing a Pointer

We can change the last example to use a pointer to demonstrate the effect:

```cpp
// Program 8.4 Modifying the original value of a function argument
#include <iostream>
#include <iomanip>
using namespace std;

double changeIt(double* pointer_to_it);   // Function prototype

int main()
{
  double it = 5.0;
  double result = changeIt(&it);            // Now we pass the address

  cout << "After function execution, it = " << it      << endl
       << "Result returned is "                << result << endl;

  return 0;
}

// Function to modify an argument and return it
double changeIt(double* pit)
{
  *pit += 10.0;                             // This modifies the original
  cout << endl
       << "Within function, *pit = " << *pit << endl;
  return *pit;
}
```

This version of the program produces the output:

```
Within function, *pit = 15
After function execution, it = 15
Result returned is 15
```

How It Works

Since the parameter type has been changed in the definition of **changeIt()**, we have altered the function prototype:

```cpp
double changeIt(double* pointer_to_it);  // Function prototype
```

We have also used a different parameter name from the one used in the function definition — just to prove that we can!

In **main()**, after declaring and initializing the variable **it**, the address of the variable is passed to the **changeIt()** function when it is called:

```cpp
double result = changeIt(&it);          // Now we pass the address
```

We don't need to create a pointer variable to hold the address of **it**. Since we only need the address to pass to the function, we are able to use the address-of operator in the function call.

The new version of the **changeIt()** function uses the dereference operator to add 10 to the value stored in the **it** variable that was defined back in **main()**:

```
*pit += 10.0;                          // This modifies the original
```

The function also returns this modified value with the statement:

```
return *pit;
```

A copy is still made of the value being returned; this always happens automatically for the value being returned from a function.

This version of **changeIt()** serves only to illustrate how a pointer parameter can allow a variable in the calling function to be modified — it is not a model of how a function should be written. Since we are modifying the value of **it** directly, returning its value is somewhat superfluous here.

Passing Arrays to a Function

Because an array name can be treated as an address, you can also pass an array as an argument to a function, just by using its name. In this case, the address of the array is copied and passed to the function being called, providing a number of advantages.

First, passing the address of an array is more efficient than passing the array by value, since copying large arrays would be very time-consuming. In fact, arrays *cannot* be passed by value. Second, and more important, because the function called does not deal with the original array address but with a copy of it, the function can treat the parameter as a pointer in the fullest sense — including modifying the address it contains. Let's try the most straightforward case first.

Try It Out – Passing an Array as a Function Argument

We can illustrate this by writing a function to compute the average of a number of values that are passed to the function in an array.

```
// Program 8.5 Passing an array
#include <iostream>
using namespace std;

double average(double array[], int count);     // Function prototype

int main()
{
  double values[] = {1.0, 2.0, 3.0, 4.0, 5.0, 6.0, 7.0, 8.0, 9.0, 10.0};

  cout << endl
       << "Average = "
       << average(values, (sizeof values) / (sizeof values[0]))
       << endl;
```

```
      return 0;
   }

   // Function to compute an average
   double average(double array[], int count)
   {
      double sum = 0.0;                        // Accumulate total in here
      for(int i = 0 ; i < count ; i++)
        sum += array[i];                       // Sum array elements

      return sum / count;                      // Return average
   }
```

This will produce the very brief output:

```
Average = 5.5
```

How It Works

The function **average()** is designed to work with an array of any length. As you can see from the prototype, it accepts two arguments: the array, and a count of the number of elements in the array:

```
double average(double array[], int count);    // Function prototype
```

The type of the first parameter is specified as an array of values of type **double**. It is not possible to specify the size of the array between the square brackets, and doing so will have no effect. This is because the size of the first dimension of an array is not part of its type (you'll remember a similar issue arising when we considered pointers to multidimensional arrays). In fact, you can pass *any* one-dimensional array as an argument to this function, which will rely on the correct value for the **count** parameter being supplied by the caller to indicate the number of elements in the array.

Within the body of the **average()** function, the computation is expressed in the way you would expect:

```
double average(double array[], int count)
{
   double sum = 0.0;                        // Accumulate total in here
   for(int i = 0 ; i < count ; i++)
     sum += array[i];                       // Sum array elements

   return sum / count;                      // Return average
}
```

There is no significant difference between this and the way we would write the same computation if we implemented it directly in **main()**. The function has no way of checking that the array actually accommodates the number of elements indicated by **count**, and it will quite happily access memory locations outside the actual array if the value of **count** is greater than the length of the array. It is up to us to ensure that this doesn't happen!

The function is called in **main()** in the output statement:

```
cout << endl
     << "Average = "
     << average(values, (sizeof values) / (sizeof values[0]))
     << endl;
```

Here, the first argument to the **average()** function is the array name, **values**, and the second argument is an expression that evaluates to the number of elements in the array.

In this example, the elements of the array passed to **average()** were accessed using normal array notation. We've said that we can also treat an array passed to a function as a pointer, and use pointer notation for the calculation. Let's try that out.

Try It Out – Using Pointer Notation When Passing Arrays

We can modify the function in Program 8.5 to work with pointer notation throughout, even though we are using an array. We will change the function prototype and header to reflect the use of pointer notation (rather than array notation) for the first parameter, although this is not strictly necessary. You could use pointer notation in the body of the function with the type of the first argument still specified as an array. Here's the modified version of the program:

```
// Program 8.6 Handling an array parameter as a pointer
#include <iostream>
using namespace std;

double average(double* array, int count);        // Function prototype

int main()
{
  double values[] = {1.0, 2.0, 3.0, 4.0, 5.0, 6.0, 7.0, 8.0, 9.0, 10.0};

  cout << endl
       << "Average = "
       << average(values, (sizeof values) / (sizeof values[0]))
       << endl;

  return 0;
}

// Function to compute an average
double average(double* array, int count)
{
  double sum = 0.0;                               // Accumulate total in here
  for(int i = 0 ; i < count ; i++)
    sum += *array++;                              // Sum array elements

  return sum / count;                             // Return average
}
```

The output will be exactly the same as the previous version of the program.

How It Works

As you can see, the program needed very few changes to make it work by using the array as a pointer. The prototype and the function header have been changed, although in fact neither change is absolutely necessary. (Try replacing the prototype and function header here with the corresponding lines from Program 8.5, but leaving the function body written in terms of a pointer. You will find that it will work just as well.)

The most interesting aspect of this version of the program is the **for** loop statement:

```
sum += *array++;                            // Sum array elements
```

Here we appear to break a rule, "that we can't modify an address specified as an array name" — by incrementing the address stored in **array**. Of course, we are not really breaking the rule at all. Remember that the pass-by-value mechanism makes a copy of the original array address, and passes that to the function. We are modifying the copy here, and the original array address will be quite unaffected. Generally, whenever we pass a one-dimensional array to a function, we are free to treat the value passed as a pointer in every sense, and change the address in any way we wish.

const Pointer Parameters

You may wish to make sure that a function does not inadvertently modify elements of the array that is passed to it. All you need to do is use **const** in the specification of the parameter type. For instance, if we wanted to prevent the function **average()** from altering elements of its first parameter, we could write the function as:

```
double average(const double* array, int count)
{
  double sum = 0.0;                         // Accumulate total in here
  for(int i = 0 ; i < count ; i++)
    sum += *array++;                        // Sum array elements

  return sum / count;                       // Return average
}
```

Now the compiler will verify that the elements of the array are not modified in the body of the function. Of course, you would also need to modify the function prototype to reflect the new type for the first parameter; remember that **const** types are quite different from **non-const** types.

When you declare a pointer parameter as **const**, you are saying to the compiler, "When this function is called, whatever the pointer argument points to should be treated as a constant." This has two consequences. The compiler will check the code in the body of the function to make sure your claim is correct, and that you don't try to change the value being pointed to. It will also allow the function to be called with an argument that points to a constant.

Note that there is no purpose in declaring an ordinary parameter type, such as an **int**, as **const**. Since the pass-by-value mechanism will make a copy of the argument when the function is called, you have no possibility of modifying the original value from within the body of the function.

Passing Multidimensional Arrays to a Function

Given what we have already seen, passing a multidimensional array to a function is quite straightforward. For a two-dimensional array, declared as follows:

```
double beans[2][4];
```

You could write the prototype of a hypothetical function **yield()** like this:

```
double yield(double beans[2][4]);
```

We have explicitly specified the size of both dimensions here, but in fact there is no way to check that the array's first dimension size is 2. With arrays, the size of the first dimension is not part of the type definition, so the type of the array **beans** is actually **double[][4]**. Any two-dimensional array with the second dimension size specified as 4 could be passed to this function.

> **FYI**
>
> How does the compiler know that this line is defining an array of the dimension sizes shown as an argument, and not a single array element? The answer is simple: you can't write a single array element as a parameter in a function definition or prototype, although of course you can pass one as an argument when you call a function. For a function accepting a single element of an array as an argument, the parameter itself would just have the type of that element. The array context doesn't apply.

When you're defining a multidimensional array as a parameter, you should omit the first dimension's size (unless you just want to indicate that your function is only intended to work with an array of a fixed size). Of course, the function will then need some way of knowing the size of the first dimension, and for this you can employ the same method we've been using for one-dimensional arrays in this chapter. You can add a second parameter to specify the size of the first dimension of the array:

```
double yield(double beans[][4], int index);
```

In case you're wondering, you can't circumvent the need for the extra parameter by using **sizeof()** within the function to determine the size of the array. Using **sizeof()** on an array parameter name within the body of a function will return the size of the pointer to which the array name is equivalent.

Let's try passing a two-dimensional array to a function with a concrete example.

Try It Out – Passing Multidimensional Arrays

We can implement the **yield()** function to sum the elements of the array that is passed to it. Here's the code to do that and exercise the function:

```
// Program 8.7 Passing a two-dimensional array to a function
#include <iostream>
using namespace std;
```

```
double yield(double values[][4], int n);

int main()
{
  double beans[3][4] = {
                          { 1.0,  2.0,  3.0,  4.0},
                          { 5.0,  6.0,  7.0,  8.0},
                          { 9.0, 10.0, 11.0, 12.0}
                       };

  cout << endl
       << "Yield = " << yield(beans, sizeof beans / sizeof beans[0])
       << endl;
  return 0;
}

// Function to compute total yield
double yield(double array[][4], int count)
{
  double sum = 0.0;
  for(int i = 0 ; i < count ; i++)       // Loop through number of rows
    for(int j = 0 ; j < 4 ; j++)         // Loop through elements in a row
      sum += array[i][j];
  return sum;
}
```

This will produce the output:

```
Yield = 78
```

How It Works

The first parameter to the **yield()** function is defined as an array of an arbitrary number of rows, with each row having four elements. When we call the function, the first argument is the array **beans**, which has three rows. The second argument is specified by dividing the total length of the array (in bytes) by the length of the first row. This will evaluate to the number of rows in the array.

The computation in the function is simply a nested **for** loop, with the inner loop summing elements of a single row, and the outer loop repeating this for each row.

In a function with a multidimensional array argument, pointer notation doesn't really apply particularly well. In the example above, when the array is passed, it passes an address that points to an array of four elements (a row). This doesn't lend itself to an easy pointer operation within the function. We would need to modify the statement in the nested **for** loop to the following:

```
sum += *(*(array+i)+j);
```

I think you will agree that the computation is clearer in array notation!

The Pass-by-Reference Mechanism

A **reference** is simply an alias for another variable. When you specify a function parameter as a reference type, your function will use the **pass-by-reference** mechanism for transferring the argument. When the function is called, the argument corresponding to a reference parameter is *not* copied, because the parameter name simply becomes an alias for the argument value in the calling program. Wherever the parameter name is used in the body of the function, it will access the argument value in the calling function directly.

To specify a reference type, you just add **&** after the type name. To specify a type as 'reference to **int**' for example, you write the type as **int&**. The diagram below shows how calling a function with a reference parameter works:

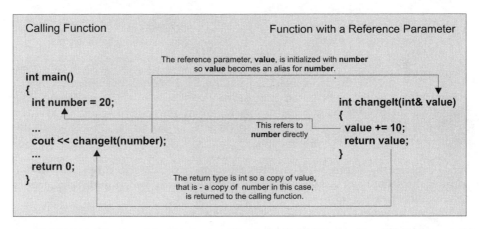

Whenever the **changeIt()** function is called, the reference parameter, **value**, is initialized with the specified argument, so while **changeIt()** is executing, **value** becomes an alternative name for the variable that was passed as an argument, **number**. If you call the function again later with a different argument, **value** will then become an alias for that argument.

Specifying a function parameter as a reference has two major effects. First, the argument is not copied, so the function accesses the argument in the caller directly. Second, the absence of the copying process makes the function call faster. This, and other aspects, will be of major importance when we consider passing class objects to a function. For now, let's look at using reference parameters a little more closely.

In the rush for the extra efficiency you get by specifying reference parameters for your functions, it's easy to forget about the other aspect of their operation. You can modify the original argument within your function, but the syntax of references makes doing so less obvious than when you use pointers for the same purpose. The potential for error by mistakenly changing an argument value is significant, and there are safer ways of changing original arguments within functions.

Function with a Pointer Parameter	Function with a Reference Parameter
``` int changeIt(int* value) { *value += 10; return *value; } ```	``` int changeIt(int& value) { value += 10; return value; } ```
An address is passed to the function, indicating clearly the possibility that the argument's value could be altered by the function.	A value is passed in the form of a reference; this gives no indication of the possibility that the arguments' value could be altered by the function.
``` int number = 20; cout << changeIt(&number); ```	``` int number = 20; cout << changeIt(number); ```

If you specify a parameter that you intend to modify as a pointer, then the argument passed when the function is called must be an address, so it becomes clear in the calling program that there is potential for the argument to be changed. An argument corresponding to a reference parameter is just an ordinary variable name, so there is no such clue. The diagram illustrates the difference between these two situations.

How do we exploit the overhead-free nature of passing references to functions without compromising the security of our arguments? The answer is to use **const** references, so let's investigate the effect of this in the next example.

Try It Out – Reference Parameters

Let's try a simple program that uses a function called **larger()**, which returns the larger of two values. We will use this function in various forms to explore how reference parameters can affect the way a function operates. Here's the first version:

```
// Program 8.8 Using reference parameters
#include <iostream>

using namespace std;

int larger(int& m, int& n);

int main()
{
  int value1 = 10;
  int value2 = 20;
  cout << endl << larger(value1, value2) << endl;

  return 0;
}
```

```
// Function to the larger of two integers
int larger(int& m, int& n)
{
  return m > n ? m : n;                  // Return the larger value
}
```

The output of this program is simply the value 20, as you might expect.

How It Works

Because the function **larger()** has reference parameters, it operates with the *original* values of the arguments **value1** and **value2** when it is called in **main()** with the statement:

```
cout << endl << larger(value1, value2) << endl;
```

If you have any doubts about this, try adding a statement in the body of the **larger()** function to alter the second parameter value:

```
int larger(int& m, int& n)
{
  n = 30;
  return m > n ? m : n;                  // Return the larger value
}
```

If you then output the value of **value2** after **larger()** has been called in **main()**, you will see that its value has indeed been changed.

Suppose we wanted to compare **value1** with some constant value: 15, say, and return the larger of these values. We might try to add the following statement to **main()**:

```
int main()
{
  int value1 = 10;
  int value2 = 20;
  cout << endl << larger(value1, value2) << endl;
  cout << endl << larger(value1, 15) << endl;

  return 0;
}
```

With this statement in place, the program will no longer compile. The compiler will not allow a reference to be created to the constant 15, because it knows that the function has direct access to it and may modify it. There is a significant conclusion from this:

> You can't pass a constant as an argument to a function when the parameter has been specified as a non-**const** reference.

Using const References

We can overcome this difficulty with **larger()** if we alter the function definition so that the parameters are **const** references. The prototype would then be:

```
int larger(const int& m, const int& n);
```

Now the function will work with variables and constants. As long as you're not intending to modify the argument that is passed, you can always define the parameter as **const**. We've got direct access to the arguments that are passed from the calling function (avoiding copying), the compiler will check that we have not included code to modify them, and that the function will work with variables and constant values. By using **const** reference parameters, we have been able to combine the greater performance and efficiency that reference parameters provide with the security of the pass-by-value method.

References versus Pointers

In most situations, using a reference parameter will be preferable to using a pointer. You should declare reference parameters as **const** wherever possible, as this provides security for the caller arguments. Of course, if you *need* to modify a reference parameter within the body of a function, you can't declare it as **const**, but you should consider whether a pointer might be a better parameter type in this situation. It is always apparent to the caller that a pointer parameter can be modified.

An important difference between a pointer and a reference is that a pointer can be null, whereas a reference always refers to something. If you want to allow the possibility of a null argument, your only option is a pointer parameter. You will begin to see in Chapter 12 that reference parameters provide some extraordinarily powerful facilities in the context of classes, and in some instances they will enable you to achieve results that would be impossible without them.

Declaring References

References don't only appear in the form of function parameters. A reference can exist in its own right, as an alias for another variable. Suppose that we have a variable declared as follows:

```
long number = 0;
```

We can declare a reference for the variable by using the following declaration statement:

```
long& rnumber = number;        // Declare a reference to variable number
```

The ampersand (**&**) following the type **long** indicates that a reference is being declared, and the initializing value following the equals sign is specified as the variable name **number**. Therefore, **rnumber** is of type 'reference to **long**'. Just as when you're declaring pointers, you can also place the **&** adjacent to the variable name, so we could have written the previous statement as:

```
long &rnumber = number;        // Declare a reference to variable number
```

> *The compiler doesn't mind which of these you use; in this book, we will use the former notation.*

The use of **&** in declaring a reference will seem a little confusing at first. Its use in the context of references looks similar to what we saw previously, when we were obtaining the address of a variable. However, with a little practice you will soon appreciate the difference.

When you declare a reference, it must *always* be initialized with the name of the variable for which it is an alias. It is not possible to declare a reference without initializing it. A further constraint is that a reference is fixed — you cannot change a reference once it has been declared;

it will always be an alias for the same variable. The reason that a reference parameter can appear to refer to different variables at different times is that the reference parameter is recreated and reinitialized each time the function is called.

A reference can always be used in place of the original variable name. For example:

```
rnumber += 10;
```

This statement has the effect of incrementing the variable **number** by 10, because **rnumber** is an alias for **number**. To make sure that you have the difference clear in your mind, let's contrast the reference **rnumber** with the pointer, **pnumber**, declared in this statement:

```
long* pnumber = &number;          // Initialize a pointer with an address
```

This declares the pointer **pnumber**, and initializes it with the address of the variable **number**. The variable can then be incremented with a statement such as:

```
*pnumber += 10;                    // Increment number through a pointer
```

There is a significant distinction here between using a pointer and using a reference: a pointer needs to be dereferenced to obtain or operate on the value of the variable to which it points. With a reference, there is no need for dereferencing. In some ways, a reference is like a pointer that has already been dereferenced, although it can't be changed to refer to another variable. The reference is the complete equivalent of the variable for which it is a reference.

That's all we need to discuss about references for now, but it's far from the end of the matter. We will be applying them extensively when we begin to look at classes in three chapters' time.

Arguments to main()

You can define the function **main()** to accept arguments that are entered on the command line when your program is executed. The types of parameters that you can specify are standardized: you can either define **main()** with no parameters, as we have done in all our examples up to now, or you can define **main()** in the form:

```
int main(int argc, char* argv[])
{
  // Code for main()
}
```

The first parameter, **argc**, is a count of the number of strings on the command line. The second parameter, **argv**, is an array that contains pointers to each of the strings that were entered on the command line, including the name of the program itself. The last element in the array **argv** (that is, **argv[argc]**) will always be 0, and the number of elements in **argv** will be **argc + 1**.

Let's take a couple of examples. Suppose that to run your program, you enter the following on the command line:

```
Myprog
```

In this case, **argc** will be 1 and **argv[]** will contain two elements. The first element will contain the address of the string **"Myprog"**, and the second element will be 0.

Alternatively, if you enter this:

```
Myprog 2 3.5 "Rip Van Winkle"
```

`argc` will be 4 and `argv[]` will have five elements. The first four elements will point to the strings `"Myprog.exe"`, `"2"`, `"3.5"`, and `"Rip Van Winkle"`. The element `argv[4]` will be 0.

What you do with the command line arguments is entirely up to you. As an illustration of how to access the command line arguments, consider the following implementation of `main()`:

```cpp
#include <iostream>

using namespace std;

int main(int argc, char* argv[])
{
  for (int i = 0 ; i < argc ; i++)
    cout << endl << argv[i];

  cout << endl;
  return 0;
}
```

This will just list all the command line arguments, including the program name. Command line arguments can be anything at all: filenames to a file copy program, for example, or a name of a person to search for in a contact file. In other words, anything that is useful to have entered for your program when it is executed.

Default Parameter Values

There are many situations where it would be useful to assign default values to one or more of your function parameters. This would mean that you only needed to specify a value for an argument when you want something different from the default.

A simple example might be a function that you use to output a standard error message. Most of the time, a default message will suffice, but on occasions you might want to specify an alternative. You can do this by specifying the default value for a parameter in the function prototype. We could write the definition for a function to output a message as:

```cpp
void showError(const char* message)
{
  cout << endl << message << endl;
}
```

To specify a default message, we would write the string to be used as the default argument value in the *prototype* for this function, which could be written as:

```cpp
void showError(const char* message = "Program Error");
```

If you want to use the function to output the default message, you call it without an argument value:

```
    showError();                    // Display default message
```

This will display the output:

```
Program Error
```

When you want to provide a particular message, you can specify the argument to the function:

```
    showError("Nothing works!");
```

We could have defined the **showError()** function using an argument of type **string**, instead of a C-style string. In this case, the prototype with a default value for the parameter would be written:

```
void showError(const string message = "Program Error");
```

> *Of course, you would need to include the **string** header in the program, to make the **string** type available.*

Specifying a default parameter value in this way can make functions simpler to use, and you are not limited to just one default parameter — you can have as many as you want. Let's explore that a little further.

Multiple Default Parameter Values

When you write your function, any parameters for which you specify default values must be placed at the *end* of the parameter list. The reason for this is simple. To use the default value of a parameter when calling the function, you omit the corresponding argument. To omit arguments from the middle of the list would give the compiler considerable cause for confusion! The compiler assumes, therefore, that any omitted arguments correspond to the rightmost parameters.

Let's contrive an example of a function with several default parameter values. Suppose that we wrote a function to display one or more data values, several to a line, as follows:

```
void showData(const int data[], int count,
                              const string& title, int width, int perLine)
{
  cout << endl << title;                    // Display the title

  // Output the data values
  for(int i = 0 ; i < count ; i++)
  {
    if(i % perLine == 0)                     // Newline before the first
      cout << endl;                          // and after perLine

    cout << setw(width) << data[i];          // Display a data item
  }
  cout << endl;
}
```

The parameter **data** specifies the data values to be displayed, and **count** indicates how many there are. The third parameter is of type **const string&** and specifies a title to head the output. The fourth parameter determines the field width for each item, and the last parameter is the number of data items per line.

This long parameter list would be quite cumbersome in calls to the function — imagine having to specify all five parameters to output a single data item! We can use default values for some of the parameters to make it easier.

Try It Out – Using Multiple Default Parameter Values

Here's how we could use the function with defaults for all but the first parameter:

```cpp
// Program 8.9 Using multiple default parameter values
#include <iostream>
#include <iomanip>
#include <string>

using namespace std;

void showData(const int data[], int count = 1,
              const string& title = "Data Values", int width = 10, int perLine = 5);

int main()
{
  int samples[] = {1, 2, 3, 4, 5, 6, 7, 8, 9, 10, 11, 12};

  int dataItem = 99;
  showData(&dataItem);

  dataItem = 13;
  showData(&dataItem, 1, "Unlucky for some!");

  showData(samples, sizeof samples / sizeof samples[0]);
  showData(samples, sizeof samples / sizeof samples[0], "Samples");
  showData(samples, sizeof samples / sizeof samples[0], "Samples", 14);
  showData(samples, sizeof samples / sizeof samples[0], "Samples", 14, 4);

  return 0;
}

// Function to output one or more integer values
void showData(const int data[],
                   int count, const string& title, int width, int perLine)
{
  cout << endl << title;                    // Display the title

  // Output the data values
  for(int i = 0 ; i < count ; i++)
  {
    if(i % perLine == 0)                     // Newline before the first
      cout << endl;                          // and after perLine
```

```
        cout << setw(width) << data[i];        // Display a data item
    }
    cout << endl;
}
```

This produces the output:

```
Data Values
        99

Unlucky for some!
        13

Data Values
        1         2         3         4         5
        6         7         8         9        10
       11        12

Samples
        1         2         3         4         5
        6         7         8         9        10
       11        12

Samples
            1               2               3               4               5
            6               7               8               9              10
           11              12

Samples
            1               2               3               4
            5               6               7               8
            9              10              11              12
```

How It Works

The prototype for the **showData()** function specifies default values for all parameters except the first:

```
void showData(const int data[], int count = 1,
          const string& title = "Data Values", int width = 10, int perLine = 5);
```

As you can see from the third parameter, you can supply default values for a reference parameter in the same way as for parameters of a non-reference type. With the last four parameters all having default values, we have five ways to call the function: we can specify all five arguments, or omit the last one, or the last two, or the last three, or the last four. Remember that we can only omit arguments at the *end* of the list: you are not, for instance, allowed to omit the second and the fifth:

```
    showData(samples, , "Samples", 15);        // Wrong!
```

In the function **main()**, we have an array of integers for sample output, defined as:

```
    int samples[] = {1, 2, 3, 4, 5, 6, 7, 8, 9, 10, 11, 12};
```

This is used to exercise the **showData()** function. The first application of the function outputs a single data value:

```
int dataItem = 99;
showData(&dataItem);
```

Because the first parameter is an array of type **int**, we must pass the address of **dataItem** as the argument. The default value for **count** of 1 applies here, and the three other default parameter values also apply.

Next, we output a modified value for **dataItem**, along with a new title:

```
dataItem = 13;
showData(&dataItem, 1, "Unlucky for some!");
```

We only want a different title, but if we specify a third argument, we must also specify the second. The value for **count** is the same as the default, as we are still outputting a single data item.

We then output the contents of the **samples** array four times in the next four statements:

```
showData(samples, sizeof samples / sizeof samples[0]);
showData(samples, sizeof samples / sizeof samples[0], "Samples");
showData(samples, sizeof samples / sizeof samples[0], "Samples", 14);
showData(samples, sizeof samples / sizeof samples[0], "Samples", 14, 4);
```

For an array, we need to specify the **count** argument; otherwise **showData** will output only the first element of the array. Each successive statement specifies an additional argument.

When you use several parameters with default values, you need to take care to sequence the parameters appropriately. The parameters should be ordered so that the one that is *least* likely to be specified comes last, with each preceding parameter being the next most likely to require an explicit value. Obviously, this will be a fine judgement in many instances.

Returning Values from a Function

As you already know, you can return a value of any type from a function. This is quite straightforward when you're returning a value of one of the basic types, but there are some pitfalls when you are returning a pointer.

Returning a Pointer

When you return a pointer from a function, you must make absolutely sure that the address it points to is either 0, or a location in memory that is still valid in the calling function. In other words, the variable pointed to must still be *in scope* after the return to the calling function. This implies the following golden rule:

> *Never return the address of an automatic local variable from a function*

Let's look at an illustration. Suppose we wanted to write a function that would return the address of the larger of two values. This function might be used on the left of an assignment, so that you could change the variable that contains the larger value:

```
    *larger(value1, value2) = 100;        // Set the larger variable to 100
```

This sort of thing can easily lead you astray. Here's an implementation that doesn't work:

```
    int* larger(int a, int b)
    {
      if(a > b)
        return &a;                    // Wrong!
      else
        return &b;                    // Wrong!
    }
```

It's fairly easy to see what's wrong with this: **a** and **b** are local variables. Copies of the original integer argument values will be transferred to the local variables **a** and **b**, but when we return **&a** or **&b**, the variables at these addresses will be out of scope in the calling program. You should get a warning from your compiler if you try to compile this implementation of the function.

What we can do is specify the parameters as pointers:

```
    int* larger(int* a, int* b)
    {
      if(*a > *b)
        return a;                     // OK
      else
        return b;                     // OK
    }
```

We could call this function with the line:

```
    *larger(&value1, &value2) = 100;    // Set the larger variable to 100
```

Writing a function to return the address of the larger of two values is unlikely to be particularly useful, but a function that returns the address of the largest element in an array might be of more interest.

Try It Out – Returning a Pointer

We could extend the idea slightly by writing two functions: one to return the address of the element in an array with the smallest value, and the other to return the element with the largest value. We can also make use of a version of our **showData()** function. This program will modify an array of **double** values so that they fall within the interval 0 to 1. You might do this if you were only interested in the relative sizes of the values — scaling values to within a fixed range can make them easier to present graphically, for example.

```
// Program 8.10 Returning a pointer
#include <iostream>
#include <iomanip>
#include <string>
```

```cpp
using namespace std;

void showData(const double data[], int count = 1,
             const string& title = "Data Values", int width = 10, int perLine = 5);
double* largest(double data[], int count);
double* smallest(double data[], int count);

int main()
{
  double samples[] = {
                       11.0,   23.0,   13.0,   4.0,
                       57.0,   36.0, 317.0,  88.0,
                        9.0,  100.0, 121.0,  12.0
                     };

  const int count = sizeof samples / sizeof samples[0];

  showData(samples, count, "Original Values");

  int min = *smallest(samples, count);

  // Shift range of values so smallest is zero
  for(int i = 0; i < count ; i++)
    samples[i] -= min;

  int max = *largest(samples, count);

  // Normalize range to 0 to 1.0
  for(int i = 0; i < count ; i++)
    samples[i] /= max;

  showData(samples, count, "Normalized Values", 12);
  return 0;
}

// Function to find the largest of an array of double values
double* largest(double data[], int count)
{
  int indexMax = 0;
  for(int i = 1; i < count; i++)
    if(data[indexMax] < data[i])
      indexMax = i;

  return &data[indexMax];
}

// Function to find the smallest of an array of double values
double* smallest(double data[], int count)
{
  int indexMin = 0;
  for(int i = 1; i < count; i++)
   if(data[indexMin] > data[i])
     indexMin = i;

  return &data[indexMin];
}
```

```
// Function to display an array of double values
void showData(const double data[],
                    int count, const string& title, int width, int perLine)
{
  cout << endl << title;
  for(int i = 0 ; i < count ; i++)
  {
    if(i % perLine == 0)
      cout << endl;
    cout << setw(width) << data[i];
  }
  cout << endl;
}
```

This program will produce the output:

```
Original Values
        11          23          13         4         57
        36         317          88         9        100
       121          12

Normalized Values
  0.0223642   0.0607029    0.028754           0   0.169329
   0.102236           1    0.268371   0.0159744   0.306709
   0.373802   0.0255591
```

How It Works

This program uses two similar functions, **largest()** and **smallest()**, which return the addresses of the largest and smallest elements in a **double** array respectively. The code for the function **largest()** is:

```
double* largest(double data[], int count)
{
  int indexMax = 0;
  for(int i = 1; i < count; i++)
    if(data[indexMax] < data[i])
      indexMax = i;

  return &data[indexMax];
}
```

This starts by assuming that the first element of the array is the largest, specified by setting the value of **indexMax** to 0. The element at index position **indexMax** is compared to each of the others in the **for** loop. If the **indexMax** element is smaller than the current element within the loop, **indexMax** is set to the current index value. The function returns the address of the largest element, given by the expression **&data[indexMax]**, which uses the address-of operator. The **smallest()** function differs only in the comparison operator used in the **if** condition.

In **main()**, we define an array called **samples**. Then, we assign the number of array elements to **count**. This means that we don't have to recalculate the value each time we need it:

```
const int count = sizeof samples / sizeof samples[0];
```

We display the original values for the elements with the statement:

```
showData(samples, count, "Original Values");
```

Apart from the type of the first argument, the definition of the **showData()** function is the same as we have seen previously. The prototype for the function defines default values for the last four parameters, and we use the defaults for the last two in this case.

We use the **smallest()** function to find the lowest value in the **samples** array with the statement:

```
int min = *smallest(samples, count);
```

To obtain the *value* of the lowest element, we apply the dereference operator, *****, to the address returned by the function.

It's possible to shift the range of values, so that the lowest value is zero, by subtracting the current lowest value from each element in the array. We do this in the **for** loop:

```
for(int i = 0; i < count ; i++)
  samples[i] -= min;
```

Now that the range runs from zero to some highest value, we can modify the values so that they fall between 0 and 1 by dividing them by the current highest value, which is obtained using the **largest()** function:

```
int max = *largest(samples, count);
```

We then modify the values in another **for** loop, by dividing them by the current highest value:

```
for(int i = 0; i < count ; i++)
  samples[i] /= max;
```

Finally, we output the new values:

```
showData(samples, count, "Normalized Values", 12);
```

This time, we override the default for the field width to accommodate the number of decimal places produced for each value.

As a final point in this section, it's worth noting that because the **largest()** and **smallest()** functions return an address, which is an *lvalue*, we could use the value they return on the left of an assignment operation by employing the dereference operator:

```
*largest(samples, count) *= 2.0;
```

The statement above, for example, would double the value of the highest element in the **samples** array.

Returning a Reference

Returning a pointer from a function certainly served its purpose, but it can be problematic, especially when you begin use the function on the left of an assignment operator, as I suggested at the end of the last section. Pointers can be null, and an attempt to dereference a null pointer will result in the failure of your program.

The solution, as you will surely have guessed from the title of this section, is to return a *reference* from a function. Because a reference is an alias for another variable, we can state a golden rule for references that's rather like our golden rule for pointers, and applies for the same reasons of scope:

> *Never return a reference to an automatic local variable from a function.*

Returning a reference allows a call to the function to be used on the left of an assignment. Suppose we define our **larger()** function as:

```
int& larger(int& m, int& n)
{
  return m > n ? m : n;          // Return a reference to the larger value
}
```

The return type is a reference to **int**, and the parameters are non-**const** references. Since we want to return one or other of the reference parameters, we cannot declare the parameters as **const**. A reference return type is an lvalue, so it can appear on the left of an assignment, and can therefore be modified. In fact, returning a reference is the *only* way you can return an lvalue from a function.

We could now use the function to change the value of the larger of two arguments with a statement like this:

```
larger(value1, value2) = 50; // Change the value of the larger one to 50
```

With the function declared in this fashion, there is no way that we can use constants as arguments. Because our parameters are non-**const** references, the compiler simply will not allow it to happen. A reference parameter clearly permits the value to be changed, and changing a constant is not something the compiler will knowingly go along with.

We're not going to examine an extended example of using reference return types just at the moment, but you can be sure that we'll be meeting them again before long. As you'll discover, reference return types become essential when we start creating our own data types using classes.

Returning a New Variable from a Function

You can create a new variable in the free store within a function, and return it to the caller by means of a pointer return value. You just use the **new** operator to allocate the space, and return the address.

The hazard with using this technique is that you run the very real risk of creating a memory leak. Every time such a function is called, more memory will be allocated in the free store, and it is up to the *calling* function to take responsibility for releasing the memory by using the **delete** operator.

Inline Functions

With functions that are very short (the **larger()** function that we have been discussing is a good example), the overhead of the code the compiler generates to deal with passing arguments and returning a result will be significant compared with the code involved in doing the actual calculation. The execution times of the two types of code may be similarly related.

In extreme cases, the code for calling the function may occupy *more* memory than the code in the body of the function. In such circumstances, you might want to suggest to the compiler that it replace a call to the function with the actual code from the body of the function, suitably adjusted to deal with local names. This could make the program shorter, or faster, or possibly both.

You can suggest that the compiler perform this task by using the **inline** keyword in the definition of the function. For example:

```
inline int larger(int m, int n)
{
  return m > n ? m : n;
}
```

With this definition, you are suggesting that the compiler should replace calls with inline code. However, it is only a suggestion, and it depends on the compiler as to whether your suggestion is taken up. When you declare a function as **inline**, the definition must be available in every source file that calls the function. For this reason, the definition of an inline function usually appears in a header file rather than a source file, and the header is included into each source file that uses the function.

Different compilers apply different rules to determine whether a function defined as **inline** will have its calls replaced by inline code. A basic prerequisite is that such functions must be short and uncomplicated. Obviously, making a long function **inline** is likely to be counterproductive, especially if it's called many times in a program. Such folly could greatly increase the size of the program, with little or no improvement in execution time.

There is actually a downside when the compiler chooses not to make inline a function that you have requested to be so. In this situation, the function call will compile as a normal function call, but the compiler will also typically treat the function as local to the source file, so each source file that uses it will have its own compiled copy of the function. The result is that you will have unnecessary duplication of the code for the function if it is used in several different source files.

Static Variables

In all the functions we have written so far, nothing is retained within the body of the function from one execution to the next. Suppose you wanted to count how many times a particular function had been called — how could you do that? One way would be to define a variable at file scope, and then to increment it from within the function. A potential pitfall of this approach, however, is that the variable can be modified by *any* function within your program file, and you can't be sure that it's only being altered when it should.

A better solution is to declare a variable within the function body as **static**, something we touched on briefly back in Chapter 3. A **static** variable is created on the first occasion that the statement that defines it is executed. Thereafter, it remains in existence until the program terminates. This means that you can carry over a value from one call of a function to the next.

To declare a variable as static, you just prefix the type name in the declaration of the variable with the keyword **static**. For example:

```
static int count = 1;
```

When this statement executes, the static variable **count** is created and initialized to 1. Subsequent executions of the same statement will have no further effect. The variable **count** will continue to exist until the program terminates. If you omit the initializing value from the declaration, the static variable will be initialized to 0.

Let's take a very simple example of a function that declares a static variable:

```
void nextInteger()
{
  static int count = 1;
  cout << endl << count++;
}
```

This function increments the static variable **count** after displaying its current value. The first time the function is called, it will display the value 1. The second time, it will display the value 2. Each time the function is called, it will display an integer that is one larger than the previous value. The static variable **count** is created and initialized only once. Subsequent calls of the function use whatever is the current value of **count**, which survives for as long as the program is executing.

You can declare any type of variable as **static**, and you can use a **static** variable for anything that you need to remember from one call of a function to the next. You might want to hold on to the number of the last file record that was read, for example, or the highest value of all the arguments that have been passed.

We can demonstrate a static variable in use with an example.

Try It Out – Using a Static Variable in a Function

The Fibonacci series is a sequence of integers in which each number is the sum of the two preceding it. We will write a function to return a number in the sequence by using static variables to recall the two previous numbers calculated by the function.

Obviously, there are no 'previous numbers' before the program starts, so we will initialize the two variables to 0 and 1. I wouldn't claim this method as a model of good programming style, but it does demonstrate the properties of static variables in a more complicated context.

```
// Program 8.11 Using a static variable
#include <iostream>
#include <iomanip>
using namespace std;
```

313

```
long nextFib();

int main()
{
  cout << endl << "The Fibonacci Series" << endl;
  for(int i = 0 ; i < 30 ; i++)
  {
    if(i % 5 == 0)                      // Every fifth number...
      cout << endl;                     // ...start a new line
    cout << setw(12) << nextFib();
  }
  cout << endl;
  return 0;
}

// Function to generate the next number in the Fibonacci series
long nextFib()
{
  static long last = 0;                 // Last number in sequence
  static long lastButOne = 1;           // Last but one number

  long next = last + lastButOne;        // Next is sum of last two
  lastButOne = last;                    // Update last but one
  last = next;                          // Last is new one
  return last;                          // Return the new one
}
```

This produces the output:

```
The Fibonacci Series

           1           1           2           3           5
           8          13          21          34          55
          89         144         233         377         610
         987        1597        2584        4181        6765
       10946       17711       28657       46368       75025
      121393      196418      317811      514229      832040
```

How It Works

The function **main()** just calls the function **nextFib()**, 30 times, in a loop:

```
for(int i = 0 ; i < 30 ; i++)
{
  if(i % 5 == 0)                      // Every fifth number...
    cout << endl;                     // ...start a new line
  cout << setw(12) << nextFib();
}
```

No arguments are passed, so the values returned are generated internally to the **nextFib()** function. The two static variables declared will hold the most recently generated number in the sequence, and the one before that:

```
static long last = 0;                 // Last number in sequence
static long lastButOne = 1;           // Last but one number
```

By judiciously initializing **last** to 0 and **lastButOne** to 1, we kick the sequence off with two 1s. At each call of **nextFib()**, the next number in the sequence is calculated by summing the previous two numbers in the sequence. The result is stored in the automatic variable **next**:

```
long next = last + lastButOne;         // Next is sum of last two
```

We can do this because **last** and **lastButOne** are static variables, which still carry the values assigned to them during the previous iteration of **nextFib()**.

Before returning the value **next**, we have to transfer the previous value in **last** to **lastButOne**, and the new value to **last**:

```
lastButOne = last;                     // Update last but one
last = next;                           // Last is new one
```

Although static variables survive as long as the program does, they are only *accessible* within the block in which they are declared, so the variables **last** and **lastButOne** can only be accessed from within the body of the function **nextFib()**.

> **FYI**
>
> The Fibonacci series may look like a bunch of rather dull numbers, but they crop up in all sorts of places. For example, plants grow successive leaves such that the angle between them is 2π times a ratio of alternate numbers in this sequence. So, plants grow their leaves at angles of 2π times 1/2 (the first and third numbers), 2π times 1/3 (the second and fourth numbers), 2π times 2/5 (the third and fifth numbers), and so on. Amazing isn't it? Maybe plants know about static variables!

Summary

This chapter has served as an introduction to writing and using functions. However, we will see more about functions in the next chapter, and more still in the context of user defined types, which we will introduce starting in Chapter 11. The important bits that you should take away from this chapter are:

- Functions are self-contained compact units of code with a well-defined purpose. A typical program will consist of a large number of small functions, rather than a small number of large functions.

- A function definition consists of a function header defining the parameters and return types, and a function body containing the executable code for the function.

- A function prototype enables the compiler to process calls to a function even though the function definition has not been processed.

- The pass-by-value mechanism for passing arguments to a function passes copies of the original argument values, so the original argument values are not accessible from within the function.

- Passing a pointer to a function allows modification of the value pointed to, even though the pointer itself is passed by value.

- Declaring a pointer parameter as **const** can prevent modification of the original value.

> ▶ You can pass the address of an array to a function as a pointer.

> ▶ Passing values to a function using a reference — the pass-by-reference mechanism — can avoid the copying implicit in the pass-by-value transfer of arguments. Any parameter that is not modified in a function should be specified as **const**.

> ▶ Specifying default values for function parameters allows arguments to be optionally omitted, whereupon the default value will be assumed.

> ▶ Returning a reference from a function allows the function to be used on the left of an assignment operator. Declaring the return type as a **const** reference will prevent this.

Exercises

Ex 8.1 Write a function that accepts two integer arguments and prompts for input until the value entered by the user falls between those of its arguments. Use the function in a program to obtain the user's date of birth, validating that the month, day and year are all sensible. Finally, output the date to the screen.

Ex 8.2 Write a function that accepts a string or array of characters as input, and reverses it. What is the best sort of argument type to use? Provide a **main()** function to test your function by prompting the user for a string of characters, reversing them, and then outputting the reversed string.

Ex 8.3 Write a program that accepts command line arguments, and which must be called with between two and four arguments. If it is called with an invalid number of arguments, output a message telling the user what they should do, and then exit. If the number of arguments is correct, print them out, one to a line.

Ex 8.4 Modify the program you wrote for Exercise 8.3 so that it will only accept two arguments, and pass the second one to the string-reversing function of Exercise 8.2. Print out the reversed string.

Ex 8.5 Write a function that returns a reference to the smaller of two integer variables. Write another that returns a reference to the larger. Use these to generate elements of the Fibonacci sequence — that's the sequence of numbers 1, 1, 2, 3, 5, 8, 13, ..., where each number is the sum of the two preceding it. (Hint: use two integer variables **val1** and **val2**, and a loop in which the smaller of these is updated to the sum of the two, whose value should then be output.)

More on Functions

In this chapter we will explore some of the subtler aspects of designing using functions. We'll examine the way that your choice of parameter types and the return type can affect how a function operates, and even where you can use it. We will also investigate ways of creating function definitions automatically.

In this chapter you will learn:

> How to implement several functions with the same name

> How you can use pointers and references as parameters

> The effect of declaring parameters with the **const** qualifier

> What function templates are, and how to use them

> How to define and use pointers to functions

> What recursive functions are and how they work

Function Overloading

Often, you will find that you need two or more functions that do essentially the *same* thing, but to *different* data types. For example, you might need several versions of our function **larger()**, for finding the larger of two variables of any of the basic numeric data types. Ideally, of course, all of these functions would have the same name, **larger()**. The alternative would be to define a function **largerInt()** for variables of type **int**, and a function **largerFloat()** for variables of type **float**, and so on — which is clumsy and laborious. This is a case for **function overloading**.

With function overloading, it is possible to have several functions in a program with the same name. The principal constraint is that each function with a given name must have a different parameter list. By this we mean that the parameter *types* distinguish one parameter list from another — it is not sufficient simply to have different parameter names. Essentially, two functions with the same name are different if

▶ the number of parameters for each function is different; or

▶ the number of parameters is the same, but at least one pair of corresponding parameters have different types

However, there are some subtleties here that we need to bring out into the open.

The Signature of a Function

The combination of the name of a function, together with its parameter types defines a unique characteristic called the **function signature**. The function signature serves to differentiate one function from another — each function in your program must have a unique function signature. It comes into play whenever you call a function in your program.

From the function prototypes or the function definitions, the compiler creates a function signature for each function in your program file. When you write a statement that includes a function call, the compiler uses the call to create a function signature, and then compares it with the set of function signatures which are available in your function prototypes and/or definitions. If it finds a match, then it has established which function you called. It is doesn't find a match, then it will check to see whether any conversions on the arguments will produce a match.

FYI   Note that the return type is *not* part of the function signature. In fact, this is logical. When you call a function, you are not obliged to store the value returned; therefore the return type of the function is not necessarily determined by the calling statement.

Try It Out – Overloading a Function

Let's try a very simple example using versions of the function **larger()** that we programmed earlier.

```
// Program 9.1 Overloading a function
#include <iostream>
#include <iomanip>
using namespace std;

double larger(double a, double b);              // Function prototypes
long larger(long a, long b);                    //


int main()
{
  cout << endl;
```

```
      cout << "Larger of 1.5 and 2.5 is " << larger(1.5, 2.5)   << endl;
      cout << "Larger of 2.5 and 3.5 is " << larger(2.5f, 3.5f) << endl;
      cout << "Larger of 15 and 25 is "   << larger(15L, 25L)   << endl;

   return 0;
   }

   // Function to return the larger of two floating point values
   double larger(double a, double b)
   {
     return a>b ? a : b;
   }

   // Function to return the larger of two integer values
   long larger(long a, long b)
   {
     return a>b ? a : b;
   }
```

This produces the output:

```
Larger of 1.5 and 2.5 is 2.5
Larger of 2.5 and 3.5 is 3.5
Larger of 15 and 25 is 25
```

How It Works

We have two overloaded versions of the function **larger()**. The first call in **main()** makes use of the version for arguments of type **double**:

```
cout << "Larger of 1.5 and 2.5 is " << larger(1.5, 2.5)   << endl; \
```

There is an exact match here so the compiler has no problem selecting the correct function to use. The next call is a little different, though:

```
cout << "Larger of 2.5 and 3.5 is " << larger(2.5f, 3.5f) << endl;
```

This statement calls a function **larger()** with parameters of type **float**. We didn't define such a function. However, the compiler can convert from **float** to **double** with no data loss; this is an acceptable automatic conversion, so the compiler can use the version of **larger()** that accepts **double** arguments.

The next statement passes arguments of type **long** to the function **larger()**:

```
cout << "Larger of 15 and 25 is "   << larger(15L, 25L)   << endl;
```

Again, there is an exact match with the version that accepts arguments of type **long**, and that is the version called. If you want to be 100% sure of which case is being called, you could add an output statement in each version of the function. For example:

```
cout << " Integer version ";
```

This will mess up the output a little, but you will be able to tell which overloaded function is called in each case.

Of course, type **int** converts to type **long** with no data loss so we could use the version with **long** parameters in this case, couldn't we? Well, give it a try by adding a few statements to **main()**:

```
int value1 = 35;
int value2 = 45;

cout << "Larger of " << value1 << " and " << value2 << " is "
     << larger(value1, value2)
     << endl;
```

Didn't work, did it? The compiler just could not decide which version of **larger()** to use. Automatic casts from **int** to **long** or from **int** to **double** are both acceptable, so there is no basis for a decision. Your code is ambiguous. The compiler is not prepared to toss a coin here and expects you to decide. You can resolve this sort of problem by putting in explicit casts:

```
cout << "Larger of " << value1 << " and " << value2 << " is "
     << larger(static_cast<long>(value1), static_cast<long>(value2))
     << endl;
```

Now there is an exact match with **long** arguments. It would have been sufficient to cast either of the arguments to **long** — the compiler would have been able to select the version with **long** parameters. However, by putting both casts in, your intentions are clear to anyone reading the code.

Overloading and Pointer Parameters

Obviously, pointers to different types are different, so the following prototypes declare two different overloaded functions:

```
int larger(int* pValue1, int* pValue2);
int larger(float* pValue1, float* pValue2);
```

You can use a parameter that is a pointer to a given type. Note that this is interpreted in the same way as an array of that type. Thus, for example, a parameter of type **int*** will be treated in the same way as a parameter type of **int[]**. Hence, the following prototypes declare the same function, not two different functions:

```
int largest(int values[], int count);
int largest(int* values, int count);
```

With either parameter type specified, the argument passed is an address, and you can implement the function using array notation or pointer notation.

Overloading and Reference Parameters

Some care is needed if you overload functions with reference parameters. For one thing, you cannot overload a function with a parameter of a given type *data_type*, with a function that has a parameter of type 'reference to *data_type*'. If you do this, the compiler will be unable to determine from a function call which function you want. To illustrate this, let's declare two function prototypes:

```
int doIt(int number);        // These are not
int& doIt(int& number);      // distinguishable
```

Now, assuming **value** is of type **int**, a statement such as:

```
doIt(value);
```

could call either function.

You should also beware when overloading a function by declaring two versions, one with a parameter 'reference to ***type1***' and one with a parameter 'reference to ***type2***'.
The function that is called will depend on the sort of arguments you use, but you may get some surprising results.

Try It Out – Overloaded Functions with Reference Parameters

Let's explore the use of reference parameters a little, with a modified version of the last example:

```
// Program 9.2 Overloading a function with reference parameters
#include <iostream>
#include <iomanip>
using namespace std;

double larger(double a, double b);
long& larger(long& a, long& b);

int main()
{
  cout << endl;
  cout << "Larger of 1.5 and 2.5 is " << larger(1.5, 2.5) << endl;

  int value1 = 35;
  int value2 = 45;

  cout << "Larger of " << value1 << " and " << value2 << " is "
       << larger(static_cast<long>(value1), static_cast<long>(value2))
       << endl;

  return 0;
}

// Function to return the larger of two floating point values
double larger(double a, double b)
{
  cout << " double version. ";
  return a>b ? a : b;
}

// Return the larger of two long references
long& larger(long& a, long& b)
{
  cout << " long ref version. ";
  return a>b ? a : b;
}
```

This version of the program produces the output:

```
double version. Larger of 1.5 and 2.5 is 2.5
double version. Larger of 35 and 45 is 45
```

How It Works

The second line of the resulting output may not have been what you were anticipating. We really want the second output statement to call the version of **larger()** with **long&** parameters:

```
cout << "Larger of " << value1 << " and " << value2 << " is "
    << larger(static_cast<long>(value1), static_cast<long>(value2))
        << endl;
```

Instead, this statement has called the version with **double** parameters — but why? After all, we *did* cast both arguments to **long**!

In fact, that is exactly where the problem lies. The arguments are not **value1** and **value2**, but the temporary locations which contain the same values, converted to type **long**. Behind the scenes, the compiler is not prepared to use a temporary address to initialize a reference — it's just too risky. The code in **larger()** has free rein on what it does with the reference parameters, and the theory is that either of the reference parameters can be modified and/or returned. Using a temporary location in this way is not sensible, so the compiler won't do it.

What can we do about this? We have a couple of choices. We could declare **value1** and **value2** as type **long**. Then the compiler will happily call the version of **larger()** which uses parameters of type 'reference to **long**'.

If circumstances don't allow this, then an alternative is to declare the reference parameters as **const**:

```
long& larger(const long& a, const long& b);
```

Remember to make this change in both the function prototype *and* the function definition. This will inform the compiler that the function will not modify the arguments; then the compiler will allow this version to be called, instead of the version with **double** parameters.

Overloading and const Parameters

It is important to realize that **const** is only sufficient to distinguish parameters for the purposes of defining the signature of a function for references and pointers. For a basic type (**int**, for example), **const int** will be identical to **int** from the point of view of overloading. Hence, the following prototypes result in the same function signature, and declare the same function:

```
long& larger(long a, long b);
long& larger(const long a, const long b);
```

The compiler will ignore the **const** aspect of the parameters in the second declaration. This is because the arguments are being passed *by value* — this means that a *copy* of each argument is passed into the function, and thus the original is protected from modification by the function.

> *For any basic type* T, *a function with parameter type* const T *is interpreted as the same as its overloaded cousin with parameter type* T — *the* const *will be ignored.*

Overloading and const Pointer Parameters

Two overloaded functions are *different*, if one of them has a parameter of type 'pointer to **type**' and the other has a parameter 'pointer to **const type**'. The corresponding parameters are pointers to different things — effectively, they are different types. For example, these prototypes have different function signatures:

```
long* larger(long* a, long* b);
long* larger(const long* a, const long* b);
```

The modifier **const** applied to the value pointed to prevents the value from being modified. Without the **const** modifier, the original value can be modified through the pointer, and the pass-by-value mechanism does not inhibit this in any way. In this example, the former function will be called with the statements:

```
int num1 = 1;
int num2 = 2;
int num3 = *larger(num1, num2);
```

The latter version of **larger()**, with **const** parameters, will be called by the following code:

```
const int num10 = 1;
const int num20 = 2;
int num3 = *larger(num10, num20);
```

The compiler will not pass a **const** value to a function where the parameter is just a pointer. To allow a **const** value to be passed through a pointer would violate the **const** declaration of the variable. Thus the compiler must select the latter version of **larger()** for this case.

By comparison, two overloaded functions are *the same*, if one of them has a parameter of type 'pointer to **type**' and the other has a parameter **const** 'pointer to **type**'. For example:

```
long* larger(long* a, long* b);
long* larger(long* const a, long* const b);
```

These two functions are not differentiated and will not compile. The reason is clear, when you consider that the first prototype has a parameter of type 'pointer to **long**', and the second has parameter of type **const** 'pointer to **long**'. If you think of 'pointer to **long**' as a type, **T**, then the parameter types are **T** and **const T** — which are not differentiated (you'll remember that we covered this case at the beginning of this section).

Overloading and const Reference Parameters

Reference parameters are more straightforward when it comes to **const**. A reference to a type **T**, and a **const** reference to a type **T** are always differentiated, so for example, type **const int&** is always different from type **int&**. This means that you can overload functions in the manner indicated by the following prototypes:

```
long& larger(long& a, long& b);
const long& larger(const long& a, const long& b);
```

Each function will have the same function body, which returns the larger of the two parameters, but the functions behave differently. The first prototype declares a function that will not accept constants as arguments, but the function can be used to modify reference parameters. The second prototype declares a function that will accept constants (and non-constants of course) as arguments, but because the return type is a **const** reference, the function cannot be used to modify reference parameters.

> *Remember that the return value has no effect on the overloading. It is not considered when the signature of a function is generated. However, as described above, it does have an effect on where the function can be used.*

Overloading and Default Argument Values

Recall from Chapter 8 that we can specify default parameter values for a function. However, if we do this for overloaded functions, it can sometimes affect the compiler's ability to distinguish one call from another and may create an ambiguous situation. For example, suppose we had two versions of the **showError()** function, which we used in Chapter 8 to display an error message. Here's one that is defined with a C-style string argument:

```
void showError(const char* message)
{
  cout << endl << message << endl;
}
```

The other is defined with a **string** argument:

```
void showError(const string& message)
{
  cout << endl << message << endl;
}
```

We cannot now define a default argument for both functions since this would create an ambiguity. The statement to output the default message in either case would be:

```
showError();
```

With this function call, the compiler has no way of knowing which function is required. Of course, this is a silly example: there would be no reason to specify defaults for both functions. A default for just one of these two functions does everything that you need. However, circumstances can arise where it is not so silly, and overall you must ensure that all function calls uniquely identify the function that should be called.

A Sausage Machine for Functions

In some of the situations above, we were writing overloaded functions that contained exactly the same code. It seems an unnecessary overhead to have to write the same code over and over, and indeed it is. In such situations, we can write the code just once, as a **function template**.

A function template is a blueprint or a recipe for a function. It is used by the compiler to generate a new member of a family of functions. The new function is created when it is first required. A more technical way of describing a function template is as a parametric function definition, where a particular function is selected by one or more parameters. The parameters are usually data types (but not always, however: for example, it can be useful to supply sizes by passing integer values). We can cast a little light into the shadows of function templates with a specific example.

The **larger()** function that we have been playing with is a good candidate for a template. A definition of a template for this function is shown below.

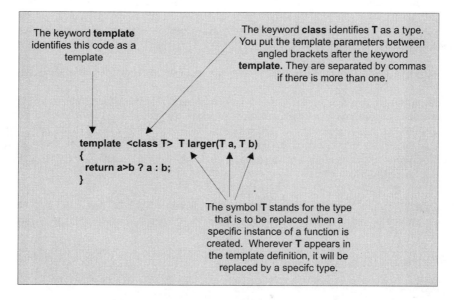

The keyword **template** identifies this code as a template

The keyword **class** identifies **T** as a type. You put the template parameters between angled brackets after the keyword **template**. They are separated by commas if there is more than one.

```
template <class T>  T larger(T a, T b)
{
    return a>b ? a : b;
}
```

The symbol **T** stands for the type that is to be replaced when a specific instance of a function is created. Wherever **T** appears in the template definition, it will be replaced by a specifc type.

The function template starts with the keyword **template** to identify it as such. This is followed by a pair of angled brackets, which contains a list of parameters. In this case we have just one, the parameter **T**. **T** is commonly used as a name for a parameter, probably because most parameters are types and because **T** is the first letter of the word *type*. In fact, you can use whatever name you like for the parameter: names such as **replaceIt** or **myType** are equally valid.

The word **class** is a keyword which identifies that **T** is a type. This implies that **T** can be one of the basic types, such as **int** or **long**, or it could be a user-defined type (a class, in other words). You will learn how to create your own types when we discuss classes.

FYI   In the context of template definitions, you may come across the keyword typename between the angled brackets. This is a common alternative to the keyword class, and has the same purpose in this context. In this book, we will use the keyword class (in preference to typename) for this purpose.

The rest of the definition is just like the definition of a normal function, except that you have the parameter, in this case **T**, sprinkled around. The compiler creates a new version of the function by replacing **T** throughout the template definition with a particular type.

You can place the template in your code in the same way as you would a normal function definition — and you can even have a template function prototype. In this case it would be:

```
template<class T> T larger(T a, T b);
```

You must ensure that either a declaration (that is, a prototype) or the definition of the template appears in the source file, prior to any use of a function generated from a template.

The compiler will create instances of the function as required from any statement that uses the function **larger()**. For example:

```
cout << "Larger of 1.5 and 2.5 is " << larger(1.5, 2.5) << endl;
```

As you see, we just use the function in the normal way. In particular, we don't specify a value for the template argument **T** — the compiler deduces the value of **T** from the arguments to the function call. Here, the arguments to **larger()** are of type **double**, so this call will cause the compiler to search for a version of **larger()** with **double** parameters. If none is found, then the compiler creates this version of **larger()** from the template, by substituting type **double** for **T** in the template definition.

The resulting template function accepts arguments of type **double** and returns a **double** value. This is sometimes called an instance or an instantiation of the template. With **double** plugged in, in place of **T**, the template instance will effectively be:

```
double larger(double a, double b)
{
   return a>b ? a : b;
}
```

 FYI This instantiation of the template will only be generated once. If a subsequent function call requires the same instance, then it will call the instance that has already been created. Your program will only ever include a single copy of the definition of each instance, even if the same instance is generated in different source files.

There are a couple of things you should keep in mind throughout the detailed discussion on function templates that follows. First, a function template does not do anything by itself. It is a recipe or blueprint that the compiler uses to create a function definition from a function call. Second, this all happens during compilation and linkage. The compiler uses a template to generate source code for a function definition, which it then compiles. The role of the linker is to link only a *single* instance of a function into the executable module, even if several different source files call the same instance. When your program executes, the existence (or otherwise) of a template in the original source code is neither apparent nor relevant.

Having said all that, let's road test a function template for real in a program.

Try It Out – Using a Function Template

Using this template is very straightforward. Here's the code to exercise it in various ways:

```cpp
// Program 9.3 Using a function template
#include <iostream>
#include <iomanip>
using namespace std;

template<class T> T larger(T a, T b);        // Function template prototype

int main()
{
  cout << endl;
  cout << "Larger of 1.5 and 2.5 is " << larger(1.5, 2.5) << endl;
  cout << "Larger of 3.5 and 4.5 is " << larger(3.5, 4.5) << endl;

  int value1 = 35;
  int value2 = 45;

  cout << "Larger of " << value1 << " and " << value2 << " is "
       << larger(value1, value2)
       << endl;


  long a = 9;
  long b = 8;

  cout << "Larger of "   << a << " and " << b << " is "
       << larger(a, b)
       << endl;

return 0;
}

// Template for functions to return the larger of two values
template <class T> T larger(T a, T b)
{
  return a>b ? a : b;
}
```

This produces the output:

```
Larger of 1.5 and 2.5 is 2.5
Larger of 3.5 and 4.5 is 4.5
Larger of 35 and 45 is 45
Larger of 9 and 8 is 9
```

How It Works

As we said before, the definition or prototype for the template must appear before you can call any instances of the function — this rule is much the same as for an ordinary function. We therefore have defined the template prototype as:

```cpp
template<class T> T larger(T a, T b);        // Function template prototype
```

This is essentially the same as the first line of the template definition, but with a semi-colon at the end.

We call the function **larger()** in **main()** for the first time in the statement:

```
cout << "Larger of 1.5 and 2.5 is " << larger(1.5, 2.5) << endl;
```

The compiler will automatically create a version of **larger()** that accepts arguments of type **double** as a result of this statement; then that version will be called here. The next statement also requires a version of **larger()** that accepts **double** arguments:

```
cout << "Larger of 3.5 and 4.5 is " << larger(3.5, 4.5) << endl;
```

Here, the compiler will do the sensible thing and use the version that it generated for the previous statement.

The next use of **larger()** is in the statement:

```
cout << "Larger of " << value1 << " and " << value2 << " is "
     << larger(value1, value2)
     << endl;
```

Here, we call the function with arguments of type **int**, so a new version of **larger()** will be generated to accept **int** arguments.

The last call of the function **larger()** has two arguments of type **long**:

```
cout << "Larger of "   << a << " and " << b << " is "
     << larger(a, b)
     << endl;
```

This time we will get a new version with two arguments of type **long**. We end up with a total of three different versions of **larger()** (in the form of three different bits of object code) from just a single piece of source code in this program.

Explicitly Specifying a Template Parameter

You can specify the parameter for the template explicitly when you call the function. This allows you to control which version of the function is used. The compiler no longer tries to deduce the type to replace **T**; it will simply accept what you specify. There are a number of situations in which this can be useful:

 In situations where the function call is ambiguous, the compilation will fail. We can use this technique to help the compiler resolve the ambiguity.

 In certain cases, the compiler is unable to deduce the template arguments, and hence is unable to choose which version of the function to use. (We'll see an example of this when we consider templates with multiple parameters.) In such cases, we must specify the template parameter explicitly.

▶ To avoid having too many versions of the function (and hence avoid excessive occupation of memory), you can force function calls to take certain versions of your function. (For example, in Program 9.3, three versions of **larger()** are used when two would probably suffice.)

Here's an example. In Program 9.3, the arguments of type **int** could be handled by the version of **larger()** which accepts arguments of type **long** (since we need that later anyway). We can force this by specifying the template parameter type to be used when we call the function:

```
cout << "Larger of " << value1 << " and " << value2 << " is "
    << larger<long>(value1, value2)
    << endl;
```

In the call in this statement, the template parameter value **long** is defined between angled brackets following the function name. Therefore, the function corresponding to type **long** will be generated and used here. The compiler will supply automatic casts for the arguments to the types required by the function parameter specifications.

Alternatively, you might decide that the version with parameters of type **double** would be satisfactory. In this case, you just specify **double** between the angled brackets; the compiler will generate and use that version. You could even force the compiler to use a version — type **short**, for example — which is likely to cause data loss. Typically, the compiler will warn you against loss of data; but the compiler will implement the version that you specify.

Here's another situation in which an explicit template parameter would be suitable:

```
cout << "Larger of " << a << " and " << value1 << " is "
    << larger(a, value1)
    << endl;
```

Here, the variables **a** and **value1** are of type **long** and **int** respectively, just as in Program 9.3. The two arguments have different types: this arrangement doesn't match the function template, and so the compiler will be unable to generate a suitable function. To overcome this, we can explicitly specify the template parameter:

```
cout << "Larger of " << a << " and " << value1 << " is "
    << larger<long>(a,value1)
    << endl;
```

Now, the compiler can make the substitution of **long** for **T** to generate the function, and then supply a cast for **value1** to make the call complete.

> *An alternative solution to this situation is to cast one of the arguments in the function call to the type of the other. Then, the compiler interprets this as having two arguments of the same type, and calls the appropriate function version.*

Specialization of Templates

Suppose that we extended Program 9.3 to call the function **larger()** with arguments that are addresses:

```
cout << "Larger of " << a << " and " << b << " is "
     << *larger(&a,&b)
     << endl;
```

As a result of this statement, the compiler will create a version of the function with the template parameter as type **long***. This version will have the prototype:

```
long* larger(long*, long*);
```

The return value will be an address, and we have to de-reference it in order to output the value. However, having done all that, *the result will only be correct by accident!* This is because the comparison in the body of the function is not correct. The function that is generated will be:

```
long* larger(long* a, long* b)
{
  return a>b ? a : b;
}
```

This is comparing the addresses, not the values! This function returns the higher-valued address, when we wanted the address containing the higher-valued long integer. This shows how easy it is to create hidden errors using templates. You need to take particular care when using pointer types as parameter values in a template.

> *When your template is designed for basic data type parameters, beware of defining versions that make little sense. The pointer argument case above is such a case.*

What could we do about this? We could define a **specialization** of our template to deal with this particular case.

For a *specific* parameter value (or set of values, in the case of a template with multiple parameters), a specialization of a template defines a behavior which is different from the standard template. The definition for a template specialization must come after a declaration or definition of the original statement. If you put a specialization first then your program won't compile.

Defining a Template Specialization

The definition of a specialization starts with the keyword **template**, but in this case the parameter is omitted. The value of the parameter for the specialization should appear between angled brackets, immediately following the template function name. The definition for a specialization of **larger()** for a value of **long*** for the parameter **T** will be:

```
template <> long* larger<long*>(long* a, long* b)
{
  return *a>*b ? a : b;
}
```

The only change to the body of the function is to de-reference the arguments **a** and **b**, so that we compare the values rather than the addresses. Let's see how it works in practice.

Try It Out – Using an Explicit Specialization

We can adapt Program 9.3, adding the problem statement above that passes addresses to **larger()** and an explicit specialization to deal with arguments of type **long***:

```
// Program 9.4 Using function template specialization
#include <iostream>
#include <iomanip>
using namespace std;

template<class T> T larger(T a, T b);              // Function template prototype
template<> long* larger<long*>(long* a, long* b); // Specialization

int main()
{
  cout << endl;
  cout << "Larger of 1.5 and 2.5 is " << larger(1.5, 2.5) << endl;
  cout << "Larger of 3.5 and 4.5 is " << larger(3.5, 4.5) << endl;

  int value1 = 35;
  int value2 = 45;

  cout << "Larger of " << value1 << " and " << value2 << " is "
       << larger(value1, value2)
       << endl;

  long a = 9;
  long b = 8;
  cout << "Larger of "   << a << " and " << b << " is "
       << larger(a,b)
       << endl;

  cout << "Larger of "   << a << " and " << b << " is "
       << *larger(&a,&b)
       << endl;

  return 0;
}

// Template for functions to return the larger of two values
template <class T> T larger(T a, T b)
{
  cout << "standard version " << endl;
  return a>b ? a : b;
}

// Template specialization definitions
template <> long* larger<long*>(long* a, long* b)
{
  cout << "specialized version " << endl;
  return *a>*b ? a : b;
}
```

Both the template and the specialization have a statement that outputs a trace when they are called, so we know which is called in each case. This produces the output:

```
standard version
Larger of 1.5 and 2.5 is 2.5
standard version
Larger of 3.5 and 4.5 is 4.5
standard version
Larger of 35 and 45 is 45
standard version
Larger of 9 and 8 is 9
specialized version
Larger of 9 and 8 is 9
```

How It Works

At the beginning of the program file we have a declaration for the template specialization, in addition to the declaration of the template that we had earlier:

```
template<> long* larger<long*>(long* a, long* b); // Specialization
```

This is necessary because **main()**, where the specialization will be used, comes before the definition. In the program, the definition of the specialization is the same as in the preceding discussion — we've just added an output statement so we can trace when it is used.

It works just as we might have anticipated. All the calls of **larger()** from the previous version of the program are repeated here. The last call is from the statement:

```
cout << "Larger of "  << a << " and " << b << " is "
     << *larger(&a,&b)
     << endl;
```

This uses the specialization of the template, as is indicated by the output.

Function Templates and Overloading

There are different ways to overload a function produced from a function template. One way, as we've just seen, is to overload the function with another function generated from the template. Alternatively, you can **overload** the function by directly defining other functions with the same name. Using overloading, you can define 'overrides' for specific cases, and these will get used in preference to the template. In this case, as always, each overloaded function must have a unique signature.

Let's reconsider the previous situation, in which we need to overload the **larger()** function to take pointer arguments. Instead of the template specialization, which we used above, we could explicitly declare an overloaded function. If we take this approach, then we would replace the specialization prototype in Program 9.4 with the following overloaded function prototype:

```
long* larger(long* a, long* b);        // overloaded function
```

In place of the specialization definition in Program 9.4, we would place the following function definition:

```
long* larger(long* a, long* b)
{
  cout << "overloaded version for long* " << endl;
  return *a>*b ? a : b;
}
```

You can make these changes to Program 9.4. When the function **larger()** is called with **long*** arguments, the compiler establishes that a suitable version of **larger()** exists, and so the template is not used. Effectively, this function definition has overridden the template.

It is also possible to overload an existing template with another template. For example, we could extend Program 9.4 by adding an **overloaded template** to find the largest value contained in an array (we will have to overlook the grammatical inaccuracy!). The definition of the template might be:

```
template <class T> T larger (const T array[], int count)
{
  cout << "template overload version for arrays " << endl;
  T result = array[0];
  for(int i = 1 ; i < count ; i++)
    if(array[i] > result)
      result = array[i];
  return result;
}
```

This will find the largest element in an array of any suitable type. You could try this out in Program 9.4 by adding a couple of statements to **main()**:

```
double x[] = { 10.5, 12.5, 2.5, 13.5, 5.5 };

cout << "Largest element has the value "
     << larger(x, sizeof x/sizeof x[0])
     << endl;
```

You will need a prototype for the additional template, of course.

Templates with Multiple Parameters

We have been using function templates with a single parameter, but you can have several parameters in a template. A classic application for a second type argument is to provide a way of controlling the return type from a function template. We could define another template for the function **larger()**, that allows the return type to be specified independently of the function parameter type:

```
// Template for functions to return the larger of two values
template <class TReturn, class TArg> TReturn larger(TArg a, TArg b)
{
  return a>b ? a : b;
}
```

Note that the compiler cannot deduce the type, **TReturn**, for the return value, so you must always specify it. However, the compiler *can* deduce the type for the arguments, so you can get away with specifying just the return type. For example:

```
cout << "Larger of 1.5 and 2.5 is "
     << larger<int>(1.5, 2.5)
     << endl;
```

The return type is specified (between the angled brackets) as **int**; and the argument type will be deduced from the arguments as **double**. The result of the function call will be 2. You can specify both **TReturn** and **TArg** if you like:

```
cout << "Larger of 1.5 and 2.5 is "
     << larger<double, double>(1.5, 2.5)
     << endl;
```

Here, the compiler will create the function that accepts arguments of type **double** and returns a result of type **double**.

Clearly, the sequence of template parameters in the template definition is important here. If we had defined the template with the return type as the second parameter, we would always have to specify *both* parameters in a function call: if we tried to specify only one parameter, it would be interpreted as the argument type, leaving the return type undefined.

Non-Type Template Parameters

So far, all the template parameters we have dealt with have been data types. In fact, your templates can also have **non-type parameters**; in this case, the function call would use non-type arguments. Arguments corresponding to non-type parameters must be either integral and compile time constant, or references/pointers to objects with external linkage.

When declaring the template, we include any non-type template parameters in the parameter list (along with any other type parameters). We'll see an example in a moment. The type of a non-type template parameter can be one of the following:

- An integral type, such as **int**, **long**, etc.
- An enumeration type
- A pointer or reference to an object type
- A pointer or a reference to a function
- A pointer to a class member

We haven't seen the last two here. We will introduce pointers to functions later in this chapter, and we will discuss references to functions and pointers to class members when we cover classes. The application of non-type template parameters to these types is beyond the scope of this book. We will only consider an elementary example here, with parameters of type **int**, just to see how it works.

Suppose we needed a function to perform range-checking on a value. We could define a template to handle a variety of types:

```
template <class T, int upper, int lower> bool isInRange(T value)
{
  return (value <= upper) && (value >= lower);
}
```

With this template, the compiler cannot deduce all of the template parameters from the use of the function. The following function call won't compile:

```
double value = 100.0;
cout << isInRange(value);                    // Won't compile - incorrect usage
```

This is because the parameters **upper** and **lower** are unspecified. To use this template, we must specify the template parameter values. The correct way to use this would be:

```
cout << isInrange<double,0,500>(value); // OK - Check between 0 and 500
```

It might well be better to use function parameters, rather than template parameters, for the limits in this case. After all, function parameters give you the flexibility of being able to pass values that are calculated when your program runs.

Pointers to Functions

As we know, a pointer stores an address value. Up to now, we have used pointers to store the address of another variable with the same basic type as the pointer. This has provided considerable flexibility in allowing us to use different variables at different times through a single pointer.

A pointer can *also* point to the address of a function. Such a pointer can point to different functions at different times during execution of your program. At any time in your program, you can use your pointer to call a function; the function that is called will be the function whose address was last assigned to the pointer.

Obviously, a pointer to a function must contain the memory address of the function that you want to call. To work properly, however, the pointer must also maintain other information — namely, the types of parameters in the parameter list for any function that it points to, and also the return type.

> *When you declare a pointer to a function, you have to specify the parameter types and the return type of the functions that it can point to, in addition to the name of the pointer.*

Clearly, this rule will restrict the number of functions to which your pointer can point. This is analogous to a pointer that stores the address of a data item. For example, a pointer to type **int** can *only* point to a location which contains a value of type **int** — if you want to store the address of a value of type **long**, then you need a different kind of pointer.

In the same way, let's suppose that we have declared a pointer to a function, for functions that accept one argument of type **int** and return a value of type **double**. This pointer can only be used to store the address of a function that has *exactly* this form. If you want to store the address of a function that accepts two arguments of type **int** and returns type **char**, then you must define another pointer that has these characteristics.

337

Function pointers are rather less common in C++ than they were in C. This is because C++ offers other facilities (classes, function overloading and so on), which are able to perform similar tasks. However, pointers to functions still hold their place in the C++ language.

Declaring Pointers to Functions

Let's declare a pointer **pfun** that we can use to point to functions that take two arguments, of type **long*** and **int**, and return a value of type **long**. The declaration would be as follows:

```
long (*pfun)(long*, int);    // Pointer to function declaration
```

This may look a little weird at first because of all the parentheses.

The parentheses around the pointer name, **pfun***, and the asterisk, are essential here — without them, this statement would declare a function rather than a pointer, because the* ***** *will bind to the* **long** *in preference to the* **pfun***.*

We can write the general form of a declaration of a pointer to a function as:

return_type **(****pointer_name***)(***list_of_parameter_types***);**

Remember that the parentheses around the pointer name are essential, otherwise you will finish up with a function prototype! The pointer can only point to functions with the same **return_type** and **list_of_parameter_types** as those specified in the declaration.

We can break the declaration down into three components that appear in sequence:

- ▶ The **return_type** of the functions that can be pointed to
- ▶ The **pointer_name** — which is preceded by an asterisk, to indicate that it's a *pointer* enclosed between the parentheses
- ▶ A **list_of_parameter_types**, enclosed between parentheses, for the functions that can be pointed to

If you attempt to assign a function to a pointer that does not conform to the types in the pointer declaration, you will get an error message from the compiler.

Of course, we should always initialize a pointer when we declare it. You can initialize a pointer to a function with the name of a function, within the declaration of the pointer. Suppose we have a function with the prototype:

```
long maxElement(const long* array, int count);    // Function prototype
```

Then we can declare and initialize a pointer to a function with the statement:

```
long (*pfun)(long*, int) = maxElement;
```

The pointer has been initialized to point to the function **maxElement()**. The pointer can be set subsequently to point to any function with the same parameter and return types.

Of course, you can also initialize a pointer to a function by using an assignment statement. Assuming the pointer **pfun** has been declared as above, we could set the value of the pointer to a different function with these statements:

```
long minElement(const long* array, int count);    // Function prototype
```

```
pfun = minElement;                 // Set pointer to function minElement()
```

As with pointers to variables, you must ensure that a pointer to a function is initialized before you use it to call a function. Without initialization, catastrophic failure of your program is guaranteed.

> *You can, if you wish, initialize a pointer to a function with the value 0. However, if the pointer is pointing to 0 when use it to 'call a function', the behavior is undefined, and catastrophic behavior will again result.*

If you now want to call the function **minElement()** using the pointer **pfun**, you just use the pointer name as though it were a function name. For example, we might use the following statements:

```
long data[] = { 23, 34, 22, 56, 87, 12, 57, 76 };
cout << "value of minimum is "
     << pfun(data, sizeof data/sizeof data[0]);
```

This will output the minimum value of the elements in the array **data**.

FYI
The ideas behind function templates and function pointers are connected in an odd sort of way. In a sense, a function pointer is actually the inverse of a function template. A particular function pointer can point to any one of a set of functions that have different names but have the same parameter and return types. Conversely, a function template defines a set of functions with the same name but where the parameter types and possibly return types may vary.

Try It Out – Pointers to Functions

To get a proper feel for these newfangled pointers and how they perform in action, let's try one out in a program:

```
// Program 9.5 Exercising pointers to functions
#include <iostream>

using namespace std;

long sum(long a, long b);                // Function prototype
long product(long a, long b);            // Function prototype

int main()
{
  long (*pDoIt)(long, long) = 0;         // Pointer to function declaration
```

```
        pDoIt = product;
        cout << endl
            << "3*5 = " << pDoIt(3, 5);                // Call product thru a pointer

        pDoIt = sum;                                   // Reassign pointer to sum()
        cout << endl
            << "3 * (4+5) + 6 = "
            << pDoIt(product(3, pDoIt(4, 5)), 6);   // Call thru a pointer twice

        cout << endl;
        return 0;
    }

    // Function to multiply two values
    long product(long a, long b)
    {
        return a*b;
    }

    // Function to add two values
    long sum(long a, long b)
    {
        return a+b;
    }
```

This example produces the output:

```
3*5 = 15
3 * (4+5) + 6 = 33
```

How It Works

This is hardly a useful program, but it does show very simply how a pointer to a function is declared, assigned a value and subsequently used to call a function.

After the usual preamble, we declare and initialize **pDoIt** — it's a pointer to a function, which can point to either of the two functions that we have defined, **sum()** or **product()**:

```
long (*pDoIt)(long, long) = 0;          // Pointer to function declaration
```

We have initialized **pDoIt** to 0, but we remember that the pointer can only call a function if it's pointing to the function. Therefore, we assign the address of the function **product()** to **pDoIt**:

```
    pDoIt = product;
```

When initializing an ordinary pointer, the name of the function can be entered just as an array name, in the sense that no parentheses or other adornments are required. The function name is automatically converted to an address, which is stored in the pointer.

The function **product()** is then called indirectly through the pointer **pDoIt** in the output statement.

```
    cout << endl
        << "3*5 = " << pDoIt(3, 5);       // Call product thru a pointer
```

The name of the pointer is used just as if it were a function name, and is followed by the arguments, between parentheses, exactly as they would appear if the original function name were being used directly.

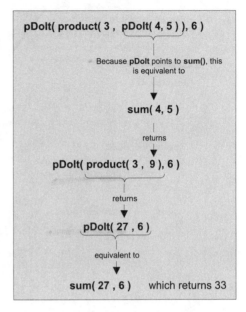

Just to show that we can do it, we change the pointer to point to the function **sum()**. We then use it again in a ludicrously convoluted expression to do some simple arithmetic. This shows that a pointer to a function can be used in exactly the same way as the function that it points to. The sequence of actions in the expression is shown in the diagram:

Passing a Function as an Argument

In fact, 'pointer to function' is a perfectly reasonable type. Therefore, we could write a function which has a 'pointer to a function' as one of its parameters. Then, when the (outer) function uses its 'pointer to function' parameter, it indirectly calls the function pointed to by the corresponding argument at the time the function is called.

Since the pointer can be made to point to different functions in different circumstances, this allows the calling program to determine the particular function that is to be called from inside the (outer) function.

When you call a function with a parameter of type 'pointer to function', the argument can be a pointer of the appropriate type containing the address of a function. Alternatively you can pass a function explicitly by just using a function name as an argument. A function that is passed to another function as an argument is sometimes referred to as a **callback function**.

Try It Out – Passing a Function Pointer

We can look at this with an example. Suppose we need a function that will process an array of numbers by producing the sum of the squares of each of the numbers on some occasions, and the sum of the cubes on other occasions. One way of achieving this is by using a pointer to a function as an argument.

```
// Program 9.6 A pointer to a function as an argument
#include <iostream>

using namespace std;

double squared(double);                      // Function prototype
double cubed(double);                        // Function prototype

double sumarray(double array[], int len, double (*pfun)(double));

int main()
{
  double array[] = { 1.5, 2.5, 3.5, 4.5, 5.5, 6.5, 7.5 };
  int len = sizeof array/sizeof array[0];

  cout << endl
       << "Sum of squares = "
       << sumarray(array, len, squared)
       << endl;

  cout << "Sum of cubes = "
       << sumarray(array, len, cubed)
       << endl;

return 0;
}

// Function for a square of a value
double squared(double x)
{
   return x*x;
}

// Function for a cube of a value
double cubed(double x)
{
   return x*x*x;
}

// Function to sum functions of array elements
double sumarray(double array[], int len, double (*pfun)(double))
{
   double total = 0.0;      // Accumulate total in here

   for(int i = 0 ; i < len ; i++)
     total += pfun(array[i]);

   return total;
}
```

[handwritten annotation: function name is passed (pointer to function)]

This example will generate the output:

```
Sum of squares = 169.75
Sum of cubes = 1015.88
```

How It Works

The first statement of interest is the prototype for the function **sumarray()**. Its third parameter is a pointer to a function which has a parameter of type **double**, and returns a value of type **double**.

```
double sumarray(double array[], int len, double (*pfun)(double));
```

The function **sumarray()** processes each element of the array passed as its first argument, using whichever function is pointed to by its third argument. The function then returns the sum of the processed array elements.

The function **sumarray()** is called twice in **main()**. For the first call, the last argument is **squared**. For the second call, the last argument is **cubed**. In each case, it's the *address* corresponding to the function name which is used as the argument, and is substituted for the function pointer in the body of the function **sumarray()**, so the appropriate function will be called within the **for** loop.

There are obviously easier ways of achieving what this example does, but using a pointer to a function provides you with a lot of generality. You could pass any function to **sumarray()** that you care to define, so long as it takes one **double** argument and returns a value of type **double**.

Arrays of Pointers to Functions

You can declare an array of pointers to functions — it's similar to declaring an array of regular pointers. You can also initialize your array of function pointers, when you declare the array. An example of declaring an array of pointers would be:

```
double sum(double, double);            // Function prototype
double product(double, double);        // Function prototype
double difference(double, double);     // Function prototype
double (*pfun[3])(double,double) =
        { sum, product, difference }; // Array of function pointers
```

Each of the elements in the array is initialized by the corresponding function address appearing in the initializing list between braces. To call the function **product()** using the second element of the pointer array, you would write:

```
pfun[1](2.5, 3.5);
```

The square brackets, which select the function pointer array element, appear immediately after the array name and before the arguments to the function being called. Of course, you can place a function call through an element of a function pointer array, within any expression in which the original function might legitimately appear. The index value selecting the pointer can be any expression producing a valid index value.

Recursion

Finally in this chapter, I'd like to delve into the world of recursive functions. We'll use recursive functions, at the end of this section, to re-examine the solution to the sorting problem that we saw in Chapter 7.

A function in C++ is permitted to call itself where this is appropriate. When a function contains a call to itself, it is referred to as a **recursive function**. A recursive function call can also be indirect — for example, where a function **fun1()** calls another function **fun2()**, which in turn calls the original function **fun1()**.

Recursion may seem like a recipe for an infinite loop, and if you are not careful it certainly can be. A prerequisite for avoiding an infinite loop is that the function contains some means of stopping the process.

What sort of things can recursion be used for? Unless you have come across the technique before, the answer may not be obvious. In physics and mathematics there are many things which can be thought of as involving recursion. A simple example is the factorial of an integer. For a given integer N, the factorial of N is the product $1\times2\times3\times...\times N$. To calculate this, we multiply 1 by 2, then multiply the result by 3, then multiply the result of that by 4 and so on.

This is very often the example given to show recursion in operation. However, we shall look at something even simpler.

Try It Out – A Recursive Function

At the start of the last chapter (see Program 8.1) we produced a function to compute the integral power of a value, that is to compute x^n. For positive values of n this is equivalent to 1 multiplied by x repeated n times; for negative values of n, it is 1 divided by x repeated n times. If n is zero the result is 1. We can implement this as a recursive function as an elementary illustration of recursion in action.

```cpp
// Program 9.7 recursive version of x to the power n
#include <iostream>
#include <iomanip>
using namespace std;

double power(double x, int n);

int main()
{
  cout << endl;

  // Calculate powers of 8 from -3 to +3
  for( int i = -3 ; i <= 3 ; i++)
    cout << setw(10) << power(8.0, i);

  cout << endl;
  return 0;
}
```

```
// Recursive function to calculate x to the power n
double power(double x, int n)
{
  if(0 == n)
    return 1.0;
  if(0 < n)
    return x*power(x, n-1);

  return 1.0/power(x, -n);
}
```

The function **main()** is exactly the same as the previous version so the output is also the same:

```
0.00195313   0.015625      0.125         1        8       64        512
```

How It Works

The first **if** statement returns the value 1.0 if **n** is zero. For positive **n**, the next **if** statement returns the result of the expression, **x*power(x, n-1)**. This causes a further call of the function **power()** with the index value reduced by 1. If, in this call, **n** is still positive, then **power()** will be called again with **n** reduced by 1. Each call of the function will be recorded in the call stack, along with the arguments for the call. This will repeat until **n** is 0, whereupon 1 will be returned and the successive outstanding calls will unwind, multiplying by **x** in each case. In fact, for a given value of **n** greater than 0, the function will call itself **n** times. The mechanism is illustrated in the figure below, assuming the value 3 for the index argument **n**.

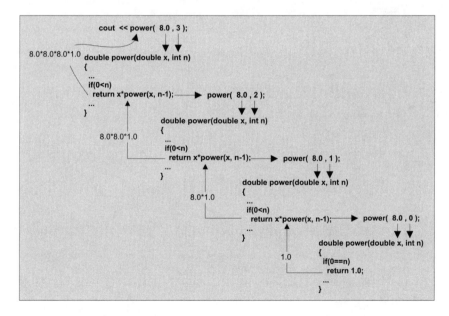

As you see, we need a total of four calls of the **power()** function to generate x^3.

For negative powers of **n**, the reciprocal of x^n is calculated, so this uses the same process that we just described.

Incidentally, you could shorten the code for the **power()** function by using the conditional operator. In fact the function body comes down to a single line:

```
double power(double x, int n)
{
  return 0 == n ? 1.0 : (0 > n ? 1.0/power(x, -n) : x*power(x, n-1));
}
```

This doesn't improve the operation particularly, and perhaps it's not quite as clear what is happening. In fact the recursive call process is very inefficient compared to a loop. Every function call involves a lot of housekeeping that includes obtaining and storing the return address, copying each of the arguments and handing over the arguments to the function being called. Implementing the function **power()** using a loop rather than recursive calls would be a lot faster:

```
double power(double x, int n)
{
  if(0 == n)
    return 1.0;
  if(0 > n)
  {
    x = 1.0/x;
    n = -n;
  }

  double result = x;
  for(int i = 1 ; i < n ; i++)
    result *= x;
  return result;
}
```

Using Recursion

Unless you have a problem which particularly lends itself to using recursive functions, or if you have no obvious alternative, it is generally better to use a different approach, such as a loop. This will be much more efficient than using recursive function calls. You also need to take care that the depth of recursion necessary to solve your problem is not itself a problem.

Sometimes, however, using recursion can considerably simplify the coding in some instances, and the gain in simplicity can sometimes be well worth the consequent loss in efficiency.

Implementing sorting and merging operations provides us with a good example in which recursion is often favored. Often, sorting and merging sets of data is a recursive process in which you reapply the same algorithm to smaller and smaller subsets of the original data. Let's look at an example.

Implementing a Sort Recursively

In Program 7.9, we extracted words from some input text and sorted them in ascending sequence by initial letter, using an array of pointers. We could implement a recursive function to sort the words using a well known sorting algorithm called *Quicksort*. Although this is an ancient method — it was invented more than 30 years ago — it is still the fastest general-purpose sorting method around.

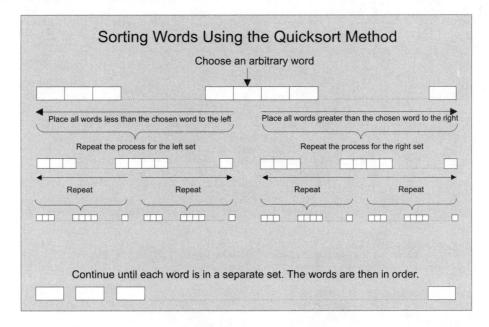

To apply the Quicksort algorithm to sorting the words, we first choose some arbitrary word from the set, such as the one in the middle. We then arrange the remaining words so all those that are 'less than' the chosen word will be to the left of the chosen word (though not necessarily in sequence), and all those that are 'greater than' the chosen word are to the right (again, not necessarily in sequence). The diagram illustrates this process.

Having performed this process once, we just repeat the process for each of the two resulting sets — to produce four sets. We repeat the process again, continuing until each word is in a separate set. The words are then in ascending order. we reach the goal by repeated subdivision of a set, always via the same process. This is a good indication that we should be able to implement the process using recursion.

Of course, we will do this by rearranging addresses in an array, not by moving words around. The diagram below shows a method for partitioning the addresses of the words into two sets, with the rearranged addresses in the original array.

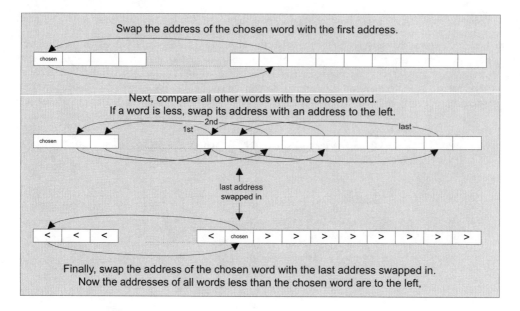

Swap the address of the chosen word with the first address.

Next, compare all other words with the chosen word.
If a word is less, swap its address with an address to the left.

Finally, swap the address of the chosen word with the last address swapped in.
Now the addresses of all words less than the chosen word are to the left,

We have to swap addresses in the array in several places, so it would be a good idea to write a function to do this:

```
// Swap address at position first with address at position second
void swap(string* pStr[], int first, int second)
{
  string* temp = pStr[first];
  pStr[first] = pStr[second];
  pStr[second] = temp;
}
```

We can use this to implement the Quicksort method by rearranging the elements in the address array in the manner illustrated in the diagram. The sorting algorithm itself should look something like this:

```
// Sort strings in ascending sequence
// Addresses of words to be sorted are from pStr[start] to pStr[end]
void sort(string* pStr[], int start, int end)
{
  // start index must be less than end index for 2 or more elements
  if(!(start<end))
    return;                          // Less than 2 elements - nothing to do

  // Choose middle address to partition set
  swap(pStr, start, (start+end)/2);          // Swap middle address with start

  // Check words against chosen word
  int current = start;
  for(int i = start+1; i<=end ; i++)
    if(*(pStr[i]) < *(pStr[start]))     // Is word less than chosen word?
      swap(pStr, ++current, i);         // Yes, so swap to the left

  swap(pStr, start, current);           // Swap the chosen word with last in
```

```
    sort(pStr, start, current-1);          // Partition the left set
    sort(pStr, current+1, end);            // Partition the right set
}
```

The function **sort()** uses three parameters: the array of addresses that we will sort, **pStr**, and the index positions of the first and last addresses in the set. The *first* time the function is called, **start** will be 0 and **end** will be the index for the last array element. In subsequent recursive calls, we will be partitioning just a part of the array, so **start** and **end** will contain interior index positions in many cases.

The steps of **sort()** are summarized as follows.

We know that recursive functions can lead to infinite loops, so we begin our function with the check that will stop the recursive function calls. If there are less than two elements in a set, they cannot be partitioned so we return. With each recursion, we partition a set into two *smaller* sets — therefore, we must end up eventually with a set that has either one or no elements.

Next, we swap the address in the middle of the set with the first address at index position **start**. The **for** loop compares the chosen word with words pointed to by the addresses following **start**. For any word which is *less than* the chosen word, its address is swapped into a position following **start**: the first goes into position **start+1**, the second to **start+2** and so on. When the loop ends, **current** contains the index position of the address of the last of these swapped words. The address of the chosen word is still at position **start**, so we swap the address of the chosen word (at position **start**) with the address at **current**. As a result, the addresses of words *less than* the chosen word are to the left of **current**; and the addresses of words *greater* are to the right.

So far we have partitioned a set of words; from here, sorting the whole set of words is easy. We simply have to sort the two subsets we have produced — to do this, we just call the **sort()** function for each subset. The addresses of words less than the chosen word run from **start** to **current-1**, and the addresses of those greater run from **current+1** to **end**.

> *Using recursion makes the code relatively easy to follow, and it is much shorter and less convoluted than if we implemented the sort using loops. A loop would still be faster, though.*

Try It Out – Sorting Words Recursively

Let's produce another version of Program 7.9 that uses the **sort()** function that we just wrote. At the same time, we can make the program more manageable by breaking it up into functions. There are three blocks of code in the original version of **main()**, which are candidates for separate functions: counting the words, creating string objects corresponding to the words and displaying the words in sequence.

The first of these functions (counting the words in the input text) will need access to the original text as well as the string object containing the separator characters. It can return the word count as an **int**. The prototype for this function will be:

```
int countWords(const string& text, const string& separators);
```

Both parameters should be **const** references, since the function does not need to modify them. The word count produced by this function will be used to create an array of pointers of the appropriate size, in the free store.

The next function (extracting words from the input) will need the array of addresses as a parameter, as well as the input text and the separators, so the prototype will be:

```
void extractWords(string* pStr[], const string& text, const string& separators);
```

Obviously, the array parameter can't be declared as **const** here, since the function will store the addresses obtained from **new** in the array. The function doesn't need to access the word count, because the extracting process doesn't require it.

The last of these functions (outputting the words) will need access to the pointer array and the word count as parameters, so its prototype will be:

```
void showWords(const string* pStr[], int count);
```

This doesn't modify the array, so we can use a **const** parameter to pass the array.

We can now use these functions together with the **sort()** and **swap()** functions that we developed earlier in the definition of **main()**:

```
// Program 9.8 Sorting strings recursively
#include <iostream>
#include <string>

using namespace std;

void swap(string* pStr[], int first, int second);
void sort(string* pStr[], int start, int end);
int countWords(const string& text, const string& separators);
void extractWords(string* pStr[], const string& text, const string& separators);
void showWords(const string* pStr[], int count);

int main()
{
  string text;                             // The string to be sorted
  const string separators = " ,.\"\n";     // Word delimiters

  // Read the string to be searched from the keyboard
  cout << endl << "Enter a string terminated by #:" << endl;
  getline(cin, text, '#');

  int word_count = countWords(text, separators);      // Get count of words stored

  if(0 == word_count)
  {
    cout << endl << "No words in text." << endl;
    return 0;
  }

  string** pWords = new string*[word_count];      // Array of pointers to the words

  extractWords(pWords, text, separators);         // Create string objects for words
```

```
      sort(pWords, 0, word_count-1);                    // Sort the words
      showWords(pWords, word_count);                    // Display the words

      // Delete words from free store
      for(int i = 0 ; i<word_count ; i++)
        delete pWords[i];

      // Now delete the array of pointers
      delete[] pWords;

      return 0;
    }
```

To complete the program we just need the definitions for the three new functions. Here's the code for the **countWords()** function:

```
int countWords(const string& text, const string& separators)
{
  int start = text.find_first_not_of(separators);   // Word start index
  int end = 0;                                       // End delimiter index
  int word_count = 0;                                // Count of words stored
  while(start != string::npos)
  {
    end = text.find_first_of(separators, start+1);
    if(end == string::npos)                          // Found one?
      end = text.length();                           // No, so set to last+1

    word_count++;                                    // Increment count

    // Find the first character of the next word
    start = text.find_first_not_of(separators, end+1);
  }
  return word_count;
}
```

It is much the same as the original code, but we have packed it into a function. The same goes for the **extractWords()** function:

```
void extractWords(string* pStr[], const string& text, const string& separators)
{
  int start = text.find_first_not_of(separators);   // Start of first word
  int end = 0;                                       // Index for the end of a word
  int index = 0;                                     // Pointer array index

  while(start != string::npos)
  {
    end = text.find_first_of(separators, start+1);   // Find end separator
    if(end == string::npos)                          // Found one?
      end = text.length();                           // No, so set to last+1
    pStr[index++] = new string(text.substr(start, end-start));

    start = text.find_first_not_of(separators, end+1); // Find start of next word
  }
}
```

To output the words in groups beginning with the same letter, with up to five words per line, we can implement **showWords()** as:

```cpp
// Output the words
void showWords(const string* pStr[], int count)
{
  const int words_per_line = 5;                    // Word_per_line
  cout << endl << "   " << *pStr[0];               // Output the first word

  int words_in_line = 0;                           // Words in the current line
  for(int i = 1 ; i<count ; i++)                   // Output remaining words
  {
    // Start newline when initial letter changes or after 5 words on a line
    if((*pStr[i])[0] != (*pStr[i-1])[0] || words_in_line++ == words_per_line)
    {
      words_in_line = 0;
      cout << endl;
    }
    cout << "   " << *pStr[i];                      // Output a word

  }
  cout << endl;
}
```

If you run the program it will work in the same way as the original version in Chapter 7, but the code is much easier to understand with the structure that the functions provide. It would also be easier to modify the program if it became necessary. Using an array here creates the requirement to traverse the text looking for words twice, because we need to know how many elements are necessary in the pointer array. There are other ways of approaching this that would remove the need to know the number of words. One possibility would be to store the addresses in a linked list. Then a single traversal of the text could create the word objects and add them to the list.

Summary

You should now have a reasonably comprehensive knowledge of writing and using functions. However, we will see more on functions in the context of user-defined types, which we will introduce starting in Chapter 11.

The important bits that you learned in this chapter are:

- Overloaded functions are functions with the same name, but with different parameter lists. Overloaded functions cannot be differentiated by the return type alone.

- The function signature is defined by the function name plus the number and types of the arguments that you specify. When you call an overloaded function, the compiler examines the function signature and compares it to the available functions, before selecting the appropriate function.

- A function template is a recipe for generating overloaded functions automatically.

- A function template has one or more parameters that are usually type variables, but can also be non-type variables. An instance of the function template — that is, a function definition — will be created by the compiler for each function call that corresponds to a unique set of template arguments.

- A function template can be overloaded with other functions or function templates.

- A pointer to a function stores the address of a function, plus information about the number and types of parameters and return type for a function.

- You can use a pointer to a function to store the address of any function with the appropriate return type, and number and types of parameters.

- You can use a pointer to a function to call the function at the address it contains. You can also pass a pointer to a function as a function argument.

- A recursive function is a function that calls itself. Implementing an algorithm recursively can sometimes result in very elegant and concise code, but usually at the expense of increased execution time compared to other methods of implementing the same algorithm.

Exercises

Ex 9.1 Create a function, **plus()**, which adds two values and returns their sum. Provide overloaded versions to work with **int**, **double** and **string** types, and test that they work with the following calls:

```
int n = plus(3, 4);
double d = plus(3.2, 4.2);
string s = plus("he", "llo");
string s1 = "aaa"; string s2 = "bbb";
string s3 = plus(s1, s2);
```

What is the most efficient way to pass the arguments to the **string** version of the function? Can you explain why the call:

```
d = plus(3, 4.2);
```

does not work?

Ex 9.2 Turn the **plus()** function into a template, and test that it works for numeric types. Does your template work for the statement (**plus("he", "llo")**) in Exercise 9.1? Can you explain this behavior? Suggest a solution to the problem.

Ex 9.3 The standard library provides trigonometry functions **sin()**, **cos()** and **tan()**; each of them takes a **double** argument and returns a **double** value. To use them you need to **#include** the standard library header file **cmath**. Write a function **calc()** that takes two arguments — a **double** value and a pointer to a trig function — and returns the result of applying the function to the value as a **double**. Write a program to test your function; when this works, set up an array of function pointers to hold the three trig functions and test it using those.

Ex 9.4 There's a recursive function, called Ackerman's function, that is popular with lecturers of computer science and mathematics courses, and can be defined like this:

If **m** and **n** are integers, then where **n >= 0** and **m >= 0**, then
ack(m,n) = n+1, if **m == 0**
ack(m,n) = ack(m-1, 1), if **n == 0** and **m > 0**
ack(m,n) = ack(m-1, ack(m, n-1)), otherwise

Write a function to compute Ackerman's function recursively, and then test it for values of **n** between 0 and 5, and **m** between 0 and 3. One particular property of this function is that the amount (or *depth*) of recursion increases dramatically for small increases in **m** and **n**, so don't try calculating it recursively for **n > 5** or **m > 3**, as there isn't a computer in existence which has enough power to do it!

Program Files and the Preprocessor

In this chapter we will look into subjects that relate to how multiple program files and header files interact, and to how you can manage and control the contents of your program files.

We have yet to discuss the major topic, classes. We will begin to define our own data types in the next chapter, and this will (in part) form a gentle introduction to classes. The material of this chapter will have implications on how we define our own data types, and we will discuss those implications as we come to them.

In this chapter you will learn:

▶ The details of how header files and program files interrelate

▶ What a translation unit is

▶ What linkage is and why it is important

▶ What namespaces are and how you create and use them

▶ What the preprocessor is, and how to use the preprocessor directives that are available

▶ The basic ideas in debugging, and what debugging help you can get from the preprocessor and the standard library

Working with Program Files

Way back in Chapter 1, we talked about how your C++ program will, in general, consist of multiple files. Let's recap on that a little. Two basic kinds of files are involved:

▶ **Header files**, which are commonly identified with the file name extension **.h** (note that some older systems use **.hpp**)

▶ **Source files**, which usually have the extension **.cpp**, and will contain your code that will compile to machine instructions — primarily function definitions.

As we have seen, the *standard* header files for library functions in ANSI C++ (for example, **iostream**) have no extension. Of course, there may be other kinds of files supporting the environment in which you are programming (defining resources of one kind or another, perhaps) but the **.h** and **.cpp** files are the ones that will contain all your C++ code.

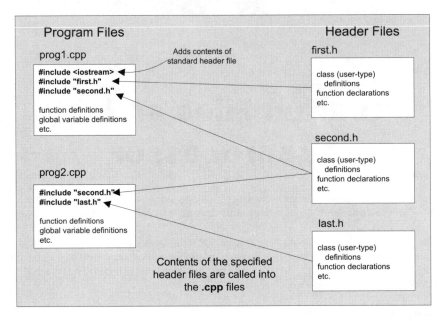

The essential difference between a header file and a **.cpp** file is in how each is used. By convention:

- **.cpp** files contain code that determines what your program does (primarily function definitions) — that is, the logic of your program.

- **.h** files contain your function declarations (that is, the prototypes, but not the definitions), type definitions and preprocessor directives.

- You should avoid putting function definitions in a **.h** file (**inline** functions are an exception to this rule).

- Each **.cpp** must **#include** any header files that it needs.

- When you compile your program, you compile just the **.cpp** files, which will incorporate the contents of the **#include**d header files as necessary.

Each **.cpp** file that you compile will produce an **object file**. The term 'object file' has nothing to do with class objects. An object file is simply a file that contains the binary output from the compiler; it is often identified with the extension **.obj**. The object files are combined by the linker into a single executable module, that usually has the extension **.exe**.

So far, we have used only header files that provide the declarations necessary for using the standard library. Our program examples have been short and simple; consequently, they have not warranted the use of separate header files, which contain our function declarations or constant definitions. In the next chapter, when we begin to define our own data types, the need for header files will become apparent. A typical practical C++ program will involve a number of header files and **.cpp** files.

Program Files and Linkage

Each **.cpp** file in your program, along with all its header files included, is called a **translation unit.** The compiler processes each **.cpp** file independently to generate an object file. These object files are then processed by the linker, which ties together any necessary connections between the object files to produce the executable program module.

The names of entities (variables, functions, parameters and so on) in a translation unit are handled in the compile/link process, in a way which is determined from a property called **linkage**. This can be a somewhat confusing property, so let's take it step by step.

Every name (or identifier) that you use in a program either has linkage, or it does not have linkage. A name has linkage when it may be used to access a variable or a function in your program from *outside* the scope in which the name is declared. Otherwise it has no linkage.

> *Remember that some names don't refer to variables or functions. A type that is declared using a* **typedef** *statement, for example, is a name that does not have linkage.*

If a name has linkage, then it can have **internal linkage** or **external linkage**. This depends on the context and scope of the name. Let's elaborate on what scope means for a moment.

The **scope**, for a name in your program, is the term used to specify the range of statements over which the name is valid. You already know that a variable name or other name declared within a statement block (enclosed between braces) has **block scope** — this is also referred to as **local scope**, because such a name is local to the block that immediately contains the declaration. A name with block scope can only be used from the point at which it is declared up to the closing brace for the block.

A name which is declared outside of all blocks (a function or a variable, for instance) is said to have **global scope**. This is also referred to as **file scope**, because the name is valid from the point of its declaration until the end of the file (translation unit) that contains it.

Now we have scope clear in our minds, let's understand what the different linkage possibilities imply, and to what kinds of names they apply. Note that a name's linkage is not affected by whether or not its declaration appears in a header file. The linkage for declarations in a translation unit is determined *after* the contents of any header files have been inserted. Linkage for a name is determined as follows:

Description	Examples
A name with **internal linkage** can be referred to from within different scopes in the same translation unit. A name with internal linkage cannot access an entity in another translation unit: so such a name is local to a translation unit.	Variables with file scope which are declared as **static.** Variables with file scope which are declared as **const.** Functions in a translation unit that are declared as **static**.

Table Continued on Following Page

Description	Examples
A name with **external linkage** can refer to an entity within any of the translation units that make up the program. In other words, a single entity can be shared and accessed throughout the program.	All names with file scope — other than names declared as **static**, names declared as **const** that have not been declared as external, **typedef** names and enumerator names. Thus, non-static function names and non-static variables with file scope have external linkage.
A name with **no linkage** refers to a unique entity.	Any variables declared within blocks that have not been declared as external. Any name that does not refer to either a function or a variable — e.g. enumerator names, **typedef** names or function parameter names in a function prototype or function definition.

Internal linkage also applies to names in another set of circumstances: we will cover this later, in our discussion of namespaces. In general, most names that have linkage are names that are declared outside of all function bodies.

Now, the interesting question is this: From within a function, how do you access a variable that is defined outside the body of the function? This comes down to how a variable is declared to be external.

External Variables

In a program which is made up of several files, the connection between a function call in one source file, and the function definition in another, is established (or **resolved**) by the linker. Before the linker acts, the compiler will compile a *call* to the function — to do this, it extracts the necessary information from the function prototype. The compiler doesn't really mind whether the function's *definition* occurs in the same file or in another **.cpp** file — the linker will sort it out. This is because functions have external linkage by default. If you want to force a function in a source file to have internal linkage, you can define it as **static**.

Variable names are different. Automatic variables defined within a function body have no linkage. If you want to use a name to access a variable from within a function body, and the variable is defined *outside* the function body, then you must declare the variable using the **extern** keyword.

Declaring a variable as **extern** implies that it is defined somewhere outside the present scope. The variable could be defined at global scope within the same file, in which case the compiler will be able to resolve the reference to the variable while compiling the translation unit. On the other hand, it could be defined in another translation unit, and in this case, all the compiler can do is inform the linker that a connection must be made — it is the linker that actually makes the connection between the name and the variable to which it refers. The diagram below illustrates the two possible situations for accessing an external variable.

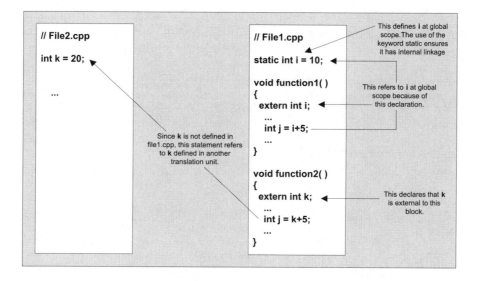

The important application of **extern** is illustrated by the name **k** in **File1.cpp**, so let's look at that first. The **extern** declaration for the name **k** in **function2()** says that any subsequent use of **k** in that function refers to **k** that is defined somewhere outside of the function block. Note that the **extern** declaration does *not* define **k**, it merely indicates that it is defined somewhere else. Here, the name **k** has external linkage, because it refers to a variable in a separate translation unit. The compiler cannot connect the name to the variable definition, and so the connection must be made by the linker.

The second case is illustrated by the name **i**. (This case is included for comparison here, although we'll see in a moment that the example would be better coded with a scope resolution operator.)

Again, the **extern** declaration for the name **i** in **function1()** says that any subsequent use of **i** in **function1()** refers to a variable **i** that is defined somewhere outside of the function block. In this case, there is a name **i** in **File1.cpp**, which is declared as **static** in that file, and therefore has internal linkage. This time, it is the compiler that makes the connection between the name **i** declared as **extern** in the function and the variable declared at global scope.

In practice, **extern** is almost never used within a function to access a variable at global scope in the same file. Such 'same-file' access is achieved by using the **scope resolution operator**, **::**. You enter this operator as two successive colons. The **function1()** example in the previous diagram would more typically be coded as:

```
static int i = 10;
void function1()
{
   // Code for the function that possibly defines a local i...
   int j = ::i + 5;                        // Refers to i at global scope
   // More code...
}
```

The expression **::i** that we use refers to the variable **i** contained in what we call the **global namespace**, and employs the *unary* form of the scope resolution operator. We'll see much more about namespaces, and the scope resolution operator, later in this chapter.

> *Names that are declared as* **extern** *are usually reserved for variables that are defined in a different file. In the case of a* static *variable, defined in the same file as the* extern *declaration, a scope resolution operator is generally preferred.*

Accessing consts in another File

Let's take another example. Suppose we have variables defined as global in a file **file1.cpp** using the statements:

```
double pi = 3.14159265;
string days[] = {
                "Sunday",   "Monday", "Tuesday", "Wednesday",
                "Thursday", "Friday", "Saturday"
             };
```

These statements define the variable **pi** and the array **days[]**, so there cannot be duplicate definitions for the same variables elsewhere. However, we can access these variables from another function in a different source file (or, for that matter, in the same source file), by declaring the variables as external. For example, a function in the file **file2.cpp** will contain the following statements:

```
extern double pi;           // Variable is defined in another file
extern string days[];       // Array is defined in another file
```

These statements do not create the variables — they merely identify that they are defined elsewhere, so the compiler does not expect to find them within the present scope. The variables are used in **file2.cpp**, but their actual locations are determined by their definitions in **file1.cpp**. This connection will be established by the linker when the object files are linked together.

> *Of course, if you declare a name as external, and its corresponding definition is not found, then you will get an error message from the linker and no executable module will be created.*

In this example, you probably want to avoid the possibility of these variables being altered. Therefore you might consider making each of them **const** when you define them in **file1.cpp**:

```
const double pi = 3.14159265;
const string days[] = {
                    "Sunday",   "Monday", "Tuesday", "Wednesday",
                    "Thursday", "Friday", "Saturday"
                 };
```

However, declaring them as **const** will have the effect of giving them internal linkage by default, and this will make them unavailable in other translation units. You can override this by using the **extern** keyword when you define them:

```
extern const double pi = 3.14159265;
extern const string days[] = {
                             "Sunday",   "Monday", "Tuesday", "Wednesday",
                             "Thursday", "Friday", "Saturday"
                            };
```

These statements still define the **const double** and the **const** array. The use of the keyword **extern** here tells the compiler that these variable names should have external linkage, even though they are **const**s.

Now, when you want to access these in **file2.cpp**, you must declare them as **const**, as well as external:

```
extern const double pi;         // Variable is defined in another file
extern const string days[];     // Array is defined in another file
```

Within the block in which these declarations appear, the use of the names **pi** and **days** will refer to the constants defined in the other file. Clearly, you can have as many declarations for external variables as you want. Of course, any external variable of a given type or non-inline function, can only have one definition in a program. (Note that a definition for an inline function must appear in every translation unit in which the function is used, but the definition must be the same in each.)

Global variables can be useful for constant values that you want to share. Indeed, by sharing constant values across all of the program files that need access to them, you can ensure that the same values are being used for the constants throughout your program. However, in general you should be aware of the disadvantages in declaring a variable as global. If your function uses a global variable, then it has an external dependency, which means that it is no longer a nice clean self-contained package of code. This makes for messy program structure, and limits the degree to which your function can be reused in another program.

Global variables are always initialized. If you don't supply an initial value for a global variable, it will be initialized with 0.

Let's see how some of what we have discussed works in practice.

Try It Out – Using External Variables

We can create a source file containing some data definitions:

```
// File data10_1.cpp
#include <string>
using namespace std;

// The next two variables have external linkage
int count;                              // Will be initialized to 0 by default
float phi = 1.618f;                     // The divine proportion or golden ratio

// Without the extern, the following would not be accessible from another file
extern const double pi = 3.14159265;
```

```
extern const string days[] = {
                             "Sunday",    "Monday", "Tuesday", "Wednesday",
                             "Thursday", "Friday", "Saturday"
                        };
```

We can now access these from another source file:

```
// Program 10.1 Accessing External Variables prog10_1.cpp
#include <iostream>
#include <string>
#include <iomanip>
using namespace std;

// Declare external variables
extern float phi;
extern const double pi;
extern const string days[];
extern int count;

int main()
{
  cout << setprecision(3) << fixed;
  cout << endl
       << "To 3 decimal places..." << endl;

  cout << "...a circle with a diameter of phi has an area of " << pi*phi*phi/4
       << endl;

  cout << "...phi squared is "         << phi*phi << endl;
  cout << "...in fact, phi+1 is also " << phi+1    << endl;

  cout << "Value of count is " << count << endl;

  count += 3;
  cout << "Today is " << days[count] << endl;
  return 0;
}
```

This example produces the output:

```
To 3 decimal places...
...a circle with a diameter of phi has an area of 2.056
...phi squared is 2.618
...in fact, phi+1 is also 2.618
Value of count is 0
Today is Wednesday
```

How It Works

Fortunately, it works exactly as we discussed. You can see that **phi** is demonstrably external since it is used in one file, in **main()**, but is defined in another file. The constant **pi** and the constant array **days** also have external linkage because they are declared as **extern**. Try removing the **extern** keyword — the code won't compile.

We display the default value for **count** so it has clearly been initialized to 0. Finally we modify the value of **count** and use it to index the **days** array.

Namespaces

With large programs, choosing unique names for all the entities that have external linkage can become difficult. This is particularly true when an application is being developed by several programmers working in parallel, or when a vendor wants to produce a library for sale to third parties. Without some kind of mechanism to prevent it, name clashes become highly likely. This is most likely in the context of user-defined types, or classes, which we will meet in the next few chapters. A **namespace** is designed to overcome this difficulty.

A namespace is a region within a program that attaches an extra name — a namespace name — to all the entity names within it. Two different namespaces can each contain entities with the same name, but the entities will be differentiated because a different namespace name is attached to each of them. The diagram illustrates two namespaces defined within a single program, possibly within the same source file.

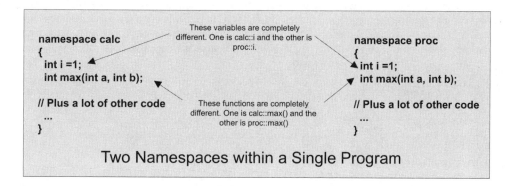

Two Namespaces within a Single Program

In each namespace, there is a variable defined with the name **i**, and a function declared with the name **max()**; however, they each refer to *distinct* entities with no possibility of a clash between them. You would typically use a separate namespace name within a single program for each collection of code that encompasses a common purpose. Each namespace would represent some logical grouping of functions, together with any related global variables and declarations. A namespace would also be used to completely contain a unit of release, such as a library.

You are already aware that the standard library is defined within the namespace **std**. This implies that every external name in the standard library is prefixed with **std**. For instance, the output stream name is **std::cout**, so to display the contents of a variable, **value**, you could write:

```
std::cout << std::endl << value;
```

The operator **::** here is the binary form of the **scope resolution operator**, that we saw earlier. The statement above **qualifies** the names **cout** and **endl** — it says to the compiler, "You'll find the definition of these names in the **std** namespace." Of course, you will immediately appreciate that this is not what we have be doing in the examples so far in this book. This is because we have been adding the following statement to our programs:

```
using namespace std;
```

In principle, this **using directive** allows all the names in the namespace, **std**, to be used without qualification. Of course, any name that you want to use must appear in a declaration in the translation unit prior to where you want to use it. So in this case, the names in the **std** namespace that you can use will be those in the standard header files that have been included into the file.

The **using** directive allows the appearance of your code to be simplified somewhat, and in all our examples so far, that has been our motivation for employing the **using** directive. However, you need to be cautious when doing this. If you employ the **using** directive for *all* your namespaces, it defeats the purpose of using namespaces at all. We will come back to the **using** directive later in this discussion.

The Global Namespace

All the programs that we have written so far have used names that we declared in the **global namespace**. The global namespace applies by default in the absence of a namespace being defined. All names within the global namespace are just as you declare them, without a namespace name being attached. In a program with multiple source files, all the names with linkage are within the global namespace.

With small programs, you can define your names within the global namespace without running into any problems. With larger applications, the potential for name clashes increases so you should use namespaces to partition your code into logical groupings. That way, each code segment will be self-contained from a naming perspective, and name clashes will be prevented.

Of course, you need to know how to declare a namespace, so let's look at that next.

Declaring a Namespace

You can declare a namespace with the statements:

```
namespace myRegion
{
    // Code you want to have in the namespace, including
    // function definitions and declarations, global variables,
    // templates, etc.
}
```

The namespace name assigned here is **myRegion**. This uniquely identifies the namespace and this name will be attached to all the entities declared within the namespace. The braces enclose the scope for the namespace **myRegion**, and every name within the namespace scope will have the name **myRegion** attached to it.

> *Of course, you would not include the function* main() *within the namespace. The runtime environment expects* main() *to be defined in the global namespace, so you must always place the function* main() *outside all your namespaces.*
>
> *Note that, at the end of the namespace declaration, there is* no *semi-colon following the closing brace.*

You can extend a namespace scope by adding a second namespace definition in a file. For example, a program file might contain:

```
namespace calc
{
  // This defines namespace calc
  // The initial code in the namespace goes here
}

namespace sort
{
  // Code in a new namespace, sort
}

namespace calc
{
  // This extends the namespace calc
  // Code in here can refer to names in the previous
  // calc namespace block without qualification
}
```

Here, we have two blocks declared as namespace **calc**, separated by a namespace **sort**. The second **calc** block is treated as a continuation of the first. Therefore, functions defined within each of the **calc** blocks all belong to the same namespace. The second block is referred to as an **extension namespace definition**, because it extends the original namespace definition. You can have further extension namespace definitions in the file, adding more code within the same namespace.

Of course, you would not usually organize a program file in this way directly. However, if you **#include** several header files into your program file, and each header file contributes some code to the same namespace, then you effectively have the sort of situation described above. A common example of this is when you **#include** a number of standard library headers (each of which contributes to the namespace **std**), interspersed with header files of your own (defined within a different namespace). For example:

```
#include <iostream>        // In namespace std
#include "mystuff.h"       // In my namespace calc
#include <string>          // In namespace std - extension namespace definition
#include "morestuff.h"     // In my namespace calc - extension namespace definition
```

Finally, note that references to names within a namespace *from inside the same namespace* do not need to be qualified. For example, names that belong to the namespace **calc** can be referenced from within **calc**, without the need to qualify them with the namespace name.

Let's take a simple example to illustrate the mechanics of declaring and using a namespace.

Try It Out – Using a Namespace

We will create a program consisting of two **.cpp** files. The first will just contain definitions of some **const**s that we defined earlier, but this time defined within a namespace:

```
// Program 10.2 Using a namespace    Data10_2.cpp
#include <string>

namespace data
{
  extern const double pi = 3.14159265;
  extern const std::string days[] = {
                              "Sunday",   "Monday", "Tuesday", "Wednesday",
                              "Thursday", "Friday", "Saturday"
                          };
}
```

Here we have defined **pi** and **days[]** within the namespace **data**. The array **days[]** is of type **string**, which is defined in the standard library, so we need to qualify the type name with the standard library namespace name, **std**.

We will use these variables in another translation unit, which will contain **main()**:

```
// Program 10.2 Using a namespace    Prog10_2.cpp
#include <iostream>
#include <string>

namespace data
{
  extern const double pi;              // Variable is defined in another file
  extern const std::string days[];     // Array is defined in another file
}

int main()
{
  std::cout << std::endl
            << "pi has the value "
            << data::pi << std::endl;

  std::cout << "The second day of the week is "
            << data::days[1] << std::endl;

  return 0;
}
```

If you compile and run this it will produce the output:

```
pi has the value 3.14159
The second day of the week is Monday
```

How It Works

In the file containing **main()**, we must declare **pi** and **days[]** as external, since they are defined in a separate translation unit. We do this with the statements:

```
namespace data
{
  extern const double pi;              // Variable is defined in another file
  extern const std::string days[];     // Array is defined in another file
}
```

We have to place the declarations for the external variables within the namespace **data**, because the variables are defined within this namespace in the first **.cpp** file. This demonstrates the point that we discussed earlier — that a namespace can be defined piecemeal. Even within a single file, there can be several namespace blocks corresponding to the same namespace name, and the contents of each will be in the same namespace. Since the type **string** is defined within the standard library namespace, we have to supply the qualified name **std::string** in the declaration.

As a general rule, you should put these declarations for **pi** and **days** in a header file, **data.h** say. The contents of this header file would just be:

```
// Declarations for globals in namespace data    data.h
namespace data
{
  extern const double pi;            // Variable is defined in another file
  extern const std::string days[];   // Array is defined in another file
}
```

Then, to make the declarations available in the file containing **main()** (or any other file that needed access to these variables), you would simply need to add a **#include** directive at the beginning:

```
#include "data.h"
```

The name has the extension **.h** to identify that it is a header file. We'll see this in action in Program 10.3.

> **FYI**
>
> The syntax for #include is slightly different here. You should omit the .h extension *only* when including *standard library* headers. We will see the significance of the double quotes rather than angled brackets when we discuss the preprocessor, later in this chapter. It's also important to ensure that the contents of a header file are not included more than once into a translation unit, and we will also see how that is done.

Back in Program 10.2, the code in the body of **main()** just consists of two output statements:

```
std::cout << std::endl
        << "pi has the value "
        << data::pi << std::endl;

std::cout << "The second day of the week is "
        << data::days[1] << std::endl;
```

The function **main()** is in the global namespace (it must be, otherwise it won't be recognized), so any name used in **main()** that is declared and defined in another namespace must be qualified — either directly, or implicitly via a **using** directive (or in some other way, that we will see later). Since we do not have a **using** directive for the namespace **std** in the source file, we must qualify each name that is from the standard library. Thus **cout** and **endl** must be qualified with the namespace name **std**, so that they can be recognized by the compiler. The constants **pi** and **days** are defined and declared within the namespace **data**, so these names must be qualified too.

Implicitly Qualifying Names

In principle, the **using** directive can make all the names in a namespace available. In the previous example, we could add a **using** directive for the namespace **std**, and avoid the necessity of qualifying **cout** and **endl** explicitly. The file contents would then be:

```
// Program 10.2 Using a namespace    Prog10_2.cpp
#include <iostream>
#include <string>

namespace data
{
  extern const double pi;            // Variable is defined in another file
  extern const std::string days[];   // Array is defined in another file
}

using namespace std;

int main()
{
  cout << endl
       << "pi has the value "
       << data::pi << endl;

  cout << "The second day of the week is "
       << data::days[1] << endl;

  return 0;
}
```

Now, we don't need to qualify **cout** and **endl**, although we still could if we wanted to. You would need to do this if you had a name of your own that clashed with a name in the standard library namespace. It would be silly to do so, but to illustrate the point you could write:

```
int cout = 10;
std::cout << Value of variable cout is " << cout;
```

In this code fragment, there is a variable **cout** defined here of type **int**, which is contained in the global namespace. There is also an output stream, **cout**, but this belongs to the **std** namespace. In the second line above, **cout** is understood to refer to the global variable, which effectively masks the output stream **cout**, even if we have a **using** directive. You can still get at the output stream **cout** by using the namespace name as a qualifier, as shown in the second statement.

> *When you use an unqualified variable name, the compiler will first try to find the definition of the variable in the current scope, prior to the point at which it is used. If it is not found, then it will look in the immediately enclosing scope. This will continue until the global scope is reached. If a declaration for the variable is not found at global scope (which could be an* extern *declaration), the compiler will conclude that the variable is not defined.*

By adding a **using** directive for the namespace data just before **main()** in the last example, we can anticipate the need to qualify any of the names, so the file contents would be:

```
// Program 10.2 Using a namespace    Prog10_2.cpp
#include <iostream>
#include <string>

namespace data
{
  extern const double pi;              // Variable is defined in another file
  extern const std::string days[];     // Array is defined in another file
}

using namespace std;
using namespace data;

int main()
{
  cout << endl
       << "pi has the value "
       << pi << endl;

  cout << "The second day of the week is "
       << days[1] << endl;

  return 0;
}
```

In this case, this makes the code much simpler. If, later, we developed this program so that **std** and **data** namespaces both contained a certain name, then we would resolve the ambiguity in the program by using the scope resolution operator. Of course, if there were lots of ambiguities then we'd lose the simplicity of the code again, even with the **using** directives. An alternative approach, which sits nicely between these extremes, is to use **using** declarations rather than **using** directives.

Applying using Declarations

A **using declaration** declares a specific name from within a given namespace. Each **using** declaration declares a single name, which can then be used unqualified following the declaration. A **using** declaration is of the form:

using *namespace_name*::*identifier*;

where **using** is a keyword, ***namespace_name*** is the name of the namespace and ***identifier*** is the name that we want to use unqualified. Note that this introduces a name from the namespace, which might refer to several different things. For instance, a set of overloaded functions defined within a namespace can be introduced with a single **using** declaration.

Instead of the **using** directive for the namespace **std** in the previous example, we could supply a **using** declaration for each name that we want to use:

```
using std::cout;
using std::endl;
```

These two declarations, preceding the definition of **main()** in the last example, would allow **cout** and **endl** to be used without qualification. Of course, you could also supply **using** declarations for the constants **pi** and **days** in the namespace **data**.

Note that although we have placed the **using** declarations and directives at global scope in all our examples, we can also place them within a namespace, or within a function, or even within a statement block. In each case the declaration or directive applies until the end of the block that contains it.

Functions and Namespaces

For a function to exist within a namespace, it is sufficient for the function prototype to appear in a namespace. The function can be defined elsewhere, by simply using the qualified name for the function — in other words, the function definition doesn't have to be enclosed in a namespace block. Let's take an example.

Suppose we want to write two functions, **max()** and **min()**, to return the maximum and minimum of an array of values. We can put the declarations for the functions in a namespace as follows:

```
// compare.h
namespace compare
{
  double max(const double* data, int size);
  double min(const double* data, int size);
}
```

This could be placed in a header file, **compare.h**, which would then be **#include**d by any file using the functions.

The definitions for the functions can now appear in a **.cpp** file. We can write the definitions without enclosing them in a namespace block, as long as the name of each function is qualified with the namespace name. The contents of the file would be:

```
// compare.cpp
#include "compare.h"

// Function to find the maximum
double compare::max(const double* data, int size)
{
  double result = data[0];
  for(int i = 1 ; i < size ; i++)
    if(result < data[i])
      result = data[i];
  return result;
}

// Function to find the minimum
double compare::min(const double* data, int size)
{
  double result = data[0];
  for(int i = 1 ; i < size ; i++)
    if(result > data[i])
      result = data[i];
```

```
      return result;
  }
```

We need the **compare.h** header file to be included so that the namespace is identified. This enables the compiler to deduce that the functions are within the namespace.

Of course you could, if you want, place the code for the function definitions within the **compare** namespace directly. In this case, the contents of **compare.cpp** would be:

```
// compare.cpp
namespace compare
{
  // Function to find the maximum
  double max(const double* data, int size)
  {
    double result = data[0];
    for(int i = 1 ; i < size ; i++)
      if(result < data[i])
        result = data[i];
    return result;
  }

  // Function to find the minimum
  double min(const double* data, int size)
  {
    double result = data[0];
    for(int i = 1 ; i < size ; i++)
      if(result > data[i])
        result = data[i];
    return result;
  }
}
```

If we were to write the function definitions in this way, then we wouldn't need to **#include** the file **compare.h** into this file. This is because the definitions are already within the namespace.

Using the functions is the same, however you have defined them. To confirm how easy it is, let's try it out with the functions that we have just defined.

Try It Out – The using Declaration

The function declarations go in the header file **compare.h** as we discussed above:

```
// compare.h
namespace compare
{
  double max(const double* data, int size);
  double min(const double* data, int size);
}
```

We will put the definitions for the functions in a separate **.cpp** file that will contain the following code:

```
// compare.cpp
#include "compare.h"

// Function to find the maximum
double compare::max(const double* data, int size)
{
  double result = data[0];
  for(int i = 1 ; i < size ; i++)
    if(result < data[i])
      result = data[i];
  return result;
}

// Function to find the minimum
double compare::min(const double* data, int size)
{
  double result = data[0];
  for(int i = 1 ; i < size ; i++)
    if(result > data[i])
      result = data[i];
  return result;
}
```

All we need is a `.cpp` file containing the definition of **main()** to try the functions out:

```
// Program 10.3 Using functions in a namespace
#include <iostream>
#include "compare.h"

using compare::max;                       // Using declaration for max
using compare::min;                       // Using declaration for min

int main()
{
  double data[] = {1.5, 4.6, 3.1, 1.1, 3.8, 2.1};

  using namespace std;                    // Using directive for standard library

  const int dataSize = sizeof data/sizeof data[0];

  cout << endl;
  cout << "Minimum double is " << min(data, dataSize) << endl;
  cout << "Maximum double is " << max(data, dataSize) << endl;

  return 0;
}
```

If you compile the two `.cpp` files and link them, when you run the program it will produce the output:

```
Minimum double is 1.1
Maximum double is 4.6
```

How It Works

The declarations for the functions are introduced into the file containing **main()** with the directive:

```
#include "compare.h"
```

> *If the file* compare.h *was in a different directory to the source files, then the* #include *directive must also contain the directory path from the source file to the header file. In this example, the header file* compare.h *is in the same directory as the source file.*

We then have a **using** declaration for each function, so that we can use the names without having to add the namespace name:

```
using compare::max;                         // Using declaration for max
using compare::min;                         // Using declaration for min
```

We could equally well have used a **using** directive for the **compare** namespace:

```
using namespace compare;
```

Since the namespace only contains the functions max() and min(), this would have been just as good, and one less line of code. However, in general the effect of a using directive is quite different from the effect of a using declaration. The using directive allows any name from the namespace that is declared in the file to be used. The using declaration on the other hand only introduces one specific name.

Within **main()** we first define an array, **data**, that we will pass as an argument to our two functions:

```
double data[] = {1.5, 4.6, 3.1, 1.1, 3.8, 2.1};
```

We then have a **using** directive for the namespace **std** that allows us to use the names declared in **<iostream>** without qualification from this point on:

```
using namespace std;                        // Using directive for standard library
```

We will need to pass the length of the array, **data**, to each function, so we compute this and store it in the constant **dataSize**:

```
const int dataSize = sizeof data/sizeof data[0];
```

Finally, we call the functions in the output statements that will display the maximum and minimum values from the array, **data**:

```
cout << "Minimum double is " << min(data, dataSize) << endl;
cout << "Maximum double is " << max(data, dataSize) << endl;
```

If we had not written the **using** declarations for the function names (or a **using** directive for the **compare** namespace), then we would have had to qualify the functions in the output statements:

```
cout << "Minimum double is " << compare::min(data, dataSize) << endl;
cout << "Maximum double is " << compare::max(data, dataSize) << endl;
```

Function Templates and Namespaces

You can define function templates in a namespace. The functions above are natural for generation from a template, so let's use those as an illustration. In this example, we'll put the template definitions in a namespace in a header file:

```
// tempcomp.h
namespace compare
{
// Function template to find the maximum element in an array
template<class T> T max(const T* data, int size)
  {
    T result = data[0];
    for(int i = 1 ; i < size ; i++)
      if(result < data[i])
        result = data[i];
    return result;
  }

// Function template to find the minimum element in an array
template<class T> T min(const T* data, int size)
  {
    T result = data[0];
    for(int i = 1 ; i < size ; i++)
      if(result > data[i])
        result = data[i];
    return result;
  }
}
```

FYI

If you wish, you can follow the recommended guidelines by placing the template definitions in a separate file, `tempcomp.cpp`, and writing only the template prototypes in the file `tempcomp.h`. Because we are using class templates, you will need to prefix each of the template definitions with the keyword `export`. The code will then be fully compatible with the ANSI/ISO standard. However, many current compilers do not support usage of `export`, and you may find that the above code is more suitable to your C++ compiler.

Of course, if you wanted to define special cases explicitly, for type **char*** for instance, you could put the prototype for the special case within the namespace above, and put the definition in a **.cpp** file, either with a qualified function name, or within a namespace block.

Try It Out – Function Templates in a Namespace

We can exercise the template in the namespace **compare** with the following code:

```
// Program 10.4 Using function templates in a namespace
#include <iostream>
#include "tempcomp.h"

using compare::max;                          // Using declaration for max
using compare::min;                          // Using declaration for min

int main()
{
  double data[] = {1.5, 4.6, 3.1, 1.1, 3.8, 2.1};
  int numbers[] = {23, 2, 14, 56, 42, 12, 1, 45};
  using namespace std;                       // Using directive for standard library

  cout << endl;

  const int dataSize = sizeof data/sizeof data[0];
  cout << "Minimum double is " << min(data, dataSize) << endl;
  cout << "Maximum double is " << max(data, dataSize) << endl;

  const int numbersSize = sizeof numbers/sizeof numbers[0];
  cout << "Minimum integer is " << min(numbers, numbersSize) << endl;
  cout << "Maximum integer is " << max(numbers, numbersSize) << endl;

  return 0;
}
```

This program produces the output:

```
Minimum double is 1.1
Maximum double is 4.6
Minimum integer is 1
Maximum integer is 56
```

How It Works

This works in much the same way as the previous example, which defined each function explicitly. There is no **.cpp** file for the **min()** and **max()** function definitions, since each necessary definition will be generated by the compiler from the appropriate template. Since the template definitions appear within the **compare** namespace, the compiler will generate the definition with that namespace.

We use the functions without qualification, since we have **using** declarations for their names within the namespace **compare**. Without the **using** declarations, we would need to qualify the function names in the output statements, as we did in the earlier example. For instance, the first two output statements would be look like this:

```
  cout << "Minimum double is " << compare::min(data, dataSize) << endl;
  cout << "Maximum double is " << compare::max(data, dataSize) << endl;
```

The first argument in each function call is an array of type **double**, so the compiler will generate definitions for versions of **max()** and **min()** that accept this argument type.

Extension Namespaces

Earlier we discussed how namespaces could be defined within several blocks. We could extend Program 10.4 to show an extension to an existing namespace in action.

Try It Out – Using an Extension Namespace

We will add another header file containing a template for a function that will normalize an array of data — that is, the function will adjust the values so that they lie between 0 and 1. Here are the contents of the header file:

```
// normal.h
// Normalize an aray of values to the range 0 to 1
#include "tempcomp.h"

namespace compare
{
  template<class Torig, class Tnorm> void normalize(Torig* data,
                                                  Tnorm* newData, int size)
  {
    Torig minValue = min(data, size);          // Get minimum element

    // Shift all elements so minimum is zero
    for(int i = 0 ; i < size ; i++)
      newData[i] = static_cast<Tnorm>(data[i] - minValue);

    Tnorm maxValue = max(newData, size);       // Get max of new set

    // Scale elements so maximum is 1
    for(int i = 0 ; i < size ; i++)
      newData[i] /= maxValue;
  }
}
```

To use this template, we can add a few statements at the end of the version of **main()** in the previous example:

```
// Program 10.5 Using a function template in a namespace extension
#include <iostream>
#include <iomanip>
#include "normal.h"

using compare::max;                    // Using declaration for max
using compare::min;                    // Using declaration for min

int main()
{
  double data[] = {1.5, 4.6, 3.1, 1.1, 3.8, 2.1};
  int numbers[] = {23, 2, 14, 56, 42, 12, 1, 45};
  using namespace std;                 // Using directive for standard library

  cout << endl;

  const int dataSize = sizeof data/sizeof data[0];
```

```
        cout << "Minimum double is " << min(data, dataSize) << endl;
        cout << "Maximum double is " << max(data, dataSize) << endl;

        const int numbersSize = sizeof numbers/sizeof numbers[0];
        cout << "Minimum integer is " << min(numbers, numbersSize) << endl;
        cout << "Maximum integer is " << max(numbers, numbersSize) << endl;
```

```
        double newData[numbersSize];                            // Array for result
        compare::normalize(numbers, newData, numbersSize);      // Normalize numbers

        // Output the normalized array values
        for(int i = 0 ; i < numbersSize ; i++)
        {
          if(i%5 == 0)
            cout << endl;
          cout << setw(12) << newData[i];
        }
        cout << endl;
        return 0;
    }
```

This will produce the output:

```
Minimum double is 1.1
Maximum double is 4.6
Minimum integer is 1
Maximum integer is 56

        0.4    0.0181818     0.236364            1    0.745455
        0.2            0          0.8
```

How It Works

Let's examine the new header file first. We have an **#include** directive for the header file containing the templates for **max()** and **min()**, so after the contents have been included, our new header will contain:

```
namespace compare
{
  // Templates for min() and max()
}
namespace compare
{
  // Template for normalize()
}
```

The second template definition is an extension to the first.

Since the **normalize()** function is to store the results as an array with values between 0 and 1, the type **Tnorm** must be able to accommodate a floating point value, regardless of the type, **Torig**, of the original data values. The template header allows both the type of the original array, and the type of the result to be flexible:

```
template<class Torig, class Tnorm> void normalize(Torig* data,
                                   Tnorm* newData, int size)
```

379

The first parameter, **data**, is an array of elements of type **Torig**, and the second parameter **newData** is an array of the same size that stores values of type **Tnorm**. Just to remind you, you could equally well use array notation for the parameters so the header could be written:

```
template<class Torig, class Tnorm> void normalize(Torig data[],
                                        Tnorm newData[], int size)
```

The function templates for **normalize()**, **max()** and **min()** are all in the same namespace; therefore the functions **max()** and **min()** can be used in **normalize()** without qualification. We use the **min()** function template to get the value of the minimum element in the array passed as the first argument:

```
Torig minValue = min(data, size);          // Get minimum element
```

We can declare **minValue** to be of type **Torig**, which is the same type as the array **data**. Next, we subtract **minValue** from each of the elements in the **data** array. We store the results of this calculation in our new array **newData**, of type **Tnorm**:

```
for(int i = 0 ; i < size ; i++)
   newData[i] = static_cast<Tnorm>(data[i] - minValue);
```

Here, the result of subtracting **minValue** from an element of the **data** array is explicitly cast to type **Tnorm**. After this operation, the minimum element in the new array will be zero and all the other elements will be positive.

We now need the value of the maximum element in the new array:

```
Tnorm maxValue = max(newData, size);          // Get max of new set
```

This uses the **max()** function template to generate a function accepting an array of type **Torig** as its first argument. In the next statement, we use a loop to divide each element of the new array by **maxValue**:

```
for(int i = 0 ; i < size ; i++)
  newData[i] /= maxValue;
```

After this operation, the minimum element will still be zero and the maximum element will be 1. All the other elements will lie in between.

Now let's look at the main part of the program. The new statements in **main()** use a manipulator, so we have to add an **#include** directive for **<iomanip>**. We have replaced the **#include** directive for **tempcomp.h** by the directive:

```
#include "normal.h"
```

Notice that we have *removed* the **#include** directive for **tempcomp.h** from the main source file. If we leave the directive in, then the definitions of **max()** and **min()** would be **#include**d twice — once directly, and once indirectly through the **#include** directive for **normal.h**. The multiple inclusion would cause a compilation error. Later in this chapter, we will see how to prevent this from occurring — even when both directives are included.

We call the **normalize()** function to normalize the integer data values in the array numbers:

```
compare::normalize(numbers, newData, numbersSize);        // Normalize numbers
```

The template for **normalize()** is within the namespace **compare**, and we have not added a **using** declaration or directive — therefore, the function name must be qualified here if the compiler is to recognize the name. The compiler will create a definition from the function template that accepts an array of type **int** as the first argument, and an array of type **double** for the second argument.

Now we have the array of normalized values, we can output them in the way that is familiar to you:

```
for(int i = 0 ; i < numbersSize ; i++)
{
  if(i%5 == 0)
    cout << endl;
  cout << setw(12) << newData[i];
}
cout << endl;
```

Unnamed Namespaces

You don't have to assign a name to a namespace, but this does not mean it doesn't have a name. You can declare an unnamed namespace with the following code:

```
namespace
{
  // Code in the namespace, functions, etc.
}
```

This creates a namespace that effectively has an internal name generated by the compiler. There is only one 'unnamed' namespace in a file, so any additional namespace declarations without a name will all be extensions to the first.

However, each unnamed namespace is unique *within a translation unit.* Unnamed namespaces within distinct translation units are distinct unnamed namespaces.

It is important to realize that an unnamed namespace is *not* within the global namespace. This fact, combined with the fact that an unnamed namespace is unique to a translation unit, has significant consequences. It means that functions, variables and anything else declared within an unnamed namespace are local to the translation unit in which they are defined. They cannot be accessed at all from any other translation unit.

Placement of function definitions within an unnamed namespace has the same effect as declaring the functions as **static** in the global namespace. Declaring functions and variables as **static** at global scope was a common way of ensuring they were not accessible outside their translation unit. An unnamed namespace is a much better way of restricting accessibility where necessary, and using **static** in this way is now deprecated.

Namespace Aliases

In a large program with multiple development groups involved, you may well need to use long namespace names in order to ensure there are no accidental name clashes. Left as they are, such long names may be unduly cumbersome in use. Having to attach names such as `SystemGroup5_Process3_Subsection2` to every function call would be more than a nuisance.

To get over this you can define an alias for a long namespace name on a local basis. The general form of statement to define an alias for a namespace name is:

namespace   *alias_name*   =   *original_namespace_name*;

You can then use **alias_name** in place of **original_namespace_name** to access names within the namespace.

For example, to define an alias for the namespace name in the previous paragraph, you could write:

```
namespace SG5P3S2 = SystemGroup5_Process3_Subsection2;
```

Now you can call a function within the original namespace with a statement such as:

```
int maxValue = SG5P3S2::max(data, size);
```

Nested Namespaces

You can define one namespace inside another. The mechanics of handling this is easiest to understand if we take a specific context. Suppose we have nested namespaces as follows:

```
// outin.h
namespace outer
{
  double max(double* data, const int& size)
  {
    // body code..
  }

  double min(double* data, const int& size)
  {
    // body code..
  }

  namespace inner
  {
    double* normalize(double* data, const int& size)
    {
      // ...
      double minValue = min(data, size);    // Calls max() in compare
      // ...
    }
  }
}
```

From within the namespace **inner**, the function **normalize()** can call the function **min()** (which is in the namespace **outer**) directly. This is because the declaration of **normalize()** is contained within the **inner** namespace, which in turn is contained within the **outer** namespace — which means that the **normalize()** declaration is contained within the **outer** namespace.

To call **min()** from the global namespace, you would qualify the function name in the usual way:

```
    int result = outer::min(data, size);
```

Of course, you could also use a **using** declaration for the function name, or specify a **using** directive for the namespace. In order to call **normalize()** from the global namespace you need to qualify the function name with both namespace names:

```
    double* newData = outer::inner::normalize(data, size);
```

The same applies if you include the function prototype within the namespace, and supply the function definition separately. We could write just the prototype of **normalize()** within the namespace **inner**, and place the definition of the function **normalize()** in the file **outin.cpp**:

```
// outin.cpp
#include "outin.h"
double* outer::inner::normalize(double* data, const int& size)
{
  // ...
  double minValue = min(data, size);     // Calls max() in compare
  // ...
}
```

Of course, in order to compile this successfully, the compiler would need to know about the namespaces. Therefore, the header **outin.h**, which is **#include**d here prior to the function definition, would need to contain the namespace declarations.

We have used a new form of the **#include** directive several times so far in this chapter. It's time we learnt a bit more about how it works, along with the other preprocessor directives that are available.

The Preprocessor

The preprocessor is usually an integral part of your compiler. It is a process that is executed by the compiler before your C++ program code is compiled into machine instructions. The job of the preprocessor is to prepare your source code for the compile phase proper, according to instructions that you have included in the source files — these instructions are called **preprocessor directives**. All preprocessor directives begin with the symbol **#**, so they are easily distinguishable from C++ language statements. Here's the complete set:

Directive	Function
`#include`	Supports header file inclusion
`#if`	Enable conditional compilation
`#else`	
`#elif`	
`#endif`	
`#if defined` (or `#ifdef`)	
`#if !defined` (or `#ifndef`)	
`#define`	Enable symbol and macro substitution
`#undef`	
`#line`	Allows redefinition of current line and filename
`#error`	Produces compile-time error messages
`#pragma`	Offers machine-specific features while retaining overall C++ compatibility

> *Although all preprocessor directives begin with* **#**, *the converse is not true: for example,* **#import** *is not a preprocessor directive.*

From your source code, the preprocessor phase analyzes, executes and then removes all the preprocessor directives, resulting in a new file that will consist purely of C++ statements. The compiler then begins the compile phase proper with this resultant file, which (assuming that there are no errors!) will generate the object file containing machine code. This object file must then be processed by the linker, along with any other object files that are part of the program, to produce the finished executable module.

We have already used preprocessor directives in all our examples, and you are very familiar with the **#include** directive by now. There are other directives, as shown above, that add considerable flexibility to the way in which you specify your programs. Keep in mind, as we proceed, that these are all preprocessor operations, which occur before your program is compiled. They modify the set of statements that constitute your program. They aren't involved in the execution of your program at all.

FYI The following discussion covers the basic syntax, examples of usage, and advice on using some of these preprocessor directives. You may wish to skip to the section on Debugging Methods, and refer back to this section as necessary.

Including Header Files in Your Programs

A header file is any external file, usually stored on disk, whose contents are included into your program by use of the **#include** preprocessor directive. We are completely familiar with statements such as:

```
#include <iostream>
```

This fetches the contents of **iostream** (the standard library header file which supports stream input/output operations) into your program. The contents of **iostream** replace the **#include** directive. This is a particular case of the general statement for including standard library header files into your program:

```
#include <standard_library_file_name>
```

Here, any standard library header file name can appear between the angled brackets. If you include a header file that you don't use, the primary effects are to take up more memory and extend the compilation time. It's also slightly confusing for anyone else who reads the program.

You can include your own source files into your program, with a slightly different **#include** statement that encloses the file name between double quotes. A typical example might be:

```
#include "myheader.h"
```

With this statement, the contents of the file named between double quotes will be introduced into the program in place of the **#include** directive. The contents of any file can be included into your program by this means. You simply specify the name of the file between quotes as we have shown in the example. With the majority of compilers you can specify the file name using upper- and lower-case characters.

In theory, you can give whatever names you like to your own header files — you don't have to use the extension **.h**. However, it is a convention adhered to by most C++ programmers, and I would recommend that you follow it.

The difference between specifying the file name between double quotes and enclosing it between angled brackets lies in the process used to find the file. The precise operation is compiler-dependent and will be described in your compiler documentation. Usually, if you use *angled brackets* then the compiler will only search the default directories containing standard library header files. If the header file name is between *double quotes* then it will search the current directory (typically the directory containing the source file that is being compiled) followed by the directories containing the standard header files. If you put a header file in some other directory, then in order for it to be found you must put the complete path, from source file to header file, between the double quotes.

You can use the **#include** mechanism for dividing your program into several files, and of course for managing the declarations for any library functions of your own. A common use of this facility is to create a header file containing all the function prototypes and global variables. These can then be managed as a separate unit and **#include**d at the beginning of the program.

If you include more than one file into your program, then you need to avoid duplicating information. Duplicate code will often cause compilation errors. We shall see later in this chapter how the preprocessor provides some facilities for ensuring that any given block of code will appear only once in your program, even if you inadvertently **#include** it several times.

> *A file introduced into your source file by an **#include** statement may also contain other **#include** statements. If so, the preprocessor will process the additional **#include** statements in the same way as the first, and continue processing until there are no more **#include** statements in the code. You can see an example of this in Program 10.5.*

Substitutions in Your Program

The simplest kind of symbol substitution you can define is to specify a sequence of characters that will replace a given symbol in a program file. You use the **#define** directive to do this. For example, you could arrange to replace the symbol **PI** by a sequence of characters that represents a numerical value, as follows:

```
#define PI 3.14159265
```

Here, although **PI** *looks* like a variable, this has nothing to do with variables, and this is a serious disadvantage. Here **PI** is a symbol or **token**, which is exchanged for the specified sequence of characters before the program code is compiled. Note also that **3.14159265** is not a numerical value, but merely a string of characters. Before compilation, the preprocessor looks through your code and replaces the string **PI** by its definition (**3.14159265**), wherever the preprocessor deems that the substitution makes sense.

> *There is room for interpretation here. For example, the preprocessor deems that the substitution should not be made wherever **PI** appears in a comment, or as part of a character string (between double quotes). We'll look at this again a little later.*

In C, the **#define** directive is often used in this way to define symbolic constants; however, in C++ it is much better to define a suitable constant using **const**. For example:

```
const long double pi = 3.14159265;
```

Now **pi** is a constant value of a particular type. The compiler will ensure that the value you have specified for **pi** is consistent with its type. If this statement appears in a source file at global scope, it can be accessed by any of the other program source files simply by declaring **pi** as external:

```
extern const long double pi;
```

In this way, the definition of **pi** can be shared throughout the program.

The general form of the **#define** preprocessor directive is:

#define   *identifier   sequence_of_characters*

Here, ***identifier*** conforms to the usual definition of an identifier in C++, as any sequence of letters and digits, the first of which is a letter, and where the underline character counts as a letter.

Note that **sequence_of_characters** can be any sequence of characters — not just digits. Let's look at one last example:

```
#define BLACK WHITE
```

The preprocessor will cause any occurrence of the five-character sequence **BLACK** in your program to be replaced by the five-character sequence **WHITE**. There is no restriction on the sequence of characters which is used to replace the token identifier.

> *There are two major disadvantages with using a* #define *directive. First,* #define *does not provide any type checking support. Second,* #define *does not respect scope and cannot be bound within a namespace.*

Removing Tokens from a Program

In a **#define** directive, if you don't specify a substitution string for an identifier then the identifier will be replaced with an empty token string — in other words, the identifier will be removed. For example, you could define an identifier with the directive:

```
#define VALUE
```

The effect of this directive is that all occurrences of the identifier **VALUE** will be removed from the statements in the program file that follow the directive.

Undefining an Identifier

It is possible that you may want to have the substitution resulting from a **#define** directive only apply to *part* of a program file. You can nullify the definition for an identifier by using the **#undef** directive. Suppose, having defined the identifier **VALUE**, you want to eliminate the effect at some point in the file. You can do this with the directive:

```
#undef VALUE
```

Subsequent to this directive, the identifier **VALUE** is undefined, so no substitutions for **VALUE** will occur. Let's take an example. Look at the following code fragment:

```
#define PI 3.142
// All occurrences of PI in code from this point will be replaced
// ...
#undef PI
// The identifier PI is no longer defined.
// Any references to PI will be left in the code from this point
```

Between the **#define** and **#undef** directives, the preprocessor will replace appropriate occurrences of **PI** in the code by **3.142**. Elsewhere, occurrences of **PI** will be left as they are.

The combination of **#define** and **#undef** directives has another use, which we will explore when we deal with decision-making preprocessor directives later in this chapter.

Macro Substitutions

A **preprocessor macro** is based on the ideas implicit in the **#define** directive examples that we have just seen, but provides a greater range of possible results by allowing what we call multiple parameterized substitutions. This not only involves replacing a token identifier by a fixed sequence of characters, but also allows parameters to be specified in the macro definition, which may themselves be replaced by argument values that you supply when you use the macro. Wherever a given parameter appears in the substitution sequence, it will be replaced by the corresponding argument. Let's look at an example:

```
#define Print(myVar) cout << (myVar) << endl
```

This directive provides for two levels of substitution. There is the substitution for **Print(myVar)** by the string immediately following it in the **#define** statement, and there is the possible substitution of alternatives for **myVar**. You could write, for example:

```
Print(ival);
```

The preprocessor will convert this to the statement:

```
cout << (ival) << endl;
```

The general form of the kind of substitution directive we have just discussed is:

#define   *identifier(list_of_identifiers)   substitution_string*

You can see from this that in the general case, any number of parameters are permitted, so we are able to define more complex substitutions.

> *You must not leave a space between the first identifier and the left parenthesis —*
> *otherwise the parentheses will be interpreted as part of the substitution string.*

We could extend the previous macro directive to add a second parameter:

```
#define Print(myVar,digits) cout << setw(digits) << (myVar) << endl
```

This directive provides for the possible substitution of alternatives for **myVar** and for **digits**. For example, you could write:

```
Print(ival,15);
```

The preprocessor will convert this to the statement:

```
cout << setw(15) << (ival) << endl;
```

Of course, the header file **<iomanip>** will need to be included for this statement to compile.

This sort of application of preprocessor macros used to be common, but in almost all cases it is better to use an **inline** function or function template. This way you ensure appropriate type checking of the arguments and you reduce the possibility of errors. Instead of the previous macro, you could use a function template defined as:

```
template<class T> inline void Print(const T& myVar, const int& digits)
{
  cout << setw(digits) << myVar << endl;
}
```

Now, if you write the statement:

```
Print(ival,15);
```

the compiler will generate an **inline** function accepting the appropriate type of argument from the template.

A very common use for this kind of macro is to allow a very simple representation of a complicated function call in order to enhance the readability of a program.

 Your C++ development system may provide further macro capabilities, such as the possibility of defining macros via the command line or within the compilation environment. These sorts of facilities are system specific and outside the scope of this book.

Macros Can Cause Errors

To show the kind of errors inherent in using macros, we can define a macro for producing the maximum of two values with the directive:

```
#define max(x, y) x>y ? x : y
```

We can then generate a substitution by putting the following statement in our program:

```
result = max(myval, 99);
```

This will be expanded by the preprocessor to:

```
result = myval>99 ? myval : 99;
```

This substitution works, and creates the illusion of a function. However, this is *not* a function, and it is important to be conscious of the substitution that is taking place. With a different statement, we can get some strange results — particularly if our substitution identifiers include explicit or implicit assignment. For example, the following modest extension of our last example can produce a result that you may not expect:

```
result = max(myval++, 99);
```

The substitution process will generate the statement:

```
result = myval++>99 ? myval++ : 99;
```

so that if the value of **myval** is larger than 99, **myval** will be incremented twice. Note that it does *not* help to use parentheses in this situation. If you write the statement as:

```
        result = max((myval++), 99);
```

then the preprocessor will convert this to:

```
        result = (myval++)>99 ? (myval++) : 99;
```

You should avoid writing macros that generate expressions of any kind. In general, you should use a template for an **inline** function, rather than a macro. In this case, the task that is intended by this macro can be achieved by using the standard library function **max()**, which returns the maximum of its two arguments. The **max()** function is defined as a template, so it works with arguments of various types.

In addition to the multiple substitution trap which we have just seen, precedence rules can also catch you out when using macros. A simple example will illustrate this. Suppose we write a macro for the product of two parameters:

```
 #define product(m, n) m*n
```

We then try to use this macro with the statement:

```
    result = product(x, y+1)
```

This compiles, but we don't get the result we want, because the macro expands to:

```
    result = x*y+1
```

Of course, this evaluates to **(x*y)+1**, not **x*(y+1)**. Finding this bug could take a long time, because there is no external indication of what's going on. In the meantime, there is almost certainly an erroneous value propagating through our program. In this case, the solution is very simple. If you must use macros to generate expressions, then put parentheses around everything. The above example should be rewritten as:

```
 #define product(m, n) ((m)*(n))
```

Now everything will work as it should. The inclusion of the outer parentheses may seem excessive, but since you don't know the context in which the macro expansion will be placed, it is better to include them.

A far better solution would be to follow the next piece of advice:

> *To repeat what I have already said — unless you have a pressing reason for doing otherwise, always use inline functions rather than preprocessor macros.*

Preprocessor Directives on Multiple Lines

A preprocessor directive must be a single logical line, but this doesn't prevent you from spreading the directive over several physical lines. You just use the continuation character \, at the end of each line except the last. We could write:

```
#define min(x, y) \
                    ((x)<(y) ? (x) : (y))
```

Here the directive definition continues on the second line, starting with the first non-whitespace character found; so you can position the text on the second line to make the most readable arrangement. Note that the **** must be the *final* character on the line, immediately before you press *Enter*.

Strings as Macro Arguments

String constants are a potential source of confusion when used with macros. The simplest string substitution is a single level definition such as:

```
#define MYSTR "This string"
```

With this macro in place, the following statement:

```
cout << MYSTR;
```

will be converted into the statement:

```
cout << "This string";
```

which should be what you are expecting. However, if we try to place the double quotes in the C++ statement (rather than in the **#define** directive), the substitution will fail. Let's illustrate what we mean. Go back to the beginning, and write the directive as:

```
#define MYSTR This string
```

Then write a statement such as:

```
cout << "MYSTR";                          // Does not invoke the macro
```

This time, there will be no substitution for **MYSTR**. Anything in quotes in your program is assumed to be a literal string, and so the preprocessor won't analyze it.

There is also a special way of specifying that an argument to a preprocessor macro is to be implemented as a string. For example, you could specify a macro to display a string as:

```
#define PrintString(arg) cout << #arg
```

The character **#**, which precedes the appearance of the parameter **arg** in the macro expansion, indicates that the argument is to be surrounded by double quotes when the substitution is generated. Therefore, if you write this statement in your program:

```
PrintString(Hello);
```

the preprocessor will convert this to:

```
cout << "Hello";
```

This apparently quirky facility was introduced into preprocessing because, without it, it's impossible to include a variable string in a macro definition. If you put the double quotes around the macro argument, then the preprocessor doesn't interpret this as a variable, but merely a string with quotes around it. On the other hand, if you put the quotes in the macro expansion, then the string between the quotes is not interpreted as a parameter variable identifier, it would be just a string constant.

One use of this mechanism is for converting a variable name to a string, such as in the directive:

```
#define show(var) cout << #var << " = " (var) << endl
```

This macro creates a shorthand way of outputting the name of a variable and its value. If we now write:

```
show(number);
```

this will generate the statement:

```
cout << "number" << " = " (number) << endl;
```

You can also generate a substitution that would allow you to display a string with double quotes included. Assuming we have defined the macro **PrintString** as above, you can write the statement:

```
PrintString("Output");
```

This will be preprocessed into the statement:

```
cout <<   "\"Output\"";
```

This is possible because the preprocessor is clever enough to recognize the need to put **\"** at each end to get a string including double quotes to be displayed correctly.

Joining the Arguments in a Macro Expansion

You might wish to generate a macro that accepts two or more arguments and joins them together with no spaces between them. In this way you could perhaps synthesize different variable names, depending on the arguments to the macro. Suppose we try to define a macro to do this as:

```
#define join(a, b) ab
```

This can't work in the way we need it to. The definition of the expansion will be interpreted as the sequence of two characters, **ab**, not as the parameter **a** followed by the parameter **b**. If we separate them with a blank, then the result will also be separated with a blank, which isn't what we want either.

In fact, the preprocessor provides us with another operator, specifically to solve this problem. The solution is to specify the macro as:

```
#define join(a, b) a##b
```

The presence of the operator comprising the two characters **##** serves to separate the macro parameters, and to indicate to the preprocessor that the result of the two substitutions are to be joined without any spaces between them. For example, writing the statement:

```
strlen(join(var, 123));
```

will result in the statement:

```
strlen(var123);
```

This appears to be a rather limited capability at first sight, since you could always have written **var123** rather that going to the trouble of using the macro. In fact, the capability to include decision-making in the instructions to the preprocessor vastly increases the potential for this kind of directive.

Logical Preprocessor Directives

The ability to execute one block of directives rather than another raises the possibility of macro substitutions in which the arguments for one macro may be selected from substitutions defined in several others, depending on conditions that can be tested in the program file.

The preprocessor provides for this, through directives that implement a logical **#if** capability. This works in essentially the same way as an **if** statement in C++, and vastly expands the scope of what you can do with the preprocessor.

The Logical #if Directive

There are two ways in which a logical **#if** directive can be used. First, you can test whether or not a symbol has been previously defined by a **#define** directive. Second, you can test whether or not a constant expression is true. Let's look at testing for a symbol definition first, since this is the most commonly used tool.

To test whether an identifier exists (as a result of having been created in a previous **#define** directive), you use a directive of the form:

#if defined *identifier*

If the specified ***identifier*** has been defined, then the set of statements following the **#if** are included in the source file to be compiled. This set of statements is ended with the directive:

```
#endif
```

If ***identifier*** has *not* been defined, then the statements between the **#if** and the **#endif** will be skipped, and will not form part of the program. This is basically the same logical process that we use in C++ programming — here we are applying it to decide whether or not a block of statements are included as part of the program.

The block of statements between the **#if** and the **#endif** can include further preprocessor directives. These directives will be executed if the ***identifier*** being tested by the **#if** is defined.

393

Let's put this into a concrete context. Suppose you put the following code in your program file:

```
// code that sets up the array data[]
double average = 0.0;

#if defined CALCAVERAGE
int count = sizeof data/sizeof data[0];
for(int i = 0 ; i < count ; i++)
  average += data[i];
average /= count;
#endif

// rest of the program...
```

Here, the **#if** directive tests whether the symbol **CALCAVERAGE** has been defined by a previous preprocessor directive. If so, the code between the **#if** and **#endif** directives will be compiled as part of the program. If the symbol **CALCAVERAGE** has not been defined, then the code will not be included.

There is a shorthand form for testing whether an identifier has been defined. Instead of writing the test as:

#if defined CALCAVERAGE

You can write it as:

#ifdef CALCAVERAGE

This is a little more concise and just as clear. A block of statements beginning with **#ifdef** should be terminated with **#endif**.

Preventing Code Duplication

You can also test for the absence of an identifier. The general form of this directive is:

```
#if !defined identifier
```

Here, the statements following the **#if** down to the **#endif** will be included in the source file to be compiled provided the **identifier** has not previously been defined. The shorthand version of this is:

```
#ifndef identifier
```

> *In fact, #ifndef tends to be used more frequently than #ifdef, since it enables you to arrange that the contents of a header file (or any file come to that) are not #included more than once.*

As we've already seen, a header file that you include into a **.cpp** file using an **#include** directive can itself contain **#include** directives to incorporate other header files — this feature is used extensively in large programs. With a complex program involving many header files, there's a good chance that a header file maybe **#include**d more than once in your source files — indeed, in many situations it becomes unavoidable. Of course, such duplication of code can

394

cause compiler errors, especially where the duplicated code contains definitions. Therefore it is imperative to guard against that possibility.

So how do we use the **#if** directive to prevent duplication of code in your program? In fact, it's very simple: we simply type the block of code that must not be duplicated and top and tail it as follows:

```
#if !defined MYHEADER_H
#define MYHEADER_H

// Block of code that must not be duplicated

#endif
```

When the preprocessor first comes across this code, the identifier **MYHEADER_H** will not have been previously been defined —therefore, the **#if** condition will be **true**. Then, the block of code following the **#if** will be included in the program. This has two consequences: first, **MYHEADER_H** will be defined through the **#define** directive. Second, our block of code will be added to the code. Any subsequent occurrence of this same group of statements won't be included — this is because the identifier **MYHEADER_H** now exists, and the **#if** condition will be **false**. Therefore, our block of statements is included only once, and is not duplicated.

Note that to define an identifier, the identifier only has to appear in a **#define** directive. It can be defined as empty as in the directive:

```
#define MYHEADER_H
```

This directive defines the identifier **MYHEADER_H**, even though it does not have a value.

It is very much standard practice to put the **#if/#endif** combination (as above) around the entire contents of each header file. This ensures that the contents of each header file will never be included into a source file more than once. It is usual to use the header file name as the identifier, since this will ensure that the identifier is unique to each header file. To take a simple practical example, the header file **data.h** (which we saw in the discussion of Program 10.2) would typically be:

```
// Declarations for globals in namespace data    data.h
#ifndef DATA_H
#define DATA_H

namespace data
{
  extern const double pi;            // Variable is defined in another file
  extern const std::string days[];   // Array is defined in another file
}
#endif
```

> *It's a good idea to get into the habit of protecting code in your own headers in this fashion as a matter of course. You will be surprised how easy it is, once you have collected a few libraries of your own functions, to end up duplicating blocks of code accidentally.*

The preprocessor **#if** is not limited to testing the existence of just one identifier. You can use logical operators to test whether multiple identifiers have been defined. For example, the statement:

```
#if defined block1 && defined block2
```

will evaluate to **true** if both **block1** and **block2** have previously been defined — so the code that follows such a directive will not be included unless this is the case. In a similar way you can use the || operator, and even more complex expressions combining several operators and using **defined** and **!defined**.

FYI

The #ifdef and #ifndef are commonly used to include code specific to an operating system environment. For instance, there are a variety of Unix systems, each of which may have its own peculiarities that must be accommodated. By using the logical directives we have been discussing here, you can provide support for a variety of environments within a single set of source files, a particular environment being selected by defining a particular symbol that identifies it.

Directives Testing For Specific Values

You can also use a form of the **#if** directive to test the value of a constant expression. If the value of the constant expression is **true** — or a non-zero value — then the following statements, down to the next **#endif**, are included. If the constant expression evaluates to **false** — or zero — then the statements down to the next **#endif** are skipped. You could write this form of the **#if** directive as:

#if *constant_expression*

The ***constant_expression*** must be an integral constant expression that does not contain casts. It can contain preprocessor macros, but after all substitutions have been made, it must end up as an integer expression. All arithmetic operations are executed with the values treated as type **long** or **unsigned long**. If the value of ***constant_expression*** is non-zero, then statements following the **#if** directive, down to the **#endif** directive, will be included in the source code to be compiled.

This is frequently applied to test for a specific value being assigned to an identifier by a previous preprocessor directive. For example, we might have the following sequence of statements:

```
#if CPU == MMX
// Code taking advantage of MMX capability
#endif
```

The statements between the **#if** directive and **#endif** will only be included in the program here if the identifier **CPU** has been defined as **MMX** in a previous **#define** directive.

Multiple Choice Code Selection

To complement the **#if** directives, we have the **#else** directive. This works in exactly the same way as the C++ **else** statement, in that it identifies a group of directives to be executed, or statements to be included, if the **#if** directive condition fails. This provides you with a choice of two blocks of code, one of which will be incorporated into the final source. For example:

```
#if CPU == MMX
cout << "MMX code version." << endl;
// MMX oriented code
#else
cout << "Regular Pentium code version." << endl;
// code for straight Pentium
#endif
```

In this case, one or other of the groups of statements will be included, depending on whether **CPU** has been defined as **MMX** or not.

The preprocessor also supports a special form of the **#if** for multiple choice selections, where you want to choose only one of several possible choices of statements for inclusion in your program, or directives to be executed. This is the **#elif** directive, which has the general form:

#elif *constant_expression*

An example of using this would be:

```
#if LANGUAGE == ENGLISH
#define Greeting "Good Morning."
#elif LANGUAGE == GERMAN
#define Greeting "Guten Tag."
#elif LANGUAGE == FRENCH
#define Greeting "Bonjour."
#else
#define Greeting "Hi."
#endif
cout << Greeting << endl;
```

With this sequence of directives the output statement will display one of a number of different greetings, which depends on the value assigned to the identifier **LANGUAGE** in a previous **#define** directive.

Another possible use for this is to include different code in a program depending on an identifier set to represent a version number:

```
#if VERSION == 3
// Code for version 3 here...
#elif VERSION == 2
// Code for version 2 here...
#else
// Code for original version 1 here...
#endif
```

This allows you to maintain a single source file that will compile to produce different versions of the program, depending on how **VERSION** has been set in a **#define** directive.

Standard Preprocessor Macros

There are several standard macros defined by the preprocessor that you can invoke when you wish. These are:

Macro Name	Description
__LINE__	The line number of the current source line as a decimal integer.
__FILE__	The name of the source file as a character string literal.
__DATE__	The date when the source file was compiled (or more strictly, when it was processed) as a character string literal in the form *mmm dd yyyy*. Here, *mmm* is the month in characters, (Jan, Feb, etc); *dd* is the day in the form of a pair of digits 01 to 31, where single digit days are preceded by a blank; and *yyyy* is the year as four digits (such as 1994).
__TIME__	The time at which the source file was compiled, as a character string literal in the form *hh:mm:ss*, which is a string containing the pairs of digits for hours minutes and seconds separated by colons.
__STDC__	This is implementation dependent. It is usually defined if a compiler option has been set to compile standard C code; otherwise it is undefined.
__cplusplus	This will be defined to the value 199711L when a C++ program is being compiled.

Note that each of the macro names start with two underscore characters, and with the exception of the macro __cplusplus, they each end with two underscore characters.

The __LINE__ and __FILE__ macros enable you to display reference information relating to the source file. You can modify the line number using the #line directive. For example, if you wanted line numbering to start from 1000 at a particular point, you would add the directive:

```
#line 1000
```

You can use the #line directive to change the string returned by the __FILE__ macro. It usually produces the fully qualified file name, but you can change it to whatever you like. For instance:

```
#line 1000 "The program file"
```

This directive changes the line number of the next line to 1000, and alters the string returned by the __FILE__ macro to **"The program file"**. This doesn't alter the actual file name — just the string returned by the macro. Of course, if you just wanted to alter the apparent file name, and leave the line numbers unaltered, you could use the __LINE__ macro in the #line directive:

```
#line __LINE__ "The program file"
```

You could use the date and time macros to record when your program was last compiled with a statement such as:

```
cout << endl
     << "Program last compiled at " << __TIME__
```

```
            << " on "                        << __DATE__
            << endl;
```

Once the program containing this statement has been compiled, the values displayed by the statement are fixed until you compile it again. On subsequent executions, the program will output the time and date of the program's compilation.

The #error and #pragma Directives

The **#error** directive is intended to enable you to produce a diagnostic message when things go wrong during the pre-processing phase. For this reason, it is normally executed as a result of a directive that tests some condition, such as an **#if** directive. The effect of executing an **#error** is to display whatever you include on the directive line as a compiler error message, and to terminate the compilation immediately. For example, you could write:

```
#ifndef __cplusplus
#error "Error - Should be C++"
#endif
```

You can, if you wish, include other preprocessor macros on the **#error** directive line. When you want to just include a string, as in the example, it is best to enclose it between double quotes. This will prevent the preprocessor from attempting to parse it as a macro. The precise form of the output is implementation defined.

The **#pragma** directive is specifically for implementation defined options, its effect will be described in your compiler documentation. Any **#pragma** directive that is not recognized by the compiler will be ignored.

Debugging Methods

Most of your programs will contain errors, or bugs, when you first complete them. You will almost always find that debugging a program represents a substantial proportion of the total time required to write it.

The larger and more complex the program, the more bugs it's likely to contain, and the more time and effort is required to make it run properly. Very large programs — operating systems, for example, or complex applications such as word processing systems, or even the C++ program development system that you may be using at the moment — can be so complex that the system will never be completely bug-free. You may already have some experience of this, with some of the systems on your own computer. Usually, residual bugs of this sort are relatively minor, and the system is programmed with ways to work around them.

Sometimes, the process of removing a bug can actually introduce new bugs into your program. Of course, this mustn't put you off — debugging is a crucial part of the programming process.

Your approach to writing a program can significantly affect how difficult it will be to test. A well-structured program consisting of compact functions, each with a well-defined purpose, is much easier to test than one without these attributes. Finding bugs will also be easier with a program that has well-chosen variable and function names, and extensive comments — which document the operation and purpose of its component functions. Good use of indentation and statement layout can also make testing and fault finding simpler.

It is beyond the scope of this book to deal with debugging comprehensively, since we are concentrating on the C++ language. In any case, you will probably be debugging your programs using tools that are specific to the C++ development system you have. Nevertheless, we will introduce some basic ideas that are general and common to most debugging systems. We will also take a look at the rather elementary debugging aids that come as standard within the C++ library.

Integrated Debuggers

Most C++ compilers are supplied with extensive debugging tools built into the program development environment. These are potentially powerful facilities, that can dramatically reduce the time required to get a program working. They typically provide a varied range of aids to testing a program. The following paragraphs discuss some of the available facilities.

By tracing **program flow**, you can execute your program by tackling the source code one statement at a time. This operates by pausing execution after each statement has been executed; execution continues with the next statement when you press a designated key. Other provisions of the debug environment will usually allow you to display information at ease, pausing to show you what's happening to the data in your program. This is also known as **stepping through** your program.

If your program is large or complex, then stepping through it one statement at a time can be very tedious. It may even be impossible to step through your program in a reasonable period of time. If your program has a loop that executes 10,000 times, then stepping through it is an unrealistic proposition. An excellent alternative is to set **breakpoints** in your code. You use breakpoints to define specific selected statements in your program; at each of these points, execution will pause and allow you to check what's happening. Execution continues to the next breakpoint when you press a specified key.

You can set **watches** in your code — this will allow you to specify variables whose values you wish to track as execution progresses. The values of the selected variables are displayed at each pause point in your program. If you step through your program statement by statement, you can see the exact point at which values are changed — and sometimes when they unexpectedly don't change.

It may be possible for you to **examine** a wide variety of **program components**. For example: at breakpoints, inspection can show details of a function, such as its return type and its arguments. You can also see details of pointers, such as the pointer's address, the address stored by the pointer and the data stored at that address. Access to the values of expressions and modifying variables may also be provided. Modifying variables can help you to bypass problem areas, allowing you to execute subsequent areas with correct data.

The Preprocessor in Debugging

While many C++ development systems provide powerful debug facilities, the addition of tracing code of your own can still be useful. By using conditional preprocessor statements, you can arrange for blocks of code to be included in your program to assist in testing. You can have complete control of the formatting of data which will be displayed for debugging purposes, and you can even arrange for the kind of output to vary according to conditions or relationships within the program.

Try It Out – Debugging With the Preprocessor

We'll illustrate how this can be done, by using a somewhat contrived program that calls functions at random through an array of function pointers. This example will also give us a chance to recap a few of the techniques that you should be familiar with by now. Just for the exercise we will declare three functions, that we will use in the example within a namespace, **fun**. We will put the namespace declaration in a header file:

```
// functions.h
#if !defined FUNCTIONS_H
#define FUNCTIONS_H
namespace fun
{
  // Function prototypes
  int sum(int, int);            // Sum arguments
  int product(int, int);        // Product of arguments
  int difference(int, int);     // Difference between arguments
}
#endif
```

We enclose the contents of the file between an **#if**/**#endif** directive combination. This prevents the contents of this file being **#include**d into a translation unit more than once.

We can put the definitions for the functions in the file **functions.cpp**:

```
// functions.cpp

//#define TESTFUNCTION             // Uncomment to get trace output

#ifdef TESTFUNCTION
#include <iostream>               // Only required for trace output
#endif

#include "functions.h"

// Definition of the function sum
int fun::sum(int x, int y)
{
  #ifdef TESTFUNCTION
  std::cout << "Function sum called." << std::endl;
  #endif

  return x+y;
}

// Definition of the function product
int fun::product(int x, int y)
{
  #ifdef TESTFUNCTION
  std::cout << "Function product called." << std::endl;
  #endif

  return x*y;
}
```

```
// Definition of the function difference
int fun::difference(int x, int y)
{
  #ifdef TESTFUNCTION
  std::cout << "Function difference called." << std::endl;
  #endif

  return x-y;
}
```

We need the standard header **<iostream>** here, because we use stream output statements to provide trace information in each function.

The standard header file **<iostream>** will only be **#include**d, and the output statements compiled, if the symbol **TESTFUNCTION** is **#define**d in the file. Note that **TESTFUNCTION** isn't **#define**d at present (the directive is commented out). We have explicit qualification of **cout** and **endl**, since we have no **using** declarations or directives in the file.

The code to call the functions goes in **main()**, which is in a separate **.cpp** file:

```
// Program 10.6 Debugging using the preprocessor
#include <iostream>
#include <cstdlib>              // For random number generator
#include <ctime>                // For time function

using namespace std;

#include "functions.h"

#define TESTINDEX

// Function to generate a random integer 0 to count-1
int random(int count)
{
  return static_cast<int>((count*static_cast<long>(rand()))/(RAND_MAX+1));
}

int main()
{
  int a = 10, b = 5;                  // Starting values
  int result = 0;                     // Storage for results

  // Declaration for an array of function pointers
  int (*pfun[])(int, int) = {fun::sum, fun::product, fun::difference};

  int fcount = sizeof pfun/sizeof pfun[0];
  int select = 0;                              // Index for function selection
  srand(static_cast<unsigned>(time(0)));       // Seed the random number generator

  // Select function from the pointer array at random
  for(int i = 0 ; i < 10 ; i++)
  {
    select = random(fcount);            // Generate random index 0 to fcount-1

    #ifdef TESTINDEX
    cout << "Random number = " << select << endl;
```

```
        if((select>=fcount) || (select<0))
        {
          cout << "Invalid array index = " << select << endl;
          return 1;
        }
        #endif

        result = pfun[select](a, b);      // Call random function

        cout << "result = " << result << endl;
      }
      result = pfun[1](pfun[0](a, b), pfun[2](a, b));
      cout << endl
           <<"The product of the sum and the difference = " << result
           << endl;
      return 0;
    }
```

When I ran it, it produced the output:

```
Random number = 2
result = 5
Random number = 2
result = 5
Random number = 1
result = 50
Random number = 0
result = 15
Random number = 1
result = 50
Random number = 1
result = 50
Random number = 0
result = 15
Random number = 1
result = 50
Random number = 2
result = 5
Random number = 1
result = 50

The product of the sum and the difference = 75
```

In general, you should get something different. If you want to get the trace output for the functions in the namespace **fun**, you must uncomment the **#define** directive at the beginning of **functions.cpp**.

How It Works

We have three **#include** directives for standard header files at the beginning of the file containing **main()**:

```
#include <iostream>
#include <cstdlib>                 // For random number generator
#include <ctime>                   // For time function
```

The header file **<cstdlib>** is necessary because we will use a standard library function **rand()** to generate random numbers. The header file **<ctime>** provides a definition for the function **time()**, which we will use to seed the random number generating process. We'll see how these work in a moment.

After the **using** directive for the namespace **std**, we have an **#include** directive for our header file:

```
#include "functions.h"
```

This will add the declarations for the functions **sum()**, **product()** and **difference()**, which we will call randomly into our source file. Remember that these are declared within the namespace **fun**.

The definition for the symbol **TESTINDEX** switches on diagnostic output in **main()**:

```
#define TESTINDEX
```

With this symbol defined, the code to output diagnostic information in **main()** will be included in the source that is compiled. If you remove this directive, then the trace code will not be included. Later on in the code, in the middle of the **for** loop, you'll find the code that is subject to this directive:

```
#ifdef TESTINDEX
cout << "Random number = " << select << endl;
if((select>=fcount) || (select<0))
{
  cout << "Invalid array index = " << select << endl;
  return 1;
}
#endif
```

This checks that we use a valid index for the array, **pfun**. Since we don't expect to generate invalid index values, we shouldn't get this output in any event!

> *It's easy to generate an invalid index value, and cause this diagnostic code to execute. To do this, we simply need to persuade the **random()** function to generate a number other than 0, 1 or 2. Try changing the definition of **random()** so that multiplies the random number by **(count+1)**, instead of **count**. Then you should get an erroneous index value produced quite regularly when the program runs, although not necessarily every time.*

The *non-erroneous* definition of the function, **random()**, which generates random integers within a specific range, is:

```
int random(int count)
{
  return static_cast<int>((count*static_cast<long>(rand()))/(RAND_MAX+1));
}
```

The standard library function **rand()** generates random numbers in the range 0 to **RAND_MAX** (where **RAND_MAX** is a constant defined in **<cstdlib>**). In this expression, the integer division results in an integer between in the range 0, 1, …, **count-1** — these are the values which index an array that of **count** elements.

You might be tempted to use the modulus operator to do this — for instance, by using the expression **rand()%count** *to get a value between 0 and* **count**. *However, this will effectively truncate the value returned from* **rand()** *to a few low order bits, and because of the way pseudo-random numbers are generated, these may not be random. By using the expression shown in the code, we effectively scale the range of values produced, so numbers in our range should be just as random as numbers in the original range.*

In **main()**, we declare and initialize an array of function pointers with the statement:

```
int (*pfun[])(int, int) = {fun::sum, fun::product, fun::difference};
```

The array is initialized with the names of the three functions declared in **functions.h**. Each function name in the initializing list is qualified with the namespace name, **fun**.

To get the size of the array, we use the statement:

```
int fcount = sizeof pfun/sizeof pfun[0];
```

Getting the number of elements in an array of function pointers is no different from getting the number of elements in any other array. There are three pointers in the array, so **fcount** will take the value 3.

After declaring and initializing the variable, **select**, that we will use to index the array, **pfun**, we call the standard library **srand()** to initialize the pseudo-random number generating process:

```
srand(static_cast<unsigned>(time(0)));        // Seed the random number generator
```

The unsigned integer that is passed to **srand()** is used to start the process off. The standard library function, **time()**, returns the current time from the system clock, in seconds — so this value will be different every time you run the program. In this way we ensure that we start the pseudo-random number generation process off with a different seed each time. Commonly, the value returned is the number of seconds elapsed since midnight on January 1, 1970 — although this is not specified by the ANSI standard and is dependent on your library.

We call the functions from the namespace **fun** at random in the **for** loop in **main()**:

```
for(int i = 0 ; i < 10 ; i++)
{
  select = random(fcount);          // Generate random index 0 to fcount-1

  #ifdef TESTINDEX
  cout << "Random number = " << select << endl;
  if((select>=fcount) || (select<0))
  {
    cout << "Invalid array index = " << select << endl;
    return 1;
  }
  #endif

  result = pfun[select](a, b);    // Call random function

  cout << "result = " << result << endl;
}
```

The function **random()** is used to generate a random index between **0** and **fcount-1**, which is stored in the variable, **select**. If **TESTINDEX** has been **#define**d in a define directive in this file, then the validation code will be executed. Within the validation code, there is a test for an invalid index value — an invalid index will cause a message to be displayed, before the program terminates in a controlled way by the **return** statement.

The program is completed with a pot-pourri of calls through function pointers, and we display the following result:

```
result = pfun[1](pfun[0](a, b), pfun[2](a, b));
cout << endl
     << "The product of the sum and the difference = " << result
     << endl;
```

If you **#define** the symbol **TESTFUNCTION** in the file **functions.cpp**, you will get trace output from each of the functions. This is a convenient way of controlling whether or not the trace statements are compiled into the program. We can see how this works by looking at one of the functions that may be called, **product()**:

```
int fun::product(int x, int y)
{
  #ifdef TESTFUNCTION
  std::cout << "Function product called." << std::endl;
  #endif

  return x*y;
}
```

The output statement simply displays a message, each time the function is called — but the output statement will *only* be compiled if **TESTFUNCTION** has been **#define**d.

FYI

Note that the #define directive for a preprocessor symbol such as TESTFUNCTION is local to the file in which it appears — so each file that requires TESTFUNCTION would need to have its own #define directive. One potential inconvenience of this is the abundance of #define directives that you start to collect in all your program files. This can be avoided by collecting all your symbols controlling trace and other debug output into a separate header file, which you then #include into *all* your .cpp files. In this way, you can alter the kind of debug output you get by making adjustments to this one header file.

Of course, you can have as many different symbolic constants defined as you wish, as we have seen previously in this chapter. If you really need to, you can use more sophisticated control mechanisms to control which blocks of debug code are included, by combining them into logical expressions that you can test using the **#ifdef** or **#ifndef** conditional directives.

All this diagnostic code is only included while you are testing the program. Once you think the program works, you quite sensibly leave it out. You therefore need to be clear that this sort of code is no substitute for error detection and recovery code that deals with unfortunate situations arising in your fully tested program (as they most certainly will).

Using the assert Macro

Another diagnostic aid is provided in the standard library. The **assert()** macro is declared in the library header **<cassert>**. This enables you to test logical expressions in your program — **assert()** causes the program to be terminated with a diagnostic message if a specified logical expression is **false**.

Try It Out – Demonstrating the assert Macro

We can demonstrate how this works with a simple example:

```
// Program 10.7 Demonstrating assertions
#include <iostream>
#include <cassert>
using namespace std;

int main()
{
  int x = 0;
  int y = 5;

  cout << endl;

  for(x = 0 ; x < 20 ; x++)
  {
    cout << "x = " << x << "   y = " << y << endl;
    assert(x<y);
  }
  return 0;
}
```

Compiling and executing this with my compiler produces the output:

```
x = 0    y = 5
x = 1    y = 5
x = 2    y = 5
x = 3    y = 5
x = 4    y = 5
x = 5    y = 5
Assertion failed: x<y, file D:\Program Files\Microsoft Visual Studio\MyProjects\
prog10_7\prog10_7.cpp, line 16
```

How It Works

Apart from the **assert()** statement, the program shouldn't need much explanation as it simply prints the values of **x** and **y** in the **for** loop.

The program is terminated by the **assert()** macro, which calls **abort()** as soon as the condition **x<y** becomes **false**. The function **abort()** is from the standard library, and its effect is to terminate the program immediately. As you can see from the output, this happens when **x** reaches the value 5. The macro displays the output on the standard error stream, **cerr**, which is always the display screen. The message contains the condition that failed, and also the file name and line number in which the failure occurred. This is particularly useful with multi-file programs, where the source of the error is pinpointed exactly.

Assertions are often used for critical conditions in a program where, if certain conditions are not met, disaster will surely ensue. You would want to be sure that the program wouldn't continue if such errors arise. You can use any logical expression as the argument to the **assert()** macro, so there's a lot of flexibility.

Program 10.6, which generates index values using a random number generator, contains exactly this kind of situation. With this sort of technique there is always the possibility of a bug somewhere, resulting in an invalid index value — and if the index is outside the limits of the array **pfun**, then the result is pretty much guaranteed to be catastrophic.

In Program 10.6, we can use the **assert()** statement to verify the validity of the index value. Instead of the **#ifdef** block, we can simply put:

```
assert((select>= 0) && (select < fcount));
```

It is very simple and effective, and when things go wrong, it provides sufficient information to pin down where the program has terminated.

You can also switch off the assertion mechanism when you recompile the program by defining the symbol **NDEBUG** at the beginning of the program file:

```
#define NDEBUG
```

This will cause all assertions in the translation unit to be ignored. If you add this **#define** at the beginning of Program 10.7, you will see that we get output for all the values of **x** from 0 to 19, and no diagnostic message. Note that this directive will only be effective if it's placed *before* the **#include** statement for **<cassert>**.

FYI

It is important to recognize that assert is not an error-handling mechanism, and that evaluation of the logical expression should not cause side effects or be based on something beyond the programmer's control (e.g. the success or otherwise of opening a file). Your program should provide appropriate code to handle such conditions.

Summary

This chapter has discussed capabilities that operate between, within and across your program files. The fact is that C++ programs typically consist of many files, and that the larger the program, the more files you have to contend with. It is therefore most important that you have a good understanding of namespaces and the preprocessor if you are able to develop real-world C++ programs.

The important points we have covered in this chapter include:

▶ Header files contain declarations, and other code that does not generate executable instructions, and **inline** function definitions. By convention, header files use file names with the extension **.h**.

▶ You put function definitions and global variables in a source file with the file name extension **.cpp**.

▶ The contents of header files containing required declarations are effectively inserted into **.cpp** files by means of **#include** directives.

▶ A **.cpp** file forms a translation unit that is processed by the compiler as a unit to generate an object file.

▶ A namespace defines a scope — all names declared within this scope have the namespace name attached to them. All declarations of names that are not in an explicit namespace scope are in the global namespace.

▶ A single namespace can be made up of separate several namespace declarations with the same name.

▶ Identical names declared within different namespaces are distinct.

▶ To refer to an identifier which is declared within a namespace, from *outside* the namespace, you need to specify the namespace name and the identifier, separated by the scope resolution operator, **::**.

▶ Names declared within a namespace can be used without qualification from inside the namespace.

▶ The preprocessor executes preprocessor directives to transform the source code in a translation unit, prior to compilation of the code proper. When all directives have been processed, the translation unit will only contain C++ code, with no preprocessor directives remaining.

▶ You can use conditional preprocessor directives to ensure that the contents of a header file are never duplicated within a translation unit.

▶ You can use conditional preprocessor directives to control whether trace or other diagnostic debug code is included in your program.

▶ The **assert()** macro enables you to test logical conditions during execution and issue a message and abort the program if the logical condition is false.

Exercises

Ex 10.1 A program calls two functions, **PrintThis(const string& s)** and **PrintThat(const string& s)**, each of which calls a third function, **Print(const string& s)**, to print the string that has been passed to it.

Implement each of the three functions and the main routine in four separate **.cpp** files, and in addition provide three header files to contain the prototypes for **PrintThis()**, **PrintThat()** and **Print()**. Make sure that the header files are adequately guarded against being included more than once, and that **main.cpp** contains the minimum number of **#include** statements.

Ex 10.2 Modify the program so that the **Print()** function uses a global integer variable to count the number of times it has been called. Print out the value of this variable in the main program after calls to **PrintThis()** and **PrintThat()**.

Ex 10.3 In the **Print.h** header file, delete the existing prototype for **Print()**, and instead create two namespaces, **print1** and **print2**, each of which contains a function **Print(const string& s)**. The fact that these have identical function signatures means that the only way they can be told apart is by using their namespace names. Implement these two functions in the **Print.cpp** file so that they print the namespace name and the string.

Now, make **PrintThis()** call the function declared in namespace **print1**, and **PrintThat()** the version in namespace **print2**. Run the program, and verify that the right functions are being called. Extra credit: you should be able to find three different ways (that is, three different forms of syntax) to call the **Print()** functions from within **PrintThis()** and **PrintThat()**.

Ex 10.4 Modify the **main()** routine so that **PrintThis()** is only called if a preprocessor symbol named **DO_THIS** is defined. If this is not the case, **PrintThat()** should be called.

Modify the code by defining a macro **PRINT()** so that **PRINT(abc)** — note the absence of quotes — calls **PrintThis("abc")** when **DO_THIS** is defined, and **PrintThat("abc")** otherwise.

Ex 10.5 Can you find a way to stop compilation if the **<iostream>** header hasn't been included in a file that needs it?

11

Creating your own Data Types

The great strength of C++ is its object-oriented nature. There's a great deal implied here, and we will spend five chapters expanding on this topic. In this chapter and the next, we will discuss the real foundation of object-oriented programming — defining your own data types. But there is much more to this than simply adding new types. Object-oriented programming provides a powerful approach to programming that is fundamentally different from what we have seen up to now. In Chapters 13 through 16 we will explore the detail of all the C++ techniques you might need to implement your own data types.

This chapter will introduce some of the basic ideas behind objects, and some of the simple ways in which you can use them. This will provide a base of knowledge for the next chapter, in which we will consider the principles of the object-oriented approach in more depth, and develop an understanding of classes and how they are defined.

In this chapter you will learn:

- ▶ What an object is
- ▶ What a structure is and how structures are declared
- ▶ How the objects of a structure are defined and used
- ▶ How to handle the members of a structure object
- ▶ What a union is

What is an Object?

The C++ language is all about exploiting the advantages of object-oriented programming, and in this chapter we will begin to develop a real understanding of the concepts involved. To begin with, we must introduce the very basic building blocks.

So what exactly is an object? In a sense, this is a difficult question to answer — precisely because an object can be anything you like. In fact, we have (in some sense) been using objects implicitly in our programs right from the start of the book.

An **object** is an instance of a data type. For example, suppose we make the following definition of a variable, as we have done so often:

```
int dollars = 0;
```

Here, we have defined a single instance of the type **int**. We have given a name to that instance, by calling it **dollars**. We might say that the variable **dollars** is an object of type **int**.

> *This is sufficiently true for the purposes of this discussion. The purists will argue that it's not quite accurate: C++ differentiates between instances of user defined types (called objects) and instances of basic data types (simply called instances).*

An object has a value — the integer **dollars** has the value 0.

The operations that we can perform on (and with) an object are precisely defined. For example, the object **dollars** (of type **int**) has a set of operations which you can apply — including arithmetic operations such as +, –, and comparison operators such as <, ==.

For a given object, there will also be operations which you *cannot* apply, because the operation is not defined for that object. Again, consider our object **dollars**. You can't add **dollars** to a string, for example, and you can't apply the subscript operator to it. This is because these operators are not defined for an object of type **int**.

As we have seen, C++ gives us a number of basic data types as standard, but it's obvious that our programming would be far less restricted if we could create our own types. So C++ gives us the tools to do exactly that — we can add new data types of our own, and specify the operations that can be applied to them. The types that you define are usually referred to as **user defined data types**, but this does not imply any particular limitations on them. Your data types can be as sophisticated and as complex as your application requires, and as we will see, they can be used with the same operators that are applied to the basic data types.

A **class** is a user defined data type, and for the most part, we define classes using the keyword **class**.

> *Don't confuse classes with the use of the* typedef *or with an enumeration. A* typedef *statement does not create a new type, but simply defines an alias for an existing type. Each enumeration is a distinct type, but it is not a class. A class is an entirely new and original type which not only has a unique set of properties, but also has operations, applicable to class objects, that are defined entirely by you.*

By way of introduction to classes, we'll be looking at two other ways of creating your own data types. They are **unions** and **structures**; we use the keywords **union** and **struct** respectively to create these. Technically, these are also classes; however, we will refer to a type defined using the keyword **class** as a class, and the other two user-defined types as unions and structures respectively.

A structure is very similar to a class, and it will help us to discuss the basics of structures first, before taking a brief look at unions, and then moving on to look at classes in depth over the next two chapters.

The Structure in C++

Historically, a **structure** was used in the C programming language — it was essentially a named aggregate of data items of different data types. For instance, you might collect together a variable **Name** of type **char***, a variable **Age** of type **int**, and a variable **Gender** of type **char**, and store this cluster of data in a structure called **Person**.

In C++, a structure is generally used for the same purpose. However, we'll see that a structure in C++ is capable of doing rather more than a structure in C. During the development of C++, the notion of a class was developed from, and vastly extended, the concept of a C structure. Structures in C++ were also blessed with these new facilities. In fact, a C++ structure is functionally replaceable by a class.

So why should we spend time and effort studying an obsolete capability such as a structure? Well, partly because it's not quite obsolete, and because, like Everest to a mountaineer, it's there as part of the C++ language. More importantly, it is still very pervasive in some environments. For instance, the Microsoft Windows operating system on a PC is positively riddled with structures — so if you want to write applications to run in that environment you will certainly need to understand the characteristics of structures, and how they are declared and used. Further, our efforts in looking at structures will not be wasted since their capabilities apply equally to classes.

There's another point to consider. In C++, a structure is undoubtedly a class. As we will see in the next chapter, the only difference between a structure and a class is in certain default characteristics, which reflect the different way that classes and structures are implemented in C++.

Understanding Structures

So far in this book, the variables and data types that we have seen have consisted of a single entity — a numeric of some kind, or a character, or a string. Life, the universe, and everything are, however, rather more complicated than these basic data types reflect — unless you are among those who believe the answer is 42, in which case all you'll ever need is an **int**!

In order to describe virtually anything in the real world, you need to define several values that are usually of a number of different types. From this idea comes the notion of a structure.

For instance, let's think about the information needed to describe something as simple as a book. You might consider the title, author, publisher, date of publication, number of pages, price, topic (or classification) and ISBN number, just for starters — you can probably come up with a few more properties, too. To identify a book in your program, you *could* specify separate variables, one to contain each of these characteristics. Ideally, though, you would prefer to have a single data type — which we'll call **Book** — which embodies *all* of these properties.

This is exactly what a structure can do for you. A structure is a data type which defines a particular kind of object of your choosing.

Defining a Structure Type

Let's stick with the notion of a book. Suppose that we just want to include the title, author, publisher and year of publication within our definition of a book. We could declare a structure type to accommodate this as follows:

```
struct Book
{
    char title[80];
    char author[80];
    char publisher[80];
    int year;
};
```

This declaration does not define any variables; it specifies a new type called Book. *The compiler will use this definition as a blueprint for creating entities of type* Book.

The keyword **struct** declares that **Book** is a structure. The elements that will make up an object of type **Book** are those that we have declared within the curly braces. Note that the definition of each element in the **struct** is terminated by a semicolon, and that a semicolon also appears after the closing brace — so it's just like an ordinary declaration.

An object of type Book	
title	The Selfish Gene
author	Richard Dawkins
publisher	Oxford University Press
year	1989

The elements **title**, **author**, **publisher** and **year**, enclosed between the braces in the definition, are usually referred to as **data members** (or, more generically, **members**) of the structure **Book**. Every variable of type **Book** will contain the members **title**, **author**, **publisher** and **year**.

The amount of memory that you need to store a structure object is the aggregate of the memory needed to store each of the data members. For example, an object of type **Book** *requires enough memory to contain three character arrays and an integer. We can use the* **sizeof()** *operator, which we introduced in Chapter 3, to measure the amount of memory occupied by a single object of a given data type. (In the next chapter, we'll discuss a subtlety of this, involving something called boundary alignment.)*

The data members of a structure can be of any type, *except* the type of the structure being defined. Thus, for example, the structure definition for **Book** must not contain a data member of type **Book**. Otherwise, consider what would happen when we initialize a variable of type **Book**: you would need to initialize the data member of type **Book** that it contained — and that would also contain a data member of type **Book** which would need initializing, and so on. In fact, the **sizeof()** your outermost variable would be infinite!

However, our declaration of the type **Book** could include a 'pointer to **Book**'; this provides a very useful capability as we shall see a little later on.

Declaring a Structure Object

Now that we have defined the structure **Book**, let's look at how to (and how not to) define variables of that type. We can define a variable of type **Book**, in exactly the same way that we would define variables of any other type:

```
Book paperback;              // Define variable paperback of type Book
```

This defines a variable **paperback**, which we can now use to store information about a book. Optionally, you can use the keyword **struct** in the definition of a variable of a structure type. We could have defined the variable **paperback** with the statement:

```
struct Book paperback;       // Define variable paperback of type Book
```

However, this is a hangover from C and is generally not practiced.

The next three statements define three variables:

```
Book novel;
Book* pTravelGuide;
Book languageGuide[10];
```

The variable **novel** is of type **Book**, **pTravelGuide** is of type 'pointer to **Book**', and **languageGuide** is an array with 10 elements of type **Book**. It's also possible (though not recommended) to define multiple variables of type **Book** in a single statement. For example, instead of the statements above, the following is legal:

```
Book novel, *pTravelGuide, languageGuide[10];
```

Just as with variables of the basic types, this single statement is error-prone, and makes for unclear code. The set of three definition statements is entirely preferable.

Finally, it's possible to define variables when you define the structure type:

```
struct Book
{
   char title[80];
   char author[80];
   char publisher[80];
   int year;
} dictionary, thesaurus;
```

This statement defines the type, **Book**, and then defines two variables of that type, called **dictionary** and **thesaurus**. However, it's good to get into the habit of writing a separate statement for the type definition, and for each of the object declarations. Typically, your type declarations would be stored in a header file, which is **#include**d into your **.cpp** files whenever the type definition is needed.

The next step is to understand how to get data into the various members that make up a variable of type **Book**.

Initializing a Structure Variable

The first way to get data into the members of a structure variable is to define the initial values for the data members in the definition. Suppose we wanted to initialize the variable **novel** with the data for a specific book. We could declare the **novel** object, and initialize its data members, with the following statement:

```
Book novel =
{
   "Feet of Clay",                // Initial value for title
   "Terry Pratchett",             // Initial value for author
   "Victor Gollanz",              // Initial value for publisher
   1996                           // Initial value for year
};
```

The initializing values appear between a set of braces, separated by commas, in much the same way that we defined initial values for members of an array. Obviously, the sequence of initial values needs to match the sequence of members in the structure definition. This statement initializes each member of the object **novel** with the corresponding value, as indicated in the comments. The name **novel** now refers to a particular object, namely the book identified by its data members.

A structure type that can be initialized with a list of values between braces is called an **aggregate** — this simply means that the structure type is composed of built-in data types, arrays and other aggregates.

> Note that we could not initialize a **Book** object in this way if the members of **Book** were of a class type such as **string**. The reason is that objects of a class type can only be created by calling a special function called a constructor, and this would imply that the structure is not an aggregate. We will see more about constructors in the next chapter.

If you supply fewer initial values in the declaration than there are data members of the structure variable, then the data members without initial values will be initialized to 0.

You can also initialize an array of structure variables, in much the same way that we initialized multi-dimensional arrays. You put the set of initial values for each array element between braces, and separate each set from the next with a comma. We could declare and initialize an array with the statement:

```
Book novels[] = {
   { "Our Game" ,               "John Le Carre" , "Hodder & Stoughton", 1995 },
   { "Trying to Save Piggy Sneed", "John Irving" ,   "Bloomsbury",          1993 },
   { "Illywhacker" ,            "Peter Carey" ,   "Faber & Faber ",      1985 }
                 };
```

This declaration creates and initializes the array, **novels**, of type **Book**, and the array will have three elements.

Accessing the Members of a Structure Variable

To access individual data members of a structure variable, you can use the **member access operator**, which is a period (and consequently sometimes known as the dot notation). To refer to a particular data member, you write the structure variable name, followed by a period, followed by the name of the member that you want to access. We can assign the value 1988 to the member **year** of our structure **novel**:

```
novel.year = 1988;
```

Variable members of a structure can be used in arithmetic expressions, in exactly the same way as you would use any other variable of the same type. To increment the member **year** by two, for example, we can write:

```
novel.year += 2;
```

Accessing members of a structure array element is also straightforward. We could calculate the time between the publication of the first and last books in the array **novels** with the statement:

```
int interval = novels[0].year - novels[2].year;
```

This calculates the difference between the **year** members of the first and last elements of the array.

Try It Out – Using Structures

We need to define a very simple real-life item, which needs more than one value to represent it, and model it as a structure.

Suppose we want to write a program to deal with boxes of various sizes. They could be candy boxes, shoe boxes, or any kind of box that is rectilinear in shape. We will use three values to define a box — length, breadth and height. The structure members reflect the representation of a box by its physical dimensions. We can declare a structure type to represent a box as shown in the diagram below.

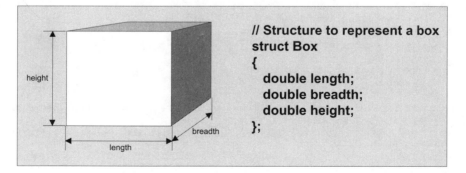

```
// Structure to represent a box
struct Box
{
    double length;
    double breadth;
    double height;
};
```

We'll use our box structure in a program that will create some boxes. We will also define and use a global function to calculate volume of a box object.

```cpp
// Program 11.1 Using a Box structure
#include <iostream>
using namespace std;

// Structure to represent a box
struct Box
{
  double length;
  double breadth;
  double height;
};

// Prototype of function to calculate the volume of a box
double volume(const Box& aBox);

int main()
{
  Box firstBox = { 80.0, 50.0, 40.0 };

  // Calculate the volume of the box
  double firstBoxVolume = volume(firstBox);
  cout << endl;
  cout << "Size of first Box object is "
       << firstBox.length  << " by "
       << firstBox.breadth << " by "
       << firstBox.height
       << endl;
  cout << "Volume of first Box object is " << firstBoxVolume
       << endl;

  Box secondBox = firstBox;    // Create a second Box object the same as firstBox

  // Increase the dimensions of second Box object by 10%
  secondBox.length *= 1.1;
  secondBox.breadth *= 1.1;
  secondBox.height *= 1.1;

  cout << "Size of second Box object is "
       << secondBox.length << " by "
       << secondBox.breadth << " by "
       << secondBox.height
       << endl;
  cout << "Volume of second box object is " << volume(secondBox)
       << endl;

  cout << "Increasing the box dimensions by 10% has increased the volume by "
       << static_cast<long>
                       ((volume(secondBox)-firstBoxVolume)*100.0/firstBoxVolume)
       << "%"
       << endl;
  return 0;
}
```

```
// Function to calculate the volume of a box
double volume(const Box& aBox)
{
  return aBox.length * aBox.breadth * aBox.height;
}
```

If you compile and run this program, you should get the output:

```
Size of first Box object is 80 by 50 by 40
Volume of first Box object is 160000
Size of second Box object is 88 by 55 by 44
Volume of second box object is 212960
Increasing the box dimensions by 10% has increased the volume by 33%
```

How It Works

In this program, the structure definition appears at global scope. Generally, the structure definition is available within the scope in which it appears. If the structure definition for **Box** had appeared within the body of **main()**, then the function **volume()** (which is also defined at global scope) would be unable to recognize the parameter type **Box&**.

FYI Putting the Box structure definition at global scope allows us to declare a variable of type Box anywhere in our .cpp file. In a program with several .cpp files, type definitions are normally stored in a .h file and then #included into each .cpp file that uses the data types.

We declare the function, **volume()**, which we define later in the source file, with the prototype:

```
double volume(const Box& aBox);
```

The parameter is a **const** reference to a **Box** object. Defining the parameter as a reference means that the original **Box** object isn't copied. This is important with complex structure types (and also classes, which we shall see in the next chapter), because the time required to copy arguments for complex objects can reduce the efficiency of your program. We make the parameter type **const** since the function should not modify the argument at all — it will just use the data members.

In **main()**, we declare and initialize a **Box** object with the statement:

```
Box firstBox = { 80.0, 50.0, 40.0 };
```

The initial values between the braces are used to initialize the corresponding members of the structure, so **length** will be 80, **breadth** will be 50, and **height** will be 40. Obviously it is important to get the initializing values in the correct order.

The volume of the box object **firstBox** is calculated by the following statement:

```
double firstBoxVolume = volume(firstBox);
```

The calculated volume is stored in the variable **firstBoxVolume**, since we will need it again later in the program. We'll come back to how the function **volume()** works in a moment.

421

The next statement in **main()** displays the dimensions of **firstBox**:

```
cout << "Size of first Box object is "
    << firstBox.length  << " by "
    << firstBox.breadth << " by "
    << firstBox.height
    << endl;
```

Here, we access each member of **firstBox** simply by prefixing the member name with the object name and the member access operator, and using this in the output statement in the normal way. The next statement displays the volume of the box that we calculated earlier:

```
cout << "Volume of first Box object is " << firstBoxVolume
    << endl;
```

Next, we want to create a new **Box** object. To begin, it will be the same as **firstBox**, but we will adjust its dimensions shortly. We do this with the statement:

```
Box secondBox = firstBox;   // Create a second Box object the same as firstBox
```

This creates a new **Box** object, **secondBox**, and sets each member of **secondBox** to the same value as the corresponding member of **firstBox**. The compiler does this by making a byte-by-byte copy of the original object.

We increment each of the dimensions of **secondBox** with the statements:

```
secondBox.length *= 1.1;
secondBox.breadth *= 1.1;
secondBox.height *= 1.1;
```

We use three separate statements to multiply the three data members by 1.1. This looks a little long-winded, doesn't it? Why can't we just write:

```
secondBox *= 1.1;                  // Wrong!!! Won't work!!!
```

The compiler would have a problem here, because **secondBox** is an object of type **Box** — and the compiler does not know how a multiply operation is supposed to work with an object of type **Box**. On the other hand, the three separate statements do compile, since the data members are all of type **double**, and the compiler knows what we mean when we multiply a **double** by 1.1.

> **FYI**
>
> Usually, an operator which is applied to a *user defined* type must be defined by the programmer. Only the assignment operator — when used to assign one object of a user defined type to another object of the same type — has a default definition. This assignment is performed by assigning values member-by-member. You will learn how to write operations for your own types in the next chapter.

With the members of **secondBox** incremented by 10%, we output the dimensions and the volume in the same way that we used for **firstBox**. Finally, we calculate the change in volume due to the increment with the statement:

```
cout << "Increasing the box dimensions by 10% has increased the volume by "
     << static_cast<long>
                   ((volume(secondBox)-firstBoxVolume)*100.0/firstBoxVolume)
     << "%"
     << endl;
```

We **static_cast** the value of the percentage increase to type **long**, so that the output is an integral percentage.

Before moving on, let's just have a look at how the function **volume()** works. The definition of the function **volume()** is:

```
double volume(const Box& aBox)
{
  return aBox.length * aBox.breadth * aBox.height;
}
```

A **Box** variable is passed into the function **volume()** as an argument, just like any other type of variable. Within the function, we deal with this variable by referring to the parameter name **aBox**. To calculate the volume, we multiply together the members of the **Box** object. In order to access each of these members we must also use the object parameter name, in conjunction with the member selection operator. This combination identifies the member of the object that you pass to the function when you call it. The resulting product is returned from the function.

Member Functions of a Structure

In Program 11.1, we designed the structure **Box** simply as a compound data item, containing three data members only. This is a common usage for structures — many programmers prefer that a structure is used merely as a collection of data items. They will compare this to their classes, which (as we shall see) generally also offer functionality. However, we have already noted that a C++ structure *is* a class, and as such, it is also possible for a C++ structure object to support functionality.

The idea of a data type which has functionality is a new concept for us. We can illustrate the ideas involved by looking again at Program 11.1, and redeveloping our **Box** data type.

In Program 11.1, you may have noticed that the **volume()** function only has relevance to **Box** objects. It has no purpose in any other context. For this reason, it is preferable to integrate the function into the type, rather than allowing it to float around as an independent entity in the global namespace.

We can define the **volume()** function within the **Box** type definition, so that it becomes an integral part of objects of that type. The function will be a member of the type **Box**. Here's how the definition would look with **volume()** as a function member of the structure:

```
struct Box
{
  double length;
  double breadth;
  double height;

  // Function to calculate the volume of a box
  double volume()
  {
```

```
        return length * breadth * height;
    }
};
```

The function is now an integral part of the type, and you can only use this function with an object of type **Box**. When you call the function, it will apply directly to the current **Box** object. This has two consequences: first, when you call the function, you don't need to include an argument. Second, the data members in the return expression don't need an object name to qualify them.

To call this function for an object, you just use the member selection operator in the same way as you did for data members. For example, with this definition for the type **Box**, we can declare an object **firstBox**, of type **Box**, and then calculate its volume as follows:

```
Box firstBox = { 80.0, 50.0, 40.0 };
double firstBoxVolume = firstBox.volume();
```

This calls the function **volume()** for the object **firstBox**. The volume of **firstBox** is calculated, and the result is stored in **firstBoxVolume**. The **length**, **breadth** and **height** data members used in the calculation will be those of the object **firstBox**.

If you call the function for a different **Box** object, then clearly the data members of that object will be used. For example, to display the volume of a **Box** variable **secondBox**, you could write:

```
cout << "Volume of second Box object is " << newBox.volume()
     << endl;
```

You could alter Program 11.1 so that it uses the **volume()** member function throughout, and the output from the program will be exactly the same.

Integrating the function with the type really changes the nature of the function. Every **Box** object now has the fundamental ability to calculate its own volume. Of course, the **volume()** function only applies to **Box** objects, and if you don't have a **Box** object then you can't use the **volume()** function. (You could write another **volume()** function at global scope. There would be no possibility of confusing them, since one can only be called when using a **Box** object, and the other can only be called using the function name by itself.)

Placing the Member Function Definition

In the example above, the member function definition is contained within the structure definition. You can, instead, put a *declaration* for the member function within the structure definition, and define the member function separately. In this case, the structure definition would be:

```
struct Box
{
  double length;
  double breadth;
  double height;

  double volume();            // Function to calculate the volume of a box
};
```

424

Here, the function definition will be separate from the definition of the structure. In the function definition, we must tell the compiler that the function being defined is a member of the structure **Box**. For this, you use the scope resolution operator, **::**, as we did with namespaces. The function definition would be:

```
double Box::volume()
{
  return length * breadth * height;
}
```

The **Box** qualifier (in conjunction with the function name) identifies that this function definition belongs to the **Box** structure. You can still use the names of the members of the **Box** structure without qualification, within the body of the function.

> *When organizing the member function definitions of your structures and classes, this method is generally recommended. We'll demonstrate it in Program 11.2, and we'll see it in the context of classes in the next chapter.*

As we've said, every object of type **Box** will have its own **volume()** function. However, the code for this function will only appear once in memory, regardless of how many objects of type **Box** exist. They all share a single copy of the function, so no memory is wasted. This raises the question of how the data members of a particular object are associated with the data member names used within the body of the function, when the function executes. We will defer answering this question until the next chapter, when we get deeper into classes.

Using Pointers with a Structure

As we have already mentioned, you can create a pointer to a variable of a structure type, or indeed to any user defined type. For example, to define a pointer to a **Box** object, the declaration is what you might expect:

```
Box* pBox = 0;            // Define a null pointer to an object of type Box
```

This pointer can hold the address of an object of type **Box**, and we have initialized it with 0 here.

Assuming that we have already defined a **Box** object called **aBox**, we can set our pointer to the address of this variable in the normal way, using the address-of operator:

```
pBox = &aBox;            // Set pointer to the address of aBox
```

The pointer **pBox** now contains the address of the object, **aBox**.

Accessing Structure Members through a Pointer

Suppose we define a **Box** object with the statement:

```
Box theBox = { 80.0, 50.0, 40.0 };
```

We can declare a pointer to a **Box** object, and initialize it with the address of **theBox**, by writing:

```
Box* pBox = &theBox;
```

We can use the pointer **pBox** to access the data members of the object to which it points. This is a two-step process: we must de-reference the pointer to obtain the object, and then use this with the member selection operator and the member name. For example, we could increment the **height** data member of **theBox** with the statement:

```
(*pBox).height += 10.0;                 // Increment the height member by 10.0
```

After executing this statement, the **height** member will have the value 60.0, and of course, the remaining members will be unchanged. Note that the parentheses in this statement are essential, since the member selection operator takes precedence over the de-referencing operator. Without the parentheses, the compiler would interpret this statement as follows:

```
*(pBox.height) += 10.0;
```

This would attempt to treat the pointer **pBox** as a **struct**, and to de-reference the expression **pBox.height**, so the statement would not compile.

The Pointer Member Access Operator

The two-step operation described above — that is, de-referencing an 'pointer to object' and accessing its members — crops up with great frequency in C++. However, the combination of the ***** and **.** operators looks clumsy; it requires judicious use of parentheses, and it doesn't immediately reflect what we're trying to do.

For all these reasons, the C++ language includes a special operator, called the **pointer member access operator**, which enables you to express the same thing in a readable and intuitive form. The pointer member access operator is used specifically for accessing members of a user-defined type through a pointer.

Instead of this clumsy-looking statement:

```
(*pBox).height += 10.0;                 // Increment the height member by 10.0
```

we can use the pointer member access operator to do the same task, as follows:

```
pBox->height += 10.0;                   // Increment the height member by 10.0
```

The operator looks like an arrow and is formed from a minus sign and a 'greater than' symbol. It's a much better expression of what is going on, isn't it? This operator is also employed in the same way when using classes, and we will be seeing a lot more of it throughout the rest of the book.

Of course, you can also use the pointer member access operator to call member functions of a structure through a pointer. Let's take pointers to objects for a test drive.

Try It Out - Using Pointers to Objects

Here's the code:

```
// Program 11.2 Using pointers to Box objects
#include <iostream>
using namespace std;

struct Box
{
  double length;
  double breadth;
  double height;

  double volume();                    // Function to calculate the volume of a box
};

int main()
{
  Box aBox = { 10, 20, 30 };
  Box* pBox = &aBox;                            // Store address of aBox
  cout << endl
       << "Volume of aBox is " << pBox->volume() << endl;

  Box* pdynBox = new Box;                       // Create Box in the free store
  pdynBox->height = pBox->height + 5.0;
  pdynBox->length = pBox->length - 3.0;
  pdynBox->breadth = pBox->breadth - 2.0;
  cout << "Volume of Box in the free store is " << pdynBox->volume() << endl;

  delete pdynBox;
  return 0;
}


// Box function to calculate volume
double Box::volume()
{
  return length * breadth * height;
}
```

This will produce the output:

```
Volume of aBox is 6000
Volume of Box in the free store is 4410
```

How It Works

Before we look at how the pointers are working, notice that the **Box** structure definition contains only a *declaration* of the **volume()** function. The *definition* of the function is listed at the end of the program. The scope resolution operator **::** indicates that the function definiton belongs to the **Box** structure.

After creating and initializing the object **aBox**, we store its address in the pointer **pBox**:

```
Box* pBox = &aBox;                            // Store address of aBox
```

We can now access the members of **aBox** indirectly, via the pointer **pBox** and the indirect member selection operator. In the following statement, we access the **volume()** function for **aBox**:

```
cout << endl
     << "Volume of aBox is " << pBox->volume() << endl;
```

Next, we create a **Box** object dynamically and store its address in another pointer:

```
Box* pdynBox = new Box;                          // Create Box in the free store
```

The address returned by **new** is stored in the pointer **pdynBox**. We have not yet initialized the data members of this new **Box** object, and so they will contain junk values. We assign values to the data members, by using expressions which involve the values of the members of **aBox**:

```
pdynBox->height = pBox->height+5.0;
pdynBox->length = pBox->length-3.0;
pdynBox->breadth = pBox->breadth-2.0;
```

In these three statements, each member is referenced using the pointer, the indirect member selection operator, and the member name. Now that we have some sensible values for the dimensions of the **Box** object, we calculate its volume:

```
cout << "Volume of Box in the free store is " << pdynBox->volume() << endl;
```

Finally, we delete the **Box** object from the free store:

```
delete pdynBox;
```

As you can see, using a pointer to an object with the indirect member selection object is quite intuitive, and the code is easy to read and understand.

Applications for Pointers to Objects

Pointers to objects of class types are very important, and in this section we'll briefly mention three situations in which they are particularly useful.

The first is an application which we briefly saw in action in Program 11.2. You must use a pointer when creating (or accessing) an object within the free store. More often than not, your programs will need to accommodate a varying number of objects, and the best way of handling this is to create objects dynamically.

The second application is a linked list. As we discussed earlier in the chapter, the data members of a structure *cannot* include a member of the same structure type — so we can't define a **Book** structure which contains a **Book** data member. However, a structure *can* contain a 'pointer to structure type'; and to take this a step further, the structure definition can include a 'pointer to a structure of the *same* type'.

This has several uses; one significant consequence is that enables the creation of a powerful mechanism for storing a collection of objects called a **linked list**.

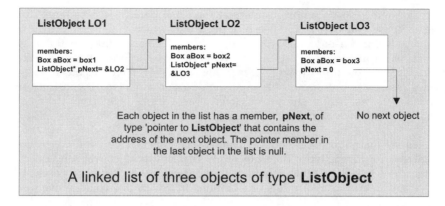

ListObject LO1

members:
Box aBox = box1
ListObject* pNext= &LO2

ListObject LO2

members:
Box aBox = box2
ListObject* pNext=
&LO3

ListObject LO3

members:
Box aBox = box3
pNext = 0

No next object

Each object in the list has a member, **pNext**, of
type 'pointer to **ListObject**' that contains the
address of the next object. The pointer member in
the last object in the list is null.

A linked list of three objects of type **ListObject**

The diagram illustrates how a sequence of objects of a given type can be chained together: each object contains a pointer member which contains the address of the next. As long as you know the address of the first object in a chain, you can get to all the others by following the chain of pointer members from one object to the next. We will look at this in more detail in the context of classes in Chapter 13.

Possible the most important application for pointers to objects is the fundamental role which they play in the way polymorphism works. Polymorphism is an essential mechanism in object-oriented programming, which we shall discuss at length in Chapter 16.

Understanding Unions

A **union** is a data type which allows you to use to the same block of memory to store values of different types at different times. The variables in a union are referred to as members of the union. There are essentially three ways in which you can use a union.

First, you can use union to enable the same block of memory to store different variables (possibly of different types), at different points in a program. The idea behind this originally was simply to economize on the use of memory, at a time when memory was limited in capacity and very expensive. However, this is happily no longer the case, and it's not worth the risk of error that is implicit in such an arrangement. Therefore this application of a union is not recommended — you can achieve the same effect by allocating memory dynamically.

The second application, which concerns memory saving on a larger scale, involves arrays. Suppose that you have a situation in which a large array of data is required, but you don't know in advance of execution what the data type will be — it will be determined by the input data. A union allows you to have several arrays of different basic types as members, and each array occupies the same block of memory (rather that each having its own memory area). At compile time, you have covered all possibilities; and at execution time, the program will use whichever array is appropriate to the type of data entered. The unused arrays do not occupy any additional space. I recommend that you don't use unions in this case either, since it's possible to achieve the same result by using a couple of pointers of different types, and again, allocating the memory dynamically.

Third, you may want to use a union to interpret the same data in two or more different ways. For example, suppose you have a variable of type **long**, which you want to treat as four characters of type **char** (in order to write it to a file as a binary value). A union provides a way of treating the **long** value as an integer when you are performing a calculation, and as a four byte block when you want to write it to a file. However, there are other ways of doing this, as we will see when we discuss file input and output. Conversely, you can use a union to do the reverse — that is, treat a string of characters as a series of integers for producing a key of some kind. Unions make both cases very easy to deal with.

Don't be misled by this third application of unions. The fact that you can access the same data through variables of different types does not imply that any type conversion is occurring. In fact, the same bit pattern is simply being interpreted in different ways, with no checks on the validity of the data — and clearly, there are lots of situations in which this could prove disastrous.

In general, a member of a union cannot be a class type unless it is an aggregate — that is, an objects which can be initialized by an initialization list. In particular, a string object cannot be a member of a union. For the most part, the data members of unions will be variables of basic types.

Let's look at how we declare a union.

Declaring Unions

As we said, a union is declared using the keyword **union**. Let's see how it works through a specific example:

```
union ShareLD            // Sharing memory between long and double
{
  double dVal;
  long lVal;
};
```

This declares a data type, **ShareLD**, which provides for the variables of type **long** and **double** to occupy the same memory. The union type name is sometimes referred to as a **tag name**. This statement is rather like a class declaration (in fact, it is a sort of class declaration) in that we haven't actually defined a union instance yet, so we don't have any variables at this point. We're now in a position to declare an instance of the union **ShareLD**. We'll call it **myUnion**:

```
ShareLD myUnion;
```

We could also have defined **myUnion** by including it in the union definition statement:

```
union ShareLD            // Sharing memory between long and double
{
  double dVal;
  long lVal;
} myUnion;
```

If we want to refer to a member of the union, we use the direct member selection operator (the period) with the union instance name, just as we have done when accessing members of a class. So, we could set the **long** variable **lVal** to 100 in the union instance **myUnion** with this statement:

```
myUnion.lVal = 100;        // Using a member of a union
```

When we use a union to store values of different types in the same memory, we encounter a basic problem. Because of the way a union works, we also need some means of determining which of the member values is current. This is usually achieved by maintaining another variable which acts as an indicator of the type of value stored.

A union can contain more than two data members, if required. We can define another union, which shares a memory location between several variables. The union will occupy the amount of memory required to store its largest member. For example, suppose we declare this union:

```
union ShareDLF
{
   double dVal;
   long lVal;
   float fVal;
};
ShareDLF uinst = {1.5};
```

On my computer, **uinst** will occupy 8 bytes, as illustrated in the diagram.

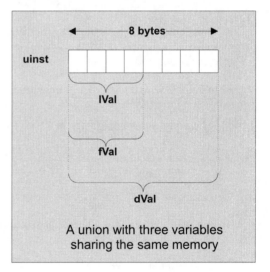

A union with three variables sharing the same memory

In the example, we defined the tag name for the union, **ShareLDF**. Then we declare an instance of the union with the name **uinst**, which we initialize with the value 1.5.

Note the way that we initialized the value of the union:

```
ShareDLF uinst = {1.5};
```

When you initialize a union within the declaration statement, it is always the *first* data member which gets initialized. In this case, it is the data member **dVal** which will contain the value 1.5. If you want to initialize the member **fVal**, then you must write separate statements for the declaration and assignment of the union:

```
ShareDLF uinst;
uinst.fVal = 1.5;
```

Anonymous Unions

You can declare a union without a union type name, in which case an instance of the union is automatically defined. For example, we can define a union like this:

```
union
{
   char* pVal;
   double dVal;
   long lVal;
};
```

This declares a union with no name, and also defines an instance of the union which has no name. Consequently, the members of the union may be referred to just by their member names, as they appear in the union definition. This can be more convenient than a union with a type name, but you need to be careful that you don't confuse the union members with ordinary variables. The members of this union will still share the same memory.

Let's illustrate how this anonymous union works. In order to use the **double** member, you could write this statement:

```
dVal = 99.5;      // Using a member of an anonymous union
```

As you can see, there is nothing here to indicate that the variable **dVal** used here is a union member. If you need to use anonymous unions, you could use a naming convention to make the members more obvious.

Note that if you declare a union without a name, but you declare objects of that type in the same statement, then the union is not anonymous. For example:

```
union
{
   char* pVal;
   double dVal;
   long lVal;
} uvalue;
```

In this case you cannot refer to the union members names by themselves, since no unnamed instance of the union exists. You just have the **uvalue** instance. You can write:

```
uvalue.dval = 10.0;
```

You can't use the member name by itself:

```
dval = 10.0;      // Error!! Unnamed union instance does not exist!!
```

More Complex Structures

The structures that we have considered have been very simple. In particular, we have used only basic data types for members of structures. In fact, the data members of a structure can be of other types, including unions and other structures. Let's take an example.

Suppose, having fallen on hard times, we were desperate to save memory and forced to make our variables share memory wherever possible. We could define a union that provided for variables of several different types to occupy the same space in memory:

```
union item
{
  double dData;
  float fData;
  long lData;
  int iData;
};
```

Now a variable of type **item** can store a value of type **double**, **float**, **long** or **int**, but only one of these at any given time. Using this is easy. We just write:

```
item value;
value.dData = 25.0;
```

This stores the floating point value in **dData**. A little later we might write:

```
value.lData = 5;
value.lData++;
```

This overwrites the floating point value by storing the value 5 in **lData**. Using this is somewhat hair-raising. One tiny mistake — such as assuming a variable of type **item** contains a **long** value when it actually stores a **double** value — and we have a disaster. If we really must get involved in this kind of thing, we must at least provide some way of checking what the type is.

In order to identify the type of the value stored, we could use an enumeration:

```
enum Type { Double, Float, Long, Int };
```

Now, we can declare a structure which has two data types. The first member is a union which is capable of holding a variable of type **double**, **float**, **long** or **int**. The second member is an enumeration variable of type **Type**. We can define the structure as:

```
struct SharedData
  {
    union                         // An anonymous union
    {
      double dData;
      float fData;
      long lData;
      int iData;
    };
    Type type;                    // Variable of the enumeration type Type
  };
```

Note that the union member of **SharedData** is anonymous. This allows us to refer to the members of the union for an object of type **SharedData** without having to specify the union name. We can declare a variable of type **SharedData** as:

```
SharedData value = {25.0, Double};    // Initializes dData to 25.0
                                      // and type to Double
```

433

This initializes the value of **dData** to 25.0. because **dData** is the first member of the union. (Since we are initializing within the declaration statement, **dData** is the only union member that the compiler will allow us to initialize.) The second value in the initializer list is the value for **type**. You can only specify one of the possibilities declared in the enumeration **Type**. Note that you can omit the initial value for type and the result will be correct, because the default 0 will correspond to **Double**:

```
SharedData value = {25.0};          // Initializes dData to 25.0 and type to Double
```

This only works because **Double** appears first in the list of enumerators in the declaration of **Type**.

We can subsequently set **value** with the statements:

```
value.lData = 10;
value.type = Long;
```

Now, as long as we remember to set the type every time we change the value, we can test the type of value which is stored, to determine how we can legally use it. For example:

```
if(value.type == Long)
  value.lData++;
```

This example is designed to illustrate how pieces of related data can be bound together, by using a structure. Of course, in this hypothetical case this whole process is rather counter-productive, because we are sharing the use of a trivially small memory area — typically 8 bytes for type **double**. *We would use more memory each time we test for the type, than we would save from sharing memory between different types!*

Structures with Structures as Members

We have seen a union as a member of a structure. As we've already mentioned, a structure can also be a data member of a structure type (provided the two structure types involved are not the same).

Suppose we wanted a type to represent a person. We might want to record some of their personal details, such as name, address, phone number, date of birth — well, let's stop there. Let's think for a moment about how to store these data items.

For example, the phone number might be stored as an integer. It's more likely, however, that you will want the area code separate from the number. You might even want a country code if you want to record information on people living overseas. We can see that storing the phone number is going to demand a structure itself. We can extend the discussion: clearly, most of the members of a **Person** structure are going to be structures themselves. Let's look at what a cut down version might look like.

We could define a **Person** structure as:

```
struct Person
{
  Name name;
  Date birthdate;
  Phone number;
};
```

There are just three data members to define a **Person** type, but each of them is a structure in its own right.

The type to store a name might be defined as:

```
struct Name
{
  char firstname[80];
  char surname[80];
};
```

> *Of course, it would be better to use **string** objects as members here, but initializing a **Name** object would then need a capability called a constructor. We will cover constructors in the next chapter; let's press on with clunky old null-terminated strings for now.*

For the **Date** structure, we can record a date as three integers, corresponding to the day in the month, the month, and the year:

```
struct Date
{
  int day;
  int month;
  int year;
};
```

For the **Phone** structure you might well want to store the number as a character string, as this would be more convenient for dialing. For our purposes, however, we can store just the area code and the number as integers:

```
struct Phone
{
  int areacode;
  int number;
};
```

You declare a variable of type **Person** in much the same way as we have declared structure objects in this chapter:

```
    Person him;
```

We can initialize a variable of type **Person** when we declare it, by using an initializer list:

```
Person her = {
                { "Letitia", "Gruntfuttock" },    // Initializes Name member
                {1, 4, 1965               },      // Initializes Date member
                {212, 5551234             }       // Initializes Phone member
              };
```

The list of initial values is arranged in a similar manner to that used for multi-dimensional arrays. The list corresponding to each member that is a structure is enclosed between braces, and each of these lists is separated from the next by commas. You are not obliged to include braces around the lists for each structure member, and if you leave them out the values are just assigned in sequence. Of course, there is more potential for error if you do it like this, and you can't omit a value for a member of an inner structure.

As it stands, there is a limited range of things you can do with a variable of type **Person**. You could use an assignment to make the members of one **Person** object the same as another:

```
Person actress;
actress = her;                    // Copy members of her
```

In this case the members of **her** (and their members) will be copied to the corresponding members of **actress**.

Of course, you can reference the value of a member using the member selection operator. For example, we could output the name of the person, **her**, with the statement:

```
cout << her.name.firstname << " " << her.name.surname << endl;
```

Displaying the name in this way is a little cumbersome, so you could include a member function for this sort of thing. Let's try that in a simple example.

Try It Out – Practicing with Persons

The structures that define the members of **Person** can contain functions as members. We could add a member to each of them to output their members. Here's the **Name** structure:

```
struct Name
{
  char firstname[80];
  char surname[80];

  // Display the name
  void show()
  {
    cout << firstname << " " << surname;
  }
};
```

We can do the same thing with the **Date** structure:

```
struct Date
{
  int day;
  int month;
  int year;
```
```
  // Display the date
  void show()
  {
    cout << month << "/" << day << "/" << year;
  }
};
```

Also with the **Phone** structure:

```
struct Phone
{
  int areacode;
  int number;
```
```
  // Display a phone number
  void show()
  {
    cout << areacode << " " << number;
  }
};
```

Now we can use the functions we have added to these structures in the definition of a similar function member of the **Person** structure:

```
struct Person
{
  Name name;
  Date birthdate;
  Phone number;
```
```
  // Display a person
  void show()
  {
    cout << endl;
    name.show();
    cout << endl;
    cout << "Born: ";
    birthdate.show();
    cout << endl;
    cout << "Telephone: ";
    number.show();
    cout << endl;
  }

  // Calculate the age up to a given date
  int age(Date& date)
  {
    if(date.year <= birthdate.year)
      return 0;
```

```
        int years = date.year - birthdate.year;
        if((date.month>birthdate.month) ||
                    (date.month == birthdate.month && date.day>= birthdate.day))
        return years;
           else
        return --years;
      }
};
```

As well as the function **show()** to output details of a **Person** object, we have also added a member function **Age()** to calculate the age of the person up to the data passed as an argument

You can put all four structure definitions in a header file **Person.h**:

```
// Person.h Definitions for Person and related structures
#ifndef PERSON_H
#define PERSON_H
#include <iostream>
using namespace std;

// Name structure definition
// Date structure definition
// Phone structure definition
// Person structure definition
#endif
```

Naturally, the definitions for each of the structures referred to in the definition of the **Person** structure must appear earlier in the file.

We can now use this in a little program:

```
// Program 11.3 Making use of a Person
#include <iostream>
using namespace std;
#include "person.h"

int main()
{
  Person her = {
                  { "Letitia", "Gruntfuttock" },      // Initializes Name member
                  {1, 4, 1965                  },      // Initializes Date member
                  {212, 5551234                }       // Initializes Phone member
              };

  Person actress;
  actress = her;                                       // Copy members of her
  her.show();
  Date today = { 15, 3, 1998 };

  cout << endl << "Today is ";
  today.show();
  cout <<  endl;

  cout << "Today " << actress.name.firstname << " is "
      << actress.age(today) << " years old."
      << endl;
  return 0;
}
```

This produces the output:

```
Letitia Gruntfuttock
Born: 4/1/1965
Telephone: 212 5551234

Today is 3/15/1998
Today Letitia is 32 years old.
```

How It Works

We first create and initialize a **Person** object, **her**, using the statement we saw earlier, and we then copy the members of **her** to the **Person** object **actress** using an assignment. To output details of **her**, we call the **show()** function for the **her** object:

```
her.show();
```

Here, when the **show()** function executes it will access the **name**, **birthdate** and **number** members of the **her** object. This function makes use of the **show()** functions for each of these objects in order to display the full details of the person, **her**.

We define a new **Date** object with the declaration:

```
Date today = { 15, 3, 1998 };
```

We then output the date that this represents with the statements:

```
cout << endl << "Today is ";
today.show();
cout <<  endl;
```

Alternatively, we could have explicitly displayed each member of the **today** object with a statement such as:

```
cout << endl << "Today is " << today.month << "/"
                           << today.day << "/"
                           << today.year << endl;
```

Finally we output the age of the object **actress** with the statement:

```
cout << "Today " << actress.name.firstname << " is "
     << actress.age(today) << " years old."
     << endl;
```

This directly accesses a member of the name member of **actress** with the expression **actress.name.firstname**. It also uses the **age()** function for the **actress** object to calculate the age up to the date represented by **today**.

In this example we have seen how to access a member of a structure that is itself a structure, and how adding functions to a structure can make objects easier to work with. This discussion is leading us closer to the notion of a class object. You may find that programmers prefer to use structures purely as collections of related data items (as in Program 11.1); and when they design data types with functionality, they turn to **classes**. Building functionality into a type is fundamental to object-oriented programming: what we have looked at so far is mere taster of the capability we will learn about in the next two chapters.

Summary

In this chapter we have used structures to introduce some of the practical aspects of programming with user defined data types and objects. In the next chapter, we will use this foundation as we further explore object-oriented techniques and principles. The key points from this chapter include:

▶ A structure type is a new data type in your program.

▶ A structure object is an object with members that are publicly accessible by default. A structure can have both data members and function members.

▶ You can refer to a member of a structure object using the object name and the member name separated by a period — the period is called the member selection operator.

▶ A union is a data type, whose objects allow you to use the same block of memory to store values for several different variables (possibly of different types) at different times.

▶ When you declare a union object, you can only supply an initial value of the type of the first member of the union.

▶ Data members of a structure can be of any type, including other structures, but a data member cannot be of the same type as the containing structure.

▶ A structure object that does not require a constructor to create it is called an aggregate: the members of an aggregate can be initialized by a list of initial values between braces.

Exercises

Ex 11.1 We're going to write a simple currency converter program. For our purposes, a *currency object* needs to tie together two things: a currency type, and a conversion factor that will convert the currency to dollars by multiplication. Design a structure that can be used to represent currency objects, and write a program that allows the user to convert between any two supported currencies by selecting 'from' and 'to' currency types from a list. The user should then be able to enter values (and get the converted value output) until they enter a negative value, at which point the program will exit.

Ex 11.2 (Harder) Provide a way for the user to add new currencies when running the program.

Ex 11.3 Implement the **SharedData** structure described in the section of the chapter called "More Complex Structures". Extend the structure (and its associated enumerated type) so that it can store *pointers* to the four types as well. Test that you can store pointers to variables.

Ex 11.4 Write a function that will accept an array of **SharedData** objects and print each one in the format **[***array_element***]** *type* **=** *value*, for example:

```
[0]   double = 37.2
[1]   float* = 2.5
```

Call the function from a suitable **main()** routine. How will you tell the function how big the array is?

Classes

In this chapter, we will expand on the discussion of types defined as structures and look into one of the most fundamental tools in the C++ programmer's toolbox: **classes**. I will also introduce some ideas that are implicit in object-oriented programming, and start to show how these are applied in practice.

As we progress, you will learn:

▶ What the basic principles in objected-oriented programming are

▶ How you define a new data type as a class, and how you can use objects of a class

▶ What class constructors are, and how you write them

▶ What the default constructor is, and how you can supply your own

▶ What the default copy constructor is

▶ What a friend function is

▶ What privileges a friend class has

▶ What the pointer **this** is, and how and when you use it

Classes and Object-Oriented Programming

Before we get into the language, syntax and programming techniques of classes, we'll start by considering how our existing knowledge relates to the concept of object-oriented programming.

The essence of **object-oriented programming** (commonly abbreviated to **OOP**) is that you write programs in terms of objects in the domain of the problem you are trying to solve, so part of the development process is designing a set of types to suit the context. If you're writing a program to keep track of your bank account, you will probably need to have data types such as **Account** and **Transaction**. For a program to analyze baseball scores, you may have types such as **Player** and **Team**. The variables of the basic types don't allow you to model real-world objects (or even imaginary objects) adequately. It's not possible to model a baseball player realistically in terms of just an **int** or a **double**, or any other basic data type. We would need several different values of different types for any meaningful representation of a baseball player.

Structures provide a possible solution. We have seen how we can define a structure type that can be a composite of variables of several other types. A structure type can also have functions as an integral part of its definition. In the last chapter, we defined a structure called **Box** to represent a box, and with this new data type we were able to define variables of type **Box**, just as we defined variables of the basic types. We were then able to create and manipulate as many **Box** objects as we needed in our program. This goes quite a long way towards making programming in terms of real world objects possible. Obviously, we can apply the idea of a structure to represent a baseball player, or a bank account, or anything else we require. By using structures we can model whatever kinds of objects we want, and write our programs around them. So, that's object-oriented programming all wrapped up then?

Well, not quite. A structure as we have defined it up to now is a big step forward, but there's more to it than that. As well as the notion of user-defined types, object-oriented programming implicitly incorporates a number of additional important ideas (famously *encapsulation* and *data hiding*, *inheritance* and *polymorphism*). The **struct**, as we've seen it, doesn't quite fit the bill. Let's get a rough, intuitive idea of what these additional OOP concepts mean right now. This will provide a reference frame for the detailed C++ programming we will be getting into in this and the next four chapters.

Encapsulation

In general, the definition of an object of a given type requires a combination of a specific number of different things — the things that make an object what it is. An object will contain a specific set of data values that describe the object in sufficient detail for your needs. For a box, it could be just the three dimensions: length, breadth, and height. For an aircraft carrier, it is likely to be rather more. An object will also contain a set of functions that operate on it — functions that will use or change the set of data values. They define the set of operations that can be applied to the object — what you can do with it, or to it. Every object of a given type will incorporate the same combination of these things: the set of data values as data members, and the set of operations as member functions.

This packaging of data values and functions within an object is referred to as **encapsulation**. The diagram below illustrates this with the example of an object that represents a loan account with a bank.

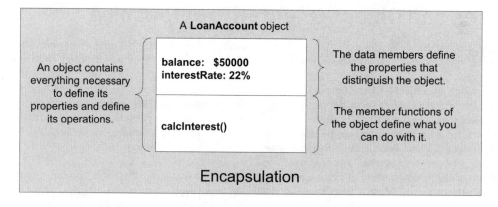

Every **LoanAccount** object will have its properties defined by the same set of data members — in this case, one to hold the outstanding balance, and the other to hold the interest rate. Each object will also contain a set of member functions that define operations on the object: the one shown here will calculate interest and add it to the balance. The properties and operations will all be encapsulated in every object of the type **LoanAccount**. Of course, this choice of what makes up a **LoanAccount** object is arbitrary. You might define it quite differently for your purposes, but however you define the **LoanAccount** type, all the properties and operations that you specify will be encapsulated within every object of the type.

Data Hiding

Of course, the bank would not want the balance for a loan account (or the interest rate for that matter) changed arbitrarily from outside an object, as we were able to do with our structure objects in the previous chapter. To permit this would be a recipe for chaos. Ideally, the data members of a **LoanAccount** object would be protected from direct outside interference, and would only be modifiable in a controlled way. The ability to make the data values for an object generally inaccessible is called **data hiding**.

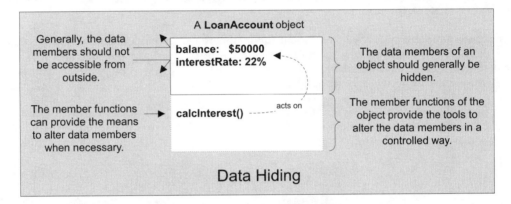

With a **LoanAccount** object, the member functions of the object can provide a mechanism that ensures any changes to the data members follow a particular policy, and that the values set are appropriate. Interest should not be negative, for instance, and generally the balance should reflect the fact that money is owed to the bank, and not the reverse.

Data hiding is important because it is necessary if you are to maintain the integrity of an object. If an object is supposed to represent a duck, it should not have four legs, and the way to enforce this is to make the leg count inaccessible — to 'hide' the data. Of course, an object may have data values that can legitimately vary, but even then you often want to control the range; after all, a duck doesn't usually weigh 300 pounds. Hiding the data belonging to an object prevents it from being accessed directly, but you can *provide* access through functions that are members of the object, either to alter a data value in a controlled way, or simply to obtain its value. Such functions can check that the change they're being asked to make is legal and within prescribed limits where necessary.

Hiding the data within an object is not mandatory, but it's generally a good idea for at least a couple of reasons. First, as I said, maintaining the integrity of an object requires that you control how changes are made. Second, direct access to the values that define an object undermines the whole idea of object-oriented programming. Object-oriented programming is supposed to be programming in terms of *objects*, not in terms of the bits that go to make up an object.

You can think of the data members as representing the **state** of the object, and the member functions that manipulate them as representing the object's **interface** to the outside world. Using the class then involves programming using the functions declared as the interface. A program using the class interface is only dependent on the function names, parameter types and return types specified for the interface. The internal mechanics of these functions do not affect the program creating and using objects of the class. That means it's important to get the interface to a class right at the design stage, but you can subsequently change the implementation to your heart's content without necessitating any changes to programs that use the class.

Inheritance

Inheritance is the ability to define one type in terms of another. For example, suppose that you have defined a type **BankAccount** that contains members to deal with the broad issues of bank accounts. Inheritance would then allow you to create the type **LoanAccount** as a specialized kind of **BankAccount**. You could define a **LoanAccount** as being like a **BankAccount**, but with a few extra properties and functions of its own. The **LoanAccount** type will **inherit** all the members of **BankAccount**, which is referred to as its **base class**. We say that **LoanAccount** is **derived** from **BankAccount**.

Each **LoanAccount** object will contain all the members that a **BankAccount** object would, but it has the option of defining new members of its own, or of *redefining* the functions it inherits, so that they are more meaningful in its context. This last ability is a very powerful one, as you will see when we explore the topic further.

Extending the example we have at the moment, you might also want to create a new type called **CheckingAccount** by adding different characteristics to **BankAccount**. This whole situation is illustrated below.

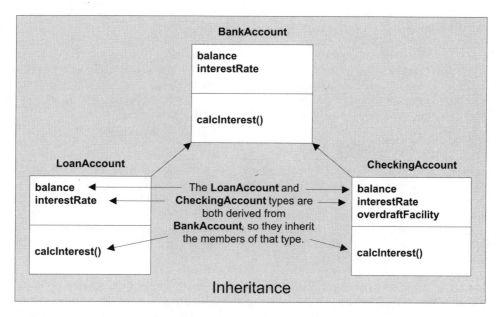

Both of the types **LoanAccount** and **CheckingAccount** would be declared such that they are derived from the type **BankAccount**. They inherit the data members and member functions of **BankAccount**, but they are free to define new characteristics that are specific to their own type.

In this example, **CheckingAccount** has added a data member called **overdraftFacility**, that is unique to itself, and both the derived classes have redefined the **calcInterest()** member function that was inherited from the base class. This is reasonable, because it's likely that calculating and dealing with the interest for a checking account will involve something rather different that doing it for a loan account.

Polymorphism

The word **polymorphism** means the ability to assume different forms at different times. Polymorphism in C++ always involves calling a member function of an object, using either a pointer or a reference. Such a function call can have different effects at different times — a sort of Jekyll and Hyde function call. The mechanism only works for objects of types that are derived from a common type, such as our **BankAccount** type. Polymorphism means that objects belonging to a 'family' of inheritance-related classes can be passed around and operated on using base class pointers and references.

In our example above, **LoanAccount** and **CheckingAccount** objects can both be passed around using a pointer or reference to **BankAccount**. The pointer or reference can then be used to call the inherited member functions of whatever object it refers to. The idea and implications of this will be easier to appreciate if we take a specific case.

Suppose we have the types **LoanAccount** and **CheckingAccount** defined as before, based on the type **BankAccount**. Suppose also that we have defined objects of these types, **debt** and **cash** respectively, as illustrated in the diagram. Because both types are based on the type **BankAccount**, a variable of type 'pointer to **BankAccount**', such as **pAcc** in the diagram, can be used to store the address of either of these objects.

The code in the diagram uses the notation we saw in the last chapter to call a function member of an object through a pointer.

The beauty of polymorphism is that the function called by **pAcc->calcInterest()** will vary depending on what **pAcc** points to. If it points to a **LoanAccount** object, then the **calcInterest()** function for that object will be called, and interest will be debited from the account. If it points to a **CheckingAccount** object, the result will be different because the **calcInterest()** function for that object will be called and interest will be credited to the account. The particular function called through the pointer is not decided when your program is compiled, but when your program executes. Thus, the same function call can do different things depending on what kind of object the pointer points to. The illustration shows just two different types, but in general you can get polymorphic behavior with as many different types as your application requires.

You need quite a bit of C++ language know-how to accomplish what I've described, and that's exactly what we'll be exploring in the rest of this chapter and through the next four chapters. You'll get hands-on experience of using polymorphism in your programs in Chapter 16. The road starts here, though, with the more modest subject of using the keyword **class** to define a new type.

Terminology

Here's a summary of the terminology that we'll be using when discussing classes in C++. It includes some terms that we have come across already:

▶ A **class** is a user-defined data type.

▶ The variables and functions declared within a class are called **members** of the class. The variables are called **data members** and the functions are called **member functions**. The member functions of a class are sometimes referred to as **methods**, but we will not use this terminology in this book.

▶ Having defined a class, we can declare variables of the class type (also called **instances** of the class). Each instance will be an **object** of the class.

▶ Defining an instance of a class is sometimes referred to as **instantiation**.

▶ **Object-oriented programming** is a programming style based on the idea of defining your own data types as classes. It involves the ideas of **encapsulation** of data, class **inheritance**, and **polymorphism**, which we have just discussed.

When we get into the detail of object-oriented programming, it may seem a little complicated in places. Getting back to the basics of what you are doing can often help to make things clearer; so use the list above to always keep in mind what objects are really about. Object-oriented programming is about writing programs in terms of the objects that are specific to the domain of your problem. All the facilities around classes in C++ are there to make this as comprehensive and flexible as possible. Let's get down to the business of understanding classes, starting with how you define a class.

Defining a Class

As I have already said, a **class**, like a **struct**, is a user-defined type. The definition of a type using the **class** keyword is, in essence, that same as one using the **struct** keyword, but the effect is different. Let's look at how we can define a class to represent a box. We'll use this to investigate how the resulting class differs from the structure that we defined earlier. To create a class, we can just use the keyword **class** in place of the keyword **struct**, so let's give this a try:

```
class Box
{
  double length;
  double breadth;
  double height;

  // Function to calculate the volume of a box
  double volume()
  {
    return length * breadth * height;
  }
};
```

We have taken the definition of the **Box** structure from the previous chapter and replaced the keyword **struct** with the keyword **class**. In any program using objects of this type, a crucial difference between structures and classes would immediately become apparent. You would be unable to reference any of the data members or call the function **volume()** from outside the class. If you tried to, the code would not compile.

When you create a class, all the members that you have defined are hidden by default, so that they are not accessible outside the class. They are said to be **private** members of the class, and private members can *only* be accessed from within a member function of the same class.

For members of a class object to be accessible in a function that is *not* part of the class, you must declare them to be **public** members of the class by using the keyword **public**. In comparison, the members of a **struct** are public by default, so that's why they were always available.

> *The keywords **class** and **struct** are used to create data types that obey the principles of object-oriented programming. By default, the members of a **class** object are private, while the members of a **struct** object are public.*

Let's see how we declare class members as public by modifying the definition of our **Box** class:

```
class Box
{
  public:
    double length;
    double breadth;
    double height;
```

```
      // Function to calculate the volume of a box
      double volume()
      {
        return length * breadth * height;
      }
  };
```

The keyword **public** is an **access specifier**. An access specifier determines whether class members are accessible in various parts of your program. Class members that are public can be accessed directly from outside the class, and therefore these members are not hidden. To specify class members as public, you use the keyword **public** followed by a colon. All class members that follow this access specifier in the class definition will be public, up to the point where another access specifier appears. Of course, objects of the class **Box** encapsulate the three data members and a function member. Every **Box** object will contain all four, and because we have declared them as public in the class, they will all be directly accessible from outside.

There are two other keywords that are access specifiers: **private** and **protected**. Class members that are private or protected are hidden — that is, they're not directly accessible from outside the class. If we were to introduce the following line into the class declaration above,

```
    private:
```

then all the members after the line would be private rather than public. We will discuss the effects of the keyword **private** in more detail later in this chapter, and see when to use the **protected** keyword in Chapter 15.

In general, you can have several appearances of any of the access specifiers in a class definition. This allows you to place data members and member functions in separate groups within the class definition, each with their own access specifier. It can be easier to see the internal structure of a class definition if you arrange to group the data members and the member functions separately, according to their access specifiers.

We can see just how close a structure is to a class by revising the first example from the previous chapter to use the latter rather than the former. This won't produce a good design for a class by any means, but we can move towards that by progressively improving our class, and seeing the positive effects of each new feature as we add it.

Try It Out – Using a Class

Here's a revised version of Program 11.1 from the previous chapter, using a class instead of a structure:

```
// Program 12.1 Using a Box class
#include <iostream>
using namespace std;

// Class to represent a box
class Box
{
  public:
    double length;
```

```
      double breadth;
      double height;

      // Function to calculate the volume of a box
      double volume()
      {
        return length * breadth * height;
      }
};
```

```
int main()
{
  Box firstBox = { 80.0, 50.0, 40.0 };

  // Calculate the volume of the box
  double firstBoxVolume = firstBox.volume();
  cout << endl;
  cout << "Size of first Box object is "
       << firstBox.length  << " by "
       << firstBox.breadth << " by "
       << firstBox.height
       << endl;
  cout << "Volume of first Box object is " << firstBoxVolume
       << endl;

  Box secondBox = firstBox;   // Create a second Box object the same as firstBox

  // Increase the dimensions of second Box object by 10%
  secondBox.length *= 1.1;
  secondBox.breadth *= 1.1;
  secondBox.height *= 1.1;

  cout << "Size of second Box object is "
       << secondBox.length << " by "
       << secondBox.breadth << " by "
       << secondBox.height
       << endl;
  cout << "Volume of second Box object is " << secondBox.volume()
       << endl;

  cout << "Increasing the box dimensions by 10% has increased the volume by "
       << static_cast<long>((secondBox.volume() - firstBoxVolume) * 100.0 /
                                                    firstBoxVolume)
       << "%"
       << endl;
  return 0;
}
```

This program produces exactly the same output as the previous version.

How It Works

The code in **main()** is exactly the same as before. This is because, having declared the class members as **public**, a class works in the same way as a structure. Everything we have discussed previously in the context of structures applies equally well to classes. You use the member access operator and the pointer member access operator in exactly the same way with classes as we did with structures.

However, one aspect of this code does not reflect the general usage of classes. In the example, we have declared and initialized a class object with the following **initializer list**:

```
Box firstBox = { 80.0, 50.0, 40.0 };
```

This statement is perfectly legal, at least in this particular case. However, the data members of class objects are typically *not* initialized in this way, because the data members are usually hidden. You can't initialize the hidden data members of a class using an initializer list. Instead, creation and initialization of class objects is done through a special kind of member function, which *can* initialize hidden data members. This member is called a class constructor.

Constructors

A **class constructor** is a special kind of function in a class that differs in significant respects from an ordinary member function. A constructor is called when a new instance of the class is defined. It provides the opportunity to initialize the new object as it is created, and to ensure that data members only contain valid values. Objects of classes in which the class definition contains a constructor cannot be initialized with a set of data values between braces.

A class constructor always has the same name as the class in which it is defined. The function **Box()**, for example, is a constructor for our class **Box**. Also, a constructor does not return a value, and therefore has no return type. It is wrong to specify a return type for a constructor; you must not even write it as **void**. The primary function of a class constructor is to assign and validate the initial values of all the data elements of the class object being created, and no return type is necessary or permitted.

Try It Out – Adding a Constructor to the Box Class

Let's extend the **Box** class from our previous example to incorporate a constructor, and then check it out with a simpler version of **main()**:

```cpp
// Program 12.2 Using a class constructor
#include <iostream>
using namespace std;

// Class to represent a box
class Box
{
  public:
    double length;
    double breadth;
    double height;

    // Constructor
    Box(double lengthValue, double breadthValue, double heightValue)
    {
      cout << "Box constructor called" << endl;
      length = lengthValue;
      breadth = breadthValue;
      height = heightValue;
    }
```

```
        // Function to calculate the volume of a box
        double volume()
        {
          return length * breadth * height;
        }
    };

    int main()
    {
      Box firstBox(80.0, 50.0, 40.0);

      // Calculate the volume of the box
      double firstBoxVolume = firstBox.volume();
      cout << endl;
      cout << "Size of first Box object is "
          << firstBox.length  << " by "
          << firstBox.breadth << " by "
          << firstBox.height
          << endl;
      cout << "Volume of first Box object is " << firstBoxVolume
          << endl;

      return 0;
    }
```

This example produces the output:

```
Box constructor called
Size of first Box object is 80 by 50 by 40
Volume of first Box object is 160000
```

How It Works

The constructor for the **Box** class has been defined with three parameters of type **double**, corresponding to the initial values for the **length**, **breadth**, and **height** members of an object:

```
        Box(double lengthValue, double breadthValue, double heightValue)
        {
          cout << "Box constructor called" << endl;
          length = lengthValue;
          breadth = breadthValue;
          height = heightValue;
        }
```

As you can see, there is no return type specified and the name of the constructor is the same as the class name. The first statement in the constructor outputs a message so that we can tell when it's been called. You wouldn't do this in production programs but, because it's helpful in showing when a constructor is called, the technique is often used when testing a program. We will use it regularly for purposes of illustration, and to trace what is happening in our examples. The rest of the code in the body of the constructor is very simple. It just assigns the arguments passed to the corresponding data members. If necessary, we could also include checks that valid, non-negative arguments are supplied for the dimensions of a box. In the context of a real application you would probably want to do this, but here our primary interest is in seeing how a constructor works, so we will keep it simple for now.

Within **main()**, we declare the object **firstBox** with the statement:

```
Box firstBox(80.0, 50.0, 40.0);
```

The initial values for the data members **length**, **breadth**, and **height** appear between the parentheses following the object name. These are passed as arguments to the constructor. When the constructor is called, it displays the message that appears as the first line of output, so we have evidence that the definition does indeed call the constructor that we have added to the class.

Since there is now a constructor declared in the class definition, we can no longer initialize the data members of an object using a list. The statement that we used to define a **Box** object in the previous example would now not compile:

```
Box firstBox = { 80.0, 50.0, 40.0 };   // Not legal! You must call a constructor.
```

> *Objects of a class whose definition includes at least one constructor must be created using a constructor.*

The next two statements in **main()** output the dimensions and volume of the box in the way we have seen previously, so we also have evidence that the data members have been set to the values specified as arguments to the constructor.

Placing Constructor Definitions Outside the Class

When we were playing with structures in the last chapter, you saw that the definition of a member function could be placed outside the structure definition. This is also true for classes, and for class constructors. We could define the class **Box** in a header file as:

```
// Box.h
#ifndef BOX_H
#define BOX_H

class Box
{
  public:
    double length;
    double breadth;
    double height;

    // Constructor
    Box(double lengthValue, double breadthValue, double heightValue);

    // Function to calculate the volume of a box
    double volume();
};

#endif
```

Now we can put the definitions of the member functions in a `.cpp` file. Each function name, including the names of any constructors, must be qualified with the class name **Box**, using the scope resolution operator:

```
// Box.cpp
#include <iostream>
#include "Box.h"

using namespace std;

// Constructor definition
Box::Box(double lengthValue, double breadthValue, double heightValue)
{
  cout << "Box constructor called" << endl;
  length = lengthValue;
  breadth = breadthValue;
  height = heightValue;
}

// Function to calculate the volume of a box
double Box::volume()
{
  return length * breadth * height;
}
```

We have to include the header file containing the declaration of the **Box** class here, otherwise the compiler won't know that **Box** is a class. Separating the declarations of classes from the declarations of their member functions is consistent with the notion of what `.h` files and `.cpp` files are for, and it makes the code easier to manage. Any source file that needs to create objects of type **Box** just needs to include the header file **Box.h**.

A programmer using this class does not need access to the definitions of the member functions, only to the class definition in the header file. As long as the *class* definition remains fixed, you are free to change the implementations of the member functions without affecting the operation of programs that use the class.

Defining a member function outside the class definition is not exactly the same as placing the definition inside the class. Function definitions that appear *within* a class definition are implicitly declared as inline functions. (This does not necessarily mean that they will turn out to be *implemented* as inline functions — the compiler still decides that, based on the characteristics of the function, as we discussed in Chapter 8.) Member functions with definitions *outside* the class can only be inline if you explicitly declare them as such.

The subsequent examples in this chapter will assume that you now have the **Box** *class split into* `.h` *and* `.cpp` *files, along with another file containing the* **main()** *function, that currently looks like this:*

```
// Program 12.2 Using a class constructor
#include <iostream>
#include "Box.h"

using namespace std;
```

```
int main()
{
  Box firstBox(80.0, 50.0, 40.0);

  // Calculate the volume of the box
  double firstBoxVolume = firstBox.volume();
  cout << endl;
  cout << "Size of first Box object is "
       << firstBox.length  << " by "
       << firstBox.breadth << " by "
       << firstBox.height
       << endl;
  cout << "Volume of first Box object is " << firstBoxVolume
       << endl;

  return 0;
}
```

The Default Constructor

Our example and experimentation with a class constructor seemed quite straightforward, but as ever, there are some subtleties lurking just beneath the surface. By defining a constructor for the class, we have modified the class in a way that is not immediately obvious. Let's look into that now.

Every class that you declare will have at least one constructor, because an object of a class is *always* created using a constructor. If you don't define a constructor for your class (as in Program 12.1), then the compiler will supply a **default constructor** that will be used to create objects of your class.

The default constructor has no parameters. When you declare a class, the compiler supplies a default constructor automatically, *but only as long as you do not define a constructor for the class yourself*. As soon as you add any constructor of your own, the compiler assumes that the default constructor is now your responsibility, and it does not supply one. The following example illustrates how the default constructor can affect your code.

Let's try defining a second **Box** object in our program, but initializing it differently from **firstBox**. Change **main()** in Program 12.2 to the following:

```
int main()
{
  Box firstBox(80.0, 50.0, 40.0);

  // Calculate the volume of the box
  double firstBoxVolume = firstBox.volume();
  cout << endl;
  cout << "Size of first Box object is "
       << firstBox.length  << " by "
       << firstBox.breadth << " by "
       << firstBox.height
       << endl;
  cout << "Volume of first Box object is " << firstBoxVolume
       << endl;
```

```
    Box smallBox;                 // Will not compile! Constructor already specified
    smallBox.length = 10.0;
    smallBox.breadth = 5.0;
    smallBox.height = 4.0;

    // Calculate the volume of the small box
    cout << "Size of small Box object is "
         << smallBox.length << " by "
         << smallBox.breadth << " by "
         << smallBox.height
         << endl;
    cout << "Volume of small Box object is " << smallBox.volume()
         << endl;

    return 0;
}
```

The new code attempts to create a new object, **smallBox**, with a declaration that does not supply initial values to the constructor. Instead, we set the data members explicitly with the three assignment statements. Unfortunately, this will not compile. The compiler's error message relates to the following line:

```
    Box smallBox;                 // Will not compile! Constructor already specified
```

Here, the compiler is looking for the default constructor — that is, the constructor with no parameters. However, this program uses the class **Box**, which includes our user-defined constructor:

```
    Box(double lengthValue, double breadthValue, double heightValue)
    {
      cout << "Box constructor called" << endl;
      length = lengthValue;
      breadth = breadthValue;
      height = heightValue;
    }
```

Because we have declared a constructor for the class, the compiler will not generate a default constructor, and this is the cause of the error.

The default constructor that's generated by the compiler does nothing — in particular, the default constructor does *not* initialize the data members of the object that is created. This is far from ideal: we must aim to have control over the values contained in our variables, so if you plan to use the default constructor to create objects, you will want to supply your own anyway. To make the new version of **main()** work, we can add our own default constructor to the class definition.

Try It Out – Supplying a Default Constructor

Let's add our version of the default constructor to the last example. For now, we will just include code to register that the default constructor is called, and come back to initializing the data members later. Here is the next version of the class definition in **Box.h**:

```
class Box
{
  public:
    double length;
    double breadth;
    double height;

    // Constructors
    Box();                                       // Default constructor
    Box(double lengthValue, double breadthValue, double heightValue);

    // Function to calculate the volume of a box
    double volume();
};
```

We must also add the definition for the default constructor to **Box.cpp**.

```
// Default constructor definition
Box::Box()
{
  cout << "Default constructor called" << endl;
  length = breadth = height = 1;         // Default dimensions
}
```

We can now use this with the following version of **main()**:

```
// Program 12.3 Defining and using a default class constructor
#include <iostream>
#include "Box.h"

using namespace std;

int main()
{
Box firstBox(80.0, 50.0, 40.0);

  // Calculate the volume of the box
  double firstBoxVolume = firstBox.volume();
  cout << endl;
  cout << "Size of first Box object is "
       << firstBox.length  << " by "
       << firstBox.breadth << " by "
       << firstBox.height
       << endl;
  cout << "Volume of first Box object is " << firstBoxVolume
       << endl;

  Box smallBox;
  smallBox.length = 10.0;
  smallBox.breadth = 5.0;
  smallBox.height = 4.0;

  // Calculate the volume of the small box
  cout << "Size of small Box object is "
       << smallBox.length << " by "
       << smallBox.breadth << " by "
```

```
         << smallBox.height
         << endl;
   cout << "Volume of small Box object is " << smallBox.volume()
         << endl;
```

```
   return 0;
}
```

We will now get the output:

```
Box constructor called
Size of first Box object is 80 by 50 by 40
Volume of first Box object is 160000
Default constructor called
Size of small Box object is 10 by 5 by 4
Volume of small Box object is 200
```

How It Works

In this version of the program, we have supplied our own constructors, so the compiler does not supply a default constructor. Crucially, we have included our own version of the default constructor. There are no error messages from the compiler, and everything works. The program output indicates that the default constructor is being called for the declaration of **smallBox**.

We have designed our default constructor to initialize the data members of any new object that it creates:

```
   length = breadth = height = 1;          // Default dimensions
```

We can now use the default constructor to define *and initialize* the **Box** object, **smallBox**:

```
   Box smallBox;
```

A significant feature of a constructor that has no parameters is that is can be called without specifying an argument list — it doesn't even need parentheses. The statement above just specifies the class type, **Box**, and the object name, **smallBox**, so this will result in a call of the constructor with no parameters.

Defining a default constructor that sets values for the data members ensures that we don't have boxes floating around in which the data members contain junk values. Having safely defined and initialized **smallBox**, we can now adjust the dimensions as appropriate:

```
   smallBox.length = 10.0;
   smallBox.breadth = 5.0;
   smallBox.height = 4.0;
```

An aspect of this example that you may have missed in all the excitement is that we have overloaded the constructor, just as we overloaded functions in Chapter 9. The **Box** class has two constructors that differ only in their parameter lists. One has three parameters of type **double**, and the other has no parameters at all.

Default Initialization Values

When we discussed 'ordinary' functions in C++, we saw how to specify **default values** for the parameters in the function prototype. We can also do this for class member functions, including constructors. If we put the definition of the member function inside the class definition, then we can put the default values for the parameters in the function header. If we only include the declaration of a function in the class definition, then the default parameter values should go in the declaration, and not in the function definition.

We decided in our default constructor that the default size for a **Box** object was a unit box, with all sides of length 1. With this in mind, we could alter the class definition in the last example to:

```
class Box
{
  public:
    double length;
    double breadth;
    double height;

    // Constructors
    Box();                                          // Default constructor
    Box(double lengthValue = 1.0, double breadthValue = 1.0,
                                    double heightValue = 1.0);

    // Function to calculate the volume of a box
    double volume();
};
```

If we make this change to the last example, what happens? We get another error message from the compiler, of course! The compiler will display a message along the lines that we have multiple default constructors defined. The code in **main()** is likely to result in a message that we have an ambiguous call to an overloaded function, caused by this line:

```
 Box smallBox;
```

The reason for the confusion is that this statement is a legal call to *either* constructor. A call made like this to the constructor with the default parameter values is indistinguishable from a call to the default constructor with no parameters. The failure to specify any parameters means that the compiler cannot differentiate one from the other. In other words, the constructor with default parameter values *also serves as a default constructor*.

The obvious solution in this case is to get rid of the constructor that accepts no parameters. If you do so, everything will compile and execute OK. However, don't assume that this is always the best way to implement the default constructor. There will be many occasions when you won't want to assign default values in this way, in which case you *will* need to write a separate default constructor. There will even be times when you don't want to have a default constructor at all, even though you've defined another constructor. This would ensure that all objects of the class must have initializing values explicitly specified in their declarations.

Using an Initializer List in a Constructor

So far, we have initialized the members of an object in the body of a class constructor using explicit assignment. However, there is a different technique available, which uses an **initializer list**. We can demonstrate this with an alternative version of the constructor for the class **Box**:

```
// Constructor definition using an initializer list
Box::Box(double lvalue, double bvalue, double hvalue) : length(lvalue),
                                                        breadth(bvalue),
                                                        height(hvalue)
{
  cout << "Box constructor called" << endl;
}
```

Now the values of the data members are not set in assignment statements in the body of the constructor. As in a declaration, they are specified as initializing values using functional notation, and appear in the initializer list as part of the function header. The member **length** is initialized by the value of **lvalue**, for example. Note that the initializer list for the constructor is separated from the parameter list by a colon, and each initializer is separated from the next by a comma.

In fact, this is more than just a different notation. There is fundamental difference in how the initialization is performed. When you initialize a data member using assignment statements in the body of the constructor, the data member is first created (using a constructor call if it is an instance of a class), and then the assignment is carried out as a separate operation. When you use an initializer list, on the other hand, the initial value is used to initialize the data member *as it is created*. This can be a much more efficient process than using assignments in the body of the constructor, particularly if the data member is a class instance. If you substitute this version of the constructor in the previous example, you will see that it works just as well.

This technique for initializing parameters in a constructor is important for another reason. As we shall see, it is the *only* way of setting values for certain types of data members.

Use of the explicit Keyword

There is a hazard with class constructors that have a *single* parameter, because the compiler can use such a constructor as an implicit conversion from the type of the parameter to the class type. This can produce undesirable results in some circumstances. Let's consider a particular situation.

Suppose we define a class that will define cubic boxes, so that all the sides will have the same length:

```
class Cube
{
  public:
    double side;

    Cube(double side);                  // Constructor
    double volume();                    // Calculate volume of a cube
    bool compareVolume(Cube aCube);     // Compare volume of a cube with another
};
```

We can define the constructor as:

```
Cube::Cube(double side) : length(side) {}
```

The function to calculate the volume of a cube will be defined as:

```
double Cube::volume() {return side * side * side;}
```

Finally, we can define the **compareVolume()** member as:

```
bool Cube::compareVolume(Cube aCube) {return volume() > aCube.volume();}
```

The constructor requires only one argument, of type **double**. Clearly, the compiler could use the constructor to convert a **double** value to a **Cube** object, but under what circumstances is that likely to happen? Let's continue examining the **Cube** class.

The class also defines a **volume()** function, and a function to compare the current object with another **Cube** passed as an argument, which returns **true** if the current object has the greater volume. You might use this in the following way:

```
Cube box1(5.0);
Cube box2(3.0);

if(box1.compareVolume(box2))
  cout << endl << "box1 is larger";
else
  cout << endl << "box1 is not larger";
```

This is all very straightforward, but look what happens if someone using this class writes:

```
if(box1.compareVolume(50.0))
  cout << endl << "Volume of box1 is greater than 50";
else
  cout << endl << "Volume of box1 is not greater than 50";
```

The person writing this code has misunderstood the **compareVolume()** function, and believes that it will compare the volume of the current object with 50.0. The compiler knows that the argument to the **compareVolume()** function should be a **Cube** object, but it will compile this quite happily because there is a constructor available that will convert the argument 50.0 to a **Cube** object. The code the compiler produces will be equivalent to:

```
if(box1.compareVolume(Cube(50.0))
  cout << endl << "Volume of box1 is greater than 50";
else
  cout << endl << "Volume of box1 is not greater than 50";
```

The function is not comparing the volume of the **box1** object with 50.0, but with 125000.0, the volume of **Cube(50.0)**! The result will be very different from what was expected. Happily, you can prevent this nightmare from ever happening by declaring the constructor as **explicit**:

```
class Cube
{
  public:
    double side;

    explicit Cube(double side);
    double volume();
    bool compareVolume(Cube aCube);
};
```

The compiler will never use a constructor declared as **explicit** for an implicit conversion. It can only be used explicitly in the program code to create an object. Since, by definition, an implicit conversion is converting from one given type to another, you only need to use the **explicit** keyword with constructors that have a single parameter.

Private Members of a Class

One of the primary purposes of a constructor is to enable you to ensure that all the data members of an object are set to appropriate values. For example, you could ensure that all the dimensions for a **Box** object are positive values by adding a few checks to the constructor:

```
Box::Box(double lvalue, double bvalue, double hvalue) : length(lvalue),
                                                        breadth(bvalue),
                                                        height(hvalue)
{
  cout << "Box constructor called." << endl;

  // Ensure positive dimensions
  if(length <= 0.0)
    length = 1.0;
  if(breadth <= 0.0)
    breadth = 1.0;
  if(height <= 0.0)
    height = 1.0;
}
```

Now we are sure that whatever the argument values to the constructor, the **Box** object will have legitimate dimensions. Of course, you might also want to output a message that this kind of adjustment is being made.

Our problem now is that having gone to such lengths to protect the integrity of the data members, there is nothing to prevent them being modified externally by statements such as:

```
Box theBox(10.0, 10.0, 5.0);
theBox.length = -20.0;                    // Set illegal box dimension
```

This is because the data members are declared using the keyword **public**. You can prevent this sort of thing by *hiding* the data members, and all that is required is to do this is to declare the data members of a class to be **private**. Class members that are private can, for the most part, only be accessed by member functions of a class. A normal function that is not a member of a given class has no direct means of accessing the **private** members of that class. This is illustrated in the diagram below.

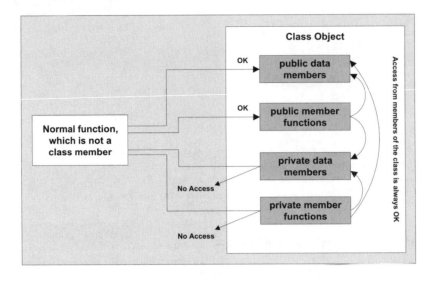

In general, it is good object-oriented programming practice to keep the data members of a class private as far as possible. After all, the whole point of object-oriented programming is to write your solutions in terms of *objects*, and to program using those objects, rather than messing around with their nuts and bolts.

The public members of a class, which typically are functions, are sometimes referred to generically as the **class interface**. The class interface provides the means for manipulating and operating on objects of the class, so it determines what you can do with an object, and what an object can do for you. By keeping the internals of a class private, you can later modify them in whatever way you want, without necessitating modifications to code that uses the class through its public interface. Thus, the public interface is effectively separated from the implementation of the class.

Try It Out – Private Data Members

We can rewrite the **Box** class once again, to make its data members private, and see how we can use it in another example. Here are the changes to the header file, **Box.h**:

```
// Box.h Definition of the Box class
#ifndef BOX_H
#define BOX_H

class Box
{
  public:
    // Constructor
    Box(double lengthValue = 1.0, double breadthValue = 1.0,
                                      double heightValue = 1.0);

    // Function to calculate the volume of a box
    double volume();
```

```
   private:
     double length;
     double breadth;
     double height;
};

#endif
```

We can also add our dimension-checking code to **Box.cpp**:

```
// Box.cpp Box class member function definitions
#include <iostream>
#include "Box.h"

using namespace std;

// Constructor
Box::Box(double lvalue, double bvalue, double hvalue) : length(lvalue),
                                                        breadth(bvalue),
                                                        height(hvalue)
{
  cout << "Box constructor called" << endl;

  // Ensure positive dimensions
  if(length <= 0.0)
    length = 1.0;
  if(breadth <= 0.0)
    breadth = 1.0;
  if(height <= 0.0)
    height = 1.0;
}

// Function to calculate the volume of a box
double Box::volume()
{
  return length * breadth * height;
}
```

The fact that the definitions of the member functions are outside the class does not affect the accessibility of the members of the class. All the members of a class can be accessed from the body of a function member of the class, regardless of where you place the definitions.

To try out the new version of the **Box** class, we can write a new **main()** function:

```
// Program 12.4 Using a class with private data members
#include <iostream>
#include "Box.h"

using namespace std;

int main()
{
  cout << endl;

  Box firstBox(2.2, 1.1, 0.5);
  Box secondBox;
  Box* pthirdBox = new Box(15.0, 20.0, 8.0);
```

```
   cout << "Volume of first box = "
        << firstBox.volume()
        << endl;

// secondBox.length = 4.0;                     // Uncomment this line to get an error

   cout << "Volume of second box = "
        << secondBox.volume()
        << endl;

   cout << "Volume of third box = "
        << pthirdBox->volume()
        << endl;

   delete pthirdBox;
   return 0;
}
```

The output from this program will be:

```
Box constructor called
Box constructor called
Box constructor called
Volume of first box = 1.21
Volume of second box = 1
Volume of third box = 2400
```

How It Works

We use the keyword **public** to start a public section where we have the declarations for the member functions: a constructor, and the function **volume()**. The placement of the declarations for the public members of the class before the private ones is quite deliberate — the public class members are usually of more interest to someone browsing the code, as they are accessible externally.

The definition of the class **Box** now declares the data members as private, by using the **private** keyword followed by a colon. All member declarations after this point, and until the next access specification, will be private and therefore inaccessible from outside the class. This is data hiding in action. If you uncomment the statement in **main()**,

```
// secondBox.length = 4.0;                     // Uncomment this line to get an error
```

then the code will not compile, because the attempt to use a private data member of a class from outside the class is not legal.

> *The only way to get a value into a private data member of a* **Box** *object is to use a constructor or a member function. It's your responsibility to make sure that all the ways in which you might want to set or modify private data members of a class are provided for through member functions.*

We can also put functions into a **private** section of a class, in which case they can only be called by other member functions. If you put the function **volume()** in the **private** section, then the statements that attempt to use it in the function **main()** will result in error messages

466

from the compiler. If you put the constructor in the **private** section, you won't be able to declare any objects of the class.

> *There are lots of reasons why you would make some functions private. For instance, you might need a 'helper' function that implements a capability that is used internally by several other member functions, but is not relevant to the use of class objects.*

Getting back to **main()**, we first declare two **Box** objects with the statements:

```
Box firstBox(2.2, 1.1, 0.5);
Box secondBox;
```

Both of these call the same constructor (well, there is only one), but the declaration for **secondBox** makes use of the default parameter values, so that **secondBox** will be a cube of dimension 1.0.

The next statement declares a pointer to a **Box** object, **pthirdBox**, and creates a **Box** object in the free store using the operator **new**:

```
Box* pthirdBox = new Box(15.0, 20.0, 8.0);
```

The operator **new** calls the same **Box** constructor, as you can see from the output, and the address returned by **new** is stored in **pthirdBox**.

We now output the volume of each **Box** object. For the object that we created dynamically, we use the pointer member access operator to call the function **volume()**:

```
cout << "Volume of third box = "
     << pthirdBox->volume()
     << endl;
```

This demonstrates that the class is still working satisfactorily now that its data members are defined as having the access specifier **private**. The major difference is that they are now completely protected from unauthorized access and modification. Since all the data members are hidden, the only way to set or change the values is through a public member function of the class. In the case of our **Box** class, that boils down to just one: the constructor.

Accessing Private Class Members

On reflection, declaring the data members of a class as **private** is rather extreme. It's all very well protecting them from unauthorized modification, but we have introduced a serious constraint: if we don't know what the dimensions of a particular **Box** object are, we have no way of finding out. Surely it doesn't need to be that secret?

Don't worry: we don't need to go back to exposing our data members with the **public** keyword. We can fix the problem by adding a member function to the class that will return the value of a data member. To provide access to the dimensions of a **Box** object, we just need to add three functions to the class definition:

```
class Box
{
  public:
```

467

```
      // Constructor
      Box(double lengthValue = 1.0, double breadthValue = 1.0,
                                          double heightValue = 1.0);

      // Function to calculate the volume of a box
      double volume();

      // Functions to provide the values of data members
      double getLength() {return length;}
      double getBreadth() {return breadth;}
      double getHeight() {return height;}

  private:
      double length;
      double breadth;
      double height;
};
```

We have added functions to the class that return the values of data members. That means the values of the data members are fully accessible, but you can't change them, so the integrity of the class is preserved without the secrecy. Functions of this kind usually have their definitions within the class definition because they are short, and this will make them inline by default. Consequently, the overhead involved in getting hold of the value of a data member will be minimal. Functions that retrieve the values of data members are often referred to as **accessor** member functions.

We could have used these accessor functions in the previous example, to output the dimensions of the **Box** object that we created dynamically:

```
   cout << "Box size is "
        << pthirdBox->getLength() << " by "
        << pthirdBox->getBreadth() << " by "
        << pthirdBox->getHeight()
        << endl;
```

You can use this approach for any class. All you need to do is to write a function for each data member that you want to make available to the outside world, and their values can be accessed without compromising the security of the class. Of course, if you put the definitions for these functions outside the class definition, you should declare them as **inline**. For instance, if we had simply declared **getLength()** in the class definition, we would have needed to define it in **Box.cpp** as:

```
   inline double Box::getLength() {return length;}
```

There may be situations in which you *do* want to allow data members to be changed from outside the class. If you supply a member function to do this, rather than exposing the data member directly, it provides you with the opportunity to perform integrity checks on the value. For example, you could add a function to allow the height of a **Box** object to be changed:

```
class Box
{
  public:
    // Constructor
    Box(double lengthValue = 1.0, double breadthValue = 1.0,
                                        double heightValue = 1.0);
```

```
// Function to calculate the volume of a box
double volume();

// Inline functions to provide the values of data members
double getLength() {return length;}
double getBreadth() {return breadth;}
double getHeight() {return height;}

// Functions to set data member values
void setHeight(double hvalue) {if(hvalue > 0) height = hvalue;}

private:
  double length;
  double breadth;
  double height;
};
```

The **if** statement ensures that we only accept new values for **height** that are positive. If a new value is supplied for the **height** member that is zero or negative, it will be ignored. Member functions that allow data members to be modified are often referred to as **mutator** member functions.

> *The **getXXX()** and **setXXX()** pair of functions for a data member is a pattern that you will see frequently in C++ programs.*

The Default Copy Constructor

Suppose we declare and initialize a **Box** object **firstBox** with this statement:

```
Box firstBox(15.0, 20.0, 10.0);
```

Suppose further that we now want to create another **Box** object, identical to the first. Putting it another way, we would like to initialize the second **Box** object with **firstBox**. Let's see what happens when we use a **Box** object as a constructor argument.

Try It Out - Creating a Copy of an Object

We can use the definition of the **Box** class from the previous example just as it is for this experiment. Here's the code to try out creating a copy of a **Box** object:

```
// Program 12.5 Creating a copy of an object
#include <iostream.h>
#include "Box.h"

int main()
{
  cout << endl;

  Box firstBox(2.2, 1.1, 0.5);
  Box secondBox(firstBox);
```

```
        cout << "Volume of first box = "
             << firstBox.volume()
             << endl;

        cout << "Volume of second box = "
             << secondBox.volume()
             << endl;

        return 0;
}
```

When you compile and run this, you should get the output:

```
Box constructor called
Volume of first box = 1.21
Volume of second box = 1.21
```

How It Works

Clearly, the program is working as we hoped it would, with both boxes having the same volume. However, as you can see from the output, our constructor was called only once (for the creation of **firstBox**). The question is, therefore, how was the **secondBox** object created?

The mechanism is similar to the situation when we had no constructor defined, and the compiler supplied a default constructor to allow an object to be created. In this case, the compiler generates a default version of what is referred to as a **copy constructor**. A copy constructor does exactly what we are doing here — it creates an object of a class by initializing it with an existing object of the same class. The default version of the copy constructor creates the new object by copying the existing object, member by member. In fact, you can use the copy constructor in this way for any data type.

> *You don't have to create an object explicitly to cause a call to the copy constructor. Whenever you pass an object by value as an argument to a function, the compiler will make a copy of the object by calling the copy constructor.*

The default copy constructor is fine for simple classes, such as the **Box** class here, but for many — classes that have pointers as members, for example — it may produce undesirable effects. Indeed, with such classes it can create serious errors in your program, and in these cases you need to define your own copy constructor for the class.

A copy constructor is a constructor that creates a new object from an existing object of the same type, and defining it requires a special approach that we will look into fully in the next chapter.

Friends

Under normal circumstances, you will hide the data members of your classes by declaring them as private. You may well have private member functions of the class too. In spite of this, it is sometimes useful to treat certain, selected functions as 'honorary members' of the class, and allow them to access non-public members of a class object, just as though they were members of the class. Such functions are called **friends** of the class. A friend can access any of the members of a class object, regardless of their access specification.

There are two situations that we need to consider. An individual function can be specified as a friend of a class, or a whole class can be specified as a friend of another class. In the latter case, all the member functions of the friend class have the same access privileges as a normal member of the class. Let's look at individual functions as friends first of all.

The friend Functions of a Class

A function that is not a member of a class but nonetheless can access all its members is called a **friend function** of that class. To make a function a friend function of a class, you must declare it as such within the class definition, using the keyword **friend**.

> *A friend function of a class can be a global function, or it can be a member of another class. However, a function **cannot** be the friend of a class of which it is a member. Consequently, the access specifiers do not apply to the friends of a class.*

I should say right now that the need for friend functions in practice is limited. They are useful in situations where a function needs access to the internals of two different kinds of objects, where making the function a friend of both classes makes that possible. I will use them here, however, in simpler contexts that do not necessarily reflect a situation where they are required, but that provide a convenient vehicle for demonstrating their operation.

Let's suppose that we wanted to implement a friend function in the **Box** class to compute the surface area of a **Box** object.

Try It Out – Using a friend to Calculate the Surface Area

To make the function a friend, we must declare it as such within the class definition. We can adapt Program 12.4, changing the definition in **Box.h** to:

```
class Box
{
  public:
    // Constructor
    Box(double lengthValue = 1.0, double breadthValue = 1.0,
                                          double heightValue = 1.0);

    // Function to calculate the volume of a box
    double volume();

    // Friend function
    friend double boxSurface(const Box& theBox);

  private:
    double length;
    double breadth;
    double height;
};
```

This example also uses the file **Box.cpp** from Program 12.4, and the following main program code:

```cpp
// Program 12.6 Using a friend function of a class
#include <iostream>
#include "Box.h"

using namespace std;

int main()
{
  cout << endl;

  Box firstBox(2.2, 1.1, 0.5);
  Box secondBox;
  Box* pthirdBox = new Box(15.0, 20.0, 8.0);

  cout << "Volume of first box = "
       << firstBox.volume()
       << endl;

  cout << "Surface area of first box = "
       << boxSurface(firstBox)
       << endl;

  cout << "Volume of second box = "
       << secondBox.volume()
       << endl;

  cout << "Surface area of second box = "
       << boxSurface(secondBox)
       << endl;

  cout << "Volume of third box = "
       << pthirdBox->volume()
       << endl;

  cout << "Surface area of third box = "
       << boxSurface(*pthirdBox)
       << endl;

  delete pthirdBox;
  return 0;
}

// friend function to calculate the surface area of a Box object
double boxSurface(const Box& theBox)
{
  return 2.0 * (theBox.length * theBox.breadth +
                theBox.length * theBox.height +
                theBox.height * theBox.breadth);
}
```

Now we will get the output:

```
Box constructor called
Box constructor called
Box constructor called
Volume of first box = 1.21
Surface area of first box = 8.14
Volume of second box = 1
Surface area of second box = 6
Volume of third box = 2400
Surface area of third box = 1160
```

How It Works

We declare the function **boxSurface()** as a friend of the **Box** class by writing the function prototype using the keyword **friend**, within the class definition:

```
friend double boxSurface(const Box& theBox);
```

We will not be altering any aspect of the **Box** object passed as an argument to the function, so it is sensible to use a **const** reference parameter specification. It's also a good idea to be consistent when placing the **friend** declaration within the definition of the class. You can see that we have chosen to position ours at the end of all the public members of the class, but before the private members. The rationale for this is that the function is part of the interface to the class, since it has full access to members of the class. Remember though that a **friend** function is *not* a member of the class, so access specifiers do not apply to it.

The **boxSurface()** function itself is a global function, and its definition follows that of **main()**. You could put it in **Box.cpp** if you wanted, since it is related to the **Box** class, but placing it in the main file helps to indicate that it's a global function.

Notice that we have to specify access to the data members of the object within the definition of **boxSurface()** by using the **Box** object that is passed to the function as a parameter. Because a friend function is *not* a class member, the data members can't be referenced by their names alone. They each have to be qualified by the object name, in exactly the same way as they might in an ordinary function accessing public members of a class. A friend function is the same as an ordinary function, except that it can access all the members of a class without restriction.

The **main()** function has been amended to call the friend function to output the surface area of each of the three objects we create. You can see from the output that it works as expected.

While this example demonstrates how you write a friend function, it is not a very realistic use of one. We could have used accessor member functions to return the values of the data members, and then **boxSurface()** need not have been a friend function at all. Perhaps the best option of all in this case would have been to make **boxSurface()** a public member function of the class, so that the capability for computing the surface area of a box becomes part of the class interface.

Friend functions are part of the interface to a class, but they undermine its security, so you should only use them when you really need to. As I explained at the beginning of this discussion, the only circumstances in which they are really necessary is where you need to access the non-public members of two different classes, and even then there may be a way of doing what you want that does not involve friend functions.

Friend Classes

You can also declare a whole class to be a friend of another class. All the member functions of the friend class will have unrestricted access to the members of the class of which it has been declared a friend.

For example, suppose we have defined a class, **Carton**, and we want to allow the member functions of the **Carton** class to have access to the members of the **Box** class. To make this happen, we just need to include a statement within the **Box** class definition that declares **Carton** to be its friend:

```
class Box
{
  // Public members of the class...

  friend class Carton;

  // Private members of the class...
};
```

Friendship is not a reciprocal arrangement. While functions in the **Carton** class can now access all the members of the **Box** class, functions in the **Box** class have no access to the private members of the **Carton** class. Friendship amongst classes is not transitive either: just because class **A** is a friend of class **B**, and class **B** is a friend of class **C**, it doesn't follow that class **A** is a friend of class **C**.

A typical use for a friend class is where the functioning of one class is highly intertwined with that of another class. A linked list (like the one we discussed in the last chapter) basically involves two class types: a **List** class that maintains a list of objects (usually called nodes), and a **Node** class that defines what a node is. The **List** class needs to stitch the **Node** objects together by setting a pointer in each **Node** object so that it points to the next. Making the **List** class a friend of the class defining a node would enable members of the **List** class to access the members of the **Node** class directly.

The 'this' Pointer

In our **Box** class, we wrote the function **volume()** in terms of the class member names in the definition of the class. When you think about it, though, *every* object of type **Box** that we create contains these members, so there must be a mechanism for the function to refer to the members of the particular object for which it has been called.

When any class member function executes, it automatically contains a hidden pointer called **this**, which contains the address of the object for which the function was called. For example, if you write:

```
cout << firstBox.volume();
```

the pointer **this** in the function **volume()** will contains the address of **firstBox**. When you call the function for another **Box** object, **this** will be set to contain the address of that object.

This means that when the data member **length** is accessed in the function **volume()** during execution, it is actually referring to **this->length**, which is the fully-specified reference to the object member that is being used. The compiler takes care of adding the necessary pointer name **this** to the member names in the function. In other words, the compiler will implement the function as:

```
double Box::volume()
{
  return this->length * this->breadth * this->height;
}
```

You could write the function explicitly using the pointer **this** if you wanted to, but it isn't necessary here. However, there are situations where you *do* need to use it: for example, when a member function has multiple parameters of the same class type, or when you need to return the address of the current object. Let's see how the **this** pointer works in practice by using it explicitly in an example.

Try It Out – Explicit Use of this

Being able to compare the volumes of **Box** objects would be a very useful addition to our class, so let's add a public function to our class **Box** to do just that. The class definition in **Box.h** will be:

```
class Box
{
  public:
    // Constructor
    Box(double lengthValue = 1.0, double breadthValue = 1.0,
                                              double heightValue = 1.0);

    // Function to calculate the volume of a box
    double volume();

    // Function to compare two Box objects
    int compareVolume(Box& otherBox);

  private:
    double length;
    double breadth;
    double height;
};
```

We will need to add the definition of **compareVolume()** to the **Box.cpp** file, alongside the other function definitions we have there:

```
// Function to compare two Box objects
// If the current Box is greater than the argument, 1 is returned
// If they are equal, 0 is returned
// If the current Box is less than the argument, -1 is returned
int Box::compareVolume(Box& otherBox)
{
  double vol1 = this->volume();          // Get current Box volume
```

```
        double vol2 = otherBox.volume();     // Get argument volume
        return vol1 > vol2 ? 1 : (vol1 < vol2 ? -1 : 0);
    }
```

We can now create a couple of **Box** objects and compare their volumes:

```cpp
// Program 12.7 Using the this pointer
#include <iostream>
#include "Box.h"

using namespace std;

int main()
{
  cout << endl;

  Box firstBox(17.0, 11.0, 5.0);
  Box secondBox(9.0, 18.0, 4.0);

  cout << "The first box is "
       << (firstBox.compareVolume(secondBox) >= 0 ? "" : "not ")
       << "greater than the second box."
       << endl;

  cout << "Volume of first box = "
       << firstBox.volume()
       << endl;

  cout << "Volume of second box = "
       << secondBox.volume()
       << endl;

  return 0;
}
```

From this program you will get the output:

```
Box constructor called
Box constructor called
The first box is greater than the second box.
Volume of first box = 935
Volume of second box = 648
```

How It Works

The implementation of the member function **compareVolume()** involves working with two **Box** objects: the one for which the function is called, and the argument. To call the function **volume()** for the object for which the **compareVolume()** function was called, we use the **this** pointer:

```cpp
    double vol1 = this->volume();          // Get current Box volume
```

> *Remember that you use the direct member access operator, ., when using an object to select a member, and the pointer member access operator, ->, when using a pointer to an object.* **this** *is a pointer, so it requires the pointer member access operator.*

476

We used the **this** pointer in this example simply to demonstrate its existence. It isn't actually necessary here, so we could equally well have written:

```
    double vol1 = volume();                    // Get current Box volume
```

Within the body of **compareVolume()**, or indeed any member function, class member names that you use by themselves will automatically be accessed using the **this** pointer, so you will always get the member belonging to the current object. You only need to use the **this** pointer explicitly in limited circumstances. One example where you might use **this** explicitly is to resolve ambiguity — if a function parameter had the same name as a data member, for example. You would also use **this** if you wanted to return the address of the current object from a member function.

To get the volume of the object passed as an argument, we just use the parameter name to call the function:

```
    double vol2 = otherBox.volume();     // Get argument volume
```

The last statement in **compareVolume()** returns the appropriate integer value:

```
    return vol1 > vol2 ? 1 : (vol1 < vol2 ? -1 : 0);
```

If **vol1** is greater than **vol2**, then the conditional operator causes 1 to be returned. Otherwise, the conditional operation within parentheses is executed and returns –1 if **vol1** is less than **vol2**, and 0 if it isn't.

The **compareVolume()** function is used in **main()** to check the relationship between the volumes of the objects **firstBox** and **secondBox** with the statement:

```
    cout << "The first box is "
         << (firstBox.compareVolume(secondBox) >= 0 ? "" : "not ")
         << "greater than the second box."
         << endl;
```

The value returned by the **compareVolume()** function is used with a conditional operator to decide whether to include the string **"not   "** in the output. The output then confirms that the **firstBox** object is larger than the **secondBox** object.

In fact, it's not essential to write the **compareVolume()** function as a class member. We could just as well have written it as an ordinary function, with the objects as arguments. Note that this is not true of the function **volume()**, since it needs to access the **private** data members of the class. Of course, if the function **compareVolume()** was implemented as an ordinary function, it wouldn't have the pointer **this**, but it would still be very simple:

```
    // Comparing two Box objects - ordinary function version
    int compareVolume(Box& box1, Box& box2)
    {
      double vol1 = box1.volume();                    // Get first Box volume
      double vol2 = box2.volume();                    // Get second Box volume
      return vol1 > vol2 ? 1 : (vol1 < vol2 ? -1 : 0);
    }
```

Let's briefly compare this function to the class member version of **compareVolume()**. In this version, both objects are arguments, but the same values are returned. You would use this version to perform the same operation as before with this statement:

```
cout << "The first box is "
     << (compareVolume(firstBox, secondBox) >= 0 ? "" : "not ")
     << "greater than the second box."
     << endl;
```

In this instance, there really isn't much to choose between these two versions. However, there is a much better way to compare objects, as we will see later.

Objects that are const and const Member Functions

Before we leave the previous example, let's consider the **compareVolume()** member function once more. Since we don't modify the parameter, we really should have declared it as **const** in the class definition:

```
class Box
{
  // Rest of the class as before...
  int compareVolume(const Box& otherBox);
};
```

Of course, you'll need to change the function definition in the same way. Try that out and run the example again. You should find that the compiler complains when it tries to link the parts of the program together. If your compiler complies with the C++ standard, you will get an error message for this statement:

```
double vol2 = otherBox.volume();       // Get argument volume
```

If you specify that an object is **const**, you are telling the compiler that you will not modify it. Here, when you call the function **volume()** for the **const** object **otherBox**, the compiler has to pass the address of **otherBox** to the function via the **this** pointer, and it has no guarantee that the function will not modify the object. The error message is likely to be in terms of being unable to convert the **this** pointer, because the compiler cannot cast away the **const** nature of the object by default.

For any object that you declare to be **const**, you can only call member functions that are also declared to be **const**. A **const** member function will not modify the object for which it is called. To declare a member function as **const**, you need to add the keyword **const** at the *end* of the function declaration in the class definition. For the **compareVolume()** function to work with a **const** parameter, we must declare the **volume()** function to be **const**. In this case, the class definition will be:

```
class Box
{
  public:
    // Constructor
    Box(double lengthValue = 1.0, double breadthValue = 1.0,
                                  double heightValue = 1.0);
```

```
      // Function to calculate the volume of a box
      double volume() const;

      // Function to compare two Box objects
      int compareVolume(const Box& otherBox);

  private:
    double length;
    double breadth;
    double height;
};
```

The keyword **const** must also appear in the function definition for **volume()** in **Box.cpp**:

```
double Box::volume() const
{
  return length * breadth * height;
}
```

The program will now compile and work as before. Declaring a member function as **const** essentially ensures that whatever the **this** pointer points to is a **const** — in other words, ***this** is **const**. You should always declare member functions that do not change the object for which they are called as **const**. This does not prevent them being called for non-**const** objects, but it does allow you to use **const** objects more widely, which will make your code more efficient and less prone to error. In fact, on this basis we should declare the **compareVolume()** function in the **Box** class to be **const** too:

```
class Box
{
  public:
    // Constructor
    Box(double lengthValue = 1.0, double breadthValue = 1.0,
                                        double heightValue = 1.0);

    // Function to calculate the volume of a box
    double volume() const;

    // Function to compare two Box objects
    int compareVolume(const Box& otherBox) const;

  private:
    double length;
    double breadth;
    double height;
};
```

Of course, it must also be **const** in the definition in **Box.cpp**:

```
int Box::compareVolume(const Box& otherBox) const
{
  double vol1 = this->volume();        // Get current Box volume
  double vol2 = otherBox.volume();     // Get argument volume
  return vol1 > vol2 ? 1 : (vol1 < vol2 ? -1 : 0);
}
```

Other member functions that are prime candidates for being declared as **const** are the accessor functions. In fact, these should always be declared as **const**, since they just provide access to the value of a data member; they do not alter it.

Note that declaring a member function as **const** affects the function signature. This means that you can overload a function by adding a **const** version of the function. For example, member functions with the following prototypes:

```
int Box::compareVolume(const Box& otherBox);

int Box::compareVolume(const Box& otherBox) const;
```

would be overloaded versions of the **compareVolume()** function. However, you should be careful about overloading a member function on the basis of **const**-ness, as it can be confusing to someone using a class.

Mutable Data Members of a Class

If you declare an object as **const**, then the **this** pointer in member functions of the object will be **const**. A direct consequence is that for an object that has been declared to be **const**, you can only call **const** member functions, as we have seen. However, there can be situations where you need to allow certain, selected data members of a class to be altered, even if the object was declared as **const**.

For an example of such a circumstance, imagine an object that obtains data from a remote source — another computer, perhaps — and stores that data in a data member that provides an internal buffer. An object of the class may well need to be able to update its internal buffer, even if it has been declared to be **const**.

To accommodate these kinds of situations, you need two things. You need to be able to exempt a particular data member from the **const**-ness of an object, and you need to be able to alter the value of the exempt data member in a **const** member function, and still have the **const** declaration of the member function unbroken. You can do both by declaring a data member as **mutable**.

To illustrate how this is applied, let's consider a simple context. Suppose that for security reasons, you wanted to record a timestamp in a data member of an object each time any member function is called. The object might represent controlled access to part of a building, for instance. You want to allow the object to be **const**, but you still want to timestamp the last use of the object.

The way to do this is to declare the data member storing the timestamp as **mutable**. This will exempt the data member from the **const**-ness implied by a **const** declaration of an object of the class, and also allow it to be altered by a **const** member function. To do this, you just use the keyword **mutable** in the member declaration. For example:

```
class SecureAccess
{
  public:
    bool isLocked() const;
    // More of the class definition...
```

```
    private:
      mutable int time;
      // More of the class definition...
  }
```

The member function **isLocked()** might be implemented something along the lines of:

```
  bool SecureAccess::isLocked() const
  {
    time = getCurrentTime();              // Store time of function call
    return lockStatus();                  // Return the state of the door
  }
```

Here, the **lockStatus()** function is assumed to return **true** if the door is locked, and **false** otherwise. Because the data member, **time**, is declared as **mutable**, it can appear on the left of an assignment statement here. Only data members that have been declared as **mutable** can appear on the left of an assignment in a member function that is declared as **const**.

Now we could create an object of the class that we declare as **const**, and call the **isLocked()** member for it:

```
    const SecureAccess mainDoor;
    bool doorState = mainDoor.isLocked();
```

Because the **mainDoor** object is **const**, you can only call its **const** member functions. Any **const** member function in the class **SecureAccess** can modify the value stored in the member **time**, regardless of whether an object is declared as **const**. If **time** is not declared as **mutable**, any **const** function member that tries to change it will cause a compilation error.

Casting Away const

Very rarely, circumstances can arise where a function is dealing with a **const** object, either passed as an argument or the object pointed to by **this**, and it is necessary to make it non-**const**. This could be because you want to pass it as an argument to another function, written by someone else, that has a non-**const** parameter. The **const_cast<>()** operator enables you to do this. The general form of using the **const_cast<>()** operator is:

const_cast<*Type*>(*expression*)

Here, the type of *expression* must be either const *Type*, or the same as *Type*. You *should not* use this operator to undermine the **const**-ness of an object. The only situations in which you should use it are those where you are sure the **const** nature of the object will not be violated as a result.

Arrays of Objects of a Class

As I indicated earlier, you can declare an array of objects of a class in exactly the same way that you declare an array of any other type. Each element of an array of class objects has to be created individually, and to do this the compiler arranges for the default constructor to be called for each element. The compiler does not allow us to initialize our array within the definition statement. We can demonstrate that this is the case with an example.

Try It Out – Creating an Array of Box Objects

We can modify the previous definition of the **Box** class to include a specific default constructor. We will illustrate the array declaration by declaring two constructors at the outset, and tracking each constructor call via lines of output. The class definition will be:

```
class Box
{
  public:
    // Constructors
    Box();
    Box(double lengthValue, double breadthValue, double heightValue);

    // Function to calculate the volume of a box
    double volume() const;

    // Function to compare two Box objects
    int compareVolume(const Box& otherBox) const;

  private:
    double length;
    double breadth;
    double height;
};
```

We have removed the default parameter values from the original constructor, so that we don't have a duplicate default constructor. The member function definitions in **Box.cpp** will be as they were at the end of the last section, although you'll need to restore the default constructor definition if you removed it when we stopped using it:

```
// Default constructor
Box::Box()
{
  cout << "Default constructor called" << endl;
  length = breadth = height = 1.0;
}
```

The code to create and use a **Box** array is very simple:

```
// Program 12.8 Creating an array of Box objects
#include <iostream>
#include "Box.h"

using namespace std;

int main()
{
  cout << endl;

  Box firstBox(17.0, 11.0, 5.0);
  Box boxes[5];

  cout << "Volume of first box = "
       << firstBox.volume()
       << endl;
```

```
        const int count = sizeof boxes / sizeof boxes[0];

        cout << "The boxes array has " << count << " elements."
            << endl;

        cout << "Each element occupies " << sizeof boxes[0] << " bytes."
            << endl;

        for(int i = 0 ; i < count ; i++)
          cout << "Volume of boxes[" << i << "] = "
               << boxes[i].volume()
               << endl;

        return 0;
    }
```

On my machine, this example generates the following output:

```
Box constructor called
Default constructor called
Default constructor called
Default constructor called
Default constructor called
Default constructor called
Volume of first box = 935
The boxes array has 5 elements.
Each element occupies 24 bytes.
Volume of boxes[0] = 1
Volume of boxes[1] = 1
Volume of boxes[2] = 1
Volume of boxes[3] = 1
Volume of boxes[4] = 1
```

How It Works

The first line of output is produced by the constructor call in the declaration:

```
Box firstBox(17.0, 11.0, 5.0);
```

The next five lines of output originate from the declaration of the array:

```
Box boxes[5];
```

You can see from the output that the default constructor is called once for each array element. This statement defines five objects, each of type **Box**. Because we are defining an array, we cannot supply arguments for a constructor. Since there are no arguments supplied, the compiler uses the default constructor to create each of the five objects of the array.

After displaying the volume of **firstBox**, just to show there is nothing special about an array of **Box** objects, we calculate the number of elements in the array using the **sizeof** operator:

```
const int count = sizeof boxes / sizeof boxes[0];
```

The value stored in **count** is displayed in the usual way by the next statement:

```
cout << "The boxes array has " << count << " elements."
    << endl;
```

The size of each element will be the size of a **Box** object, which is displayed by this statement:

```
cout << "Each element occupies " << sizeof boxes[0] << " bytes."
    << endl;
```

You can see from the output that the size of a **Box** object is 24 bytes, which corresponds to the memory required for storing three values of type **double** on my machine. The presence or otherwise of member functions has no influence on the size of an object.

Finally in this example, we display the volume of each element of the **Boxes** array in a loop:

```
for(int i = 0 ; i < count ; i++)
  cout << "Volume of boxes[" << i << "] = "
        << boxes[i].volume()
        << endl;
```

It's clear from the output that the default constructor initialization is working satisfactorily, as the volume of each array element is 1.

The Size of a Class Object

As we saw in the last example, you can obtain the size of a class object by using the **sizeof** operator in exactly the way we have done previously with the basic data types. You can apply the operator either to a particular object, or to the class type. The size of a class object is generally the sum of the sizes of the data members of the class, although on some machines it may turn out to be greater than this on occasion. This isn't something that should bother you, but it's nice to know why.

On some computers, for performance reasons, two-byte variables must be placed at an address that is a multiple of two, four byte variables must be placed on a boundary that is a multiple of four, and so on. A consequence of this is that sometimes, the compiler must leave gaps between the memory for one value and the next. If, on such a machine, you have three variables that occupy two bytes, followed by a variable that requires four bytes, a gap of two bytes may need to be left in order to place the fourth variable on the correct boundary. In this case, the total space required by all four is greater than the sum of the individual sizes. We can create an example that will illustrate this on a PC and other systems that require **boundary alignment**.

Try It Out – Object Sizes Affected by Boundary Alignment

We can define a variation on the **Box** class we will call **SizeBox**, designed specifically to show the effect of boundary alignment on object sizes:

```
// SizeBox.h
#ifndef SIZEBOX_H
#define SIZEBOX_H

class SizeBox
{
  public:
    SizeBox();
    int totalSize();                    // Sum of sizes of members
```

```
    private:
      char* pMaterial;
      double length;
      double breadth;
      double height;
};

#endif
```

```
// SizeBox.cpp
#include "SizeBox.h"

SizeBox::SizeBox() : length(1.0),
                     breadth(1.0),
                     height(1.0),
                     pMaterial("Cardboard")
{}

// Sum of sizes of members
int SizeBox::totalSize()
{
  return sizeof(length) + sizeof(breadth) + sizeof(height) + sizeof(pMaterial);
}
```

We don't need the class to do very much other than be able to create instances of itself and supply the number of bytes occupied by its members, so the only member functions are the constructor and the function **totalSize()**. We have an extra data member that is a pointer to a null-terminated string that records the type of the material the box is made of. We can create objects and report the amount of memory they occupy with the following code:

```
// Program 12.9 Trying object sizes
#include <iostream>
#include "SizeBox.h"
using namespace std;

int main()
{
  SizeBox box;
  SizeBox boxes[10];
  cout << endl            << "The data members of a Box object occupy "
       << box.totalSize() << " bytes.";

  cout << endl            << "A single Box object occupies "
       << sizeof SizeBox << " bytes.";

  cout << endl            << "An array of 10 Box objects occupies "
       << sizeof(boxes)   << " bytes."
       << endl;
  return 0;
}
```

This will produce the output:

```
The data members of a Box object occupy 28 bytes.
A single Box object occupies 32 bytes.
An array of 10 Box objects occupies 320 bytes.
```

How It Works

The output demonstrates that things don't quite add up. The memory for a **SizeBox** object is made up of 24 bytes for the three **double** members, plus 4 bytes for the pointer member, **pMaterial**, which makes a total of 28 bytes, as reported in the first line of output. When we output the size of a **SizeBox** object, however, it turns out to be 32 bytes, and this is confirmed by the array of 10 objects.

The extra 4 bytes are due to boundary alignment, which has the effect you can see here from time to time. As I described before, on many machines the compiler has to allocate addresses for 8-byte variables that are a multiple of 8, addresses for 4-byte variables that are a multiple of 4, and so on for performance reasons.

4 bytes	4 bytes	8 bytes	8 bytes	8 bytes
pMaterial	not used	**length**	**breadth**	**height**

The **SizeBox** object consists of a pointer and three members of type **double**. The pointer **pMaterial** will be at an address that is a multiple of 4, because it occupies 4 bytes. The three 8-byte members must each occupy an address that is a multiple of 8. If the next available address is *not* a multiple of 8, then the compiler has to leave a gap — 4 bytes in this case — to make the **length** member lie on an 8-byte boundary.

You might think that by rearranging the data members — by putting **pMaterial** last, for instance — you could make class objects occupy less space, but this is not usually the case. The compiler must take account of what happens in the case of an array of objects, and this will require that the object is on a boundary that is a multiple of 8 bytes.

Now we have got that out of the way, let's get back to what we can do with a class!

Static Members of a Class

Both data members and member functions of a class can be declared as **static**. Static data members of a class are used to provide class-wide storage of data that is independent of any particular object of the class type, but is accessible by any of them. They record properties of the class as a whole, rather than of individual objects. You can use static data members to store constants that are specific to a class, or you could store information about the objects of a class in general, such as how many there are in existence.

A static member function provides a computational ability that's independent of any individual class object, but can be invoked by any class object if necessary. It can also be invoked from outside the class if it is a public member. A common use of static member functions is to operate on static data members, regardless of whether any objects of the class have been declared.

Because the context is a class definition, there is a little more to this topic than the effect of the keyword **static** outside of a class, so we need to consider it in greater detail. Let's look into static data members first.

Static Data Members of a Class

Static data members of a class are associated with the class as a whole, not with any particular object of the class. When you declare a data member of a class as **static**, the effect is that the static data member is defined only once, and will exist *even if no objects of the class have been created*. Each static data member is accessible in any object of the class that has been created, and is shared amongst however many objects there are. An object gets its own independent copies of each of the ordinary data members of a class, but only one instance of each static data member ever exists, regardless of how many class objects have been defined.

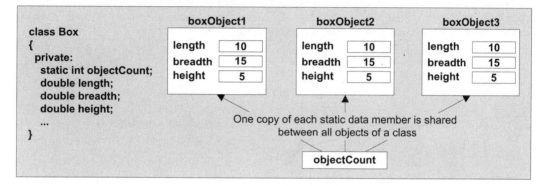

You use static data members to record class-wide information. One use for a static data member is to count how many objects of a class actually exist. We could add a static data member to our **Box** class by adding the following statement to our class definition:

```
static int objectCount;          // Count of objects in existence
```

We now have a problem. How do we initialize the static data member? We can't put it in the class declaration — that's simply a blueprint for an object, and initializing values are not allowed. We don't want to initialize it in a constructor, because we want to increment it every time the constructor is called; and anyway, it exists even if no objects exist (and therefore no constructors have been called). Similarly, we can't initialize it in another member function, because a member function is associated with an object, and we want it initialized before any object is created.

The answer is to write the initialization outside of the class declaration with a statement like this one:

```
int Box::objectCount = 0;          // Initialize static member of class Box
```

Even though the static data member is specified as private, you can still initialize it in this fashion. Indeed, this is the *only* way you can initialize it. Of course, because it's private, you cannot then access **objectCount** directly from outside the class

Since this statement defines and initializes the static member of the class, there must only be one occurrence of it in your program. The logical place to put it is therefore the **Box.cpp** file.

> *Notice that the keyword* **static** *is not included in the definition — indeed, you must not include it. However, we do need to qualify the member name by using the class name and the scope resolution operator, so that the compiler understands we are referring to a static member of the class. Otherwise, we would simply create a global variable that was nothing to do with the class.*

Try It Out – Counting Instances

Let's add the **static** data member and the object counting capability to Program 12.8. We will need just two extra statements in the class definition: one to declare the new static data member, and another to define a function that will retrieve its value:

```
class Box
{
  public:
    // Constructors
    Box();
    Box(double lengthValue, double breadthValue, double heightValue);

    // Function to calculate the volume of a box
    double volume() const;

    // Function to compare two Box objects
    int compareVolume(const Box& otherBox) const;

    int getObjectCount() const {return objectCount;}

  private:
    static int objectCount;            // Count of objects in existence
    double length;
    double breadth;
    double height;
};
```

The **getObjectCount()** function has been declared as **const** because it does not modify any of the data members of the class. You can add the statement to initialize the static member **objectCount** at the end of the **Box.cpp** file:

```
// Initialize static member of class Box
int Box::objectCount = 0;
```

We must also modify both constructors to update the count when an object is created:

```
// Default constructor
Box::Box()
{
  cout << "Default constructor called" << endl;
  ++objectCount;
  length = breadth = height = 1.0;
}
```

```
// Constructor definition using an initializer list
Box::Box(double lvalue, double bvalue, double hvalue) : length(lvalue),
                                                        breadth(bvalue),
                                                        height(hvalue)
{
  cout << "Box constructor called" << endl;
  ++objectCount;

  // Ensure positive dimensions
  if(length <= 0)
    length = 1.0;
  if(breadth <= 0)
    breadth = 1.0;
  if(height <= 0)
    height = 1.0;
}
```

We can modify the version of **main()** from Program 12.8 to output the object count:

```
// Program 12.10 Counting Box objects
#include <iostream>
#include "Box.h"

using namespace std;

int main()
{
  cout << endl;

  Box firstBox(17.0, 11.0, 5.0);
  cout << "Object count is " << firstBox.getObjectCount() << endl;
  Box boxes[5];
  cout << "Object count is " << firstBox.getObjectCount() << endl;

  cout << "Volume of first box = "
       << firstBox.volume()
       << endl;

  const int count = sizeof boxes / sizeof boxes[0];

  cout <<"The boxes array has " << count << " elements."
       << endl;

  cout <<"Each element occupies " << sizeof boxes[0] << " bytes."
       << endl;

  for(int i = 0 ; i < count ; i++)
    cout << "Volume of boxes[" << i << "] = "
         << boxes[i].volume()
         << endl;

  return 0;
}
```

489

The program will now produce the output:

```
Box constructor called
Object count is 1
Default constructor called
Default constructor called
Default constructor called
Default constructor called
Default constructor called
Object count is 6
Volume of first box = 935
The boxes array has 5 elements.
Each element occupies 24 bytes.
Volume of boxes[0] = 1
Volume of boxes[1] = 1
Volume of boxes[2] = 1
Volume of boxes[3] = 1
Volume of boxes[4] = 1
```

How It Works

This code shows that there is indeed only one copy of the static member **objectCount**, and both of the constructors are updating it. We called the function **getObjectCount()** for the **firstBox** object on both occasions, but for the second call, we could have used any of the array elements and we would have got the same result.

Note that the size of a **Box** object is unchanged in the output compared to the previous example, even though we have added **objectCount** to the class definition. This is because static data members are not part of any object — they belong to the class. Since static data members are not part of a class object, member functions that you have declared as **const** can modify static data members of a class without violating their **const**-ness.

> *You* must *define a static data member, or the compiler will complain. The declaration in the class definition doesn't define the static variable, so until you define it, it doesn't exist.*

Accessing Static Data Members

Suppose that in a reckless moment, we declared the **objectCount** data member as public:

```
class Box
{
  public:
    static int objectCount;             // Count of objects in existence

    // Constructors
    Box();
    Box(double lengthValue, double breadthValue, double heightValue);

    // Function to calculate the volume of a box
    double volume() const;

    // Function to compare two Box objects
    int compareVolume(const Box& otherBox) const;
```

```
          int getObjectCount() const {return objectCount;}

      private:
        double length;
        double breadth;
        double height;
    };
```

Now we don't need to use the **getObjectCount()** function. To output the number of objects in **main()**, we could just write:

```
    cout << "Object count is " << firstBox.objectCount << endl;
```

There's more: I claimed that a static variable exists even if no objects have been created. This means that we should be able to get the count *before* we create the **firstBox** object, but how do we refer to the data member? The answer is that you just use the class name, **Box**, as a qualifier with the scope resolution operator:

```
    cout << "Object count is " << Box::objectCount << endl;
```

In fact, you can always use the class name to access a public static member of a class. It doesn't matter whether any objects exist or not. Try it out by modifying the last example; you'll see that it works as described.

The Type of a Static Data Member

A static data member is not part of each object of the class, so it can be of the same type as the class. The **Box** class can contain a static data member of type **Box**, for example. This might seem a little strange at first, but it can be useful. We can use the **Box** class to illustrate just how.

Suppose we want to have a standard 'reference' box available for some purpose. We might want to relate **Box** objects in various ways to a standard box, for example. Of course, you could define a standard **Box** object outside the class, but if you are going to use it within member functions of the class, it creates an external dependency that it would be better to get rid of. The alternative solution is to make the standard **Box** a static member of the class:

```
    class Box
    {
      public:
        // Constructors
        Box();
        Box(double lengthValue, double breadthValue, double heightValue);

        // Function to calculate the volume of a box
        double volume() const;

        // Function to compare two Box objects
        int compareVolume(const Box& otherBox) const;

      private:
        const static Box refBox;            // Standard reference box
        double length;
        double breadth;
        double height;
    };
```

Since **refBox** is a standard **Box** object that should not be changed, we also declare it as **const**. However, we must still initialize it outside the class for it to be defined. We could put a statement in **Box.cpp** to define **refBox**:

```
const Box Box::refBox(10.0, 10.0, 10.0);
```

This calls the constructor of the **Box** class to create **refBox**. Since the static data member of the class will be created before any objects are created in the program, there will always be at least one **Box** object in existence.

Any of the member functions for objects of the class can access **refBox**, so it is available to all, but it is not accessible outside the class because we declared it to be a private member. A class constant is one situation where you might want to make the data member public if it has a useful role outside the class. As long as it is declared as **const**, it cannot be modified.

Static Member Functions of a Class

By declaring a function member as **static**, you make it independent of any particular object of the class. Just like a static data member, a static function member of a class exists even if no class objects have been created. Declaring a static function in a class is easy: you simply use the keyword **static**, as we did with the data member **objectCount**. In fact, we could have declared the **getObjectCount()** function as static in the previous example:

```
class Box
{
  public:
    // Constructors
    Box();
    Box(double lengthValue, double breadthValue, double heightValue);

    // Function to calculate the volume of a box
    double volume() const;

    // Function to compare two Box objects
    int compareVolume(const Box& otherBox) const;

    static int getObjectCount() {return objectCount;}

  private:
    static int objectCount;               // Count of objects in existence
    double length;
    double breadth;
    double height;
};
```

> *Static member functions cannot be declared as **const**. Because a static member function is not associated with any object of a class, it has no **this** pointer, so the idea of **const** does not apply.*

Static member functions have the advantage that they exist and can be called even if no objects of the class exist. You can call a static member function using the class name as a qualifier. For example:

```
cout << "Object count is " << Box::getObjectCount() << endl;
```

Of course, if you have created objects of the class, you can call a static member function through an object of the class in the same way as you call any other member function. For instance:

```
cout << "Object count is " << firstBox.getObjectCount() << endl;
```

The difference between this and an ordinary member function is that the static function has no access to the object for which it is called. In order for a static member function to access an object of the class, it would need to be passed as an argument to the function. Referencing members of a class object from within a static function must then be done using qualified names (as you would do with an ordinary global function accessing a public data member).

Of course, a static member function is a full member of the class in terms of access privileges. If an object of the same class is passed as an argument to a static member function, it can access **private** as well as **public** members of the object. It would not make sense to do so, but just to illustrate the point you could include a definition of a static function in the **Box** class as:

```
static double sum(Box theBox)
{
  return theBox.length + theBox.breadth + theBox.height;
}
```

Even though we are passing the **Box** object as an argument, the private data members can be accessed. Of course, it would make more sense to do this with a member function, rather than a static function.

Summary

In this and the previous chapter we have covered the basic ideas behind classes in C++, and the ground rules for defining and using them. However, this is just the start. There is a great deal more to learn about implementing the operations applicable to objects of your classes, and about the subtleties of the internals of a class. In subsequent chapters, we will be building on what you have learnt here and seeing more about how you can extend the capabilities of your classes, as well as exploring more sophisticated ways of using classes in practice. The key points to keep in mind from this chapter are:

- A **class** provides a means of defining your own data types. Classes can reflect whatever types of **objects** your particular problem requires.

- A class can contain **data members** and **member functions**. The member functions of a class always have free access to the data members of the same class.

- Objects of a class are created and initialized using functions called **constructors**. A constructor is called automatically when an object declaration is encountered.
- Constructors may be overloaded to provide different ways of initializing an object.

- Members of a class can be specified as **public**, in which case they are freely accessible from any function in a program. Alternatively, they may be specified as **private**, in which case they may only be accessed by member functions or **friend** functions of the class.

▶ Data members of a class can be defined as **static**. Only one instance of each static data member of a class exists, no matter how many objects of the class are created.

▶ While static data members of a class are accessible in a member function of a class object, they are not part of the class object, and do not contribute to its size.

▶ Static function members of a class exist, and can be called, even if no objects of the class have been created.

▶ Every non-static function member of a class contains the pointer **this**, which points to the current object for which the function was called.

▶ A static function member of a class does not contain the pointer **this**.

▶ Member functions of a class declared as **const** cannot modify data members of an object of the class, unless the data members have been declared as **mutable**.

▶ Using references to class objects as arguments to function calls can avoid substantial overheads in passing complex objects to a function.

▶ A copy constructor is a constructor for an object that is initialized with an existing object of the same class. The compiler generates a default copy constructor for a class if you do not define one.

Exercises

Ex 12.1 Create a simple class called **Integer** that has an **int** as its single, private data member. Provide a constructor and destructor for the class, and use them to output messages that tell you when objects are created and destroyed. Write a test program to manipulate **Integer** objects, and verify that you cannot assign directly into the data member.

Provide member functions of the class to get and set the data member, and to print out its value. Exercise these functions in your test program.

Ex 12.2 Modify the default constructor so that the data member is initialized to zero in the initialization list. Provide a second constructor to allow **Integer** objects to be created and initialized with a value.

In your test program, write a function that takes an **Integer** object as an argument, first by value and then by reference. What do you see printed from the constructors and destructors when the function is called? Make sure that you understand why this is so.

Ex 12.3 Write a class called **Sequence** to store an ascending, incremental sequence of integer values, the length and starting value of which are provided in the constructor. Make the default a sequence of 10 values, starting at zero (0, 1, 2, 3, 4, 5, 6, 7, 8, 9). You will need to allocate enough memory to hold the sequence, and then fill the memory with the requisite values.

Provide a **Print()** function to list the sequence, so that you can be sure **Sequence** objects are being created correctly.

Make sure that any memory you allocate to hold the sequence is freed when **Sequence** objects are destroyed. (Note: be certain that you release *all* the memory!)

Ex 12.4 Write a function to compare two sequences. **Sequence** objects are different if they are different lengths, or if they are the same length but their corresponding values differ. Write this function as a member of the **Sequence** class.

Ex 12.5 Rewrite the comparison function to be a friend of the **Sequence** class. How will you have to change the arguments and the way in which you call it? Which technique do you think is better?

13

Class Operations

There are a number of subtleties in the creation and destruction of class objects, and you will need to understand them if operations on objects of your classes are to work safely and effectively. In this chapter, we'll cover the groundwork on the creating and destroying class objects.

To make clear the reasons why some things need to be done in a particular way, we will be developing our classes incrementally over this chapter and the next. The intermediate stages we go through will sometimes have shortcomings that need to be overcome.

In this chapter you will learn:

> How to use pointers and references with class types

> What a class destructor is, and when you should implement one

> How to deal with dynamic memory allocation within a class

> When you must implement a copy constructor, and how you do it

> How to limit access to a class

> What a nested class is

Pointers and References to Class Objects

In the last chapter, we saw how to declare and use pointers and references to class objects, in the same way that we use them for basic data types. Pointers and references to class objects are key features of object-oriented programming, and they each provide particular advantages.

There are three basic contexts in which you can use a pointer to a class object:

> As a means of invoking operations on an object — that is, calling functions using the pointer member access operator, `->`

> As an argument to a function

> As a data member of a class

The first of these is the means by which calling a function polymorphically becomes possible, where the function called will depend on the type of the object pointed to. We will investigate this capability extensively in Chapter 16.

Passing a pointer to an object as an argument to a function avoids the copying implicit in the pass-by-value mechanism. This can vastly improve the efficiency of your program — especially if large objects are involved, because copying large objects is a time-consuming process.

If a class contains a pointer to an object as one of its data members, it enables a series of objects to be linked together, and it can even allow objects of different types to be linked. This is essential for organizing data into structures like graphs or trees, or into the linked lists that we referred to briefly in Chapter 11. We will come back to look at linked lists in a moment.

References to objects have importance as parameter types for functions. In general, passing an object by reference is much faster than passing it by value, because copying inherent in the pass-by-value mechanism is avoided. They are also fundamental in the implementation of the copy constructor — as we shall see.

Pointers as Data Members

Declaring a pointer as a data member of a class is simple. Here, we'll see how pointer data members can be applied in practice.

Let's look at an example that we introduced back in Chapter 11: a linked list of objects. We can use this idea to put together a working example that uses a pointer as a data member of a class, and also to draw together some of the topics covered in Chapter 12. Further, we will also see how even a simple class can produce unexpected complications, that we have to recognize and deal with.

FYI — I should say here and now that you don't *need* to create your own linked list classes; there are very flexible versions already defined in the standard library, as we shall see. However, we can learn a lot by trying to put our own classes together to do this, and we'll get a good understanding of how linked lists work as well.

We will define a class that represents a collection of an arbitrary number of **Box** objects (where **Box** is the class that we introduced in Chapter 11). A **Box** object will represent a unit of a product to be delivered, and our collection of **Box** objects will represent a truckload of boxes, so we'll call the class **TruckLoad**. The **TruckLoad** class will help us to plan how the truck should be loaded, so that the driver can unload his deliveries in the right order.

Ultimately, this arrangement might be used, for example, in a program which is used in a distribution office. For example, the office takes orders for a product and arranges for their dispatch. The method of dispatch is by truck. In this model, the order of loading the truck at the depot is crucial, because the truck-driver must be able to unload the boxes in the correct order at the various destinations on his route.

A linked list is appropriate for such an application. We might have used an array, but a linked list has two significant advantages. First, an array must be fixed in size when we declare it, while a linked list can be as long or as short as we need — this makes for efficient memory management. Second, as the distribution office employees plan each consignment, they may need to add to the list at the beginning, or the end, or in the middle. This facility can be efficiently implemented in a linked list, but not in array.

We want to be able to create a new **TruckLoad** object from a single **Box** object, or from an array of **Box** objects. We also want to be able to add **Box** objects to a **TruckLoad** object, and to retrieve all the **Box** objects in the **TruckLoad**. Let's build the class step by step.

We need to consider how we are going to collect **Box** objects together, so that they represent a coherent whole — a truckload. We need a programming device that can tie an arbitrary number of **Box** objects together. A **Box** object has no in-built facility for linking it with another **Box** object, and to start altering the definition of the **Box** class to incorporate this capability would be inconsistent with the idea of a box — boxes aren't like that.

One way to collect **Box** objects into a group is to define another kind of object, which we'll call a **Package**. A **Package** object has two key facilities — it can 'contain' a **Box** object, and it can be linked to another **Package** object.

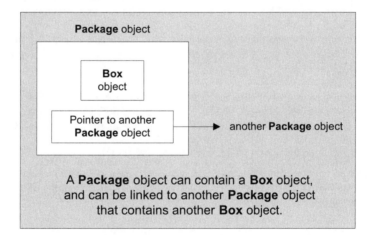

The diagram shows how each **Package** object contains a **Box** object, and also forms a link in a chain of **Package** objects, which are strung together using pointers. Hence, a **Package** object is simply an element that forms part of a list.

> *The Box/Package relationship here illustrates how, in order to organize basic objects into structures of various kinds, we inevitably must design some other encompassing object that allows us to obtain the contained basic object, and also provides the links between objects.*

In this case, a collection of **Package** objects, each containing a **Box** object, will be created and managed by a **TruckLoad** object. The **TruckLoad** object will represent an instance of a truckload of boxes — there may be any number of boxes in the truckload. The **Package** object provides the mechanism whereby the **TruckLoad** object can keep track of the **Box** objects it contains. The relationship between these objects is illustrated in the diagram.

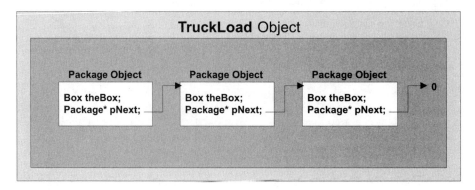

The diagram shows a **TruckLoad** object, containing a list of **Package** objects: each **Package** object contains a **Box** object and a pointer to the next **Package** object. This **TruckLoad** object holds three **Package** objects, but it could hold one object or a thousand objects.

In this elementary implementation, we will only add **Package** objects at the end of the list. In this case, the constructor for the **Package** class will need to create an object that's detached — that is, with a null pointer.

To add a **Package** to the end of the list, we can define a function in the **Package** class that enables the pointer member, **pNext**, of the last object in the list to be updated with the address of the new object. The process that manages this will be in the **TruckLoad** class, which represents the list.

> *In a more advanced implementation, it would be relatively easy to implement a function that allows us to add **Package** objects at any point in the list. The standard library linked list, **list**, supports this facility.*

Defining the Package Class

From the discussion above, our first instinct when writing the **Package** class may be to design a class which has two data members, one of type **Box** and one of type 'pointer to **Package**':

```
class Package
{
  public:
    Package(Box* pBox): theBox(*pBox), pNext(0){}      // Constructor

    Box getBox() const { return theBox; }              // Retrieve the Box object
    Package* getNext() const { return pNext; }         // Get next package address
    void setNext(Package* pPackage){ pNext = pPackage; }
                                                       // Add package to end of list
```

```
    private:
      Box theBox;                                    // The Box object
      Package* pNext;                                // Pointer to the next Package
  };
```

Before we look into the other features of this class, we should seriously consider the consequences of implementing this class definition. When the **Package** constructor creates a **Package** object from a **Box** object, it initializes the data member **theBox** by de-referencing the pointer that's passed as an argument. There is a very important issue here: it is that the **Package** constructor creates a *duplicate* **Box** object.

Let's think about the physicality of this for a moment. The **Package** constructor creates a **Package** object by a copying a **Box** object (which already exists) and adding a 'pointer to **Package**'. The first problem with this is the obvious waste of memory: why should a **Package** object have its own copy of a **Box** object, which already exists?

The second problem is a practical one, involving the copying procedure involved in this **Package** constructor. Every time we create a **Package** object, a **Box** object is copied, byte-by-byte, from its original location to the new object. The process of copying is generally a time-consuming one. If the objects being copied are large, or a large number of objects are copied within a single program, then our program is likely to be terribly inefficient. If we decide to increase the scale of our program in the future then this could become a costly problem.

The third problem is also practical: if we have multiple copies of a single **Box** object, how can we be sure that they all carry the same values? Suppose, for some reason, the values of one **Box** object must be adjusted. The effort behind locating and adjusting all copies of a **Box** object will make for clumsy program code and further inefficiency at runtime, and is prone to bugs.

The diagram illustrates what would happen if we tried to implement this version of the **Package** class. As you can see, there are multiple copies of each **Box** object in existence. One copy is generated by the **Package** constructor. Note that the **getBox()** member function (which makes the **private Box** data member available outside the **Package** class) also generates a copy of the **Box** data member, each time it is called.

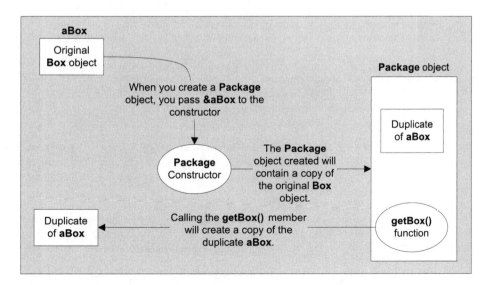

To say this could get confusing is something of an understatement. It's clear that a **Package** class that contains a copy of an original **Box** object is not the way forward. We need to reconsider this aspect of the class design.

One solution is to design the **Package** class so that each **Package** object contains a *pointer* to the original **Box** object (rather than a copy of the **Box** object). The class definition then becomes:

```
class Package
{
  public:
    Package(Box* pNewBox):pBox(pNewBox), pNext(0){}    // Constructor
    Box* getBox() const { return pBox; }               // Retrieve the Box pointer
    Package* getNext() const { return pNext; }          // Get next package address
    void setNext(Package* pPackage) { pNext = pPackage; }
                                                        // Add package to end of list

  private:
    Box* pBox;                                          // Pointer to the Box
    Package* pNext;                                     // Pointer to the next
Package
};
```

Now we deal in pointers to **Box** objects throughout, so that the **Box** objects in the list are not duplicates.

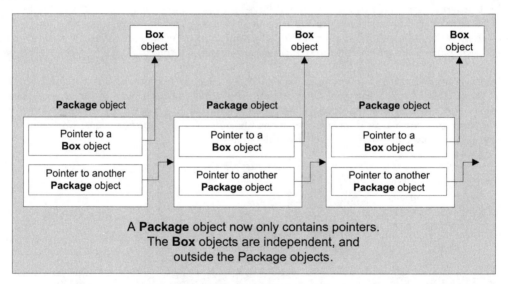

A **Package** object now only contains pointers.
The **Box** objects are independent, and
outside the Package objects.

The **getBox()** function now allows access to the private **Box*** member of the **Package** class from outside the class. The function **getNext()**, called for a particular **Package** object, will return the address of the next **Package** object in the list (or the null pointer, if it reaches the end of the list).

In order to update the pointer to the next **Package** in the list, we have defined the **setNext()** function, which stores the address passed as an argument in the **pNext** pointer. To add a new new **Package** object to end of the list, you simply pass its address to the **setNext()** function.

The **Package** class has enough capability for our needs at the moment. We can now use it to implement a list in the **TruckLoad** class.

> **FYI**
>
> When developing container classes, such as this TruckLoad class, you will need to consider carefully whether or not the data members of your class should be duplicates of the original objects. Sometimes it doesn't matter, but usually it does — if you don't take account of it you can get some very obscure bugs in your program. When using containers, it is often wise to avoid duplication. Use of pointers, as we have applied here, is not the only solution. Later, we will see how we can use references to avoid copying objects.

Defining the TruckLoad Class

A **TruckLoad** class represents a list of **Package** objects. The class must provide everything necessary to create and extend the list, and also the means by which **Box** objects can be retrieved. If we store the address of the first **Package** object in the list as a data member of a **TruckLoad** object, then we can get to any of the other **Package** objects in the list by stepping through the chain of **pNext** pointers, using the **getNext()** function from the **Package** class. It will also be useful to store the address of the last **Package** object, as this will make it easy to add a new object to the end of the list.

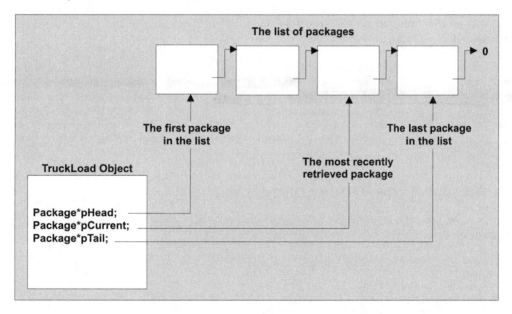

Let's think about how the process for retrieving **Box** objects should work. The starting point is the first object in the list — so we will need a function in the **TruckLoad** class to retrieve this. We could call it **getFirstBox()**.

If we keep track of the **Package** that was retrieved most recently from a **TruckLoad** object, we can then use a function **getNextBox()** to retrieve the **Box** object from the *next* **Package** object in the list, and to update the record of the last **Package** object retrieved.

Another essential capability is adding a **Box** to the list, so we will also need a member function to do that — we'll call it **addBox()**.

Here's an initial definition for the **TruckLoad** class, based on the ideas we have just discussed:

```
class TruckLoad
{
  public:
    TruckLoad(Box* pBox = 0, int count = 1);    // Constructor

    Box* getFirstBox();                         // Retrieve the first Box
    Box* getNextBox();                          // Retrieve the next Box
    void addBox(Box* pBox);                     // Add a new Box to the list

  private:
    Package* pHead;                             // First in the list
    Package* pTail;                             // Last in the list
    Package* pCurrent;                          // Last retrieved from the list
};
```

We have declared all the data members as **private**, since there is no need for any of them to be available outside the class. We have also declared one constructor for the class, but with the default values for the parameters, it will serve as three. If you omit both arguments to the constructor, then it will act as a default constructor and create an empty list. Omitting just the **count** argument will create a list containing a single **Box** object, because **count** will default to 1. Specifying both arguments will create a list containing the given number (**count**) of **Box** objects from the array **pBox**. We'll see how these are implemented in the definition for the **TruckLoad** constructor in a moment.

The mechanism for retrieving **Box** objects is implemented through the member functions **getFirstBox()** and **getNextBox()**. Each of these will need to modify the **pCurrent** pointer, so we can't declare them as **const** member functions. The **addBox()** function also changes the list, so we can't declare that as **const** either.

All of the member functions of the class require external definitions, so let's see how we put those together.

Implementing the TruckLoad Class

We can start with the constructor. This either creates a list of one or more **Package** objects from an array of **Box** objects, or it creates an empty list:

```
TruckLoad::TruckLoad(Box* pBox, int count)
{
  pHead = pTail = pCurrent = 0;

  if((count > 0) && (pBox != 0))
    for(int i = 0 ; i<count ; i++)
      addBox(pBox+i);
}
```

This sets the data members of the class to 0, so that we start out with an empty list. If there are objects to be added then **pBox** will be non-null, and **count** will be positive, so we check for this in the **if** condition. If both conditions are **true**, we add the **Box** objects using the

addBox() function member, which we will come to in a moment. Each call of **addBox()** will create a **Package** object containing the **Box** object pointed to by the argument, and will add this **Package** object to the list. Thus, in the **for** loop, we add to the list the **Box** object pointed to by **pBox**, then **pBox+1**, then **pBox+2**, and so on.

> *Remember that incrementing a pointer by 1 increments it to point to the next object, so the address contained by **pBox** will be incremented by **sizeof(Box)**.*

Defining the Member Functions

Let's define the **addBox()** function first, since we call that in the constructor:

```
void TruckLoad::addBox(Box* pBox)
{
  Package* pPackage = new Package(pBox);    // Create a Package

  if(pHead)                                 // Check list is not empty
    pTail->setNext(pPackage);               // Add the new object to the tail
  else                                      // List is empty
    pHead = pPackage;                       // so new object is the head
  pTail = pPackage;                         // Store its address as tail
}
```

The function creates a new **Package** object in the free store and stores the address returned in the local variable **pPackage**.

> *There is the possibility that the operator **new** will be unable to allocate the memory required here, but we will ignore that problem here. We will see how to deal with this when we discuss exception handling in Chapter 17.*

When we add an object to the list, we have to consider whether or not the list is empty. If **pHead** is non-null then the list is not empty, in which case we can add the new object to the end of the list by storing its address in the **pNext** member of the current tail **pTail**. If **pHead** is null then the list is empty, so we can just store the address of the new object as the first member of the list. In this example, the new **Package** object is always added to the end of the list, so the data member **pTail** is updated to reflect this.

The **getFirstBox()** function definition is a piece of cake:

```
Box* TruckLoad::getFirstBox()
{
  pCurrent = pHead;
  return pCurrent->getBox();
}
```

The address of the first **Package** object in the list is stored in **pHead**, and so we store that address in **pCurrent**. We then call the **getBox()** function for the **Package** object to obtain the address of the **Box** object, which we return.

The **getNextBox()** function needs to get access to the *next* **Package** object via the **getNext()** function of the most recent **Package** object that was retrieved, but we also need to accommodate the situation when **pCurrent** is null. The code defining **getNextBox()** is:

```
Box* TruckLoad::getNextBox()
{
  if(pCurrent)
    pCurrent = pCurrent->getNext();        // pCurrent is not null so set to next
  else                                     // pCurrent is null
    pCurrent = pHead;                      //  so set to the first list element

  return pCurrent ? pCurrent->getBox() : 0;
}
```

In the normal course of events, when **pCurrent** contains the valid address of a **Package** object, we call the **getNext()** function of the current **Package** object to obtain the address of the next one. If **pCurrent** is null, then we simply go back to the beginning of the list. All this is handled in the **if-else** statement. Of course, it is possible that we have run off the end of the list, and in this case **pCurrent** will have been set to null; we use a conditional statement to return 0 in this case. If we attempted to call the function **getBox()** with a null value in **pCurrent**, then the program would fail. (We have not yet considered deleting elements from the list, but when we do, we will also be able to end up with an empty list.) The null value returned will enable you to detect when you have reached the end of a list: you simply check the pointer returned from the **getNextBox()** function.

Although we seem to have assembled all the bits and pieces, we need to create and use our list, and we'll soon discover that there's still a serious problem with the **TruckLoad** class. However, let's throw caution to the wind, try it out in an example, and then come back to the outstanding problem afterwards.

Try It Out – Using a Linked List

We can put together a complete definition for the **Box** class in the header file, **Box.h**:

```
// Box.h - Definition of the Box class
#ifndef BOX_H
#define BOX_H
class Box
{
  public:
    Box(double aLength = 1.0, double aBreadth = 1.0,
                            double aHeight = 1.0);  // Constructor

    double volume() const;                          // Calculate Box volume

    double getLength()  const;
    double getBreadth() const;
    double getHeight()  const;

    int compareVolume(const Box& otherBox) const;   // Compare volumes of boxes

  private:
    double length;
    double breadth;
    double height;
};
#endif
```

We have added functions to access the dimensions of a **Box** object, as we will need them in our example. We will define the constructor and functions in a separate **.cpp** file for this class, **Box.cpp**:

```cpp
// Box.cpp Implementation of the Box class
#include "Box.h"

// Constructor
Box::Box(double aLength, double aBreadth, double aHeight)
{
  length = aLength > 0.0 ? aLength : 1.0;
  breadth = aBreadth > 0.0 ? aBreadth : 1.0;
  height = aHeight > 0.0 ? aHeight : 1.0;
}

// Calculate Box volume
double Box::volume() const{ return length*breadth*height; }

// getXXX() functions
double Box::getLength()  const { return length; }
double Box::getBreadth() const { return breadth; }
double Box::getHeight()  const { return height; }

// Function to compare two Box objects
// If the current Box is greater than the argument, 1 is returned
// If they are equal, 0 is returned
// If the current Box is less than the argument -1 is returned
int Box::compareVolume(const Box& otherBox) const
{
  double vol1 = volume();                  // Get current Box volume
  double vol2 = otherBox.volume();         // Get argument volume
  return vol1>vol2 ? 1 : (vol1<vol2 ? -1 : 0);
}
```

We can put the definitions for the two classes that implement a linked list in the same header file, **List.h**. To be consistent, we'll rearrange the **Package** class definition so that the constructor and functions are defined out-of-line. The file contents will be:

```cpp
// List.h classes supporting a linked list
#ifndef LIST_H
#define LIST_H

#include "Box.h"

// Class defining a list element
class Package
{
  public:
    Package(Box* pNewBox);                    // Constructor
    Box* getBox() const;                      // Retrieve the Box pointer
    Package* getNext() const;                 // Get next package address
    void setNext(Package* pPackage);          // Add package to end of list

  private:
    Box* pBox;                                // Pointer to the Box
    Package* pNext;                           // Pointer to the next
Package
};
```

```
// Class defining a TruckLoad - implements the list
class TruckLoad
{
  public:
    TruckLoad(Box* pBox = 0, int count = 1);    // Constructor

    Box* getFirstBox();                         // Retrieve the first Box
    Box* getNextBox();                          // Retrieve the next Box
    void addBox(Box* pBox);                     // Add a new Box to the list

  private:
    Package* pHead;                             // First in the list
    Package* pTail;                             // Last in the list
    Package* pCurrent;                          // Last retrieved from the list
};
#endif
```

Note that the definition for the **Package** class precedes that of the **TruckLoad** class. If the order were reversed, then the code would not compile, because the **TruckLoad** class refers to the **Package** type.

> *Sometimes, you can find a situation with two classes **A** and **B**, where each class definition contains references to the other class. In such a scenario, class **A** must be declared before class **B** is defined; subsequently, class **A** can also be defined. The declaration of class **A** can be made with the following statement:*
>
> **class A;**
>
> *This tells the compiler that **A** is a class — so it can go ahead and compile class **B**; then the compiler will also know about class **B** so it can compile the definition of class **A**.*

The member function definitions can go in a file with the name **List.cpp**:

```
// List.cpp
#include "Box.h"
#include "List.h"

// Package class definitions
// Package constructor
Package::Package(Box* pNewBox):pBox(pNewBox), pNext(0){}

// Retrieve the Box pointer
Box* Package::getBox() const { return pBox; }

// Get next package address
Package* Package::getNext() const { return pNext; }

// Add package to end of list
void Package::setNext(Package* pPackage) { pNext = pPackage; }


// TruckLoad class member definitions
// TruckLoad constructor
TruckLoad::TruckLoad(Box* pBox, int count)
{
  pHead = pTail = pCurrent = 0;
```

```
    if((count > 0) && (pBox != 0))
      for(int i = 0 ; i<count ; i++)
        addBox(pBox+i);
}

// Retrieve the first Box
Box* TruckLoad::getFirstBox()
{
  pCurrent = pHead;
  return pCurrent->getBox();
}

// Retrieve the next Box
Box* TruckLoad::getNextBox()
{
  if(pCurrent)
    pCurrent = pCurrent->getNext();        // pCurrent is not null so set to next
  else                                     // pCurrent is null
    pCurrent = pHead;                      //  so set to the first list element

  return pCurrent ? pCurrent->getBox() : 0;
}

// Add a new Box to the list
void TruckLoad::addBox(Box* pBox)
{
  Package* pPackage = new Package(pBox);   // Create a Package

  if(pHead)                                // Check list is not empty
    pTail->setNext(pPackage);              // Add the new object to the tail
  else                                     // List is empty
    pHead = pPackage;                      // so new object is the head
  pTail = pPackage;                        // Store its address as tail
}
```

FYI

Member functions declared as const in the class definition must be declared as const
when you define them. The function signature includes const — this means that, if
you forget to specify them as const in the function definitions, the compiler will think
that they are different functions from those that appear in the class definition.

Notice that the file List.h contains a #include directive for the definition of the Box
class. In fact, there are a number of #include directives for header files. In particular,
the file List.cpp contains #include directives for Box.h and List.h. The #ifndef/
#endif preprocessor directives in each header file — which we introduced in Chapter
10 — will prevent any definitions from appearing in a source file more than once. Without
them, the file List.cpp will not compile, because it would #include the definitions
of Box.h twice: once directly, and once indirectly, by #include-ing List.h.

We can define **main()** in the file **Prog13_1.cpp** to create some **Box** objects and organize them
in a linked list. We will generate two lists: one by generating a list containing a single **Box**
object and adding further objects, and the other from an array of **Box** objects. We can use a
version of the **random()** function that we wrote in Chapter 10 to generate **Box** dimensions. To
exercise the lists, we will search each for the largest **Box** object. Here's the code:

509

```cpp
// Program 13.1 Exercising a linked list of Box objects
#include <iostream>
#include <cstdlib>                    // For random number generator
#include <ctime>                      // For time function

using namespace std;

#include "Box.h"
#include "List.h"

// Function to generate a random integer 1 to count
inline int random(int count)
{
  return 1 + static_cast<int>((count*static_cast<long>(rand()))/(RAND_MAX+1));
}

int main()
{
  const int dimLimit = 100;                   // Upper limit on Box dimensions
  srand((unsigned)time(0));                    // Initialize the random number generator

  // Create an empty list
  TruckLoad load1;

  // Add 10 random sized Box objects to the list
  for(int i = 0 ; i < 10 ; i++)
    load1.addBox(new Box(random(dimLimit), random(dimLimit), random(dimLimit)));

  // Find the largest Box in the list
  Box* pBox = load1.getFirstBox();
  Box* pNextBox;
  while(pNextBox = load1.getNextBox()) // Assign and then test pointer to next Box
    if(pBox->compareVolume(*pNextBox) < 0)
      pBox = pNextBox;

  cout << endl
       << "The largest box in the first list is "
       << pBox->getLength() << " by "
       << pBox->getBreadth() << " by "
       << pBox->getHeight() << endl;

  const int boxCount = 20;                    // Number of elements in Box array
  Box boxes[boxCount];                        // Array of Box objects

  for(int i = 0 ; i < boxCount ; i++)
    boxes[i] = Box(random(dimLimit), random(dimLimit), random(dimLimit));

  TruckLoad load2(boxes, boxCount);

  // Find the largest Box in the list
  pBox = load2.getFirstBox();
  while(pNextBox = load2.getNextBox())
    if(pBox->compareVolume(*pNextBox) < 0)
      pBox = pNextBox;

  cout << endl
       << "The largest box in the second list is "
       << pBox->getLength() << " by "
```

```
                    << pBox->getBreadth() << " by "
                    << pBox->getHeight() << endl;

  // Delete the Box objects in the first list
  pNextBox = load1.getFirstBox();
  while(pNextBox)
  {
    delete pNextBox;
    pNextBox = load1.getNextBox();
  }
  return 0;
}
```

When I ran this example, I obtained the output:

The largest box in the first list is 94 by 68 by 55

The largest box in the second list is 80 by 73 by 78

You will almost certainly get something different from this, because of the random numbers generated for the dimensions of the **Box** objects. You will recall (from Chapter 10) that the random number generator is seeded from your computer's clock.

How It Works

The function **main()** creates two lists of **Box** objects. In the absence of any real **Box** object, we'll generate some randomly-sized ones, whose dimensions are pseudo-random integer values between 1 and 100. The random dimensions are generated by the function defined as:

```
inline int random(int count)
{
  return 1 + static_cast<int>((count*static_cast<long>(rand()))/(RAND_MAX+1));
}
```

This calls the standard library function **rand()**, which (as we saw in Chapter 10) produces pseudo-random integers between 0 and **RAND_MAX**. The process is initialized by calling the standard library function **srand()** with a seed value, which is often specified as the current clock time. The value returned by the function **rand()** is scaled to produce values between 0 and 99 and 1 is added so that numbers between 1 and 100 are returned by **random()**. We cast the value returned by **rand()** to **long** to ensure that the multiplication is done with **long** values. Otherwise we could get a value that exceeds the capacity of **int** when **int** is only two bytes.

We use the default version of the constructor for **TruckLoad** to create an empty list:

```
TruckLoad load1;
```

We then use a **for** loop to add ten **Box** objects, with random dimensions, to the list **load1**:

```
for(int i = 0 ; i < 10 ; i++)
  load1.addBox(new Box(random(dimLimit), random(dimLimit), random(dimLimit)));
```

On each loop iteration, we create a **Box** object in the free store, and add it to the list using the **addBox()** function. We don't need to keep track of any of these objects because they are available from the list.

Next, we scan the list to find the **Box** object with the largest volume:

```
Box* pBox = load1.getFirstBox();
Box* pNextBox;
while(pNextBox = load1.getNextBox()) // Assign and then test pointer to next Box
  if(pBox->compareVolume(*pNextBox) < 0)
    pBox = pNextBox;
```

In this part of the program, the pointer **pBox** is used to store the address of the *largest* object. To begin, **pBox** is arbitrarily set to the first object in the list. The **while** loop is controlled by the address returned by the **getNextBox()** function for **load1**. It's important to notice that the **while** loop condition contains an assignment (**=**) rather than the comparison (**==**): hence, the expression tested in the **while** loop is the resulting **pNextBox** *after* the assignment has been made. The comment in the code indicates this — otherwise, it's easy for another programmer to misinterpret the code. When the value of **pNextBox** is zero, this indicates that we have reached the end of the list, and so the loop terminates.

Within the loop, we use the **compareVolume()** function in the **Box** class to compare the volumes of the **Box** pointed to by **pBox** and the **Box** object at the current position in the list, which is pointed to by **pNextBox**. We must use the **->** operator to call **compareVolume()**, since we are calling it through a pointer, **pBox**. The function requires an object as an argument, so we have to de-reference the **pNextBox** pointer. If the return value is negative then the argument is greater than the object pointed to by **pBox**, so we store its address in **pBox** as the new largest object. When the loop ends, **pBox** will contain the address of the **Box** object in the list with the largest volume.

We then display the dimension of this **Box** object, with the statement:

```
cout << endl
     << "The largest box in the first list is "
     << pBox->getLength() << " by "
     << pBox->getBreadth() << " by "
     << pBox->getHeight() << endl;
```

We repeat the same process with a second list, **load2**, which we create from an array of **Box** objects.

Note that the **Box** objects in the first list were created in the free store, whereas the **Box** objects in the array are local objects. We therefore need to delete the **Box** objects in the first list when we are done.

Well, everything seems to work OK, and we get the right answers, so what's wrong with the **TruckLoad** class? In fact, there are three problems that need looking at:

▶ The least significant problem is that the **Package** class is accessible to all, even though we only want to use this class in the context of the **TruckLoad** class.

▶ A somewhat more serious problem (although it's not evident in our particular example) concerns the duplication of a **TruckLoad** object. Suppose we take a **TruckLoad** object **load1**, and create a direct copy of it, **load2**. The result of this is that **load2** is *not* be independent of **load1** — because not only will both lists contain pointers to the same **Box** objects, but they will also contain pointers to the same **Package** objects. If we then deleted **load2**, the objects that belonged to the **load1** list would cease to exist because they would be deleted as a part of **load2**.

▶ The third problem is one of memory management. Look again at how we create **Package** objects in the **TruckLoad** class. They are created in the free store, and yet no provision has been made for deleting them. Every time we add a new **Box** to a list, a new **Package** object will be created that is never deleted, even when the **TruckLoad** object goes out of scope. This is a very serious memory leak that should never be overlooked.

Let's look at how we can deal with each of these problems, starting with the first.

Controlling Access to a Class

The need to limit the accessibility of a class arises quite often in practice. We designed the **Package** class to be used specifically with the **TruckLoad** class, and therefore we should really make sure that **Package** objects can only be created by functions in the **TruckLoad** class. What we really need is a mechanism by which we can declare **Package** objects as public to the **TruckLoad** class but private to the rest of the world. The best way to do this is by using the concept of a nested class.

Nested Classes

A **nested class** is a class that has its definition inside the definition of another class. The name of the nested class is limited to the scope of the enclosing class. We could put the definition of the **Package** class inside the definition of the **TruckLoad** class, like this:

```
class TruckLoad
{
 public:
   TruckLoad(Box* pBox = 0, int count = 1);   // Constructor

   Box* getFirstBox();                        // Retrieve the first Box
   Box* getNextBox();                         // Retrieve the next Box
   void addBox(Box* pBox);                    // Add a new Box to the list

 private:
   // Class defining a list element
   class Package
   {
     public:
       Box* pBox;                             // Pointer to the Box
       Package* pNext;                        // Pointer to the next Package

       void setNext(Package* pPackage);       // Add package to end of list
       Package(Box* pNewBox);                 // Constructor
   };
```

513

```
      Package* pHead;                        // First in the list
      Package* pTail;                        // Last in the list
      Package* pCurrent;                     // Last retrieved from the list
};
```

The **Package** type is now local to the scope of the **TruckLoad** class definition. Because we have put the definition of the **Package** class in the **private** section of the **TruckLoad** class, it is not possible to create **Package** objects from outside the **TruckLoad** class.

Since the **Package** class is entirely private to the **TruckLoad** class, we can make the **Package** members **public**. Hence, they are directly accessible to function members of a **TruckLoad** object, so we can dispense with the **Package** member functions **getBox()** and **getNext()**. All of the **Package** members will be inaccessible outside the class.

We also need to modify the definitions of the member functions of the **TruckLoad** class. The **addBox()** function can add a new object to the end of the list by accessing the **pNext** member of the last object directly:

```
void TruckLoad::addBox(Box* pBox)
{
  Package* pPackage = new Package(pBox);   // Create a Package

  if(pHead)                                // Check list is not empty
    pTail->pNext = pPackage;               // Add the new object to the tail
  else                                     // List is empty
    pHead = pPackage;                      // so new object is the head
  pTail = pPackage;                        // Store its address as tail
}
```

The function to retrieve the first **Box** object no longer requires a function to get at the pointer to the **Box** object, so the definition now becomes:

```
Box* TruckLoad::getFirstBox()
{
  pCurrent = pHead;
  return pCurrent->pBox;
}
```

The function to obtain the address of the next **Box** object in the list can now be defined as:

```
Box* TruckLoad::getNextBox()
{
  if(pCurrent)
    pCurrent = pCurrent->pNext;            // pCurrent is not null so set to next
  else                                     // pCurrent is null
    pCurrent = pHead;                      //  so set to the first list element

  return pCurrent ? pCurrent->pBox : 0;
}
```

> *Nesting the* Package *class inside the* TruckLoad *class simply defines the* Package *type. Objects of type* TruckLoad *aren't affected in any way — they will have exactly the same members as before. Function members of a nested class can directly reference static members of the enclosing class, as well as any other types or enumerators that are defined in the enclosing class. Other members of the enclosing class can only be accessed from the nested class in the normal ways: via a class object, or a pointer or a reference to a class object.*

Nested Classes with public Access Specifiers

Let's briefly mention what would happen if we put the **Package** class definition in the **public** section of the **TruckLoad** class. Then, the program *would* be possible to create **Package** objects externally, as long as you qualified the class name. For example:

```
TruckLoad::Package aPackage(aBox);       // Define a variable of type Package
```

Of course, making the type **Package** public would rather defeat our reason for making it a nested class in the first place!

Friend Classes

It's also possible to limit the accessibility of a class by using **friend** classes. In this case, we would declare all the data members of the **Package** class as **private**, and also declare the class to be a friend of the **TruckLoad** class, by including the following statement in the **Package** class definition:

```
friend class TruckLoad;
```

This ensures that all the members of **Package** objects are available to the **TruckLoad** class, and makes them inaccessible otherwise.

> **FYI**
>
> In subsequent examples in this chapter, however, we shall employ the concept of nested classes. It reinforces the idea that Package class is not an independent entity, and only has a role in the context of TruckLoad objects.

The Importance of the Copy Constructor

A copy constructor is used to create a brand new object that's identical to an existing object. We mentioned in the context of Program 12.5 that the compiler supplies a default copy constructor when necessary, if you don't include one in the class definition. The default copy constructor works by copying the values of the data members of the original object into the corresponding data members of the newly-created object.

This can cause problems in some circumstances, and certainly does so in the case of the **TruckLoad** class. Suppose that we want to duplicate a **TruckLoad** object — say, if we were to repeat the same delivery schedule on two different days. When you duplicate a **TruckLoad** class object, the default copy constructor simply copies the addresses stored in the data members **pHead**, **pTail** and **pCurrent** to the new object, so that both **TruckLoad** objects share the same chain of **Package** objects.

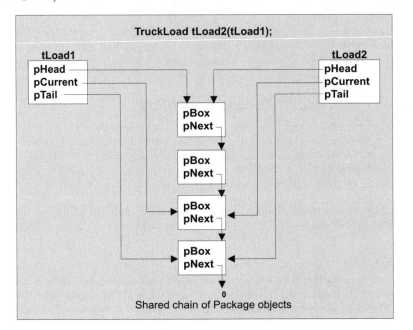

We don't really have two lists here at all, but just one. However, we do have two different ways to access the list, and this is where the danger lies. A modification to the list using **tLoad1**, say, will affect the chain of **Package** objects, but this change will not be reflected in the data members of **tLoad2**. In particular, if you add to the list **tLoad1**, then the **pTail** member of **tLoad2** will point to a **Package** object which is no longer the last in the list.

In fact, there is a further subtlety. We are likely to experience similar problems if we create a function that takes a **TruckLoad** argument. Remember that the copy constructor is called when a function receives an argument via the pass-by-value mechanism. Therefore, the function call would use the **TruckLoad** copy constructor to create a duplicate of the original **TruckLoad** object — then the function only needs to add an object to the list to invalidate the original **TruckLoad** object.

Implementing the Copy Constructor

The copy constructor for an object must accept an argument of the same class type, and create a duplicate in an appropriate manner. There is an immediate problem that we must overcome, and we can see it clearly if we try to write the copy constructor for the **TruckLoad** class as follows:

```
TruckLoad::TruckLoad(TruckLoad Load)
{
  // Code to create a duplicate of the object Load
}
```

This looks OK at first sight, but consider what happens when the constructor is called. The argument is passed *by value*, so the compiler will arrange to call the copy constructor to make a copy of the argument. Of course, the argument to the copy constructor is passed by value, so another call to the copy constructor is required; and so on. In short, we have set up a recursive call to the copy constructor.

In fact, your compiler will not allow this code to compile. The solution is to specify the parameter as a reference.

Reference Parameters

The copy constructor should be defined, with a **const** reference parameter, as:

```
TruckLoad::TruckLoad(const TruckLoad& Load)
{
  // Code to create a duplicate of the object Load
}
```

Now the argument is no longer passed by value, so the recursive calls to the copy constructor are avoided. Instead, the compiler simply initializes the parameter with the object that is passed to it by reference. The parameter should be **const**, because a copy constructor is only in the business of creating duplicates — it should not modify the original. You can conclude from this that the parameter type for a copy constructor is *always* a **const** reference to an object of the same class. In other words, the form of the copy constructor is the same for any class:

```
Type::Type(const   Type&  object)
{
   // Code  to  produce  a  duplicate  of  object
}
```

In this general form of the copy constructor, **Type** is the class type name.

So, how would the copy constructor for our **TruckLoad** class be implemented? We must create a chain of duplicate **Package** objects for the new **TruckLoad** object that we are creating. You could do this with the following code for the **TruckLoad** class that has the **Package** class nested within it:

```
TruckLoad::TruckLoad(const TruckLoad& load)
{
  pHead = pTail = pCurrent = 0;
  if(load.pHead == 0)
    return;

  Package* pTemp = load.pHead;           // Saves addresses for new chain
  do
  {
    addBox(pTemp->pBox);
  }while(pTemp = pTemp->pNext);          // Assign and then test pointer to next Box

}
```

The process is to create a copy of the first **Package** by calling its copy constructor, and then to copy each of the subsequent **Package** objects, but updating the **pNext** pointer in each duplicate **Package** object with the address of the next object in the new chain.

As it stands, the **Package** objects of the original and duplicate lists still point to the same **Box** objects. In order to create a completely *independent* duplicate **TruckLoad** object, whose **Package** objects point to their own **Box** objects, we would also have to implement our own copy constructor for the **Package** class. For our purposes, we will simply implement the **TruckLoad** copy constructor, to see that working.

Let's see if our version works for real.

Try It Out – Using a Copy Constructor

We will need the files **Box.h** and **Box.cpp** just as in Program 13.1. We'll use the nested **TruckLoad/Package** class discussed above, and add the copy constructor, so that **List.h** will contain the following class definition:

```
class TruckLoad
{
  public:
    TruckLoad(Box* pBox = 0, int count = 1);     // Constructor
    TruckLoad(const TruckLoad& load);            // Copy constructor

    Box* getFirstBox();                          // Retrieve the first Box
    Box* getNextBox();                           // Retrieve the next Box
    void addBox(Box* pBox);                      // Add a new Box to the list

  private:
    // Class defining a list element
    class Package
    {
      public:
        Box* pBox;                               // Pointer to the Box
        Package* pNext;                          // Pointer to the next Package

        void setNext(Package* pPackage);         // Add package to end of list
        Package(Box* pNewBox);                   // Constructor
    };

    Package* pHead;                              // First in the list
    Package* pTail;                              // Last in the list
    Package* pCurrent;                           // Last retrieved from the list
};
```

The prototype for the **TruckLoad** copy constructor has been added here, as a **public** member of the class. The file **List.cpp** must be updated to contain its definition; we must also update the definitions of the **TruckLoad** member functions **addBox()**, **getFirstBox()** and **getNextBox()**, and remove the definitions of **Package** member functions **getBox()** and **getNext()**. The final amendment to **List.cpp** is to update the qualifications of the other **Package** member definitions:

```
// Package constructor
TruckLoad::Package::Package(Box* pNewBox):pBox(pNewBox), pNext(0){}

// Add package to end of list
void TruckLoad::Package::setNext(Package* pPackage) { pNext = pPackage; }
```

We'll create a **TruckLoad** object with just three box objects this time. We can use the copy constructor to copy the existing **TruckLoad** object, and then extend it. Because we will find the **Box** object with the largest volume from several lists, we can hive off the code to do that into a separate function. Here's the code:

```cpp
// Program 13.2 Exercising the copy constructor
#include <iostream>
#include <cstdlib>                   // For random number generator
#include <ctime>                     // For time function

using namespace std;

#include "Box.h"
#include "List.h"

// Function to generate a random integer 1 to count
inline int random(int count)
{
  return 1 + static_cast<int>((count*static_cast<long>(rand()))/(RAND_MAX+1));
}

// Find the Box in the list with the largest volume
Box* maxBox(TruckLoad& Load)
{
  Box* pBox = Load.getFirstBox();
  Box* pNextBox;
  while(pNextBox = Load.getNextBox())  // Assign and then test pointer to next Box
    if(pBox->compareVolume(*pNextBox) < 0)
      pBox = pNextBox;
  return pBox;
}

int main()
{
  const int dimLimit = 100;                 // Upper limit on Box dimensions
  srand((unsigned)time(0));                 // Initialize the random number generator

  // Create a list
  TruckLoad load1;

  // Add 3 Boxes to the list
  for(int i = 0 ; i < 3 ; i++)
    load1.addBox(new Box(random(dimLimit), random(dimLimit), random(dimLimit)));

  Box* pBox = maxBox(load1);                 // Find the largest Box in the first list

  cout << endl
      << "The largest box in the first list is "
      << pBox->getLength()  << " by "
      << pBox->getBreadth() << " by "
      << pBox->getHeight()  << endl;

  TruckLoad load2(load1);                     // Create a copy of the first list

  pBox = maxBox(load2);                       // Find the largest Box in the second list
```

```
              cout << endl                        // Display it
                   << "The largest box in the second list is "
                   << pBox->getLength()  << " by "
                   << pBox->getBreadth() << " by "
                   << pBox->getHeight()  << endl;

              // Add 5 more boxes to the second list
              for(int i = 0; i<5; i++)
                load2.addBox(new Box(random(dimLimit), random(dimLimit), random(dimLimit)));

              pBox = maxBox(load2);                // Find the largest Box in the extended list

              cout << endl                        // Display it
                   << "The largest box in the extended second list is "
                   << pBox->getLength()  << " by "
                   << pBox->getBreadth() << " by "
                   << pBox->getHeight()  << endl;

              // Count the number of boxes in the first list and display the count
              Box* pNextBox = load1.getFirstBox();
              int count = 0;                       // Box count
              while(pNextBox)                      // While there is a box
              {
                count++;                           // Increment the count
                pNextBox = load1.getNextBox();     // and get the next box
              }
              cout << endl << "First list still contains " << count << " Box objects."<< endl;

              // Delete the Box objects in the free store
              pNextBox = load2.getFirstBox();
              while(pNextBox)
              {
                delete pNextBox;
                pNextBox = load2.getNextBox();
              }
              return 0;
            }
```

When I ran this it produced the output:

```
The largest box in the first list is 44 by 92 by 87

The largest box in the second list is 44 by 92 by 87

The largest box in the extended second list is 55 by 83 by 85

First list still contains 3 Box objects.
```

You will certainly get something different, and you may have to run the example a few times to get the largest box in the extended list to be different from that in the first list.

How It Works

Our new function, **maxBox()**, accepts a **TruckLoad** object as its parameter. It returns a pointer, which points to the **Box** object in this truckload that has the greatest volume. The code for this function is taken from the body of the **main()** function of Program 13.1. Note that the parameter is a reference, and so we don't incur the overhead of copying what might be a substantial list.

To demonstrate that the **TruckLoad** class copy constructor works as it should, we first create an empty **TruckLoad** object, **load1**:

```
TruckLoad load1;
```

Then, as we did in Program 13.1, we add **Box** objects to the list. Each **Box** object is created in the free store:

```
for(int i = 0 ; i < 3 ; i++)
  load1.addBox(new Box(random(dimLimit), random(dimLimit), random(dimLimit)));
```

For checking purposes, we obtain the most voluminous **Box** object in the list by calling the **maxBox()** function:

```
Box* pBox = maxBox(load1);                 // Find the largest Box in the first list
```

After displaying the dimensions of this **Box** object, we create a copy of **load1** using the **TruckLoad** class copy constructor:

```
TruckLoad load2(load1);                    // Create a copy of the first list
```

As an indication that **load2** is the same as the original, we use **maxBox()** again to obtain the largest **Box** object contained in **load2**, and we display its dimensions. We then add a further five **Box** objects to the list **load2**:

```
for(int i = 0; i<5; i++)
  load2.addBox(new Box(random(dimLimit), random(dimLimit), random(dimLimit)));
```

Next, we use the **maxBox()** function again with **load2**, to find the largest of all eight boxes in the list; and we display its dimensions.

The crucial part is that **load1** has not been modified, and to demonstrate this we count the number of **Box** objects contained in **load1**:

```
Box* pNextBox = load1.getFirstBox();
int count = 0;                             // Box count
while(pNextBox)                            // While there is a box
{
  count++;                                 // Increment the count
  pNextBox = load1.getNextBox();           // and get the next box
}
```

The loop is controlled by the pointer **pNextBox**. To begin, it contains the address of the first **Box** object; as long as **pNext** doesn't point past the end of the list (that is, as long as **pNext** is not null) then we increment **count** and move **pNext** along the list. When we get to the end of the list, **getNextBox()** will return null, so the loop will end.

Finally, after displaying the value of **count**, we delete all the **Box** objects in **load2** from the free store. Of course, this will include the objects contained in **load1** so we don't have to worry further about them.

Our **TruckLoad** *class is put together on the assumption that the user takes responsibility for the* **Box** *objects stored. They can be created in the free store, as we have done in the example, or they could be automatic objects — our class will work just as well. Giving the user responsibility for* **Box** *objects means that he has the power to invalidate a* **TruckLoad** *object by deleting a* **Box** *object from the free store. One way to do this would be to duplicate and then delete a* **TruckLoad** *object. You can prevent the user doing this, quite simply, by declaring the* **TruckLoad** *copy constructor as a* **private** *member of the class — this prevents its use outside the class and inhibits the compiler from generating a default version. Since it could not be used in that case, there would be no need to provide a definition for it.*

Dynamic Memory Allocation within an Object

Let's move on to the third of the problems with the **TruckLoad** class that we identified earlier. It's another serious problem — a memory leak — and it arises because the **TruckLoad** class constructors (including the copy constructor) and the **addBox()** function allocate memory dynamically.

We need a means of releasing this memory when a **TruckLoad** object is destroyed. In fact, there *is* another class member, which we haven't met so far — it's called a **destructor**. When a **TruckLoad** object is destroyed, the compiler calls the class destructor in to do the job. We can define our own destructor for the **TruckLoad** class; if we don't then the compiler supplies a default destructor.

What is a Destructor?

A class destructor is a special kind of class member, that destroys an object when it goes out of scope or (for an object that was created dynamically) when it is deleted from the free store. The destructor for an object is called automatically whenever the object should be destroyed. It is almost never necessary to call a destructor explicitly, but it is often necessary to define one.

Destroying Objects

Destroying an object involves freeing the memory occupied by the non-static data members of the object. Static members, of course, continue to exist even when there are no class objects in existence, so they are not affected. For data members that occupy memory allocated statically, the destructor takes care of things automatically and you don't need to worry about them.

Members that are declared dynamically are allocated memory in the free store. Since your code allocated the memory, your code is responsible for freeing it. When you delete such an object, you must release the free store memory *at the same time* — otherwise, the address of the memory occupied will be lost. There's no way to release the memory subsequently. If you repeatedly fail to release free store memory (in a loop for instance) and you succeed in filling the free store, then your program will fail.

Of course, the memory will always be reclaimed by the operating system when your program finishes executing, but that's not much help to your program.

The Destructor

Whenever a class object is destroyed, the compiler calls the class's destructor. The class destructor always has the same form. It is a **public** member function with the same name as the class, preceded by a tilde ~. The class destructor does not have any parameters, and it does not return a value. While a class can have several constructors, it can only ever have one destructor. For the **TruckLoad** class, the class destructor would be defined like this:

```
TruckLoad::~TruckLoad()
{
  // Code to destroy the object
}
```

It's an error to specify a return type or parameters for a destructor.

The Default Destructor

Just like the default constructor, the compiler generates the default destructor in the absence of any explicit destructor being provided with a class. If you don't define a destructor for a class, the compiler will always supply one that is **public** and **inline**.

Each of the objects that we have used up to now has caused its default destructor to be called when it was explicitly deleted from the free store, or (if it was an automatic variable) when it went out of scope. We can see this happening by adding an explicit destructor to each of the classes in the previous example.

Try It Out – The Destructor in Action

We can modify Program 13.2 by adding a definition of a destructor to each of the classes. You need to amend the **Box** class definition by adding the following destructor definition to the file **Box.cpp**:

```
// Box destructor
Box::~Box()
{
  cout << "Box destructor called." << endl;
}
```

You also need to add the destructor prototype to the **public** section of the **Box** class definition, in **Box.h**:

```
class Box
{
  public:
    // Box destructor
    ~Box();

    // Rest of the class as before....
};
```

In a similar way, add destructor definitions for the **Package** and **TruckLoad** classes to **List.cpp**:

```
// TruckLoad destructor
TruckLoad::~TruckLoad()
{
  cout << "TruckLoad destructor called." << endl;
}

// Package destructor
TruckLoad::Package::~Package()
{
  cout << "Package destructor called." << endl;
}
```

and we need to add the prototypes to the class definition in the **List.h** header file:

```
class TruckLoad
{
  public:
    // TruckLoad destructor
    ~TruckLoad();

    // other TruckLoad public member declarations

  private:
    class Package
    {
      public:
        // Destructor
        ~Package();

        // Rest of Package class definition...
    };

    // Rest of TruckLoad class definition...
};
```

For each **.cpp** file, you'll also need to **#include** the standard header file **iostream**, and add a **using** declaration for the namespace **std**.

Try It Out – Tracing the Destructor

We'll use much the same **main()** function that we used in Program 13.2.

```
// Program 13.3 Exercising the destructor

// Code as Program 13.2 ...
```

If you compile and run this example, you'll get a trace of all the destructor calls that occur during program execution.

How It Works

Let's go through the output to see what is happening in the program. You may find some of what is going on surprising. The first part of the output is something like:

```
The largest box in the first list is 52 by 83 by 93

The largest box in the second list is 52 by 83 by 93

The largest box in the extended second list is 52 by 83 by 93

First list still contains 3 Box objects.
```

There's nothing surprising so far. Next, we have a record of eight **Box** destructor calls, followed by two **TruckLoad** destructors call:

```
Box destructor called.
Box destructor called.
Box destructor called.
Box destructor called.
Box destructor called.
Box destructor called.
Box destructor called.
Box destructor called.
TruckLoad destructor called.
TruckLoad destructor called.
```

The eight **Box** destructor calls occur because we explicitly delete the **Box** objects that we allocated in the free store for the first list, **load1**:

```
pNextBox = load2.getFirstBox();
while(pNextBox)
{
  delete pNextBox;
  pNextBox = load2.getNextBox();
}
```

Without this code, the memory would not be released until after the program was terminated. When **return** is executed in **main()**, the two **TruckLoad** objects go out of scope, which causes the **TruckLoad** class destructor calls above.

Notice that there are no **Package** destructor calls. This means that all those **Package** objects were created, but never deleted. The memory for all the **Package** objects was allocated dynamically, so it is our responsibility to delete these objects. Since we did not, their destructors are never called. This is a serious defect; let's fix it now.

Implementing a Destructor

The responsibility for deleting the **Package** objects should lie with the object that created them. Since **Package** objects are created by **TruckLoad** objects, we need to address the problem by implementing a suitable destructor for the **TruckLoad** class. A **TruckLoad** object will need to delete each **Package** object in its list when it is destroyed. We can implement this within the **TruckLoad** class destructor. Replace the destructor definition in the **List.cpp** file with the following:

```
TruckLoad::~TruckLoad()
{
   cout << "TruckLoad destructor called." << endl;
   while(pCurrent = pHead->pNext)
   {
     delete pHead;                        // Delete the previous
     pHead = pCurrent;                    // Store address of next
   }
     delete pHead;                        // Delete the last
}
```

If you run the example with this version of the **TruckLoad** destructor, you will get the following output:

```
The largest box in the first list is 98 by 79 by 78

The largest box in the second list is 93 by 68 by 99

The largest box in the extended second list is 89 by 98 by 78

First list still contains 3 Box objects.
Box destructor called.
Box destructor called.
Box destructor called.
Box destructor called.
Box destructor called.
Box destructor called.
Box destructor called.
Box destructor called.
TruckLoad destructor called.
Package destructor called.
Package destructor called.
Package destructor called.
Package destructor called.
Package destructor called.
Package destructor called.
Package destructor called.
Package destructor called.
TruckLoad destructor called.
Package destructor called.
Package destructor called.
Package destructor called.
```

After each **TruckLoad** destructor call, we now call the **Package** destructor the appropriate number of times: once for each **Package** object that was created. This is due entirely to the code that we have just added to the destructor for the **TruckLoad** class. Since there were three objects in the first list and eight in the second, it is clear from the output that the **TruckLoad** objects are being destroyed in the reverse order from which they were created.

Out of all this comes a golden rule:

> *If you allocate memory dynamically within an object, you must implement a destructor for the class.*

References in Classes

We have seen how being able to use a reference as a function parameter type is fundamental to writing a copy constructor – it's the only way it can be done. There will be lots of other situations where using a reference parameter is highly advantageous, because it avoids the copying that is implicit in the pass-by-value mechanism. In the next chapter, we will see that returning a reference from a member function can be important too.

Another possibility is that you can use a reference as a data member of a class. This does not come up very often, but we need to take a closer look at this, since references require special consideration in this context.

References as Members of a Class

To demonstrate how to declare a data member as a reference, we can use a reference to a **Box** object (instead of a 'pointer to **Box**') as a data member of the **Package** class. The basic definition of the amended **Package** class within the **TruckLoad** class will be:

```
class Package
{
    public:
        Box& rBox;                              // Reference to the Box
        Package* pNext;                         // Pointer to the next Package

        ~Package();                             // Destructor

        void setNext(Package* pPackage);        // Add package to end of list
        Package(Box& rNewBox);                  // Constructor
};
```

The definition of the constructor, in **List.cpp**, should be changed to:

```
TruckLoad::Package::Package(Box& rNewBox):rBox(rNewBox), pNext(0){}
```

We know that you should always initialize ordinary data members in the initializer list where you can, as it's more efficient; but with reference data members, you do not have a choice. A reference is an alias for another name, so you cannot initialize it in an assignment within a constructor — you must use the initializer list.

Let's consider how storing a reference to a **Box** object affects the function members of the **TruckLoad** class. We'll look at the **addBox()** member first. We can change the parameter to a reference, and pass the reference to the **Package** class constructor:

```
void TruckLoad::addBox(Box& rBox)
{
    Package* pPackage = new Package(rBox);    // Create a Package

    if(pHead)                                 // Check list is not empty
        pTail->pNext = pPackage;              // Add the new object to the tail
    else                                      // List is empty
        pHead = pPackage;                     // so new object is the head
    pTail = pPackage;                         // Store its address as tail
}
```

The function prototype should also be adjusted appropriately. This will change the way that the **addBox()** function is used. It now requires an object as an argument, not a pointer — a disadvantage of this is that there is no clue in the function call that the argument is passed by reference. You must also change the parameter for declaration of this function in the definition of the **TruckLoad** class.

We will still want the possibility of passing an array to the **TruckLoad** class constructor so we could leave the parameter list as it is, but we must now pass the array to the **addBox()** function as a reference:

```
TruckLoad::TruckLoad(Box* pBox, int count)
{
  pHead = pTail = pCurrent = 0;

  if((count > 0) && (pBox != 0))
    for(int i = 0 ; i<count ; i++)
      addBox(*(pBox+i));
}
```

The only change is to de-reference the pointer **pBox+i**, so that we pass an object to **addBox()** rather than an address.

The copy constructor calls the **addBox()** member, so we must change the definition of that, too;

```
TruckLoad::TruckLoad(const TruckLoad& load)
{
  pHead = pTail = pCurrent = 0;
  if(load.pHead == 0)
    return;

  Package* pTemp = load.pHead;         // Saves addresses for new chain
  do
  {
    addBox(pTemp->rBox);
  }while(pTemp = pTemp->pNext);        // Assign and then test pointer to next Box

}
```

The **getFirstBox()** and **getNextBox()** currently return pointers: should we change these so that they return a reference? The answer is determined from how we use the return value. We access successive **Box** objects in a list by successive calls to the **getNextBox()** function in the **TruckLoad** class, and we detect the end of a list by a null return value. We can't do this with a reference return type, since there is no such thing as a null reference. Therefore, we shuld ensure that these functions continue to return a 'pointer to **Box**'.

The following adjustment to the definition of **getFirstBox()** must be made:

```
Box* TruckLoad::getFirstBox()
{
  pCurrent = pHead;
  return &pCurrent->rBox;
}
```

We just return the address of the reference to the **Box** object in the **Package** object. We don't need parentheses in the expression that does this, because the **->** operator is of higher precedence than the address-of operator.

The definition of **getNextBox()** should be changed to:

```
Box* TruckLoad::getNextBox()
{
  if(pCurrent)
    pCurrent = pCurrent->pNext;          // pCurrent is not null so set to next
  else                                   // pCurrent is null
    pCurrent = pHead;                    //  so set to the first list element

  return pCurrent ? &pCurrent->rBox : 0;
}
```

The constructor for the **TruckLoad** class is unaffected so that completes all the changes necessary to use a reference in the **Package** class.

If you want to run the last version of **main()** with this version of the classes, you must alter the argument passed to **addBox()** in **main()** to an object — you just need to de-reference the address returned by the operator new in both instances. The first of these statements will become:

```
loadl.addBox(*(new Box(random(dimLimit), random(dimLimit), random(dimLimit))));
```

> *Also, don't forget that we've changed the function signature for the **addBox()** function, so you'll need to reflect that change in the function prototype!*

This has demonstrated some of the implications of using reference as a class member, but it does not improve the classes. The solution using pointers is preferable. When using references to dynamic objects, there is always a risk that the object may be deleted; so the reference becomes an alias for a non-existent object.

Summary

In this chapter, you have learned about the basic set of parts that you can put together in implementing your own classes. What you need to implement in a particular class is down to you. You need to decide the nature and scope of the facilities that each of your classes should provide. Always keep in mind that you are defining a data type — a coherent entity — and your class needs to reflect its nature and characteristics.

The important points we have seen in this chapter include:

▶ You can only initialize class members that are references through the constructor's initializer list. A reference cannot be initialized with an assignment statement.

▶ A copy constructor is called whenever you pass an object by value to a function. The consequence of this is that the parameter to the copy constructor for a class must be a reference.

▶ If you allocate memory dynamically within a member function of a class, always implement a destructor to release memory, a copy constructor, and the copy assignment operator.

▶ You can limit access to a class by declaring all its members as **private**. Then, only **friend** classes can create objects of the class type.

▶ A nested class is a class that has its definition inside that of another class. The nested class name is within the scope of the enclosing class. To refer to the nested class type from outside the enclosing class, the type name must be qualified by the name of the enclosing class.

▶ If a nested class definition is placed in the **private** section of the enclosing class, objects of the nested class type cannot be created outside the enclosing class.

Exercises

Ex 13.1 Although the standard library includes a **string** class, creating your own provides a very good introduction to the issues involved in designing and writing a 'real' C++ class. You can write one using the basic **char** data type, and you'll see as you progress how it's possible to hide much of the complexity involved in using C-style strings.

Create a header file for a **mystring** class, putting it into its own namespace. Give the class two private data members: an integer length, and a **char*** that will point to the string that the object is managing. Why is it useful to store the length as a data member of the class?

Ex 13.2 Create an implementation (**.cpp**) file for your class, and provide constructors so that **mystring** objects can be constructed from the following data types:

▶ A string literal (e.g. **const char***), so that you can write **mystring s1("hello")**.

▶ A single character repeated a number of times. The default repeat value should be one. An example of using this constructor would be **mystring s2('c', 5)**.

▶ An integer value, so that **mystring s3(10)** would store the string **"10"**. (Hint: use the **_itoa()** function from the **<cstdlib>** header file.) As an optional extra, you could add a second argument that specifies the number base to be used for conversion.

Do you think that these constructors ought to be **explicit** or not? Make sure that the constructors provide error handling wherever necessary.

Ex 13.3 The constructors will allocate memory to hold the string; provide a destructor so that the memory is properly released when the object is destroyed.

Ex 13.4 Write a copy constructor for the class, so that your **mystring** objects can be created and initialized from other strings.

Ex 13.5 Add some member functions to the class that:

▶ Return the length of the string
▶ Print the string
▶ Find the zero-based position of a character or substring within the string, returning –1 if it isn't found

Now you can write a test program to create and manipulate **mystring** objects in various ways. Satisfy yourself that everything works the way it should.

14

Operator Overloading

In this chapter, we will be exploring how you can add functionality to your classes, so that they behave more like C++'s basic data types.

We have already seen how our classes can have member functions that operate on the data members of an object — we can think of this as the member function 'operating on the objects that it is applied to' — but we can do much more than that. With operator overloading, you can arrange for the basic operators of C++ to operate in a well-defined way on your class objects.

In this chapter you will learn:

- ▶ What C++ operators you can implement for your own data types
- ▶ How to implement functions in your classes that overload operators
- ▶ How to implement operator functions as class members and as ordinary functions
- ▶ When you must implement the assignment operator
- ▶ How to define type conversions as operator functions
- ▶ What smart pointers are

Implementing Operators for your Classes

Our **Box** class was designed so that it could be applied in an application that is primarily concerned with the volume of a box. For such an application, it would be fundamental to be able to compare box volumes. In Chapter 12, we implemented the **compareVolume()** function in the **Box** class for comparing the volume of two objects, but wouldn't it be nice if you could write:

```
if(Box1 < Box2)
   // Do something...
```

instead of that rather clumsy-looking call:

```
if(Box1.compareVolume(Box2) < 0)
   // Do something...
```

You might also like to add the volumes of two **Box** objects with an expression such as **Box1 + Box2**, or even select the third **Box** in a list of **Box** objects with an expression like **load1[2]**. Well, it's quite possible to do all of this and more — all you have to do is write the code to implement what you want. The facility for doing this in C++ is called **operator overloading**.

Operator Overloading

Operator overloading enables you to apply standard operators (such as **+, -, *, <** and so on) to objects of your own data types. To do this, you write a function that redefines a particular operator so that it performs a particular action every time it is applied to objects of your class.

For example, in order to determine how the **<** operator should work with **Box** objects, you could write a member function in the **Box** class that defines the operator's behavior. In our case, we're interested in the volume of a **Box** object — so we could define the function to return **true** if the volume of the first **Box** object is smaller than that of the second. The name of such a function in this case would be **operator<()**.

> **FYI**
>
> In general, the name of a function that overloads a given operator is composed of the keyword operator, followed by the operator that you are overloading. In the case of operators that use alphabetic characters, such as new and delete, there must be at least one space between the keyword and the operator itself. For other operators, the space is optional.

Operators that can be Overloaded

Operator overloading doesn't allow you to invent new operators. Also, you can't change the precedence of an operator or the number of operands, so your overloaded version of an operator will have the same priority in the sequence of evaluating an expression as the original base operator. You can find a table showing the precedence of all the operators in Appendix D.

Although you can't overload all the operators, the restrictions aren't particularly oppressive. These are the operators that you *can't* overload:

The scope resolution operator	**::**
The conditional operator	**?:**
The direct member access operator	**.**
The de-reference pointer to class member operator	**.***
The **sizeof** operator	**sizeof**

We haven't met the pointer to class member operator yet, but we will — in Chapter 16.

Also, you cannot overload the pre-processor directive symbol **#**, or the token pasting symbol **##**. Anything else is fair game, which gives you quite a bit of scope. As we will see, a function that overloads an operator for a particular class does not necessarily have to be a member of the class — it can be an ordinary function. We will look at examples of both.

> *Obviously, it's a good idea to ensure that your version of a standard operator is reasonably consistent with its normal usage, or at least reasonably intuitive in its meaning and operation in the context of your class. It wouldn't be a very sensible approach to produce an overloaded + operator for a class that performed the equivalent of a multiply on class objects.*

The best way to understand how operator overloading works is to step through an example, so let's implement what we just referred to: the less-than operator, **<**, for the **Box** class.

Implementing an Overloaded Operator

To overload an operator for a class, we just have to write an operator function. A binary operator implemented as a member of a class has one parameter, which I'll explain in a moment, and we can add the following prototype for the function to overload the **<** operator to the **Box** class definition:

```
class Box
{
  public:
    bool operator<(const Box& aBox) const;        // Overloaded 'less-than' operator

    // The rest of the Box class
};
```

Since we are implementing a comparison here, the return type is **bool**. Our operator function **operator<()** will be called as a result of comparing two **Box** objects using **<**. The parameter is the right operand of the **<** operator, and the left operand will correspond to the **this** pointer. Since the function does not change either operand, we have specified the parameter and the function as **const**.

To see how this works, suppose we have the following **if** statement:

```
if(box1 < box2)
  cout << "box1 is less than box2" << endl;
```

The test expression, between parentheses, will result in our operator function being called. It is equivalent to the function call **box1.operator<(box2)**. Indeed, if you were so inclined, you could write it like this in the **if** statement:

```
if(box1.operator<(box2))
    cout << "box1 is less than box2" << endl;
```

You can see that using the **operator<** function will make the code much more readable.

Now we know how the operands in the expression **box1 < box2** map to the function call, we can implement the overloaded operator quite easily. The definition of the member function to overload the **<** operator is shown in the diagram on the next page.

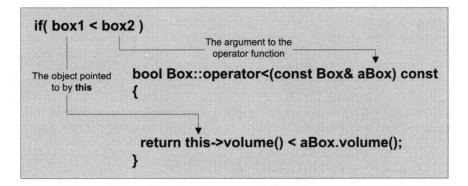

We use a reference parameter to the function to avoid unnecessary copying of the argument when the function is called. The **return** expression uses the member function **volume()** to calculate the volume of the **Box** object pointed to by **this**, and compares the result (using the basic < operator) with the volume of the **aBox** object. Thus, the Boolean value **true** is returned if the **Box** object pointed to by the **this** pointer has a smaller volume than the **aBox** object passed as a reference argument — and **false** is returned otherwise.

FYI   Here, the this pointer is used just to show the association with the first operand. It is not necessary to use this explicitly.

Try It Out – Using an Overloaded < Operator

We can exercise the overloaded less-than operator for **Box** objects with an example. The definition of the **Box** class will be contained in the header file **Box.h**, and will include the definition of the overloaded operator function **operator<()**:

```
// Box.h - Definition of the Box class
#ifndef BOX_H
#define BOX_H

class Box
{
  public:
    // Constructor
    Box(double aLength = 1.0, double aBreadth = 1.0, double aHeight = 1.0);

    double volume() const;                    // Calculate Box volume

    double getLength()  const;
    double getBreadth() const;
    double getHeight()  const;

    bool operator<(const Box& aBox) const     // Overloaded 'less-than' operator
    {                                          // Defined inline
      return volume() < aBox.volume();
    }
```

```
  private:
    double length;
    double breadth;
    double height;
};
#endif
```

Notice that we've defined the overloaded operator as an inline function, as it will be more efficient if it is compiled as such. We've also got prototypes for the other members of the **Box** class. The definitions are contained in **Box.cpp** as follows:

```
// Box.cpp
#include "Box.h"

// Box constructor
Box::Box(double aLength, double aBreadth, double aHeight):
      length(aLength), breadth(aBreadth), height(aHeight) {}

// Calculate Box volume
double Box::volume() const
{
  return length * breadth * height;
}


// getXXX() functions
double Box::getLength()  const { return length; }
double Box::getBreadth() const { return breadth; }
double Box::getHeight()  const { return height; }
```

Overloading comparison operators will make the **compareVolume()** member superfluous, so we can dispense with it.

We will exercise the overloaded **<** operator by finding the largest element in an array of **Box** objects. Here's the code to do that:

```
// Program 14.1 Exercising the overloaded 'less-than' operator
#include <iostream>
#include <cstdlib>                // For random number generator
#include <ctime>                  // For time function
using namespace std;

#include "Box.h"

// Function to generate random integers from 1 to count
inline int random(int count)
{
  return 1 + static_cast<int>((count*static_cast<long>(rand()))/(RAND_MAX+1));
}

int main()
{
  const int dimLimit = 100;        // Upper limit on Box dimensions
  srand((unsigned)time(0));        // Initialize the random number generator

  const int boxCount = 20;         // Number of elements in Box array
  Box boxes[boxCount];             // Array of Box objects
```

```
        for(int i = 0 ; i < boxCount ; i++)
          boxes[i] = Box(random(dimLimit), random(dimLimit), random(dimLimit));

        // Find the largest Box object in the array
        Box* pLargest = &boxes[0];

        for(int i = 1 ; i < boxCount ; i++)
          if(*pLargest < boxes[i])
            pLargest = &boxes[i];

        cout << endl
             << "The box with the largest volume has dimensions: "
             << pLargest->getLength()  << " by "
             << pLargest->getBreadth() << " by "
             << pLargest->getHeight()  << endl;
        return 0;
      }
```

When I ran this example, it produced the output:

```
The box with the largest volume has dimensions: 76 by 92 by 90
```

Random numbers being what they are, you will most probably get a different result.

How It Works

The function **main()** first creates an array of **Box** objects. We arbitrarily assume that the first array element is the largest, and store its address with the statement:

```
Box* pLargest = &boxes[0];
```

We then compare the **Box** object at the address contained in the pointer **pLargest** with each of the succeeding array elements:

```
for(int i = 1 ; i < boxCount ; i++)
  if(*pLargest < boxes[i])
    pLargest = &boxes[i];
```

The comparison in the **if** will result in our **operator<()** function being called. The argument to the function will be **boxes[i]**, and the **this** pointer will point to the **Box** object pointed to by **pLargest**. If **boxes[i]** has a larger volume than the **Box** object pointed to by **pLargest**, then the result of the comparison is **true**, so we save the address of **boxes[i]** as the new largest **Box** object. We use a pointer here because it's much more efficient than the alternative:

```
Box largest = boxes[0];
for(int i = 1 ; i < boxCount ; i++)
  if(largest < boxes[i])
    largest = boxes[i];        // Copies the object from the array
```

In this code, there is extra overhead compared with the original. Every time a **Box** object is stored in the variable **largest** within the loop, the object in the **boxes** array has to be copied to the **largest** object, member by member. Exactly how much time this requires depends on the size and complexity of the objects, but when you use a pointer, only the address is copied.

When we exit the loop, the pointer **pLargest** will contain the address of the largest **Box** object in the array, so we output the dimensions of the largest object using the pointer:

```
cout << endl
     << "The box with the largest volume has dimensions: "
     << pLargest->getLength()  << " by "
     << pLargest->getBreadth() << " by "
     << pLargest->getHeight()  << endl;
```

Global Operator Functions

The **volume()** function is a **public** member of the **Box** class, so we could implement the overloaded **<** operator as an ordinary function — a **global operator function** — outside of the class. In this case, the definition of the function would be:

```
inline bool operator<(const Box& Box1, const Box& Box2)
{
  return Box1.Volume() < Box2.Volume();
}
```

We have declared **operator<()** to be an inline function, as we want it to be compiled as such if possible. With the operator defined in this fashion, the code in **main()** in the previous example would work in exactly the same way. Of course, you must not declare this version of the operator function as **const** — **const** can only be applied to functions that are members of a class.

> *When you specify a member function as* **const***, you are saying it does not modify the object for which it is called — so* **const** *in this context is specifically about the object to which it belongs.*

Even if an operator function needed access to **private** members of the class, it would still be possible to implement it as an ordinary function by declaring it as a **friend** function of the class. Generally, though, if a function must access **private** members of a class then it's better practice to define it as a class member.

Implementing Full Support for an Operator

Implementing an operator such as **<** for a class creates an expectation. You can write expressions like **Box1 < Box2**, but what about **Box1 < 25.0**, or **10 < Box2**? Our operator function **operator<()** won't handle either of these. When you start to implement an overloaded operator for a class, you need to consider the likely range of circumstances in which the operator might be used.

FYI

When we use the basic < operator, for example to compare a float with an int, the compiler automatically converts one of the operands to the same type as the other before implementing the comparison — and the basic < operator is overloaded to compare two data elements of the same type. The situation here discussed above is a little different — we need to overload the < operator so that the demands of the comparisons above make sense.

We can quite easily support the types of expression that we have just seen. Let's first add a function that compares the volume of a **Box** object (the **Box** object is the first operand) with a second operand of type **double**. We will define it as an inline function outside the class, just to see how it's done. We need to add the following prototype to the **public** section of the **Box** class definition:

```
bool operator<(double aValue) const;        // Compare Box volume < double value
```

The **Box** object will be passed to the function as the implicit pointer **this**, and the **double** value is passed as an argument. Implementing this function is as easy as the first operator function — there's just one statement in its body:

```
// Function to compare volume of a Box object with a constant
inline bool Box::operator<(double aValue) const
{
  return volume() < aValue;
}
```

FYI This definition should follow the class declaration in Box.h. **An inline function should not be defined in a separate** .cpp **file, because its definition must appear in every source file that uses the function. Putting it together with the class definition ensures this will always be so.**

Dealing with an expression like **10 < box2** isn't any harder; it's just different. A *member* operator function always provides the **this** pointer as the left operand. Since the left operand in this case is of type **double**, we can't implement the operator as a member function. That leaves us with two choices: to implement the function as a global operator function, or as a **friend** function.

Since we don't need to access any **private** members of the class, we can implement it as an ordinary function:

```
// Function comparing a constant with volume of a Box object
inline bool operator<(const double aValue, const Box& aBox)
{
  return aValue < aBox.volume();
}
```

We now have three overloaded versions of the **<** operator for **Box** objects, so as well as expressions like **box1 < box2**, we can handle things such as **box1 < 2.5 * box2.volume()**, or even **0.5 * (box1.Volume() + box2.Volume()) < box3**. Either operand for the **<** operator can be any expression that results in a value of type **double**, or a **Box** object.

Try It Out – Complete Overloading of the < Operator

We can put all this together into an example to show that it really works! As well as the operator function, we will add a function to the **Box** class that will display the dimensions of an object. This will make the code in **main()** more compact. To update the **Box.h** file from Program 14.1, first remove the old **operator<()** function definition, and then add the following prototypes to the public section of the class definition:

```
    bool operator<(const Box& aBox) const;         // Compare Box < Box
    bool operator<(const double aValue) const;     // Compare Box < double value
```

Then add the following inline member function definitions to **Box.h**:

```
// Function comparing Box object < Box object
inline bool Box::operator<(const Box& aBox) const
{
  return volume() < aBox.volume();
}
```

```
// Function comparing Box object < double value
inline bool Box::operator<(const double aValue) const
{
  return volume() < aValue;
}
```

Finally, add the global operator function definition to the end of **Box.h**:

```
// Function comparing double value < Box object
inline bool operator<(const double aValue, const Box& aBox)
{
  return aValue < aBox.volume();
}
```

These three operator function definitions should be placed between the end of the **Box** class definition and the **#endif** directive. We have included the definitions for all the operator functions in the header file, **Box.h**, because they are all inline. Only definitions for member functions that are not inline should go in a **.cpp** file. Therefore, the **Box.cpp** file is unchanged from Program 14.1.

We can apply the new operators to finding all the **Box** objects in an array that have a volume between specified limits. Here's the code to do that:

```
// Program 14.2 Exercising the overloaded 'less-than' operators
#include <iostream>
#include <cstdlib>                  // For random number generator
#include <ctime>                    // For time function
using namespace std;

#include "Box.h"

// Function to generate random integers from 1 to count
inline int random(int count)
{
  return 1 + static_cast<int>((count* static_cast<long>(rand())) / (RAND_MAX+1));
}
```

541

```
// Display box dimensions
void show(const Box& aBox)
{
  cout << endl
       << aBox.getLength() << " by "
       << aBox.getBreadth() << " by " << aBox.getHeight();
}
```

```
int main()
{
  const int dimLimit = 100;        // Upper limit on Box dimensions
  srand((unsigned)time(0));        // Initialize the random number generator

  const int boxCount = 20;         // Number of elements in Box array
  Box boxes[boxCount];             // Array of Box objects

  for(int i = 0 ; i < boxCount ; i++)
    boxes[i] = Box(random(dimLimit), random(dimLimit), random(dimLimit));

  // Find the largest Box object in the array
  Box* pLargest = &boxes[0];

  for(int i = 1 ; i < boxCount ; i++)
    if(*pLargest < boxes[i])
      pLargest = &boxes[i];

  cout << endl
       << "The largest box in the array has dimensions:";
  show(*pLargest);

  int volMin = 100000.0;                  // Lower Box volume limit
  int volMax = 500000.0;                  // Upper Box volume limit
  // Display details of Box objects between the limits
  cout << endl << endl
       << "Boxes with volumes between "
       << volMin << " and " << volMax << " are:";
  for(int i = 0 ; i < boxCount ; i++)
    if(volMin < boxes[i] && boxes[i] < volMax)
      show(boxes[i]);

  cout << endl;
  return 0;
}
```

When I ran the example, I got the following output:

```
The largest box in the array has dimensions:
100 by 79 by 99

Boxes with volumes between 100000 and 500000 are:
92 by 38 by 46
76 by 83 by 44
83 by 78 by 18
31 by 87 by 83
93 by 15 by 90
62 by 64 by 88
```

How It Works

The function **show()** just displays the dimensions of the **Box** object that is passed as an argument. This is just a convenient function that we will use in **main()**.

The first part of **main()** creates an array of **Box** objects and finds the **Box** with the largest volume, as before. This exercises the original version of **operator<()** that we defined as a member of the **Box** class. We try out the two new operator functions we have added with the code to list all **Box** objects with volumes between **volMin** and **volMax**. These are found in the loop:

```
for(int i = 0 ; i < boxCount ; i++)
  if(volMin < boxes[i] && boxes[i] < volMax)
    show(boxes[i]);
```

The **if** expression will call both new versions of the operator. The sub-expression **volMin < boxes[i]** is equivalent to **operator<(volMin, boxes[i])**, while **boxes[i] < volMax** is equivalent to calling the member function with the expression **boxes[i].operator < (volMax)**. To display the dimensions of a **Box** object that meets the criteria, we simply pass it to the **show()** function.

> **FYI**
>
> *Any* comparison operator can be implemented in much the same way as we have implemented the less-than operator. They would only differ in the minor details; the general approach to implementing them would be exactly the same.

Operator Function Idioms

All the binary operators that can be overloaded always have operator functions of the form that we have seen in the previous section. When an operator **X** is being overloaded, and the left operand is an object of the class for which **X** is being overloaded, the *member* function defining the overload will be of the form:

Return_Type operator *X*(*Type RightOperand*);

The **Return_Type** will depend on what the operator does. For comparison and logical operators, it will typically be **bool** (although you could use **int**). Operators such as **+** and ***** will need to return an object in some form, as we will see.

When you implement a binary operator using a *non-member* function, it will be of the form:

Return_Type operator *X*(*Class_Type LeftOperand*, *Type RightOperand*);

Here, **Class_Type** is the class for which you are overloading the operator **X**.

If the left operand, of type **Type**, for a binary operator is not implemented as a member of the class **Type**, then it must be implemented as a *global* operator function that will be of this form:

Return_Type operator *X*(*Type LeftOperand*, *Class_Type RightOperand*);

When you implement unary operators as member functions of a class, they do not require a parameter in general — although the increment and decrement operators are an exception to this, as we will see. For example, the general form of a unary operator function for the operation **Op** as a member of the class **Class_Type** would be:

```
Class_Type& operator Op();
```

Unary operators implemented as *global* operator functions have a single parameter that is the operand. As a non-member function, the operator function for the unary operator **Op** could be declared as:

```
Class_Type& operator Op(Class_Type&);
```

Note that for all operator functions —either as member functions or as global operator functions — you have no flexibility in the number of parameters. You must use the number of parameters specified for the particular operator.

We won't go through examples of overloading every operator, as most of them are similar to the ones we have already seen. However, we *will* take a close look at those operators that have particular idiosyncrasies when you overload them.

Overloading the Assignment Operator

The assignment operator is the operator **=**, and is referred to as such to distinguish it from the operators **+=**, ***=**, and so on. The assignment operator copies from an object of a given type (on the right of an assignment) to another of the same type (on the left). You call the assignment operator when you write:

```
Box box1;
Box box2(10, 10, 10);
box1 = box2;              // Call the assignment operator
```

If you don't provide an overloaded assignment operator function to copy objects of your class, the compiler will provide a default version: **operator=()**.

It's interesting to note what happens if you define an extremely simple class — such as a class with just a single data member:

```
class Data
{
  public:
    int value;
};
```

Depending on how you use it, what you may actually be getting is:

```
class Data
{
  public:
    int value;
```

```
        Data(){}                                        // Default constructor
        ~Data(){}                                       // Destructor

        Data(const Data& aData) : Value(aData.value) {} // Copy constructor

        Data& operator=(const Data& aData)              // Assignment operator
        {
          value = aData.value;
          return *this;
        }
    };
```

The default version of the assignment operator will simply provide a member-by-member copying process, similar to that of the default copy constructor.

> *Don't confuse the copy constructor with the assignment operator — they are definitely not the same. The copy constructor is called when a class object is created and initialized with an existing object of the same class, or when an object is passed to a function by value. The assignment operator is called when the left-hand side and the right-hand side of an assignment statement are objects of the same class.*

For our **Box** class, the default assignment operator works with no problem, but for any class that has members allocated dynamically, you need to look carefully at the requirements placed on it. There is potential for chaos in your program if you don't implement an assignment operator under these circumstances.

The problems are similar to those we discussed when we covered the copy constructor. Suppose we apply the default assignment operator to objects with dynamic memory allocation. This will result in two objects sharing objects in the free store, so that the two become interdependent. Then, a change to one can render the other invalid.

Our **TruckLoad** class, from Chapter 13, is a case in point. Member-wise copying of one **TruckLoad** to another will result in both objects sharing the same list; that was the problem we had to overcome in Chapter 13. The solution is simple: implement the copy assignment operator so that the parts of an object that were created dynamically are duplicated properly. This is not all that it needs to do though, as we shall see.

> *In fact, any class that has problems with the default copy constructor will also have problems with the default assignment operator. If you need to implement one, you also need to implement the other — and also the destructor.*

Implementing the Assignment Operator

Let's look at what the function has to do. An assignment has two operands: the right operand is the object being copied, while the left operand is the destination for the assignment, which will end up as a copy of the right operand. We will do the copying within the operator function, so what should the return type be? Do we actually need to return anything?

Let's look at how our function will be applied in practice. With normal usage of the assignment operator, we would be able to write:

```
    load1 = load2 = load3;
```

These are three variables of type **TruckLoad**, and we are making **load1** and **load2** copies of **load3**. Because the assignment operator is right associative, this is equivalent to:

```
load1 = (load2 = load3);
```

In terms of the member function **operator=()**, this is equivalent to:

```
load1.operator=(load2.operator=(load3));
```

It should be clear from this that whatever we return from **operator=()** may end up as the argument to another **operator=()** call. Since the parameter for **operator=()** will be a reference to an object, we can conclude that the function must return the object that is the left operand. Further, if we are to avoid unnecessary copying, the return type must be a reference to this object.

The process for duplicating the right operand is the same as that used for the copy constructor, and since we now know what the return type should be, we can have a first stab at defining the = operator for the **TruckLoad** class. Take a moment to consider the following, and then we'll discuss what's wrong with it:

```
TruckLoad& TruckLoad::operator=(const TruckLoad& load)
{
  pHead = pTail = pCurrent = 0;
  if(load.pHead == 0)
    return;

  Package* pTemp = load.pHead;        // Saves addresses for new chain
  do
  {
    addBox(pTemp->pBox);
  }while(pTemp = pTemp->pNext);

  return *this;                       // Return the left operand
}
```

The **this** pointer contains the address of the left argument, so returning ***this** will return the object. Apart from that, this code is the same as we had for the copy constructor. The function looks OK, and it will appear to work most of the time, but there are two problems with it.

The first problem is with the left operand. It is a **TruckLoad** object that potentially contains a list. By setting its data member **pHead** to 0 we cast adrift any **Package** objects owned by the **TruckLoad** object. We must first delete any **Package** objects owned by the left operand:

```
TruckLoad& TruckLoad::operator=(const TruckLoad& load)
{
  while(pCurrent = pHead)             // Copy and check pointer for null
  {
    pHead = pHead->pNext;            // Move pHead to the address of the next object
    delete pCurrent;                 // Delete current object
  }

  pHead = pTail = pCurrent = 0;
  if(load.pHead == 0)
    return;
```

```
      Package* pTemp = load.pHead;        // Saves addresses for new chain
      do
      {
        addBox(pTemp->pBox);
      }while(pTemp = pTemp->pNext);

      return *this;                        // Return the left operand
    }
```

If the left operand contains a list, **pHead** will be non-null. The **while** loop saves the pointer to the first **Package** object in the list and checks it for null. If it is not null, the body of the loop is executed, which moves **pHead** to the address of the next **Package** object in ths list, then deletes the current head of the list. In this way, we progress down the list, repeatedly deleting the object at the head until we reach a null pointer.

That takes care of the left operand, but there's still a problem. Suppose someone were to write:

```
    load1 = load1;
```

This doesn't look like a very sensible assignment, but the situation could arise as a consequence of a more complex statement, where it is not obvious that this will be the outcome. In this situation, because of our fix for the first problem, we will delete the list contained in the object and then attempt to copy the now non-existent list! We need to check for the possibility of both operands being the same. To do this, we can modify the function to:

```
    TruckLoad& TruckLoad::operator=(const TruckLoad& load)
    {
      if(this == &load)                    // Compare operand addresses
        return *this;                      // if equal return the 1st operand

      while(pCurrent = pHead)              // Copy and check pointer for null
      {
        pHead = pHead->pNext;              // Move pHead to the address of the next object
        delete pCurrent;                   // Delete current object
      }

      pHead = pTail = pCurrent = 0;
      if(load.pHead == 0)
        return;

      Package* pTemp = load.pHead;         // Saves addresses for new chain
      do
      {
        addBox(pTemp->pBox);
      }while(pTemp = pTemp->pNext);

      return *this;                        // Return the left operand
    }
```

If both operands are the same object, they will have the same address, so comparing **this** with the address of the argument passed to **operator=()** does the trick.

> *Whenever you write an assignment operator, you should always check for the possibility of both operands being the same object.*

We can now extend the golden rule for classes that allocate memory dynamically that we started to develop at the end of Chapter 13:

> *If your class functions allocate memory in the free store, always implement a copy constructor, an assignment operator, and a destructor.*

You're not limited to overloading the copy assignment operator just to copy an object. In general, you can have several overloaded versions of the assignment operator for a class. Additional versions of the assignment operator would have a parameter type that was different from the class type — so they would effectively be conversions. In any event, the return type should be a reference to the left operand. Of course, you can also overload the other operators of the form **op=** if you want.

It is likely in many cases that you specifically *don't* want to allow certain assignment operations on the objects of your class. If this is the case, you can prevent them by declaring the assignment operator as a **private** member of the class.

Try It Out – Implementing the Assignment Operator

Let's put together a simple working example that will illustrate how class objects behave with and without an assignment operator defined, and therefore exactly why they're so important. We can define a class **ErrorMessage** to represent an error message — with a copy constructor, an assignment operator, and a destructor in the first instance:

```
// ErrorMessage.h
#ifndef ERRORMESSAGE_H
#define ERRORMESSAGE_H
#include <iostream>
using namespace std;

class ErrorMessage
{
  public:
    ErrorMessage(const char* pText = "Error");              // Constructor
    ~ErrorMessage();                                        // Destructor
    void resetMessage();                                    // Change the message
    ErrorMessage& operator=(const ErrorMessage& Message);   // Assignment operator

    char* what() const{ return pMessage; }                  // Display the message

  private:
    char* pMessage;
};
#endif
```

Of course, this class must define a copy constructor, a copy assignment operator, and a destructor as it allocates memory dynamically. By removing the copy assignment operator from the class, we will be able to see what happens when we forget to implement it.

The definitions required for the constructor, destructor and other member functions can go in **ErrorMessage.cpp**:

```
// ErrorMessage.cpp ErrorMessage class implementation
#include <cstring>
#include "ErrorMessage.h"
using namespace std;

// Constructor
ErrorMessage::ErrorMessage(const char* pText)
{
  pMessage = new char[ strlen(pText) + 1 ];          // Get space for message
  strcpy(pMessage, pText);                           // Copy to new memory
}

// Destructor to free memory allocated by new
ErrorMessage::~ErrorMessage()
{
  cout << endl << "Destructor called." << endl;
  delete[] pMessage;                                 // Free memory for message
}

// Change the message
void ErrorMessage::resetMessage()
{
  // Replace message text with asterisks
  for(char* temp = pMessage ; *temp != '\0' ; *(temp++) = '*')
    ;
}

// Assignment operator
ErrorMessage& ErrorMessage::operator=(const ErrorMessage& message)
{
  if(this == &message)                               // Compare addresses, if equal
    return *this;                                    // return left operand

  delete[] pMessage;                                 // Release memory for left operand
  pMessage = new char[ strlen(message.pMessage) + 1];

  // Copy right operand string to left operand
  strcpy(this->pMessage, message.pMessage);

  return *this;                                      // Return left operand
}
```

We can put this version of the error message class through its paces with the following source file:

```
// Program 14.3 Overloading the copy assignment operator
#include <iostream>
#include <cstring>
using namespace std;

#include "ErrorMessage.h"

int main()
{
  ErrorMessage warning("There is a serious problem here");
  ErrorMessage standard;
```

```
        cout << endl << "warning contains - " << warning.what();
        cout << endl << "standard contains - " << standard.what();

        standard = warning;                          // Use copy assignment operator

        cout << endl << "After assigning the value of warning, standard contains - "
            << standard.what();

        cout << endl << "Resetting warning, not standard" << endl;
        warning.resetMessage();                      // Reset the Warning message

        cout << endl << "warning now contains - " << warning.what();
        cout << endl << "standard now contains - " << standard.what();
        cout << endl;

        return 0;
    }
```

If we compile and run this as it is, we will get the output:

```
warning contains - There is a serious problem here
standard contains - Error
After assigning the value of warning, standard contains - There is a serious
problem here
Resetting warning, not standard

warning now contains - ******************************
standard now contains - There is a serious problem here

Destructor called.

Destructor called.
```

As you can see, everything works as it should. We are able to reset the message contained in the first **ErrorMessage** object without affecting the object that was copied.

Now remove or comment out the declaration of the assignment operator in the class definition, and its definition in **ErrorMessage.cpp**. Recompiling the program and running it again will produce this output:

```
warning contains - There is a serious problem here
standard contains - Error
After assigning the value of warning, standard contains - There is a serious
problem here
Resetting warning, not standard

warning now contains - ******************************
standard now contains - ******************************

Destructor called.

Destructor called.
```

You may well get other error messages because, as it stands, the program attempts to release memory in the free store twice for the same object.

How It Works

The interesting aspect of this example is its peculiar operation without the assignment operator. In the **main()** function we create an object, **warning**, containing a specific text string with the statement:

```
ErrorMessage warning("There is a serious problem here");
```

This calls the **ErrorMessage** constructor with the string passed as an argument. Next we create an **ErrorMessage** object using the default message string:

```
ErrorMessage standard;
```

After displaying both objects' messages, we call the assignment operator for the **ErrorMessage** class with the statement:

```
standard = warning;                              // Use copy assignment operator
```

The second time we ran the program, this was the *default* assignment operator provided by the compiler, so both objects' **pMessage** members contained the same address. As a consequence, when we modified the **warning** object with the statement:

```
warning.resetMessage();                          // Reset the Warning message
```

we were modifying the string common to both objects — the output clearly showed the **standard** string to be the same as the **warning** string.

At the end of the program the two **ErrorMessage** objects go out of scope and their destructors are called, as indicated by the output. The first destructor call will delete the string pointed to by **pMessage** from the free store. In the defective version, when the second destructor call occurs it will attempt to delete the same string again, because the **pMessage** members of both **ErrorMessage** objects contain the same address — your system may produce a warning of its own. And all for the want of an assignment operator!

The first time we ran the program, using the **ErrorMessage** class with the assignment operator implemented, an independent copy of the right operand was created and **standard** was not affected by the modification of **warning**. The **pMessage** pointers in the two objects point to separate strings, so no problem arises with the destructors.

Overloading the Arithmetic Operators

Let's look at how to overload the addition operator for our **Box** class. This is an interesting case, because addition is a binary operation that involves creating and returning a new object. The new object will be the sum (whatever we define that to mean) of the two **Box** objects that are its operands.

What do we want the sum to mean? There are a number of possibilities, but because the primary purpose of a box is to hold something, and its volumetric capacity is of primary interest to us, we might reasonably expect that the sum of two boxes is a box that can hold as much as both together.

On that basis, let's define the sum of two **Box** objects to be a **Box** object that's large enough to contain the two original boxes stacked on top of each other. This is consistent with the notion that our class might be used for packaging, since adding a number of **Box** objects together results in a **Box** object that can contain them.

We can do this in a simple-minded way, as follows. The new object will have a **length** member that is the larger of the **length** members of the objects being summed; and a **breadth** member derived in a similar way. The **height** member will be the sum of the **height** members of the two operands, so that the resultant **Box** object can contain the other two **Box** objects. By altering the constructor, we'll also arrange that the **length** member of a **Box** object is always greater than or equal to the **breadth** member.

The diagram illustrates the **Box** object produced by adding two **Box** objects together:

Since the result of addition will be a new **Box** object, the function implementing addition must return a **Box** object. If the function that overloads the **+** operator is to be a member function, then the declaration of the function in the **Box** class definition can be:

```
Box operator+(const Box& aBox) const;        // Adding two Box objects
```

We can define the *parameter* as **const**, since the function will not modify it, and as a reference to avoid unnecessary copying of the right operand when the function is called. We can declare the *function* as **const** because it does not alter the left operand. The definition of the member function will be:

```
// Function to add two Box objects
inline Box Box::operator+(const Box& aBox) const
{
    // New object has larger length and breadth, and sum of heights
    return Box( length  > aBox.length  ? length  : aBox.length,
                breadth > aBox.breadth ? breadth : aBox.breadth,
                height + aBox.height );
}
```

552

Notice particularly that we don't create a **Box** object in the free store to return to the caller. This would be a very poor way of implementing the function, because it is hard to see how you could ensure that the memory was released. Returning a pointer would also affect how other operators, such as **operator=()**, are written. The way the function is written, a local **Box** object is created and a copy is returned to the calling program. Since these are automatic variables, the memory management is taken care of automatically.

Try It Out – Overloading the Addition Operator

Let's see how our new addition operator works in an example. We'll add to the **Box** class that we used in Program 14.3. We need to add the declaration of the operator function to the **public** section of the **Box** class definition in **Box.h**:

```
class Box
{
  public:
    Box(double aLength = 1.0, double aBreadth = 1.0, double aHeight = 1.0);
                                          // Constructor

    double volume() const;                    // Calculate Box volume

    double getLength()  const;
    double getBreadth() const;
    double getHeight()  const;

    bool operator<(const Box& aBox) const;     // Compare Box < Box
    bool operator<(const double aValue) const; // Compare Box < double value
    Box operator+(const Box& aBox) const;      // Function to add two Box objects

  private:
    double length;
    double breadth;
    double height;
};
```

You need to add the inline definition of the **operator+()** function, that we saw just now, to the **Box.h** file, following the class definition.

We will modify the definition of the constructor in **Box.cpp** to:

```
Box::Box(double aLength, double aBreadth, double aHeight)
{
  double maxSide = aLength > aBreadth ? aLength : aBreadth;
  double minSide = aLength < aBreadth ? aLength : aBreadth;
  length = maxSide > 0.0 ? maxSide : 1.0;
  breadth = minSide > 0.0 ? minSide : 1.0;
  height = aHeight > 0.0 ? aHeight : 1.0;
}
```

The constructor has been changed to ensure that the **length** member always contains the longer of the length and breadth of a **Box** object. This will present the objects in a consistent orientation, although our addition operator may produce some very tall, narrow boxes.

553

Let's exercise the addition operator together with the `<` operator by finding the pair of **Box** objects from an array that have the least volume when they are added together. With an array of 20 **Box** objects this will involve checking 380 pairs of objects. Here's the code to do that:

```
// Program 14.4 Adding Box objects
#include <iostream>
#include <cstdlib>                 // For random number generator
#include <ctime>                   // For time function
using namespace std;

#include "Box.h"

// Function to generate random integers from 1 to count
inline int random(int count)
{
  return 1 + static_cast<int>((count* static_cast<long>(rand()))/(RAND_MAX + 1));
}

// Display box dimensions
void show(const Box& aBox)
{
  cout << endl
       << aBox.getLength() << " by "
       << aBox.getBreadth() << " by " << aBox.getHeight();
}

int main()
{
  const int dimLimit = 100;        // Upper limit on Box dimensions
  srand((unsigned)time(0));        // Initialize the random number generator

  const int boxCount = 20;         // Number of elements in Box array
  Box boxes[boxCount];             // Array of Box objects

  // Create 20 Box objects
  for(int i = 0 ; i < boxCount ; i++)
    boxes[i] = Box(random(dimLimit), random(dimLimit), random(dimLimit));

  int first = 0;                   // Index of first Box object of pair
  int second = 1;                  // Index of second Box object of pair
  double minVolume = (boxes[first] + boxes[second]).volume();

  for(int i = 0 ; i < boxCount - 1 ; i++)
    for(int j = i + 1 ; j < boxCount ; j++)
      if(boxes[i] + boxes[j] < minVolume)
      {
        first = i;
        second = j;
        minVolume = (boxes[i] + boxes[j]).volume();
      }

  cout << "The objects that sum to the smallest volume are:";
  cout << endl << "boxes[" << first << "] ";
  show(boxes[first]);
  cout << endl << "boxes[" << second << "] ";
  show(boxes[second]);
  cout << endl << "Volume of the sum is " << minVolume << endl;
```

```
        return 0;
    }
```

I got the output:

```
The objects that sum to the smallest volume are:
boxes[8]
15 by 15 by 23
boxes[16]
21 by 15 by 41
Volume of the sum is 20160
```

You should typically get a different result each time you run the program.

How It Works

We record the pair of elements of the array, whose **Box** objects give the smallest volume when summed, by storing the index values in the variables **first** and **second**. We arbitrarily set the first two array elements as the initial pair and store their combined volume with the statement:

```
double minVolume = (boxes[first] + boxes[second]).volume();
```

Because **operator+()** returns a **Box** object, we can call the **volume()** function for the **Box** object that results from adding **boxes[first]** and **boxes[second]**. The parentheses around the sum of the two **Box** objects are essential, as the precedence of the member access operator is higher than that of **+**. Of course, if we had wanted to *save* the combined **Box** object, we could have written:

```
Box combined = boxes[first] + boxes[second];    // Assigns sum to new Box object
double minVolume = combined.volume();
```

The pair that combines to form the smallest **Box** object is found in the nested loop:

```
for(int i = 0 ; i < boxCount - 1 ; i++)
  for(int j = i + 1 ; j < boxCount ; j++)
    if(boxes[i] + boxes[j] < minVolume)
    {
      first = i;
      second = j;
      minVolume = (boxes[i] + boxes[j]).volume();
    }
```

The outer loop, controlled by **i**, iterates through the array elements from the first to the last but one. The inner loop, controlled by **j**, combines the **Box** object selected by **i** with each of the following objects in the array in turn. For each pair of **Box** objects, the volume of the sum is compared with **minVolume** using the overloaded operator **<** in the **if** expression. This expression is equivalent to:

```
(boxes[i].operator+(boxes[j])).operator<(minVolume)
```

The **operator+()** returns a **Box** object whose **operator<()** function is then called. If the **operator<()** function returns **true**, we record the current index values in **first** and **second**, and store the volume of the sum of the **Box** objects in **minVolume**.

Finally, we use the **show()** function to output the results for the **Box** objects we have found with the statements:

```
cout << "The objects that sum to the smallest volume are:";
cout << endl << "boxes[" << first << "] ";
show(boxes[first]);
cout << endl << "boxes[" << second << "] ";
show(boxes[second]);
cout << endl << "Volume of the sum is " << minVolume << endl;
```

Of course, the overloaded **+** operator can be used in more complex expressions to add **Box** objects. For example, you could write:

```
Box box4 = box1 + box2 + box3;
```

The result of this is a **Box** object **box4** that can contain the other three **Box** objects stacked on top of each other.

We could equally well have implemented the addition operation for the class as a normal (that is, non-member) function, since the dimensions of a **Box** object are accessible through **public** member functions. The prototype of such a function would be:

```
Box operator+(const Box& aBox, const Box& bBox);
```

If the values of the data members were not accessible in this way, you could still write it as a normal function that you declared as a friend function within the **Box** class. Of these choices, the friend function is always the least desirable, so always take the alternative to a friend function when there is one. Operator functions are quite a fundamental class capability, so I generally prefer to implement them as class members — it represents that the operation is an integral part of the type.

Implementing One Operator in Terms of Another

If you implement addition for a class, you inevitably create the expectation that the **+=** operator will work too. Of course, in practice there's no connection between **+** and **+=**, but if you're going to implement both, it's worth noting that you can implement **+** in terms of **+=** very economically.

First, let's define the function to implement **+=** for the **Box** class. Because assignment is involved, it will need to return a reference. Using the notion that we used for adding **Box** objects together in the addition operator, the definition might be:

```
// Overloaded += operator
inline Box& Box::operator+=(const Box& right)
{
  length =  length  > right.length ? length  : right.length;
  breadth = breadth > right.breadth ? breadth : right.breadth;
  height += right.height;
  return *this;
}
```

This is a straightforward implementation of modifying the left operand, which is ***this**, by adding the right operand. Once again, the resulting object can contain the original objects placed one on top of the other.

We can now implement **operator+()** using **operator+=()**, so the function simplifies to:

```
// Function to add two Box objects
inline Box Box::operator+(const Box& aBox) const
{
    return Box(*this) += aBox;
}
```

Here, the expression **Box(*this)** calls the copy constructor to create a copy of the left operand for the addition. Then the **operator+=()** function is called to add the right operand object, **right**.

You could apply the same ideas to implement overloaded versions of **-=**, ***=**, and so on for a class. While we are on the topic of defining one operator in terms of another, you can do the same sort of thing with comparisons. Since we have defined the **operator<()** function, you could define the function to overload **>=** in terms of that:

```
inline bool Box::operator>=(const Box& aBox) const
{
    return !(*this<(aBox));
}
```

The negation of *less than* is *greater than or equal to*, so that's why you could define the function like this.

Overloading the Subscript Operator

The subscript operator **[]** provides very interesting possibilities for certain kinds of classes. Clearly, this operator is aimed primarily at selecting one of a number of objects that you can interpret as an array — but in fact, the objects could be contained in any one of a number of different containers. You can overload the subscript operator to access the elements of sparse array (where many of the elements are empty), or an associative array, or even a linked list. The data might even be stored in a file, and you could use the subscript operator to hide the complications of file input and output operations. Since you control what goes on inside the operator function, you could even improve on the way the standard subscript operator works — for instance, by checking that a given index value is legal.

Our **TruckLoad** class, from Chapter 13, is an example of a class that would support an implementation of the subscript operator. Each **TruckLoad** object contains an ordered set of objects — rather than making users write their own code to iterate through the **Box** objects in the list, you could provide a means of accessing them through an index value. An index of 0 would return the first object in the list; an index of 1 would return the second; and so on. The inner workings of the subscript operator would take care of iterating through the list to find the object required.

Let's think about how the **operator[]()** function might work in this case. It will need to accept an index value that is interpreted as a position in the list, and return the **Box** object at that position. We must return an object (not a pointer) if we are to be consistent with the normal meaning of an expression such as **load[3]**, which ought to refer to the fourth object in the list represented by the object **load**. The declaration for the function in the **TruckLoad** class might therefore be:

```
class TruckLoad
{
  public:
    Box operator[](int index) const;        // Overloaded subscript operator
    // Rest of the class as before...
};
```

We could implement the function as follows:

```
// Subscript operator
Box TruckLoad::operator[](int index) const
{
  if(index<0)                              // Check for negative index
  {
    cout << endl << "Negative index";
    exit(1);
  }

  Package* pPackage = pHead;               // Address of first Package
  int count = 0;                           // Package count
  do
  {
    if(index == count++)                   // Up to index yet?
      return *pPackage->pBox;              // If so return the Box
  } while(pPackage = pPackage->pNext);

  cout << endl << "Out of range index";    // If we get to here index is too high
  exit(1);
}
```

FYI Some older compilers may not support this use of `exit()` — they may complain that there is no value returned from the function. If you have this problem, then try replacing each of the two statements `exit(1);` with `return *pTail->pBox;` — it defeats the object of testing the index value, but your code should at least compile successfully.

If the value of **index** is negative, we terminate the program after displaying a message. In the **do-while** loop we traverse the list, incrementing **count** as we go. When the value of **count** is the same as **index**, the loop has reached the **Package** object we're looking for: we return the **Box** object that corresponds to that **Package** object. If we traverse the entire list without **count** reaching the value of **index**, then **index** must be out of range so we terminate the program after issuing a message.

> *Just terminating the program here is not a good way of handling this kind of problem. You really want to allow the program to continue if possible, while also signaling that an error has occurred. C++ provides exceptions to handle exactly this kind of problem — and we will be discussing these in Chapter 17.*

Let's see how this pans out in practice by trying another example.

Try It Out – Overloading the Subscript Operator

We will use the **Box** class as defined for Program 14.4. We can extend the **TruckLoad** class definition in **List.h** to include our overloaded subscript operator function:

```
// List.h classes supporting a linked list
#ifndef LIST_H
#define LIST_H

#include "Box.h"

class TruckLoad
{ public:
    // Constructors
    TruckLoad(Box* pBox = 0, int count = 1);        // Constructor
    TruckLoad::TruckLoad(const TruckLoad& Load);    // Copy constructor

    ~TruckLoad();                                    // Destructor

    Box* getFirstBox();                              // Retrieve the first Box
    Box* getNextBox();                               // Retrieve the next Box
    void addBox(Box* pBox);                          // Add a new Box to the list
    Box operator[](int index) const;                 // Overloaded subscript operator

  private:
   class Package
    {
      public:
        Box* pBox;                                   // Pointer to the Box
        Package* pNext;                              // Pointer to the next Package

        Package(Box* pNewBox);                       // Constructor
};

    Package* pHead;                                  // First in the list
    Package* pTail;                                  // Last in the list
    Package* pCurrent;                               // Last retrieved from the list
};

#endif
```

The implementation of the function will go in the **List.cpp** file. Just to make sure you have it all, the complete file contents appear here:

```
// List.cpp Implementations for the Package and TruckLoad classes
#include <iostream>
#include "Box.h"
#include "List.h"
using namespace std;

// Package class functions
// Package constructor
TruckLoad::Package::Package(Box* pNewBox):pBox(pNewBox), pNext(0){}
```

559

```
// TruckLoad class functions
// Constructor
TruckLoad::TruckLoad(Box* pBox, int count)
{
  pHead = pTail = pCurrent = 0;

  if(count > 0 && pBox != 0)
  for(int i = 0 ; i<count ; i++)
    addBox(pBox+i);
  return;
}

// Copy constructor
TruckLoad::TruckLoad(const TruckLoad& Load)
{
  pHead = pTail = pCurrent = 0;
  if(Load.pHead == 0)
    return;

  Package* pTemp = Load.pHead;                    // Saves addresses for new chain
  do
  {
    addBox(pTemp->pBox);
  }while(pTemp = pTemp->pNext);
}

// Destructor
TruckLoad::~TruckLoad()
{
  while(pCurrent = pHead->pNext)
  {
    delete pHead;                    // Delete the previous
    pHead = pCurrent;                // Store address of next
  }
    delete pHead;                    // Delete the last
}

// Get the first Box in the list
Box* TruckLoad::getFirstBox()
{
  pCurrent = pHead;
  return pCurrent->pBox;
}

// Get the next Box in the list
Box* TruckLoad::getNextBox()
{
  if(pCurrent)
    pCurrent = pCurrent->pNext;    // pCurrent is not null so set to next
  else                             // pCurrent is null
    pCurrent = pHead;              //  so set to the first list element

  return pCurrent ? pCurrent->pBox : 0;
}

// Add a list element
void TruckLoad::addBox(Box* pBox)
{
  Package* pPackage = new Package(pBox);          // Create a Package
```

```
    if(pHead)                                     // Check list is not empty
      pTail->pNext = pPackage;                    // Add the new object to the tail
    else                                          // List is empty
      pHead = pPackage;                           // so new object is the head
    pTail = pPackage;                             // Store its address as tail
  }
```

```
  // Subscript operator
  Box TruckLoad::operator[](int index) const
  {
    if(index<0)                                   // Check for negative index
    {
      cout << endl << "Negative index";
      exit(1);
    }

    Package* pPackage = pHead;                    // Address of first Package
    int count = 0;                                // Package count
    do
    {
      if(index == count++)                        // Up to index yet?
        return *pPackage->pBox;                   // If so return the Box
    } while(pPackage = pPackage->pNext);

    cout << endl << "Out of range index";         // If we get to here index is too high
    exit(1);
  }
```

Note that the output from the destructor for the **TruckLoad** class has been removed, as we no longer need it.

To try out our subscript operator, we can create a linked list of **Box** objects (as we did in Program 13.1), and then use the subscript operator to find the largest:

```
// Program 14.5 Using the overloaded subscript operator
#include <iostream>
#include <cstdlib>              // For random number generator
#include <ctime>                // For time function
using namespace std;

#include "Box.h"
#include "List.h"

// Function to generate random integers from 1 to count
inline int random(int count)
{
  return 1 + static_cast<int>((count*static_cast<long>(rand()))/(RAND_MAX + 1));
}

// Display box dimensions
void show(const Box& aBox)
{
  cout << endl
       << aBox.getLength() << " by " << aBox.getBreadth()
                           << " by " << aBox.getHeight();
}
```

```
int main()
{
  const int dimLimit = 100;        // Upper limit on Box dimensions
  srand((unsigned)time(0));        // Initialize the random number generator

  const int boxCount = 20;         // Number of elements in Box array
  Box boxes[boxCount];             // Array of Box objects

  // Create 20 Box objects
  for(int i = 0 ; i < boxCount ; i++)
    boxes[i] = Box(random(dimLimit), random(dimLimit), random(dimLimit));

  TruckLoad load = TruckLoad(boxes, boxCount);

  // Find the largest Box in the list
  Box maxBox = load[0];

  for(int i = 1 ; i < boxCount ; i++)
    if(maxBox < load[i])
      maxBox = load[i];

  cout << endl
       << "The largest box in the list is ";
  show(maxBox);
  cout << endl;
  return 0;
}
```

When I ran this example, it produced the output:

```
The largest box in the list is
90 by 79 by 77
```

How It Works

The **main()** function now uses the subscript operator to retrieve **Box** objects from the linked list. The first **Box** object in the list is retrieved with the statement:

```
Box maxBox = load[0];
```

This statement is equivalent to:

```
Box maxBox = load.operator[](0);
```

Using the subscript operator, we can use an index to iterate through the remaining objects in the list to find the largest:

```
for(int i = 1 ; i < boxCount ; i++)
  if(maxBox < load[i])
    maxBox = load[i];
```

We also use the overloaded **<** operator to compare the current largest object, namely **maxBox**, with the list object at index position **i**, namely **load[i]**. This is not a particularly efficient process, since our overloaded subscript operator has to iterate through the list every time we refer to an object in the list. It could be improved by keeping track of the index position of the last recorded element, and using that for getting to subsequent elements. However, it's always going to be slower than iterating through the list as we did previously. Looks neat though, doesn't it?

Lvalues and the Overloaded Subscript Operator

There are circumstances under which you might want to overload the subscript operator and use the object returned from it as an lvalue — that is, on the left of an assignment statement. With our present implementation, you will get a bug in your program if you write:

```
load[0] = load[1];
```

The problem is the return value from **operator[]()**. The object returned is a temporary object that is created by the compiler, which could cause you problems if you use it on the left of an assignment.

Beware — this is legal C++, so the compiler won't necessarily produce an error message. There are some circumstances in which assigning to a temporary variable is useful, but such circumstances should be carefully controlled.

However, we can redefine the operator so that it returns a reference — and that *can* be used as an lvalue (obviously, you must not return a reference to a local object in this situation). We can change the definition of the subscript operator to:

```
Box& TruckLoad::operator[](int index)
{
  if(index<0)                              // Check for negative index
  {
    cout << endl << "Negative index";
    exit(1);
  }

  Package* pPackage = pHead;               // Address of first Package
  int count = 0;                           // Package count
  do
  {
    if(index == count++)                   // Up to index yet?
      return *pPackage->pBox;              // If so return the Box
  } while(pPackage = pPackage->pNext);

  cout << endl << "Out of range index";    // If we get to here index is too high
  exit(1);
}
```

None of the code in the body of the function needs to be changed — just the signature. We have to remove **const** from the definition because by returning a reference to a **Box**, we're allowing a **TruckLoad** object to be changed. Of course, the declaration within the **TruckLoad** class definition must also be altered. Now we can use statements such as:

```
load[0] = load[1] + load[2];
```

Just to be sure we understand what is really happening here, let's see what this translates to in terms of function calls. The statement will be equivalent to:

```
load.operator[](0) = (load.operator[](1)).operator+(load.operator[](2));
```

If we had overloaded the assignment operator for the **Box** class, this would have broken down further to:

```
load.operator[](0).operator=((load.operator[](1)).operator+(load.operator[](2)));
```

Overloading on const

In some circumstances, you may not want to allow **Box** objects to be used as lvalues. On the other hand, sometimes you do. How can we differentiate between the two situations?

One way is to use a **TruckLoad** object that is **const** when you don't want to allow modification of the **Box** objects it contains, and a non-**const** object when you do. You can overload a member function that is non-**const** with another that is **const**, so we can have two versions of our subscript operator. The **const** version will be called for **const TruckLoad** objects, and the non-**const** version otherwise — this is what **const** implies when applied to a member function. The non-**const** version would be defined as in the previous example. Here's how we could define the **const** version:

```
const Box& TruckLoad::operator[](int index) const
{
  // Body of the function the same as before...
}
```

The body of the function is exactly the same, but the function and the return type are both **const** — so the reference cannot be used on the left of an assignment. The effect is that **Box** objects returned by the **operator[]()** function for a **const TruckLoad** object cannot be used on the left of an assignment.

Overloading Type Conversions

You can define an operator function to convert from one class type to another type. The type you are converting to can be a basic type or a class type. Operator functions that are conversions for objects of an arbitrary class, **Object**, are of the form:

```
class Object
{
  public:
    operator Type();                // Conversion from Object to Type
  // Rest of Object class definition ...
};
```

Here, **Type** is the destination type for the objects of the class. Note that there is no return type specified. The target type is always implicit, so here the function must return an object of type **Type**.

As an example, you might want to define an operator function to convert from type **TruckLoad** to type **Box*** – a pointer to an array of **Box**es. The declaration of the function within the **TruckLoad** class would be:

```
class TruckLoad
{
  public:
    operator Box*() const;
  // Rest of TruckLoad class definition ...
};
```

The return type — **Box*** — is implicit in the nature of the operator, so you don't need to specify it. Implementing this particular function would have its problems. You would need to create the array in the free store, so the caller would need to assume responsibility for deleting it, which is not generally a good approach.

Another possibility might be to define a conversion from type **Box** to type **double**. For application reasons, we might decide that this conversion would result in the volume of the **Box** being converted. We could define this as:

```
class Box
{
  public:
    operator double() const
    { return volume(); }
  // Rest of Box class definition ...
};
```

Then, given a **Box** object named **theBox**, the operator function would be called if you wrote:

```
double boxVolume = theBox;
```

You could also cause the operator function to be called explicitly with a statement that induced the cast specifically, such as:

```
double total = 10 + static_cast<double>(theBox);
```

> *You can also invoke this kind of conversion with the old-style casts, by writing an expression such as* **double(TheBox)***.*

Ambiguities with Conversions

You need to be conscious of the possibility of creating ambiguities that will cause compiler errors when implementing conversion operators for your classes. As we have said, constructors can also effectively implement a conversion. A conversion from type **Type1** to type **Type2** is implemented by including a constructor in class **Type2** with the declaration:

```
Type2(const Type1& theObject);        // Constructor converting Type1 to Type2
```

If you now implemented a conversion operator in class **Type2** to do the same as this constructor, declared as:

```
operator Type1();                     // Conversion from type Type1 to Type2
```

then the compiler may not be able to decide which function to use when a conversion is required. To remove the ambiguity between the conversion operator and the constructor, you can declare the constructor as **explicit**, as we discussed in Chapter 12. This will prohibit the use of the constructor for implicit conversions, so the conversion operator will be selected by the compiler.

> *An obvious consequence of this is that conversion operators should be used with great caution.*

Overloading the Increment and Decrement Operators

The **++** and **--** operators present a new problem for the functions that implement overloading them, as they behave differently depending on whether or not they prefix their operand. We therefore need two functions for each operator: one to be called in the prefix case, the other to be called for postfix case.

The postfix form of the operator function is distinguished from the prefix form by the presence of a parameter of type **int**, which is not otherwise used. The declarations for the functions to overload **++** for an arbitrary class, **Object**, class will be:

```
class Object
{
  public:
    Object& operator++();          // Overloaded prefix increment operator
    const Object operator++(int);  // Overloaded postfix increment operator
    // Rest of Object class definition ...
};
```

The return type for the prefix form normally needs to be a reference to the current object after it has been incremented.

For the postfix form, we create a copy of the object in its original form before we modify it, then return the *copy* of the original after the increment has been performed. The return value for the postfix operator is declared as **const** to prevent expressions such as **theObject++++** from compiling. Such expressions are inelegant, confusing, and inconsistent with the normal behavior of the operator. However, if you don't declare the return type as **const**, such usage would be possible.

> *For any class implementation of these overloaded operators, the return type for the prefix form will therefore always be a reference to the current object, and the return type for the postfix form will be a new object of the same type.*

Smart Pointers

Since we have the ability to overload the de-reference operator, *****, and the indirect member access operator, **->**, it is possible to define a type that represents a **smart pointer** — something that behaves like a pointer but is really a class object. The standard library makes extensive use of a form of smart pointers, referred to as a **class iterator,** as we will see in Chapter 20 — but what exactly are smart pointers used for?

A smart pointer is an object that can act as an intelligent pointer to objects that may be organized in a complicated way. It can hide the complication in the organization of the objects it points to. Hence, it can simply return the object when de-referenced, or access its member through the **->** operator, just like an ordinary pointer.

Each smart pointer class is designed to suit the context in which it is to be applied. It may be, for example, that the objects you want to refer to are stored in a container class of some kind, which stores objects in a complex structure such as a tree or a list. You might want to use a smart pointer to access and step through them without worrying about the internal organization.

The objects that you access through a smart pointer may not even be all in one place. In a very complex application context, you might have objects that are stored in files or databases across multiple systems on a network, but within your program you want a smart pointer object to take care of sorting out how to retrieve the objects when you iterate through them. From the perspective of your program code, local objects will look just the same as remote objects. All of the complexity of accessing the objects pointed to by a smart pointer is buried inside the class that defines it. Externally, you would expect use a smart pointer pretty much as you would an ordinary pointer.

We could create a class defining a smart pointer, that we could use with the **TruckLoad** class to access the **Box** objects it contains. This will provide us with an opportunity to see a simple implementation of a smart pointer, and see examples of some more practical examples of overloaded operators. We can also include a practical demonstration of overloading the increment operator.

Defining a Smart Pointer Class for Box Objects

Our smart pointer should work like a regular **Box** pointer, except that it will point to **Box** objects within a **TruckLoad** object. We can call it the **BoxPtr** class. We could create a **BoxPtr** object from a reference to a **TruckLoad** object, and have it automatically point to the first **Box** in the linked list. This implies that the **BoxPtr** object will need to keep track of the current **Box** object pointed to in the **TruckLoad** object, and the **TruckLoad** object itself. We could put these in an outline definition for the **BoxPtr** class that we will put in the header file **BoxPtr.h**:

```
#ifndef BOXPTR_H
#define BOXPTR_H
#include "List.h"

class BoxPtr
{
  public:
    BoxPtr(TruckLoad& load);                    // Constructor

  private:
    Box* pBox;                                  // Points to current Box in rLoad
    TruckLoad& rLoad;

    // Not accessible so not implemented
    BoxPtr();                                   // Default constructor
    BoxPtr(BoxPtr&);                            // Copy constructor
    BoxPtr& operator=(const BoxPtr&);           // Assignment operator
};
#endif
```

By only allowing a **BoxPtr** object to be created from a **TruckLoad** object, we can be sure that the **TruckLoad** object exists — although it might be empty. We don't want to allow **BoxPtr** objects to be created using a default constructor, so we declare it as a **private** member of the class. Having copies of **BoxPtr** objects would also complicate things, but we can avoid that too by declaring the copy constructor and the assignment operator in the **private** section of the class.

We won't need to modify the **TruckLoad** or **Box** classes at all. We can use the versions that we employed in Program 14.5. What else do we need in our **BoxPtr** class? We certainly need to implement the ***** and **->** operators if a **BoxPtr** object is going to behave like a pointer, so let's add those to the definition:

```
class BoxPtr
{
  public:
    BoxPtr(TruckLoad& load);              // Constructor
    Box& operator*();                     // * overload
    Box* operator->();                    // -> overload

  private:
    Box* pBox;                            // Points to current Box in rLoad
    TruckLoad& rLoad;

    // Not accessible so not implemented
    BoxPtr();                             // Default constructor
    BoxPtr(BoxPtr&);                      // Copy constructor
    BoxPtr& operator=(const BoxPtr&);     // Assignment operator
};
```

Since it is to behave like a **Box*** pointer, de-referencing a **BoxPtr** object should return a reference to a **Box** object, and that's why the return type is **Box&**. The ***** operator is a unary operator, so there is no parameter to the function.

The **operator->()** function is a little odd, so let's see how it works when it is used. It will be called in situations like this:

```
BoxPtr pLoadBox(aTruckLoad);
double boxVol = pLoadBox->volume();
```

Here, **aTruckLoad** is a **TruckLoad** object. Since the **pLoadBox** will initially represent a pointer to the first **Box** object in **aTruckLoad**, the second statement should call the **volume()** member of that object. The second statement will actually be equivalent to:

```
double boxVol = (pLoadBox.operator->())->volume();
```

An extra **->** operator gets inserted to access the member, **volume()**, so the **operator->()** function must return a pointer of type **Box***.

We want to be able to increment a **BoxPtr** object so that an expression such as **++pLoadBox** should point to the next **Box** object in the **TruckLoad** object. We can add both the prefix and the postfix forms to the class:

```
class BoxPtr
{
  public:
    BoxPtr(TruckLoad& load);                // Constructor
    Box& operator*();                       // * overload
    Box* operator->();                      // -> overload
    Box* operator++();                      // Prefix increment
    const Box* operator++(int);             // Postfix increment

  private:
    Box* pBox;                              // Points to current Box in rLoad
    TruckLoad& rLoad;

    // Not accessible so not implemented
    BoxPtr();                               // Default constructor
    BoxPtr(BoxPtr&);                        // Copy constructor
    BoxPtr& operator=(const BoxPtr&);       // Assignment operator
};
```

Each of these returns type **Box*** of course, since we are incrementing a stand-in for a pointer. The postfix form returns a **const** object to prevent repeated applications of the operator such as **pLoadBox++++**.

Do we need anything else? We most certainly do. We will want to use a **BoxPtr** object to control loops, so that we can write statements such as:

```
if(pLoadBox)
{
  // Do something...
}
```

We need the object to behave like a normal pointer here, and have it automatically translated into something that is a valid **if** test expression. One way to do this is to implement a conversion to **bool** for objects of type **BoxPtr**. If we do that, the compiler will automatically insert the conversion operator when we use a **BoxPtr** as an **if** test expression. We can add a declaration for that to the class:

```
class BoxPtr
{
  public:
    BoxPtr(TruckLoad& load);                // Constructor
    Box& operator*();                       // * overload
    Box* operator->();                      // -> overload
    Box* operator++();                      // Prefix increment
    const Box* operator++(int);             // Postfix increment
    operator bool();                        // Conversion to bool

  private:
    Box* pBox;                              // Points to current Box in rLoad
    TruckLoad& rLoad;

    // Not accessible so not implemented
    BoxPtr();                               // Default constructor
    BoxPtr(BoxPtr&);                        // Copy constructor
    BoxPtr& operator=(const BoxPtr&);       // Assignment operator
};
```

569

Note that no return type is required or allowed here, as it is implicit in the nature of the operator function for the conversion. There are other ways to make objects work as an **if** test expression, and you will meet those in the context of the standard library classes for stream input/output, that we will explore in Chapter 19.

That's enough for our purposes, so let's see how we can put together the definitions for the member functions of our **BoxPtr** class.

Implementing the Smart Pointer Class

The constructor is very easy. All we have to do is to initialize the member that is a reference to a **TruckLoad** object, and store the address of the first **Box** object that it contains. You can put the definition in a source file, **BoxPtr.cpp**:

```
// BoxPtr.cpp
#include "List.h"
#include "BoxPtr.h"
#include <iostream>
using namespace std;

BoxPtr::BoxPtr(TruckLoad& load) : rLoad(load)
{
  pBox = rLoad.getFirstBox();
}
```

The **rLoad** member must be initialized in the initialization list for the constructor — it is the only way you can initialize a member that is a reference. To get the address of the first **Box** object, we just call the **getFirstBox()** member of the object passed as an argument.

The de-reference operator function should return the object that is pointed to by the **pBox** member of the **BoxPtr** object, but we have to consider the possibility that there may not be one. We can define the function as:

```
Box& BoxPtr::operator*()
{
  if(pBox)
    return *pBox;
  else
  {
    cout << endl << "Dereferencing null BoxPtr";
    exit(1);
  }
}
```

If **pBox** is null, we can't return an object in the normal way at all. De-referencing a null pointer is a disaster situation so we display a message and end the program. This is not a good way to deal with this. You will learn about a better way to handle this kind of error in Chapter 17.

FYI Again, you may find that your compiler does not support this use of exit(). If so, try replacing the statement exit(1); with the statement return *pBox; — just as a short term fix.

The indirect member selection operator is much simpler. We just need to return the **pBox** member:

```
Box* BoxPtr::operator->()
{
  return pBox;
}
```

This returns whatever address is contained in **pBox**, so when **pBox** is null the return value will be null. The user of our class needs to verify that the smart pointer is not null before using it — just like using a regular pointer.

The prefix increment operator for **BoxPtr** objects also returns a pointer, just like incrementing an ordinary pointer:

```
Box* BoxPtr::operator++()
{
  return pBox = rLoad.getNextBox();
}
```

Remember that the prefix operator increments *before* it is used in an expression, so we just return the address of the next pointer in the **TruckLoad** object, and that is returned by the **getNextBox()** member. This will return null if we increment beyond the end of the last **Box** object.

The postfix version of the increment operator must increment the smart pointer *after* using the current value in the expression. This sounds difficult, but it isn't. We can implement it as follows:

```
const Box* BoxPtr::operator++(int)
{
  Box* pTemp = pBox;
  pBox = rLoad.getNextBox();
  return pTemp;
}
```

We save a copy of the current address in **pBox**, then increment **pBox** to point to the next **Box** object, before returning the original. Easy, isn't it?

The last member function we must define is the conversion operator. This is almost as close to trivial as it gets:

```
BoxPtr::operator bool()
{
  return pBox != 0;
}
```

We want to return **true** if **pBox** is not null, and the expression in the return does exactly that.

Let's make sure all this works by running another example.

Try It Out – Using a Smart Pointer

We can try out our smart pointer class by creating a **TruckLoad** object containing a set of random **Box** objects, as we have done before. We can then try out most of our operator functions. Here's the code:

```cpp
// Program 14.6 Using a smart pointer
#include <iostream>
#include <cstdlib>              // For random number generator
#include <ctime>               // For time function
using namespace std;

#include "Box.h"
#include "List.h"
#include "BoxPtr.h"

// Function to generate random integers from 1 to count
inline int random(int count)
{
  return 1 + static_cast<int>((count*static_cast<long>(rand()))/(RAND_MAX + 1));
}

int main()
{
  const int dimLimit = 100;       // Upper limit on Box dimensions
  srand((unsigned)time(0));       // Initialize the random number generator

  const int boxCount = 20;        // Number of elements in Box array
  Box boxes[boxCount];            // Array of Box objects

  // Create 20 Box objects
  for(int i = 0 ; i < boxCount ; i++)
    boxes[i] = Box(random(dimLimit), random(dimLimit), random(dimLimit));

  TruckLoad load = TruckLoad(boxes, boxCount);

  // Find the largest Box in the list
  BoxPtr pLoadBox(load);                          // Create smart pointer

  Box maxBox = *pLoadBox;                // Intialize maxBox object using * operator
  if(pLoadBox)                           // Try the bool conversion
    cout << endl << "Volume of first Box is " << pLoadBox->volume();  // ...and ->

  while(++pLoadBox)                      // Prefix increment smart pointer
    if(maxBox < *pLoadBox)
      maxBox = *pLoadBox;

  cout << endl
       << "The largest box in the list is "
       << maxBox.getLength()  << " by "
       << maxBox.getBreadth() << " by "
       << maxBox.getHeight()  << " with volume "
       << maxBox.volume()     << endl;
  return 0;
}
```

This example produces the output:

```
Volume of first Box is 110880
The largest box in the list is 100 by 74 by 91 with volume 673400
```

How It Works

Let's walk through how the operator functions are applied in this example. After setting up a **TruckLoad** object to contain 20 **Box** objects, we create a smart pointer with the statement:

```
BoxPtr pLoadBox(load);                          // Create smart pointer
```

When it is created, the **pLoadBox** object is a surrogate for a pointer to the first **Box** object in the **TruckLoad** object, **load**. We can therefore de-reference it to initialize the **maxBox** object:

```
Box maxBox = *pLoadBox;                 // Intialize maxBox object using * operator
```

This statement calls the default constructor for the **Box** class to create **maxBox**. It then calls the **operator*()** function for the **pLoadBox** object, and uses the reference to the **Box** object that is returned as the argument to the **operator=()** function for the **Box** object **maxBox**.

Next, the **if** statement calls two member functions of the **BoxPtr** class:

```
if(pLoadBox)                                   // Try the bool conversion
   cout << endl << "Volume of first Box is " << pLoadBox->volume();  // ...and ->
```

The **if** expression implicitly calls the **operator bool()** function, and the output statement calls the **operator->()** function that returns the address of the current **Box** object.

The **while** loop uses the prefix increment operator in the loop control expression:

```
while(++pLoadBox)                              // Prefix increment smart pointer
   if(maxBox < *pLoadBox)
      maxBox = *pLoadBox;
```

The **operator++()** function returns the pointer to the next **Box** object. Assuming it is not null we use the **operator*()** function to de-reference it, and then the **operator<()** member of the **maxBox** object to compare volumes. If the latest **Box** object has a greater volume, we store it in **maxBox** — using **operator*()** for the **pLoadBox** object class and **operator=()** for the **maxBox** object.

At the end of the loop, **pLoadBox** will represent a null pointer, so we can no longer use it. We finally output information about the **maxBox** object in the usual way.

Overloading Operators new and delete

You can overload the operators **new** and **delete** for a particular class, and if you implement **new** you must implement **delete**. The usual reason for overloading these operators is to make memory allocation and de-allocation faster and more economical for a particular class of objects. This can arise when you need to allocate space for very large numbers of objects that each require a small amount of memory. Allocating space for small objects one at a time can carry a considerable penalty in terms of overhead in the actual amount of memory allocated to each object, and the time it takes to allocate and release the memory.

The standard approach to implementing **new** is to allocate a big chunk of memory using the default **new** operator, and then to farm this out in small chunks of the size required. Obviously, the class **delete** operation must then be implemented to handle releasing the small chunks of memory. Typical declarations for a class-specific **new** and **delete** are:

```
class Data
{
  public:
    void* operator new(size_t Size);
    void operator delete(void* Object, size_t size);
  // Rest of Data class definition ...
};
```

To call the global operators from within class-specific operator functions, you just use the scope resolution operator, **::**. For example, to call global **new** from within the class-specific **new** operator, you would write something like:

```
void* operator new(size_t size)
{
  // ...
  pSpace = ::new char(size);                  // size bytes allocated
  // ...
}
```

Implementing these operators is not for the faint-hearted, as managing out-of-memory and other error conditions can get a little complicated — you should not attempt it unless it is absolutely essential. Since overloading these operators is a rare necessity, we will not dwell on it further.

Summary

In this chapter, you have learned about how you can add functions to make objects of your own data types work with the basic operators in C++. What you need to implement in a particular class is down to you. You need to decide the nature and scope of the facilities each of your classes should provide. Always keep in mind that you are defining a data type — a coherent entity — and that your class needs to reflect its nature and characteristics. You should also make sure that your implementation of an overloaded operator is not in conflict with what the operator does in its standard form.

The important points we have seen in this chapter include:

▶ You can overload any operator — except for the scope resolution operator, the conditional operator, the member access operator, the de-reference pointer to class member operator, and the **sizeof** operator — within a class, to provide class-specific behavior.

▶ Operator functions can be defined as members of a class, or as global operator functions.

▶ For a unary operator defined as a class member function, the operand is the class object.

▶ For a unary operator defined as a global operator function, the operand is the function parameter.

▶ For a binary operator function declared as a member of a class, the left operand is the class object and the right operand is the function parameter.

▶ For a binary operator defined as a global operator function, the first parameter specifies the left operand, and the second parameter specifies the right operand.

▶ To overload the increment operator, two functions are required in order to provide for the prefix and postfix forms of the operators. The function to implement a postfix operator has an extra parameter of type **int** that serves only to distinguish the function from the prefix version. The same is true of the decrement operator.

▶ Functions that implement the overloading of the **+=** operator can be used in the implementation of the **+** function. This is true for all the **op=** operators.

▶ A smart pointer is an object that behaves like a pointer. One form of smart pointer is used to iterate through a complex collection of objects of a given type, in much the same way that you use an ordinary pointer. The standard template library uses this extensively.

Exercises

Ex 14.1 These exercises are going to build on the ones from the previous chapter, so begin by providing an overloaded assignment operator for your **mystring** class. Make sure that you guard against self-assignment! Test that your operator works correctly with the following statements, where **s1**, **s2** and **s3** are **mystring** objects:

```
s1 = s2;
s1 = s1;
s1 = s2 = s3;
```

Ex 14.2 Overload the **+** operator to provide string concatenation. Test that **s1 = s2 + s3;** works correctly. Provide the **+=** operator — what should this operator return?

Ex 14.3 Overload **[]** to provide access to individual characters in the string, so that **s1[4]** returns the fifth character of **s1**. How will you ensure that this can be used on either side of an assignment?

Ex 14.4 Provide overloads for the **==, !=, >** and **<** operators, which can be used to compare your **mystring** objects. What types should these Boolean operators return? Check that expressions such as **if (s1 == s2)** work correctly.

Ex 14.5 (Harder) Overload the **()** operator to return a substring from a **mystring** object, so that **s1(2, 3)** returns the three characters starting at **s1[2]**.

15

Inheritance

In this chapter, we are going to look into a topic that lies at the heart of object-oriented programming — **inheritance**. Inheritance is the means by which we can create new classes by reusing and expanding on existing class definitions.

There are other ways of creating new class definitions from old ones — for example, we saw how to nest classes in Chapter 13. However, inheritance is rather more subtle than nesting classes — as we will see in the next chapter, inheritance is fundamental to making polymorphism possible. Inheritance is at the very heart of object-oriented programming, and this chapter does not cover the whole story by any means. You should also consider the next chapter to be an integral part of what inheritance is all about.

In this chapter you will learn about:

▶ How inheritance fits into the idea of object-oriented programming

▶ What base and derived classes are, and how they are related

▶ Defining a new class in terms of an existing one

▶ The use of the keyword **protected** to define a new access specification for class members

▶ How constructors behave in a derived class and what happens when they are called

▶ What happens with destructors when using a derived class

▶ Multiple inheritance and how it works

▶ Conversions between class types in a class hierarchy

Classes and Object-Oriented Programming

Let's start from what we have learned so far, and see how that leads us to the ideas we will explore in this chapter.

In Chapter 12, we introduced the concept of a class. A class is a data type that you define to suit your own application requirements. When you use object-oriented programming to solve a problem, your first step is to establish the definitions of the types of entities to which your program relates. Then you must code these types by writing class definitions. Finally, you program the solution to your problem in terms of objects (the instances of the classes that you have defined), using operations that work directly with those objects.

Any type of entity can be represented by a class — from the completely abstract (such as the mathematical concept of a complex number) to something as decidedly physical as a tree or a truck. Your class definition should characterize a *set* of entities, which are identified by a common set of properties. So, as well as being a data type, a class can also be a definition of a real-world object (or, at least, an approximation which is useful for solving a given problem).

In many real-world problems, the *types* of the entities involved are related. For example, a dog is a special kind of animal, which has all the properties of an animal plus a few more. Consequently, our class definitions of **Animal** and **Dog** should be related in some way. A different case is illustrated by the idea that an automobile has an engine, so there should really be some way of using our **Engine** class when defining the **Automobile** class. In this chapter we'll see how these two essentially different relationships are implemented in C++.

Hierarchies

In previous chapters, we have used the **Box** class to describe a rectangular box — our definition of a **Box** object consisted of just the three orthogonal dimensions. We can apply this basic definition to the many different kinds of rectangular box which we find in the real world — cardboard cartons, wooden crates, candy boxes and cereal boxes, and so on. Each of these objects has three orthogonal dimensions, and in this way they are just like our generic **Box** objects. In addition, each of them has other properties — for example, the things they are designed to hold, or the materials from which they are made. In fact, you could describe them as specialized kinds of **Box** objects.

For example, we might describe a **Carton** class, which has the same properties as a **Box** object — namely the three dimensions — plus the additional property of its composite material. We might then specialize even further, by using the **Carton** definition to describe a class called **FoodCarton** — this will be a special kind of **Carton** which is designed to hold food. It will have all the properties of a **Carton** object, and an additional member to model the intended contents.

The relationship between such a hierarchy of classes is shown in the diagram.

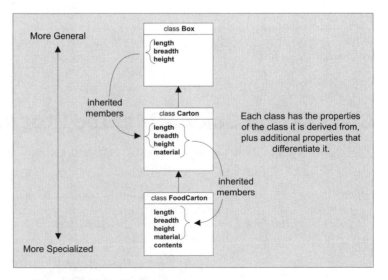

The **Carton** class is an extension of the **Box** class — you might say that the **Carton** class is *derived* from the specification of the **Box** class. In a similar way, the **FoodCarton** class has been derived from the **Carton** class. It is common to indicate this relationship diagrammatically by using an arrow which points towards the more general class in the hierarchy — we have used this convention in the diagram above.

> *We'll also see later that we can* combine *the definitions of existing classes to create a new class definition. The new class will possess all the features of the original classes. For example, we might create a* **Packed_Sandwich** *type by combining the* **FoodCarton** *definition with a definition for a class called* **Sandwich** *(that describes the constituent parts of a sandwich object).*

By following this process, we develop a hierarchy of interrelated classes. In the hierarchy, one class is derived from another by adding extra properties — in other words, by specializing. In the diagram above, each class has *all* the properties of the **Box** class (on which it is based), and this illustrates precisely the mechanism of class inheritance in C++. We could define the **Box**, **Carton** and **FoodCarton** classes quite independently of each other, but by defining them as related classes we gain a tremendous amount. Let's look at how this works in practice.

Inheritance in Classes

To begin with, let's establish the terminology that we will use for related classes. Given a class **A**, suppose that we create a new, specialized class **B**. The class **A** is called the **base class**, and the class **B** is called the **derived class**. You might think of **A** as being the 'parent', and **B** as the 'child'. The derived class automatically contains all of the data members of the base class, and (with some restrictions which we'll discuss) all the function members. The derived class is said to **inherit** the data members and function members of the base class.

If class **B** is a derived class defined *directly* in terms of class **A**, then we say that class **A** is a **direct base class** of **B**. We also say that **B** is **derived from A**. In the example above, the class **Carton** is a direct base class of **FoodCarton**. Because **Carton** is itself defined in terms of the class **Box**, we say that the class **Box** is an **indirect base class** of the class **FoodCarton**. An object of the **FoodCarton** class will have inherited members from **Carton** — including the members that the **Carton** class inherited from the **Box** class.

The way in which a derived class inherits members from a base class is illustrated in the following diagram.

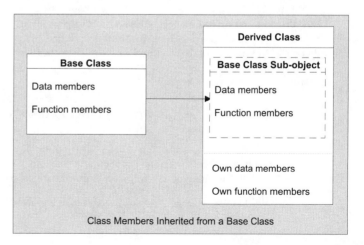

Class Members Inherited from a Base Class

As you can see, the derived class has a complete set of data members and member functions from the base class, plus its own data members and member functions. Thus, each derived class object contains a complete base class sub-object, plus other members.

Inheritance vs Aggregation

The process of class inheritance is not merely a means of getting members of one class to appear in another. There is a very important idea that underpins the whole concept: derived class objects should represent sensible base class objects.

To illustrate what I mean, there are a number of simple tests that you can employ. The first is the *is a kind of* test: any derived class object *is a kind of* base class object. In other words, a derived class object should describe a subset of the objects represented by the base class. For example: a class **Dog** might be derived from a class **Animal**. This makes sense because a dog *is a kind of* animal — or rather, a **Dog** object is a reasonable representation of a particular kind of **Animal** object. On the other hand, a **Table** class should not be derived from the **Dog** class: although **Table** objects and **Dog** objects usually have four legs, a **Table** object cannot really be considered to be a **Dog** in any way.

The *is a kind of* test is an excellent first check, but it's not infallible. For example, suppose that we defined a class, **Bird**, that (among other things) reflected the fact that most birds can fly. Now, an ostrich *is a kind of* bird; but it's nonsense to derive a class **Ostrich** from the **Bird** class, because ostriches can't fly! If your classes pass the *is a kind of* test, then you should double check by asking the following question: Is there anything I can say about (or demand of) the base class that's inapplicable to the derived class? If there is, then the derivation probably isn't safe. Thus, deriving **Dog** from **Animal** is sensible, but deriving **Ostrich** from **Bird** isn't — instead, you'd probably need to implement the classes **Flighted_Birds** and **Flightless_Birds**.

If your classes fail the *is a kind of* test, then you almost certainly shouldn't use class derivation. In this case, you could instead implement the *has a* test. A class object passes the *has a* test if it contains an instance of another class. You can implement this situation by including an object of the second class as a data member of the first. This type of dependence is called **aggregation**.

For example, consider a class **Automobile**. This class is likely to contain major automobile components as its class members. Clearly, an automobile *has an* engine, *has a* transmission, *has a* chassis and *has* suspension — so it makes sense for the **Automobile** class to contain objects of type **Engine**, **Transmission**, **Chassis**, **Suspension**. Note that, for example, it's not true to say that an engine is a kind of automobile. Hence, these classes fail the *is a kind of* test, so inheriting **Automobile** from **Engine** would be nonsensical.

To summarize the three tests:

▶ The *is a kind of* test is a first-stop test to check whether inheritance is an appropriate way to implement your classes.

▶ If the classes pass the *is a kind of* test, then double check by asking the question: Is there anything I can say about (or demand of) the base class that's inapplicable to the derived class? If the answer is 'no', then inheritance is usually appropriate.

▶ If the classes fail the *is a kind of* test, then try the *has a* test. If they pass the *has a* test, then aggregation is usually the answer.

Of course, the appropriate implementation is dependent on your application, and these rules are a guide rather than gospel. Sometimes, class derivation is used simply to assemble a set of capabilities, so that the derived class is an envelope for packaging a given set of functions. Even then, the derived class generally represents a set of functions that are related in some way.

It's time to see what the code looks like when we derive one class from another.

Deriving Classes from a Base Class

Let's go back to a simplified version of the **Box** class, which has three **private** data members and a **public** constructor:

```
// Box.h - defines Box class
#ifndef BOX_H
#define BOX_H
class Box
{
  public:
    Box(double lv=1.0, double bv=1.0, double hv=1.0);

  private:
    double length;
    double breadth;
    double height;

};
#endif
```

Because we have specified default values for the parameters in the constructor, it will also serve as the default constructor. You can save this definition in a header file **Box.h**, and add it to the example with a **#include** directive. To be consistent, the definition for the **Box** constructor is contained in the file **Box.cpp**:

```
// Box.cpp
#include "box.h"

// Constructor
Box::Box(double lv, double bv, double hv) : length(lv), breadth(bv), height(hv)
{}
```

Now, we shall define another class, called **Carton**. A **Carton** object will be much as we described earlier — similar to a **Box** object, but with an extra data member that indicates the composite material of the object. We can declare the new data member to be a null-terminated string that describes the sort of material the box is made of. (In practice we may prefer to to use a **string** object for this, but by using a null-terminated string we will demonstrate some of the implications of dynamic memory allocation). We will define **Carton** as a derived class, using the **Box** class as the base class:

```
// Carton.h - defines the Carton class with the Box class as base
#ifndef CARTON_H
#define CARTON_H
#include "Box.h"                              // For Box class definition
#include <cstring>
```

```
class Carton : public Box
{
  public:
    Carton(const char* pStr = "Cardboard");     // Constructor

    ~Carton();                                   // Destructor

  private:
    char* pMaterial;
};
#endif
```

We must **#include** the **Box** class definition into this file because it is the base class for **Carton**. The definitions are out-of-line, and contained in the file **Carton.cpp**:

```
// Carton.cpp
#include "Carton.h"
#include <cstring>

// Constructor
Carton::Carton(const char* pStr)
{
  pMaterial = new char[strlen(pStr)+1];     // Allocate space for the string
  strcpy( pMaterial, pStr);                 // Copy it
}

// Destructor
Carton::~Carton()
{
  delete[] pMaterial;
}
```

The first line of the **Carton** class definition indicates that **Carton** is derived directly from **Box**:

```
class Carton : public Box
```

The keyword **public** is the base class access specifier, and it indicates how the members of **Box** are to be accessed within the **Carton** class. We'll discuss this further in a moment.

In all other respects, the **Carton** class definition looks like any other. It contains a new member, **pMaterial**, which is a pointer to a null-terminated string. It is initialized, by the class constructor, to the address of a string that is created in the free store. This will ensure the object has its own string describing the material. We must also supply a destructor, to release the memory for the string object that **pMaterial** points to. Notice that the constructor includes a default value for the string describing the contents of a **Carton** object, so that this is also the default constructor for the **Carton** class. Objects of the class **Carton** contain all the data members of the base class, **Box**, plus the additional data member, **pMaterial**.

Let's see how this operates in a working example.

Try It Out — Using a Derived Class

Here is the code for our first example using a derived class:

```
// Program 15.1 Defining and using a derived class
#include <iostream>
#include "Box.h"                    // For the Box class
#include "Carton.h"                 // For the Carton class

using namespace std;

int main()
{
   // Create a Box and two Carton objects
   Box myBox(40.0, 30.0, 20.0);
   Carton myCarton;
   Carton candyCarton("Thin cardboard");

   // Check them out - sizes first of all
   cout << endl
        << "myBox occupies "       << sizeof myBox       << " bytes" << endl;
   cout << "myCarton occupies "    << sizeof myCarton    << " bytes" << endl;
   cout << "candyCarton occupies " << sizeof candyCarton << " bytes" << endl;

// myBox.length = 10.0;            // uncomment this for an error

// candyCarton.length = 10.0;     // uncomment this for an error

   return 0;
}
```

On my machine I get the output:

```
myBox occupies 24 bytes
myCarton occupies 32 bytes
candyCarton occupies 32 bytes
```

How It Works

First, we **#include** the header files that contain the definitions for the **Box** and **Carton** classes. Of course, the file containing the definition of the **Carton** class also includes **Box.h**, but the **#ifndef**/**#endif** preprocessor directives will prevent the **Box** class definition from being duplicated.

We declare a **Box** object and two **Carton** objects in **main()**, then output the number of bytes occupied by each object. The output shows what we would expect — that a **Carton** object is larger than a **Box** object. A **Box** object has three data members of type **double**; each of these occupies 8 bytes on my machine, so that's 24 bytes in all. Both of our **Carton** objects are the same size: 32 bytes. The additional memory occupied by each **Carton** object is down to the data member **pMaterial** (the length of the string doesn't affect the size of a **Carton** object, because **pMaterial** is a pointer).

583

If we uncomment either of the next two statements, the program will no longer compile. The first of these statements is:

```
//  myBox.length = 10.0;            // uncomment this for an error
```

Of course, we'd expect this statement to cause an error. The **length** member of the **Box** object **myBox** was declared as a **private** data member, and so it's not accessible to this output statement. By uncommenting the next statement, we'll see that we can't access the **length** member of the **Carton** object either:

```
//  candyCarton.length = 10.0;    // uncomment this for an error
```

The compiler will generate a message to the effect that the **length** member from the base class is not accessible. This is perhaps a little unexpected — after all, when we defined the **Carton** class, didn't we inherit the **Box** class members as **public**?

The reason for the error is that **length** in a **private** data member in the base class. In the derived class **Carton**, the **length** member is a **public**ly inherited **private** data member. The compiler interprets this by making **length** a **private** member of **Carton**. Consequently, when we attempt to access the member **candyCarton.length**, the compiler immediately flags up the error.

> *If you really wanted to access these* **private** *data members, then you could use a* **public** *function member such as* **getLength()**, *as we discussed in Chapter 12.*

> **Access to the inherited members of a derived class object is determined by both** *the access specifier of the data member in the base class* **and** *the access specifier of the base class in the derived class.*

The whole question of the access of inherited members in a derived class needs to be looked at more closely. A third access specifier, **protected**, will come into play shortly. Let's discuss some more examples; and later on, I'll present a summary of how base class access specifiers affect the access level of inherited class members.

Access Control Under Inheritance

The **private** data members of a base class are also members of the derived class, but they remain **private** to the *base* class within the derived class. This means that the inherited data members are accessible to the inherited function members from the base class, but they are *not* accessible to the member functions declared within the derived class definition.

For example, let's add a function **volume()** to the derived class **Carton**. The file **Carton.h** would update to this:

```
// Carton.h - defines the Carton class with the Box class as base
#ifndef CARTON_H
#define CARTON_H
#include "Box.h"                              // For Box class definition
#include <cstring>
```

```
class Carton : public Box
{
  public:
    Carton(const char* pStr = "Cardboard");      // Constructor

    ~Carton();                                   // Destructor

    double volume() const;                       // Error - members not accessible

  private:
    char* pMaterial;
};
#endif
```

and the file **Carton.cpp** would update to this:

```
// Carton.cpp
#include "Carton.h"
#include <cstring>

// Constructor
Carton::Carton(const char* pStr)
{
  pMaterial = new char[strlen(pStr)+1];      // Allocate space for the string
  strcpy( pMaterial, pStr);                  // Copy it
}

// Destructor
Carton::~Carton()
{
  delete[] pMaterial;
}

// Function to calculate the volume of a Carton object
double Carton::volume() const
{
  return length*breadth*height;
}
```

Suppose we try to run a program using this class and the **Box** class definition from Program 15.1. Any program which uses these classes will not compile. The function **volume()** in the **Carton** class attempts to access the **private** members of the base class, which is not legal — even though they will be inherited members of the derived class.

However, it *is* legal to use the **volume()** function if it's a base class member. So if you move the definition of the function **volume()** to the **public** section of the base class **Box**, then not only will the program compile, but you can use the function to obtain the volume of a **Carton** object. Let's see that working.

585

Try It Out — Base Class Member Functions

First change the class definition in **Box.h** to:

```
class Box
{
  public:
    Box(double lv=1.0, double bv=1.0, double hv=1.0);

// Function to calculate the volume of a Box object
    double volume() const;

  private:
    double length;
    double breadth;
    double height;
};
```

We can declare the **volume()** function as **const** because it does not alter any data members of the class — it just uses them to calculate the volume of an object. Add the function definition to the file **Box.cpp**:

```
// Box.cpp
#include "box.h"

// Constructor
Box::Box(double lv, double bv, double hv) : length(lv), breadth(bv), height(hv)
{}

// Function to calculate the volume of a Box object
double Box::volume() const
{
  return length*breadth*height;
}
```

For this program, we use the files **Carton.h** and **Carton.cpp** which we used in Program 15.1. Thus, the **Carton** class inherits the **Box** class **public**ly, and also has a constructor, a destructor and a **private** data member **pMaterial**.

We can now calculate the volumes of the **Box** and **Carton** objects that we created in Program 15.1, to see how using a base class function in a derived class works out:

```
// Program 15.2 Using a function inherited from a base class
#include <iostream>
#include "Box.h"                              // For the Box class
#include "Carton.h"                           // For the Carton class

using namespace std;

int main()
{
  // Create a Box and two Carton objects
  Box myBox(40.0, 30.0, 20.0);
  Carton myCarton;
  Carton candyCarton("Thin cardboard");
```

```
        cout << endl;
        cout << "myBox volume is "       << myBox.volume()       << endl;
        cout << "myCarton volume is "    << myCarton.volume()    << endl;
        cout << "candyCarton volume is " << candyCarton.volume() << endl;
        return 0;
    }
```

I get the output:

```
    myBox volume is 24000
    myCarton volume is 1
    candyCarton volume is 1
```

How It Works

This demonstrates that the **volume()** function defined in the **Box** class works equally well for objects of the **Carton** class. It is able to access the base class data members, even though they are **private**, and not accessible from derived class functions. The volume of both **Carton** objects is 1, so evidently we have the default dimensions that are set in the base class constructor.

The **Carton** class constructor is called when we create an object of the class; but clearly the base class constructor must also be called somehow, since the derived class constructor offers no provision (and indeed no possibility) for initializing the data members inherited from the base class. You can confirm that the base class constructor is called for a **Carton** object by adding output statements to trace when each constructor is called. For **Box** you could add the following statement to the body of the constructor:

```
    cout << "Box constructor" << endl;
```

You could put a similar statement in the **Carton** class constructor. Don't forget to include the **iostream** header file, and to add a **using** statement in each **.cpp** file. If you run the program again you will get the output:

```
    Box constructor
    Box constructor
    Carton constructor
    Box constructor
    Carton constructor

    myBox volume is 24000
    myCarton volume is 1
    candyCarton volume is 1
```

The first line of output is due to the creation of the **Box** object, **myBox**. The next two lines are generated by the creation of the **Carton** object, **myCarton**. You can see that to create a **Carton** object, there is an automatic call of the **Box** class constructor (in fact the default constructor) before the **Carton** class constructor is executed, and it is this that initializes the base class members.

Later in this chapter, we'll have a closer look at base class constructors, and in particular, how we can have more control over how base class data members are initialized.

Declaring Members of a Class as protected

The **private** members of a base class are only accessible to function members of the base class, but this isn't always convenient. There will doubtless be many occasions when we want the members of a base class to be *accessible* from within the derived class, but nonetheless *protected* from outside interference. As you will surely have anticipated by now, C++ provides a way to do this.

In addition to the **public** and **private** access specifiers for members of a class, you can also declare members of a class as **protected**. Within the class, the keyword **protected** has exactly the same effect as the keyword **private**. Members of a class that are **protected** can only be accessed by member functions of the class, **friend** classes and **friend** functions of the class. These **protected** class members can't be accessed from outside the class, so they behave like **private** class members.

The difference between **protected** and **private** members only becomes apparent in a derived class. Members of a base class that are declared as **protected** are freely accessible in function members of a derived class, whereas the **private** members of the base class are not.

We could redefine our **Box** class to have **protected** data members as follows:

```
class Box
{
  public:
    Box(double lv=1.0, double bv=1.0, double hv=1.0);

  protected:
    double length;
    double breadth;
    double height;
};
```

Now the data members of **Box** are still effectively **private**, in that they can't be accessed by ordinary global functions, but they are now accessible within member functions of a derived class. Let's use an example to demonstrate.

Try It Out – Using Inherited protected Members

We can use this version of the **Box** class to derive a new version of the **Carton** class that accesses the members of the base class through its own member function, **volume()**.

We need to remove the **volume()** function prototype from the **Box** class definition (as above), and also remove the **volume()** function definition from **Box.cpp**.

Then we'll add the **volume()** function prototype to the **Carton** class definition, and add the **volume()** function definition to **Carton.cpp**.

We'll also declare the data member of the **Carton** class as **protected**, so that it will have the same specification as the data members inherited from **Box**. Here's the class definition:

```
class Carton : public Box
{
  public:
    Carton(const char* pStr = "Cardboard");      // Constructor

    ~Carton();                                    // Destructor

      // Function to calculate the volume of a Carton object
      double volume() const;

    protected:
      char* pMaterial;
};
```

Here's the function definition, to be added to **Carton.cpp**:

```
// Function to calculate the volume of a Carton object
double Carton::volume() const
{
  return length*breadth*height;
}
```

We can try out the new **Carton** class with the following program:

```
// Program 15.3 Using inherited protected members in a derived class
#include <iostream>
#include "Box.h"                                 // For the Box class
#include "Carton.h"                              // For the Carton class

using namespace std;

int main()
{
  // Create a Box and two Carton objects
  Box myBox(40.0, 30.0, 20.0);
  Carton myCarton;

  cout << endl;
//cout << "myBox volume is "      << myBox.volume()      << endl;
                                                         // Uncomment for error
  cout << "myCarton volume is " << myCarton.volume()  << endl;
//cout << "myCarton length is " << myCarton.length    << endl;
                                                         // Uncomment for error

  return 0;
}
```

The comments are for demonstrating aspects of our new versions of the **Box** and **Carton** classes. This program displays the output:

```
Box constructor
Box constructor
Carton constructor

myCarton volume is 1
```

How It Works

If you uncomment the output statement that purports to calculate the volume of **myBox**, then the program will not compile:

```
//cout << "myBox volume is " << myBox.volume() << endl;  // Uncomment for error
```

This is because the **Box** class now has no function **volume()** defined. You can only calculate the volume of **Carton** objects.

The volume of the **Carton** object, **myCarton**, is calculated by invoking the function **volume()** that is defined in the derived class:

```
cout << "myCarton volume is " << myCarton.volume()  << endl;
```

This function accesses the inherited members **length**, **breadth**, and **height** to produce the result. These members were declared as **protected** in the base class and remain **protected** in the derived class. The output shows that the volume is being calculated properly for **myCarton**. Its volume turns out to be 1, because default values are assigned to the members inherited from **Box**.

> *Since we specified **pMaterial** in the **Carton** class as **protected**, all the data members of this class will now be **protected**, and therefore they all could be accessed in another class derived from **Carton**.*

You can demonstrate that the **protected** members of the base class remain **protected** in the derived class, by uncommenting the following statement

```
//cout << "myCarton length is " << myCarton.length    << endl;
                                                    // Uncomment for error
```

If you do this, you will get an error message from the compiler, to the effect that the member **length** is **protected**, and so it cannot be accessed from outside the derived class.

The Access Level of Inherited Class Members

As we've seen, when you derived a class from a base class, you must choose the base class access specifier. There are three possibilities: **public**, **protected** or **private**.

FYI

In fact, the *default* base class access specifier is `private`. So if you omit the specifier altogether — for example, by writing `class Carton : Box` at the top of the `Carton` class definition in Program 15.1 — then the `private` access specifier is assumed.

We also know that the access specifiers for the data members of the base class come in three flavors — again, the choice is **public**, **protected** or **private**.

By using the base class to create a derived class, the base class access specifier affects the access status of the inherited members. There are nine different combinations; we have seen some of them in the examples in this chapter. We'll cover all of the possible circumstances in the following paragraphs, although the usefulness of some of these will only become apparent in the next chapter, when we move on to discuss polymorphism.

First, we'll look at how **private** members of a base class are inherited into a derived class. Regardless of the base class access specifier (**public**, **protected** or **private**), a **private** base class member always remains **private** to the base class. There are two consequences of this. First, inherited **private** members are **private** members of the derived class (so they're inaccessible outside the derived class). Second, they are also inaccessible to member functions of the derived class (because they're **private** to the base class).

Now, we'll see how **public** and **protected** base class members are inherited. In all of the remaining cases, the derived members are accessible to member functions of the derived class. Let's see how the members are inherited.

The most common form of inheritance is **public** inheritance. In this case, the access status of the inherited members is unchanged. Thus, inherited **public** members are **public**, and inherited **protected** members are **protected**.

When the inheritance of the base class is **protected**, inherited **public** members become **protected** in the derived class. The **protected** inherited members retain their original access level in the derived class.

Finally, when the inheritance of the base class is **private**, inherited **public** and **protected** members become **private** to the derived class — so they are accessible by member functions of the derived class, but cannot be accessed if they are inherited in another derived class.

This is summarized in the following illustration:

Being able to change the access level of inherited members in a derived class gives you a degree of flexibility, but remember that you can only make the access level more stringent — you can't relax the access level specified in the base class.

Using Access Specifiers in Class Hierarchies

As we've just seen, you have two aspects to consider when defining a hierarchy of classes — the class member access specifiers and the base class access specifier. As we said in Chapter 12, the **public** members of a class define the external interface to the class — which should not normally include data members. Class members that are not part of the class interface should not be directly accessible from outside the class, and this means that they should be **private** or **protected**. Which you choose for a particular member depends on whether or not you want to allow access in a derived class. If you do, use **protected**, otherwise use **private**. It's generally wise to keep things as locked away as possible.

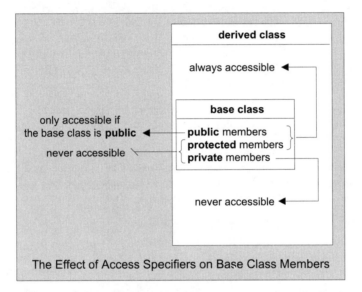

The Effect of Access Specifiers on Base Class Members

As the diagram above shows, the accessibility of inherited members is only affected by the access specifiers of these members in the base class definition. Within the derived class, the **public** and **protected** base class members are always accessible, and the **private** base class members are never accessible. From outside the derived class, only **public** base class members may be accessed — and this is only the case when the base class is declared as **public**.

As we've seen, if the base class access specifier is **public** then the access status of inherited members remains unchanged. By using the **protected** and **private** base class access specifiers, you are able to do two things.

First, you can prevent access to **public** base class members from outside the derived class — either specifier will do this. If the base class has **public** function members then this is a serious step — because the class interface for the base class is being removed from public view in the derived class.

Second, you can affect how the inherited members of the derived class are inherited in another class, which uses the derived class as its base.

592

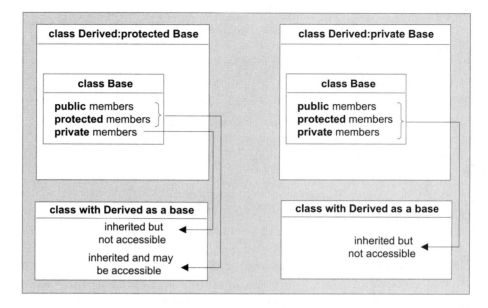

As the diagram shows, the **public** and **protected** members of a base class can be handed on as **protected** members of another derived class. Members of a **private**ly inherited base class will not be accessible in any further derived class.

In the majority of instances, as our examples reflect, you will find that the **public** base class access specifier is most appropriate, with the base class data members declared as either **private** or **protected**. By using either the **protected** or **private** base class access specifiers, the base class sub-object is internal to the derived class object, and is therefore not part of the public interface to a derived class object. In practice, since the derived class object *is a kind of* base class object, you will want the base class interface to be inherited in the derived class, and this implies that the base class must be specified as **public**.

Changing the Access Specification of Inherited Members

You might want to exempt a particular base class member from the effects of a **protected** or **private** base class access specifier. Let's take an example. Suppose we define the **Box** class with a **public** member function, **volume()**:

```
class Box
{
  public:
    // Constructor
    Box(double lv=1.0, double bv=1.0, double hv=1.0);

    // Function to calculate the volume of a Box object
    double volume() const;

  protected:
    double length;
    double breadth;
    double height;
};
```

Just for the record, here are the out-of-line function definitions for this class:

```
// Constructor
Box::Box(double lv, double bv, double hv) : length(lv), breadth(bv), height(hv)
{
  cout << "Box constructor" << endl;
}

// Function to calculate the volume of a Box object
double Box::volume() const
{
  return length*breadth*height;
}
```

We now want to derive a new class, **Package**, using **Box** as a **private** base class — but we'd really like the **volume()** function to be **public** in the derived class. Of course, the default result of **private** inheritance is that all the **public** and **protected** members will be **private** in the derived class. We can alter this for a particular inherited member by employing a **using declaration**.

This is essentially the same as the **using** declaration that we saw in Chapter 10, when we discussed namespaces. We can force the **volume()** function to be **public** in the derived class by writing the following class definition:

```
class Package : private Box
{
  public:
    using Box::volume;              // Inherit as public

  // Rest of the class definition
};
```

The class definition defines a scope — and the **using** declaration within the class definition introduces a name into that class scope. The **using** declaration here overrides the **private** base class access specifier just for the base class member function, **volume()**. The function will be inherited as **public** in the **Package** class, not as **private**.

There are two points of syntax to note here. First, when you apply a **using** declaration to a member of a base class, you must qualify the member name with the base class name, as we have done above, because the class name specifies the context for the member name. Second, note that you don't supply a parameter list or a return type here — just the qualified name of the member function.

Here, we have used a using declaration to override the effect of the base class specifier an inherited member function — but the same technique also works for inherited data members. Simply use the base class name and the scope resolution operator before the member name.

It's also possible to use a **using** declaration to override a original **public** or **protected** base class access specificier. Hence, you can use this technique to allow a base class member more accessibility, or less accessiblility, in the derived class. For example, if the **volume()** function were **protected** in the **Box** base class, then you could make it **public** in the derived class, **Package**, with the same **using** declaration that we used above.

Note that you cannot apply a **using** declaration in this way to a **private** member of a base class, because **private** members cannot be accessed in a derived class.

Now that we know how we can hide members of a base class and still access them in a derived class, let's return to the question of constructors.

Constructor Operation in a Derived Class

Although, in Programs 15.2 and 15.3, the default base class constructor was called automatically, this doesn't have to be the case. We can arrange to call a particular base class constructor from the derived class constructor. This will enable us to initialize the base class data members with a constructor other than the default. It also allows us to choose one or other base class constructor, depending on the data supplied to the derived class constructor.

Try It Out – Calling Base Class Constructors

We can demonstrate this by using a modified version of Program 15.3. We'll keep the trace statements in the existing class constructors. To show how we can call a base class constructor explicitly, we will add a second constructor for the **Carton** class that allows you to specify the dimensions of the object. You need to alter the **Carton** class definition in **Carton.h** to:

```
class Carton : public Box
{
  public:
    // Constructor which can also act as default constructor -
    //           calls default base constructor automatically
    Carton(const char* pStr = "Cardboard");

    // Constructor explicitly calling the base constructor
    Carton(double lv, double bv, double hv, const char* pStr = "Cardboard");

    ~Carton();                                    // Destructor

    // Function to calculate the volume of a Carton object
    double volume() const;

  protected:
    char* pMaterial;
};
```

As ever, the out-of-line function definitions will be contained in **Carton.cpp**:

```
// Carton.cpp
#include "Carton.h"
#include <cstring>
#include <iostream>
using namespace std;
```

```cpp
// Constructor which can also act as default constructor -
//          calls default base constructor automatically
Carton::Carton(const char* pStr)
{
  pMaterial = new char[strlen(pStr)+1];     // Allocate space for the string
  strcpy( pMaterial, pStr);                 // Copy it
  cout << "Carton constructor 1" << endl;
}
```

```cpp
// Constructor explicitly calling the base constructor
Carton::Carton(double lv, double bv, double hv, const char* pStr): Box(lv, bv, hv)
{
  pMaterial = new char[strlen(pStr)+1];     // Allocate space for the string
  strcpy(pMaterial, pStr);                  // Copy it
  cout << "Carton constructor 2" << endl;
}
```

```cpp
// Destructor
Carton::~Carton()
{
  delete[] pMaterial;
}

// Function to calculate the volume of a Carton object
double Carton::volume() const
{
  return length*breadth*height;
}
```

So that we can track when the default constructor in the **Box** class is called, we will modify the definition to provide a separate default constructor:

```cpp
class Box
{
  public:
    Box();                              // Default constructor

    Box(double lv, double bv, double hv);     // Constructor

  protected:
    double length;
    double breadth;
    double height;
};
```

Again, we'll put the out-of-line definitions into the file **Box.cpp**:

```cpp
// Box.cpp
#include "box.h"
#include <iostream>
using namespace std;
```

```cpp
// Default constructor
Box::Box() : length(1.0), breadth(1.0), height(1.0)
{
  cout << "Default Box constructor" << endl;
}
```

```
// Constructor
Box::Box(double lv, double bv, double hv) : length(lv), breadth(bv), height(hv)
{
  cout << "Box constructor" << endl;
}
```

We will write a version of **main()** that will call both **Carton** class constructors:

```
// Program 15.4 Calling a base class constructor from a derived class constructor
#include <iostream>
#include "Box.h"                              // For the Box class
#include "Carton.h"                           // For the Carton class

using namespace std;

int main()
{
  // Create two Carton objects
  Carton myCarton;
  Carton candyCarton(50.0, 30.0, 20.0, "Thin cardboard");

  cout << endl << "myCarton volume is "    << myCarton.volume();
  cout << endl << "candyCarton volume is " << candyCarton.volume()
       << endl;

  return 0;
}
```

Compiling and running this version of the program produces the output:

```
Default Box constructor
Carton constructor 1
Box constructor
Carton constructor 2

myCarton volume is 1
candyCarton volume is 30000
```

How It Works

The output statement in each constructor provides us with a clear understanding of the sequence of events. For the **Carton** object **myCarton**, the compiler first calls the default **Box** constructor, followed by the first **Carton** constructor. The default **Box** constructor call is the automatic call that we have seen before.

For the second **Carton** object, the **Box** constructor is called as a result of an explicit constructor call, in the header of the second **Carton** constructor:

```
Carton::Carton(double lv, double bv, double hv, const char* pStr): Box(lv, bv, hv)
```

The explicit call of the constructor for the **Box** class appears after a colon in the header of the derived class constructor. The call appears only in the constructor definition, and not in the prototype. The parameters of the **Carton** constructor are passed to the base class constructor as arguments.

597

*You may have noticed that the notation for calling the base class constructor is exactly the same as that used for initializing data members in a constructor. We have used this notation in the constructors for the **Box** class. This is perfectly consistent with what we are doing here, since essentially we are initializing the **Box** sub-object of the **Carton** object using the arguments passed to the **Carton** constructor.*

The table below explains what each of the constructors calls recorded in the output is responsible for:

Program output	Object being constructed
`Default Box constructor`	**Box** sub-object of **myCarton**
`Carton constructor 1`	Remainder of **myCarton** object
`Box constructor`	**Box** sub-object of **candyCarton**
`Carton constructor 2`	Remainder of **candyCarton** object

When a derived class object is created, the base class constructor must be called before the derived class constructor. This is a general rule. When several levels of inheritance are involved, the class constructor of the most general base class is called first; subsequent constructor calls are made in order of derivation, until finally, the derived class constructor is called.

While base class data members that are not **private** to the base class can be *accessed* from the derived class, they can't be *initialized* in the initialization list for the derived class constructor. For example, try replacing the second **Carton** class constructor with the following (you'll only need to change the file **Carton.cpp**):

```
// Constructor that won't compile!
Carton::Carton(double lv, double bv, double hv, const char* pStr):
                                    length(lv), breadth(bv), height(hv)
{
  pMaterial = new char[strlen(pStr)+1];    // Allocate space for the string
  strcpy(pMaterial, pStr);                 // Copy it
  cout << "Carton constructor 2" << endl;
}
```

At first sight, we'd expect this to work, since **length**, **breadth** and **height** are protected base class members that are inherited **public**ly — so the **Carton** class constructor should be able to access them. However, the compiler complains that **length**, **breadth** and **height** are *not* members of the **Carton** class. So what's really happening here?

The answer is that the derived class constructor *can* refer to **protected** base class members, but not in the initialization list — because at that stage, they still don't exist. The initialization list is processed before the base class constructor is called, and before the base part of the object has been created. If you want to initialize the inherited data members explicitly, you must do it in the body of the constructor. You could, instead, use the following constructor definition in the file **Carton.cpp**:

```
// This constructor doesn't cause a compiler error
Carton::Carton(double lv, double bv, double hv, const char* pStr)
{
  length = lv;
  breadth = bv;
  height = hv;
  pMaterial = new char[strlen(pStr)+1];          // Allocate space for the string
  strcpy(pMaterial, pStr);                        // Copy it
  cout << "Carton constructor 2" << endl;
}
```

By the time the body of the constructor is executed, the base part of the object has been created. In this case, base part of the **Carton** object is created by an automatic call of the default base class constructor. We can subsequently refer to the names of the non-**private** base class members without a problem.

The Copy Constructor in a Derived Class

We've already seen what happens when an object of a user-defined class is declared and initialized with another object of the same class. Let's briefly look over this again. Consider these statements:

```
Box myBox(2.0, 3.0, 4.0);                        // Calls constructor
Box copyBox(myBox);                              // Calls copy constructor
```

Here, we declare a **Box** object **myBox**, but the key statement here is the second statement, in which the copy object, **copyBox**, is declared and initialized. In Chapter 13 we saw how, for such an initialization, the copy constructor is called automatically by the compiler. In Program 12.5 we also saw that, if you haven't defined your own copy constructor for the **Box** class, the compiler will supply a default version, that creates the new object by copying the original object member by member.

Now, let's exercise copy constructors in a derived class situation. To do this, we'll add to the class definitions that we used in Program 15.4. First, we'll add a copy constructor to the base class **Box**, by inserting the following code into **Box.cpp**:

```
// Copy constructor
Box::Box(const Box& aBox) :
                 length(aBox.length), breadth(aBox.breadth),
height(aBox.height)
{
  cout << "Box copy constructor called" << endl;
}
```

> *Recall, from Chapter 13, that you must specify the parameter for the copy constructor as a reference.*

This simply initializes the data members by copying the original values, and generates output so that we can track when the **Box** copy constructor is being called. We'll also need to add the copy constructor prototype to the **public** section of the **Box** class declaration in **Box.h**:

```
Box(const Box& aBox);                            // Copy constructor
```

For the **Carton** class, we also add our own copy constructor. For a first effort, we'll try adding the following definition to **Carton.cpp**:

```
// Copy constructor
Carton::Carton(const Carton& aCarton)
{
  pMaterial = new char[strlen(aCarton.pMaterial)+1];
                                        // Allocate space for the string
  strcpy(pMaterial, aCarton.pMaterial);           // Copy it
  cout << "Carton copy constructor" << endl;
}
```

Of course, we also need to add the prototype to the class definition in **Carton.h**:

```
    Carton(const Carton& aCarton);                 // Copy constructor
```

> *In fact, the copy constructor for the **Carton** class is important, because the class contains a data member, **pMaterial**, which is a pointer. Our copy constructor must duplicate the string pointed to by **pMaterial**, rather than just copying the pointer. Otherwise, the original and copy objects would each contain a pointer that points to the same string — and when one of the objects is deleted, the string is also deleted, and the pointer in the remaining object would be useless.*

Let's see if this works.

Try It Out — The Copy Constructor in Derived Classes

We can try to exercise the copy constructors that we have just defined in the **Box** and **Carton** classes by creating a **Carton** object, and then creating a duplicate:

```
// Program 15.5 Using a derived class copy constructor
#include <iostream>
#include "Box.h"                              // For the Box class
#include "Carton.h"                           // For the Carton class

using namespace std;

int main()
{
   Carton candyCarton(20.0, 30.0, 40.0, "Glassine board");
                                              // Declare and initialize
   Carton copyCarton(candyCarton);                    // Use copy constructor

   cout << endl
        << "Volume of candyCarton is " << candyCarton.volume()
        << endl
        << "Volume of copyCarton is " << copyCarton.volume()
        << endl;

   return 0;
}
```

This produces the output:

```
Box constructor
Carton constructor 2
Default Box constructor
Carton copy constructor

Volume of candyCarton is 24000
Volume of copyCarton is 1
```

How It Works (or Why It Doesn't)

A cursory inspection of the output will show that all is not as it should be. Clearly the volume of **copyCarton** is not the same as **candyCarton**, which is strange since one is supposed to be a copy of the other. The output also shows the reason for this.

In order to copy the **candyCarton** object, we call the copy constructor for the **Carton** class. As part of the copy process, the **Carton** copy constructor must make a copy of the **Box** sub-object of **candyCarton**, and to do this it should call the **Box** copy constructor. However, the output clearly shows that the *default* **Box** constructor is being called instead.

The **Carton** copy constructor doesn't call the **Box** copy constructor, simply because we didn't tell it to. The compiler knows that it has to create a **Box** sub-object for the object **copyCarton**, but we didn't specify how it should be done, and the compiler can't second-guess our intentions. The best it can do is create a default base object.

> *When you write a constructor for an object of a derived class, remember that you are responsible for ensuring that the members of the derived class object are properly initialized. This includes all the inherited data members, as well as the data members specific to the derived class.*

The fix for this is to call the **Box** copy constructor in the initialization list of the **Carton** copy constructor. Simply change the copy constructor definition in **Carton.cpp** to:

```
// Copy constructor
Carton::Carton(const Carton& aCarton) : Box(aCarton)
{
  pMaterial = new char[strlen(aCarton.pMaterial)+1];
                                      // Allocate space for the string
  strcpy(pMaterial, aCarton.pMaterial);          // Copy it
  cout << "Carton copy constructor" << endl;
}
```

Now, the **Box** class copy constructor is called with the **aCarton** object as an argument. The object **aCarton** is of type **Carton**, but the parameter for the **Box** class copy constructor is a reference to a **Box** object. The compiler will insert a conversion for **aCarton** — from type **Carton** to type **Box** — and this will result in only the base part of **aCarton** being passed to the **Box** class copy constructor. Now, if you compile and run the example again, the output will be:

```
Box constructor
Carton constructor 2
Box copy constructor called
Carton copy constructor
```

601

```
Volume of candyCarton is 24000
Volume of copyCarton is 24000
```

The output shows that the constructors are called in the correct sequence. In particular, the **Box** copy constructor (for the **Box** sub-object of **copyCarton**) is called before the **Carton** copy constructor. By way of a check, we can see that the volumes of the **candyCarton** and **copyCarton** objects are now identical.

To summarize, here's another golden rule to remember:

> *You can write your own definition for any kind of constructor for a derived class. When you do so, you are responsible for the initialization of all members of the derived class object, including all its inherited members.*

Destructors under Inheritance

Destroying a derived class object — either when it goes out of scope or, in the case of an object in the free store, when you delete it — involves both the derived class destructor *and* the base class destructor.

We can demonstrate this by employing statements in the **Box** and **Carton** destructor definitions, that will allow us to trace exactly when they are called. We'll amend the class definitions which we used in Program 15.5. Add the destructor definition to the file **Box.cpp**:

```
// Destructor
Box::~Box()
{
   cout << "Box destructor" << endl;
}
```

Don't forget to add the prototype to the class definition in **Box.h**:

```
~Box();                                  // Destructor
```

The **Carton** class already has a destructor, so we just need to add the trace statement to the destructor definition. Add the following line to **Carton.cpp**:

```
// Destructor
Carton::~Carton()
{
   cout << "Carton destructor. Material = " << pMaterial << endl;
   delete[] pMaterial;
}
```

The trace output displays the composite material, so we can tell which **Carton** object is being destroyed by assigning a different composite material to each one. Let's see how these classes behave in practice.

Try It Out — Destructors in a Class Hierarchy

We can see how class destructors behave with objects of a derived class with the following version of **main()**:

```
// Program 15.6 Destructors in a class hierarchy
#include <iostream>
#include "Box.h"                                // For the Box class
#include "Carton.h"                             // For the Carton class

using namespace std;

int main()
{
  Carton myCarton;
  Carton candyCarton(50.0, 30.0, 20.0, "Thin cardboard");

  cout << endl << "myCarton volume is "    << myCarton.volume();
  cout << endl << "candyCarton volume is " << candyCarton.volume()
       << endl << endl;

  return 0;
}
```

If you recompile the program with the changes to the header files containing the class definitions, you will get the output:

```
Default Box constructor
Carton constructor 1
Box constructor
Carton constructor 2

myCarton volume is 1
candyCarton volume is 30000

Carton destructor. Material = Thin cardboard
Box destructor
Carton destructor. Material = Cardboard
Box destructor
```

How It Works

We create two **Carton** objects here: the first is an object with default dimensions, and the second has explicit dimensions and a material description. Then we output the volume of each object, for no particular reason.

The point of the exercise is to see how the destructors behave. The output from the destructor calls indicates two aspects about how the objects are destroyed. First, you can see the sequence in which destructors are called for a particular object; and second, you can see the order in which the objects are destroyed.

The destructor calls recorded by the output correspond to the following actions:

603

Destructor output	Object destroyed
`Carton destructor. Material = Thin cardboard`	`candyCarton` object
`Box destructor`	`Box` sub-object of `candyCarton`
`Carton destructor. Material = Cardboard`	`myCarton` object
`Box destructor`	`Box` sub-object of `myCarton`

You can see from this that the objects are destroyed in the *reverse* order from which they were created. The object **myCarton** is first and destroyed last; the **candyCarton** object is declared last and destroyed first.

This sequence is chosen to ensure that we never end up with an object in an illegal state. An object can only be used after it has been declared — this means that any given object can only contain pointers (or references) which point (or refer) to objects that have already been created. By destroying the given object *before* any objects that it might point (or refer) to, we ensure that the destructor execution cannot result in any invalid pointers or references.

For a particular derived class object, the sequence of destructor calls is the reverse of the constructor call sequence for the object — the derived class destructor is called first, then the base class destructor, just as in the example. The case of a three level class hierarchy is illustrated below.

For an object with several levels of base class, this sequence of destructor calls runs through the hierarchy of classes, starting with the derived class destructor and ending with the destructor for the most general base class.

Duplicate Member Names

It's possible you could find a situation where a base class and derived class each have a data member with the same name. If you're really unlucky, you might even have names duplicated in the base class and an indirect base.

Of course, this situation is confusing, and you should never deliberately set out to create such an arrangement in your own classes. However, circumstances may dictate that this is how things turn out. For example, if you are deriving your class from a base class designed by another programmer, you would almost certainly know nothing about the **private** data members of his class — you would only know about the base class interface. What happens if, by coincidence, the base and derived classes use the same data member names?

In fact, duplication of names is no bar to inheritance. Let's look at how to differentiate between identically-named base and derived class members.

Suppose we have a class **Base**, defined as:

```
class Base
{
  public:
    Base(int number = 10){ value = number; }        // Constructor
  protected:
    int value;
};
```

This just contains a single data member, **value**, and a constructor. We can derive a class **Derived** from **Base** as follows:

```
class Derived: public Base
{
  public:
    Derived(int number = 20){ value = number; }      // Constructor
    int total() const;                               // Total value of data members
  protected:
    int value;
};
```

The derived class has a data member called **value**, and will also inherit the member **value** from the base class. As you can see, it's already starting to look confusing! We'll show how the compiler tells the difference, within the derived class, by writing a definition for the **total()** function.

Within the derived class member function, the name **value** by itself refers to the data member declared within that scope — that is, the derived class member. The base class member is declared within a different scope, and to access it from the derived class member function you must qualify the member name (using the base class name and the scope resolution operator). Thus, we can write the implementation of the **total()** function as:

```
int Derived::total() const
{
  return value + Base::value;
}
```

The expression **Base::value** specifies the base class data member, and the name **value** by itself refers to the member declare in the **Derived** class.

Duplicate Function Member Names

What happens when base class and derived class member functions share the same name? We can distinguish two situations in relation to functions in a derived class that share a common name as a base class member function.

In the first case, the functions have the same name but different parameter lists. Although the function signatures are different, this is *not* a case for function overloading. This is because overloaded functions must be defined within the same scope, and each class, base or derived, defines a separate scope.

In fact, the scope is the key to the situation. The derived class function member will hide the inherited function member with the same name. Thus, when the base and inherited member functions have the same name, we must introduce the qualified name of the base class member function into the scope of the derived class with a **using** declaration. Either function can then be called for a derived class object, as illustrated in the diagram.

```
class Base
{
  public:
    void doThat(int arg);
    ...
};




class Derived: public Base
{
  public:
    void doThat(double arg);
    using Base::doThat;
    ...
};
```

By default the derived class function **doThat()** would hide the inherited function with the same name. The **using** declaration introduces the function name, **doThat**, from the base class into the derived class's scope, so the derived class scope includes both versions of the function.

```
Derived object;
object.doThat(2);        // Call inherited base function
object.doThat(2.5);      // Call derived function
```

The second possibility is that the inherited functions are the same in all respects, so they even have the same function signature. We could still differentiate the inherited function from the derived class function by using the class name and the scope resolution operator to call the base class function:

```
Derived object;              // Object declaration
object.Base::doThat(3);      // Call base version of the function
```

However, there's a lot more to it than that; this subject is closely related to polymorphism, so we will defer further discussion of this possibility until the next chapter.

Multiple Inheritance

So far, our derived classes have all been derived from a *single* direct base. However, we're not limited to this structure — a derived class can have as many direct base classes as your application requires. This concept is referred to as **multiple inheritance** (as opposed to **single inheritance**, when a single base class is used), and it opens vast new dimensions of potential complexity in inheritance.

Multiple inheritance is used much less frequently than single inheritance, and so we will not explore it here in great depth. We will simply examine the basic ideas behind how multiple inheritance works, and see where the complications come in.

Multiple Base Classes

Multiple inheritance involves the use of two or more direct base classes to derive a new class, so things are immediately more complicated. The idea of a derived class being a specialization of its base leads in this case to the notion that the derived class defines an object that is a specialization of two or more different and independent class types concurrently.

In practice, multiple inheritance is not often used in this way. More often, multiple base classes are used to add the features of the base classes together to form a composite object containing the capabilities of its base classes — sometimes referred to a 'mix-in programming'. This is usually for the convenience of implementation, rather than to reflect any particular relationships between objects. For an example, we night consider a programming interface of some kind — for graphics programming, perhaps. A comprehensive interface could be packaged in a set of classes, each of which defines a self-contained interface that provides some specific capability — such as drawing two-dimensional shapes. You can then use several of these classes as bases to derive a new class, which provides precisely the set of capabilities that you need for your application.

To explore some of the implications of multiple inheritance, let's start with a hierarchy that includes the **Box** and **Carton** classes we've used so far. Suppose that we want to define a class that represents a package containing dry contents, such as a carton of cereal. It's possible to do this by using single inheritance, deriving a new class from the Carton class and adding a data member to represent contents; but we could also do it using the hierarchy illustrated below.

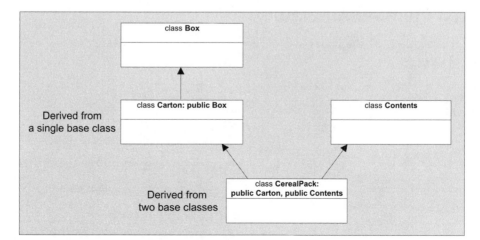

The definition of the **CerealPack** class would look like this:

```
class CerealPack: public Carton, public Contents
{
  // Details of the class...
};
```

Each of the base classes is specified after the colon in the class header; they are separated by commas. Each base class has its own access specifier (as with single inheritance, if you omit the access specifier, then the default **private** is assumed).

The **CerealPack** class will now inherit *all* the members of *both* classes. As in the case of single inheritance, the access level of each inherited member is determined by two factors: the access specifier of the member in the base class, and the base class access specifier.

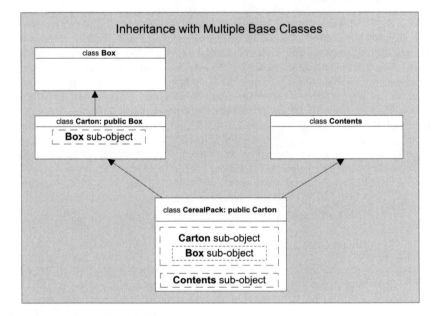

Inherited Member Ambiguity

Let's put some flesh on the bones and define our classes in more detail. We can define the **Box** class in **Box.h** as:

```
// Box.h - defines Box class
#ifndef BOX_H
#define BOX_H
class Box
{
  public:
    Box(double lv=1, double bv=1, double hv=1); // Constructor

    Box(const Box& aBox);                        // Copy constructor

    ~Box();                                      // Destructor
```

```
    // Function to calculate the volume of a Box object
    double volume() const;

  protected:
    double length;
    double breadth;
    double height;
};
#endif
```

The definitions are out-of-line, and contained in the file **Box.cpp**:

```
// Box.cpp
#include "box.h"
#include <iostream>
using namespace std;

// Default constructor
Box::Box(double lv, double bv, double hv) : length(lv), breadth(bv), height(hv)
{
  cout << "Box constructor" << endl;
}

// Copy constructor
Box::Box(const Box& aBox) :
                    length(aBox.length), breadth(aBox.breadth),
height(aBox.height)
{
  cout << "Box copy constructor called" << endl;
}

// Destructor
Box::~Box()
{
  cout << "Box destructor" << endl;
}

// Function to calculate the volume of a Box object
double Box::volume() const
{
  return length*breadth*height;
}
```

This version of the **Box** class is very similar to previous versions. We have a single constructor, which also acts as the default constructor by supplying default parameter values. The volume function is now back in the base class, where it should be.

We will extend the **Carton** class definition slightly from the previous versions. The header file **Carton.h** should contain:

```
// Carton.h - defines the Carton class with the Box class as base
#ifndef CARTON_H
#define CARTON_H
#include "Box.h"                              // For Box class definition
#include <cstring>
```

```
class Carton : public Box
{
  public:
    Carton(double lv = 1, double bv = 1, double hv = 1,   // Constructor
           const char* pStr = "Cardboard",
           double dense = 0.125, double thick = 0.2);

    // Constructor explicitly calling the base constructor

    ~Carton();                                 // Destructor

    double getWeight() const;                  // "Get carton weight" function

  protected:
    char* pMaterial;                           // Carton material
    double thickness;                          // Material thickness inches
    double density;                            // Material density in pounds/cubic inch
};
#endif
```

There are two new data members, that record the thickness and density of the material from which the **Carton** object is made. The constructor provides defaults for all the **Carton** class data members. There is a new function in the class, **getWeight()**, which uses the new data members to calculate the weight of an empty **Carton** object. The definitions, in **Carton.cpp**, are as follows:

```
// Carton.cpp
#include "Carton.h"
#include <cstring>
#include <iostream>
using namespace std;

// Constructor
Carton::Carton(double lv, double bv, double hv,
               const char* pStr, double dense, double thick):
                   Box(lv, bv, hv), density(dense), thickness(thick)
{
  pMaterial = new char[strlen(pStr)+1];      // Allocate space for the string
  strcpy( pMaterial, pStr);                  // Copy it
  cout << "Carton constructor" << endl;
}

// Destructor
Carton::~Carton()
{
  cout << "Carton destructor" << endl;
  delete[] pMaterial;
}

// "Get carton weight" function
double Carton::getWeight() const
{
  return 2*(length*breadth + breadth*height + height*length)*thickness*density;
}
```

610

The **Contents** class will describe an amount of a dry product, such as breakfast cereal, which can then be contained in a carton. The **Contents** class has three data members: name, volume and density (in pounds per cubic inch). In practice, you would probably want to include a set of possible cereal types, complete with their densities, so that you could validate the data in the constructor — but we will ignore such niceties in the interests of keeping things simple.

Here's the class definition along with the pre-processor directives that you need to put in the header file **Contents.h**:

```
// Contents.h - Dry contents
#ifndef CONTENTS_H
#define CONTENTS_H
#include <cstring>

class Contents
{

  public:
    Contents(const char* pStr = "cereal", double weight =0.3, double vol = 0);
                                     // Constructor

    ~Contents();                     // Destructor

    double getWeight() const;        // "Get contents weight" function

  protected:
    char* pName;                     // Contents type
    double volume;                   // Cubic inches
    double unitweight;               // Pounds per cubic inch
};
#endif
```

In addition to the constructor and the destructor, we have a public function **getWeight()** to calculate the weight of the volume of the material. The definitions are contained in **Contents.cpp**:

```
// Contents.cpp
#include "contents.h"
#include <cstring>
#include <iostream>
using namespace std;

// Constructor
Contents::Contents(const char* pStr, double weight, double vol):
                                     unitweight(weight), volume(vol)
{
  pName = new char[strlen(pStr)+1];
  strcpy(pName, pStr);
  cout << "Contents constructor" << endl;
}

// Destructor
Contents::~Contents()
{
  delete[] pName;
  cout << "Contents destructor" << endl;
}
```

```
// "Get Contents weight" function
double Contents::getWeight() const
{
  return volume*unitweight;
}
```

Now we can define the **CerealPack** class with the **Carton** and **Contents** classes as public base classes. Put the definition in a header file, **CerealPack.h**:

```
// Cerealpack.h - Class defining a carton of cereal
#ifndef CEREALPACK_H
#define CEREALPACK_H
#include <iostream>
#include "Carton.h"
#include "Contents.h"

using namespace std;
class CerealPack: public Carton, public Contents
{
  public:
    CerealPack(double length, double breadth, double height,
                                         const char* cerealType);
                                // Constructor

    ~CerealPack();              // Destructor
};
#endif
```

Once again, the definitions go in the **Cerealpack.cpp** file:

```
// Cerealpack.cpp
#include <iostream>
#include "Carton.h"
#include "Contents.h"
#include "Cerealpack.h"
using namespace std;

// Constructor
CerealPack::CerealPack(double length, double breadth, double height,
                                         const char* cerealType):
                Carton(length, breadth, height, "cardboard"),
                Contents(cerealType)
{
  cout << "CerealPack constructor" << endl;
  Contents::volume = 0.9*Carton::volume();        // Set contents volume
}

// Destructor
CerealPack::~CerealPack()
{
  cout << "CerealPack destructor" << endl;
}
```

This class inherits from both the **Carton** and **Contents** class. The constructor requires only the external dimensions and the cereal type. The material for the **Carton** object is set in the **Carton** constructor call, in the initialization list.

The **CerealPack** object will contain two sub-objects corresponding to the two base classes. Each sub-object is initialized through constructor calls in the initialization list for the **CerealPack** class constructor. Note that the **volume** data member of the **Contents** class is zero by default so, in the body of the **CerealPack** constructor, we calculate its value from the **Carton volume** member. The reference to the **volume** data member inherited from the **Contents** class must be qualified here because it is the same as the name of the function inherited from **Box** via **Carton**. We will be able to trace the sequence of constructor and destructor calls from the output statements here, and in the other classes.

Try It Out — Using Multiple Inheritance

We could try creating a **CerealPack** object and calculate its volume and weight with the following very simple program:

```
// Program 15.7 Using multiple inheritance
#include <iostream>
#include "CerealPack.h"                              // For the CerealPack class

using namespace std;

int main()
{
  CerealPack packOfFlakes(8.0, 3.0, 10.0, "Cornflakes");

  cout << endl;
  cout << "packOfFlakes volume is " << packOfFlakes.volume() << endl;
  cout << "packOfFlakes weight is " << packOfFlakes.getWeight() << endl
       << endl;

  return 0;
}
```

Unfortunately, this program won't compile. The difficulty is that we have rather foolishly used some non-unique function names in the base classes — so the name **volume** (inherited as a function from **Box** and as a data member from **Contents**) and the **getWeight()** function (inherited from **Carton** and from **Contents**) are not unique in the **CerealPack** class. In short, we have an ambiguity problem.

Of course, when writing classes for use in inheritance, we should avoid duplicating member names in the first instance. The ideal solution to this problem is to rewrite our classes.

If we were unable to rewrite the classes — for example, if the base classes were taken from a library of some sort — then we would be forced to qualify the function names of our **main()** function. We could amend the program to:

```
// Program 15.7 Using multiple inheritance
#include <iostream>
#include "CerealPack.h"                              // For the CerealPack class

using namespace std;
```

```
int main()
{
  CerealPack packOfFlakes(8.0, 3.0, 10.0, "Cornflakes");

  cout << endl;
  cout << "packOfFlakes volume is " << packOfFlakes.Carton::volume() << endl;
  cout << "packOfFlakes weight is "
       << packOfFlakes.Carton::getWeight()+packOfFlakes.Contents::getWeight()
       << endl
       << endl;

  return 0;
}
```

Now the program will compile, and when you run it, it will produce the output:

```
Box constructor
Carton constructor
Contents constructor
CerealPack constructor

packOfFlakes volume is 240
packOfFlakes weight is 71.5

CerealPack destructor
Contents destructor
Carton destructor
Box destructor
```

How It Works

You can see from the output that this cereal will give you a solid start to the day — a single packet weighs over four pounds. You can also see that the constructor and destructor call sequence follows the same pattern that we observed in the single inheritance context — the constructors run down the hierarchy from most base to most derived, and the destructors run in the opposite sequence.

The object of type **CerealPack** has sub-objects from both legs of its inheritance chain, and all the constructors for these sub-objects are involved in the creation of a **CerealPack** object.

Repeated Inheritance

In the example above, we demonstrated how ambiguities can occur when member names of base classes are duplicated. You should also be aware of another ambiguity which can arise in multiple inheritance — when a derived object contains multiple versions of a sub-object of one of the base classes.

When using multiple inheritance, you must not use a class more than once as a direct base class. However, it is clearly still possible to end up with duplication of an *indirect* base class. Suppose that the **Box** and **Contents** classes were themselves derived from a class **Common**. The diagram shows the class hierarchy that we've created here.

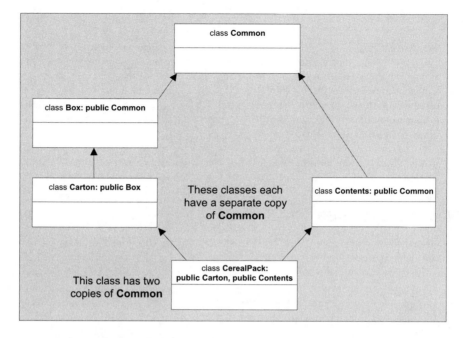

The **CerealPack** class inherits all the members of both the **Contents** class and the **Carton** class. The **Carton** class inherits all the members of the **Box** class, and both the **Box** and **Contents** classes inherit the members of the **Common** class. Thus, as the diagram shows, the **Common** class is duplicated in the **CerealPack** class. The effect of this on objects of type **CerealPack** is illustrated below.

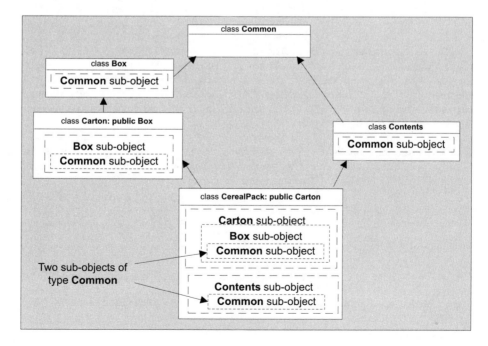

As the diagram shows, every **CerealPack** object will have two sub-objects of type **Common**.

It is conceivable — just — that you actually want to *allow* the duplication of the **Common** class. In this case, you must qualify each reference to the **Common** class member, so that the compiler can tell which inherited member you're referring too. In this case, you could do this by using the **Carton** and **Contents** class names as qualifiers — since each of these classes contains a unique sub-object of type **Common**. Of course, to call the **Common** class constructors when creating a **CerealPack** object, you would also need qualifiers to specify which of the two base objects you were initializing.

More typically, though, you would want to *prevent* the duplication of a base class, so let's see how to do that.

Virtual Base Classes

To avoid duplication of a base class, you must identify to the compiler that the base class should only appear once within any derived class. You do this by declaring the class as a **virtual base class** using the keyword **virtual**. The **Contents** class would be defined as:

```
class Contents: public virtual Common
{
    ...
};
```

The **Box** class would also be defined with a virtual base class:

```
class Box: public virtual Common
{
    ...
};
```

Now, any class which uses the **Contents** and **Box** classes as (direct or indirect) bases will inherit the other members of the base classes as usual — but will inherit only one instance of the **Common** class. So, in our example above, the derived **CerealPack** class would inherit only a single instance of the **Common** base class. Since there is no duplication of the members of **Common** in the **CerealPack** class, no qualification of the member names is needed when referring to them in the derived class.

Declaring the **Common** class as a virtual base class for the **Contents** and **Box** classes does not preclude the possibility of another class having **Common** as a non-virtual base class, and that class being a third base class for **CerealPack**. For example:

```
class Freebie: public Common
{
    ...
};
```

The **CerealPack** class could be:

```
class CerealPack: public Carton, public Contents, public Freebie
{
    ...
};
```

Now the **CerealPack** class has two sub-objects of type **Common** — one is inherited from the **Carton** and **Contents** classes, and the other is inherited from the **Freebie** class. In order to reference members of **Common** for a particular sub-object, you would have to qualify the member name by the name of the direct base class from which it came. If we declared **Common** as a *virtual* base class of **Freebie**, then the **CerealPack** class would predictably inherit just one sub-object of type **Common**.

Converting between Related Class Types

Every derived class object has at least one base class object inside it, waiting to get out. Conversions from a derived type to its base are always legal and automatic. Define a **Carton** object with the declaration:

```
Carton aCarton(40, 50, 60, "fiberboard");
```

We can convert this object to a base class object of type **Box** and store the result with the statement:

```
Box aBox;
aBox = aCarton;
```

This converts the **aCarton** object to a new automatic object of type **Box**, and stores a copy of it in the variable **aBox**. Of course, it's only the **Box** portion of **aCarton** which is used here — the **Carton** portion is sliced off and discarded. The assignment operator being used is the default assignment operator for the **Box** class. Remember that the statements above are not equivalent to:

```
Box aBox = aCarton;
```

The end result is the same, but in this case the statement involves the copy constructor for the **Box** class, rather than the assignment operator. The **aCarton** object is converted to a **Box** object, and that is passed to the copy constructor for **Box**.

As this example demonstrates, conversions up the class hierarchy (that is, towards the base class) are legal and automatic as long as there is no ambiguity. Ambiguity can arise when two base classes each have the same type of sub-object. For example, if we use the definition of the **CerealPack** class that contains two **Common** sub-objects (as we saw in the previous section), and initialize an object **packOfFlakes**, of type **CerealPack**, then the following will be ambiguous:

```
Common commonObject = packOfFlakes;
```

The compiler will try to initialize the value of **commonObject**, but will not be able to determine whether the conversion of **packOfFlakes** should be to the **Common** sub-object of **Carton**, or to the **Common** sub-object of **Contents**.

You cannot obtain automatic conversions for objects down the class hierarchy (that is, towards the more specialized classes). An object of type **Box** contains no information about any class type that may be derived from **Box**, so the conversion does not have a sensible interpretation.

Summary

In this chapter, you have learnt how to define a class based on one or more existing classes, and how class inheritance determines the make-up of a derived class. Inheritance is a fundamental characteristic of object-oriented programming and makes polymorphism possible. We'll be looking into polymorphism in the next chapter. The important points to take from this chapter include:

> A class may be derived from one or more base classes, in which case the derived class inherits members from all of its bases.

> Single inheritance involves deriving a class from a single base class. Multiple inheritance involves deriving a class from two or more base classes.

> Access to the inherited members of a derived class is controlled by two factors: the access specifier of the member in the base class, and the access specifier of the base class in the derived class declaration.

> A constructor for a derived class is responsible for initializing all members of the class, including the inherited members.

> Creation of a derived class object always involves the constructors of all of the direct and indirect base classes, which are called in sequence (from the most base through to the most direct) prior to the execution of the derived class constructor.

> A derived class constructor can explicitly call constructors for its direct bases in the initialization list for the constructor.

> A member name declared in a derived class, which is the same as an inherited member name, will hide the inherited member. To access the hidden member, use the scope resolution operator to qualify the member name with its class name.

> When a derived class with two or more direct base classes contains two or more inherited sub-objects of the same class, the duplication can be prevented by declaring the duplicated class as a virtual base class.

Exercises

Ex 15.1 Define a base class called **Animal** that contains two private data members: a **string** to store the **name** of the animal (e.g. "Fido"), and an integer member called **weight** that will contain the weight of the **Animal** in pounds. Also include a public member function, **who()**, that displays a message giving the name and weight of the **Animal** object. Derive two classes named **Lion** and **Aardvark**, using **Animal** as a public base class. Then, write a **main()** function to create **Lion** and **Aardvark** objects ("Leo" at 400 lbs, and "Algernon" at 50 lbs, say). Demonstrate that the **who()** member is inherited in both derived classes by calling it for the derived class objects.

Ex 15.2 Change the access specifier for the **who()** function in the **Animal** class to **protected**, but leave the rest of the class as before. Now modify the derived classes so that the original version of **main()** still works without alteration.

Ex 15.3 In the solution to the previous exercise, change the access specifier for the **who()** member of the base class back to **public**, and implement the **who()** function as a member of each derived class so that the output message also identifies the name of the class. Now change the function **main()** to call the base class version of **who()** as well as the derived class version, for each of the derived class objects.

Ex 15.4 Define a **Person** class containing data members for **age**, **name** and **gender**. Derive a class called **Employee** from **Person** that adds a data member to store a personnel **number**. Derive a further class **Executive** from **Employee**. Each derived class should define a function that displays information about what it is. (Name and type will do — something like, "Fred Smith is an Employee.") Write a **main()** function to generate an array of 5 executives and an array of 5 ordinary employees, and then display information about them. In addition, display the information on the executives by calling the member function inherited from the **Employee** class.

16

Virtual Functions and Polymorphism

Polymorphism is such a powerful feature of object-oriented programming that you will use it in the majority of your C++ programs. Polymorphism requires the use of derived classes, and the content of this chapter relies heavily on the concepts related to inheritance that you saw introduced in the last chapter.

In this chapter you will learn:

▶ What polymorphism is, and how you can get polymorphic behavior with your classes

▶ What a virtual function is

▶ When and why you need virtual destructors in a class hierarchy

▶ How default parameter values for virtual functions are used

▶ What a pure virtual function is, and how you declare a function as such

▶ What an abstract class is

▶ How you can cast between class types in a hierarchy

▶ How you can determine the type of a pointer to an object at runtime

▶ What pointers to members are, and how you can use them

Understanding Polymorphism

As we will see, polymorphism always involves the use of a pointer to an object, or a reference to an object, when calling a function. Also, polymorphism only operates within a class hierarchy, so the ability to derive one class from another is fundamental to making polymorphism possible.

What exactly does polymorphism entail? We can get a rough idea of how it works by considering an example with more boxes, but first we need to understand the role of a pointer to a base class.

Using a Base Class Pointer

One thing you learned in the previous chapter is that the objects of a derived class represent a subset of objects of the base class — in other words, every derived class object is also a base class object. Consequently, you can always use a 'pointer to base class' to store the address of a derived class object — in fact, you can even use a 'pointer to an indirect base class' for this purpose.

In the diagram below, the **Carton** class is derived from the **Box** base class by single inheritance, and the **CerealPack** class is derived by multiple inheritance from the **Carton** and **Contents** base classes. The diagram illustrates how pointers to base classes could be used to store addresses of the derived objects within such a class structure.

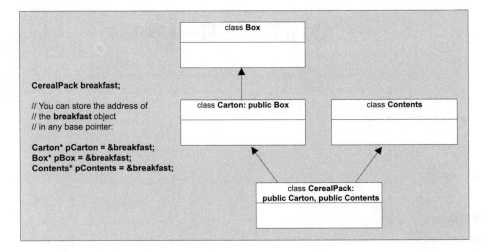

The reverse of this is not true. For instance, you can't use a pointer of type **CerealPack*** to store the address of any (direct or indirect) base class object. This is logical, because the base classes do not describe a complete derived class object. A derived class object always contains a complete sub-object of each of its bases, but each base class only represents a part of a derived class object.

Let's take a specific example. Suppose we were to derive two classes from the **Box** class that featured in the previous chapter, to represent different kinds of containers. The **Carton** class definition will be of the form:

```
class Carton: public Box
{
    // Details of the class...
};
```

A new class called **ToughPack** will have a similar definition:

```
class ToughPack: public Box
{
    // Details of the class...
};
```

Now, for the sake of discussion, let's suppose that the volume of each of these derived types is calculated differently. For a **Carton** made of cardboard, you might just reduce the volume slightly, to take account of the thickness of the material. For a **ToughPack** object, on the other hand, you might have to reduce the usable internal volume by a considerable amount, to allow for protective packaging.

Given these class definitions, we can declare and initialize a pointer as:

```
Carton aCarton(10.0, 10.0, 5.0);
Box* pBox = &aCarton;
```

The pointer **pBox**, of type 'pointer to **Box**', has been initialized with the address of **aCarton** (which is of type **Carton**). This is possible because **Carton** is derived from **Box**, and therefore contains a sub-object of type **Box**. We can use the same pointer to store the address of a **ToughPack** object, as the **ToughPack** class is also derived from **Box**:

```
ToughPack hardcase(12.0, 8.0, 4.0);
pBox = &hardcase;
```

At any given time, the pointer **pBox** might contain the address of an object of any class that has **Box** as a base. The type of the pointer at the time of its declaration is called its **static type** — the static type of **pBox** is 'pointer to **Box**'. Because **pBox** is a pointer to a base class, it also has a **dynamic type**, which varies according to the type of object it points to. When **pBox** is pointing to a **Carton** object, its dynamic type is 'pointer to **Carton**'. When **pBox** is pointing to a **ToughPack** object, its dynamic type is 'pointer to **ToughPack**'. When **pBox** points to an object of type **Box**, its dynamic type is the same as its static type.

From this comes the magic of **polymorphism**. Under conditions that we will come to shortly, you can use the pointer **pBox** to call a function that's defined in the base class and in each derived class. The function will then be selected on the basis of the dynamic type of **pBox**. Consider this statement:

```
pBox->volume();
```

If **pBox** contains the address of a **Carton** object, then we can use this statement to call the **volume()** function for a **Carton** object. If **pBox** points to a **ToughPack** object, then it will call the **volume()** function for **ToughPack**. This would work just as well for other classes derived from **Box**, if we were to create them.

The statement **pBox->volume();** can result in different behavior depending on what **pBox** is pointing to. Perhaps more importantly, the behavior that is *appropriate* to the object pointed to by **pBox** is selected automatically at runtime. (It's as though the pointer has a built-in **switch** statement that tests for the type, and selects the function to be called accordingly.)

This is an extremely powerful mechanism. Situations often arise in which the specific type of the object you will be dealing with cannot be determined in advance — when the type cannot be determined at design time or at compile time, but only at runtime — and they can be handled easily using polymorphism. It's commonly used with interactive applications, where the type of input is down to the whim of the user.

623

For instance, a graphics application that allows different shapes to be drawn — circles, lines, curves and so on — may define a derived class for each shape type, and these classes will all have a common base class called **Shape**. The program will store the address of whichever object the user creates in a base class pointer **pShape**, of type 'pointer to **Shape**', and then draw the appropriate shape with an statement such as **pShape->draw();**. This will call the **draw()** function that corresponds to the particular shape being pointed to, and so this one expression is capable of drawing any kind of shape.

In order to operate in this way, it is essential that the function being called is a member of the base class. Let's take a more in-depth look at how inherited functions behave.

Calling Inherited Functions

Before we get to specifics of polymorphism, we need to look more closely at the behavior of inherited member functions, and the relationship that they have with derived class member functions. To help with this, we'll revise the **Box** class to include a function that calculates the volume of a **Box** object, and another function that displays the resulting volume. The new version of the class in files **Box.h** and **Box.cpp** will be:

```
// Box.h
#ifndef BOX_H
#define BOX_H

class Box
{
  public:
    Box(double lengthValue = 1.0, double breadthValue = 1.0,
                                      double heightValue = 1.0);

    // Function to show the volume of an object
    void showVolume() const;

    // Function to calculate the volume of a Box object
    double volume() const;

  protected:
    double length;
    double breadth;
    double height;
};

#endif
```

```
// Box.cpp
#include <iostream>
using namespace std;

Box::Box(double lvalue, double bvalue, double hvalue) : length(lvalue),
                                                        breadth(bvalue),
                                                        height(hvalue)
{}

void Box::showVolume() const
{
```

```
      cout << "Box usable volume is " << volume() << endl;
}

double Box::volume() const
{
  return length * breadth * height;
}
```

We no longer need the user-defined destructor, or the trace statement in the constructor, so they have both been omitted. With the **Box** class in this form, we can display the usable volume of a **Box** object just by calling the **showVolume()** function for that object. We use the same data members (**length**, **breadth** and **height**), and they are specified as **protected** so that they will be accessible to the member functions of any derived class.

We'll also define the **ToughPack** class, with **Box** as a base. A **ToughPack** object incorporates packing material to protect its contents, so its capacity is only 85% of the capacity of a basic **Box** object. We therefore need a different **volume()** function in the derived class to account for this:

```
// ToughPack.h
#ifndef TOUGHPACK_H
#define TOUGHPACK_H

#include "Box.h"

class ToughPack : public Box               // Derived class
{
  public:
    // Constructor
    ToughPack(double lengthValue, double breadthValue, double heightValue);

    // Function to calculate volume of a ToughPack allowing 15% for packing
    double volume() const;
};

#endif
```

```
// ToughPack.cpp
#include "ToughPack.h"

ToughPack::ToughPack(double lVal, double bVal, double hVal) : Box(lVal, bVal,
hVal)
{}

double ToughPack::volume() const
{
  return 0.85 * length * breadth * height;
}
```

Conceivably there could be other additional members in this derived class, but for the moment we'll keep it simple, concentrating on how the inherited functions work. The derived class constructor simply calls the base class constructor in its initializer list, to set the data member values. No statements are necessary in the body of the derived class constructor. We also have a new version of the **volume()** function to replace the version from the base class. The idea here is that we can get the inherited function **showVolume()** to call the derived class version of **volume()** when we call it for an object of the **ToughPack** class. Let's see if it works.

Try It Out – Using an Inherited Function

We can test our new derived class very simply by creating a **Box** object and a **ToughPack** object that have identical dimensions, and then verifying that the correct volumes are being calculated. The **main()** function to do this would be as follows:

```
// Program 16.1 Behavior of inherited functions in a derived class
#include <iostream>
#include "Box.h"                              // For the Box class
#include "ToughPack.h"                        // For the ToughPack class

using namespace std;

int main()
{
  Box myBox(20.0, 30.0, 40.0);               // Declare a base box
  ToughPack hardcase(20.0, 30.0, 40.0);      // Declare derived box - same size

  cout << endl;
  myBox.showVolume();                        // Display volume of base box
  hardcase.showVolume();                     // Display volume of derived box

  return 0;
}
```

When I run the program, I get this rather disappointing output:

```
Box usable volume is 24000
Box usable volume is 24000
```

How It Works

The derived class object is supposed to have a smaller capacity than the base class object, so our program is obviously not working as we intend it to. Let's try and establish what's going wrong. The second call to **showVolume()** is for an object of the derived class, **ToughPack**, but evidently this is not being taken into account. The volume of a **ToughPack** object should 85% of that of a basic **Box** object with the same dimensions.

The trouble is that in this program, when the **volume()** function is called by the **showVolume()** function, the compiler sets it once and for all as the version of **volume()** defined in the base class. No matter *how* you call **showVolume()**, it will never call the **ToughPack** version of the **volume()** function.

When function calls are fixed in this way, before the program is executed, it is called **static resolution** of the function call, or **static binding**. The term **early binding** is also commonly used. In this example, a particular **volume()** function is *bound* to the call from the function **showVolume()** during the compilation of the program. Every time **showVolume()** is called, it uses the base class **volume()** function that's bound to it.

> **FYI** The same kind of resolution would occur in the derived class **ToughPack**, if we set the conditions appropriately. That is, by adding a function **showVolume()** (which called **volume()**) to the **ToughPack** class, the **volume()** call would be resolved statically to the derived class function.

What if we call the **volume()** function for the **ToughPack** object directly? As a further experiment, let's add statements to call the **volume()** function of a **ToughPack** object directly, and also through a pointer to the base class:

```
cout << "hardcase volume is " << hardcase.volume() << endl;
Box *pBox = &hardcase;
cout << "hardcase volume through pBox is " << pBox->volume() << endl;
```

Place these statements just before the **return** statement in **main()**. When you run the program now, you'll get this output:

```
Box usable volume is 24000
Box usable volume is 24000
hardcase volume is 20400
hardcase volume through pBox is 24000
```

This is quite informative. We can see that a call to **volume()** for the derived class object, **hardcase**, calls the derived class **volume()** function, which is what we want. The call through the base class pointer **pBox**, however, is resolved to the base class version of **volume()**, even though **pBox** contains the address of **hardcase**. In other words, both calls are resolved statically. The compiler will implement these calls as:

```
cout << "hardcase volume is " << hardcase.ToughPack::volume() << endl;
Box *pBox = &hardcase;
cout << "hardcase volume through pBox is " << pBox->Box::volume() << endl;
```

A static call of a function through a pointer is determined solely by the type of the pointer, and not by the object to which it points. The pointer **pBox** is of type 'pointer to **Box**', so any static call using **pBox** can only call a function member of **Box**.

> *Any call to a function through a base class pointer that is resolved statically will call a base class function.*

What we really want from our example is for the question of which **volume()** function to use in any given instance to be resolved when the program is executed. So, if we call **showVolume()** with a derived class object, we would like it to determine that the derived class **volume()** function should be called, not the base class version. Similarly, if we call the **volume()** function through a base class pointer, then we want it to choose the **volume()** function that is appropriate to the object pointed to. This sort of operation is referred to as **dynamic binding**, or **late binding**.

The program doesn't achieve our aims yet because we have to tell the compiler that the **volume()** function in **Box** and the classes derived from **Box** is special, and that we want calls to it to be resolved dynamically. We need to specify that **volume()** is a **virtual function**.

Virtual Functions

When you declare a function as **virtual** in a base class, you indicate to the compiler that you want dynamic binding for the function in any class that's derived from this base class. A virtual function is declared in a base class by using the keyword `virtual`.

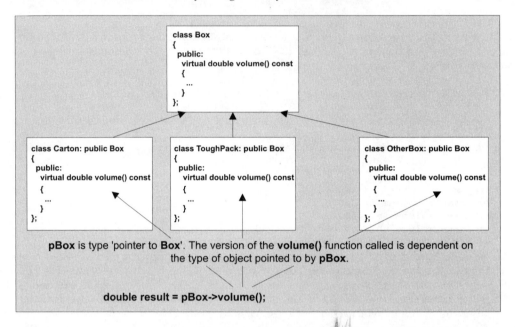

class Box
{
  public:
    virtual double volume() const
    {
      ...
    }
};

class Carton: public Box
{
  public:
    virtual double volume() const
    {
      ...
    }
};

class ToughPack: public Box
{
  public:
    virtual double volume() const
    {
      ...
    }
};

class OtherBox: public Box
{
  public:
    virtual double volume() const
    {
      ...
    }
};

pBox is type 'pointer to **Box**'. The version of the **volume()** function called is dependent on the type of object pointed to by **pBox**.

double result = pBox->volume();

A function that you declare as `virtual` in a base class will also be a virtual function in all classes derived (either directly or indirectly) from the base. To obtain polymorphic behavior, each derived class may implement its own version of the virtual function (although it's not obliged to; we'll look into that later). Virtual function calls can be made using a variable that is a pointer or a reference to a base class object. The diagram above illustrates how a call to a virtual function through a pointer is resolved dynamically. The pointer to base is used to store the address of an object with a type corresponding to one of the derived classes. It could point to an object of any of the three derived classes shown, or of course to a base class object. Which `volume()` function is called will depend on the type of the object to which the pointer points when the call is executed.

> *Describing a class as polymorphic means that it's a derived class that contains at least one virtual function.*

Before we go on, note that a call to a virtual function using an object will *always* be resolved statically. You only get dynamic resolution of calls to virtual functions through a pointer or a reference. That said, let's give virtual functions a whirl.

Try It Out – Using a Virtual Function

To make our example work as we originally hoped, we need a very small change to the **Box** class. We just need to add the keyword **virtual** to the declaration of the **volume()** function in that class:

```
class Box
{
  public:
    Box(double lengthValue = 1.0, double breadthValue = 1.0,
                                      double heightValue = 1.0);

    // Function to show the volume of an object
    void showVolume() const;

    // Function to calculate the volume of a Box object
    virtual double volume() const;

  protected:
    double length;
    double breadth;
    double height;
};
```

> *Note that you don't need to add the* **virtual** *keyword to the function definition, and in fact it would be an error to do so.*

To make it more interesting, let's implement the **volume()** function in a new class called **Carton** a little differently:

```
// Carton.h
#ifndef CARTON_H
#define CARTON_H

#include <string>
#include "Box.h"
using std::string;

class Carton : public Box
{
  public:
    // Constructor explicitly calling the base constructor
    Carton(double lv, double bv, double hv, string material = "Cardboard");

    // Copy constructor
    Carton(const Carton& aCarton);

    // Destructor
    ~Carton();

    // Function to calculate the volume of a Carton object
    double volume() const;
```

```
    private:
      string* pMaterial;
};

#endif
```

```
// Carton.cpp
#include "Carton.h"

Carton::Carton(double lv, double bv, double hv, string material) : Box(lv, bv, hv)
{
  pMaterial = new string(material);
}

Carton::Carton(const Carton& aCarton)
{
  length = aCarton.length;
  breadth = aCarton.breadth;
  height = aCarton.height;
  pMaterial = new string(*aCarton.pMaterial);
}

Carton::~Carton()
{
  delete pMaterial;
}

double Carton::volume() const
{
  double vol = (length - 0.5) * (breadth - 0.5) * (height - 0.5);
  return vol > 0.0 ? vol : 0.0;
}
```

The **volume()** function for a **Carton** assumes the thickness of the material is 0.25, so 0.5 is subtracted from each dimension to account for the sides of the carton. If, for some reason, a **Carton** object has been created with any of its dimensions less than 0.5, then the carton's volume will be calculated to be 0.

We'll also be using the **ToughPack** class as we defined it in Program 16.1. We can modify the **main()** function from the previous example to make use of a **Carton** object, and also to call the **showVolume()** function using the pointer **pBox**:

```
// Program 16.2 Using virtual functions
#include <iostream>
#include "Box.h"                          // For the Box class
#include "ToughPack.h"                    // For the ToughPack class
#include "Carton.h"                       // For the Carton class

using namespace std;

int main()
{
  Box myBox(20.0, 30.0, 40.0);           // Declare a base box
  ToughPack hardcase(20.0, 30.0, 40.0);  // Declare derived box - same size
  Carton aCarton(20.0, 30.0, 40.0);      // A different kind of derived box
```

```
        cout << endl;
        myBox.showVolume();                             // Display volume of base box
        hardcase.showVolume();                          // Display volume of derived box
        aCarton.showVolume();                           // Display volume of derived box
        cout << endl;

        // Now try using a base pointer for the Box object
        Box* pBox = &myBox;                             // Points to type Box
        cout << "myBox volume through pBox is " << pBox->volume() << endl;
        pBox->showVolume();
        cout << endl;

        // Now try using a base pointer for the ToughPack object
        pBox = &hardcase;                               // Points to type ToughPack
        cout << "hardcase volume through pBox is " << pBox->volume() << endl;
        pBox->showVolume();
        cout << endl;

        // Now try using a base pointer for the Carton object
        pBox = &aCarton;                                // Points to type Carton
        cout << "aCarton volume through pBox is " << pBox->volume() << endl;
        pBox->showVolume();

        return 0;
}
```

You can now recompile the example with these changes. When you run it, the output produced should be:

```
Box usable volume is 24000
Box usable volume is 20400
Box usable volume is 22722.4

myBox volume through pBox is 24000
Box usable volume is 24000

hardcase volume through pBox is 20400
Box usable volume is 20400

aCarton volume through pBox is 22722.4
Box usable volume is 22722.4
```

How It Works

The keyword **virtual** in the base class definition of the function **volume()** is sufficient to determine that *all* declarations of the function in derived classes will also be understood to be virtual. You can (optionally) use the **virtual** keyword for your derived class functions as well — this was illustrated in the previous diagram.

> **FYI**
>
> In this example, we omitted the keyword **virtual** from the declarations of **volume()** to demonstrate that it is not necessary to use it. However, I recommend that you *do* use the keyword **virtual** with *all* declarations of virtual functions in derived classes, since it makes it clear to anyone reading the derived class definition that the functions are indeed virtual, and that they will be linked to dynamically.

The program is now clearly doing what we wanted in the first place. The first call to the function **showVolume()** with the **Box** object **myBox** is:

```
myBox.showVolume();                                // Display volume of base box
```

This simply calls the base class version of **volume()**, since **myBox** is of type **Box**. The second call to **showVolume()** is with the **ToughPack** object, **hardcase**:

```
hardcase.showVolume();                             // Display volume of derived box
```

This statement calls the **showVolume()** function defined in the **Box** class — in fact, there aren't any other versions of **showVolume()**. The function is inherited as a public member of the **ToughPack** class, so there is no problem calling it in this way. However, the call to **volume()** in **showVolume()** is resolved to the version defined in the derived class, because **volume()** is a virtual function. We get the volume calculated appropriately for a **ToughPack** object.

The third call of **showVolume()** is for a **Carton** object:

```
aCarton.showVolume();                              // Display volume of derived box
```

The function **showVolume()** is inherited in **Carton** and the call to **volume()** is resolved to the **Carton** class version, so again we get the correct volume for the object.

Next, we use the pointer **pBox** to call the **volume()** function directly, and also indirectly through the **showVolume()** function. The pointer first contains the address of the **Box** object **myBox**, then the addresses of the two derived class objects in turn. The resulting output for each object shows that the appropriate version of the **volume()** function is selected automatically in each case, so we have a clear demonstration of polymorphism in action.

Requirements for a Function to be Virtual

For a function to behave 'virtually', you must declare and define it with the same name and parameter list in any derived class as it has in the base class. Further, if you have declared the base class function as **const**, then you must declare the derived class function to be **const** as well. Generally, the return type of the function in a derived class must also be the same as that in the base class, but there is an exception when the return type in the base class is a pointer or a reference to a class type. In this case, the derived class version of a virtual function may return a pointer or a reference to a more specialized type than that of the base. We won't be going into this further, but in case you come across it elsewhere, the technical term used in relation to these return types is **covariance**.

You can conclude from the rules for virtual function definitions that if you try to use different parameters for a virtual function in a derived class from those in the base class, then the virtual function mechanism won't work. The function in the derived class will operate with static binding that is established and fixed at compile time. This will be also the case if you forget to declare a derived class function as **const** when the base class function is **const**.

You can test this out by deleting the **const** keyword from the declaration of **volume()** in the **Carton** class, and running the last example again. This action means that the **volume()** function in **Carton** no longer matches the virtual function declared in **Box**, and so the derived class **volume()** function is not virtual. Consequently, the resolution is static, so that the function called for **Carton** objects through a base pointer, or even indirectly through the **showVolume()** function, is the base class version.

If the function name and parameter list of a function in a derived class are the same as those of a virtual function declared in the base class, then the return type *must* be consistent with the rules for a virtual function. If it isn't, the derived class function will not compile.

I should add a warning at this point that you should *never* declare a virtual function as **inline**, implicitly or otherwise. An inline function call is supposed to be replaced at compile time by inline code, so a function being virtual is not consistent with it being inline. You must always arrange for virtual functions to be declared as virtual within the class, and then for the definitions to appear separately in a **.cpp** file.

Virtual Functions and Class Hierarchies

If you want your function to be treated as virtual via a base class pointer, then you *must* declare it as virtual in the base class. You can declare as many virtual functions as you need in a base class, but it's not the case that all virtual functions need to be declared within the 'most' base class in a hierarchy of several levels. This is shown in the illustration below.

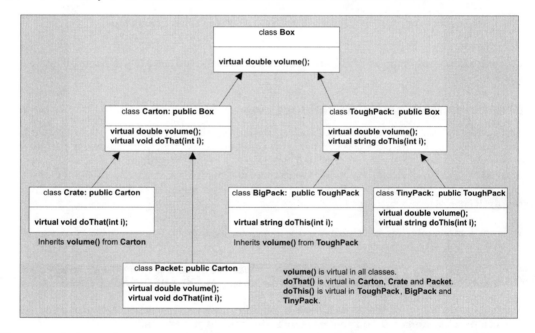

When you declare a function as **virtual** in one class, the function is virtual in all classes derived directly or indirectly from that class. For example, all of the classes derived from the **Box** class above inherit the **virtual** nature of the **volume()** function. You could call the **volume()** function for any of these classes through a pointer **pBox** of type **Box***, since the pointer could contain the address of an object of any class in the hierarchy:

```
double result = pBox->volume();          // Call for any class in the hierarchy
```

The **Crate** class does not declare the virtual function **volume()**, so the version inherited from **Carton** would be called for **Crate** objects. It is inherited as a virtual function, and therefore can be called polymorphically.

633

A pointer **pCarton**, of type **Carton***, could also be used to call the **volume()** function, but only for objects of the **Carton** class and the two classes that have **Carton** as a base: **Crate** and **Packet**:

```
   result = pCarton->volume();                    // Call for Carton, Crate, or Packet
```

The **Carton** class and the classes derived from it also contain the virtual function **doThat()**. This function can also be called polymorphically using a pointer of type **Carton***:

```
   pCarton->doThat(12);                           // Call for Carton, Crate, or Packet
```

Note that you could not call **doThat()** for these classes using the pointer **pBox**, because the **Box** class does not contain the function **doThat()**.

Similarly, the virtual function **doThis()** could be called for objects of type **ToughPack**, **BigPack** and **TinyPack** using a pointer to the base class, **pToughPack**:

```
   string answer = pToughPack->doThis(3); // Call for ToughPack,
                                          // BigPack or TinyPack
```

Of course, the same pointer could also be used to call the **volume()** function for objects these classes.

Access Specifiers and Virtual Functions

The access specification of a virtual function declaration in a derived class *can* be different from the specification in the base class. When you call the virtual function through a pointer, the access specification in the base class will determine whether the function is accessible in the derived class. If the virtual function is public in the base class, it can be called for any derived class through a pointer (or a reference) to the base class, regardless of the access specification in the derived class.

We can demonstrate this by modifying the previous example.

Try It Out – The Effect of Access Specifiers on Virtual Functions

Modify the definition of the **ToughPack** class from the previous example to make the **volume()** function **protected**, and add the **virtual** keyword to its declaration:

```
class ToughPack : public Box          // Derived class
{
  public:
    // Constructor
    ToughPack(double lengthValue, double breadthValue, double heightValue);

  protected:
    // Function to calculate volume of a ToughPack allowing 15% for packing
    virtual double volume() const;
};
```

We must change the **main()** function just slightly:

```
// Program 16.3 Access specifiers and virtual functions
#include <iostream>
#include "Box.h"                                // For the Box class
#include "ToughPack.h"                          // For the ToughPack class
#include "Carton.h"                             // For the Carton class

using namespace std;

int main()
{
  Box myBox(20.0, 30.0, 40.0);                  // Declare a base box
  ToughPack hardcase(20.0, 30.0, 40.0);         // Declare derived box - same size
  Carton aCarton(20.0, 30.0, 40.0);             // A different kind of derived box

  cout << endl;
  myBox.showVolume();                           // Display volume of base box
  hardcase.showVolume();                        // Display volume of derived box
  aCarton.showVolume();                         // Display volume of derived box
  cout << endl;

//   cout << "hardcase volume is " << hardcase.volume() << endl;
                                                // Uncomment for error

  // Now try using a base pointer for the Box object
  Box *pBox = &myBox;                           // Points to type Box
  cout << "myBox volume through pBox is " << pBox->volume() << endl;
  pBox->showVolume();
  cout << endl;

  // Now try using a base pointer for the ToughPack object
  pBox = &hardcase;                             // Points to type ToughPack
  cout << "hardcase volume through pBox is " << pBox->volume() << endl;
  pBox->showVolume();
  cout << endl;

  // Now try using a base pointer for the Carton object
  pBox = &aCarton;                              // Points to type Carton
  cout << "aCarton volume through pBox is " << pBox->volume() << endl;
  pBox->showVolume();

  return 0;
}
```

It should come as no surprise to you when this code produces exactly the same output as the last example.

How It Works

Even though **volume()** is declared as protected in the **ToughPack** class, we can still call it for the **hardcase** object through the **showVolume()** function inherited from the **Box** class. We can also call it directly through a pointer to the base class, **pBox**. However, if you uncomment the line that calls the **volume()** function directly, using the **hardcase** object, the code won't compile.

What matters here is whether the call is resolved dynamically or statically. When you use a class object, the call is determined statically (that is, by the compiler), and since the **volume()** function is protected in the **ToughPack** class, the call using the **hardcase** object will not compile. All the other calls are resolved when the program executes — they are polymorphic calls. In this case, the access specification for a virtual function in the base class will be inherited in all the derived classes. This is regardless of the explicit specification in the derived class: the explicit specification will *only* affect calls that are resolved statically.

Default Parameter Values in Virtual Functions

Because default values are dealt with at compile time, you can get unexpected results when using default values with virtual function parameters. If the base class declaration of a virtual function has a default parameter value, and you call the function through a base pointer, you will *always* get the default parameter value from the base class version of the function. Any default parameter values in derived class versions of the will have no effect.

We can demonstrate this by altering the previous example to include a parameter with a default value for the **volume()** function.

Try It Out – Default Parameter Values

Modify the declaration for the **volume()** function in file **Box.cpp** to:

```
double Box::volume(const int i) const
{
  cout << "Parameter = " << i << endl;
  return length * breadth * height;
}
```

You'll also have to adjust the function member declaration in the **Box** class:

```
    // Function to calculate the volume of a Box object
    virtual double volume(const int i = 5) const;
```

The parameter serves no purpose other than to demonstrate how default values are assigned. Modify **Carton** in the same way, but make the default parameter value 50, and in the **ToughPack** class make the default 500. You can also restore the **public** access specification for the **volume()** function in the **ToughPack** class, and don't forget that you'll need to include the **iostream** header in the two **.cpp** files.

With these changes to the class definitions, we can try out the default parameter values with an amended **main()** function, in which we simply uncomment the line that calls the **volume()** member for the **hardcase** object directly. You will get this output:

```
Parameter = 5
Box usable volume is 24000
Parameter = 5
Box usable volume is 20400
Parameter = 5
Box usable volume is 22722.4

Parameter = 500
hardcase volume is 20400
Parameter = 5
```

```
myBox volume through pBox is 24000
Parameter = 5
Box usable volume is 24000

Parameter = 5
hardcase volume through pBox is 20400
Parameter = 5
Box usable volume is 20400

Parameter = 5
aCarton volume through pBox is 22722.4
Parameter = 5
Box usable volume is 22722.4
```

How It Works

In every instance of calling the **volume()** function except one, the default value output is that for the base class function. The exception is when we call **volume()** using the **hardcase** object. This will be resolved statically, so the default parameter value for the **ToughPack** class is used. All the other calls are resolved dynamically, so the base class default value applies.

Using References to Call Virtual Functions

You can also call a virtual function through a reference, and reference parameters are a powerful aid to applying polymorphism. Calling a virtual function through a variable that's a reference doesn't have the same magic as a call through a pointer, because a reference variable is initialized once and only once, and therefore can only call the functions for that object. Reference parameters to a function, however, are a different matter.

Suppose you define a function with a parameter that's a reference to a base class. You can then pass a *derived* class object to the function as an argument. Within the function, you can use the reference parameter to call a virtual function. When your function executes, the appropriate virtual function for the object passed will be selected automatically. We could show this in action by modifying the function **main()** from Program 16.2 to call a function that has a parameter of type 'reference to **Box**'.

Try It Out – Using References with Virtual Functions

In this example, we're going to add a new function called **showVolume()**, which outputs the volume of an object, as a separate global function. We can pass it a reference argument and use that to call the **showVolume()** function for an object. The function definition will be:

```
void showVolume(const Box& rBox)
{
  rBox.showVolume();
}
```

We can call this function from **main()** with some derived class arguments to see how it works. The only changes you need to make to the class definitions are to do with the **volume()** member functions, from which you should remove the **i** parameters and the lines that output **i** in their definitions.

We just need to alter the source file containing **main()** to:

```
// Program 16.5 Using virtual functions through a reference to the base class
#include <iostream>
#include "Box.h"                                 // For the Box class
#include "ToughPack.h"                           // For the ToughPack class
#include "Carton.h"                              // For the Carton class

using namespace std;

void showVolume(const Box& rBox);                // Prototype for global
function

int main()
{
  Box myBox(20.0, 30.0, 40.0);                   // Declare a base box
  ToughPack hardcase(20.0, 30.0, 40.0);          // Declare derived box - same size
  Carton aCarton(20.0, 30.0, 40.0);              // A different kind of derived box

  cout << endl;
  showVolume(myBox);                             // Display volume of base box
  showVolume(hardcase);                          // Display volume of derived box
  showVolume(aCarton);                           // Display volume of derived box

  // Lines deleted

  return 0;
}

// Global function to display the volume of a box
void showVolume(const Box& rBox)
{
  rBox.showVolume();
}
```

Running this program should produce the output:

```
Box usable volume is 24000
Box usable volume is 20400
Box usable volume is 22722.4
```

How It Works

In the function **main()**, we create a base class object **myBox**, and two different derived class objects, **hardcase** and **aCarton**. We then call the global **showVolume()** function with each of these objects as an argument. As you see from the output, the correct **volume()** function is being used in each case, confirming that polymorphism works through a reference parameter.

Each time the function is called, a reference parameter is initialized with the object passed as an argument. Because the parameter is a reference to a base class, the compiler arranges for the binding to the virtual function **volume()** to occur at runtime. If you had specified the parameter as a reference to a derived class, the call would have been resolved statically, because it would have been completely determined. Only calls of a virtual function through a base class reference will result in dynamic binding.

Calling the Base Class Version of a Virtual Function

We've seen that it's easy to call the derived class version of a virtual function though a pointer or reference to a derived class object — the call is made dynamically. However, what do we do in the same situation, when we actually want to call the *base class* function for the derived class object?

Our **Box** class provides an opportunity to see why such a call might be required. It could be useful to calculate the loss of total volume in a **Carton** or **ToughPack** object, and one way to do this would be to calculate the difference between the results returned from the base class and derived class versions of the **volume()** function.

You can force the virtual function for a base class to be called statically by using the class name, with the scope resolution operator, to specify the particular function you want. Suppose we have a pointer **pBox** that's defined as follows:

```
Carton aCarton(40.0, 30.0, 20.0);
Box* pBox = &aCarton;
```

We can now calculate the loss in total volume for a **Carton** object with the statement:

```
double difference = pBox->Box::volume() - pBox->volume();
```

The expression **pBox->Box::volume()** calls the *base* class version of the **volume()** function. The class name, together with the scope resolution operator, identifies a particular **volume()** function, so this will be a static call resolved at compile time.

Using the scope resolution operator, you can call the base class implementation of any member function, provided the access specifiers allow you access to the function.

Note that you cannot use this technique to force the selection of a particular *derived* class function in a call through a pointer. The expression **pBox->Carton::volume()** will not compile, because **Carton::volume()** is not a member of the **Box** class. A call of a function through a pointer is either a static call to a function member of the class type for the pointer, or it is a dynamic call to a virtual function.

To call the base class version of a virtual function through an *object* of a derived class is also simple. You can use a **static cast** to convert the derived class object to the base class, and use the result to call the base class function. We could calculate the loss in volume for the **aCarton** object with the statement:

```
double difference = static_cast<Box>(aCarton).volume() - aCarton.volume();
```

Both calls in this statement are resolved statically. Casting **aCarton** to type **Box** results in an object of type **Box**, so the function call will be to the **Box** version of **volume()**. Calls to virtual functions using an object are always resolved statically.

Converting Between Pointers to Class Objects

If your program contains a pointer to a *derived* class, you can easily make an implicit conversion to a pointer to a *base* class, and you can do this for both direct and indirect base classes. For example, let's first declare a pointer to a **Carton** object as:

```
Carton* pCarton = new Carton(30, 40, 10);
```

We can convert this pointer implicitly to a pointer to a direct base class of **Carton** (recall that **Box** is a direct base class of **Carton**):

```
Box* pBox = pCarton;
```

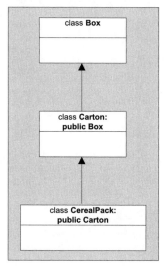

The result is a 'pointer to **Box**', which is initialized to point to the new **Carton** object. We could also implicitly convert a pointer to a derived class type into a pointer to an *indirect* base. Suppose we have the hierarchy shown in this diagram:

Here, **Box** is a direct base class of **Carton**, so it is an indirect base class of **CerealPack**. We can therefore write the following:

```
Box* pBox = pCerealPack;
```

This statement converts the address in **pCerealPack** from type 'pointer to **CerealPack**' to 'type pointer to **Box**'. If you need to specify the conversion explicitly, you can use the **static_cast<>()** operator:

```
Box* pBox = static_cast<Box*>(pCerealPack);
```

The compiler can usually expedite this cast, because it can determine that **Box** is a base class of **CerealPack**. Since a **CerealPack** object will contain a **Box** object, the cast is possible. The circumstances where it would not be legal are if the **Box** class was inaccessible, or if the **Box** class was a virtual base class, but the compiler should be able to spot these. The diagram below shows the possible static casts for pointers up the hierarchy from the most derived class, **CerealPack**.

Casting Pointers up a Class Hierarchy

As you can see, the result in each case is a pointer to the sub-object corresponding to the destination type. It is easy to get confused when thinking about casting pointers to class types. Don't forget that a pointer to a class type can only point to objects of that type, or to objects of a derived class type, and not the other way round. To be specific, the pointer **pCarton** could contain the address of an object of type **Carton** (which could be a sub-object of a **CerealPack** object), or an object of type **CerealPack**. It could *not* contain the address of an object of type **Box**. This is because a **CerealPack** object is a specialized kind of **Carton**, but a **Box** object is not.

Despite what you might think from the things we've seen so far, it's sometimes possible to make casts in the opposite direction. Casting a pointer *down* a hierarchy, from a base class to a derived class, is different because whether the cast works depends on what the base pointer is pointing to. For a static cast from a base class pointer such as **pBox** to a derived class pointer such as **pCarton** to be legal, the base class pointer must be pointing to a **Box** sub-object of a **Carton** object. If that's not the case, the result of the cast is undefined.

Casting Pointers down a Class Hierarchy

The diagram shows static casts from a pointer, **pBox**, which contains the address of a **Carton** object. The cast to type **Carton*** will work, because the object is of type **Carton**. The result of the cast to type **CerealPack***, on the other hand, is undefined because no object this type exists.

If you are in any doubt about its legitimacy, you should not use a static cast. The success of an attempt to cast a pointer down a class hierarchy depends on whether the pointer contains the address of an object of the destination type. A static cast does not check whether this is the case, so if you attempt it in circumstances where you don't know what the pointer points to, you risk an undefined result. Therefore, when you want to cast down a hierarchy, you need to do it a different way: a way where the cast can be checked at runtime.

Dynamic Casts

A **dynamic cast** is a cast that's performed at runtime. To specify a dynamic cast, you use the **dynamic_cast<>()** operator. You can *only* apply this operator to pointers and references to polymorphic class types — that is, class types that contain at least one virtual function. The reason for this is that only pointers to polymorphic class types contain the information that the **dynamic_cast<>()** operator needs to check the validity of the cast. This operator is specifically for the purpose of converting between pointers or between references to class types in a hierarchy.

Note that the types between which you are casting must be pointers or references to classes within the same class hierarchy. You can't use **dynamic_cast<>()** for anything else. To begin our exploration of the operator, we will take a look at casting *pointers* dynamically.

Casting Pointers Dynamically

There are two basic kinds of dynamic cast that we can distinguish. The first is a cast down a hierarchy, *from* a pointer to a direct or indirect base type, *to* a pointer to a derived type. This is referred to as a **downcast**. The second possibility is a cast *across* a hierarchy; this is referred to as a **crosscast**. Examples of both of these sorts of cast are illustrated below.

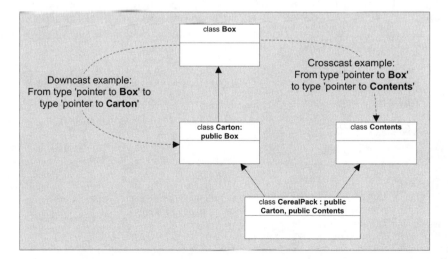

For a pointer **pBox**, of type 'pointer to **Box**', we could write the downcast shown in the diagram as:

```
Carton* pCarton = dynamic_cast<Carton*>(pBox);
```

As you can see, the **dynamic_cast<>()** operator is written in the same way as the **static_cast<>()** operator. The destination type goes between the angled brackets following **dynamic_cast**, and the expression that you want to be cast to the new type goes between the parentheses. For this cast to be legal, the classes **Box** and **Carton** must contain virtual functions, either as declared or inherited members. For the cast to *work*, **pBox** must point to either a **Carton** object or a **CerealPack** object, since only objects of these types contain a **Carton** sub-object. If the cast does not succeed, the pointer **pCarton** will be set to 0.

The crosscast shown above could be written:

```
Contents* pContents = dynamic_cast<Contents*>(pBox);
```

As in the previous case, both the **Contents** class and the **Box** class must be polymorphic for the cast to be legal. The cast can only succeed if **pBox** contains the address of an object of type **CerealPack**, because this is the only type that contains a **Contents** object and can be referred to using a pointer of type **Box***. Again, if the does not succeed, 0 will be stored in **pContents**.

Using **dynamic_cast<>()** to cast down a class hierarchy may fail, but in contrast to the static cast, the result will be a null pointer rather than just 'undefined'. This provides a clue as to how you can use this. Suppose you have some kind of object pointed to by a pointer to **Box**, and you want to call a non-virtual function member of the **Carton** class. A base class pointer only allows you to call the *virtual* functions of a derived class, but the **dynamic_cast<>()** operator can enable you to call a non-virtual function. Suppose that **surface()** is a non-virtual function member of the **Carton** class. You could call it with the statement:

```
dynamic_cast<Carton*>(pBox)->surface();
```

This is obviously hazardous. You still need to be sure that **pBox** is pointing to a **Carton** object, or to an object of a class that has the **Carton** class as a base. If it isn't, the **dynamic_cast<>()** operator will return null, and the call will fail. To fix this, you can use the **dynamic_cast<>()** operator to determine whether what you intend to do is valid. For example:

```
if(Carton* pCarton = dynamic_cast<Carton*>(pBox))
  pCarton->surface();
```

Now we will only attempt the function call if the result of the cast is not null.

Note that you cannot remove **const**-ness with **dynamic_cast<>()**. If the pointer type you are casting from is **const**, then the pointer type you are casting to must also be **const**. If you want to cast from a **const** pointer to a non-**const** pointer, you must first cast to a non-**const** pointer of the same type as the original by using the **const_cast<>()** operator.

Converting References

You can also apply the **dynamic_cast<>()** operator to a reference parameter in a function, in order to cast down a class hierarchy to produce another reference. In the following example, the parameter to the function **doThat()** is a reference to a base class (**Box**) object. In the body of the function, we can cast the parameter to a reference to a derived type:

```
double doThat(Box& rBox)
{
  ...

  Carton& rCarton = dynamic_cast<Carton&>(rBox);

  ...
}
```

This statement casts from 'reference to **Box** to 'reference to **Carton**'. Of course, in general, the object passed as an argument may not be a **Carton** object, and if so the cast will not succeed. There is no such thing as a null reference, so this fails in a different way from a failed pointer cast: execution of the function will stop, and an exception of type **bad_cast** will be thrown. You haven't met exceptions yet, but you'll find out what this means in the next chapter.

The Cost of Polymorphism

There's no such thing as a free lunch, and this tenet certainly applies to polymorphism. You have to pay for polymorphism in two ways: it requires more memory, and virtual function calls result in an additional overhead. Each of these arises because of the way that virtual function calls are typically implemented in practice.

Suppose that two classes **A** and **B** contain identical data members, but that **A** contains virtual functions, while **B**'s functions are non-virtual. Then, an object of type **A** will require more memory than an object of type **B**.

> *You can create a simple program with two such class objects, and use* **sizeof()** *to see the memory difference for yourself. Also, the* **.exe** *file of a program containing virtual functions will be larger than the equivalent program with non-virtual functions.*

The reason for the increase in memory requirements is that when we create an object of a polymorphic class (such as class **A** above), a special pointer is created in the object. This pointer is then used to call any of the virtual functions in the object. The special pointer points to a table of function pointers that gets created for the class, and this table, usually called a **vtable**, has one entry for each virtual function in the class.

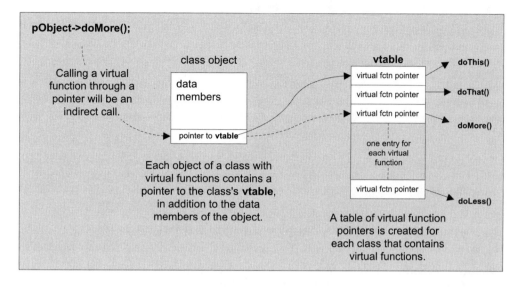

When a function is called through a pointer to a base class object, the following sequence of events occurs. First, the pointer to the vtable in the object being pointed to is used to find the beginning of the vtable for the class. Then, the entry for the function to be called is found in the vtable for the class, usually by using an offset. Finally, the function is called *indirectly* through the function pointer in the vtable. This indirect call is a little slower than a direct call of a non-virtual function, so each call of a virtual function carries some overhead in execution time.

However, this overhead is quite cheap, and should not give you cause for concern. A few extra bytes per object, and slightly slower function calls, is a small price to pay for the power and flexibility that polymorphism offers. I offer this explanation, then, for the time when you notice that the size of an object that has virtual functions is larger than that of an equivalent object that doesn't!

Pure Virtual Functions

You might envisage a situation that demands a base class with a number of derived classes, and a virtual function that's redefined to suit each of your derived classes, but in which there is no meaningful definition that you could give to the function in the base class itself.

For example, you might define a base class, **Shape**, from which you would derive classes defining specific shapes, such as **Circle**, **Ellipse**, **Rectangle**, **Curve** and so on. The **Shape** class might include a virtual function **draw()** that you would call to draw a particular shape, but the **Shape** class itself is abstract: there is no meaningful implementation of the **draw()** function for the **Shape** class. This is a job for a **pure virtual function**.

The primary purpose of a pure virtual function is to enable the derived class versions of the function to be called polymorphically. To declare a pure virtual function rather than an 'ordinary' virtual function, you use the same syntax, but add **= 0** to its declaration within the class. A pure virtual function usually has no implementation.

If all that sounds confusing, we can see how to declare a pure virtual function by defining the **Shape** class I just alluded to:

```
// Generic base class for shapes
class Shape
{
  public:
    // Pure virtual function to draw a shape
    virtual void draw() const = 0;

    // Pure virtual function to move a shape
    virtual void move(const Point& newPosition) = 0;

  protected:
    Point position;                          // Position of a shape

    Shape(const Point& shapePosition) : position(shapePosition) {}
};
```

The **Shape** class contain a data member of type **Point** (which is another class type) that will store the position of a shape. It's in the base class because every shape must have a position, and the constructor will initialize it. The **draw()** function is *virtual* because we have used the keyword **virtual**, and *pure* because the '**= 0**' (following the parameter list) specifies that the function is not defined for this class. In other words, the **draw()** function is a *pure virtual* function. You can see that **move()** is also a pure virtual function.

A class that contains a pure virtual function is called an **abstract class**. In this case, the **Shape** class contains two pure virtual functions — **draw()** and **move()** — so it is most definitely an abstract class. Let's look a little more at exactly what this means.

Abstract Classes

Even though it has a data member and a constructor, the **Shape** class is an incomplete description of an object, because the **draw()** and **move()** functions are not defined. We are therefore not allowed to create instances of the **Shape** class; it exists purely for the purpose of defining any classes that are derived from it. Since you cannot create objects of an abstract class, you can't use it as a function parameter type, or as a return type. Note however that pointers or references to an abstract class *can* be used as parameter or return types.

This begs the question, "If you can't create an instance of an abstract class, then why does the abstract class contain a constructor?" The answer is that the constructor for an abstract class is there to initialize its data members. To allow this, the constructor for an abstract class can be called from the initializer list of a derived class constructor. If you try to call the constructor for an abstract class from anywhere else, you will get an error message from the compiler.

Since the constructor for an abstract class cannot be used generally, it's a good idea to declare it as a protected member of the class, as I have done for the **Shape** class. Note that the constructor for an abstract class must not call a pure virtual function; the effect of calling a pure virtual function is undefined.

Any class that derives from the **Shape** class must define both the **draw()** function and the **move()** function if it is not also to be an abstract class. More specifically, if any pure virtual function of an abstract base class is *not* defined in the derived class, then the pure virtual function will be inherited as such, and the derived class will *also* be an abstract class.

To illustrate this, we could define a new class called **Circle**, which has the **Shape** class as a base:

```
// Class defining a circle
class Circle: public Shape
{
  public:
    Circle(Point center, double circleRadius) : Shape(center),
                                          radius(circleRadius) {}

    virtual void draw() const
    {
      // Circle center is at point 'position', inherited from the base class
      cout << " Circle center " << position << " radius " << radius << endl;
    }

    virtual void move(const Point& newCenter) {position = newCenter;}

  private:
    double radius;                              // Radius of a circle
};
```

The **draw()** function and the **move()** function are defined, so this class is not abstract. If either function were not defined here, then the **Circle** class would be abstract. The class includes a constructor, which initializes the base class sub-object by calling the base class constructor.

> *You can call the constructor of an abstract base class in the initializer list of a derived class constructor.*

Of course, an abstract class can also contain non-pure and non-virtual functions. It can also contain any number of pure virtual functions, as our example illustrates. The presence of at least *one* pure virtual function is what makes a given class abstract. A derived class must have definitions for every pure virtual function in its base; otherwise, it will also be an abstract class. Let's look at a working example of using an abstract class.

Try It Out – An Abstract Class

We could define a new version of the **Box** class with the **volume()** function declared as a pure virtual function:

```
class Box
{
  public:
    Box(double lengthValue = 1.0, double breadthValue = 1.0,
                                          double heightValue = 1.0);

    // Function to calculate the volume of a Box object
    virtual double volume() const = 0;
```

647

```
  protected:
    double length;
    double breadth;
    double height;
};
```

We no longer need the definition of **volume()** in the file **Box.cpp**, and we can get rid of the **showVolume()** function for this example as well. Since **Box** is now an abstract class, we can no longer create objects of this class. Both the **Carton** and **ToughPack** classes define the **volume()** function, so they are not abstract, and we can use objects of these classes to confirm that the virtual **volume()** functions are still working as before:

```cpp
// Program 16.6 Using an abstract base class
#include <iostream>
#include "Box.h"                          // For the Box class
#include "ToughPack.h"                    // For the ToughPack class
#include "Carton.h"                       // For the Carton class

using namespace std;

int main()
{
  cout << endl;

  ToughPack hardcase(20.0, 30.0, 40.0);
  Box* pBox = &hardcase;                         // Store address of ToughPack object
  cout << "Volume of hardcase is " << pBox->volume() << endl;

  Carton aCarton(20.0, 30.0, 40.0);
  pBox = &aCarton;                               // Store address of a Carton object
  cout << "Volume of aCarton is " << pBox->volume() << endl;

  return 0;
}
```

This generates the following output:

```
Volume of hardcase is 20400
Volume of aCarton is 22722.4
```

How It Works

The pure virtual declaration of **volume()** in the **Box** class ensures that the **volume()** functions in the **Carton** and **ToughPack** classes are also virtual. Therefore we can call them through a pointer to the base class, and the call will be resolved dynamically. We define and initialize first a **ToughPack** object, and then the pointer **pBox**:

```cpp
ToughPack hardcase(20.0, 30.0, 40.0);
Box* pBox = &hardcase;                         // Store address of ToughPack object
```

pBox will now contain the address of the **ToughPack** object, **hardcase**. We use the pointer to the base class, **Box**, to call the **ToughPack** class version of the **volume()** function:

```cpp
cout << "Volume of hardcase is " << pBox->volume() << endl;
```

You can see from the output that the function call is resolved dynamically to the **ToughPack** version of the **volume()** function. Next, we store the address of a **Carton** object in **pBox**:

```
Carton aCarton(20.0, 30.0, 40.0);
pBox = &aCarton;                                // Store address of a Carton object
```

The address of the **ToughPack** object contained in **pBox** is overwritten by the address of the **Carton** object. We then use **pBox** to display the volume of the **Carton** object:

```
cout << "Volume of aCarton is " << pBox->volume() << endl;
```

Since **pBox** contains the address of the **Carton** object, the call is resolved dynamically to the **volume()** function in the **Carton** class.

Abstract Classes as Interfaces

Sometimes, an abstract class arises simply because a function has no sensible definition in the context of the class, and only has a meaningful interpretation in a derived class. However, there is another way of using abstract classes.

An abstract class that contains *only* pure virtual functions can be used to define a **standard class interface**. It would typically represent a declaration of a set of related functions that supported a particular capability — a set of functions for communications through a modem, for example. As we've discussed, a class that derives from such an abstract base class must define an implementation for each virtual function, but the way in which each virtual function is implemented is specified by whoever is implementing the derived class. The abstract class fixes the interface, but the implementation (via the derived class) is flexible.

Indirect Abstract Base Classes

I briefly mentioned indirect inheritance earlier in this chapter. Given a base class and a derived class, it may be that the base itself is derived from a more general base class. In this situation, the most-derived class inherits *indirectly* from the most-base class. You can create as many levels of derivation as you need. A small extension of the last example will demonstrate indirect inheritance involving an abstract class, and will also illustrate the use of a virtual function across a second level of inheritance.

Try It Out – More Than One Level of Inheritance

We could define a **Vessel** class to represent a generic container that we could use as an abstract base class for the **Box** class. This would allow for classes representing other types of storage containers (**Bottle** or **Can**, for instance) to be derived from **Vessel**, so that we could deal with calculating volumes of these types of object polymorphically. We could put a definition for the **Vessel** class in a new header file called **Vessel.h**:

```
// Vessel.h - Abstract class defining a vessel
#ifndef VESSEL_H
#define VESSEL_H
```

```
class Vessel
{
  public:
    virtual double volume() const = 0;
};

#endif
```

This is an abstract class because it contains the pure virtual function, **volume()**. We can now modify the **Box** class to define the **Vessel** class as a base:

```
// Box.h
#ifndef BOX_H
#define BOX_H

#include "Vessel.h"

class Box : public Vessel
{
  public:
    Box(double lengthValue = 1.0, double breadthValue = 1.0,
                                          double heightValue = 1.0);

    // Function to calculate the volume of a Box object
    virtual double volume() const;

  protected:
    double length;
    double breadth;
    double height;
};

#endif
```

In addition to including the header for the **Vessel** class and making **Box** derive from **Vessel**, we have returned the **volume()** function to its virtual (rather than pure virtual) status, so we can reinstate the function definition to **Box.cpp**:

```
double Box::volume() const
{
  return length * breadth * height;
}
```

While we're about it, we can add another class derived from **Vessel** that will define a can, placing the definition in **Can.h** and the implementation in **Can.cpp**:

```
// Can.h Class defining a cylindrical can of a given height and diameter
#ifndef CAN_H
#define CAN_H

#include "Vessel.h"

class Can : public Vessel
{
  public:
    Can(double canDiameter, double canHeight);
    virtual double volume() const;
```

```
    protected:
      double diameter;
      double height;
      static const double pi;
  };

  #endif

  // Can.cpp
  #include "Can.h"

  Can::Can(double canDiameter, double canHeight) : diameter(canDiameter),
                                                   height(canHeight)
  {}
```

This class defines **Can** objects that represent regular cylindrical cans, such as a beer can. The class defines **pi** as a **const** static member, because it's required within function members of the class. Static class members exist even if the constructor is never called, so we must initialize **pi** at global namespace scope. We can do this by placing the definition in **Can.cpp**, along with the definition of the **volume()** function:

```
// Function to calculate the volume of a Can object
double Can::volume() const
{
  return pi * diameter * diameter * height / 4;
}

// Definitions for the Can class
const double Can::pi = 3.14159265;                 // Initialize static member
```

We could put the definition for **pi** in the header file after the class definition, but we would need to ensure that the definition appeared between the **#ifndef**/**#endif** pair of directives, because there must be only one definition for each static data member in a program.

Believe it or not, we can exercise all the classes, new and old, with a very short **main()** function:

```
// Program 16.7 Using an indirect base class
#include <iostream>
#include "Box.h"                      // For the Box class
#include "ToughPack.h"                // For the ToughPack class
#include "Carton.h"                   // For the Carton class
#include "Can.h"                      // for the Can class

using namespace std;

int main()
{
  Box aBox(40, 30, 20);
  Can aCan(10, 3);
  Carton aCarton(40, 30, 20);
  ToughPack hardcase(40, 30, 20);

  Vessel* pVessels[] = { &aBox, &aCan, &aCarton, &hardcase };
```

651

```
    cout << endl;
    for(int i = 0 ; i < sizeof pVessels / sizeof(pVessels[0]) ; i++)
      cout << "Volume is " << pVessels[i]->volume() << endl;

    return 0;
}
```

This generates the following output:

```
Volume is 24000
Volume is 235.619
Volume is 22722.4
Volume is 20400
```

How It Works

We have a three-level class hierarchy in this example, as shown in the illustration below.

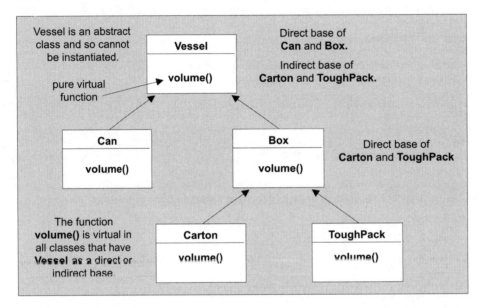

The **volume()** function is virtual in all the classes that have **Vessel** as a direct or indirect base. If a derived class fails to define a function that's declared as a pure virtual function in the base class, then the function will be inherited as a pure virtual function, and this will make the derived class an abstract class. You can demonstrate this effect by removing the **const** declaration from either the **Can** or the **Box** class. This will make the function different from the pure virtual function in the base class, so the derived class will inherit the base class version, and the program will not compile.

This time around, we use an array of pointers of type 'pointer to **Vessel**' to exercise the virtual functions:

```
Box aBox(40, 30, 20);
Can aCan(10, 3);
Carton aCarton(40, 30, 20);
ToughPack hardcase(40, 30, 20);
```

```
Vessel* pVessels[] = { &aBox, &aCan, &aCarton, &hardcase };
```

The array elements are initialized with the addresses of the four different types of vessel we have defined: this will declare and initialize an array with four elements. We then call the virtual function **volume()** in the **for** loop:

```
for(int i = 0 ; i < sizeof pVessels / sizeof(pVessels[0]) ; i++)
  cout << "Volume is " << pVessels[i]->volume() << endl;
```

This calls the **volume()** function of the object pointed to by each of the elements in the array of pointers, **pVessels**. You can see from the output that the function calls are all resolved dynamically.

Destroying Objects through a Pointer

The use of pointers to a base class when working with derived class objects is very common, because that's how you can take advantage of virtual functions. A problem arises, though, when you want to destroy objects through a base class pointer. We can see the problem if we implement the classes in the previous example with destructors that display a message.

Try It Out – Destroying Objects through a Pointer

Add a destructor to the **Vessel** class that just displays a message when it gets called:

```
class Vessel
{
  public:
    virtual double volume() const = 0;
    ~Vessel();
};
```

```
// Vessel.cpp
#include <iostream>
#include "Vessel.h"
using namespace std;

Vessel::~Vessel()
{
  cout << "Vessel destructor" << endl;
}
```

Do the same for the **Can**, **Box** and **ToughPack** classes, and add an output statement to the destructor for the **Carton** class. You'll need to **#include** the **iostream** header file to several of the **.cpp** files involved, as well.

We now need to modify **main()** from the previous example to initialize the **pVessels** array with the addresses of objects created in the free store. We also need to use the operator **delete** to release the memory when we're done.

```
// Program 16.8 Destroying objects through a pointer
#include <iostream>
#include "Box.h"                        // For the Box class
#include "ToughPack.h"                  // For the ToughPack class
#include "Carton.h"                     // For the Carton class
#include "Can.h"                        // for the Can class

using namespace std;

int main()
{
  Vessel* pVessels[] = { new Box(40, 30, 20),    new Can(10, 3),
                      new Carton(40, 30, 20), new ToughPack(40, 30, 20) };

  cout << endl;
  for(int i = 0 ; i < sizeof pVessels / sizeof(pVessels[0]) ; i++)
    cout << "Volume is " << pVessels[i]->volume() << endl;

  // Delete the objects from the free store
  for(int i = 0 ; i < sizeof pVessels / sizeof(pVessels[0]) ; i++)
    delete pVessels[i];

  return 0;
}
```

If you run this, you'll get the output:

```
Volume is 24000
Volume is 235.619
Volume is 22722.4
Volume is 20400
Vessel destructor
Vessel destructor
Vessel destructor
Vessel destructor
```

How It Works

We clearly have yet another failure on our hands: the wrong destructors are being called in each case. Once again, the problem occurs because the binding to the destructor is being set at compile time, and since we're applying the **delete** operator to an object pointed to by a pointer to **Vessel**, the **Vessel** class destructor is called every time. To fix this, we need dynamic binding for the destructors.

Virtual Destructors

To ensure that the correct destructor is called for objects allocated in the free store, we need to employ **virtual class destructors**. To implement a virtual class destructor, we just add the keyword **virtual** to the destructor declaration in the class. This signals to the compiler that destructor calls through a pointer or a reference parameter should have dynamic binding, and so the destructor will be selected at runtime. This works in spite of the fact that all the destructors have different names; destructors are treated as a special case for this purpose.

Try It Out – Calling Virtual Destructors

We can show this effect by modifying the last example: we just need to add the keyword **virtual** to the destructor declaration in the base class, like this:

```
class Vessel
{
  public:
    virtual double volume() const = 0;
    virtual ~Vessel();
};
```

The destructors of all the derived classes will automatically be virtual as a result of declaring a virtual base class destructor. If you run the example again, you will now get this output:

```
Volume is 24000
Volume is 235.619
Volume is 22722.4
Volume is 20400
Box destructor
Vessel destructor
Can destructor
Vessel destructor
Carton destructor
Box destructor
Vessel destructor
ToughPack destructor
Box destructor
Vessel destructor
```

How It Works

What a difference one little keyword makes! The output shows that deleting the **Box** object results in two destructor calls: one for the **Box** destructor, and one for the **Vessel** destructor. Deleting the **Can** object also results in two destructor calls. Deleting the **Carton** and **ToughPack** objects results in three destructor calls for each: the class destructor for the object, then the destructor for the direct base class, and finally the destructor for the indirect base.

You saw earlier in the book that objects are *always* destroyed in this way, with destructor calls for each successive base class, until the 'ultimate' base is reached. This is the reverse of the sequence of constructor calls when a derived class object is created.

> *When you're using inheritance, you should always declare your base class destructor as* **virtual**, *as a matter of course. There is a small overhead in the execution of the class destructors, but you won't notice it in the majority of circumstances. Using virtual destructors ensures that your objects will be properly destroyed, and avoids potential problems that might otherwise occur.*

Identifying Types at Runtime

You know by now that a pointer to a base class can contain the address of an object of any derived type. This means that, at a given moment in time, it may not necessarily be obvious to what type of object the pointer is pointing. The pointer may be passed as an argument or may be a class member; in either case, the address is set elsewhere. The same is true for reference parameters — a parameter of type 'reference to **Base**' may be used with an argument that is an object of any class type derived from **Base**.

In these situations, it could be helpful to know the type of the pointer or reference — your course of action might depend on the result. This may be particularly useful where there are two or more 'limbs' in a hierarchy, such as the one we used earlier that contained the **Can** class in one limb and the **Carton** class in another.

The **typeid()** operator allows you to discover a type at runtime. To use the operator, you must **#include** the standard header file **typeinfo** into your source file; the header contains the definition of the **type_info** class. The **typeid()** operator returns an object of type **type_info** — or more strictly, of type **const std::type_info**. The **type_info** class implements the **==** operator, allowing you to compare one **type_info** object with another.

For a particular type, you get the **type_info** object by using the expression **typeid(type)**. For example, the expression **typeid(Box*)** returns the **type_info** object that represents the type **Box***. You could check whether a particular pointer, **pVessel**, is pointing to a derived class object of type **Carton** with the statement:

```
if(typeid(*pVessel) == typeid(Carton))
  cout << "Pointer is type Carton" << endl;
else
  cout << "Pointer is not type Carton" << endl;
```

In practice, you'll be using **typeid()** to perform rather more exciting actions than this: for example, you might be calling a non-virtual function for a particular class.

A top-level **const** qualifier is ignored here, just as it is with parameter types in function overloading, so that type **const Carton** will result in the same **type_info** object as type **Carton**.

When you apply **typeid()** to determining dynamic types, you will usually need to de-reference a pointer to a base class in order to test the type of the object pointed to, as in the code snippet above. With reference parameters, of course, you just use the parameter name to get the **type_info** object for the type of the argument. For example:

```
void Box::doThat(Vessel& rVessel)
{
  ...

  if(typeid(rVessel) == typeid(Carton))
    cout << "Type Carton was passed" << endl;
  else
    cout << "Type Carton was not passed" << endl;

  ...
}
```

Here, **doThat()** is a hypothetical function, defined in the **Box** class, which accepts an object of any class derived from **Vessel**. The code determines whether the object referenced by the parameter is of type **Carton**. Of course, you could test for any or all of the class types that have **Vessel** as a base.

> *Don't forget that if you want to use the **typeid()** operator, you must **#include** the **typeinfo** header file into your source file.*

You should find that you don't need to use **typeid()** extensively in your programs. If you're overusing **typeid()**, then you are probably not using polymorphism where you should. Using **typeid()** too often makes your program very inflexible — you inevitably introduce tests for specific class types into your program, and such tests will need to be changed if you introduce new classes into your hierarchy.

By contrast, virtual functions are very flexible — you can add new classes to your hierarchy without the need to change any existing code that calls virtual functions in the hierarchy. Consequently, any new class type that implements existing virtual functions will be accommodated automatically.

Pointers to Class Members

We've seen how to define a pointer to a variable of any type. We have also seen how to define pointers to functions. You can even use a pointer to store the address of a data member of a given class object (assuming it is accessible). However, you *can't* use a pointer to a function to store the address of a member function, even when the pointer type reflects the same function signature as the member function. This is because a member function uses the class type as part of its type, so the type of a member function is always different from the type of an ordinary function with the same parameter list.

You can, however, define pointers to members of a *class*, and such pointers can point to data members or member functions.

Pointers to class members provide an additional level of generalization in your programs. A pointer to a class member can point to any of several compatible members, and can be used to access the member it points to for *any* object of that class. Let's look at pointers to data members first, as they are simpler than pointers to member functions.

Pointers to Data Members

A *regular* pointer contains the address of a specific variable. It could be an ordinary variable, or a data member of a class object, but in either case the pointer contains the address of a specific location in memory.

A pointer to a data member of a class works differently. It contains the address of a data member of a class *type*, and *only* refers to a particular location in memory when it is combined with a class object.

To illustrate what that means, we can return to code we had in Program 16.5, and modify the **Box** class to see how pointers to data members work. Let's alter the access specification for the data members to **public**. (This is for demonstration only; they'll revert to **protected** access again shortly.) The class definition will be:

```
class Box
{
  public:
    Box(double lengthValue = 1.0, double breadthValue = 1.0,
                                        double heightValue = 1.0);

    // Function to show the volume of an object
    void showVolume() const;

    // Function to calculate the volume of a Box object
    virtual double volume() const;

  public:
    double length;
    double breadth;
    double height;
};
```

Since the three data members are all of type **double**, we can declare a pointer to a data member that could be used to refer to any of them. The pointer type will be **double Box::***. The declaration will be:

```
double Box::* pData;
```

> *For a clumsy-looking type name like* **double Box::***, *it wouldn't be a bad idea to use* **typedef** *to create a synonym. You could use this statement:*
>
> **typedef double Box::* pBoxMember;**
>
> *to create a synonym* **pBoxMember**, *which you could then use in place of* **double Box::***.

You could now assign the address of the **breadth** member of the class to this pointer with this statement:

```
pData = &Box::breadth;
```

Of course, **pData** does not point to a specific item of data, because it isn't a pointer to a data member of a class object. It is a pointer to a class member *in general*. It will only refer to a particular location in memory when you combine it with an object of type **Box**.

FYI — A pointer to a data member is most useful when your class contains several data members of the same type. If there is only one such class member, then you might as well refer to it directly.

To make use of a pointer to a data member of a class, we need to look at some new operators.

'Pointer to Member' Selection Operators

So far, we have set up a pointer to a data member of a class. As I mentioned, though, you can only use it to access members of a particular *object*. You will always use pointers such as this in conjunction with an object, a reference to an object or a pointer to an object. Let's declare and define an object of type **Box**:

```
    Box myBox(20.0, 30.0, 40.0);                        // Declare a box
```

Given that **pData** is still defined as above, we can now use it to refer to the **breadth** member of the **myBox** object. First, we'll work in conjunction with the **myBox** object name directly. We can refer to the **breadth** member of **myBox** by using the expression **myBox.*pData**. We could use this expression to display the value of the **breadth** data member of **myBox** with the statement:

```
    cout << "Data member value is " << myBox.*pData << endl;
```

This uses the **'direct pointer to member' selection operator**, **.***. You can see that this is a combination of the member selection operator (**.**) and the de-reference operator (*****), applied to the pointer to data member. The **.*** operator is always is used to select a member of a class object, by combining a class object (or a reference to a class object) with a pointer to a member. Here, the pointer **pData** is de-referenced to access the **breadth** member of the **Box** class, and the member selection operator applies this to the **myBox** object — so we effectively get **myBox.breadth**.

Next, we can work in conjunction with a pointer to **myBox**. To do so, we need to declare and initialize a 'pointer to **Box**' with the declaration:

```
    Box* pBox = &myBox;
```

We will access the data member of **myBox** via this pointer, with the help of a pointer to data member, **pData**. To do this, we must use the **'indirect pointer to member' selection operator**, **->***, as follows:

```
    cout << "Data member value is " << pBox->*pData << endl;
```

This is a combination of the indirect member selection operator, (**->**), and the de-reference operator, (*****). Let's see how all this fits together within a working example.

Try It Out – Using a Pointer to a Data Member

With the data members of the **Box** class declared as **public**, as we discussed above, we can try out a pointer to a data member with the following program:

```
// Program 16.9 Using a pointer to a data member
#include <iostream>
#include "Box.h"                            // For the Box class
#include "ToughPack.h"                      // For the ToughPack class
#include "Carton.h"                         // For the Carton class

using namespace std;
```

```
        typedef double Box::* pBoxMember;                    // Define pointer to data member type

        int main()
        {
          Box myBox(20.0, 30.0, 40.0);                       // Declare a base box
          ToughPack hardcase(35.0, 45.0, 55.0);              // Declare a derived box
          Carton aCarton(48.0, 58.0, 68.0);                  // A different kind of derived box

          pBoxMember pData = &Box::length;                   // Define pointer to Box data member

          cout << endl;

          // Using a pointer to class data member with class objects
          cout << "length member of myBox is " << myBox.*pData << endl;
          pData = &Box::breadth;

          cout << "breadth member of myBox is " << myBox.*pData << endl;
          pData = &Box::height;

          cout << "height member of myBox is " << myBox.*pData << endl;
          cout << "height member of hardcase is " << hardcase.*pData << endl;
          cout << "height member of aCarton is " << aCarton.*pData << endl;

          Box* pBox = &myBox;                                          // Define pointer to Box

          // Using a pointer to class data member with a pointer to the base class
          cout << "height member of myBox is " << pBox->*pData << endl;
          pBox = &hardcase;
          cout << "height member of hardcase is " << pBox->*pData << endl;

          cout << endl;
          return 0;
        }
```

If you compile and run this, you will get the output:

```
length member of myBox is 20
breadth member of myBox is 30
height member of myBox is 40
height member of hardcase is 55
height member of aCarton is 68
height member of myBox is 40
height member of hardcase is 55
```

How It Works

Prior to the definition of **main()**, we define the type **pBoxMember** with the statement:

```
typedef double Box::* pBoxMember;                    // Define pointer to data member type
```

This defines **pBoxMember** as a synonym for the type 'pointer to a **double** member of **Box**'.

After defining objects of each of the classes **Box**, **Carton** and **ToughPack**, we declare and initialize a pointer to a **double** member of the **Box** class with the declaration:

```
pBoxMember pData = &Box::length;                     // Define pointer to Box data member
```

pData now points to the length member of the **Box** class, so we can use it to refer to the **length** member of any **Box** object. We display the **length** member of **myBox** with this statement:

```
cout << "length member of myBox is " << myBox.*pData << endl;
```

Since **pData** is a pointer, we can reassign it to point to a different member of the **Box** class:

```
pData = &Box::breadth;
```

Now **pData** points to the **breadth** member of the class. Remember that **pData** can only store the address of a data member of type **double**. If there were a data member of a different type, **string** say, we would have to declare a different pointer to class data member to store the address.

We are now able to display the value of the **breadth** member of **myBox** with a very similar statement to the earlier one:

```
cout << "breadth member of myBox is " << myBox.*pData << endl;
```

Just to prove that it wasn't a fluke, we store the address of the height member of **Box** and display the value of that member for the **myBox** object with these statements:

```
pData = &Box::height;
cout << "height member of myBox is " << myBox.*pData << endl;
```

Of course, every object of a class derived from **Box** contains a **Box** sub-object, so we are also able to use the pointer to data member with **Carton** and **ToughPack** objects.

After declaring and initializing **pBox**, we use the indirect pointer to member selection operator to display the value of the **height** member of **myBox**:

```
Box* pBox = &myBox;
cout << "height member of myBox is " << pBox->*pData << endl;
```

Of course, this also works when the pointer to the base class contains the address of a derived class object:

```
pBox = &hardcase;
cout << "height member of hardcase is " << pBox->*pData << endl;
```

This displays the value of the **height** member of the object pointed to by **pBox**, so we effectively get the value of **hardcase.height**.

Pointers to Member Functions

The type of a 'pointer to a member function of a class' involves the class type, as well as the function parameter list and return type. This means that such a pointer is specific to a class, and cannot be used to store addresses of function members of any other class. Apart from that, they follow the same principles as the pointers to functions that we discussed in Chapter 9. The declaration of a pointer to a member function gets a little messy, so let's get down to a specific instance.

Let's reset the **Box** class data members to be **protected**, and add **public** functions to retrieve the values of the data members:

```
class Box
{
  public:
    Box(double lengthValue = 1.0, double breadthValue = 1.0,
                                        double heightValue = 1.0);

    // Function to show the volume of an object
    void showVolume() const;

    // Function to calculate the volume of a Box object
    virtual double volume() const;

    // Get values of data members
    double getLength() const { return length; }
    double getBreadth() const { return breadth; }
    double getHeight() const { return height; }

  protected:
    double length;
    double breadth;
    double height;
};
```

We can now declare a pointer to member function, which we can use to store the address of any of the three functions we've added. The pointer is declared as:

```
double(Box::*pGet)() const;
```

As with the pointer to data member, this points to a function member of the class, and only translates to a specific function when combined with a class object. The class name qualifies the pointer name within the parentheses, and identifies the pointer with the class. In general, to declare a pointer to a function for a class ***class_type***, you would write:

return_type(*class_type*::*pointer_name*)(*parameter_type_list*);

This is a complicated declaration! For this reason, such types are very often declared using a **typedef** for use within the program code. Instead of the above declaration, we can begin again by defining a synonym for the type of the pointer **pGet** with the statement:

```
typedef double(Box::*pBoxFunction)() const;
```

The general form of declaration of a synonym for a pointer to a member function is:

typedef *return_type*(*class_type*::*ptr_typename*)(*parameter_type_list*);

This defines the type ***ptr_typename***. Pointers of this type can store the address of any member function of the class ***class_type*** that has a return type ***return_type***, and the parameter types listed in ***parameter_type_list***.

Now we can use the type **pBoxFunction**, defined above, to declare a pointer:

```
pBoxFunction pGet = &Box::getLength;
```

As well as declaring the pointer **pGet**, this statement also initializes **pGet** with the address of the function **getLength()**. Of course, **pGet** can only point to functions that are members of the **Box** class, and that have the return type and parameter list as specified in the **typedef** statement. This also means that **pGet** can only point to **const** member functions.

You use pointers to member functions in combination with a class object, a reference to an object or a pointer, and use the same operators we saw in the context of pointers to class data members. Let's give pointer to member functions a whirl in another example.

Try It Out – Pointers to Member Functions

With the **Box** class defined as you have just seen, we can call members of the **Box** class through a pointer to the member function with the following code:

```
// Program 16.10 Using a pointer to a function member
#include <iostream>
#include "Box.h"                               // For the Box class
#include "ToughPack.h"                         // For the ToughPack class
#include "Carton.h"                            // For the Carton class

using namespace std;

typedef double (Box::*pBoxFunction)() const;   // Pointer to member function type

int main()
{
  Box myBox(20.0, 30.0, 40.0);                 // Declare a base box
  ToughPack hardcase(35.0, 45.0, 55.0);        // Declare a derived box
  Carton aCarton(48.0, 58.0, 68.0);            // A different kind of derived box

  pBoxFunction pGet = &Box::getLength;         // Pointer to member function

  cout << endl;

  // Call member function for an object through the pointer
  cout << "length member of myBox is " << (myBox.*pGet)() << endl;

  pGet = &Box::getBreadth;
  cout << "breadth member of myBox is " << (myBox.*pGet)() << endl;

  pGet = &Box::getHeight;
  cout << "height member of myBox is " << (myBox.*pGet)() << endl;

  // It works for derived class objects too
  cout << "height member of hardcase is " << (hardcase.*pGet)() << endl;
  cout << "height member of aCarton is " << (aCarton.*pGet)() << endl;

  Box* pBox = &myBox;                                  // Pointer to the base class

  // Calling a function with a pointer to a class object
  cout << "height member of myBox is " << (pBox->*pGet)() << endl;

  pBox = &hardcase;
  cout << "height member of hardcase is " << (pBox->*pGet)() << endl;
```

```
        cout << endl;
        return 0;
    }
```

This program generates the output:

```
length member of myBox is 20
breadth member of myBox is 30
height member of myBox is 40
height member of hardcase is 55
height member of aCarton is 68
height member of myBox is 40
height member of hardcase is 55
```

How It Works

The **typedef** defines a synonym for a pointer to **Box** member function type:

```
typedef double(Box::*pBoxFunction)() const;       // Pointer to member function type
```

Pointers of this type can only point to function members of the **Box** class that have no arguments, return a value of type **double** *and* are **const**. Another function member that differs in *any* respect requires a different pointer type.

We use the type that we have defined in **main()**, to declare the pointer **pGet**:

```
pBoxFunction pGet = &Box::getLength;               // Pointer to member function
```

We can use **pGet** to store the address of any of the three functions in **Box** that retrieve the values of the data members, since they all have the same signature and return type. Here, it is initialized with the address of the **getLength()** function member.

To call the **getLength()** function for the **myBox** object, we just use the direct pointer member selection operator:

```
cout << "length member of myBox is " << (myBox.*pGet)() << endl;
```

The parentheses around the expression **myBox.*pGet** are mandatory — without them, the statement will not compile. This is because the precedence of the function call operator, **()**, is higher that the precedence of the operator **.***. Without the parentheses, the expression would be equivalent to **myBox.*(pGet())**. In this case, we would be trying to apply the direct member selection operator to the value return by a function called **pGet()** in the global namespace. The same applies later in the program, when we use the indirect member selection operator to call a function member through a pointer to a class object:

```
cout << "height member of myBox is " << (pBox->*pGet)() << endl;
```

Once again, the function call operator is of a higher precedence than the indirect member selection operator, and so we must include the parentheses. As you can see from the output from the rest of the code in the example, we can call functions for derived class objects through the pointer **pGet** in the same way as we did for a pointer to a class data member.

Passing Pointers to Members to a Function

The parameters of member functions can be 'pointer to a member'. They can be pointers to data members, or pointers to function members. Let's look at an example of the latter.

By applying the proverbial sledgehammer to crack a nut, we could write a function to calculate the area of any side of a **Box** object as a function member of the **Box** class with two parameters that are pointers to member functions:

```
class Box
{
  public:
    double sideArea(double (Box::*pGetSide1)() const,
                                          double (Box::*pGetSide2)() const)
    {
      return (this->*pGetSide1)() * (this->*pGetSide2)();
    }

  // Rest of the class as before
};
```

The code above shows the parameter types in their full glory, although you can make the same code look rather simpler by first defining the type, **pBoxFunction**, from the previous example using **typedef**:

```
typedef double (Box::*pBoxFunction)() const;      // Pointer to member function type
```

Now the function definition in the class becomes:

```
class Box
{
  public:
    double sideArea(pBoxFunction pGetSide1, pBoxFunction pGetSide2)
    {
      return (this->*pGetSide1)() * (this->*pGetSide2)();
    }

  // Rest of the class as before
};
```

Given a **Box** object **myBox**, you could obtain the area of a side with a statement such as:

```
cout << "Side area is "
     << myBox.sideArea(&Box::getHeight, &Box::getLength) << endl;
```

This passes the addresses of the member functions **getHeight()** and **getLength()** as arguments, so these will be used to obtain the values for the side lengths in the area calculation.

You could equally well call this function for a derived class object, since the function will be inherited. Of course, you could also call it through a base class pointer for a **Box** object, or an object of the **Carton** or **ToughPack** classes.

Summary

In this chapter, we've covered the principal ideas involved in using inheritance. The fundamentals that you should keep in mind are these:

- Polymorphism involves calling a function through a pointer or a reference, and having the call resolved dynamically — that is, when the program is executing.

- A function in a base class may be declared as **virtual**. This forces all occurrences of the function in classes derived from the base to be virtual as well. When you call a virtual function through a pointer or a reference, the function call is resolved dynamically: the type of object for which the function call is made will determine the particular function that is used.

- A call of a virtual function using an object and the direct member selection operator is resolved statically — that is, at compile time.

- If a base class contains a virtual function, then you should declare the base class destructor as **virtual**. This will ensure correct selection of a destructor for dynamically created derived class objects.

- A pure virtual function has no definition. A virtual function in a base class can be specified as pure by placing **= 0** at the end of the function declaration.

- A class with one or more pure virtual functions is called an abstract class, for which no objects can be created. In any derived class, all the inherited pure virtual functions must be defined. If they're not, it too becomes an abstract class, and no objects of the class can be created.

- Default parameter values for virtual functions are assigned statically, so if there are default values for a base version of a virtual function, default values specified in a derived class will be ignored for dynamically resolved function calls.

- You can declare pointers to class members. These can be pointers to data members, or pointers to function members. You can use such a pointer in conjunction with an object, a reference or a pointer to an object, to refer to the class member of the object defined by the pointer to member.

Exercises

Ex 16.1 As in last chapter's exercises, define a base class called **Animal** that contains two private data members: a **string** member to store the name of the animal (e.g. "Fido"), and an integer member, **weight**, that will contain the weight of the **Animal** in pounds. Also include a virtual public member function, **who()**, that returns a **string** object containing the name and weight of the **Animal** object, and a pure virtual function called **sound()** that in a derived class should return a **string** representing the sound the animal makes. Derive at least three classes — **Sheep**, **Dog**, and **Cow** — with the class **Animal** as a public base, and implement the **sound()** function appropriately in each class.

Define a class called **Zoo** that can store up to 50 animals of various types in an array (use an array of pointers). Write a **main()** function to create a random sequence of a given number of derived class objects and store pointers to them in a **Zoo** object. Use a member function of the **Zoo** object to output information about each animal in the **Zoo**, and the sound that it makes.

Ex 16.2 Define a class called **BaseLength** that stores a length as an integral number of millimeters, and which has a member function **length()** that returns a **double** value specifying the length. Derive classes called **Inches**, **Meters**, **Yards**, and **Perches** from the **BaseLength** class that override the base class **length()** function to return the length as a **double** value in the appropriate units. (1 inch is 25.4 millimeters; 1 meter is 1000 millimeters; 1 yard is 36 inches; 1 perch (US) is 5.5 yards.) Define a **main()** function to read a series of lengths in various units and create the appropriate derived class objects, storing their addresses in an array of type **BaseLength***. Output each of the lengths in millimeters as well as the original units.

Ex 16.3 Define conversion operator functions to convert each of the derived types in the previous example to any other derived type. For example, in the **Inches** class, define members **operator Meters()**, **operator Perches()** and **operator Yards()**. Add code to **main()** to output each measurement in the four different units. (Remember that conversion operators do not need to have a return type specified, because it is implicit in their name.)

Ex 16.4 Repeat the previous exercise using constructors for the conversions instead of conversion operators.

17

Program Errors and Exception Handling

Exceptions are a way of signaling errors or unexpected conditions in your C++ programs. Using exceptions to signal errors is not mandatory, and you will sometimes find it more convenient to handle them in other ways. However, it is important to understand how exceptions work, because they can arise in the use of standard language features such as the operators **new** and **dynamic_cast**, and they are used extensively within the standard library.

In this chapter you will learn:

> What an exception is

> How you can use exceptions to signal error conditions in your program

> How you handle exceptions

> What exceptions are defined within the standard library

> How you can limit the types of exceptions that a function can throw

> How to deal with exceptions that are thrown in a constructor

> How an exception being thrown can affect a destructor for a class

Handling Errors

Error handling is a fundamental element of successful programming. You need to equip your program to deal with potential errors and abnormal events, and this can take more effort than writing the code that executes when things work the way they should. The quality of the error handling code you write will determine how robust your program is, and is usually a major factor in making a program user-friendly. It will also have a substantial impact on how easy it is to correct errors in the code, and to extend it.

Not all errors are equal though, and the nature of the error will determine how it is best dealt with in your program. In many cases, you'll want to deal with errors directly where they occur. For example, consider the task of reading input from the keyboard: mistyping can result in erroneous input, but this is not really a serious problem. It's usually quite easy to detect an input error, and the most appropriate course of action is often simply to discard the input and prompt the user to enter the data again. The error-handling code in this case is integrated with the code that handles the overall input process.

More serious errors are often recoverable, and can be dealt with in a manner that does not prejudice other activity within a program. When an error is discovered within a function, it is often convenient to return an error code of some kind to impart information to the caller about the error, and to allow the caller to determine how best to proceed.

Exceptions provide us with an *additional* approach to handling errors — they don't replace the kinds of mechanisms I have just described. The primary advantage of using exceptions to signal errors is that the error handling code is separated completely from the code that caused the error.

Understanding Exceptions

An **exception** is a temporary object, of any type, that is used to signal an error. An exception could be a basic type of object, such as **int** or **char***, but it's usually an object of a class that you define specially for the purpose. An exception object is intended to carry information from the point at which the error occurred to the code that is to handle the error, and this is best done with an object of a class.

When you identify an error in your code, you can signal the error by '**throwing**' an exception. Code that may throw exceptions must be enclosed within a special block bounded by braces, called a **try block**. If a statement that is not within a **try** block throws an exception, your program will terminate. We'll discuss this a little further in a moment.

A **try** block is followed by one or more **catch blocks**. Each **catch** block contains the code to handle a particular kind of exception; for this reason, a **catch** block is sometimes referred to as a **handler**. Thus, if you throw exceptions when errors occur, all the code that deals with the errors is within **catch** blocks, completely separate from the code that is executed when nothing is wrong. The code to handle 'normal' events is completely separated from the code that handles 'exceptional' events.

Code that may throw exceptions must be within a **try** block.

When an exception is thrown, the **catch** blocks are examined in sequence. Control is transferred to the first **catch** block that has a parameter that can match the type of the exception, by automatic conversion of the exception if necessary.

```
try
{
  // Code that may throw exceptions...
}

catch(parameter specifying exception type 1)
{
  // Code to handle the exception...
}
catch(parameter specifying exception type 2)
{
  // Code to handle the exception...
}

...

catch(parameter specifying exception type n)
{
  // Code to handle the exception...
}
```

As illustrated above, a **try** block is a normal block between braces, preceded by the keyword **try**. Each time the **try** block is executed, it may throw any one of several different kinds of exception. Therefore, it may be followed by a number of different **catch** blocks, each of which is intended to handle a different type of exception. The type of exception that a handler deals with is identified by a single parameter between parentheses, following the **catch** keyword that is placed immediately before the braces for the **catch** block, as illustrated above.

A **catch** block is only executed when an exception of a matching type is thrown. If a **try** block doesn't throw an exception, then none of the corresponding **catch** blocks are executed. You cannot branch into a **try** block — by using a **goto**, for instance. The only way to execute a **try** block is to start from the beginning, with the first statement following the opening brace.

Throwing an Exception

It is high time we threw an exception, to find out what happens when we do so. Although you should always use class objects for exceptions (as we'll do later in the chapter), we can begin by using basic types, since it will keep the code very simple while we explore what's going on.

You throw an exception using a **throw expression**, which you write using the keyword **throw**. Here's an example of how to throw an exception:

```
try
{
  // Code that may throw exceptions...

  if(test > 5)
    throw "test is greater than 5";              // Throws an exception

  // This code will execute if the exception is not thrown
}
catch(const char* message)
{
  // Code to handle the exception...
  // This code is executed if an exception of type 'char*'
  // or 'const char*' is thrown
  cout << message << endl;
}
```

If the value of **test** is greater than 5, the **throw** statement throws an exception. In this case, the exception is, **"test is greater than 5"**. Control is immediately transferred out of the **try** block, to the first handler for the type of the exception being thrown: **const char***. We have just the one handler here, which happens to catch exceptions of type **const char***, so the statement in the **catch** block will be executed, and the exception will be displayed.

FYI The compiler actually ignores the keyword **const** when matching the exception type with the **catch** parameter type. We'll examine this more thoroughly later.

671

Try It Out – Throwing and Catching Exceptions

Let's try exceptions out in a working example, in which we'll have a go at throwing exceptions of type **int** and **const char***. We can include a few output statements that will help us see the flow of control:

```
// Program 17.1 Throwing and catching exceptions
#include <iostream>

using namespace std;

int main()
{
  cout << endl;
  for(int i = 0 ; i < 7 ; i++)
  {
    try
    {
      if(i < 3)
        throw i;
      cout << " i not thrown - value is " << i << endl;

      if(i > 5)
        throw "Here is another!";
      cout << " End of the try block." << endl;
    }
    catch(const int i)
    {
      cout << " i caught - value is " << i << endl;
    }
    catch(const char* pmessage)
    {
      cout << "  \"" << pmessage << "\" caught" << endl;
    }

    cout << "End of the for loop (after the catch blocks) - i is " << i << endl;
  }

  return 0;
}
```

This example will produce the output:

```
   i caught - value is 0
End of the for loop (after the catch blocks) - i is 0
   i caught - value is 1
End of the for loop (after the catch blocks) - i is 1
   i caught - value is 2
End of the for loop (after the catch blocks) - i is 2
   i not thrown - value is 3
   End of the try block.
End of the for loop (after the catch blocks) - i is 3
   i not thrown - value is 4
   End of the try block.
End of the for loop (after the catch blocks) - i is 4
   i not thrown - value is 5
   End of the try block.
```

```
End of the for loop (after the catch blocks) - i is 5
  i not thrown - value is 6
  "Here is another!" caught
End of the for loop (after the catch blocks) - i is 6
```

How It Works

Within the **for** loop, we have a **try** block containing code that will throw an exception of type **int** if **i** (the loop counter) is less than 3, and an exception of type **const char*** if **i** is greater than 5:

```
try
{
  if(i < 3)
    throw i;
  cout << "  i not thrown - value is " << i << endl;

  if(i > 5)
    throw "Here is another!";
  cout << "  End of the try block." << endl;
}
```

Throwing an exception *immediately* transfers control out of the **try** block, so the output statement at the end of the block will only be executed if no exception is thrown. You can see from the output that this is the case. We only get output from the last statement when **i** has the value 3, 4 or 5. For all other values of **i**, an exception is thrown, so the output line is not executed.

The first **catch** block immediately follows the **try** block:

```
catch(const int i)
{
  cout << "  i caught - value is " << i << endl;
}
```

The handlers for a **try** block must immediately follow the **try** block. If you place any code between the **try** block and the first **catch** block, or between successive **catch** blocks for a **try** block, then the program will not compile. This **catch** block handles exceptions of type **int**, and you can see from the output that it executes when the first **throw** statement is executed. You can also see that the next **catch** block is *not* executed in this case. After this handler executes, control passes directly to the last statement at the end of the loop.

The second handler deals with exceptions of type **char***:

```
catch(const char* pmessage)
{
  cout << "  \"" << pmessage << "\" caught" << endl;
}
```

When we throw the exception **"Here is another!"**, control passes from the **throw** statement directly to this handler, skipping the previous **catch** block. If no exception is thrown, then neither of the **catch** blocks is executed. You could put this **catch** block before the previous handler, and the program would work just as well. On this occasion, the sequence of the handlers doesn't matter, but that's not always the case. You'll see examples where the order of the handlers is important later in the chapter.

673

The statement marking the end of an iteration of the loop is:

```
cout << "End of the for loop (after the catch blocks) - i is " << i << endl;
```

This code is executed whether or not a handler is executed. As you can see, throwing an exception does not end the program — unless you want it to, of course. If you can fix the problem that caused the exception within the handler, then your program can continue.

The Exception Handling Process

Having seen the example, you should have a fairly clear idea of the sequence of events when an exception is thrown. Some other things happen in the background, though, and you might be able to guess some of them if you think about how control is transferred from the **try** block to the **catch** block. The **throw**/**catch** sequence of events is illustrated conceptually in the diagram below.

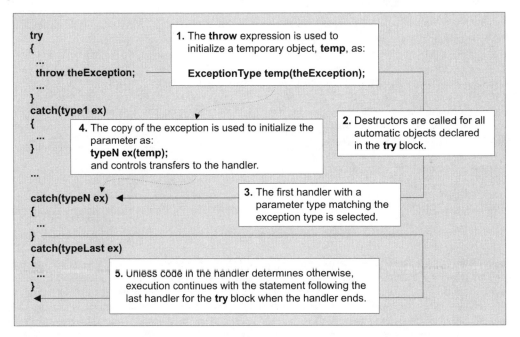

Of course, a **try** block is a statement block, and you know already that a statement block always defines a scope. Throwing an exception leaves the **try** block immediately, and at that point, all the automatic objects that have been declared within the **try** block (up to the point when the exception is thrown) are destroyed. None of them exists by the time the handler code is executed. This is most important — it implies that you must not throw an exception object that's a pointer to an object that is local to the **try** block. It is also the reason why the exception object is copied.

> *An exception object must be of a type that can be copied. An object of a class that has a private copy constructor **cannot** be used as an exception.*

Since the **throw** expression is used to initialize a temporary object — and therefore creates a copy of the exception — you *can* throw objects that are local to the **try** block. The copy of the thrown object will then be used to initialize the parameter for the **catch** block when the handler has been selected.

The **catch** block is *also* a statement block, so when the **catch** block has completed execution, all automatic objects that are local it (including the parameter) will be destroyed. Unless a **goto** or a **return** is used to transfer control out of the **catch** block, execution continues with the statement immediately following the last **catch** block for this **try** block.

Once a handler has been selected for an exception, and control has been passed to it, the exception that was thrown is considered to have been handled. This is true even if you leave the **catch** block empty and it does nothing.

Unhandled Exceptions

If an exception thrown in a **try** block is not handled by any of its **catch** blocks, then (subject to the possibility of nested **try** blocks, which we will discuss shortly) the standard library function **terminate()** is called. This function calls a predefined **default terminate handler function**, which in turn calls the standard library function **abort()**.

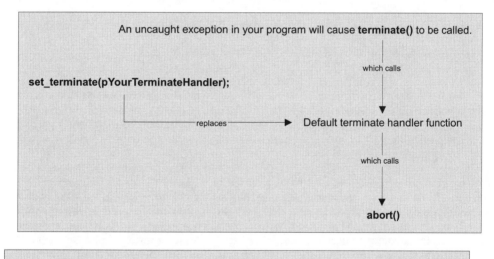

*The **abort()** function terminates the entire program immediately. Unlike **exit()**, it does not call destructors for any constructed static objects.*

The default action provided by the default terminate handler could be disastrous in some situations — for example, it may leave your files in an unsatisfactory state, or you may have a connection to a telephone line left open. In such cases, you would really want to make sure that things are tidied up properly. You can do this by replacing the default terminate handler function with your own version, as illustrated above. To replace the default handler, you call the standard library function **set_terminate()**, which accepts an argument of type **terminate_handler**, and returns a value of the same type. This type is defined in the **exception** standard header file as:

```
typedef void (*terminate_handler)();
```

675

terminate_handler is a pointer to a function that has no parameters and does not return a value, so your replacement function must be of this form. You can do what you want within your version of the terminate handler, but it *must not* return — it must ultimately terminate the program. Your definition of the function could take this form:

```
void myHandler()
{
   // Do necessary clean-up to leave things in an orderly state...
   exit(1);
}
```

Calling the **exit()** standard library function is a more satisfactory way of terminating your program than calling **abort()**.

> *Calling **exit()** ensures that destructors for global objects are called, and any open input/output streams are flushed if necessary, and closed. Any temporary files created using the standard library will be deleted.*

The integer argument that you pass to the **exit()** function is returned to the operating system as a status code. A non-zero value indicates abnormal program termination.

To set up the above function as the terminate handler, you could write:

```
terminate_handler pOldHandler = set_terminate(myHandler);
```

The return value is a pointer to the previous handler that was set, so by saving it you will be able to restore it later if necessary. The first time you call **set_terminate()**, the return value will be a pointer to the default handler. Each subsequent call to instate a new handler will return a pointer to whatever handler is in effect. This means that you can have your handler in effect for a particular part of your program, and then restore the default handler when your handler no longer applies.

Of course, you can set different terminate handlers at various points in your program to provide shutdown actions that suit the particular conditions that apply at any given time. For example, when your program is involved in database operations, you might need to make sure that there is an orderly shutdown of the database when a fatal error occurs, so you would define a terminate handler to take care of this. Another part of your program might be managing communications using a modem, in which case you will probably want your terminate handler to close the communications link. Different terminate handlers accommodating different shutdown requirements can be used whenever you need them.

Code that Causes an Exception to be Thrown

I said right at beginning of this discussion that **try** blocks enclose code that may throw an exception. However, this does not mean that the code that throws the exception must *physically* be between the braces bounding the **try** block. It only needs to be *logically* within the **try** block. This means that if a function is called from within a **try** block, any exception thrown from within that function can be caught by one of the **try** block's **catch** blocks. An example of this is illustrated below.

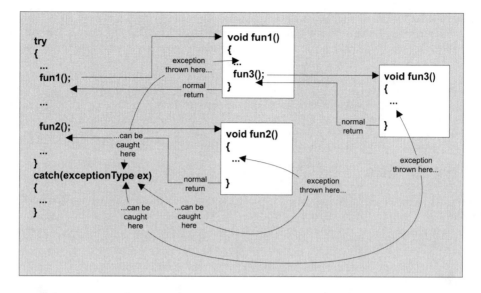

There are two function calls shown within the **try** block, to **fun1()** and **fun2()**. Exceptions of type **exceptionType** that arise within either function can be caught by the **catch** block following the **try** block. An exception thrown within a function that is not also caught by that function may be passed on to the calling function at the next level up. If it is not caught there, it can be passed on up to the next level — this is illustrated above by the exception thrown in **fun3()**. If an exception reaches a level where there are no further **catch** handlers and it is still uncaught, then the terminate handler will be called to end the program.

Of course, if the same function is called from different points in a program, the exceptions that the code in the body of the function may throw could be handled by different **catch** blocks at different times. You can see an example of this situation in the diagram below.

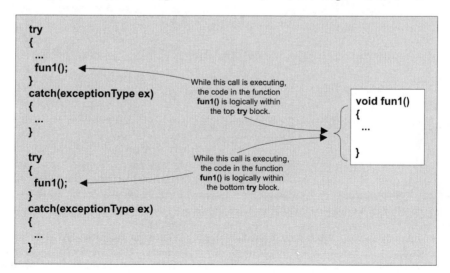

While the function is executing as a consequence of the call in the first **try** block, any exceptions of type **exceptionType** thrown by **fun1()** can be handled by the **catch** block for that **try** block. When it is called from within the second **try** block, the catch handler for that **try** block will deal with any exception of type **exceptionType** that is thrown.

You should be able to see from this that you can choose to handle exceptions at the level that is most convenient to your program structure and operation. If it suited you, in an extreme case you could catch all the exceptions that arose anywhere in a program in **main()**, just by enclosing the code in **main()** in a **try** block and appending a suitable variety of **catch** blocks.

Nested try Blocks

You can nest a **try** block inside another **try** block. Each of these will have its own set of **catch** blocks to handle the exceptions that may be thrown within it, and the **catch** blocks for a **try** block will *only* be invoked for exceptions that are thrown within the corresponding **try** block. It works like this:

```
try          // outer try block
{
  ...
  try          // inner try block
  {
    ...
  }
  catch(exceptionType ex)  ◄──────────── This handler can catch exceptions thrown
  {                                        in the inner try block.
    ...
  }
  ...
}
catch(exceptionType ex)  ◄──────────── This handler can catch exceptions thrown
{                                      anywhere in the outer try block, as well
  ...                                  as uncaught exceptions from the inner
}                                      try block.
```

The diagram shows one handler for each **try** block, but in general there may be several. When the code within inner **try** block throws an exception, its handlers get the first chance to deal with it. Each of its handlers is checked for a matching exception type, and if none of them matches, the handlers for the outer **try** block will have a chance to catch the exception. You can nest **try** blocks in this way to whatever depth is appropriate for your application.

When an exception is thrown by the code in the outer **try** block, that block's **catch** handlers will handle it, even if the statement originating the exception precedes the inner **try** block. The **catch** handlers for the inner **try** block can never be involved in dealing with exceptions thrown by code within the outer **try** block.

Naturally, the code within both **try** blocks may call functions, in which case, while the function is executing, the code within the body of the function is logically within the **try** block that called it. Any or all of the code within the body of the function could also be within its own **try** block, in which case this **try** block would be nested within the **try** block that called the function.

Try It Out – Nested try Blocks

That all sounds rather complicated in words, but it's much easier in practice. We can put together a simple example in which we throw an exception and then see where it ends up. Once again, we're going for explanation rather than gritty realism at this stage, so we will throw exceptions of type **int** and type **long**. The code for this program, which demonstrates both nested **try** blocks and throwing an exception within a function, is as follows:

```cpp
// Program 17.2 Throwing exceptions in nested try blocks
#include <iostream>
using namespace std;

void throwIt(int i)
{
  throw i;                                       // Throws the parameter value
}

int main()
{
  for(int i = 0 ; i <= 5 ; i++)
  {
    try
    {
      cout << endl << "outer try: ";
      if(i == 0)
        throw i;                                 // Throw int exception

      if(i == 1)
        throwIt(i);                              // Call the function that throws int

      try                                        // Nested try block
      {
        cout << endl << " inner try: ";
        if(i == 2)
          throw static_cast<long>(i);            // Throw long exception

        if(i == 3)
          throwIt(i);                            // Call the function that throws int
      }                                          // End nested try block
      catch(int n)
      {
        cout << endl << "Catch int for inner try. "
             << "Exception " << n;
      }

      cout << endl << "  outer try: ";

      if(i == 4)
        throw i;                                 // Throw int
      throwIt(i);                                // Call the function that throws int
    }
    catch(int n)
    {
      cout << endl << "Catch int for outer try. "
           << "Exception " << n;
    }
```

```
      catch(long n)
      {
        cout << endl << "Catch long for outer try. "
             << "Exception " << n;
      }
    }

    cout << endl;
    return 0;
  }
```

This will produce the output:

```
outer try:
Catch int for outer try. Exception 0
outer try:
Catch int for outer try. Exception 1
outer try:
  inner try:
Catch long for outer try. Exception 2
outer try:
  inner try:
Catch int for inner try. Exception 3
    outer try:
Catch int for outer try. Exception 3
outer try:
  inner try:
    outer try:
Catch int for outer try. Exception 4
outer try:
  inner try:
    outer try:
Catch int for outer try. Exception 5
```

How It Works

The **throwIt()** function throws its parameter value. If you were to call this function outside a **try** block, it would immediately cause the program to end, as the exception will go uncaught and the default terminate handler will be called.

All the exceptions are thrown within the **for** loop. Within the loop, we determine when to throw an exception, and what kind of exception to throw, by testing the value of the loop variable, **i**, in successive **if** statements. At least one exception is thrown on each iteration. Entry to each **try** block is recorded in the output, and since each exception has a unique value, we can easily see where each exception is thrown and caught.

The first exception is thrown from the outer **try** block when the loop variable, **i**, is 0:

```
if(i == 0)
    throw i;                                  // Throw int exception
```

You can see from the output that the **catch** block for exceptions of type **int** that follows the outer **try** block catches this. The **catch** block for the inner **try** block has no relevance here, as it can only catch exceptions thrown in the inner **try** block.

The next exception is thrown in the outer **try** block as a result of calling **throwIt()**:

```
if(i == 1)
  throwIt(i);                        // Call the function that throws int
```

This is also caught by the **catch** block for **int** exceptions that follows the outer **try** block. The next two exceptions, however, are thrown in the inner **try** block:

```
if(i == 2)
  throw static_cast<long>(i);        // Throw long exception

if(i == 3)
  throwIt(i);                        // Call the function that throws int
```

The first of these is an exception of type **long**. There is no **catch** block for the inner **try** block for this type of exception, so it propagates to the outer **try** block. Here, the **catch** block for type **long** handles it, as you can see from the output. The second exception is of type **int**, and is thrown in the body of the **throwIt()** function. There is no **try** block in this function, so the exception propagates to the point where the function was called in the inner **try** block. The exception is then caught by the **catch** block for **int** exceptions following the inner **try** block.

When one of the handlers for the inner **try** block catches an exception, execution continues with the remainder of the outer **try** block. Thus, when **i** is 3, we get output from the **catch** block for the inner **try** block, *plus* output from the handler for **int** exceptions for the outer **try** block. The latter exception is thrown as a result of the **throwIt()** function call at the end of the inner **try** block.

Finally, we throw two more exceptions in the outer **try** block:

```
if(i == 4)
  throw i;                           // Throw int
throwIt(i);                          // Call the function that throws int
```

The handler for **int** exceptions for the outer **try** block catches both of these exceptions. The second exception here is thrown within the body of the function **throwIt()**, and since it is called in the outer **try** block, it's the **catch** block following the outer **try** block that handles it.

Although none of these was a realistic exception — exceptions in real programs are invariably class objects — they did show the mechanics of throwing and catching exceptions, and what happens with nested **try** blocks. Let's move on to take a closer look at exceptions that *are* objects.

Class Objects as Exceptions

You can throw any kind of class object as an exception. However, you should bear in mind that the idea of an exception object is to communicate information to the handler about what went wrong. Therefore, it is usually appropriate to define a specific exception class designed to represent a particular kind of problem. This is likely to be application-specific, but your exception class objects will almost invariably contain a message of some kind, and possibly some sort of error code as well. You could also arrange for an exception object to provide additional information about the source of the error in whatever form was appropriate.

We could define a simple exception class of our own. Put it in a header file with the fairly generic name **MyTroubles.h**, as we will be adding to this file later:

```
// MyTroubles.h Exception class definition
#ifndef MYTROUBLES_H
#define MYTROUBLES_H

class Trouble
{
  public:
    Trouble(const char* pStr = "There's a problem") : pMessage(pStr) {}
    const char* what() const {return pMessage;}

  private:
    const char* pMessage;
};

#endif
```

This class just defines an object representing an exception that stores a message indicating that there is a problem. There is a default message defined in the parameter list for the constructor so you can use the default constructor to get an object containing the default message. The **what()** member function returns the current message. As we don't allocate memory in the free store, the default copy constructor will be satisfactory in this case. To keep the logic of exception handling manageable, you need to ensure that the member functions of an exception class do not throw exceptions. You'll see later in this chapter how you can explicitly prevent a member function from doing so.

Let's find out what happens when a class object is thrown, by trying a few. As in our previous examples, we won't bother to create errors most of the time. We will just throw exception objects so that we can follow what happens to them under various circumstances. Let's first make sure we know how to throw an object.

Try It Out – Throwing an Exception Object

We can exercise our exception class with a very simple example that throws some exception objects in a loop:

```
// Program 17.3 Throw an exception object
#include <iostream>
#include "MyTroubles.h"
using namespace std;

int main()
{
  for(int i = 0 ; i < 2 ; i++)
  {
    try
    {
      if(i == 0)
        throw Trouble();
      else
        throw Trouble("Nobody knows the trouble I've seen...");
    }
```

```
      catch(const Trouble& t)
      {
        cout << endl << "Exception: " << t.what();
      }
    }
    return 0;
}
```

This will produce the output:

```
Exception: There's a problem
Exception: Nobody knows the trouble I've seen...
```

How It Works

We throw two exception objects in the **for** loop. The first object thrown is created by the default constructor for the **Trouble** class, and contains the default message string. The second exception object is thrown in the **else** clause of the **if**, and contains a message that we pass as an argument to the constructor. The **catch** block catches both of these exception objects.

Remember that an exception object is *always* copied when it is thrown, so if you don't specify the parameter in the **catch** block as a reference, it will be copied a second time — quite unnecessarily. The sequence of events when an exception object is thrown is that the object is first copied (to create a temporary object), and the original is then destroyed because the **try** block is exited and the object goes out of scope. The copy is then passed to the catch handler — by reference, if the parameter is a reference. If you want to observe these events taking place, just add a copy constructor and a destructor to the **Trouble** class.

Matching a Catch Handler to an Exception

I said earlier that the handlers following a **try** block are examined in the sequence in which they appear in your code, and that the first handler whose parameter type matches the type of the exception will be executed. With exceptions that are basic types (rather than class types), an exact type match with the parameter in the **catch** block is necessary. With exceptions that are class objects, on the other hand, automatic conversions may be applied to match the exception type with the parameter type of a handler.

When matching the parameter (caught) type to the exception (thrown) type, the following are considered to be a match:

▶ The parameter type is the same as the exception type, ignoring **const**

▶ The type of the parameter is a direct or indirect base class of the exception class type, or a reference to a direct or indirect base class of the exception class, ignoring **const**

▶ The exception and the parameter are pointers, and the exception type can be converted automatically to the parameter type, ignoring **const**

The possible type conversions listed here have implications for how you sequence the handlers for a **try** block. If you have several handlers for exception types within the same class hierarchy, then the most *derived* class type must appear first and the most *base* class type last. If a handler for a base type appears before a handler for a type derived from that base, then the base type will always be selected to handle the derived class exceptions. In other words, the handler for the derived type will never be executed.

683

Let's add a couple more exception classes to the header containing the **Trouble** class, and use **Trouble** as a base class for them. Here's how the contents of the header file **MyTroubles.h** will look with the extra classes defined:

```
// MyTroubles.h Exception class definition
#ifndef MYTROUBLES_H
#define MYTROUBLES_H

// Base exception class
class Trouble
{
  public:
    Trouble(const char* pStr = "There's a problem");
    virtual ~Trouble();
    virtual const char* what() const;

  private:
    const char* pMessage;
};

// Derived exception class
class MoreTrouble : public Trouble
{
  public:
    MoreTrouble(const char* pStr = "There's more trouble");
};

// Derived exception class
class BigTrouble : public MoreTrouble
{
  public:
    BigTrouble(const char* pStr = "Really big trouble");
};

#endif
```

Note that the **what()** member and the destructor of the base class have been declared as **virtual**. The **what()** function will therefore also be virtual in the classes derived from **Trouble**. It doesn't make much of a difference here, but remembering to declare a virtual destructor in a base class is a good habit to get into.

Other than different default strings for the message, the derived classes don't add anything to the base class. Often, just having a different class name can be used to differentiate one kind of problem from another. You just throw an exception of a particular type when that kind of problem arises; the internals of the classes don't have to be different. Using a different **catch** block to catch each class type provides the means of distinguishing one kind of problem from another.

We can put the definitions of the member functions of the three classes in **MyTroubles.cpp**:

```
// MyTroubles.cpp
#include "MyTroubles.h"

// Constructor for Trouble
Trouble::Trouble(const char* pStr) : pMessage(pStr)
{}
```

```
// Destructor for Trouble
Trouble::~Trouble()
{}

// Returns the message
const char* Trouble::what() const
{
  return pMessage;
}

// Constructor for MoreTrouble
MoreTrouble::MoreTrouble(const char* pStr) : Trouble(pStr)
{}

// Constructor for BigTrouble
BigTrouble::BigTrouble(const char* pStr) : MoreTrouble(pStr)
{}
```

We can now try this out in an example.

Try It Out – Throwing Exception Types that are in a Hierarchy

Here's the code to throw exceptions of the **Trouble**, **MoreTrouble** and **BigTrouble** types, and the handlers to catch them:

```
// Program 17.4 Throwing and Catching Objects in a Hierarchy
#include <iostream>
#include "MyTroubles.h"

using namespace std;

int main()
{
  Trouble trouble;
  MoreTrouble moreTrouble;
  BigTrouble bigTrouble;

  cout << endl;
  for(int i = 0 ; i < 7 ; i++)
  {
    try
    {
      if(i < 3)
        throw trouble;
      if(i < 5)
        throw moreTrouble;
      else
        throw bigTrouble;
    }
    catch(BigTrouble& rT)
    {
      cout << "  BigTrouble object caught: " << rT.what() << endl;
    }
    catch(MoreTrouble& rT)
    {
      cout << " MoreTrouble object caught: " << rT.what() << endl;
```

```
        }
    catch(Trouble& rT)
    {
      cout << "Trouble object caught: " << rT.what() << endl;
    }

    cout << "End of the for loop (after the catch blocks) - i is " << i << endl;
  }

  cout << endl;
  return 0;
}
```

This will produce the output:

```
Trouble object caught: There's a problem
End of the for loop (after the catch blocks) - i is 0
Trouble object caught: There's a problem
End of the for loop (after the catch blocks) - i is 1
Trouble object caught: There's a problem
End of the for loop (after the catch blocks) - i is 2
 MoreTrouble object caught: There's more trouble
End of the for loop (after the catch blocks) - i is 3
 MoreTrouble object caught: There's more trouble
End of the for loop (after the catch blocks) - i is 4
  BigTrouble object caught: Really big trouble
End of the for loop (after the catch blocks) - i is 5
  BigTrouble object caught: Really big trouble
End of the for loop (after the catch blocks) - i is 6
```

How It Works

After creating one object of each class type, we have a **for** loop that contains the following **try** block:

```
try
{
  if(i < 3)
    throw trouble;
  if(i < 5)
    throw moreTrouble;
  else
    throw bigTrouble;
}
```

For values of the loop variable **i** less than 3, we throw an exception of type **Trouble**. For **i** equal to 3 and 4, we throw an exception of type **MoreTrouble**. When **i** is 5 or greater, we throw an exception of type **BigTrouble**.

We have a handler for each class type, starting with exceptions of type **BigTrouble**:

```
catch(BigTrouble& rT)
{
  cout << " BigTrouble object caught: " << rT.what() << endl;
}
```

The other handlers are essentially the same, although they do contain slightly different messages. In the handlers for the two derived types, the inherited **what()** function will still return the message. Note that the parameter type for each of the **catch** blocks is a reference here, as in the previous example. One reason for using a reference is to avoid making *another* copy of the exception object. In the next example, we will see another good reason why you should *always* use a reference parameter in a handler.

Each handler displays the message contained in the object thrown, and you can see from the output that each handler is called to correspond with the type of the exception thrown. The ordering of the handlers is important because of the way the exception is matched to a handler, and because the types of our exception classes are related. Let's explore that in a little more depth.

Catching Derived Class Exceptions with a Base Class Handler

Since exceptions of derived class types will be automatically converted to a base class type for the purposes of matching the handler parameter, we could catch all the exceptions thrown in the previous example with a single handler. Let's modify the previous example to see this happening.

Try It Out – Using a Base Class Handler

All you need to do is to delete (or comment out) the two derived class handlers from the previous example.

```
// Program 17.5 Catching exceptions with a base class handler
#include <iostream>
#include "MyTroubles.h"

using namespace std;

int main()
{
  Trouble trouble;
  MoreTrouble moreTrouble;
  BigTrouble bigTrouble;

  cout << endl;
  for(int i = 0 ; i < 7 ; i++)
  {
    try
    {
      if(i < 3)
        throw trouble;
      if(i < 5)
        throw moreTrouble;
      else
        throw bigTrouble;
    }
```

```
    catch(Trouble& rT)                                    // Base class handler only
    {
      cout << "Trouble object caught: " << rT.what() << endl;
    }
```

```
    cout << "End of the for loop (after the catch blocks) - i is " << i << endl;
  }

  cout << endl;
  return 0;
}
```

The program now produces the output:

```
Trouble object caught: There's a problem
End of the for loop (after the catch blocks) - i is 0
Trouble object caught: There's a problem
End of the for loop (after the catch blocks) - i is 1
Trouble object caught: There's a problem
End of the for loop (after the catch blocks) - i is 2
Trouble object caught: There's more trouble
End of the for loop (after the catch blocks) - i is 3
Trouble object caught: There's more trouble
End of the for loop (after the catch blocks) - i is 4
Trouble object caught: Really big trouble
End of the for loop (after the catch blocks) - i is 5
Trouble object caught: Really big trouble
End of the for loop (after the catch blocks) - i is 6
```

How It Works

The **Trouble&** handler now catches all the exceptions. If the parameter in a **catch** block is a reference to a base class, then it will match any derived class exception. So, while the output proclaims **Trouble object caught** for each exception, the last four catches actually correspond to objects *derived* from **Trouble**.

Because the dynamic type is retained when the exception is passed by reference, you could also get the dynamic type and display it using the **typeid()** operator. Just modify the code for the handler to:

```
    catch(Trouble& rT)
    {
      cout << typeid(rT).name() << " object caught: " << rT.what() << endl;
    }
```

Some compilers do not enable run-time type identification by default, so if this doesn't work, check for a compiler option to switch it on. With this modification to the code, the output will show that the derived class exceptions still retain their dynamic types, even though a reference to the base class is being used. You will recall that the **typeid()** operator returns an object of the **type_info** class; the **name()** member of the class returns the class name as **const char***.

For the record, the output from this version of the program should look like this:

```
class Trouble object caught: There's a problem
End of the for loop (after the catch blocks) - i is 0
class Trouble object caught: There's a problem
```

```
End of the for loop (after the catch blocks) - i is 1
class Trouble object caught: There's a problem
End of the for loop (after the catch blocks) - i is 2
class MoreTrouble object caught: There's more trouble
End of the for loop (after the catch blocks) - i is 3
class MoreTrouble object caught: There's more trouble
End of the for loop (after the catch blocks) - i is 4
class BigTrouble object caught: Really big trouble
End of the for loop (after the catch blocks) - i is 5
class BigTrouble object caught: Really big trouble
End of the for loop (after the catch blocks) - i is 6
```

You could now try changing the parameter type for the handler to **Trouble**, so the exception is passed by value rather than by reference:

```
catch(Trouble t)
{
    cout << typeid(t).name() << " object caught: " << t.what() << endl;
}
```

When you run *this* version of the program, you will get the output:

```
class Trouble object caught: There's a problem
End of the for loop (after the catch blocks) - i is 0
class Trouble object caught: There's a problem
End of the for loop (after the catch blocks) - i is 1
class Trouble object caught: There's a problem
End of the for loop (after the catch blocks) - i is 2
class Trouble object caught: There's more trouble
End of the for loop (after the catch blocks) - i is 3
class Trouble object caught: There's more trouble
End of the for loop (after the catch blocks) - i is 4
class Trouble object caught: Really big trouble
End of the for loop (after the catch blocks) - i is 5
class Trouble object caught: Really big trouble
End of the for loop (after the catch blocks) - i is 6
```

The **Trouble** handler is still being selected for the derived class objects, but the dynamic type is not being preserved. This is because the parameter is initialized using the base class copy constructor, so any properties associated with the derived class are lost.

In this situation, only the base class sub-object of the original derived class object is retained. All derived class members are removed from the object. This is an example of **object slicing**, which results because the base class copy constructor knows nothing about derived objects. Object slicing is a common source of error when passing objects by value, and it can happen with ordinary functions as well as with exception handlers. You should *always* use reference parameters in your **catch** blocks.

Rethrowing an Exception

When a handler catches an exception, it can **rethrow** it to allow a handler for an outer **try** block to catch it. You can rethrow the current exception with a statement consisting of just the keyword **throw**, with no throw expression:

```
throw;              // Rethrow the exception
```

This will rethrow the existing exception object without copying it. You might rethrow an exception if the handler discovers the nature of the exception requires it to be passed on to another level of **try** block. You might also want to register the point in the program where an exception was thrown, and then rethrow it for handling in some central location in the program, such as in **main()**.

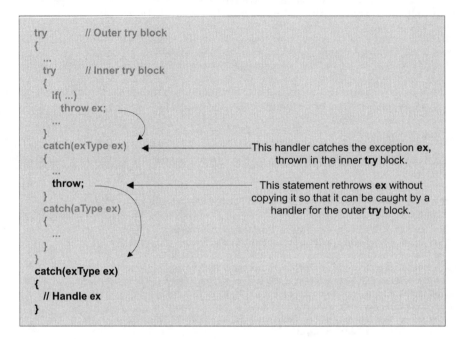

```
try        // Outer try block
{
  ...
  try        // Inner try block
  {
    if( ...)
      throw ex;
    ...
  }
  catch(exType ex)          ◄────────  This handler catches the exception ex,
  {                                     thrown in the inner try block.
    ...
    throw;   ◄────────────  This statement rethrows ex without
  }                          copying it so that it can be caught by a
  catch(aType ex)            handler for the outer try block.
  {
    ...
  }
}
catch(exType ex)
{
  // Handle ex
}
```

Note that rethrowing an exception from the inner **try** block does not make the exception available to other handlers for the inner **try** block. When a handler is executing, any exception that is thrown (including the current exception) needs to be caught by a handler for a **try** block that encloses the current handler, as illustrated above.

The fact that a rethrown exception is *not* copied is important, especially when the exception is a derived class object that initialized a base class reference parameter. Let's demonstrate this with an example.

Try It Out – Rethrowing an Exception

We can throw some **Trouble**, **MoreTrouble** and **BigTrouble** exception objects, and then rethrow some of them to see how the mechanism works:

```
// Program 17.6 Rethrowing exceptions
#include <iostream>
#include "MyTroubles.h"

using namespace std;

int main()
{
  Trouble trouble;
```

```
        MoreTrouble moreTrouble;
        BigTrouble bigTrouble;

        cout << endl;
        for(int i = 0 ; i < 7 ; i++)
        {
          try
          {
            try
            {
              if(i < 3)
                throw trouble;
              if(i < 5)
                throw moreTrouble;
              else
                throw bigTrouble;
            }
            catch(Trouble& rT)
            {
              if(typeid(rT) == typeid(Trouble))
                cout << "Trouble object caught: " << rT.what() << endl;
              else
                throw;                              // Rethrow current exception
            }
          }
          catch(Trouble& rT)
          {
            cout << typeid(rT).name() << " object caught: " << rT.what() << endl;
          }
          cout << "End of the for loop (after the catch blocks) - i is " << i << endl;
        }

        cout << endl;
        return 0;
      }
```

This example will display the output:

```
Trouble object caught: There's a problem
End of the for loop (after the catch blocks) - i is 0
Trouble object caught: There's a problem
End of the for loop (after the catch blocks) - i is 1
Trouble object caught: There's a problem
End of the for loop (after the catch blocks) - i is 2
class MoreTrouble object caught: There's more trouble
End of the for loop (after the catch blocks) - i is 3
class MoreTrouble object caught: There's more trouble
End of the for loop (after the catch blocks) - i is 4
class BigTrouble object caught: Really big trouble
End of the for loop (after the catch blocks) - i is 5
class BigTrouble object caught: Really big trouble
End of the for loop (after the catch blocks) - i is 6
```

How It Works

The **for** loop works as in the previous program, but this time we have one **try** block nested inside another. The exception objects are thrown in the inner **try** block:

```
try
{
  if(i < 3)
    throw trouble;
  if(i < 5)
    throw moreTrouble;
  else
    throw bigTrouble;
}
```

This throws the same sequence of objects as the previous examples. The handler will catch them all, because its parameter is a reference to the base class:

```
catch(Trouble& rT)
{
  if(typeid(rT) == typeid(Trouble))
    cout << "Trouble object caught: " << rT.what() << endl;
  else
    throw;                                    // Rethrow current exception
}
```

This handler will catch **Trouble** objects, and any objects of the classes derived from **Trouble**. The **if** statement here tests the class type of the object passed, and executes the output statement if it is of type **Trouble**. For any other type of exception, the exception is rethrown. You can distinguish the output from this **catch** block because it doesn't start with the word **class**.

The rethrown exception is available to be caught by the handler for the outer **try** block:

```
catch(Trouble& rT)
{
  cout << typeid(rT).name() << " object caught: " << rT.what() << endl;
}
```

The parameter here is also a reference to **Trouble**, so it will catch all the derived class objects. You can see from the output that it catches the rethrown objects, and they are still in pristine condition.

Now, you might imagine that the **throw;** statement in the handler for the inner **try** block is equivalent to the following statement:

```
throw rT;                                    // Rethrow current exception
```

After all, we're just rethrowing the exception, aren't we? The answer is no; in fact, there's a major difference. Make this modification to the program code and run it again. You will get this output:

```
Trouble object caught: There's a problem
End of the for loop (after the catch blocks) - i is 0
Trouble object caught: There's a problem
```

```
End of the for loop (after the catch blocks) - i is 1
Trouble object caught: There's a problem
End of the for loop (after the catch blocks) - i is 2
class Trouble object caught: There's more trouble
End of the for loop (after the catch blocks) - i is 3
class Trouble object caught: There's more trouble
End of the for loop (after the catch blocks) - i is 4
class Trouble object caught: Really big trouble
End of the for loop (after the catch blocks) - i is 5
class Trouble object caught: Really big trouble
End of the for loop (after the catch blocks) - i is 6
```

Throwing the exception in this manner results in the exception being *copied*, using the copy constructor for the **Trouble** class. We have the object slicing problem again. The derived portion of each object is sliced off, so you are left with just the base class sub-object in each case. You can see from the output that the **typeid()** operator identifies all the exceptions as type **Trouble**.

Catching All Exceptions

You can use an ellipsis (three periods) as the parameter specification for a **catch** block, to indicate that the block should handle any exception:

```
catch(...)
{
  // Code to handle any exception...
}
```

This **catch** block will handle an exception of any type, so a handler like this must always be last in the sequence of handlers for a **try** block. Of course, you have no idea what the exception is, but at least you can prevent your program terminating because of an uncaught exception. Note that even though you don't know anything about it, you can rethrow the exception as we did in the previous example.

Try It Out - Catching Any Exception

We can modify the last example to catch all the exceptions for the inner **try** block by using ellipses in place of the parameter:

```
// Program 17.7 Catching any exception
#include <iostream>
#include "MyTroubles.h"

using namespace std;

int main()
{
  Trouble trouble;
  MoreTrouble moreTrouble;
  BigTrouble bigTrouble;

  cout << endl;
  for(int i = 0 ; i < 7 ; i++)
```

```
    {
      try
      {
        try
        {
          if(i < 3)
            throw trouble;
          if(i < 5)
            throw moreTrouble;
          else
            throw bigTrouble;
        }
        catch(...)
        {
          cout << "We caught something! Let's rethrow it." << endl;
          throw;                                    // Rethrow current exception
        }
      }
      catch(Trouble& rT)
      {
        cout << typeid(rT).name() << " object caught: " << rT.what() << endl;
      }

      cout << "End of the for loop (after the catch blocks) - i is " << i << endl;
    }

    cout << endl;
    return 0;
}
```

This produces the output:

```
We caught something! Let's rethrow it.
class Trouble object caught: There's a problem
End of the for loop (after the catch blocks) - i is 0
We caught something! Let's rethrow it.
class Trouble object caught: There's a problem
End of the for loop (after the catch blocks) - i is 1
We caught something! Let's rethrow it.
class Trouble object caught: There's a problem
End of the for loop (after the catch blocks) - i is 2
We caught something! Let's rethrow it.
class MoreTrouble object caught: There's more trouble
End of the for loop (after the catch blocks) - i is 3
We caught something! Let's rethrow it.
class MoreTrouble object caught: There's more trouble
End of the for loop (after the catch blocks) - i is 4
We caught something! Let's rethrow it.
class BigTrouble object caught: Really big trouble
End of the for loop (after the catch blocks) - i is 5
We caught something! Let's rethrow it.
class BigTrouble object caught: Really big trouble
End of the for loop (after the catch blocks) - i is 6
```

How It Works

The only changes from the previous example are shown shaded. The **catch** block for the inner **try** block has been changed to:

```
catch(...)
{
  cout << "We caught something! Let's rethrow it." << endl;
  throw;                                    // Rethrow current exception
}
```

This is a genuine 'catch-all' that can catch anything you throw at it. Every time an exception is caught, a message is displayed and the exception is rethrown to be caught by the **catch** block for the outer **try** block. There, its type is properly identified and the string returned by its **what()** member is displayed.

Functions that Throw Exceptions

A function can throw an exception that will be caught in the calling function, as we saw in Program 17.2. For this to occur, you just need an exception to be *thrown* within the function, and not caught there. Of course, if you don't want to have the program terminated, the exception needs to be caught *somewhere*, and for that to happen the function call must be enclosed within a **try** block. The handlers for this **try** block should then catch the exception.

Of course, a function body can contain its own **try** blocks to handle its own exceptions. Any that are uncaught will propagate to the point at which the function was called. It is sometimes convenient to make the whole body of a function a **try** block with its own set of handlers, and you can do this by means of a **function try block**.

Function try Blocks

You define a function **try** block by putting the keyword **try** before the opening brace of the body of the function. You then put the handlers for the function **try** block after the closing brace of the function body. For example:

```
void doThat(int argument)
try
{
  // Code for the function...
}
catch(BigTrouble& ex)
{
  // Handler code for BigTrouble exceptions...
}
catch(MoreTrouble& ex)
{
  // Handler code for MoreTrouble exceptions...
}
catch(Trouble& ex)
{
  // Handler code for Trouble exceptions...
}
```

The entire body of the function is now a **try** block, while the **catch** blocks follow the closing brace for the function body.

Of course, a function that throws exceptions does not *need* to have a function **try** block, or indeed any **try** block at all. However, any *call* of a function that throws exceptions should be enclosed by a **try** block, otherwise the uncaught exception will end the program. It would be as well to indicate in such cases that the function might throw exceptions.

Specifying the Exceptions that a Function may Throw

By default, a function can throw any type of exception. This is not particularly helpful, because if you want to be certain of catching all exceptions, you have to use 'catch-all' **catch** blocks with ellipses for *every* **try** block that calls such a function. There are also situations in which throwing *any* exception would be a serious inconvenience, and you may want to ensure (and enforce) that a function throws no exceptions.

You can specify the set of exceptions that a function might throw by adding an **exception specification** to the function header. You have three options for the exception specification:

Exception Specification	Possible Exceptions
No exception specification	Your function allows exceptions of any type to be thrown.
throw()	No exceptions may be thrown.
throw(*exception_type_list*)	Exceptions of the types specified between the parentheses, separated by commas, may be thrown.

The exception specification limits the types of exception that a function can throw. If a function has an exception specification, it must appear in any function declaration as well as in the function definition.

Here is an example of a function definition that includes an exception specification:

```
void doThat(int argument) throw(Trouble, MoreTrouble)
try
{
  // Code for the function...
}
catch(BigTrouble& ex)
{
  // Handler code for BigTrouble exceptions...
}
```

This function handles any **BigTrouble** exceptions, but **Trouble** and **MoreTrouble** ones must be caught by the calling function. The declaration for the above function would also need to include the exception specification:

```
void doThat(int argument) throw(Trouble, MoreTrouble);
```

If you declare a pointer to a function that includes an exception specification, then you must also include the exception specification. For example:

```
    void (*pFunction)(int) throw(Trouble, MoreTrouble); // Pointer to function
                                                        // declaration
    pFunction = doThat;                                 // Store function address
```

If you use a **typedef** to define the pointer to function type, then you must *not* include the exception specification, because the exception specification is not part of the type. However, you must include it when you use the type in the declaration of the pointer, like this:

```
    typedef void (*FunctionPtrType)(int);                     // Define pointer to
                                                              // function type
    FunctionPtrType pFunction throw(Trouble, MoreTrouble);    // Pointer to function
                                                              // declaration
```

The first statement defines the type, which is then used in the second statement. You only include the exception specification in the pointer declaration.

Unexpected Exceptions

A function should only throw exceptions of the types allowed by its exception specification, but there is no general way for the compiler to verify that this is the case. A function with an exception specification limiting the types of exceptions that it can throw can quite legitimately call other functions without exception specifications. Any of these could throw exceptions that are not within the set of types specified by the exception specification. This possibility is recognized in C++ through the notion of an **unexpected exception**.

If a function does throw an exception that is not one of the types specified within its exception specification, it will not be propagated outside the function, as this would render the exception specification ineffective. Instead, the exception will initiate a chain of events starting with the standard library function **unexpected()** being called. The complete chain is illustrated below.

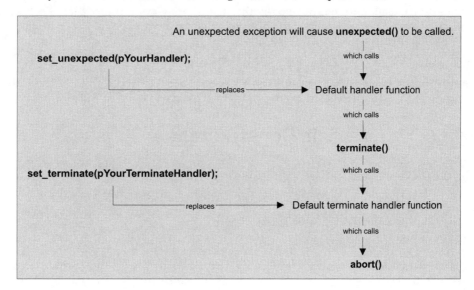

The purpose of this sequence of calls is to provide you with an opportunity to deal with unexpected exceptions a little more gracefully than just bringing the program to an abrupt halt. The **unexpected()** function calls a handler function, the default action of which is to call the standard library function **terminate()** (which is called for uncaught exceptions). As we saw earlier, **terminate()** then calls a default terminate handler function, which calls **abort()** to end the program.

You can replace the default handler function to be called by **unexpected()** with your own version — the technique is similar to the one used to replace the default terminate handler called by **terminate()**. You just call the **set_unexpected()** function with the address of your handler function as an argument. The parameter type for the **set_unexpected()** function is defined as:

```
typedef void (*unexpected_handler)();
```

From the definition of the **unexpected_handler** type, you can see that your function must have no parameters, and must not return a value. Within your unexpected handler function you can do whatever you want, but you must end the function in one of the following ways:

▶ By throwing an exception that conforms to the exception specification for the function that threw the unexpected exception

▶ By throwing an exception of type **bad_exception** — this is a standard type, which is defined in the **exception** header file

▶ By calling **terminate()**, **exit()** or **abort()**

Just as with the terminate handler, you can have different handlers to suit different situations, and this gives you the freedom to deal with unexpected exceptions in your own way. The idea behind the **std::bad_exception** type is that you can always include a handler for this type to deal with unexpected exceptions. All functions that have an exception specification would then need to include this type as a permitted exception. In this way, you control how unexpected exceptions are dealt with, rather than accepting the rather crude handling provided by the default action of calling **terminate()**, which then calls **abort()**. However, if your unexpected handler function throws a **bad_exception** exception, and this type is not in the exception specification for the function, then the function **terminate()** will be called anyway.

Throwing Exceptions in Constructors

A constructor cannot return a value, but it *can* throw exceptions. When you're in the process of creating an object, throwing exceptions provides a way for you to signal that all is not as it should be. The **Box** class that we have used in previous chapters is a case in point. You might want to throw an exception if invalid dimensions are supplied as constructor arguments. We will come back to this point a little later in the chapter.

However, care is needed when you throw exceptions in a constructor, particularly if the constructor allocates memory dynamically. If an exception is thrown from within a constructor, then the object under construction will not have been created properly, and therefore the destructor for the object will never be called. At best, the destructor for any complete sub-objects will be called. At worst, it is possible that any memory that has been allocated in the free store is not released in the normal way. When that happens, the free store memory must be released as part of the exception handling process.

One obvious way in which exceptions can be thrown in a constructor is due to the default behavior of the operator **new**. If operator **new** fails to allocate the required memory, it will throw an exception of type **bad_alloc**.

A constructor is a function, so it can have a function **try** block. What's more, the **try** block in a constructor can include the initialization list, so that exceptions thrown by constructors for sub-objects can also be caught. If your constructor might throw an exception, a good way to deal with it is to provide the constructor with a function **try** block, and add handlers to clean up when bad things happen. A class constructor to do this could be of the form:

```
Example::Example(int count) throw(bad_alloc)
try : BaseClass(count)
{
  // Allocate some memory...
  // Rest of the constructor...
}
catch(...)
{
  // Release memory as necessary...
}
```

Here, the constructor for the **Example** class calls a constructor for a base class, **BaseClass**, in the initialization list. This call and the body of the constructor are within the function **try** block, so the handler will be invoked for any exception thrown by the base class constructor or the constructor for the current object. Note that we don't need to rethrow the exception in the **catch** block here. Exceptions that are thrown in a constructor **try** block are rethrown automatically.

Exceptions and Destructors

Since automatic objects are destroyed when an exception is thrown, some class destructors may be called before the handler for the exception is executed. Within a destructor, it can be important to know that the destructor is being called because an exception was thrown (rather than for an object going out of scope, for example). When this is the case, *any* exception that is thrown within the destructor will cause **terminate()** to be called, which will end the program immediately. This will prevent the **catch** block for the original exception ever being reached, which could be disastrous in many circumstances. In this situation, you need to be sure that no exceptions are thrown from the destructor in order to allow the handler for the original exception to execute.

As a general rule, your destructors should not throw exceptions, but if they must there's a function you can call to detect when a destructor is being called because an exception was thrown. The function **uncaught_exception()** will return **true** if an exception was thrown and the corresponding **catch** block has not been executed, so this will allow a suitable course of action within your destructor. Of course, to prevent exceptions from escaping beyond the bounds of a destructor, you can enclose the code in a **try** block and use a handler that will catch any exception.

Standard Library Exceptions

Several exception types are defined in the standard library. They are all derived from the standard class **std::exception**, which is defined in the **exception** header file. The **exception** class includes a default constructor and copy constructor, the copy assignment operator and a virtual function **what()** that returns a null-terminated string describing the exception. None of these functions will throw an exception. The standard exception classes derived from **exception** are shown in the diagram below.

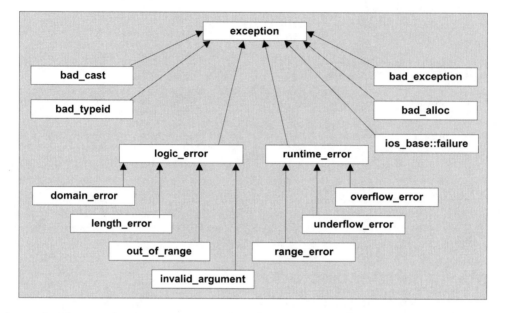

We have already seen the **bad_cast** exception that can be thrown by the **dynamic_cast<>()** operator; I referred to the **bad_alloc** exception when we were discussing the operator **new** in Chapter 7; and we saw the **bad_exception** class a little earlier in this chapter. A **bad_typeid** exception will be thrown if you use the **typeid()** operator with a null pointer, and the **ios_base::failure** exception is thrown by functions in the standard library that support stream input-output. We will discuss streams in Chapter 19.

The other types of exceptions are in two groups, with each group having a base class derived from **exception**. They are all defined in the header file **stdexcept**. The types that have **logic_error** as a base are exceptions thrown for errors that could (at least in principle) have been detected before the program executed, because they are caused by defects in the program logic. The other group, derived from **runtime_error**, is for errors that are generally data dependent and can only be detected at runtime. The exception types thrown by standard library functions indicate errors of various kinds. For instance, if you access characters in a **string** object using the **at()** member function, and the index value is outside the legal range for the object, an exception of type **out_of_range** will be thrown.

Because giving **catch()** a base class parameter will match any derived class exception, you could catch any of the standard exceptions by using a parameter of type **exception&** for a **catch** block. Of course, you could also a parameter of type **logic_error&** or **runtime_error&** to catch exceptions of one or the other group that is thrown by standard library functions.

Standard Library Exception Classes

All the standard exception classes have **exception** as a base, so you need to understand what members this class has, as they are inherited by all the other exception classes. The definition of the **exception** class is in the standard library header file, **exception**, and is as follows:

```
class exception
{
  public:
    exception() throw();                        // Default constructor
    exception(const exception&) throw();        // Copy constructor
    exception& operator=(const exception&) throw();  // Assignment operator
    virtual ~exception() throw();               // Destructor
    virtual const char* what() const throw();   // Return a message string
};
```

Like the rest of the standard library, the **exception** class is defined within the namespace **std**. The **throw()** that appears in the declaration of each member is the function exception specification that we discussed earlier. This ensures that the member functions of the **exception** class do not throw exceptions themselves.

Notice that there are no data members. The null-terminated string returned by the member **what()** is defined within the body of the function definition, and is implementation dependent. This function is declared as virtual, so it will also be virtual in any classes derived from **exception**. Having a virtual function that can deliver a message corresponding to each exception type can be used to provide a basic, economical way of recording any exception that's thrown. You can provide your **main()** function with a function **try** block, plus a **catch** block for exceptions of type **exception**:

```
int main()
try
{
   // Code for main...
}
catch(exception& rEx)
{
   cout << endl << typeid(rEx).name() << " caught in main: " << rEx.what();
}
```

The **catch** block will catch all exceptions that have the **exception** class as a base, and will display the class type and the message returned by the **what()** function. Thus, this simple mechanism will give you information about an exception that is thrown anywhere in the program but not caught elsewhere. If your program uses exception classes that are *not* derived from **exception**, an additional **catch** block with an ellipsis in place of a parameter type will catch all other exceptions, but in this case you will have no information as to what they are.

While this is a handy 'catch-all' mechanism, more local **try** blocks will provide a direct way to localize the source code that is the origin of an exception when it is thrown.

Using Standard Exceptions

There is no reason why you shouldn't use the exception classes defined in the standard library, and several very good reasons why you should. You can use the standard library exceptions in two ways: you can throw exceptions of standard types in your own programs, and you can use the standard exception classes as a base for your own exception classes.

Obviously, if you are going to throw standard exceptions, you need to throw them in circumstances consistent with their purpose. This means that you should not be throwing **bad_cast** exceptions, for instance, since these have a very specific role already. However, you will find that you can use some of the exception classes derived from **logic_error** and **runtime_error** directly in your programs. To use a familiar example, you might throw the **range_error** exception in a **Box** class constructor when invalid dimensions are supplied as arguments:

```
Box::Box(double lv, double bv, double hv) throw(std::range_error)
{
  if(lv <= 0.0 || bv <= 0.0 || hv <= 0.0)
    throw std::range_error();

  length = lv;
  breadth = bv;
  height = hv;
}
```

Of course, the source file would need to include the **stdexcept** header file that defines the **range_error** class. If you had a **using** directive for the namespace name **std**, you could omit the qualifier on the base class name. The body of the constructor will throw a **range_error** exception if any of the arguments are zero or negative. The constructor definition includes an exception specification restricting the exceptions that are thrown to **range_error** exceptions alone. Don't forget that the class definition must also include the same exception specification for the constructor.

Deriving your own Exception Classes

A major point in favor of always deriving your own classes from one of the standard exception classes is that your classes become part of the same family as the standard exceptions. This makes it possible for you to catch standard exceptions as well as your own exceptions within the same **catch** blocks. For instance, if your exception class is derived from **logic_error**, then a **catch** block with a parameter type of **logic_error&** will catch your exceptions as well as the standard exceptions with that base. A **catch** block with **exception&** as its parameter type will always catch standard exceptions — including yours, as long as your classes have **exception** as a base.

We could have incorporated our **Trouble** exception class (and the exception classes derived from it) quite simply, by deriving it from the **exception** class. We just need to modify our class definition as follows:

```
class Trouble : public std::exception
{
  public:
    Trouble(const char* pStr = "There's a problem") throw();
    virtual ~Trouble() throw();
```

```
        virtual const char* what() const throw();

  private:
    const char* pMessage;
};
```

This provides its own implementation of the virtual **what()** member defined in the base class. Our version will display the message from the class object, as before. With our new knowledge of the exception specification for functions, we have added an exception specification to each member function, so that no exceptions are thrown from within them. You would also need to update the member functions of the classes **MoreTrouble** and **BigTrouble** that are derived from **Trouble** in a similar fashion. Each of the definitions for the member functions must include the same exception specification that appears for the function in the class definition.

Summary

Exceptions are an integral part of C++. Several operators throw exceptions, and we have seen that they are used within the standard library to signal errors. It is therefore important that you have a good grasp of how they work, even if you don't plan to use your own exception classes. The important points that we have covered in this chapter are:

- ▶ Exceptions are objects used to signal errors in a program.

- ▶ Code that may throw exceptions is usually contained within a **try** block.

- ▶ The code to handle exceptions of various types that may be thrown in a **try** block is placed in one or more **catch** blocks following the **try** block.

- ▶ A **try** block, along with its **catch** blocks, can be nested inside another **try** block.

- ▶ A handler with a parameter of a base class type can catch an exception of a derived class type.

- ▶ If an exception is not caught by any **catch** block, then the **terminate()** function will be called, and this will call **abort()**.

- ▶ The standard library defines a range of standard exceptions.

- ▶ An exception specification limits the types of exceptions that a function can throw.

- ▶ If an exception is thrown within a function that is not permitted by the exception specification for the function, the **unexpected()** function will be called.

- ▶ You can change the default behavior of the **unexpected()** function by implementing your own unexpected handler, and establishing it by passing a pointer to your function to the **set_unexpected()** function.

- ▶ A function **try** block for a constructor can enclose the initialization list as well as the body of the constructor.

- ▶ The **uncaught_exception()** function allows you to detect when a destructor was called as a result of an exception being thrown.

Exercises

Ex 17.1 Derive your own exception class called **CurveBall** from the standard **exception** class, to represent an arbitrary error, and write a function that will throw this exception approximately 25% of the time. (One way to do this is by generating a random number between 1 and 20, and if the number is 5 or less, throw the exception.) Define the function **main()** to call this function 1000 times, and to record and display the number of times an exception was thrown.

Ex 17.2 Define another exception class called **TooManyExceptions**, and throw an exception of this type from the **catch** block for **CurveBall** exceptions in previous example when the number of exceptions caught exceeds 10.

Ex 17.3 Implement your own terminate handler in the code for the previous example so that a message is displayed when the **TooManyExceptions** exception is thrown.

Ex 17.4 A **sparse array** is one in which most of the element values are zero or empty. Define a class for a one-dimensional sparse array of elements of type pointer to **string** such that only the non-zero elements are stored. The potential number of elements should be specified as a constructor argument, so a sparse array to store up to 100 **string** objects could be declared with the statement:

```
SparseArray words(100);
```

Implement the subscript operator for the **SparseArray** class so that array notation can be used to retrieve or store elements. Throw exceptions if the legal index range is exceeded in the subscript operator functions. (Hints: use a linked list internally so that each node stores each element along with its subscript. Remember that you can overload the subscript operator with respect to **const** — the non-**const** version will be called when an element is on the left of an assignment.)

18

Class Templates

Templates are a powerful mechanism for generating new class types automatically. A significant portion of the standard library, called the **Standard Template Library**, is built entirely on the ability to define class templates, so it's clear that an understanding of the techniques involved is an important thing to have. By the end of this chapter, you will have learned:

▶ What a class template is and how it is defined

▶ What an instance of a class template is, and how one is created

▶ How to define templates for member functions of a class template outside the body of the class template definition

▶ How type parameters differ from non-type parameters

▶ How static members of a class template are initialized

▶ What a partial specialization of a class is, and how it is defined

▶ How a class template can be nested inside another class template

Understanding Class Templates

Class templates are based on the same idea as the function templates that we saw back in Chapter 9. A class template is a **parameterized type** — that is, a recipe for creating a family of classes using one or more parameters, where the argument corresponding to each parameter is typically (but not always) a type. When you declare a variable using a class template, the compiler will use the template to produce a definition for a class corresponding to the template arguments that you use in your declaration. You can use a class template in this way to generate any number of different classes.

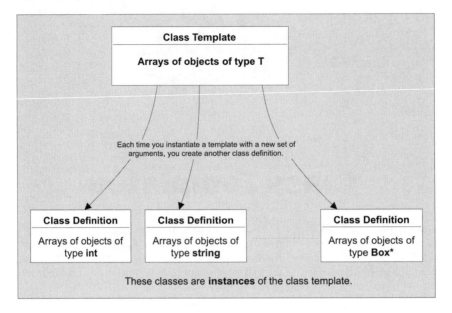

Class Template

Arrays of objects of type T

Each time you instantiate a template with a new set of
arguments, you create another class definition.

Class Definition	**Class Definition**	**Class Definition**
Arrays of objects of type **int**	Arrays of objects of type **string**	Arrays of objects of type **Box***

These classes are **instances** of the class template.

A class template has a name, just like an ordinary class, and a set of parameters. The name of a class template must be unique within a namespace, so you can't have another class or another template with the same name in the namespace in which the template is declared. A class *definition* is generated from a class template by supplying an argument for each of the template's parameters.

Each class that is generated from a template by the compiler is called an **instance** of the template. As you will see, declaration of a variable using a template type will result in the creation of an instance of the template, but you can also declare instances of a class template explicitly, without declaring a variable at the same time. Classes instantiated from a template will not be duplicated, so once a given template instance has been created, it will be used for any subsequent declarations of variables of its type.

Applications of Class Templates

Although there are many applications for class templates, perhaps their most common use is in the definition of **container classes**. These are classes that can contain sets of objects of a given type, organized in a particular way. That might simply mean an array, for example, or a pushdown stack, or a linked list of objects; the important point is that the storage method used is independent of the type of objects being stored.

A class template provides exactly the tool you need to define a container that can store any kind of object. The template parameter can be used to specify the kinds of objects that the container will store. The Standard Template Library, which comes as part of a standard C++ implementation, has many templates that define containers of various kinds. We'll be looking at how you can use some of those in Chapter 20.

Let's consider a specific situation where a class template can help. Suppose that you were unhappy with the fact that arrays in C++ do not check whether the index value you supply is a legal value, because this allows you inadvertently to overwrite memory locations that are not within the bounds of the array. Of course, one solution would be for you to write your own

Array class that would check that an index value was within legal limits. All you would have to do is define the **operator[]()** function for the class so that it checked the array index value, and perhaps threw an exception if it was not legal.

But what *kind* of array would your **Array** class represent? In one situation you might need an array of type **double**, and another time you might need an array of **string** objects — or indeed, an array of any type of object. You would need a separate class to be defined for each type of array that you use, even though the classes would be very similar. Having to write several, essentially identical classes seems rather tedious and unnecessary, and indeed it is. Not only that, each of your classes would also need a different name, so you could end up with a range of classes with names like **ArrayOfDouble**, **ArrayOfString**, **ArrayOfBox** and so on.

This is where a class template comes riding to the rescue, because it can be used to generate an **Array** class to suit any type that you require. Once you've defined **Array** as a class template, new **Array** classes that will manage any kind of object your heart desires will be created quite automatically.

Defining Class Templates

When you first see class template definitions, they tend to look more complicated than they really are, largely because of the appearance of the notation used to define them, and the parameters sprinkled around the code in the definition. Class template definitions are basically very similar to those of ordinary classes, but like so many things, the devil is in the details.

You define a class template with the keyword **template**, and you place the parameters for the template between angled brackets following the **template** keyword. After that, you write the template class definition using the keyword **class**, followed by the class name and then the body of the definition between braces. Just like a regular class, the whole definition ends with a semicolon. Thus, the general form of a class template is:

```
template <template parameter list> class ClassName
{
    // Template class definition...
};
```

In this conceptual definition, *ClassName* is the name of the *template*. You write the code for the body of the template just as you would write the body of an ordinary class, except that some of the member declarations and definitions will be in terms of the template parameters. The parameters for the template appear between the angled brackets, separated by commas. To create a class from this template, each of the parameters in the list needs to be specified.

Template Parameters

A template parameter list can contain two kinds of parameters — **type parameters** and **non-type parameters** — and there can be any number of parameters in the list. The argument corresponding to a type parameter is a type, such as **int**, or **string**, or **Box**, whereas the argument for a non-type parameter is either a value of a given type, such as 200, or a variable of a given type, such as **ivalue**. Type parameters in templates are much more common that non-type parameters, so we will defer further discussion of non-type parameters until later in this chapter.

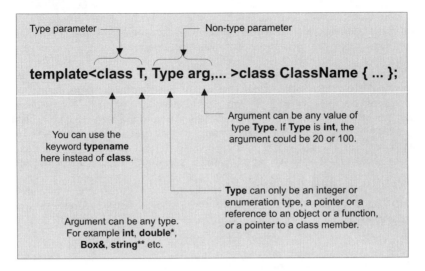

Type parameter — Non-type parameter

```
template<class T, Type arg,... >class ClassName { ... };
```

You can use the keyword **typename** here instead of **class**.

Argument can be any value of type **Type**. If **Type** is **int**, the argument could be 20 or 100.

Argument can be any type. For example **int**, **double***, **Box&**, **string**** etc.

Type can only be an integer or enumeration type, a pointer or a reference to an object or a function, or a pointer to a class member.

Type parameters are usually written using the keyword **class** followed by the parameter name (**class T** in the illustration above), but you can also use the keyword **typename** instead of **class**, so **typename T** would be just as good here. **T** is often used as a type parameter name (or **T1**, **T2**, and so on when there are several type parameters for a template), but you can use whatever name you want.

> *Although the keyword* **class** *seems to imply that the argument for a type parameter has to be a class, you can actually supply any type as an argument, so you can use the keyword* **typename** *if it makes it clearer in this context.*

We can see what the reality of class templates is like by looking at how a simple template with a single type parameter works in practice.

A Simple Class Template

Let's take the example that we had in our introduction and define a class template for arrays that will do bounds checking on index values to make sure that they are legal. Our array template will just have a single type parameter, so in outline its definition will be:

```
template <typename T> class Array
{
  // Definition of the template...
};
```

The **Array** template has just one type parameter, **T**. You can tell that it's a type parameter because it's preceded by the keyword **typename**. Whatever is 'plugged in' for this parameter when we instantiate the template — **int**, **double***, **string**, etc. — will determine the type of the elements stored in an object of the resultant class. The definition in the body of the template will be much the same as a class definition, with data members and member functions that can be declared as **public**, **protected** or **private**, and it will typically have constructors and a destructor. You can use **T** to declare variables or to specify the parameters or return types for member functions, either by itself or in types such as **T*** (pointer to type **T**). Furthermore, you can use the template name — **Array**, in this case — as a type name, as well as in the declaration of constructors and the destructor.

The very least we will need by way of a class interface is a constructor, plus a copy constructor (because we will be allocating the space for the array dynamically), a copy assignment operator (because the compiler will supply one if we don't), an overloaded subscript operator and finally a destructor. With this in mind, we can write the initial definition of the template as follows:

```
template <typename T> class Array
{
  private:
    T* elements;                              // Array of type T
    size_t size;                              // Number of elements in the array

  public:
    explicit Array<T>(size_t arraySize);     // Constructor
    Array<T>(const Array<T>& theArray);      // Copy Constructor
    ~Array<T>();                             // Destructor
    T& operator[](long index);               // Subscript operator
    const T& operator[](long index) const;   // Subscript operator for const arrays
    Array<T>& operator=(const Array<T>& rhs); // Assignment operator
};
```

The body of the template looks much like a regular class definition, except that it's sprinkled with **T** in various places. For example, there is a data member, **elements**, which is of type 'pointer to **T**' (equivalent to 'array of **T**'). When the class template is instantiated to produce a specific class definition, **T** will be replaced by the actual type used to instantiate the template. If we create an instance of the template for type **double**, **elements** will be of type 'array of **double**'.

We use type **size_t** for the member, **size**, that stores the number of elements in the array. This is a standard integer type defined in the standard header file **cstddef** and corresponds to the type of value returned by the **sizeof()** operator. It is the preferred type for specifying array dimensions.

Notice the way the first constructor is declared as **explicit**. Because this function takes a single integer argument, we have two ways to write a constructor call:

```
Array<int>one(5);      // explicit constructor notation
Array<int>two = 5;     // assignment-like notation
```

By declaring the constructor as **explicit**, we prohibit the second (and rather unintuitive) form of syntax. We also prevent you from passing integers to functions expecting arrays.

The subscript operator has been overloaded on **const**. The non-**const** version will apply to non-**const** array objects, and can return a non-**const** reference to an element of the array. Thus this version can appear on the left of an assignment. The **const** version will be called for **const** objects and will return a **const** reference to an element. Obviously this cannot appear on the left of an assignment.

711

In the copy assignment operator declaration, we use the type **Array<T>&**. This type is 'reference to **Array<T>**'. When a class is synthesized from the template — when **T** is type **double**, for example — this will be a reference to the class name for that particular class, which will be **Array<double>**. More generally, the class name for a specific instance of a template is formed from the template name followed by the actual type argument between angled brackets. The template name followed by the list of parameter names between angled brackets is called the **template ID**.

You don't need to use the full template ID within the template definition. Within the body of our class template, **Array** by itself will be taken to mean **Array<T>**, while **Array&** will be interpreted as **Array<T>&**, so we could simplify the class template definition to:

```
template <typename T> class Array
{
  private:
    T* elements;                              // Array of type T
    size_t size;                              // Number of elements in the array

  public:
    explicit Array(size_t arraySize);         // Constructor
    Array(const Array& theArray);             // Copy Constructor
    ~Array();                                 // Destructor
    T& operator[](long index);                // Subscript operator
    const T& operator[](long index) const;    // Subscript operator
    Array& operator=(const Array& rhs);       // Assignment operator
};
```

> *If you need to identify the template outside the body of the template, you must use the template ID. We'll see this situation when we're defining class template member functions later in the chapter.*

The assignment operator will allow one array object to be assigned to another — something that you can't do with ordinary arrays in C++. If you wanted to inhibit this capability for some reason, you would still need to declare the **operator=()** function as a member of the template. If you don't, a public default assignment operator will be created when necessary for any template instance. To inhibit use of the assignment operator, you can just declare it as a **private** member of the class — then it can't be accessed. Of course, no implementation for the member function would be necessary in this case, since C++ doesn't require you to implement a member function unless it is used, and this one will never be used.

Defining Member Functions of a Class Template

You can include the definitions for the member functions of the class template within its body. In this case, they will be implicitly **inline** in any instance of the template, just like in an ordinary class. However, you will certainly want to define members outside of the template body from time to time, especially if they involve a lot of code. When you do that, the syntax is a little different, and appears rather daunting at first sight, so let's take a look at it.

The clue to understanding the syntax is that definitions for the member functions of a template class will themselves be function templates. The parameter list for the function template that defines a member function must be identical to that of the class template. If that sounds a little confusing, it will help to get down to specifics. We can write definitions for the member functions of our **Array** template, starting with the constructor.

When you're defining it outside the class template definition, the constructor's name must be qualified by the class template name, in a similar way to an ordinary class member function. However, this isn't a function definition, it's a *template* for a function definition, so that has to be expressed as well. Here's the definition of the constructor:

```
template <typename T>                        // This is a template with parameter T
Array<T>::Array(size_t arraySize) : size(arraySize)
                                             // Array<T> identifies the class template
{
  elements = new T[size];
}
```

The first line here identifies this as a template, and also specifies the template parameter as **T**. Splitting the template function declaration into two lines, as we're doing here, is only for illustrative purposes, and is not necessary if the whole construct will fit on one line.

In the qualification of the constructor name, **Array<T>**, the template parameter is essential because it is this that ties the function definition to the class template. Note that you *don't* use the **typename** keyword here — that's only used in the template parameter list. No parameter list is necessary after the constructor name itself. When the constructor is instantiated for an instance of the class template, for type **double** for example, the type name will replace **T** in the constructor qualifier, so the qualified constructor name for the class **Array<double>** will be **Array<double>::Array()**.

In the constructor, we must allocate memory in the free store for an **elements** array that contains **size** elements of type **T**. If **T** is a class type, a public default constructor must exist in the class **T**. If it doesn't, the instance of this constructor will not compile. The operator **new** will throw a **bad_alloc** exception if the memory cannot be allocated for any reason, so the **Array** constructor should usually be used within a **try** block.

The destructor must release the memory for the **elements** array, so its definition will be:

```
template <typename T> Array<T>::~Array()
{
  delete[] elements;
}
```

We are releasing memory allocated for an array, so we must use the appropriate form of the **delete** operator here.

The copy constructor has to create an array for the object being created that's the same size as that of its argument, and then copy the latter's data members to the former. We can define the code for this as:

```
template <typename T> Array<T>::Array(const Array& theArray)
{
  size = theArray.size;
  elements = new T[size];
  for(int i = 0 ; i < size ; i++)
    elements[i] = theArray.elements[i];
}
```

This assumes that the assignment operator works for type **T**. You can see how important it is to define the assignment operator for classes that allocate memory dynamically. If the class **T** doesn't define it, the default copy constructor for **T** will be used, with undesirable side effects for such classes as we discussed back in Chapter 13. Without looking at the code for the template before you use it, you may not realize the dependency on the assignment operator.

The **operator[]()** function is quite straightforward, but we should ensure that illegal index values can't be used. For an index value that is out of range, we can throw an exception:

```
template <typename T> T& Array<T>::operator[](long index)
{
  if(index < 0 || index >= size)
    throw out_of_range(index < 0 ? "Negative index" : "Index too large");

  return elements[index];
}
```

We could define our own exception class to use here, but it's easier to borrow the **out_of_range** class that's already defined in the standard library in the **stdexcept** header file. This is thrown if you index a **string** object with an out-of-range index value, for example, so our usage is consistent with that. We throw an exception of type **out_of_range** if the value of **index** is not between **0** and **size-1**. The argument to the constructor is a **string** object that describes the error. A null-terminated string (type **const char***) corresponding to the **string** object is be returned by the **what()** member of the exception object. The argument that we pass to the **out_of_range** constructor is a simple message in each case, but you could contrive to include information in the string object about the index value and the size of the array to make tracking down the source of the problem a little easier.

The **const** version of the subscript operator function will be almost identical:

```
template <typename T> const T& Array<T>::operator[](long index) const
{
  if(index < 0 || index >= size)
    throw out_of_range(index < 0 ? "Negative index" : "Index too large");

  return elements[index];
}
```

The last function template we need to define is for the assignment operator. This will need to release any memory allocated in the destination object and then do what the copy constructor did — after checking that the objects are not identical, of course. Here's the definition:

```
template <typename T> Array<T>& Array<T>::operator=(const Array& rhs)
{
  if(&rhs == this)                        // If lhs == rhs
    return *this;                         //   just return lhs

  if(elements)                            // If lhs array exists
    delete[]elements;                     // then release the free store memory

  size = rhs.size;
  elements = new T[rhs.size];
  for(int i = 0 ; i < size ; i++)
    elements[i] = rhs.elements[i];
}
```

The check for the left operand being identical to the right is essential here, otherwise we would free the memory for the common **elements** member, then attempt to copy it when it no longer exists. With different operands we release any memory for the left operand before creating a copy of the right operand.

All the definitions we have written here are for function templates and they are inextricably bound to the class template They are not function definitions, they are templates to be used by the compiler when the code for one of them needs to be generated, so they need to be available in any source file that uses the template. For this reason, you would normally put all the definitions of the member functions for a class template in the header file containing the class template itself.

Even though you may define the member functions of a template as separate function templates, they can still be inline functions. To request that the compiler should consider them as candidates for inline implementation, you just add the keyword **inline** to the beginning of the definition immediately following **template<>**, like this:

```
template <typename T> inline const T& Array<T>::operator[](long index) const
{
  if(index < 0 || index >= size)
    throw out_of_range(index < 0 ? "Negative index" : "Index too large");

  return elements[index];
}
```

Creating Instances of a Class Template

An instance of a class template is created by the compiler as a result of a declaration of an object that has a type produced by the template. For example:

```
Array<int> data(40);
```

To compile this statement two things are required — the type **Array<int>** must be declared so that the type is identified, and the constructor must exist because that will be called to create the object. This statement will create an instance of our class template, which is the class **Array<int>**, and an instance of the constructor for that class. That is all that is necessary to create the object **data** so that is all that the compiler provides at this point.

The class definition that will be included in your program is generated by substituting **int** in place of **T** in the template definition, but there is one complication. The compiler will only compile the member functions that your program uses, not necessarily the entire class that would be produced from a simple substitution for the template parameter. On the basis of the declaration for the object, **data**, it will be equivalent to:

```
class Array<int>
{
  private:
    int* elements;                        // Array of type int
    size_t size;                          // Number of elements in the array
```

```
   public:
     Array(size_t arraySize);                              // Constructor
};
```

You can see that that apart from the constructor, the member functions of the class are missing here. The compiler will not create instances of anything that is not required to create the object, and it will not include parts of the template that are not needed in your program. This implies that there can even be coding errors in a class template, and your program may still compile link and run successfully. If the errors are in parts of the template that are not required by your program, they may not be detected by the compiler because they will not be included in the code that is compiled. Obviously, you are almost certain to have other statements in a program besides the declaration of an object that use other member functions — the destructor will always be required to destroy the object in any event — so the final version of the class in the program will include more than that shown above. The point is, though, that what is finally in the class generated from the template will be precisely those parts that are actually used in the program.

The instantiation of a class template from a declaration is referred to as an **implicit instantiation** of the template, because it arises as a by-product of declaring an object. This terminology is also to distinguish it from an **explicit instantiation** of a template, which we will come to in a moment, and which behaves a little differently.

As we said, the declaration of **data** will also cause the class constructor, **Array<int>::Array()**, to be called, so the function template that defines the constructor will be used by the compiler to create a definition for the constructor for the class:

```
Array<int>::Array(long arraySize) : size(arraySize)
{
  elements = new int[size];
}
```

Each time you use a class template with a different type argument to declare a variable, a new class will be defined and included in your program. Since the creation of the class object requires a constructor to be called, the definition of the appropriate class constructor will also be generated. Of course, creating an object of a type that you have created before does not necessitate any new template instances being created. The compiler will just make use of any previously created template instances as required.

As you use the member functions of a particular instance of the class template — by calling functions on the object that you defined using the template, for example — the code for each member function that you use will be generated. If there are member functions that you don't use, no instances of their templates will be created. The creation of each function definition is an implicit template instantiation, since it arises out of the use of the function. The template itself is not part of your executable code. All it is doing is enabling the compiler to generate the code that you need automatically.

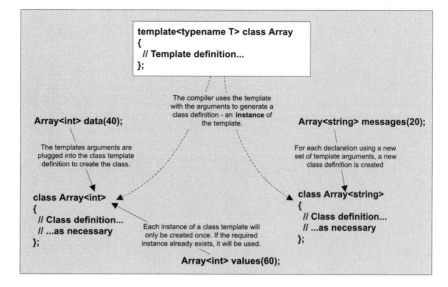

Note that a class template is only implicitly instantiated when an object type needs to be created. Declaring a pointer to an object type will not cause an instance of the template to be created. For example:

```
Array<string>* pObject;
```

This declares **pObject** to be of type 'pointer to type **Array<string>**'. No object of type **Array<string>** is created as a result of this statement, and so no template instance is created either. Contrast this with the declaration:

```
Array<string*> pMessages(10);
```

This does result in the creation of an instance of the class template. This declares an object of type **Array<string*>**, so each element of **pMessages** can store a pointer to a **string** object. An instance of the template defining the class constructor will also be generated.

Let's try out our **Array** template in a working example.

Try It Out – Using a Class Template

We can put the class template and the templates defining the member functions of the template all together in a header file **Array.h**:

```
// Array class template definition
#ifndef ARRAY_H
#define ARRAY_H

#include <iostream>
#include <stdexcept>                                    // For the exception classes
using namespace std;
```

```cpp
template <typename T> class Array
{
  private:
    T* elements;                             // Array of type T
    size_t size;                             // Number of elements in the array

  public:
    explicit Array(size_t arraySize);        // Constructor
    Array(const Array& theArray);            // Copy Constructor
    ~Array();                                // Destructor
    T& operator[](long index);               // Subscript operator
    const T& operator[](long index) const;   // Subscript operator
    Array& operator=(const Array& rhs);      // Assignment operator
};

// Constructor
template <typename T>                        // This is a template with parameter T
Array<T>::Array(size_t arraySize) : size(arraySize)
                                             // Array<T> identifies the class template
{
  elements = new T[size];
}

// Copy Constructor
template <typename T>
Array<T>::Array(const Array& theArray)
{
  size = theArray.size;
  elements = new T[size];
  for(int i = 0 ; i < size ; i++)
    elements[i] = theArray.elements[i];
}

// Destructor
template <typename T>
Array<T>::~Array()
{
  delete[] elements;
}

// Subscript operator
template <typename T>
T& Array<T>::operator[](long index)
{
  if(index < 0 || index >= size)
    throw out_of_range(index < 0 ? "Negative index" : "Index too large");

  return elements[index];
}

// Subscript operator for const objects
template <typename T>
const T& Array<T>::operator[](long index) const
{
  if(index < 0 || index >= size)
    throw out_of_range(index < 0 ? "Negative index" : "Index too large");

  return elements[index];
}
```

```
// Assignment operator
template <typename T>
Array<T>& Array<T>::operator=(const Array& rhs)
{
  if(&rhs == this)                                // If lhs == rhs
    return *this;                                 //   just return lhs

  if(elements)                                    // If lhs array exists
    delete[]elements;                             // then release the free store memory

  size = rhs.size;
  elements = new T[rhs.size];
  for(int i = 0 ; i < size ; i++)
    elements[i] = rhs.elements[i];
}

#endif
```

To use the template, we just need a program that will declare some arrays using the template and try them out. We shall endeavor to use some out-of-range index values, just to see that it works:

```
// Program 18.1 Using a class template
#include "Box.h"
#include "Array.h"
#include <iostream>
#include <iomanip>
using namespace std;

int main()
{
  const int doubleCount = 50;
  Array<double> values(doubleCount);              // Class constructor instance created

  try
  {
    for(int i = 0 ; i < doubleCount ; i++)
      values[i] = i + 1;                          // Member function instance created

    cout << endl << "Sums of pairs of elements:";
    int lines = 0;
    for(int i = doubleCount - 1 ; i >= 0 ; i--)
      cout << (lines++ % 5 == 0 ? "\n" : "") << setw(5)
           << values[i] + values[i - 1];
  }
  catch(const out_of_range& ex)
  {
    cout << endl <<"out_of_range exception object caught! " << ex.what();
  }

  try
  {
    const int boxCount = 10;
    Array<Box> boxes(boxCount);                   // Template instance created
    for(int i = 0 ; i <= boxCount ; i++)
      cout << endl << "Box volume is " << boxes[i].volume();
                                                  // Member instance created
```

```
     }
     catch(const out_of_range& ex)
     {
        cout << endl << "out_of_range exception object caught! " << ex.what();
     }

     cout << endl;
     return 0;
  }
```

The header file **Box.h** contains the definition of the **Box** class from Chapter 16, and you will need to have **Box.cpp** containing the definitions for the **Box** class member functions as part of this program too.

This example will produce the output:

```
Sums of pairs of elements:
    99    97    95    93    91
    89    87    85    83    81
    79    77    75    73    71
    69    67    65    63    61
    59    57    55    53    51
    49    47    45    43    41
    39    37    35    33    31
    29    27    25    23    21
    19    17    15    13    11
     9     7     5     3
out_of_range exception object caught! Negative index
Box volume is 1
Box volume is 1
Box volume is 1
Box volume is 1
Box volume is 1
Box volume is 1
Box volume is 1
Box volume is 1
Box volume is 1
Box volume is 1
out_of_range exception object caught! Index too large
```

How It Works

At the beginning of **main()**, we create an object of type **Array<double>** using our class template with a parameter type of **double**:

```
    Array<double> values(doubleCount);                    // Template instance created
```

This statement declares **values** as type **Array<double>**, and the number of elements in the array is specified as **doubleCount**. When the compiler processes this statement, it will create a definition for the class **Array<double>** from the class template. To create the object, **values**, a constructor call is necessary (**Array<double>::Array(doubleCount)**), so the compiler will use the function template for the constructor to create the definition for the constructor in our program.

Within the **try** block, we initialize the elements of **values** with values from **1** to **doubleCount** in a **for** loop:

```
for(int i = 0 ; i < doubleCount ; i++)
  values[i] = i + 1;                     // Member function instance created
```

The expression **values[i]** will result in an instance of the subscript operator function being created. This is called implicitly by this expression as **values.operator[](i)**. As **values** is not **const**, the non-**const** version will be called.

We use a second **for** loop in the **try** block to output the sums of successive pairs of elements, starting at the end of the array:

```
for(int i = doubleCount - 1 ; i >= 0 ; i--)
  cout << (lines++ % 5 == 0 ? "\n" : "") << setw(5)
          << values[i] + values[i - 1];
```

This also calls the subscript operator function, but the instance of the function template has already been created, so no new instance is generated. Clearly, the expression **values[i - 1]** will have an illegal index value when **i** is 0, so this causes an exception to be thrown by the **operator[]()** function. The handler catches this:

```
catch(const out_of_range& ex)
{
  cout << endl <<"out_of_range exception object caught! " << ex.what();
}
```

The **what()** function for the **out_of_range** exception returns a null-terminated string corresponding to the **string** object passed to the constructor when the exception object was created. You can see from the output that a **Negative index** was thrown by the overloaded operator function.

When the exception is thrown by the subscript operator function, control is passed immediately to the handler, so the illegal element reference is not used, and nothing will be stored at the location indicated by the illegal index. Of course, the loop also ends immediately at this point.

In the next **try** block, we define an object that can store an array of **Box** objects:

```
Array<Box> boxes(boxCount);                      // Template instance created
```

This time, the compiler will generate an instance of the class template, **Array<Box>**, which stores an array of **Box** objects, because the template has not previously been instantiated for **Box** objects. The statement will also call the constructor for this class to create the object **boxes**, so an instance of the function template for the constructor will be created. The constructor for the **Array<Box>** class will call the default constructor for the **Box** class when the **elements** member of the class is created in the free store. Of course, all the **Box** objects in the **elements** array will have the default dimensions of 1 by 1 by 1.

We display the volume of each **Box** object in a **for** loop:

```
for(int i = 0 ; i <= boxCount ; i++)
  cout << endl << "Box volume is " << boxes[i].volume();
                                          // Member instance created
```

The expression **boxes[i]** calls the overloaded subscript operator, so again an instance of the function template will be used by the compiler to produce a definition of this function. When **i** has the value **boxCount**, the subscript operator function will throw an exception because **boxCount** is beyond the end of the **elements** array. The **catch** block following the **try** block catches the exception:

```
catch(const out_of_range& ex)
{
  cout << endl <<"out_of_range exception object caught! " << ex.what();
}
```

Since the **try** block is exited, all locally declared objects will be destroyed, including the **boxes** object. The **values** object still exists at this point, since it was not created within the previous **try** block, and it is still in scope.

Exporting Templates

A disadvantage of placing the code for member functions of a class template in a header file is that all this code has to be processed by the compiler in every source file into which it is included. This can represent a substantial processing overhead in a large program that makes extensive use of templates. An alternative approach allows you to place templates for member functions in a separate source file and make them available in any other source file that requires access to them. All you need to do is to export the function template definitions by using the keyword **export** with each template. For example:

```
// ArrayTemplate.cpp file
#include <iostream>
#include <stdexcept>                          // For the exception classes
#include "Array.h"
using namespace std;

// Constructor
export template <typename T>           // This is a template with parameter T
Array<T>::Array(size_t arraySize) : size(arraySize)
                                       // Array<T> identifies the class template
{
  elements = new T[size];
}

// Copy Constructor
export template <typename T>
Array<T>::Array(const Array& theArray)
{
  size = theArray.size;
  elements = new T[size];
  for(int i = 0 ; i < size ; i++)
    elements[i] = theArray.elements[i];
}

// Plus templates for other member functions as before, but with export keyword...
```

This file can now be compiled separately, and the object file produced can be used as part of any program that uses the class template.

The header file, **Array.h**, will contain the class template as before, but only declarations for the function templates are necessary:

```
// Array class template definition
#ifndef ARRAY_H
#define ARRAY_H

// Class template definition as before
template <typename T> class Array
{
  private:
    T* elements;                                 // Array of type T
    size_t size;                                 // Number of elements in the array

  public:
    explicit Array(size_t arraySize);            // Constructor
    Array(const Array& theArray);                // Copy Constructor
    ~Array();                                    // Destructor
    T& operator[](long index);                   // Subscript operator
    const T& operator[](long index) const;       // Subscript operator
    Array& operator=(const Array& rhs);          // Assignment operator
};

#endif
```

Now any program that wants to use the class template just needs to include the shorter version of **Array.h** into any source file that requires it, and have **ArrayTemplate.cpp** as a source file, or access to the object files produced from it when it is linked.

Only function templates that are not inline can be exported. If you use the keyword **export** with an inline function template, it will be ignored. If you *do* export a template definition, you must not repeat the definition anywhere else in the program. Only declarations of an exported template can appear in other source files. You cannot export a template that you have defined in an unnamed namespace.

Static Members of a Class Template

A class template can have static members, just as an ordinary class can. Static member functions of a template class are quite straightforward. Each instance of a class template will instantiate the static member function of the class as needed. Such a member function has no **this** pointer and therefore cannot refer to non-static members of the class. The rules for defining static member functions of a class template are the same as those for a class, and a static member function of a class template will behave in each instance of the template just as if it were in an ordinary class.

A static data member is a little more interesting because it needs to be initialized outside the template definition. Suppose our **Array** template contained a static data member. The declaration of the member, and the template to initialize it, would be:

```
template <typename T> class Array
{
  private:
    static T value;                              // Static data member
    T* elements;                                 // Array of type T
    size_t size;                                 // Number of elements in the array
```

```
   public:
      explicit Array(size_t arraySize);              // Constructor
      Array(const Array& theArray);                  // Copy Constructor
      ~Array();                                      // Destructor
      T& operator[](long index);                     // Subscript operator
      const T& operator[](long index) const;         // Subscript operator
      Array& operator=(const Array& rhs);            // Assignment operator
   };
```

```
template < typename T > T Array<T>::value;         // Initialize static data member
```

The initialization is accomplished through a template. A static data member is always dependent on the parameters of the template of which it is a member, so we must initialize **value** as a template with parameter **T**. The static variable name must also be qualified with the type name **Array<T>**, so that it's identified with the instance of the class template. You can't use **Array** by itself here, as this definition is outside the body of the template, and the template ID is **Array<T>**.

Non-Type Class Template Parameters

A non-type parameter looks like a function parameter — a type name followed by the name of the parameter. The argument for a non-type parameter will therefore be a value of the given type. However, you can't use just any type for a non-type parameter in a class template. Non-type parameters are intended to be used to define values that might be useful in specifying a container, such as array dimensions or other size specification, or possibly upper and lower limits for index values.

A non-type can only be an integral type, such as **int** or **long**, an enumeration type, a pointer or a reference to an object, such as **string*** or **Box&**, a pointer or a reference to a function, or a pointer to a member of a class. You can conclude from this that a non-type parameter *can't* be a floating point type or any class type, so types **double**, **Box** and **string** are not allowed, and neither is **string****. Remember that the primary rationale for non-type parameters is to allow sizes and range limits for containers to be specified. Of course, the argument corresponding to a non-type parameter *can* be an object of a class type, as long as the parameter type is a reference. For a parameter of type **Box&**, for example, you could use any object of type **Box** as an argument.

A non-type parameter is written just like a function parameter, with a type name followed by a parameter name. For example:

```
template <typename T, size_t size> class ClassName
{
  // Definition using T and size...
};
```

This template has a type parameter, **T**, and a non-type parameter, **size**. The definition will be expressed in terms of these two parameters and the template name. If you need it, the *name* of a type parameter can also be the *type* of a non-type parameter. For example:

```
template <typename T,           // T is the name of the type parameter
          size_t size,
          T value>              // T is also the type of this non-type parameter
class ClassName
```

```
{
  // Definition using T, size, and value...
};
```

This template has a non-type parameter, **value**, of type **T**. The parameter **T** must appear before its use in the parameter list, so **value** could not precede the type parameter **T** here. Note that using the same symbol with the type and non-type parameters implicitly restricts the possible arguments for the **typename** parameter to the types permitted for a non-type argument (in other words, **T** must be an integral type).

To show how you could use non-type parameters, suppose you defined the class template for arrays as:

```
template <typename T, int arraySize, T value> class Array
{
  // Definition using T, size, and value...
};
```

You could now use the non-type parameter, **value**, to initialize each element of the array in the constructor:

```
template <typename T, int arraySize, T value>
Array<T, size, value>::Array(size_t arraySize) : size(arraySize)
{
  elements = new T[arraySize];
  for(int i = 0 ; i < arraySize, i++)
    elements[i] = value;
}
```

Because a non-type parameter can only be an integral type, a pointer or a reference, you cannot create **Array** objects to store **double** values, so the usefulness of the template is somewhat restricted.

Non-Type Parameter Example

As a more tangible example, we could consider adding a non-type parameter to the **Array** template to allow a bit more flexibility in indexing the array:

```
template <typename T, long startIndex> class Array
{
private:
    T* elements;                                    // Array of type T
    size_t size;                                    // Number of elements in the array

public:
    explicit Array(size_t arraySize);               // Constructor
    Array(const Array& theArray);                   // Copy Constructor
    ~Array();                                       // Destructor
    T& operator[](long index);                      // Subscript operator
    const T& operator[](long index) const;          // Subscript operator
    Array& operator=(const Array& rhs);             // Assignment operator
};
```

This adds a non-type parameter, **startIndex** of type **long**. The idea of this is that you can specify that you want to use index values that vary over a given range, for example from –10 to +10, in which case you would declare the array with the non-type parameter value as –10 and the argument to the constructor as 21, since the array would need 21 elements.

Because the class template now has two parameters, the function templates defining the member functions of the class template must have the same two parameters. This would be necessary even if some of the functions were not going to use the non-type parameters. The parameters are part of the identification for the template, so to match the class template, they must have the same parameter list.

There are some serious disadvantages to what we have done. A consequence of adding the new **startIndex** template parameter is that different values for the argument generate different template instances. This means that an array of **double** values indexed from 0 will be a different type from an array of **double** values indexed from 1. If you use both in a program, two independent class definitions will be created from the template, each with whatever member functions you use. This has at least two undesirable consequences — firstly, you will get a lot more compiled code in your program than you might have anticipated (a condition often known as 'code bloat'). Secondly (and worse), you will not be able to intermix elements of the two types in an expression. We would be much better off if we provided flexibility for the range of index values by adding a parameter to the constructor rather than using a non-type template parameter. For example:

```
template <typename T> class Array
{
  private:
    T* elements;                                    // Array of type T
    size_t size;                                    // Number of elements in the array
    long start;                                     // Starting index value

  public:
    explicit Array(size_t arraySize, long startIndex = 0); // Constructor
    Array(const Array& theArray);                   // Copy Constructor
    ~Array();                                       // Destructor
    T& operator[](long index);                      // Subscript operator
    const T& operator[](long index) const;          // Subscript operator for const
    Array& operator=(const Array& rhs);             // Assignment operator
};
```

The extra member, **start**, is intended to store the starting index for the array specified by the second constructor argument. The default value for the **startIndex** parameter is zero, so normal indexing is obtained by default.

However, in the interest of seeing how the member functions are defined when we have a non-template parameter, let's complete the set of function templates that we need for the **Array** class template.

Templates for Member Functions

Because we have added a non-type parameter to the class template definition, the code for the function template for the constructor, and the templates for the other member functions will also need to be changed. The template for the constructor will be:

```
template <typename T, long startIndex>
Array<T, startIndex>::Array(size_t arraySize) : size(arraySize)
{
  elements = new T[size];
}
```

The template ID is now **Array<T, startIndex>**, so this is used to qualify the constructor name. This is the only change apart from adding the new template parameter to the template.

For the copy constructor, we need to make similar changes to the function template:

```
template <typename T, long startIndex>
Array<T, startIndex>::Array(const Array& theArray)
{
  size = theArray.size;
  elements = new T[size];
  for(int i = 0 ; i < size ; i++)
    elements[i] = theArray.elements[i];
}
```

Of course, the external indexing of the array doesn't affect how we manage things internally.

The destructor also only needs to have the extra template parameter added:

```
template <typename T, long startIndex>
Array<T, startIndex>::~Array()
{
  delete[] elements;
}
```

You need to change the template definition for the non-**const** subscript operator function to:

```
template <typename T, long startIndex>
T& Array<T, startIndex>::operator[](long index)
{
  if(index < startIndex || index > startIndex + static_cast<long>(size) - 1)
    throw out_of_range(index < startIndex ?
                                   "Index too small" : "Index too large");

  return elements[index - startIndex];
}
```

There are significant changes here. The validity checks on the **index** value now verify that it's between the limits determined by the non-type template parameter, and the number of elements in the array. Index values can only be from **startIndex** to **startIndex+size-1**. Because **size_t** is usually an unsigned integer type we need to explicitly cast it to **long**, otherwise the other values will be converted automatically to **size_t** and this will produce a wrong result if they are negative. The choice of message for the exception, and the expression selecting it have also been changed.

We need to change the **const** version in a similar fashion:

```
template <typename T, long startIndex>
const T& Array<T, startIndex>::operator[](long index) const
{
```

727

```
      if(index < startIndex || index > startIndex + static_cast<long>(size) -1)
        throw out_of_range(index < startIndex ?
                                       "Index too small" : "Index too large");

      return elements[index - startIndex];
    }
```

Finally, we need to alter the function template for the assignment operator, but only the template parameter list and the template ID qualifying the operator name need to be modified here:

```
    template <typename T, long startIndex>
    Array<T, startIndex>& Array<T, startIndex>::operator=(const Array& rhs)
    {
      if(&rhs == this)                    // If lhs == rhs
        return *this;                     //  just return lhs

      if(elements)                        // If lhs array exists
        delete[]elements;                 // then release the free store memory

      size = rhs.size;
      elements = new T[rhs.size];
      for(int i = 0 ; i < size ; i++)
        elements[i] = rhs.elements[i];
    }
```

There are restrictions on how you use a non-type parameter within a template. In particular, you must not modify the value of a parameter within the template definition. Thus, a non-type parameter cannot be used on the left of an assignment, or have the increment or decrement operator applied to it — in other words it is treated as a constant.

Back in Chapter 9, we saw how the template arguments to function templates could be deduced from the function arguments. This is not the case with class templates. All parameters in a class template must always be specified, unless there are default values for parameters — a technique we will discuss later in the chapter.

Arguments for Non-Type Parameters

An argument for a non-type parameter that is not a reference or a pointer must be a compile-time constant expression. This means that you cannot use an expression containing a non-**const** integer variable as an argument, which is a slight disadvantage, but the compiler can validate the argument, which is a compensating plus. For example, the following statements will not compile:

```
    long start = -10;
    Array<double, start> values(21);    // Won't compile
```

The compiler will generate a message to the effect that the second argument here is invalid. A correct version of these two statements is:

```
    const long start = -10;
    Array<double, start> values(21);
```

Now that **start** has been declared as **const**, the compiler can rely on its value, and both template arguments are now legal.

The compiler will also provide standard conversions on arguments if they are necessary to match the parameter type. For example, if we had a non-type parameter declared as type **const size_t**, the compiler will convert an integer literal such as 10 to the required argument type.

Pointers and Arrays as Non-Type Parameters

The argument for a non-type parameter that is a pointer must be an address, but it can't be any old address. It must be the address of an object or function with external linkage, so for example, you can't use addresses of array elements or addresses of non-static class members as arguments. This also means that if your non-type parameter is of type **const char***, you cannot use a string literal as an argument when you instantiate the template. If you want to use a string literal as an argument in this case, you must initialize a pointer variable with the address of the string literal, and pass the pointer as the template argument.

Because a pointer is a legal non-type template parameter, you can specify an array as a parameter, but an array and a pointer are not always interchangeable when supplying arguments to a template. For example, you could define a template as:

```
template <long* pNumber> class MyClass
{
  // Template definition...
};
```

You can now create instances of this template with the following code:

```
long data[10];                         // Global
long* pData = data;                    // Global

MyClass<pData> values;
MyClass<data> values;
```

Either an array name or a pointer of the appropriate type can be used as an argument corresponding to a parameter that is a pointer. However, the converse is not the case. Imagine that we have defined a template as:

```
template <long number[10]> class AnotherClass
{
  // Template definition...
};
```

The parameter here is an array with 10 elements, and the argument must be of the same type. In this case, using the array **data** that we declared above, you can write:

```
AnotherClass<data> numbers;            // OK
```

However, you *can't* use a pointer, so the following won't compile:

```
AnotherClass<pData> numbers;           // Not allowed!
```

In spite of the shortcomings of our **Array** template, let's see non-type parameters in action in a working example.

Try It Out – Using Non-Type Parameters

You just need to plug the changes we discussed above into the header file containing the **Array** template definition. We can then exercise the new features with the following example:

```cpp
// Program 18.2 Using non-type parameters in a class template
#include "Box.h"
#include "Array.h"
#include <iostream>
#include <iomanip>
using namespace std;

int main()
{
  try
  {
    const int size = 21;                       // Number of array elements
    const int start = -10;                     // Index for first element
    const int end = start+size-1;              // Index for last element

    Array<double, start> values(size);         // Declare array for double values

    for(int i = start;  i<= end ; i++)         // Initialize the elements
      values[i] = i - start + 1;

    cout << endl<< "Sums of pairs of elements: ";
    int lines = 0;
    for( int i = end ; i >= start ; i--)
      cout << (lines++ % 5 == 0 ? "\n" : "")
           << setw(5) << values[i] + values[i - 1];
  }
  catch(const out_of_range& ex)
  {
    cout << endl << "out_of_range exception object caught! " << ex.what();
  }
  catch(const exception& ex)
  {
    cout << endl << ex.what();
  }

  try
  {
    const int start = 0;
    const int size = 11;

    Array<Box, start - 5> boxes(size);

    for(int i = start - 5 ; i <= start + size - 5 ; i++)
      cout << endl << "Box volume is " << boxes[i].volume();
  }
  catch(const exception& ex)
  {
    cout << endl << typeid(ex).name() << " exception caught! "<< ex.what();
  }

  cout << endl;
  return 0;
}
```

This will display the output:

```
Sums of pairs of elements:
   41   39   37   35   33
   31   29   27   25   23
   21   19   17   15   13
   11    9    7    5    3
out_of_range exception object caught! Index too small
Box volume is 1
Box volume is 1
Box volume is 1
Box volume is 1
Box volume is 1
Box volume is 1
Box volume is 1
Box volume is 1
Box volume is 1
Box volume is 1
Box volume is 1
class std::out_of_range exception caught! Index too large
```

How It Works

In the first **try** block, we start by defining some constants that specify the range of index values and the size of the array:

```
const int size = 21;                       // Number of array elements
const int start = -10;                     // Index for first element
const int end = start+size-1;              // Index for last element
```

We then create an instance of our template to store 21 values of type **double**:

```
Array<double, -10, 10> values;
```

The second argument corresponds to the non-type parameter for the template, and specifies the lower limit for the index values of the array. The size of the array is specified as the constructor argument.

We assign values to the elements of the **values** object within the **for** loop:

```
for(int i = start;  i<= end ; i++)         // Initialize the elements
   values[i] = i - start + 1;
```

The index value, **i**, runs from the lower limit **start**, which will be –10, to the upper limit **end**, which will be +10. Within the loop, we define the initial values for the array elements, so that they run from 1 to 21.

With the array initialized, we output sums of pairs of successive elements, starting at the end of the array and counting down.

```
int lines = 0;
for( i = end ; i >= start ; i--)
  cout << (lines++ % 5 == 0 ? "\n" : "")
       << setw(5) << values[i] + values[i - 1];
```

The **lines** variable is just to enable us to output the sums five to a line. As in the earlier example, our sloppy control of the index value results in the expression **values[i - 1]** causing an **out_of_range** exception to be thrown. The first handler for the **try** block catches it:

```
catch(const out_of_range& ex)
{
  cout << endl << "out_of_range exception object caught! " << ex.what();
}
```

This displays the message you see in the output. We also have a second handler for the **try** block:

```
catch(const exception& ex)
{
  cout << endl << ex.what();
}
```

This will actually catch *any* exception of type **exception**, or indeed of any type that has **exception** as a base, so all of the standard exceptions will be caught by this. It will therefore catch a **bad_alloc** exception if one were to be thrown by the **Array<double>** constructor. Remember that the parameter must be a reference here, otherwise derived class exceptions will be converted to the base class, and we'll get the object slicing problem that we discussed in the last chapter.

Since **out_of_range** also has the **exception** class as a base, we could have caught either exception with a single handler. For example, we could use the same handler that we have used for the third **try** block:

```
catch(const exception& ex)
{
  cout << endl << typeid(ex).name() << " exception caught! "<< ex.what();
}
```

In fact, as we learned in the previous chapter, we could have used the same handler with all three **try** blocks, reducing the source code and the size of the executable module. We'd still get full information about what exception was thrown. I wish I'd thought of it sooner!

In any case, the next **try** block creates an array to store **Box** objects:

```
Array<Box, start-5 > boxes(size);
```

You can see from this that expressions are acceptable as argument values for non-type parameters in a template instantiation. Such an expression must either evaluate to the type of the corresponding parameter, or it must be possible to convert the result to the appropriate type by means of a standard conversion. You need to take care if the expression includes the **>** symbol. For example:

```
Array<Box, start > 5 ? start : 5> boxes;
```

The intent of the expression for the second argument using the conditional operator is to supply a value of at least 5, but as it stands, this won't compile. The **>** in the expression will be paired with the opening angled bracket, and will close the parameter list. Parentheses are needed to make the statement valid:

```
Array<Box, (start > 5 ? start : 5)> boxes;
```

FYI

> The same fix applies to expressions involving the indirect member access operator (->), or the shift right operator (>>).

The next **for** loop will throw another exception, just like the previous example, and the handler will catch it.

Try It Out - The Better Solution

You must always keep in mind that non-type parameter arguments in a class template are part of the type that corresponds to an instance of the template. Every unique combination of template arguments produces another class type. As we indicated earlier, in the case of our **Array<T>** template this is particularly inefficient, and the usefulness of the template is restricted. We can't assign one array of **double**s, say, to another array of **double**s, if the starting indexes for the arrays are different — the arrays will be of different types. The class template with an extra data member and an extra constructor parameter will be much more effective. Here's the preferred version of the template that we saw earlier. The highlighted code shows the differences from the original template class:

```
template <typename T> class Array
{
  private:
    T* elements;                         // Array of type T
    size_t size;                         // Number of elements in the array
    long start;                          // Starting index value

  public:
    explicit Array(size_t arraySize, long startIndex = 0); // Constructor
    Array(const Array& theArray);        // Copy Constructor
    ~Array();                            // Destructor
    T& operator[](long index);           // Subscript operator
    const T& operator[](long index) const;  // Subscript operator for const
    Array& operator=(const Array& rhs);  // Assignment operator
};
```

The constructor will be changed slightly from the original version to initialize the new data member:

```
template <typename T>
Array<T>::Array(size_t arraySize, long startIndex) : size(arraySize),
start(startIndex)
{
  elements = new T[size];
}
```

The copy constructor will also have to take care of the extra data member:

```
template <typename T>
Array<T>::Array(const Array& theArray)
{
```

```
      size = theArray.size;
      start = theArray.start;
      elements = new T[size];
      for(int i = 0 ; i < size ; i++)
        elements[i] = theArray.elements[i];
    }
```

Similarly for the assignment operator:

```
template <typename T>
Array<T>& Array<T>::operator=(const Array& rhs)
{
  if(&rhs == this)                          // If lhs == rhs
    return *this;                           //   just return lhs

  if(elements)                              // If lhs array exists
    delete[]elements;                       // then release the free store memory

  size = rhs.size;
  start = rhs.start;
  elements = new T[rhs.size];
  for(int i = 0 ; i < size ; i++)
    elements[i] = rhs.elements[i];
}
```

Both subscript operator functions need to be changed in the same way – here's the non-**const** version as an example:

```
template <typename T>
T& Array<T>::operator[](long index)
{
  if(index < start || index > static_cast<long>(size) + start - 1)
    throw out_of_range(index < start ? "Index too small" : "Index too large");

  return elements[index - start];
}
```

We could try this out with the following program:

```
// Program 18.3 A better Array class template
#include "Box.h"
#include "Array.h"
#include <iostream>
#include <iomanip>
using namespace std;

int main()
{
  try
  {
    const int size = 21;                        // Number of array elements
    const int startValues = -10;                // Index for first element
    const int endValues = startValues + size - 1;  // Index for last element

    Array<double> values(size, startValues);    // values[-10] to values[10]
```

```
      for(int i = startValues; i <= endValues ; i++)       // Initialize the elements
        values[i] = i - startValues + 1;
      const int startData = startValues+5;                 // Index for first element
      const int endData = endValues+5;                     // Index for last element

      Array<double> data(size, startData);                 // Data[-5] to Data[15]

      for(int j = startData, i = startValues ; i <= endValues ; i++, j++)
                                                            // Initialize

        data[j] = values[i];

      cout << endl << "Sums of pairs of elements: ";
      int lines = 0;
      for(int i = endData ; i >= startData ; i--)
        cout << (lines++ % 5 == 0 ? "\n" : "") << setw(5) << data[i] + data[i - 1];
    }
    catch(const exception& ex)
    {
      cout << endl << typeid(ex).name() << " exception caught! "<< ex.what();
    }

    cout << endl;
    return 0;
  }
```

This program will display the following output:

```
Sums of pairs of elements:
    41    39    37    35    33
    31    29    27    25    23
    21    19    17    15    13
    11     9     7     5     3
class std::out_of_range exception caught! Index too small
```

How It Works

Because we set the **start** index by means of a constructor parameter rather than a class template parameter, we can work with arrays that use different index ranges, as long as they store values of the same type. Since the constructor has a default of 0 for the start index for the array, the template can be used in exactly the same way as the original when you want to use arrays indexed from zero.

The code in **main()** creates an object, **values**, that can be indexed from –10 to +10, and an object, **data**, that be indexed from –15 to +10. Both objects store values of type **double**. We initialize the elements of the **data** object using elements of the **values** object, thus demonstrating that we can mix them in an expression. This would have been impossible with the class template with a non-type parameter as the non-type parameter would have resulted in the objects being of different types.

This suggests that you should always think twice about using non-type parameters in a class template to be sure that they are really necessary. There is often an alternative approach that can provide you with more flexible templates and more efficient code.

Default Template Parameter Values

You can supply default values for both type and non-type parameters in a class template. If a given class template parameter has a default value, then all subsequent parameters in the list must also have default values specified. If you omit an argument for a class template parameter that has a default value specified, the default will be used, just like default parameter values in a function. Similarly, when you omit the argument for a given parameter in the list, then all subsequent arguments must also be omitted.

The default values for class template parameters are written in the same way as defaults for function parameters — following an **=** after the parameter name. We could supply defaults for both the parameters in the version of the **Array** template with a non-type parameter. For example:

```
template < typename T = int, long startIndex = 0> class Array
{
  // Template definition as before...
};
```

Of course, the same default values would also have to appear in the templates for the member functions. We could omit all the template arguments to declare an array of **int** indexed from 0.

```
Array<> numbers(101);
```

The legal index values run from 0 to 100, as determined by the default value for the non-type template parameter and the argument to the constructor. We must still supply the angled brackets, even though no arguments are necessary in the case. The other possibilities open to us are to omit the second argument, or to supply them all. For example:

```
Array<string, -100> messages(200);          // Array of 200 string objects
Array<Box> boxes(101);                       // Array of 101 Box objects
```

> *You can't omit just the first argument. In general, all the template arguments that would have appeared to the right of the first one to be left out must also be omitted.*

If a class template has default values for any of its parameters, they are only specified in the first declaration of the template in a source file (which, of course, can also be the definition of the template).

Explicit Template Instantiation

So far, we have created instances of a class template *implicitly*, as a result of declaring a variable of a template type. You can also *explicitly* instantiate class templates and function templates. The effect of an explicit instantiation of a template is that the compiler will create the instance determined by the parameter values that you specify.

We have already seen how to explicitly instantiate *function* templates back in Chapter 9. To instantiate a class template, you just use the keyword **template** followed by the template class name and the template arguments that you want to use. You could explicitly create an instance of the **Array** template with the declaration:

```
template class Array<double, 1>;
```

This creates an instance of the template that can store values of type **double**, indexed from 1. Explicitly instantiating a class template generates the class type definition, and it instantiates all of the member functions of the class from their templates.

Friends of Class Templates

Since a class can have friends, you won't be surprised to learn that a class template can also have friends that can be classes, functions or other templates. If a class is a friend of a template, then all its member functions are friends of every instance of the template. A function that is a friend of a template is a friend of any instance of the template.

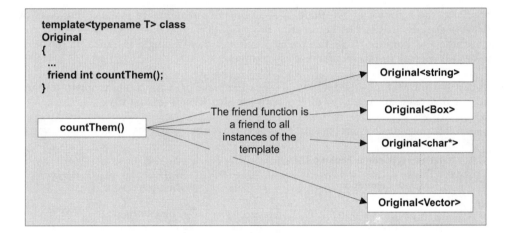

Templates that are friends of a template are a little different. Since they have parameters, the parameter list for the template class usually contains all the parameters to define the friend template. This is necessary to identify the instance of the friend template that is the friend of the particular instance of the original class template. However, the function template for the friend is only instantiated when you use it in your code. In the diagram below, **getBest()** is a function template.

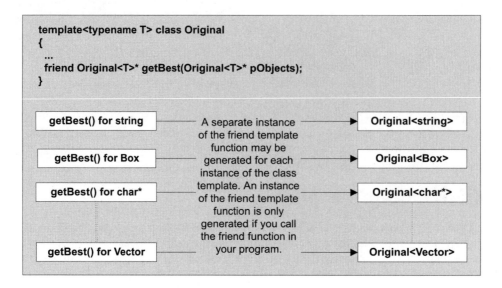

Although in the example above there is a unique friend template instance for each of the class template instances, this is not necessarily the case. If the class template has some parameters that are not also parameters of the friend template, then a single instance of the friend template may service several instances of the class template.

Note that an ordinary class may have a class template or a function template declared as a friend. In this case, all instances of the template are friends of the class.

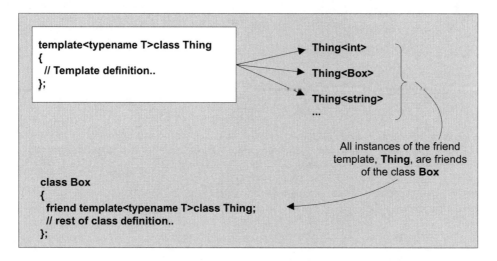

With the example in the diagram, every member function of every instance of the **Thing** template is a friend of the class **Box**, because the template has been declared as a friend of the class.

Special Cases

There are going to be many situations where a class template definition won't be satisfactory for every conceivable argument type. For example, you can compare **string** objects by using overloaded comparison operators, but you can't do the same thing with null-terminated strings. If your template compares objects using the comparison operators, it will work for type **string** but not for type **char***. To compare objects of type **char***, you'll need to use the comparison functions declared in the **cstring** header file.

To deal with this sort of problem, you can define a **class template specialization**. This provides a class definition that is specific to a given set of arguments for the template parameters. Note that this is a class definition — not a class template. Instead of using the template to generate the class for a particular type, **char*** say, the compiler will use your specialization instead. Thus a class template specialization provides a way for you to define specific versions of a class to be used by the compiler for specific class template argument values.

Suppose that we wanted to create a specialization of the first version of our **Array** template for type **char***. We will further suppose that it includes member functions for comparing objects of a template type — these might work by comparing the **elements** members of the two objects involved, element by element, but the detail of this is unimportant. We would write the class template definition as:

```
template <> class Array<char*>
{
  // Definition of a class to suit type char*...
};
```

This definition of the specialization of the **Array** template for type **char*** must be preceded by the original template definition, or by a declaration for the original template.

Because all the parameters are specified in the specialization here, it is called a **complete specialization** of the template, and that's why the first set of angle brackets are empty. Since we're taking care of specifying all the arguments, there's no room for any template arguments. There is no flexibility here — for type **char*** as the **Array** template argument, the compiler will use the specialization rather than apply the argument to the template.

It may be that just one or two member functions in a class template need to have code specific to a particular type. If the member functions are defined by separate function templates, rather than within the body of the class template, you can just provide specializations for the function templates.

Partial Template Specialization

If we were specializing the version of the template with two parameters, we would only want to specify the type parameter for the specialization, leaving the non-type parameter open. We could do this with a **partial specialization** of the **Array** template that we could define as:

```
template <long start> class Array<char*, start>
{
  // Definition to suit type char*...
};
```

739

The parameter list following the **template** keyword indicates the parameters that need to be specified for an instance of this template specialization — just one in this case. The first parameter is omitted because it is now fixed. The angled brackets following the template name specify how the parameters in the original template definition are specialized. The list here must have the same number of parameters as appear in the original, unspecialized template. The first parameter for this specialization is **char***. The other parameter is specified as the corresponding parameter name in this template, and is therefore not specialized in any way.

Apart from the special considerations you might need to give to a template instance produced by using **char*** for a type parameter, it may well be that pointers in general are a specialized subset that need to be treated differently from objects and references. In order to obtain a suitable comparison when your template is instantiated using a pointer type, you will need to dereference the variables before comparing them, otherwise you will be just comparing addresses, and not the objects or values stored at those addresses.

For this situation, you can define another partial specialization of the template. The first parameter is not completely fixed in this case, but it must fit within a particular pattern that we can specify in the list following the template name. For example, a partial specialization of the **Array** template for pointers would look like this:

```
template <typename T, long start> class Array<T*, start>
{
   // Definition to suit pointer types other than char*...
};
```

The first parameter is still **T**, but the **T*** between angled brackets following the template name indicates that this definition is to be used for instances where **T** is specified as a pointer. The other two parameters are still completely variable, so this specialization will apply to any instance that corresponds to the first argument being a pointer.

Selecting from Multiple Partial Specializations

Suppose we had created both of the partial specializations of the **Array** template that we just discussed — the one for type **char***, and the one for any pointer type. How could we be sure that the version for type **char*** will be selected by the compiler when this is appropriate for any particular instantiation? For example, consider this declaration:

```
Array<Box*, -5> boxes(11);
```

Clearly, this only fits with the specialization for pointers in general, but both partial specializations would fit the declaration if we wrote:

```
Array<char*, 1> messages(100);
```

In this case, the compiler will determine that the **char*** partial specialization is a better fit because it is more specialized than the alternative. The partially specialized template for **char*** is determined to be more specialized than the specialization for pointers in general because while anything that selects the **char*** specialization — which happens to be just **char*** — will also select the **T*** specialization, the reverse is not the case.

Class Templates with Nested Classes

A class template definition can contain a nested class or a **nested class template**. A nested class template is independently parameterized, so you have a two-dimensional ability to generate classes. Dealing with this is outside the scope of this book, but we can explore some aspects of a class template with a nested class.

Let's take a particular example. Suppose we want to implement a stack, which is a 'last in, first out' storage mechanism. A 'push' operation stores an item at the top of a stack, while a 'pop' operation takes the item at the top of the stack off the stack. We would want a stack to be able to hold objects of any given kind, so this is a natural for a template.

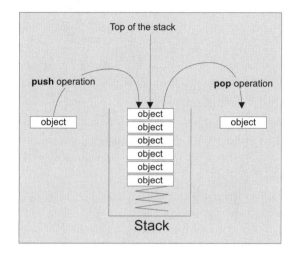

The template parameter for a **Stack** template will be a type parameter that specifies the type of objects in the stack, so the initial template definition is going to be:

```
template <typename T> class Stack
{
   // Detail of the Stack definition...
};
```

If we want the stack's capacity to grow automatically, we can't use fixed storage for objects within the stack. One way of providing the ability to automatically grow and shrink the stack as objects are pushed onto it or popped off it, is to implement the stack as a linked list. The nodes in the linked list can be created in the free store, and the stack will only need to remember the node at the top of the stack. This is illustrated below.

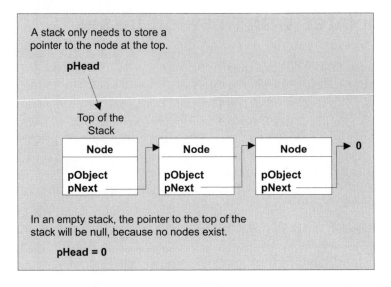

A stack only needs to store a pointer to the node at the top.

pHead

Top of the Stack

Node		Node		Node
pObject		pObject		pObject
pNext		pNext		pNext

0

In an empty stack, the pointer to the top of the stack will be null, because no nodes exist.

pHead = 0

When we create an empty stack, the pointer to the head of the list will be null, so we can use the fact that it doesn't contain any **Node** objects as an indicator that the stack is empty.

We will need a nested class in each instance of the **Stack** template that will define nodes in the list, and since a node must hold an object of type **T**, the **Stack** template parameter type, we can define it as a nested template. We can add this to our initial outline of the **Stack** template:

```
template <typename T> class Stack
{
  private:
    class Node
    {
      public:
        T* pItem;                              // Pointer to object stored
        Node* pNext;                           // Pointer to next node

        // Construct a node from an object
        Node(T& rItem) : pItem(&rItem), pNext(0) {}
        Node() : pItem(0), pNext(0) {}         // Construct an empty node
    };

    // Rest of the Stack definition...
};
```

Since the **Node** class is declared as **private**, we can afford to declare all the members as **public**, so they are directly accessible from member functions of the **Stack** template. We will assume that objects of type **T** are the responsibility of the user, so we will just store a pointer to an object of type **T** in a **Node** object. We will further assume that the user of the **Stack** is entirely responsible for destroying the objects that are stored. The default constructor just sets both data members to null, so this will be used to create a **Node** in an empty stack. The other constructor will be used when an object is pushed onto the stack. The parameter to this constructor is a reference to an object of type **T**.

We can now fill out the rest of the **Stack** class template to support the linked list of **Node** objects shown in the previous diagram:

```
template <typename T> class Stack
{
  private:
    class Node
    {
      public:
        T* pItem;                               // Pointer to object stored
        Node* pNext;                            // Pointer to next node

        // Construct a node from an object
        Node(T& rItem) : pItem(&rItem), pNext(0) {}
        Node() : pItem(0), pNext(0) {}          // Construct an empty node
    };

    Node* pHead;                                // Points to the top of the stack

  public:
    Stack():pHead(0){}                          // Default constructor
    Stack(const Stack& aStack);                 // Copy constructor
    ~Stack();                                   // Destructor
    Stack& operator=(const Stack& aStack);      // Assignment operator

    void push(T& rItem);                        // Push an object onto the stack
    T& pop();                                   // Pop an object off the stack
    bool isEmpty() {return pHead == 0;}         // Empty test
};
```

As I explained earlier, a stack only needs to 'remember' the top node, so there's only one data member, **pHead**, of type **Node**. We have a default constructor, plus a copy constructor, a destructor and the assignment operator because nodes will be created dynamically. We also have the **push()** and **pop()** members to transfer objects to and from the stack, and the **isEmpty()** function that returns **true** if the stack is empty.

To complete the implementation of our stack, we just need the templates for the member functions of the **Stack** template.

Defining Function Templates for Members

The default constructor is defined within the template as all it has to do is initialize **pHead** to 0. The copy constructor must replicate the **Stack<T>** object being copied, and we can do this by walking through the nodes, copying them as we go:

```
template <typename T> Stack<T>::Stack(const Stack& aStack)
{
  pHead = 0;
  if(aStack.pHead)
  {
    pHead = new Node(*aStack.pHead);      // Copy the top node of the original
    Node* pOldNode = aStack.pHead;        // Points to the top node of the original
    Node* pNewNode = pHead;               // Points to the node in the new stack
```

```
          while(pOldNode = pOldNode->pNext)    // If it is null, it is the last node
          {
            pNewNode->pNext = new Node(*pOldNode);     // Duplicate it
            pNewNode = pNewNode->pNext;                // Move to the node just created
          }
        }
      }
```

The assignment operator will be very similar to the copy constructor, but two extra things must be done. First, we must check that the objects involved are not identical. Second, we must release memory for nodes in the object on the left of the assignment. Here's the template to define that:

```
template <typename T> Stack<T>& Stack<T>::operator=(const Stack& aStack)
{
  if(this == &aStack)                          // If objects are identical
    return *this;                              // return the left object

  // Release memory for nodes in the left object
  Node* pTemp;
  while(pHead)                                 // While current pointer is not null
  {
    pTemp = pHead->pNext;                      // Get the pointer to the next
    delete pHead;                              // Delete the current
    pHead = pTemp;                             // Make the next current
  }

  if(aStack.pHead)
  {
    pHead = new Node(*aStack.pHead);           // Copy the top node of the original
    Node* pOldNode = aStack.pHead;             // Points to the top node of the original
    Node* pNewNode = pHead;                    // Points to the node in the new stack

    while(pOldNode = pOldNode->pNext)          // If it is null, it is the last node
    {
      pNewNode->pNext = new Node(*pOldNode);   // Duplicate it
      pNewNode = pNewNode->pNext;              // Move to the node just created
    }
  }
  return *this                                 // Return the left object
}
```

If the objects in the assignment are the same, we just dereference the **this** pointer to get the left-hand object, and return it. If the objects are different, the first step is to delete all the nodes for the left-hand object before we replace them with copies of the nodes from the right-hand object. Having done that, we just copy the right-hand object with code identical to the copy constructor. The code to do the copying is common to both the copy constructor and the assignment operator, so we could put it in a separate member function.

The code to delete nodes in the destructor will be exactly the same as the code in the assignment operator function:

```
template <typename T> Stack<T>::~Stack()
{
  Node* pTemp;
  while(pHead)
```

```
    {
      pTemp = pHead->pNext;
      delete pHead;
      pHead = pTemp;
    }
  }
```

FYI As with the copying code, could put this code in separate helper function that is private to the **Stack** class template, and then just call it when the capability is required. This reduces the size of the executable.

The template for the **push()** operation is very easy:

```
template <typename T> void Stack<T>::push(T& rItem)
{
  Node* pNode = new Node(rItem);                  // Create the new node
  pNode->pNext = pHead;                           // Point to the old top node
  pHead = pNode;                                  // Make the new node the top
}
```

To create the node, we pass a reference to the object to the **Node** constructor. The **pNext** member of this node needs to point to the node that was previously at the top. We then make the new node the top of the stack.

The **pop()** operation is slightly more work because we must delete the top node:

```
template <typename T> T& Stack<T>::pop()
{
  T* pItem = pHead->pItem;                        // Get pointer to the top node object
  if(!pItem)                                      // If it is empty
    throw std::logic_error("Stack empty");        // Pop is not valid so throw exception

  Node* pTemp = pHead;                            // Save address of top node
  pHead = pHead->pNext;                           // Make next node the top
  delete pTemp;                                   // Delete the previous top node
  return *pItem;                                  // Return the top object
}
```

There is the possibility of someone attempting a pop operation on an empty stack. Since we return a reference, we can't signal an error through the return value, so we have to throw an exception in this case.

Once we've retrieved the pointer to the object in the top node, we delete the top node, promote the next node to the top, and return the object. Now we have completed all the templates we need to define the stack, we can exercise our nested templates in a working example.

Try It Out – Using Nested Class Templates

You need to gather all the templates into a header file, **Stack.h**. Here's how it would look with the helper functions that we mentioned in the text:

```cpp
// Stack.h Templates to define stacks
#ifndef STACKS_H
#define STACKS_H
#include <stdexcept>

template <typename T> class Stack
{
  private:
    class Node
    {
      public:
        T* pItem;                           // Pointer to object stored
        Node* pNext;                        // Pointer to next node

        // Construct a node from an object
        Node(T& rItem) : pItem(&rItem), pNext(0) {}
        Node() : pItem(0), pNext(0) {}      // Construct an empty node
    };

    Node* pHead;                            // Points to the top of the stack
    void copy(const Stack& aStack);         // Helper to copy a stack
    void freeMemory();                      // Helper to release free store memory

  public:
    Stack():pHead(0){}                      // Default constructor
    Stack(const Stack& aStack);             // Copy constructor
    ~Stack();                               // Destructor
    Stack& operator=(const Stack& aStack);  // Assignment operator

    void push(T& rItem);                    // Push an object onto the stack
    T& pop();                               // Pop an object off the stack
    bool isEmpty() {return pHead == 0;}     // Empty test
};

// Copy constructor
template <typename T> Stack<T>::Stack(const Stack& aStack)
{
  copy(aStack);
}

// Helper to copy a stack
template <typename T> void Stack<T>::copy(const Stack& aStack)
{
  pHead = 0;
  if(aStack.pHead)
  {
    pHead = new Node(*aStack.pHead);        // Copy the top node of the original
    Node* pOldNode = aStack.pHead;          // Points to the top node of the original
    Node* pNewNode = pHead;                 // Points to the node in the new stack

    while(pOldNode = pOldNode->pNext)       // If it is null, it is the last node
```

```
    {
      pNewNode->pNext = new Node(*pOldNode);          // Duplicate it
      pNewNode = pNewNode->pNext;                     // Move to the node just created
    }
  }
}


// Assignment operator
template <typename T> Stack<T>& Stack<T>::operator=(const Stack& aStack)
{
  if(this == &aStack)                                 // If objects are identical
    return *this;                                     // return the left object

  freeMemory();                                       // Release memory for nodes in lhs
  copy(aStack);                                       // Copy rhs to lhs

  return *this                                        // Return the left object
}

// Helper to release memory for a stack
template <typename T> void Stack<T>::freeMemory()
{
  Node* pTemp;
  while(pHead)                                        // While current pointer is not null
  {
    pTemp = pHead->pNext;                             // Get the pointer to the next
    delete pHead;                                     // Delete the current
    pHead = pTemp;                                    // Make the next current
  }
}


// Destructor
template <typename T> Stack<T>::~Stack()
{
  freeMemory();
}

// Push an object onto the stack
template <typename T> void Stack<T>::push(T& rItem)
{
  Node* pNode = new Node(rItem);                      // Create the new node
  pNode->pNext = pHead;                               // Point to the old top node
  pHead = pNode;                                      // Make the new node the top
}

// Pop an object off the stack
template <typename T> T& Stack<T>::pop()
{
  T* pItem = pHead->pItem;                            // Get pointer to the top node object
  if(!pItem)                                          // If it is empty
    throw std::logic_error("Stack empty");  // Pop is not valid so throw exception

  Node* pTemp = pHead;                                // Save address of top node
  pHead = pHead->pNext;                               // Make next node the top
  delete pTemp;                                       // Delete the previous top node
  return *pItem;                                      // Return the top object
}
#endif
```

We can then use them in the following program that messes strings about a bit, using stacks:

```cpp
// Program 18.4 Using a stack defined by nested class templates
#include "Stack.h"
#include <iostream>
#include <string>
using namespace std;

int main()
{
  const char* words[] = {"The", "quick", "brown", "fox", "jumps"};
  Stack<const char*> wordStack;                  // A stack of null terminated strings

  for(int i = 0 ; i < 5 ; i++)
    wordStack.push(words[i]);

  Stack<const char*> newStack(wordStack);    // Create a copy of the stack

  // Display the words in reverse order
  while(!newStack.isEmpty())
    cout << newStack.pop() << " ";
  cout << endl;

  // Reverse wordStack onto newStack
  while(!wordStack.isEmpty())
    newStack.push(wordStack.pop());

  // Display the words in original order
  while(!newStack.isEmpty())
    cout << newStack.pop() << " ";
  cout << endl;

  cout << endl << "Enter a line of text:" << endl;
  string text;
  getline(cin, text);                            // Read a line into the string object

  Stack<const char> characters;                  // A stack for characters

  for(int i = 0 ; i < text.length() ; i++)
    characters.push(text[i]);              // Push the string characters onto the stack

  cout << endl;
  while(!characters.isEmpty())
    cout << characters.pop();                   // Pop the characters off the stack

  cout << endl;
  return 0;
}
```

This example will produce output something like:

```
jumps fox brown quick The
The quick brown fox jumps

Enter a line of text:
A nod is as good as a wink to a blind horse

esroh dnilb a ot kniw a sa doog sa si don A
```

How It Works

We first define an array of 5 objects that are null-terminated strings, initialized with the words shown. We then declare a stack object to store **const char*** objects with the statement:

```
Stack<const char*> wordStack;                 // A stack of null terminated strings
```

This will create an instance of the **Stack** template and an instance of the constructor for **Stack<const char*>**. We push the array elements onto the stack in the **for** loop:

```
for(int i = 0 ; i < 5 ; i++)
  wordStack.push(words[i]);
```

The stack will have the first word at the bottom of the **wordStack** stack, and the last word at the top. We then create a copy of the stack with the statement:

```
Stack<const char*> newStack(wordStack);    // Create a copy of the stack
```

This calls the copy constructor, so an instance of the function template for this will be created. **newStack** will be a duplicate of **wordStack**. In the next **while** loop, we display the words in reverse order by popping them off the stack and outputting them:

```
while(!newStack.isEmpty())
  cout << newStack.pop() << " ";
```

This uses **isEmpty()** to continue popping objects off the stack; the function returns **false** as long as the stack is not empty. Using the **isEmpty()** function is a safe way of getting the complete contents of a stack. The **newStack** is empty by the end of the loop, but we still have the original in **wordStack**.

In the next **while** loop, we retrieve the words from **wordStack** and pop them onto **newStack**:

```
while(!wordStack.isEmpty())
  newStack.push(wordStack.pop());
```

The pop and push operations are combined in a single statement, where the object returned by **pop()** for **wordStack** is the argument for **push()** for **newStack()**. At the end of this loop, **wordStack** will be empty and **newStack** will contain the words in their original sequence — with the first word at the top of the stack. We then output the words by popping them off **newStack**, so at the end of this loop both stacks are empty:

```
while(!newStack.isEmpty())
  cout << newStack.pop() << " ";
```

The next part of the program reads a line of text into a string object using the **getline()** function:

```
cout << endl << endl << "Enter a line of text:" << endl;
string text;
getline(cin, text);                           // Read a line into the string object
```

749

This reads the input into the **string** object, **text**. We then create a stack to hold characters:

```
Stack<const char> characters;               // A stack for characters
```

This will create a new instance of the **Stack** template, **Stack<const char>**, and a new instance of the constructor for this type of stack. At this point, the program will contain two classes from the **Stack** template each with a nested **Node** class.

We peel off the characters from **text**, and push them onto our new stack in a **for** loop:

```
for(int i = 0 ; i < text.length() ; i++)
   characters.push(text[i]);               // Push the string characters onto the stack
```

The **length()** function of the **text** object is used to determine when the loop ends; we can now display the input string in reverse by popping the characters off the stack:

```
cout << endl;
while(!characters.isEmpty())
   cout << characters.pop();               // Pop the characters off the stack
```

You can see from the output that my input was not even slightly palindromic, but you could try, "Ned, I am a maiden".

More Advanced Class Templates

More advanced aspects of applying class templates are outside the scope of this book — a full discussion of this could be the topic for a complete book, but we will just mention a couple of capabilities without going into more detail.

As you would expect, a class template can have base classes, and as you'd expect, these can be ordinary classes or they can be templates themselves. For example, you might want a template that was derived from the **Stack** template in order to provide some additional capabilities not available in the basic **Stack** template. You could define the template like this:

```
template <typename T> class SpecialStack: public Stack<T>
{
  public:
    SpecialStack();
    ~SpecialStack();
    SpecialStack(const SpecialStack& aStack);

    int ObjectCount();                    // Count the objects
};
```

This is a trivial example that just adds a function to determine how many objects are in the stack, but it illustrates that specifying a template as a base to a template is quite straightforward. An instance of this template will derive from the **Stack<T>** instance, so it works in the same way as for ordinary derived classes.

Note also that a type parameter in a template can itself be a template, so we could define a template like this:

```
template <typename T1, template <typename T2> Array> class ClassName
{
  // Template definition...
};
```

The first template parameter, **T1**, is a type parameter, the second parameter is also a type parameter but this time it is a template. The parameter **T2** will determine a specific instance of the **Array** template that will be used as the second argument for the **ClassName** template.

Summary

An understanding of how class templates are defined and used is fundamental to understanding how to apply the capabilities of the Standard Template Library that we will discuss in Chapter 20. It is also a powerful augmentation of the basic language facilities for defining classes. The essential points we have discussed in this chapter include:

▶ A class template defines a family of class types.

▶ An instance of a class template is a class definition produced from the template by a given set of template arguments.

▶ An implicit instantiation of a class template arises out of a declaration for an object of a class template type.

▶ An explicit instantiation of a class template defines a class for a given set of arguments for the template parameters.

▶ An argument corresponding to a type parameter in a class template is a type that can be a basic type or a class type, or a pointer or a reference type.

▶ A non-type parameter can be of an integral or enumeration type, or a pointer or a reference.

▶ A partial specialization of a class template defines a new template that is to be used for a specific, restricted subset of the possible arguments for the original class template.

▶ A complete specialization of a class template defines a new template for a specific, complete set of parameter arguments for the original class template.

▶ A friend of a class template can be a function, a class, a function template or a class template.

▶ An ordinary class can declare a class template or a function template as a friend.

Exercises

Ex 18.1 You created a sparse array class in the exercises at the end of the previous chapter. This time, define a *template* for one-dimensional sparse arrays that will store objects of any type, so that only the elements stored in the array occupy memory. The potential number of elements that can be stored by an instance of the template should be unlimited. The template might be used to define a sparse array containing pointers to elements of type **double** with the statement:

```
SparseArray<double> values;
```

Define the subscript operator for the template so that element values can be retrieved and set just like a normal array. If an element does not exist at an index position, the subscript operator should return an object created by the default constructor for the object class. Exercise the template with a **main()** function that stores 20 random element values of type **int** within the range 32 to 212 at random positions in a sparse array with an index range from 0 to 499, and output the non-zero element values along with their index positions.

Ex 18.2 Define a template for a linked list that allows the list to be traversed backwards, from the end of the list, as well as forwards from the beginning. (Each node will need a pointer to the previous node as well as a pointer to the next.) Apply the template in a program to store individual words from some arbitrary prose or poetry as string objects, and then to display them 5 to a line in reverse order.

Ex 18.3 Use the linked list and sparse array templates to produce a program that stores words from a prose or poetry sample in a sparse array of up to 26 linked lists, where each list contains words that have the same initial letter. Output the words, starting each group with a given initial letter on a new line. (Remember to leave a space between successive **>** characters when specifying template arguments — otherwise **>>** will be interpreted as a shift right operator.)

Ex 18.4 Add an **insert()** function to the **SparseArray** template that adds an element following the last element in the array. Use this function and a **SparseArray** instance that has elements that are **SparseArray** objects storing **string** objects to perform the same task as the previous exercise.

19

Input and Output Operations

The C++ language itself has no provision for input and output. The subject of this chapter is the input and output capabilities that are available in the standard library, which provides you with support for device independent input and output operations in your programs. We have used elements of these facilities to read from the keyboard and write to the screen in all the examples you've seen so far. Here we will expand on that, and also look at how we can read and write disk files. By the end of this chapter, you will have learned:

▶ What a stream is

▶ What the standard streams are

▶ How binary streams differ from text streams

▶ How to create and use file streams

▶ How errors in stream operations are recorded, and how you can manage them

▶ How to use unformatted stream operations

▶ How to write numerical data to a file as binary data

▶ How objects can be written to and read from a stream

▶ How to overload the insertion and extraction operators for your classes

▶ Implementing stream support for template classes

▶ How to create string streams

Input and Output in C++

As you create your C++ programs, you'll find yourself requiring many different kinds of input and output capability. Your application might need to store and retrieve data in a database, to create and display graphics on the screen, to communicate over a telephone line through a modem, or to communicate over a network. All of these examples have one thing in common, at least: they are totally outside the remit of the C++ language and library facilities.

This implies that in the majority of situations, you will be using input-output capability that is not part of the C++ standard, although they may well be provided as part of your C++ development environment. It may also be the case that some of the facilities provided by C++ are not consistent with the environment in which your program is to execute. Your computer's operating system controls communication with the screen and the keyboard, and it could be that reading from **cin** and writing to **cout** is not possible. This is the case if you're programming for Microsoft Windows on a PC, for example, although the facility is emulated in many C++ development systems for Windows.

Of course, the capabilities that are defined within C++ are still important, as they represent a substantial standard library facility with extensive functionality. Not only do they provide you with file input-output capability, but they also include facilities for data formatting using string-based I/O.

Understanding Streams

The input and output functionality provided by the standard library involves using **streams**. A **stream** is an abstract representation of an input or output device that's a source or destination for data in your program. You can visualize a stream as a sequence of characters flowing between an external device and the main memory of your computer. You can write data to an **output stream** and read data from an **input stream**; some streams can provide the capability for both input and output of data.

There are two modes for transferring data to and from streams: **text mode** and **binary mode**. While a stream of characters is read or written in both modes, in text mode the stream may transform certain characters as they are read from or written to the physical device. Whether this occurs, and how characters are changed, is system dependent. On some systems, for example, a single newline character written to a stream will be replaced by *two* characters: a carriage return and a line feed. In binary mode, such transformations of characters in the stream are suppressed, and the original characters are transferred without conversion.

In addition to the two modes of data transfer, there are two ways in which you can read from and write to a stream. Firstly, you can read and write various types of data using the extraction and insertion operators, as we have been doing throughout the book when reading from the keyboard or writing to the screen. These are **formatted input/output operations**. Binary numerical data, such as integers and floating point values, are converted to a character representation before they are written to the stream, and the inverse process occurs when data values are read. These operations can be in text mode or binary mode, but generally they are carried out in text mode. All the operations writing to **cout** and reading from **cin** in this book are formatted I/O operations in text mode.

The second way of working with a stream is to read or write character-based data. A read or write operation can be for just a single character, a given number of characters, or a sequence of characters terminated by a delimiter of some kind, but the most significant point about this method is that you only read or write *bytes*. These are **unformatted input/output operations**. Even though these operations do not format the data themselves, the data in the stream may still be transformed by text mode, depending on the system environment.

The primary reason for using streams as the basis for input and output operations in C++ is to make your source code for these operations independent of the physical device involved. This has a couple of advantages. Firstly, you don't have to worry about the detailed mechanics of each device, as that is all taken care of behind the scenes. Secondly, your program will work with a variety of disparate input/output devices without necessitating any changes to the source code.

The physical reality of an output stream — in other words, where the data goes when you write to it — can be any device to which a sequence of bytes can be transferred. It will typically be the screen, a file on your hard disk, or possibly your printer. The standard library defines three output streams, **cout**, **cer** and **clog**, all of which are typically associated with your display screen. **cout** is the standard output stream, while **cerr** and **clog** are both connected to the **standard error stream**, which is used for error reporting from your program. The difference between the last two streams is that **cerr** is unbuffered (so data is written immediately to the output device) whereas **clog** is buffered (so data will only be written when the buffer is full).

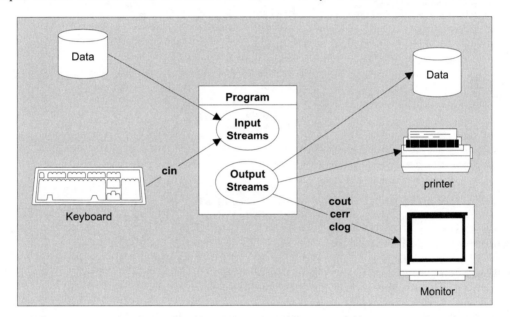

In principle, an **input stream** can also be any serial source of data, but it is typically a disk file or the keyboard. The standard library defines a standard input stream, **cin**, which is usually associated with the keyboard.

As you might have guessed by now, streams in C++ are objects of classes, and the standard streams are predefined objects that are already associated with specific external devices on your system. When we've been reading objects from **cin** using the extraction operator, **>>**, or writing objects to **cout** using the insertion operator, **<<**, we have been using overloaded versions of the **operator<<()** and **operator>>()** functions for these objects. As far as the standard streams are concerned, everything is set up and ready to go. However, when you want to use something other than the standard streams — for *file* input and output, for instance — you must create the stream objects that you need and associate them with the physical source or destination for the data. To set us on our way, let's take a look at the classes that define streams.

Stream Classes

There are quite a few classes involved in stream input-output, but the main ones we'll be interested in, and the relationships between them, are illustrated in the diagram below.

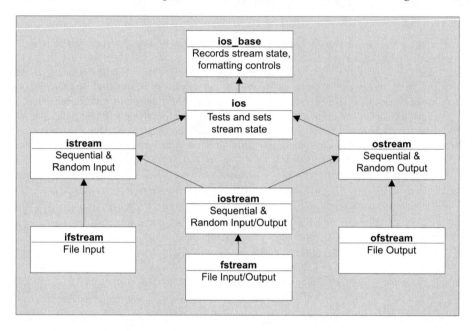

This is a simplified representation, but it's all we need to understand the principles. **ios_base** is an 'ordinary' class, while the others are instances of templates — the **istream** class, for example, is an instance of the **basic_istream** template, and the **ios** class is an instance of the **basic_ios** template. However, we are interested in the classes rather than their templates, because we will be using the classes in our programs. The stream classes share a common base, **ios**, which inherits flags recording the state of a stream and the formatting modes in effect from the **ios_base** class. Thus, all the stream classes that provide the input-output operations share a common set of status and formatting flags, and functions to query and set them.

The standard input stream, **cin**, is an object of type **istream**, while the standard output streams **cout**, **cerr**, and **clog** are **ostream** objects. You can see that the stream classes for file handling, **ifstream**, **fstream**, and **ofstream**, all have **istream**, **ostream**, or both as base classes, so the facilities that we have used with the standard streams are going to be available with file streams too.

The template classes generally have type parameters that specify the character sets for a particular stream, and the classes identified in the diagram apply to streams that deal with characters of type **char**. There are instances of these templates that define streams that can handle characters of type **wchar_t**, called **wistream**, **wostream**, **wiostream**, **wifstream**, **wofstream** and **wfstream**. We won't discuss these wide character stream classes specifically in this chapter, but they work in the same way as the byte stream classes.

Since you'll sometimes see references to the original templates, rather than to the abbreviated class type names we had in the diagram, you need to be aware of the template names. The stream classes are defined using **typedef**s, as follows:

```
typedef basic_ios<char>        ios;
typedef basic_istream<char>    istream;
typedef basic_ostream<char>    ostream;
typedef basic_iostream<char>   iostream;
typedef basic_ifstream<char>   ifstream;
typedef basic_ofstream<char>   ofstream;
typedef basic_fstream<char>    fstream;
```

The corresponding wide character streams just have **wchar_t** as the type parameter argument to the template, in place of **char**. We will use the abbreviated class names in the rest of this chapter rather than the full template names, as it's considerably less to type!

Standard Streams

The standard streams are defined as stream class objects within the **std** namespace. These definitions appear in the header file **iostream**:

```
extern istream cin;
extern ostream cout;
extern ostream cerr;
extern ostream clog;
```

The **iostream** header file also defines the corresponding wide character stream objects as:

```
extern wistream wcin;
extern wostream wcout;
extern wostream wcerr;
extern wostream wclog;
```

We have already made extensive use of the standard input stream **cin**, and the standard output stream **cout**. The **cerr** and **clog** streams are used in exactly the same way as **cout**. I won't repeat in this chapter what we've covered in previous chapters about how reading from and writing to the standard streams is handled. Instead, we'll concentrate on understanding more of the background of how they work, and how the same techniques and mechanisms apply to other stream types.

To begin with, we will revisit the formatted stream operations you're already familiar with, and we'll explore how you can use them for files as well as for the standard streams. We will then look into how unformatted stream operations work, and how and when we can use those to our advantage.

Stream Insertion and Extraction Operations

The insertion and extraction operators that we have been using with standard stream objects work just the same with other types of stream objects. All the standard streams operate in text mode, because this mode ensures that the data is presented correctly on output.

The insertion and extraction operators are principally concerned with converting between internal binary representations of data values and their external character representations. When you use these operators with streams other than the standard streams, you'll still usually want to use them in text mode, since they're geared to working with a text-based representation of the data. Text mode is concerned with ensuring that the visual presentation of the data is correct.

759

Stream Extraction Operations

The function **operator>>()** is implemented as a set of overloaded members of the **istream** class to support reading basic types of data from any input stream. There will be an overloaded version of this operator for each of the basic data types in C++. Let's look at how the code we have been writing connects to these operator functions by considering what happens when we write statements such as these:

```
int i = 0;
double x = 0.0;
cin >> i >> x;
```

Remember that **cin** is an object of type **istream**. The last statement, which reads the two variables from the standard stream, **cin**, translates to:

```
(cin.operator>>(i)).operator>>(x);
```

As you might expect, the **operator>>()** function is called once for each time you use the extraction operator. The **operator>>()** function for streams returns a reference to the stream object for which it was called (in this case **cin**), so the return value is used to call the next operator function. The parameter to the **operator>>()** function has to be a reference, to allow the function to store the data value read from the stream in the variable that is passed as an argument.

A whitespace character is always regarded as a delimiter between values, so you cannot read whitespace characters into your program using the **operator>>()** members of the **istream** class. Excess whitespace characters are generally ignored. You will recall that we had to use the **getline()** function for **cin** when we wanted to read a line of text from the keyboard.

The **operator>>()** function is implemented as an overloaded set of members of the **istream** class, for the following basic types:

short	int	long
unsigned short	unsigned int	unsigned long
float	double	long double
bool	void*	

The function supporting the last of these types, **void***, enables you to read address values into a pointer of any type, *except* for a pointer to type **char**, which refers to a null-terminated string and is treated as a special case. A pointer of any type can be passed as an argument to a function with a parameter of type 'reference to **void***', but there are non-member versions of **operator>>()** that accept arguments that are pointers to null-terminated strings. They have the prototypes:

```
istream& operator>>(istream& in, signed char* pStr);
istream& operator>>(istream& in, unsigned char* pStr);
```

One of these functions will always be selected when you use a pointer to a null-terminated string with the extraction operator. If you want to read an address and store it in a pointer of type **char***, you must read it as type **void***, then cast the address to type **char*** to store it.

Reading a single character using the extraction operator is also supported through **operator>>()** functions that are not members of the **istream** class, because they can be implemented using the **get()** function defined for **istream** objects. There are three versions, corresponding to reading a single character as type **char**, **signed char**, and **unsigned char**. We'll come back to the **get()** function later in the chapter.

Stream Insertion Operations

The **operator<<()** function is overloaded in the **ostream** class for formatted stream output of data values of the basic types. Output to **cout** works analogously to input with **cin**. You could write the data values **i** and **x** to **cout** with the statement:

```
cout << i << ' ' << x;
```

This statement translates to three calls of **operator<<()** functions:

```
operator<<(cout.operator<<(i), ' ').operator<<(x);
```

All versions of the **operator<<()** function return a reference to the stream object for which they are called, so the return value can always be used to call the next **operator<<()** function. As I've explained, the **operator<<()** functions that write single characters and null-terminated strings to the stream are implemented as non-member functions. That's why the operator function call to write **i** to the stream appears as the first argument to the operator function call to write the space. The latter returns the stream object, and that's used to call the member function that writes the value of **x**.

The **operator<<()** function is overloaded in the **ostream** class for the same set of types as the **operator>>()** functions in the **istream** class, listed above. In addition, outputting of a single character or a null-terminated string is catered for by non-member versions of **operator<<()**. The functions that output a single character to an output stream have the prototypes:

```
ostream& operator<<(ostream& out, char ch);
ostream& operator<<(ostream& out, signed char ch);
ostream& operator<<(ostream& out, unsigned char ch);
```

There are similar functions defined that will output null-terminated strings:

```
ostream& operator<<(ostream& out, const char* pStr);
ostream& operator<<(ostream& out, const signed char* pStr);
ostream& operator<<(ostream& out, const unsigned char* pStr);
```

You can see now why you can output a string using a pointer, when pointers to other types are always written to a stream as an address. Because these functions exist, sending a variable of type **const char*** to an output stream writes the string to which the pointer points to the stream, rather than the address stored in the pointer variable. If for some reason you want the address contained in the pointer to be output rather than the string, you must explicitly cast it to type **void***. Then, the member function of **ostream** that has a parameter of that type will be called, and the address will be sent to the stream. Thus, if you have the statements:

```
const char* pMessage = "More is less and less is more.";
cout << pMessage;
```

you will display the message. To output the address contained in **pMessage**, you must write the output statement as:

```
cout << static_cast<void*>(pMessage);
```

Stream Manipulators

We have already made extensive use of manipulators to control formatting of a stream. In particular, the following basic manipulators can be inserted into a stream:

Manipulator	Meaning
dec	Set the default radix for integers to decimal.
oct	Set the default radix for integers to octal.
hex	Set the default radix for integers to hexadecimal.
fixed	Output floating point values in fixed point notation without an exponent.
scientific	Output floating point values in scientific notation with an exponent.
boolalpha	Represent **bool** values as alphabetic — **true** and **false** in English.
noboolalpha	Represent **bool** values as **1** and **0**.
showbase	Indicate the base for octal (**0** prefix) and hexadecimal (**0x** prefix) integers.
noshowbase	Omit the base indication for octal and hexadecimal integers.
showpoint	Always output floating point values to the stream with a decimal point.
noshowpoint	Output integral floating point values without a decimal point.
showpos	Display a **+** prefix for positive integers.
noshowpos	No **+** prefix for positive integers.
skipws	Skip whitespace on input.
noskipws	Do not skip whitespace on input.
uppercase	Use upper case for hexadecimal digits **A** to **F**, and **E** for an exponent.
nouppercase	Use lower case for hexadecimal digits **a** to **f**, and **e** for an exponent.
internal	Insert 'fill characters' to pad the output to the field width.
left	Align values left in an output field.
right	Align values right in an output field.
endl	Write a newline character to the stream buffer and writes the contents of the buffer to the stream.
flush	Write data from the stream buffer to the stream.

All of these manipulators can be placed directly into the stream. For example:

```
int i = 1000;
cout << hex << uppercase << i;
```

This will output the value of the integer, **i**, as a hexadecimal value, using upper case hexadecimal digits. In other words, what you'd see on the screen is **3E8**.

It's interesting to see how this works. You know that using an insertion operator results in a version of **operator<<()** being called, but none of the versions we have seen so far can be involved here, since they only deal with values being output to the stream. The effect of these manipulators does not involve sending data to a stream, so they can't be data values. In fact, all of the manipulators in the above list are pointers to functions of the same type. When you use one of these manipulators, a special version of **operator<<()** that accepts a pointer to a function is called, and the manipulator is passed as an argument.

To make this clearer, the manipulator **hex** is the name of this function:

```
ios_base& hex(ios_base& str);
```

You might use this manipulator in a statement such as:

```
cout << hex << i;
```

This translates to:

```
(cout.operator<<(hex)).operator<<(i);
```

The first call of **operator<<()** has the pointer to function, **hex**, as an argument. Within the operator function, the function **hex()** will be called to set the output formatting to transfer the value of **i** to the stream in hexadecimal format.

The **ios_base** class that cropped up in the prototype for **hex()** is the base class of the **ios** class, as you saw at the beginning of this chapter. Since this is inherited by all of the stream classes the type **ios_base&** can reference any stream object. All of the manipulators are pointers to functions that have a parameter and a return type of type 'reference to **ios_base**', so they all result in the same version of **operator<<()** being called, which will call the function pointed to by the argument. **ios_base** defines flags that control the stream, and the function that is called when you use a manipulator modifies the appropriate flags to produce the desired result. You can modify these flags directly using functions **setf()** and **unsetf()** for a stream object, but it's much easier to use the manipulators.

Manipulators with Arguments

There are some manipulators that accept an argument when you use them. To access these, you must **#include** the **iomanip** header file into your source file, since it contains their declarations. You use these manipulator functions in the same way as the other manipulators, by effectively inserting a function call into the stream. These manipulators are:

Manipulator	Meaning
setprecision(int n)	Set the precision for floating point output to **n** digits. This remains in effect until you change it.
setw(int n)	Set the field width for the next output value to **n** characters. This will reset on each output to the default setting, which is to output value in a field width that is just sufficient to accommodate the value.
setfill(char ch)	Set the fill character to be used as padding within the output field to **ch**. This is modal, so it remains in effect until you change it again.
setbase(int base)	Set the output representation for integers to octal, decimal or hexadecimal, corresponding to values for the argument of 8, 10 and 16. Any other values will leave the number base unchanged.

The return type for each of these manipulators is implementation defined. An example of using them is:

```
cout << endl << setw(10) << setfill('*') << left << i;
```

This statement outputs the value **i** left-justified in a field that's 10 characters wide. The field will be padded with **'*'** in any unused character positions to the right of the value. The fill character will be in effect for any following output values, but you must set the field width explicitly prior to each output value.

> It is an error to include parentheses for the manipulators that are function pointers (such as **left**), so don't mix them up with the four we have discussed here.

The **iomanip** header also declares the functions **setiosflags()** and **resetiosflags()** that you can use to set or reset the flags controlling stream formatting by specifying a mask. You construct the mask that you pass as an argument by using the bitwise OR operator to combine the flags that are defined in the **ios_base** class. The name of each flag is the same as the name of the manipulator that sets it, so you could set the flags for left-justified, hexadecimal output as follows:

```
cout << endl << setw(10) << setiosflags(ios::left | ios::hex) << i;
```

This will output **i** as a left-justified, hexadecimal value in a field that's 10 characters wide. We can use **ios** as the qualifier for the flag names here, because the flags are inherited in the **ios** class from **ios_base**.

File Streams

There are three types of stream class objects that you can use for working with files: **ifstream**, **ofstream** and **fstream**. As we saw earlier, these have **istream**, **ostream** and **iostream** as base classes respectively. An **istream** object represents a file stream that you can read from, an **ofstream** object represents a file output stream that you can write to, and **fstream** is a file stream that you can read or write.

You can associate a file stream object with a physical file on disk when you create it. Alternatively, you can create a file stream object that is not associated with a particular file, and then use a member function to establish the connection with the physical file later on. In order to read or write a physical file, the file must be 'opened', attaching it to your program via the operating system with a set of permissions that describe how you are going to use it. If you create a file stream object with an initial association to a particular file, the file is opened and available for use in your program immediately. Note that it's possible to change the physical file that a file stream object is associated with, so you could use a single **ofstream** object to write to different files at different times.

A file stream has some important properties. It has a length, which corresponds to the number of characters in the stream; it has a beginning, which is the first character in the stream; and it has an end, which is the position *after* the last character in the stream. It also has a current position, which is the index position of the character in the stream where the next read or write operation will start. The first character in a file stream is at position 0. These properties provide a way for you to move around a file to read the particular parts that you're interested in, or to overwrite selected areas of the file.

Writing to a File

To begin our investigation of file streams, let's look at how we can write to a file output stream. An output file will be represented by an **ofstream** object, which we can create like this:

```
ofstream outFile("filename");
```

The file called **filename** will automatically be opened for writing, so you can write to it immediately in the default mode, text mode. If the file called **filename** does not exist, it will be created. If it already exists, any data that was in the file is discarded, and the data that you write to the file will form its new contents. Even if you *don't* write to the file after opening it, the original contents will be discarded and you will have an empty file. The object **outFile** has an **ostream** sub-object, so all of the stream operations we have been discussing in the context of the standard stream, **cout**, apply equally well to **outFile**. We can exercise this with a version of the example back in Chapter 7 that generated primes, Program 7.6.

Try It Out – Writing to a File

We can write the primes to a file instead of to the screen. All we need to do is define an **ostream** object for a file, and use that in place of **cout** in the example. Here's the modified code, with the altered lines shaded:

```
// Program 19.1 Writing primes to a file
#include <fstream>                           // For file streams
#include <iomanip>
using namespace std;

int main()
{
  const int max = 100;                       // Number of primes required
  long primes[max] = {2, 3, 5};              // First three primes defined
  int count = 3;                             // Count of primes found
  long trial = 5;                            // Candidate prime
  bool isprime = true;                       // Indicates when a prime is found

  do
  {
    trial += 2;                              // Next value for checking
    int i = 0;                               // Index to primes array

    // Try dividing the candidate by all the primes we have
    do
    {
      isprime = trial % *(primes + i) > 0;   // False for exact division
    } while(++i < count && isprime);

    if(isprime)                              // We got one...
      *(primes + count++) = trial;           // ...so save it in primes array
  } while(count < max);

  ofstream outFile("C:\\JunkData\\primes.txt"); // Define file stream object
```

```
  // Output primes 5 to a line
  for(int i = 0 ; i < max ; i++)
  {
    if(i % 5 == 0)                                // New line after every 5th prime
      outFile << endl;
    outFile << setw(10) << *(primes + i);
  }

  return 0;
}
```

This program doesn't send any output to the screen. The only output is the file that gets written. Note that if you use the path specified in the program, you must create the **JunkData** directory before you run it. The program only creates the file, not the directory.

How It Works

First of all, we have a **#include** directive for the **fstream** header file that defines the file stream classes:

```
#include <fstream>                               // For file streams
```

We no longer need the **iostream** header, since we don't use any of the standard streams in this example. All of the calculations are the same as in Chapter 7, so the first change to **main()** is the addition of a declaration for the file output stream object:

```
ofstream outFile("C:\\JunkData\\primes.txt");   // Define file stream object
```

This defines an **ofstream** object, **outFile**, and associates it with the file called **primes.txt** in the **JunkData** directory on your **C:** drive. This code uses MSDOS notation, so you should use a file path and name to suit your environment here. Remember that you need to use **** for a single backslash in the path, because a single **** starts an escape sequence. On this occasion, I have used the extension **.txt** in the file name because we're writing the file in text mode, and it should therefore be viewable by applications that handle **.txt** files. We haven't added checks for success in this program, but we'll cover those possibilities later.

If you don't specify a path, the file will be assumed to be in the current directory. If it doesn't already exist there, it will be created in that directory. If you want to err on the side of caution, you could do as I have done and set aside a directory somewhere that you will use to experiment with file operations. As long as you use fully qualified file names in all your programs, there is then no risk of corrupting important files by accident.

The final modification to the program is to make it write to the file in exactly the same way as we originally wrote to **cout**, using the insertion operator, **<<**:

```
for(int i = 0 ; i < max ; i++)
{
  if(i % 5 == 0)                                // New line after every 5th prime
    outFile << endl;
  outFile << setw(10) << *(primes + i);
}
```

When the program is done, you should find the file **primes.txt** in the **C:\JunkData** directory (or whatever path you specified). If you view the contents using a text editor, you will see that the file contains the same data as was displayed by the original version of the program.

Of course, if we just wanted to use the file as a medium for intermediate storage, and we didn't want to look at the contents directly, we could dispense with the newline characters. We still need whitespace between one value and the next if we want to read them back using the extraction operator, but we could reduce this to a single space. In that case, the output statement could be:

```
for(int i = 0 ; i < max ; i++)
   outFile << ' ' << *(primes + i);
```

Notice that we didn't have to do anything to close the file. When an **ostream** object is destroyed, the file that it is associated with is closed automatically, so our file will be closed when the **outFile** object goes out of scope. If you want to close the file explicitly, you can call the **close()** function for the object, so this statement would close the file represented by our **outFile** object:

```
outFile.close();
```

On my system, an **ostream** object overwrites any existing file contents. You can verify that this is the case for your system by running the program again with a different value for the number of primes, and taking another look at the file contents.

> *Don't worry: you don't always have to overwrite the file each time; that just happens to be the default setting. We'll look at how to control the way a file is written a little later in the chapter.*

Reading from a File

To read from a file, you can create an object of type **ifstream** and associate it with the file on your disk. For example:

```
const char* filename = "C:\\JunkData\\primes.txt";
ifstream inFile(filename);
```

This defines the object **inFile**, associates it with the file **primes.txt** in the **JunkData** directory on the **C:** drive, and opens the file. If you're going to read a file, it must already exist, but we both know that things don't always go as planned. What happens if you try to read from a file that you haven't prepared earlier?

As far as this definition is concerned, the answer is absolutely nothing: we just have a file stream object that won't work. To find out if everything is as it should be, we must test the status of the file, and there are several ways to do this. One possibility is for you to call the **is_open()** member of the **ifstream** object, which returns **true** if the file is open, and **false** if it is not. Another option is to call the **fail()** function inherited in the file stream classes from the **ios** class, which returns **true** if any file error occurred. Alternatively, you can use the **!** operator with the file stream object. This operator is overloaded in the **ios** class to check the stream status indicators that are defined in that class. When applied to the stream object, it returns **true** if the stream is not in a satisfactory state. Using the overloaded **!** operator is equivalent to calling the **fail()** function, and so to make sure our stream object is in a satisfactory condition and ready for use, we could write:

```
if(!inFile)
{
  cout << endl << "Failed to open file " << filename;
  return 1;
}
```

You can test that an output file stream object is available for use in exactly the same way, as the **ofstream** class inherits the overloaded **!** operator too. It also inherits the **fail()** function, and implements the **is_open()** function. We'll look further into stream error states a little later in the chapter.

Reading a file in text mode is just like reading from **cin** — you use the extraction operator in exactly the same way. However, we don't necessarily know how many data values there are in a file, so how do we know when we have reached the end? The **eof()** function that is inherited from **basic_ios** in the **ofstream** class provides a neat solution. It returns **true** when the end of file is reached, so we can just continue to read data until that happens.

Try It Out – Reading a File

We now have enough knowledge about how input file streams work to have a go at reading back the file that we wrote in the previous example. We will just read the file and output the values to the screen. Here's the code:

```
// Program 19.2 Reading the primes file
#include <fstream>
#include <iostream>
#include <iomanip>
using namespace std;

int main()
{
  const char* filename = "C:\\JunkData\\primes.txt"; // Name of the file to read
  ifstream inFile(filename);                         // Create input stream object

  // Make sure the file stream is good
  if(!inFile)
  {
    cout << endl << "Failed to open file " << filename;
    return 1;
  }

  long aprime = 0;
  int count = 0;
  while(!inFile.eof())                               // Continue until EOF is found
  {
    inFile >> aprime;                                // Read a value from the file
    cout << (count++ % 5 == 0 ? "\n" : "") << setw(10) << aprime;
  }
  cout << endl;
```

```
    return 0;
}
```

I get the following output from this example:

2	3	5	7	11
13	17	19	23	29
31	37	41	43	47
53	59	61	67	71
73	79	83	89	97
101	103	107	109	113
127	131	137	139	149
151	157	163	167	173
179	181	191	193	197
199	211	223	227	229
233	239	241	251	257
263	269	271	277	281
283	293	307	311	313
317	331	337	347	349
353	359	367	373	379
383	389	397	401	409
419	421	431	433	439
443	449	457	461	463
467	479	487	491	499
503	509	521	523	541

How It Works

We create the file stream object from the filename with the statements:

```
const char* filename = "C:\\JunkData\\primes.txt";   // Name of the file to read
ifstream inFile(filename);                            // Create input stream object
```

Before we use the file, we need to check that it has been opened successfully:

```
if(!inFile)
{
  cout << endl << "Failed to open file " << filename;
  return 1;
}
```

The **operator!()** function for the object **inFile** that is inherited from the base class, **ios**, will return **true** if the constructor was not able to create the stream object properly and open the file. This will be the case if the file does not exist, for instance. If something has gone wrong, we display an error message and end the program.

Once we're sure the file is open, it's just a question of reading values from the file and outputting them to the standard stream, **cout**:

```
long aprime = 0;
int count = 0;
while(!inFile.eof())                                  // Continue until EOF is found
{
  inFile >> aprime;                                   // Read a value from the file
  cout << (count++ % 5 == 0 ? "\n" : "") << setw(10) << aprime;
}
```

769

The **while** loop continues until the value returned from the **eof()** member of **inFile** is **true**. Within the loop, we read a value from the **inFile** stream into **aprime**, and we output the value to **cout**. The conditional operator outputs a newline character after every five values. After the last value has been read from the file, the **eof()** member will return **true**, because the current file position will be at the end of file.

Setting the File Open Mode

The **file open mode** for an **ifstream** or **ofstream** object determines what you can do with a file. It is determined by a combination of bit mask values that are defined in the **ios_base** class and inherited in the **ios** class as values of type **openmode**. The mask values that can be set are:

Value	Meaning
ios::app	Move to the end of the file before each write (**app**end). This ensures that you can only add to what is already in a file; you cannot overwrite it.
ios::ate	Move to the end of the file when opening it (**at** end). You can move the current position to elsewhere in the file subsequently.
ios::binary	Set binary mode rather than text mode. In binary mode, all characters are unchanged when they are transferred to or from the file.
ios::in	Open the file for reading.
ios::out	Open the file for writing.
ios::trunc	**Trunc**ate the existing file to zero length.

Because these are bit masks, you generate a specification for the open mode by bitwise-ORing combinations of these values. For a file that is to be opened for writing in binary mode, such that data can only be added at the end of the file, you would specify the mode by using the expression **ios::out | ios::app | ios::binary**. You can also open a file for reading *and* writing by specifying both **ios::in** and **ios::out**; for this, you use an object of type **fstream**, as we shall see shortly.

You set the file open mode by specifying it as a second argument to the file stream class constructor. Both the **ifstream** and **ofstream** constructors have a second parameter of type **openmode** that has a default value specified. The default value for the file open mode for an **ifstream** object is **ios::in**, which just opens the file for input. The default for an **ofstream** object is **ios::out | ios::trunc**, which specifies that the file is to be opened for output. If it already exists, its length is set to zero, thus ensuring that any existing contents are overwritten.

Suppose you wanted to specify the file open mode for a file output stream such that you could only append data to the file. You could do this with the following statement:

```
const char* filename = "C:\\JunkData\\primes.txt";
ofstream outFile(filename, ios::out | ios::app);
```

If you explicitly close a file stream by calling the **close()** function for the stream object, you can open the file again with a new open mode by calling the stream object's **open()** function. The **open()** function accepts two arguments, the first being the file name, and the second being the open mode mask. The default values for the second parameter to the **open()** member of a file stream class are the same as for the class constructor. We could close the **outFile** stream and reopen it with a different open mode setting with the following statements:

```
outFile.close();
outFile.open(filename);
```

This reopens the file to overwrite the original contents, as **ios::out | ios::trunc** is the default value for the second parameter.

Try It Out – Specifying the File Open Mode

We could amend the prime numbers example once again, so that it will generate and display the number of primes that you specify, but so that the primes are stored in a file for reuse in the future. That way, the program need only generate primes in excess of those already in the file. Any that are already in the file can be displayed immediately. Here's the code to do that:

```
// Program 19.3 Reading and writing the primes file
#include <fstream>
#include <iostream>
#include <iomanip>
#include <cmath>
#include <string>
using namespace std;

long nextprime(long lastprime, const char* filename);  // Find the prime
                                                        // after lastprime

int main()
{
  const char* filename = "C:\\JunkData\\primes.txt";
  int nprimes = 0;                                      // Number of
                                                        // primes required
  int count = 0;                                        // Count of primes found
  long lastprime = 0;                                   // Last prime found

  // Get number of primes required
  int tries = 0;                                        // Number of input tries
  cout << "How many primes would you like (at least 3)?: ";
  do
  {
    if(tries)
      cout << endl << " You must request at least 3, try again: ";
    cin >> nprimes;

    if(++tries == 5)                                    // Five tries is generous
    {
      cout << endl << " I give up!" << endl;
      return 1;
    }
  } while(nprimes < 3);
```

```
    ifstream inFile;                                   // Create input file
                                                       // stream object
    inFile.open(filename);                             // Open the file as an
                                                       // input stream

  cout << endl;
  if(!inFile.fail())
  {
    do
    {
      inFile >> lastprime;
      cout << (count++ % 5 == 0 ? "\n" : "") << setw(10) << lastprime;
    } while(count < nprimes && !inFile.eof());
    inFile.close();
  }
  inFile.clear();                                      // Clear any errors

  try
  {
    ofstream outFile;
    if(count == 0)
    {
      outFile.open(filename);                          // Open file to create it
      if(!outFile.is_open())
        throw ios::failure(string("Error opening output file ") +
                           string(filename) +
                           string(" in main()"));
      outFile << " 2 3 5";
      outFile.close();
      cout << setw(10) << 2 << setw(10) << 3 << setw(10) << 5;
      lastprime = 5;
      count = 3;
    }

    while(count < nprimes)
    {
      lastprime = nextprime(lastprime, filename);
      outFile.open(filename, ios::out | ios::app);     // Open file to append data
      if(!outFile.is_open())
        throw ios::failure(string("Error opening output file ") +
                           string(filename) +
                           string(" in main()"));
      outFile << " " << lastprime;
      outFile.close();
      cout << (count++ % 5 == 0 ? "\n" : "") << setw(10) << lastprime;
    }
    cout << endl;
    return 0;
  }
  catch(exception& ex)
  {
    cout << endl << typeid(ex).name() << ": " << ex.what();
    return 1;
  }
}
```

This uses the **nextprime()** function, which returns the next prime after the first argument value. The second argument is the name of the file containing the primes found so far. The definition of this function is:

```cpp
// Find the next prime after the argument
long nextprime(long lastprime, const char* filename)
{
  bool isprime = false;                        // Indicator that we have a prime
  long aprime = 0;                             // Stores primes from the file
  ifstream inFile;                             // Local input stream object

  // Find the next prime
  for( ; ; )
  {
    lastprime += 2;                            // Next value for checking
    long limit = static_cast<long>(sqrt(lastprime));

    // Try dividing the candidate by all the primes up to limit
    inFile.open(filename);                     // Open the primes file
    if(!inFile.is_open())
      throw ios::failure(string("Error opening input file ") +
                         string(filename) +
                         string(" in nextprime()"));
    do
    {
      inFile >> aprime;
    } while(aprime <= limit &&
            !inFile.eof() &&
            (isprime = lastprime % aprime > 0));

    inFile.close();
    if(isprime)                                // We got one...
      return lastprime;                        // ...so return it
  }
}
```

This program will output the number of primes that you request, and write them to the file **primes.txt**.

How It Works

The program is now structured a little differently. Since we will keep all the primes in a file, we no longer need to store them in memory. Primes are now found by the **nextprime()** function, but before we explore that, let's look at how the code in **main()** works.

After getting the number of primes required from the user, we open the **primes.txt** file as an input stream with the statements:

```cpp
ifstream inFile;                    // Create input file stream object
inFile.open(filename);              // Open the file as an input stream
```

The **ifstream** object, **inFile**, is created using the default constructor. The object will not be associated with a particular file at this point. To use the stream object to open the **primes.txt** file, we call the **open()** function with the filename as the argument. The function will accept a second argument — the open file mode — but since we did not specify it, the default value of **ios::in** will be used.

Of course, it could be that the file does not yet exist, so we must verify that the file stream is in a good state before we try to read it. We test the file stream object using its **fail()** function:

```
if(!inFile.fail())
{
  do
  {
    inFile >> lastprime;
    cout << (count++ % 5 == 0 ? "\n" : "") << setw(10) << lastprime;
  } while(count < nprimes && !inFile.eof());
  inFile.close();
}
```

We only read the file if **fail()** returns **false**. Within the **if** block, we read up to **nprimes** numbers from the file in the **do-while** loop. We check for end-of-file in the loop condition by calling the **eof()** function for **inFile**. The complement of the **bool** value returned is ANDed with the comparison of **count** and **nprimes**, and so the loop ends either when we have read the required number of primes from the file, or when we reach the end of file.

After the **if** statement, there could be errors set for the file stream object — either because the file does not exist, or because the end of file was reached. These are not reset when you close the file, so because we may want to use the object again, we reset any error flags by calling the **clear()** function for the stream object:

```
inFile.clear();                                       // Clear any errors
```

We will discuss what else you can do with the **clear()** function a little later in the chapter.

The remainder of the code in **main()** comes within a **try** block, because we will throw exceptions if we encounter problems with opening files. The **catch** block will catch any exception type that has **exception** as a base, and gives us a convenient way to handle errors of the same type in the same place.

At this point, we can use the value of **count** as an indicator of whether any primes were read from the file. If not, then we can write the file from scratch with the first three primes. This is done by the following code:

```
ofstream outFile;
if(count == 0)
{
  outFile.open(filename);                               // Open file to create it
  if(!outFile.is_open())
    throw ios::failure(string("Error opening output file ") +
                       string(filename) +
                       string(" in main()"));
  outFile << " 2 3 5";
  outFile.close();
  cout << setw(10) << 2 << setw(10) << 3 << setw(10) << 5;
```

```
            lastprime = 5;
            count = 3;
    }
```

We create an output file stream object named **outFile**, and then call its **open()** function to open the **primes.txt** file. This will open the file with the open mode specified as **ios::out | ios::trunc**, so any previous contents of the file will be erased and we will write the file from the beginning. In the code, we call the **is_open()** function member of **outFile** in an **if** statement to verify that the file is open and ready to be written. If nothing went wrong, we write the first three primes to the file and close it. We then write the same three primes to **cout**, and set the **lastprime** value and the count of the number of primes appropriately. If we cannot open the file to write it for some reason, we throw an exception of type **ios::failure**. This exception class is actually defined in the **ios_base** class, and is therefore inherited in **ios** and all the stream classes. Of course, being a standard exception class, it has the **exception** class as a base. The constructor accepts an argument of type **string**, and whatever you pass to the constructor will be returned by the **what()** member function of the object, so you can use that to identify the exception in a **catch** block, as we do in **main()**.

At this point, we may need to calculate more primes, if the number of primes from the file is lower than the number requested. This is taken care of in the **while** loop that continues until **count** is equal to **nprimes**:

```
        while(count < nprimes)
        {
          lastprime = nextprime(lastprime, filename);
          outFile.open(filename, ios::out | ios::app);    // Open file to append data
          if(!outFile.is_open())
            throw ios::failure(string("Error opening output file ") +
                               string(filename) +
                               string(" in main()"));
          outFile << " " << lastprime;
          outFile.close();
          cout << (count++ % 5 == 0 ? "\n" : "") << setw(10) << lastprime;
        }
```

The **nextprime()** function calculates the next prime number after the value of the first argument. The second argument specifies the name of the file from which to retrieve existing primes for use in the calculation. The file is then opened for output, but this time the file open mode determines that whatever we write to the file will always be appended to the end. Again, if we have a problem opening the file, we throw an exception.

After writing the prime returned from **nextprime()**, we close the file. This is necessary because on the next iteration, **nextprime()** will need to open the file again to read it. On each iteration, the prime number found is also written to **cout**. The loop continues until **nprimes** numbers have been displayed, and after the loop the file will contain at least the same set of primes as it contained at the start, since any new primes will just have been added to it.

Finding a new prime in the **nextprime()** function involves using the primes from the file as divisors, so a local **ifstream** object is created. The process for finding the next prime is in the indefinite **for** loop. The first value to be checked is obtained by incrementing **lastprime** by two:

```
        lastprime += 2;                                    // Next value for checking
```

The value passed to the function as **lastprime** will be the last prime number found, so we don't need to check that it is odd. To check whether the value is a prime number, we must try dividing by all the primes up to the square root of the value, so we calculate this as the integer value **limit** with the statement:

```
long limit = static_cast<long>(sqrt(lastprime));
```

This uses the standard library **sqrt()** function that's declared in the **cmath** header file. The argument will automatically be converted to **double**, and we cast the **double** result from the **sqrt()** function back to **long**.

We open the file stream and verify that the file was opened successfully with the statements:

```
inFile.open(filename);                              // Open the primes file
if(!inFile.is_open())
    throw ios::failure(string("Error opening input file ") +
                        string(filename) +
                        string(" in nextprime()"));
```

If opening the file fails, we throw the same type of exception that we threw in **main()** for a file problem. Here we have a slightly different argument to the constructor, so we will be able to identify where the problem occurred in the program. The exception will be caught by the **catch** block in **main()**, so all file problems will be handled in the same place.

After opening the input file stream, the candidate prime is checked in the **do-while** loop:

```
do
{
  inFile >> aprime;
} while(aprime <= limit &&
            !inFile.eof() &&
            (isprime = lastprime % aprime > 0));
```

A prime is read from the file within the loop, but all the rest of the work is done in the loop condition. This has three logical expressions ANDed together, so if any of the three is false, the loop ends.

The first condition is that the divisor is less than **limit**, the square root of the candidate value. If it isn't, we have checked all divisors up to this value without finding an exact division, so we must have a prime. The second condition is that we have not reached end of file, and this should never occur. If it does, there is a serious defect in the program somewhere, or with the file. The third condition checks the remainder after the division. If it is zero, we have an exact division, so **lastprime** is not prime and we need to try another candidate.

When the loop ends, we close the file so that we can open it again at the beginning of the next iteration:

```
inFile.close();
```

Whether or not we have found a prime is indicated by **isprime**, set in the loop condition. If it's **true**, we have a prime and we can return the value. If not, we just go round the **for** loop again.

```
if(isprime)                                         // We got one...
   return lastprime;                                // ...so return it
```

Our program works, but this process of opening and closing the file every time we go round the loop is very inefficient. It would be much better if we could just read the file from the beginning each time, so let's see how we could do that.

Managing the Current Stream Position

You control the current stream position using functions defined in the **istream** and **ostream** classes, but they don't apply to the standard streams because the standard streams don't relate to physical devices for which a stream position would be meaningful. They *do* apply, however, to objects of the file stream classes that are associated with a physical file. The functions in **istream** and **ostream** are inherited in **ifstream** and **ofstream** respectively, and both sets of functions will be inherited by the **fstream** class via **iostream**.

Basically, there are two things that you can do in relation to the stream position: you can obtain and record the current position in the stream, and you can change the current position. The current position is returned by the **tellg()** function for input stream objects, and by the **tellp()** function for output stream objects. The 'g' in **tellg()** is for 'get' and the 'p' in **tellp()** is for 'put', so this indicates whether you get data from the stream the function relates to, or put data to it. Both functions return a value of type **pos_type**, which represents an absolute position in a stream.

For example, you might obtain the current position in an input file stream object called **inFile** with the following statement:

```
pos_type here = inFile.tellg();                    // Record current file position
```

You can define a new position in a stream by passing a position that you earlier recorded using **tellg()** or **tellp()** to the **seekg()** member function for an input stream object, or to the **seekp()** member function for an output stream object. You just call the function corresponding to the stream type with a previously recorded stream position. For example, you could reset the stream position for **inFile** back to **here** with the statement:

```
inFile.seekg(here);                                // Set current position to here
```

The **pos_type** value, **here**, is an integral value that corresponds to a character index position in the stream, where the first character is at index position 0. It is therefore possible to use numerical values to move to specific positions in a stream. This can be hazardous in text mode because the number of bytes stored in the stream may be different from the number of characters written. However, seeking to position 0 is always going to move to the beginning of the stream, so we could have used that in the **nextprime()** function:

```
long nextprime(long lastprime, const char* filename)
{
  bool isprime = false;                            // Indicator that we have a prime
  long aprime = 0;                                 // Stores primes from the file
  ifstream inFile(filename);                       // Local input stream object

  if(!inFile.is_open())
    throw ios::failure(string("Error opening input file ") +
                       string(filename) +
                       string(" in nextprime()"));
```

```
// Find the next prime
for( ; ; )
{
  lastprime += 2;                                        // Next value for checking
  long limit = static_cast<long>(sqrt(lastprime));

  // Try dividing the candidate by all the primes up to limit
  do
  {
    inFile >> aprime;
  } while(aprime <= limit &&
          !inFile.eof() &&
          (isprime = lastprime % aprime > 0));

  if(isprime)                                            // We got one...
  {
    inFile.close();                                      // ...so close the file...
    return lastprime;                                    // ...and return the prime
  }
  inFile.seekg(0);                                       // Move to beginning of
                                                         // file
}
}
```

With this version of the function, we open the file when we create the **ifstream** object, and simply reset the file position to the first character in the file at the end of the **for** loop.

As an alternative to moving to a new position in a stream that you specify with a positive value of type **pos_type**, you can also move by using an offset value relative to one of three specific positions in a stream. The offset can be positive or negative. You can define a new position relative to the first character in the stream (the offset must be positive), relative to the last character in the stream (the offset must be negative), or relative to the current position. In the latter case, the offset can be either positive or negative, as long as you're not at one of the ends.

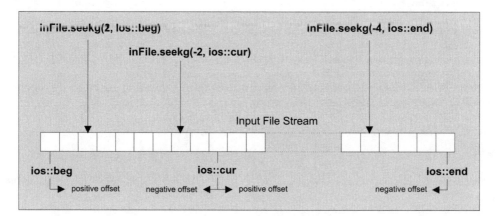

To set a relative position, you use versions of **seekg()** or **seekp()** that accept two arguments. The first argument is the offset, which is an integral value of type **off_type**, and the second argument must be one of the following values that are defined in the **ios** class:

Value	Description
ios::beg	Offset is relative to the first character in the file.
ios::cur	Offset is relative to the current file position.
ios::end	Offset is relative to the last character in the file.

As I explained, the offset value must be positive relative to **ios::beg** and negative relative to **ios::end**. You can go in either direction relative to **ios::cur** by using positive or negative values for the offset. You can specify the offset as an explicit integer constant, or you could provide the value of the offset as an expression that evaluates to an integer.

The **seekg()** functions return a reference to the file stream object, so you can combine the seek operation with an input operation by using an extraction operator. For example:

```
inFile.seekg(10, ios::beg) >> value;
```

This statement will move the file position to an offset of 10 characters from the beginning of the file, and read from that point into **value**.

Similarly, you can use the **seekp()** function to move to a position where you want to start the next *output* operation, and the function arguments are exactly the same as for **seekg()**. The next write to the stream will overwrite characters, starting with the character at the new position.

Relative seek operations can be a dubious operation in text mode, particularly when you're writing characters to the stream. This is because the number of characters that are actually stored may be different from the number of characters that you wrote.

We are not done with the operations we have discussed here, and we'll come back to them later in this chapter, when we discuss random read/write operations on a stream.

Unformatted Stream Operations

In addition to the insertion and extraction operators for formatted stream input-output, there are member functions in the stream classes for transferring character-based data to or from a stream without any formatting of the data. The extraction operator treats whitespace characters as delimiters, but otherwise ignores them. In general, the unformatted stream input functions do not skip whitespace characters — they are read and stored just like any others.

An important use of some of the unformatted input-output functions is reading and writing file streams in binary mode, as we will see later. While these functions only specifically provide a way to write character-based data, you can still use some of them to read and write binary numeric data. First of all, let's look at what the unformatted input functions can do for us.

Unformatted Stream Input

There is a wealth of unformatted input functions defined in the **istream** class, and they're inherited in the **ifstream**, **iostream** and **fstream** classes. For a start, there are four varieties of the member function **get()**, the first two of which read a single character from a stream:

▶ **int_type get();**
This version reads a single character from the stream and returns it as type **int_type**. The type **int_type** is implementation defined, and will be an integral type capable of storing any character. It will usually correspond to type **int**. If the end of file is reached, the function returns the character **EOF**, which is defined in the **iostream** header file. If a character cannot be read from the stream, for whatever reason, the error flag **ios::failbit** will be set. (We'll discuss this and other error flags later in the chapter, when we discuss I/O errors.)

▶ **istream& get(char& ch);**
This function also reads a single character from the stream, but this time the character read is stored in **ch**. The function returns a reference to the stream object, so you can combine calling this function with other member function calls. As with the previous function, if a character cannot be read from the stream, the **failbit** error flag will be set, and **EOF** will be stored in **ch**.

There is another member function, called **peek()**, which is the equivalent of the first **get()** function above in that it reads the next character from the stream, but the character is left *in* the stream, so you can read it again. **peek()** returns a character read from a stream as a value of type **int_type**, as described for the **get()** function.

You can write the last character read from the stream back to the stream using the member function **unget()**. This function returns a reference to the **istream** object for which it was called. It is typically used in combination with one of the **get()** functions that reads a single character, when you are parsing input from a stream. For example, you might need a function to skip non-digits in a file input stream in order to position the stream at the next digit:

```
void skipnondigits(ifstream& in)
{
  int_type ch = 0;
  while((ch = in.get()) != EOF)     // Read while not EOF
    if(isdigit(ch))                 // If a digit is read...
    {
      in.unget();                   // ...put back the digit...
      return;                       // ...and return
    }
}
```

The **putback()** member function has a similar effect to **unget()**, but in this case you specify the character to put back in the stream as an argument. In the example above, instead of the statement calling **unget()**, we could have written:

```
    in.putback(ch);                 // ...put back the digit...
```

The character specified as the argument to **putback()** must be the same as the last character read, otherwise the result is undefined. Both functions return a reference to the stream.

The other two **get()** functions read a sequence of characters as a null-terminated string:

> **istream& get(char* pArray, streamsize n);**
> This function reads up to **n**-1 characters from the stream and stores them in the array **pArray**, adding a null terminator at the end to make **n** characters in total. Characters are read until a newline character is read, end of file is reached, or **n**-1 characters have been read and stored. If a newline character is reached, it is not stored in the array, but a null byte is always appended at the end of the sequence of characters read. The effect of this function is to read a whole line of text without storing the **'\n'** character marking the end of the line, but terminating the string stored with a null character. It also leaves the **'\n'** character as the next character in the stream to be read. Since a total of **n** characters may be stored in the array, the array pointed to by **pArray** should have at least **n** elements. The **ios::failbit** is set if no characters are stored. The type **streamsize** for the second parameter is a signed integral type that is implementation defined, usually as **long**.

> **istream& get(char* pArray, streamsize n, char delim);**
> This works in the same way as the previous function, except that you can specify a delimiter, **delim**, that will be used in place of newline to end the input process. If the delimiter is found, it is not stored in the array, and it is left in the stream.

In addition, there are two **getline()** function members that are almost equivalent to the two **get()** functions that read a line of text:

```
istream& getline(char* pArray, streamsize n);
istream& getline(char* pArray, streamsize n, char delim);
```

The difference between **getline()** and the corresponding **get()** function is that **getline()** removes the delimiter from the input stream, so the next character to be read is the character following the delimiter.

When you use one of these unformatted input functions, you can determine the number of characters actually read from the stream by calling the member function **gcount()**. This will return the count of characters read by the last unformatted input operation as a value of type **streamsize**.

It's also possible to read a specified number of characters from a stream, assuming they are available, with the **read()** member function:

```
istream& read(char* pArray, streamsize n);
```

This function reads **n** characters of any kind into **pArray**, including newlines and null characters. If the end of the file is reached before **n** characters have been read, **ios::failbit** is set in the input object.

You would typically use the **read()** function when you expect that **n** characters *are* available in the stream. There is another member function that you might use when this is not the case. The **readsome()** function operates similarly to **read()**, but returns the count of the number of characters read:

```
streamsize readsome(char* pstr, streamsize n);
```

781

If fewer than **n** characters are available in the stream, the function sets the flag **ios::eofbit**.

You can skip over a number of characters in an input stream with the function:

```
istream& ignore(streamsize n, int_type delim);
```

Up to **n** characters are read from the stream and discarded. Reading a **delim** character or reading **n** characters ends the process. There are default values for the parameters **n** and **delim** of 1 and **EOF** respectively. Thus, you can skip a single character with the statement:

```
inFile.ignore();            // Skip one character
```

To skip 20 characters, you would write:

```
inFile.ignore(20);          // Skip 20 characters up to the end of the file
```

Reading the end of file will stop the process in this case, but you could skip 20 characters in the current line with the statement:

```
inFile.ignore(20, '\n');   // Skip 20 characters up to the end of the current line
```

Unformatted Stream Output

In stark contrast to the plethora of input functions, for unformatted output to a stream you have just two functions available: **put()** and **write()**. The **put()** function takes the form:

```
ostream& put(char ch);
```

This writes the single character, **ch**, to the stream, and returns a reference to the stream object. To write a sequence of characters to a stream, you use the **write()** function, which has this form:

```
ostream& write(const char* pArray, streamsize n);
```

This writes **n** characters to the stream from the array, **pArray**. Any kind of characters can be written, including null characters.

Generally, output to a steam will be buffered, and on occasion you will want the contents of the stream buffer written to the stream regardless of whether the buffer is full. In such cases, you call the **flush()** member of **ostream**. This function will write the contents of the stream buffer to the stream and return a reference to the stream object.

Errors in Stream Input/Output

All the stream classes store the state of the stream in three flags that record different kinds of errors for a stream. These flags are defined as bit masks of type **iostate** in the base class **ios**. The meanings of these flags are:

Flag	Meaning
`ios::badbit`	Set when a stream is in a state where it cannot be used further — if an I/O error occurred, for example. This is not recoverable.
`ios::eofbit`	Set when end of file is reached.
`ios::failbit`	Set if an input operation did not read the characters expected, or an output operation failed to write characters successfully. This is typically due to a conversion or formatting error. Any subsequent operations will fail while the bit is set, but the situation may be recoverable.

Thus, if **EOF** is read in a stream, the stream state will be `ios::eofbit`. If a serious error occurred while reading from a stream and no characters could be read from it, both the **badbit** and **failbit** flags would be set, so the stream state would be the result of `ios::badbit | ios::failbit`.

You can test the state of a stream by using a stream object in an **if** statement or a loop condition. The stream object by itself in these contexts calls the overloaded **void*()** operator. For example:

```
while(inFile)
{
  // Read from inFile...
}
```

We haven't discussed overloading **operator void*()** previously because it's rather specialized. The operator function does not have a return type specified because it is implicit — as **void***, of course. The **operator void*()** function for a stream object returns a pointer that is intended to be used as a Boolean test of the state of that object.

Because the object is used as the **if** test expression, the **operator void*()** member of **inFile** will be called automatically. This returns null if either **failbit** or **badbit** is set, and non-null otherwise. Note that the non-null pointer that's returned is not intended to be de-referenced. You can use this kind of loop to read to the end of a file, because when the end of file is reached, the read operation will set **failbit**.

As we discussed earlier, you can also use the overloaded **!** operator to test the state of the stream, as it returns **true** if either **badbit** or **failbit** is set.

The stream classes inherit function members that you can use to test their flags individually — they each return a value of type **bool**:

Function	Action
`bad()`	Returns **true** if **badbit** is set in the stream object.
`eof()`	Returns **true** if **eofbit** is set in the stream object.
`fail()`	Returns **true** if **failbit** or **badbit** is set in the stream object.
`good()`	Returns **true** if none of the bits is set in the stream object.

Once a flag is set, it remains set unless you reset it. You will sometimes want to reset the flags — when you reach the end of a file, for example — as a means of terminating reading from a file stream that you may subsequently want to read again. Calling the **clear()** function member for an object resets all three flags. In fact, **clear()** accepts an argument of type **iostate** that corresponds to all three flags bitwise ORed together, but it has a default of 0. (Actually, the default is **ios::goodbit**, which is defined as 0.) So, once you have read end-of-file for an input stream, **inFile**, you can reset the stream state with the statement:

```
inFile.clear();
```

The **clear()** function has a return type of **void**.

I/O Errors and Exceptions

When errors occur in stream input and output operations, exceptions may be thrown. The exceptions for stream errors are of type **ios::failure**; as we discussed earlier, this is a nested class of **ios** inherited from **ios_base**. A mask that is a member of a stream object determines whether an exception will be thrown when a particular stream state flag is set. You can set this mask by passing a mask to the **exceptions()** member of the stream object, with bits set to specify which flags you want to throw exceptions. For example, if you would like to have exceptions thrown when *any* of the flag bits is set for a stream called **inFile**, you could enable this with the following statement:

```
inFile.exceptions(ios::badbit | ios::eofbit | ios::failbit);
```

Now if anything goes wrong at all, even when the end of a file is reached, an exception of type **ios::failure** will be thrown.

Generally, it's better to test the error flags in one of the ways we have discussed, rather than to use exceptions for handling I/O errors, at least as far as the **eofbit** and **failbit** flags are concerned. Most of the time, you will be involved in dealing with **failbit** and **eofbit** flags, since these are a part of the normal process of handling stream input and output. The default position in most development environments is that exceptions are *not* thrown for stream errors. You can check whether exceptions will be thrown by calling a version of **exceptions()** with no arguments that returns a value of type **iostate**. The value returned reflects which error flags will result in an exception being thrown, so you can test whether a given flag being set will throw exceptions as follows:

```
iostate willthrow = inFile.exceptions();
if(willthrow & ios::badbit)
  cout << "Setting badbit will throw an exception";
```

The result of ANDing **ios::badbit** with **willthrow** will be 0 unless **ios::badbit** is set to 1 in **willthrow**.

Using Binary Mode Stream Operations

There are situations where text mode is not appropriate or convenient, and it can sometimes cause you difficulties. The transformation of newline characters into two characters on some systems and not others makes relative seek operations unreliable for programs that are to run in both environments. By using **binary mode**, you avoid these complications and make your stream operations much simpler. We have already seen how to open a stream in binary mode: you just need to specify the open mode flags appropriately. We could try this in an example.

Try It Out – Copying Files in Binary Mode

We can copy any file using the **get()** and **put()** functions that read and write a single character:

```cpp
// Program 19.4 Copying files
#include <iostream>              // For standard streams
#include <fstream>               // For file streams
#include <string>                // For strings
#include <stdexcept>             // For standard
exceptions

using namespace std;

int main(int argc, char* argv[])
{
  try
  {
    // Verify correct number of arguments
    if(argc != 3)
      throw invalid_argument("Input and output file names required.");

    const string source = argv[1];
    const string target = argv[2];

    // Check for output file identical to input file
    if(source == target)
      throw invalid_argument(string("Cannot copy ") +
                             source +
                             string(" to itself."));

    ifstream in(source.c_str(), ios::in | ios::binary);// Create input file stream
    if(!in)                                            // Stream object OK?
      throw ios::failure(string("Input file ") +
                         string(source) +
                         string(" not found"));

    // Check if output file exists
    ifstream temp(target.c_str(), ios::in | ios::binary); // Try to create as
                                                          // input file
    char ch = 0;                            // Stores a character
    if(temp)                                // If the file stream object is ok
    {                                       //   then the output file exists
      temp.close();                         // Close the stream
      cout << endl
           << target << " exists, do you want to overwrite it? (y or n): ";
      ch = cin.get();
      if(toupper(ch) != 'Y')
        return 0;
    }
```

```
    // Create output file stream
    ofstream out(target.c_str(), ios::out | ios::binary | ios::trunc);

    // Copy the file
    while(in.get(ch))
      out.put(ch);

    if(in.eof())
      cout << endl << source << " copied to " << target << " successfully.";
    else
      cout << endl << "Error copying file";
    return 0;
  }
  catch(exception& ex)
  {
    cout << endl << typeid(ex).name() << ": " << ex.what();
    return 1;
  }
}
```

This program requires the name of the input file and the name of the output file as command line arguments. I applied it to copying the executable module for this program, so it produced the output:

```
FileCopy.exe copied to FullCopy.exe successfully.
```

How It Works

The array **argv** will have **argc** elements, the first of which will contain the program name. Thus, **argv** should have three elements, accommodating the program name plus the two filenames, so we first verify that to be the case with the statements:

```
if(argc != 3)
  throw invalid_argument("Input and output file names required.");

const string source = argv[1];
const string target = argv[2];
```

If there are no command line arguments, we throw a standard exception of type **invalid_argument** that will be caught by the **catch** block at the end of **main()**. Having checked the arguments, we then assign them to a pair of **string** objects that will make for easier manipulation and recognition in the remainder of the code.

We don't want to be copying a file to itself, so we check that the files are not the same by comparing them. If they are the same, we don't continue — we throw another exception:

```
// Check for output file identical to input file
if(source == target)
  throw invalid_argument(string("Cannot copy ") +
                         source +
                         string(" to itself."));
```

Once we're past the validity checks on the command line arguments, we're ready to create the file stream object corresponding to the input file:

```
ifstream in(source.c_str(), ios::in | ios::binary); // Create input file stream
```

786

This uses the **string::c_str()** function, which returns the null-terminated string contained within the **source** object. The file is opened as a binary input file, as specified by the second constructor argument. We must verify that the stream object was created properly before we try to use it:

```
if(!in)                                         // Stream object OK?
   throw ios::failure(string("Input file ") +
                      source +
                      string(" not found"));
```

This uses the overloaded **!** operator for the stream object. The **istream** constructor will set **failbit** if the file cannot be found and opened.

Next, we need to see whether the output file exists. If so, we should verify that it is to be overwritten:

```
ifstream temp(target.c_str(), ios::in | ios::binary); // Try to create as
                                                      // input file
char ch = 0;                                // Stores a character
if(temp)                                    // If the file stream object is ok
{                                           //   then the output file exists
  temp.close();                             // Close the stream
  cout << endl
       << target << " exists, do you want to overwrite it? (y or n): ";
  ch = cin.get();
  if(toupper(ch) != 'Y')
    return 0;
}
```

When you create an **ifstream** object for a file, the file must exist. If the file cannot be found and opened, the constructor will set **failbit**, so the **operator void*()** member that is called implicitly by using the stream object in the **if** condition will return null. Thus, the code in the **if** block will only be executed if the file exists. Once we've established that, we can close the file, since we have no intention of reading it. We just offer the option of not overwriting it.

We create the output file stream object next:

```
// Create output file stream
ofstream out(target.c_str(), ios::out | ios::binary | ios::trunc);
```

Now we can proceed with the copy, which is done in a very simple loop:

```
while(in.get(ch))
  out.put(ch);
```

In the loop condition, we read a character from **in** using the **get()** function. This returns **EOF** when the end of file is reached, which will cause the loop to end. On each iteration, the character that was stored in **ch** is written to the output file stream, **out**.

Finally, we verify that we did reach the end of the file, so that we're sure the entire file was copied properly:

```
if(in.eof())
   cout << endl << source << " copied to " << target << " successfully.";
```

```
    else
        cout << endl << "Error copying file";
```

The **eof()** function returns **true** if **eofbit** is set in the file stream object, **in**.

Writing Numeric Data in Binary Form

When using binary mode, it is often more convenient to use unformatted stream input-output operations than the insertion and extraction operators. This provides the possibility of writing numerical values as binary values, with no conversion to a text string representation of a number. Doing this neatly avoids the errors that may be introduced when converting binary floating point values to decimal representation, and takes up less space in the file. Furthermore, we don't need to write whitespace to a file to separate one value from the next; this will also make the file shorter, and therefore faster to read. As long as we know what kind of data was written, we can read back exactly what we wrote.

Beware, however, that these benefits only apply if you are reading the data on the same sort of computer that wrote it. There is a whole range of potential disparities between binary data produced by different machines. The representation of characters can vary — IBM mainframes use EBCDIC, for example, whereas PCs use ASCII. Equally, there can be differences in the representations of binary floating point values, and even binary integers can be stored differently on different machine architectures.

There are no stream functions in the standard library that will write numerical data values to a file in binary, or read them back, but we can write some of our own. We can use the **read()** and **write()** functions to implement a set of functions that will write any of the numerical types as binary data. The best way to see how this might work is, as ever, to consider an example.

Let's suppose we want to write values of type **double** to a file. We could implement our own **write()** function to do this as follows:

```
void write(ostream& out, double value)
{
  out.write(reinterpret_cast<char*>(&value), sizeof(double));
}
```

To write a floating point value to a file, we just want to write the succession of bytes that the value occupies in memory. This is illustrated below, assuming that type **double** occupies 8 bytes:

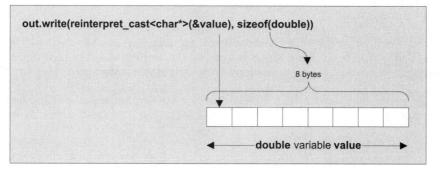

We force the conversion of the address of the first byte of the **double** value to **char***, and then pass that to the **write()** member function of the stream object, **out**. The **reinterpret_cast<>()** operator just alters the *interpretation* of the pointer, without converting the value that it points to in any way. The **sizeof()** operator provides the number of bytes to be written for type **double**, so we pass that value to the **write()** member of the stream object as the count of the number of bytes to be written.

Clearly, any of the numeric types are going to work in exactly the same way, so we could consider defining a template that will generate these functions when required. However, such a template would also create functions for class types, creating the illusion that they would work with any class object. Unfortunately, this is not the case. Any class object that contained a pointer data member would not be valid when it was read back from a file, because the address in the pointer member would almost certainly be invalid. You should never violate encapsulation, and you should *only* use the copying capabilities provided by a class. Thus, you must write an overloaded function for each numeric type that you want to support, and avoid the potential misuse that a function template would present.

Returning to our theme, a function to read a binary value back from the file is also easily implemented:

```
void read(istream& in, double& value)
{
  in.read(reinterpret_cast<char*>(&value), sizeof(double));
}
```

This reads the number of bytes that a **double** variable occupies into the memory locations occupied by the **double** variable, **value**. The second argument here must be a reference, because we are going to store the data read from the file at this location.

Notice that we used a reference to an **istream** object as the first parameter type here, rather than a reference to an **ifstream** object. Similarly, with the **write()** function we used **ostream&** as the type for the stream parameter. Although we'll only want to use these functions with file streams, making the parameters references to file streams has a distinct disadvantage. The **fstream** class is derived from **iostream**, and so has **istream** and **ostream** as indirect base classes. It is not derived from **ifstream** or **ofstream** at all. By using **istream&** and **ostream&** as the parameter types, we ensure that both functions will work with **fstream** as well as **ifstream** in the case of **read()**, or **ofstream** in the case of **write()**.

Implementing functions to read and write *arrays* of values of the basic types is also not difficult, although you would need to pass a length as an argument to each function, as you cannot deduce the length of an array passed to a function.

We can see some versions of the functions we have just discussed in action with an alternative version of Program 19.3 that works with binary files.

Try It Out – Writing Binary Numeric Data to a File

The only changes we need to make to the original program will be to create the file stream objects as binary streams, and to replace the formatted I/O operations with our own read and write functions:

```cpp
// Program 19.5 Reading and writing the primes file as binary
#include <fstream>
#include <iostream>
#include <iomanip>
#include <cmath>
#include <string>
using namespace std;

long nextprime(long lastprime, const char* filename);    // Find the prime after
                                                          // lastprime
void write(ostream& out, long value);                    // Write binary long value
void read(istream& in, long& value);                     // Read binary long value

int main()
{
  const char* filename = "C:\\JunkData\\primes.bin";
  int nprimes = 0;                               // Number of primes required
  int count = 0;                                 // Count of primes found
  long lastprime = 0;                            // Last prime found

  // Get number of primes required
  int tries = 0;                                 // Number of input tries
  cout << "How many primes would you like (at least 3)?: ";
  do
  {
    if(tries)
      cout << endl << " You must request at least 3, try again: ";
    cin >> nprimes;

    if(++tries == 5)                             // Five tries is generous
    {
      cout << endl << " I give up!" << endl;
      return 1;
    }
  } while(nprimes < 3);

  ifstream inFile;                               // Create input file stream object
  inFile.open(filename, ios::in | ios::binary);  // Open the file as an input
                                                 // stream

  cout << endl;
  if(!inFile.fail())
  {
    do
    {
      read(inFile, lastprime);
      cout << (count++ % 5 == 0 ? "\n" : "") << setw(10) << lastprime;
    } while(count < nprimes && !inFile.eof());
    inFile.close();
  }
  inFile.clear();                                // Clear any errors

  try
  {
    ofstream outFile;
```

```
    if(count == 0)
    {
      // Open file to create it
      outFile.open(filename, ios::out | ios::binary | ios::app);
      if(!outFile.is_open())
        throw ios::failure(string("Error opening output file ") +
                           string(filename) +
                           string(" in main()"));
      write(outFile, 2);                              // Write 2 as binary long
      write(outFile, 3);                              // Write 3 as binary long
      write(outFile, 5);                              // Write 5 as binary long
      outFile.close();
      cout << setw(10) << 2 << setw(10) << 3 << setw(10) << 5;
      lastprime = 5;
      count = 3;
    }

    while(count < nprimes)
    {
      lastprime = nextprime(lastprime, filename);

      // Open file to append data
      outFile.open(filename, ios::out | ios::binary | ios::app);
      if(!outFile.is_open())
        throw ios::failure(string("Error opening output file ") +
                           string(filename) +
                           string(" in main()"));
      write(outFile, lastprime);                      // Write prime as binary
      outFile.close();
      cout << (count++ % 5 == 0 ? "\n" : "") << setw(10) << lastprime;
    }
    cout << endl;
    return 0;
  }
  catch(exception& ex)
  {
    cout << endl << typeid(ex).name() << ": " << ex.what() << endl;
    return 1;
  }
}
```

We need very few changes to the definition of the **nextprime()** function:

```
long nextprime(long lastprime, const char* filename)
{
  bool isprime = false;                 // Indicator that we have a prime
  long aprime = 0;                      // Stores primes from the file
  ifstream inFile;                      // Local input stream object

  // Find the next prime
  for( ; ; )
  {
    lastprime += 2;                                 // Next value for checking
    long limit = static_cast<long>(sqrt(lastprime));
```

```
      // Try dividing the candidate by all the primes up to limit
      inFile.open(filename, ios::in | ios::binary);          // Open the primes file
      if(!inFile.is_open())
        throw ios::failure(string("Error opening input file ") +
                           string(filename) +
                           string(" in nextprime()"));

      do
      {
        read(inFile, aprime);                                // Read prime as binary
      } while(aprime <= limit &&
              !inFile.eof() &&
              (isprime = lastprime % aprime > 0));

      inFile.close();
      if(isprime)                                       // We got one...
        return lastprime;                               // ...so return it
    }
  }
```

Of course, we must add definitions for the **read()** and **write()** functions to the source file:

```
// Read a long value from a file as binary
void read(istream& in, long& value)
{
  in.read(reinterpret_cast<char*>(&value), sizeof(value));
}

// Write a long value to a file as binary
void write(ostream& out, long value)
{
  out.write(reinterpret_cast<char*>(&value), sizeof(value));
}
```

The program will output as many primes as you specify when you run it.

How It Works

We will only look at the specifics of the file operations, as we've seen the other code before. First, we have the prototypes for the binary **read()** and **write()** functions:

```
void write(ostream& out, long value);          // Write binary long value
void read(istream& in, long& value);           // Read binary long value
```

The filename has a different extension to distinguish it from the **primes.txt** file that we created earlier:

```
const char* filename = "C:\\JunkData\\primes.bin";
```

Were you to read the text file as binary, it would create a significant amount of confusion in the program!

When we open the input file, we specify the open mode as binary:

```
inFile.open(filename, ios::in | ios::binary);     // Open the file as an input
                                                  // stream
```

The second argument to the constructor is now explicit, rather than assuming the default value of an input file in text mode. If the file doesn't already exist, we open it as a binary output file to create it:

```
outFile.open(filename, ios::out | ios::binary | ios::app);
```

We then write the first three primes to the new file as binary values:

```
write(outFile, 2);                          // Write 2 as binary long
write(outFile, 3);                          // Write 3 as binary long
write(outFile, 5);                          // Write 5 as binary long
```

When we're adding primes to the file, we also open it as a binary output file:

```
// Open file to append data
outFile.open(filename, ios::out | ios::binary | ios::app);
```

Of course, writing to the file now uses our own **write()** function that will write the bytes:

```
write(outFile, lastprime);                  // Write prime as binary
```

Within the **nextprime()** function definition, the file is opened as a binary input file, and we use our own version of **read()** to read each of the prime values. If type **long** occupies 4 bytes, then each value will only occupy four character positions (bytes) in the file, regardless of the actual value, and there are no spaces between one value and the next. Thus, any value greater than 999 will occupy less file space in our new regime, and if we were writing floating point values to the file, the reduction in file space may be even greater. Binary files are in general more compact than text files, and faster to read. There is no additional processing overhead due to formatting, either.

Read/Write Operations on a Stream

You can open a stream for both input and output. For general streams, the **iostream** class implements the capability, but you will usually be using **fstream** class objects, since they specifically support input-output with files. As we saw early on in this chapter, **fstream** inherits from **iostream**, which in turn inherits from **istream** and **ostream**, so all the input and output functions we have discussed so far are available for an **fstream** object.

You can declare an **fstream** object with a file name as argument, just like an **ifstream** or **ofstream** object. For example:

```
const char* filename = "C:\\Junk Data\\primes.txt";
fstream bothways(filename);
```

The default open mode is **ios::in | ios::out**, so like the other streams it will be in text mode by default. If you want to specify it as a binary stream, just use the second parameter, exactly as we have done before. For example:

```
fstream bothways(filename, ios::in | ios::out | ios::binary);
```

This opens the file for both input and output operations in binary mode. If the file cannot be opened for any reason, **ios::failbit** will be set. Note that you cannot use **ios::app** with **fstream** objects, but you can use **ios::trunc**, which will discard any previous file contents. In fact, you can't use **ios::app** in combination with **ios::in** at all, so you can't use it for **ifstream** objects either. This is not unreasonable, since **ios::app** implies that you'll *write* at the end of the file, which is not particularly meaningful for a read operation.

The default constructor creates a stream object with no associated file. You can then open a particular physical file by using the **open()** member of the **fstream** object. For example:

```
fstream inout;
inout.open(filename, ios::in | ios::out | ios::binary | ios::trunc);
```

The first statement creates an **fstream** object without associating it with a particular file. The second statement will open the file specified by **filename** for both input and output in binary mode, and discard any existing file contents. If you omit the second argument specifying the open file mode, the default is the same as for the constructor: **ios::in | ios::out**.

If you are both writing and reading a file, then almost by definition you will want to access the file at random positions within it, so let's look at how you do that.

Random Access to a Stream

Although we'll be exploring random access to a file in the context of **fstream**, you can apply the same techniques to reading an **ifstream**, or (a less likely possibility) to writing an **ofstream**. Once you have opened a file stream for input and output, you can read from or write to any position in the stream. However, you do need to know where you are in the stream and where you want to go next. For a stream that was written using formatted write operations with the insertion operator, this may be decidedly tricky.

The difficulty stems from the fact that unless you always set the width of the field, you really don't know in general how many bytes will be written to the stream. If you write an integer to the stream, the number of bytes written will depend on the number of decimal digits, and whether a sign is included. A width specification just sets a minimum, so unless you set it to a value that is at least as many characters as the maximum width you're going to output, you still can't be sure. Text mode provides an added layer of complication in that there may be more bytes written on some systems than on others for a given output. For this reason, random access is easiest and safest in binary mode, using unformatted read and write operations. Let's see how we might access a binary file randomly.

Random Access to a Binary Stream

We could modify Program 19.5 that wrote prime numbers to a binary file to provide the possibility of requesting a particular prime — the 25th or 432nd prime, for instance. The idea is that if the prime is in the file, it just fetches it and displays it. If it isn't, it should calculate up to the prime required and add the new ones to the file.

This time, the file will be a little different. If we can keep track of how many primes are in the file, we can easily determine whether a requested prime is already there. The easiest way to record this is to always write a count of the number of primes as the last data item in the file.

The input to the program will be the sequence number of the prime required: 3 for the third prime, 101 for the 101st prime, and so on. The basic logic of the program is shown below:

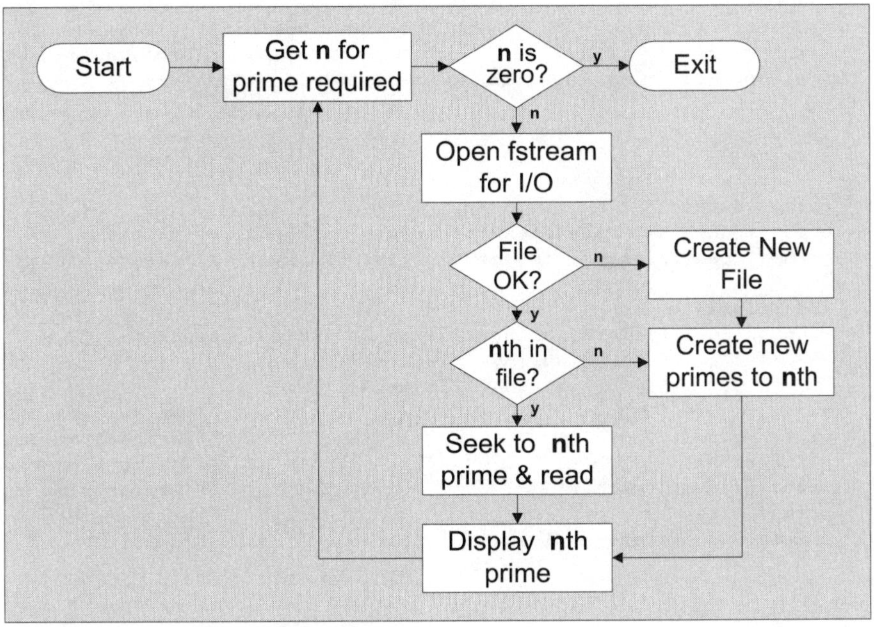

Let's work through the logic of this and put the code together piecemeal. Apart from some dialog with the user, the first step is to open the file — or if it doesn't exist, to create it. We will use an **fstream** object for the file. Since we can both read and write an **fstream**, once we have opened it at the beginning of the program, we can use it anywhere for input or output as necessary:

```cpp
int main()
{
  const char* filename = "C:\\JunkData\\nuprimes.bin";
  fstream primes;                                    // Create file stream object
  primes.open(filename, ios::in | ios::out | ios::binary); // Open the file
  long count = 0;                                    // Count of primes found

  // Rest of the code...
}
```

Aside from the simple but important task of setting up a **long** variable to hold the number of primes found so far, this code opens the file in binary mode for both read and write operations. Because the open mode is specified as input as well as output, this will fail if the file does not exist, so we must check that the stream is good:

```
int main()
{
  try
  {
    const char* filename = "C:\\JunkData\\nuprimes.bin";
    fstream primes;                                    // Create file stream object
    primes.open(filename, ios::in | ios::out | ios::binary); // Open the file
    long count = 0;                                    // Count of primes found

    if(!primes)
    {
      primes.clear();
      cout << endl << "File doesn't exist - creating..." << endl;
      primes.open(filename, ios::out | ios::binary);  // Create binary file

      if(!primes)
        throw ios::failure(string("Failed to create output file ") +
                           string(filename) +
                           string(" in main()"));
      write(primes, 2);                                // Write 2 as binary long
      write(primes, 3);                                // Write 3 as binary long
      write(primes, 5);                                // Write 5 as binary long
      write(primes, count = 3);                        // Write prime count
      primes.close();
      primes.open(filename, ios::in | ios::out | ios::binary);
    }

    // Rest of the code...
  }
  catch(exception& ex)
  {
    cout << endl << typeid(ex).name() << ": " << ex.what() << endl;
    return 1;
  }
}
```

If the file was not opened successfully, we clear the **ios** error flags and attempt to open the file again, but this time in binary mode for output only. This should create a new file, but we still check to make sure. If an error flag was set, we throw an **ios::failure** exception that contains a string explaining the error.

When we get past this check, we write the first three prime numbers and the count to the file. Then we close the stream, so that it can be reopened for both input and output. We're ready to start the process of finding the required prime.

First, we must read the sequence number of the prime required. If we put the whole process inside an indefinite **for** loop, we'll be able to repeat the cycle of finding specific primes as often as required, and we can use a zero or negative value entered as the signal to terminate the program:

```
int main()
{
  try
  {
    // Code to open the file...

    long nprime = 0;                          // Sequence no. of prime required
    long lastprime = 0;                       // Last prime found
    for( ; ; )
    {
      cout << "Which prime (e.g. enter 15 for the 15th prime, zero to end)?: ";
      cin >> nprime;
      if(nprime <= 0)                         // Zero or negative?
        return 0;                             // ...yes, so we are done

      // Rest of the code for finding the prime to follow...
    }
    cout << endl;
    return 0;
  }
  catch(exception& ex)
  {
    cout << endl << typeid(ex).name() << ": " << ex.what() << endl;
    return 1;
  }
}
```

The rest of the code will follow the existing code inside the **for** loop. To determine whether the requested prime is in the file, we need to obtain the count of the number of primes in the file:

```
primes.seekg(-static_cast<int>(sizeof(long)), ios::end); // Go to start of
                                                         // last item
read(primes, count);                                     // Read the last item
```

The **count** is the last item in the file. You might argue that placing it at the start would give you an easier ride, but this way we get to give some of the functions we've seen a stiffer workout — we'll have to seek relative to the end of the file. The **count** value will be at a position that's **sizeof(long)** bytes back from the end of the file, but **sizeof()** returns a value of **size_t** which is usually defined as an unsigned integer, so we need to cast it to **int** before changing its sign. After seeking to that position, we read **count** using the version of **read()** from Program 19.5 that reads binary **long** values.

Now we must check whether **nprime** is less than this value — if it is, we can just read the prime from the appropriate position in the file:

```
if(nprime <= count)
{
  cout << endl << "Prime in file";
  primes.seekg((nprime - 1) * sizeof(long), ios::beg); // Seek to position
                                                       // of nth
  read(primes, lastprime);                             // ...and read it
}
```

We can get to any prime number by seeking directly to its position in the file, relative to the beginning. The offset from **ios::beg** for the first prime is 0 bytes, for the second prime it's **sizeof(long)** bytes, for the third prime it's **2 * sizeof(long)** bytes, and so on. Thus the one we are looking for will be **(nprime - 1) * sizeof(long)** bytes from the beginning of the file. When we get there, we just read it using our binary **read()** function.

If **nprime** is greater than **count**, we must calculate new primes and continue to add them to the file until we have a total of **nprime** primes in it. We do this in the **else** part of the **if**:

```
if(nprime <= count)
{
  cout << endl << "Prime in file";
  primes.seekg((nprime - 1) * sizeof(long), ios::beg); // Seek to position
                                                        // of nth
  read(primes, lastprime);                             // ...and read it
}
else
  while(count < nprime)
  {
    lastprime = nextprime(primes);
    primes.seekp(-static_cast<int>(sizeof(long)), ios::end);  // Move to the
                                                              // end
    write(primes, lastprime);                    // Write prime as binary
    write(primes, ++count);                      // Write prime as binary
  }
```

This uses a revised version of **nextprime()** that accepts a single argument: the file stream. This function will calculate and return the prime following the last prime in the file, but let's come back to how that works in a moment. When we *have* the next prime, we seek to the position of the count at the end of the file, and overwrite it with the new prime. We then write the incremented count to the file. Note that we use **seekp()** here rather than **seekg()** because we're going to write to the file. This is essential because **fstream** has separate internal, synchronized buffers for input and output; **seekg()** applies to one and **seekp()** applies to the other.

The last step in the **for** loop is to display the prime required, before going round for another choice. The following statement will do this:

```
cout << endl << "The " << nprime << " prime is " << lastprime << endl;
```

If you're a stickler for detail, you can use conditional operators to figure out here whether it should be **"st"**, **"nd"**, **"rd"** or **"th"** after the value of **nprime** in the output:

```
cout << endl    << "The "
        << nprime << ((nprime%10 == 1) && (nprime != 11) ? "st" :
                      (nprime%10 == 2) && (nprime != 12) ? "nd" :
                      (nprime%10 == 3) && (nprime != 13) ? "rd" : "th")
        << " prime is " << lastprime << endl;
```

We can implement the **nextprime()** function as follows:

```
long nextprime(fstream& primes)
{
  bool isprime = false;                    // Indicator that we have a prime
```

```
      long aprime = 0;                                      // Stores primes from the file
      long candidate = 0;                                   // Value to be tested

      primes.seekg(-static_cast<int>(2 * sizeof(long)), ios::end);  // Go to last
                                                            // prime in file
      read(primes, candidate);                              // ...and read it

      // Find the next prime
      for( ; ; )
      {
        candidate += 2;                                     // Next value for checking
        long limit = sqrt(candidate);                       // Upper limit for divisors
        primes.seekg(0, ios::beg);                          // Go to the start of the file

        // Try dividing the candidate by all the primes up to limit
        do
        {
          read(primes, aprime);                             // Read prime as binary
        } while(aprime <= limit && (isprime = candidate % aprime > 0));

        if(isprime)                                         // We got one...
          return candidate;                                 // ...and return the prime
      }
    }
```

The interesting parts here are the file access sections; the actual calculation is essentially as before. We first seek to where the last prime is in the file. Each item has **sizeof(long)** bytes, so we back off twice that number of bytes from the end of the file using **seekg()**. This takes account of that fact that the count of the number of primes in the file is the last item stored in the file. We then store the last prime in **candidate** using our own binary **read()** function.

To check the candidate, we seek to the beginning of the file — which corresponds to an offset of zero bytes relative to **ios::beg** — and read consecutive prime divisors from the file. We use these to test the candidate in the loop condition. The **limit** check ensures we never reach the end of the file, so no **ios** flags for the stream should ever be set.

Try It Out – Randomly Accessing a File

We can package all that we've seen together and give it a whirl. The complete version of **main()** is as follows:

```
// Program 19.6 Reading and writing the primes file as binary
#include <fstream>
#include <iostream>
#include <cmath>
#include <string>
using namespace std;

long nextprime(fstream& primes);            // Find the prime after lastprime
void write(ostream& out, long value);       // Write binary long value
void read(istream& in, long& value);        // Read binary long value
```

799

```cpp
int main()
{
  try
  {
    const char* filename = "C:\\JunkData\\nuprimes.bin";
    fstream primes;                                       // Create file stream object
    primes.open(filename, ios::in | ios::out | ios::binary); // Open the file
    long count = 0;                                       // Count of primes found

    if(!primes)
    {
      primes.clear();
      cout << endl << "File doesn't exist - creating..." << endl;
      primes.open(filename, ios::out | ios::binary);      // Create binary file

      if(!primes)
        throw ios::failure(string("Failed to create output file ") +
                           string(filename) +
                           string(" in main()"));
      write(primes, 2);                                   // Write 2 as binary long
      write(primes, 3);                                   // Write 3 as binary long
      write(primes, 5);                                   // Write 5 as binary long
      write(primes, count = 3);                           // Write prime count
      primes.close();
      primes.open(filename, ios::in | ios::out | ios::binary);
    }

    long nprime = 0;                                      // Sequence no. of prime required
    long lastprime = 0;                                   // Last prime found
    for( ; ; )
    {
      cout << "Which prime (e.g. enter 15 for the 15th prime, zero to end)?: ";
      cin >> nprime;
      if(nprime <= 0)                                     // Zero or negative?
        return 0;                                         //  ...yes, so we are done

      primes.seekg(-static_cast<int>(sizeof(long)), ios::end); // Go to start of
                                                               // last item
      read(primes, count);                               // Read the last item

      if(nprime <= count)
      {
        cout << endl << "Prime in file";
        primes.seekg((nprime - 1) * sizeof(long), ios::beg); // Seek to position
                                                             // of nth
        read(primes, lastprime);                         //  ...and read it
      }
      else
        while(count < nprime)
        {
          lastprime = nextprime(primes);
          primes.seekp(-static_cast<int>(sizeof(long)), ios::end);  // Move to the
                                                                    // end
          write(primes, lastprime);                      // Write prime as binary
          write(primes, ++count);                        // Write prime as binary
        }
```

```
       cout << endl   << "The "
           << nprime << ((nprime%10 == 1) && (nprime != 11) ? "st" :
                         (nprime%10 == 2) && (nprime != 12) ? "nd" :
                         (nprime%10 == 3) && (nprime != 13) ? "rd" : "th")
           << " prime is " << lastprime << endl;
    }
    cout << endl;
    return 0;
  }
  catch(exception& ex)
  {
    cout << endl << typeid(ex).name() << ": " << ex.what() << endl;
    return 1;
  }
}
```

You need to add the definitions for **nextprime()**, and the **read()** and **write()** functions. A sample of the sort of output you can get is:

```
File doesn't exist - creating...
Which prime (e.g. enter 15 for the 15th prime, zero to end)?: 9

The 9th prime is 23
Which prime (e.g. enter 15 for the 15th prime, zero to end)?: 99

The 99th prime is 523
Which prime (e.g. enter 15 for the 15th prime, zero to end)?: 1001

The 1001st prime is 7927
Which prime (e.g. enter 15 for the 15th prime, zero to end)?: 5000

The 5000th prime is 48611
Which prime (e.g. enter 15 for the 15th prime, zero to end)?: 3456

Prime in file
The 3456th prime is 32213
Which prime (e.g. enter 15 for the 15th prime, zero to end)?: 0
```

How It Works

We covered all the detail of developing the code. All input and output operations are carried out with the same file stream object, and we seek directly to the position that we require. Since we are using unformatted I/O operations in binary mode, this is a snap, as we always know how many bytes each item in the file occupies. Even with various kinds of data in the file, as long as you know what data items were written, and what the sequence was, you can figure out where things are in an unformatted binary file.

String Streams

There are three **string stream classes** that connect a stream to a **string** object: **istringstream**, **ostringstream**, and **stringstream**, which have **istream**, **ostream** and **iostream** as base classes, respectively. Operations on these classes are essentially the same as for the file streams, except of course that the input and output operations are to **string** objects.

Although they can use any of the input/output functions that are inherited from their corresponding base class, string streams are used most often with the insertion and extraction operators. The reason for this is that their primary application is formatting data in memory, or analyzing input. For example, you might have an application where the format of the input is not known in advance. In such a case, you could read the data into a **string** object, and then use the stream input operations with an **istringstream** object attached to your **string** object containing the input. This provides the possibility to read the input as many times as necessary to figure out its format.

Suppose you read a line of input from **cin** with the statements:

```
string buffer;
getline(cin, buffer);
```

Having read the input into **buffer**, you can create an **istringstream** object with the statement:

```
istringstream inStr(buffer);
```

You can now read from **buffer** via the stream **inStr** just like any other stream, and make use of the conversion capability from character representation to binary:

```
long value = 0;
double data = 0.0;
inStr >> value >> data;
```

You can use an **ostringstream** object to format data into a string. For instance, you could create a **string** object and an output string stream with the statements:

```
string outBuffer;
ostringstream outStr(outBuffer);
```

You can now use the insertion operators to write to **outBuffer** via **outStr**:

```
double number = 2.5;
outStr << "number = " << (number / 2);
```

As a result of the write to the string stream, **outBuffer** will contain **"number = 1.25"**. The string **outBuffer** will automatically expand to accommodate however many characters you write to the stream, so it is a very flexible way of forming strings or complex output messages.

The **string** parameter to the string stream constructors is a reference in each case, so write operations for **ostringstream** and **stringstream** objects act directly on the **string** object. There is also a default constructor for each of the string stream classes. When you use these, the string stream object will maintain a **string** object internally, and you can obtain a copy of this using the **str()** member. For example:

```
ostringstream outStr;
double number = 2.5;
outStr << "number = " << (3 * number / 2);
string output = outStr.str();
```

After these statements, **output** will contain the string **"number = 3.75"**.

Objects and Streams

So far we have talked primarily about transferring basic data types to and from a stream. However, in previous chapters I've been telling you how great object-oriented programming is, so what about writing objects to a file? I just knew that question would come up.

As far as the C++ standard library is concerned, you are on your own. While this is inconvenient, it's not altogether surprising — by nature, a class is completely open-ended, and therfore by definition it's an unknown quantity. Input and output operations are going to be class specific, whether we like it or not. In spite of the difficulties implicit in this, some C++ development systems do provide a framework of support for reading and writing objects, sometimes at the small expense of having to use a particular base class. However, if yours doesn't provide anything, don't worry — you *can* do it yourself. What's more, you don't need to go to the trouble of deriving your own stream classes to do it.

Ideally, you want to be able to read and write objects of your classes using the same extraction and insertion operators that you use for the basic data types. All that's required is for you to supply functions to overload these operators for your class types. How easy or difficult this will be depends on the complexity of your classes. Once you know how to do it for formatted I/O, you should have little trouble implementing unformatted operations for use in binary mode. First of all, then, let's see how we might implement formatted I/O for class objects in a simple case.

Overloading the Insertion Operator for Class Objects

You can implement an overloaded version of **operator<<()** that will write objects of a given class to a stream as a friend of the class. Let's take a version of the **Box** class that we have used from time to time in the book, and enable **Box** objects to be written to a stream.

To start with, we need to declare the function as a friend of the **Box** class, so that it has access to its data members:

```
// Box.h
#ifndef BOX_H
#define BOX_H

class Box
{
  public:
    // Constructor
    Box(double lv = 1, double bv = 1, double hv = 1);

    // Virtual Destructor
    virtual ~Box();

    // Function to show the volume of an object
    void showVolume() const;

    // Function to calculate the volume of a Box object
    virtual double volume() const;

    // Friend insertion operator
    friend ostream& operator<<(ostream& out, const Box& rBox);
```

```
    protected:
      double length;
      double breadth;
      double height;
  };

  #endif
```

Since the function returns a reference to the stream object, we will be able to use it to write **Box** objects to a stream in the same way as any of the basic data types. This applies to a file stream just as well as it does to **cout**. We can implement the function using the overloaded insertion operations for standard types:

```
ostream& operator<<(ostream& out, const Box& rBox)
{
  return out << ' ' << rBox.length << ' ' << rBox.breadth << ' ' << rBox.height;
}
```

This just writes the three data members to the stream, each preceded by a space, and returns the stream object that was passed to it, **out**. If you only intend the operator to be used to output objects to **cout**, then you might want to embellish the output with more descriptive information, such as the member names. However, if you intend to use it for writing to a file, such formatting would make reading objects back rather messier, so it's better to keep it simple in this case.

If the class contains query functions that retrieve the values of the data members (such as **getLength()** etc. that we have used in other chapters), then the **operator<<()** function does not need to be a friend of the class — you could implement it using the **public** query functions. For now, though, let's see how to work with what we've got.

Try It Out – Writing Objects to a Stream

Box.h, which contains the friend declaration for **operator<<()**, is listed above. You'll also need to define the function in **Box.cpp**, which looks like this:

```
// Box.cpp
#include <iostream>
using namespace std;

#include "Box.h"

// Constructor
Box::Box(double lv, double bv, double hv) : length(lv),
                                            breadth(bv),
                                            height(hv)
{}

// Destructor
Box::~Box()
{}

// Function to show the volume of an object
void Box::showVolume() const
```

```
  {
    cout << endl << "Box usable volume is " << volume();
  }

  // Function to calculate the volume of a Box object
  double Box::volume() const
  {
    return length * breadth * height;
  }

  // Friend operator function for Box
  ostream& operator<<(ostream& out, const Box& rBox)
  {
    return out << ' ' << rBox.length << ' ' << rBox.breadth << ' ' << rBox.height;
  }
```

In **main()**, we'll just create a couple of **Box** objects and output them:

```
  // Program 19.7 Writing Box object to cout
  #include <iostream>
  using namespace std;

  #include "Box.h"

  int main()
  {
    Box bigBox(50, 60, 70);
    Box smallBox(2, 3, 4);
    cout << endl << "bigBox is " << bigBox;
    cout << endl << "smallBox is " << smallBox;
    cout << endl;
    return 0;
  }
```

This example produces the output:

```
  bigBox is   50 60 70
  smallBox is  2 3 4
```

How It Works

After declaring the two **Box** objects, we output them with the statements:

```
    cout << endl << "bigBox is " << bigBox;
    cout << endl << "smallBox is " << smallBox;
```

The first of these is equivalent to the statement:

```
    operator<<((cout.operator<<(endl)).operator<<("bigBox is "), bigBox);
```

In other words, we're calling the friend version of **operator<<()** with
(cout.operator<<(endl)).operator<<("bigBox is ") as the first argument, and **bigBox**
as the second argument. The expression for the first argument calls the member function for
cout to output the newline, followed by the member function to output the string. This latter
call returns the stream object, **out**, which is passed as the first argument to our friend function.
The second statement works in exactly the same way. Easy, isn't it?

Overloading the Extraction Operator for Class Objects

Reading objects from a stream just requires an implementation of **operator>>()** for your class, which will need to be a friend if the data members are **private** or **protected**. Of course, you can avoid the requirement for a friend function if you implement **public** member functions to set the data members' values, but I'm trying to keep the class as small as possible for the purposes of this discussion. It goes without saying that the insertion and extraction operators for a class object have to be implemented consistently, with the members' values being read in the same sequence in which they are written. We could implement the operator for the **Box** class as:

```
istream& Box::operator>>(istream& in, Box& rBox)
{
  return in >> rBox.length >> rBox.breadth >> rBox.height;
}
```

Because we're modifying the members of **rBox**, the second parameter cannot be **const**. This is a very simple-minded implementation that takes no account of input errors. In practice, you would not only want to deal with errors such as 'end-of-file' occurring before you have read all the values you need, but you would also want to do some validity checking on the values themselves to ensure you end up with a valid **Box** object. However, this simple version will be sufficient to show the mechanics. Let's try it out, along with the insertion operator.

Try It Out – Reading and Writing Objects

Of course, we could just read a **Box** object from the keyboard, but let's be more adventurous and try writing **Box** objects to a file and then reading them back. You need to add a friend declaration for **operator>>()** to the **Box** class definition in **Box.h**:

```
class Box
{
  ...

    // Friend insertion and extraction operators
    friend ostream& operator<<(ostream& out, const Box& rBox);
    friend istream& operator>>(istream& in, Box& rBox);

  ...
};
```

You must also add the definition of the **operator>>()** function, as shown above, to **Box.cpp**. The program to use our new operator function will be:

```
// Program 19.8 Writing Box objects to a file
#include <fstream>
#include <iostream>
#include <string>
using namespace std;

#include "Box.h"

int main()
{
  try
  {
```

```
          const string filename = "C:\\JunkData\\boxes.txt";

          ofstream out(filename.c_str());
          if(!out)
            throw(ios::failure(string("Failed to open output file ") + filename));

          Box bigBox(50, 60, 70);
          Box smallBox(2,3,4);

          out << bigBox << smallBox;
          out.close();

          cout << endl << "Wrote two Box objects to the file:";
          cout << endl << "bigBox is " << bigBox;
          cout << endl << "smallBox is " << smallBox;
          cout << endl;

          ifstream in(filename.c_str());
          if(!in)
            throw(ios::failure(string("Failed to open input file ") + filename));

          cout << endl << "Reading objects from the file:";
          Box newBox;                                      // Default Box object

          in >> newBox;
          cout << endl << "First Box read is " << newBox;
          in >> newBox;
          cout << endl << "Second Box read is " << newBox;
          cout << endl;
          return 0;
        }
      catch(exception& ex)
        {
          cout << endl << typeid(ex).name() << ": " << ex.what() << endl;
          return 0;
        }
    }
```

This produces the output:

```
Wrote two Box objects to the file:
bigBox is   50 60 70
smallBox is   2 3 4

Reading objects from the file:
First Box read is   50 60 70
Second Box read is   2 3 4
```

How It Works

There is really very little to say about this code, because it works in the same way as reading and writing the basic types. We use a new file to hold **Box** objects:

```
const string filename = "C:\\JunkData\\boxes.txt";
```

After creating two **Box** objects, we write them to the file with this statement:

```
out << bigBox << smallBox;
```

This is equivalent to the statement:

```
operator<<(operator<<(out, bigBox), smallBox);
```

Because **ofstream** has **ostream** as a base class, returning the **ofstream** object **out** as type **ostream&** in the first argument to the outer **operator<<()** call works perfectly well. Having written the file, we then close it, and use our **operator<<()** function with the standard stream, **cout**:

```
cout << endl << "bigBox is " << bigBox;
cout << endl << "smallBox is " << smallBox;
```

This outputs the two **Box** objects to the screen, just as it did in our last example. To prove that there's no sleight of hand going on, we can now read a **Box** object back from the file into a new **Box** object, **newBox**, with the statement:

```
in >> newBox;
```

This is making use of our new extraction operator to retrieve a **Box** object from the file stream, **in**. The statement is equivalent to:

```
operator>>(in, newBox);
```

The use of separate input statements isn't significant — we could equally well have read both **Box** objects from the file into separate **Box** objects in memory with a single statement. Last of all, each **Box** object is read from the file and displayed on **cout** to show that the program has worked correctly.

More Complex Objects in Streams

With the **Box** object, I chose a deliberately simple case. Handling derived class objects is a little more complicated because our **operator>>()** and **operator<<()** functions are not class members, and therefore cannot be virtual. We really do *need* a virtual input and output mechanism to ensure that derived class objects are handled properly when they are referred to using a base pointer or a reference to a base class, but there's no way we can make the operator functions class members.

The insertion and extraction operators are binary operators, and binary operator functions that are members of a class can only have one parameter. We would have no way to pass the stream object *and* the right operand to the function. The operator functions *could* call a virtual class member though, and that provides a way to deal with the difficulty. For our **Box** class, we could implement it like this:

```
class Box
{
  public:
    // Constructor
    Box(double lv = 1, double bv = 1, double hv = 1);

    // Virtual Destructor
    virtual ~Box();

    // Function to show the volume of an object
    void showVolume() const;
```

```
    // Function to calculate the volume of a Box object
    virtual double volume() const;

    // Member stream I/O functions
    virtual ostream& put(ostream& out) const;
    virtual istream& get(istream& in);

  protected:
    double length;
    double breadth;
    double height;
};

// Insertion and extraction operators
ostream& operator<<(ostream& out, const Box& rBox);
istream& operator>>(istream& in, Box& rBox);
```

We have added two virtual members to the class that will perform the stream I/O operations, and because our insertion and extraction operators will now call functions in the class's public interface, they no longer need to be friend functions. All we have to do is implement the operator functions to make use of the new members. We can define the **put()** member function like this:

```
ostream& Box::put(ostream& out) const
{
  return out << ' ' << length << ' ' << breadth << ' ' << height;
}
```

This does exactly the same thing as the earlier version of the **operator<<()** function, which we can now implement as:

```
ostream& operator<<(ostream& out, const Box& rBox)
{
  return rBox.put(out);
}
```

This just calls the virtual function **put()** to perform the output operation, and returns the stream object. Similarly, the **get()** function definition will be:

```
istream& Box::get(istream& in)
{
  return in >> length >> breadth >> height;
}
```

Once again, we can use this in the implementation of the friend function **operator>>()**:

```
istream& operator>>(istream& in, Box& rBox)
{
  return rBox.get(in);
}
```

To provide stream support for a derived class of **Box**, such as **Carton**, you just need to define member functions that override the virtual **get()** and **put()** functions in the base class. The derived class member functions can call the corresponding base class versions where necessary.

You'll remember our **Carton** class that inherited from **Box**, implementing a different **volume()** function and adding a **string*** data member that held a pointer to a **string** containing the name of the material from which the **Carton** was made. The prototypes of the **get()** and **put()** member functions for this class would be:

```
class Carton: public Box
{
  public:
    virtual ostream& put(ostream& out) const;
    virtual istream& get(istream& in);

  // Rest of the class definition...
};
```

The **put()** function could be implemented as:

```
ostream& Carton::put(ostream& out) const
{
  out << ' ' << *pMaterial;
  return Box::put(out);
}
```

We could implement the **get()** function as:

```
istream& Carton::get(istream& in)
{
  pMaterial = new string;                    // Allocate for new string
  in >> *pMaterial;                          // Read the string
  return Box::get(in);
}
```

Now, whether you output an object of the base class, **Box**, or of the derived class, **Carton**, the base class member **operator<<()** will select the appropriate virtual **put()** function for the object, even when the object is referenced by a base class reference. This will work for any class that has **Box** as a base, as long as the **get()** and **put()** members are implemented for the class.

Classes that contain pointers to objects of other classes add a further complication. One fundamental prerequisite is that the class type of the object being pointed to has overloaded operators to do the business. You can then use these to write or retrieve the objects pointed to. Another prerequisite is that there has to be a way of constructing the object from the data read from the stream. One way to do this requires that the class pointed to must have a default constructor. You can then use this when you're reading objects from a stream, to synthesize objects in the free store, and then initialize them with data from the stream. Another possibility is to provide a class constructor that accepts an input stream as an argument, and constructs an object using data from the stream.

As bad as that sounds, it can get even trickier if the object pointed to by a member of a class *also* has pointers to class objects. We could explore some of the ramifications of this with an example, so let's really stick our necks out and try to implement a modicum of stream support for a version of the **Stack** template that we defined in the previous chapter. We won't do a comprehensive job on this, but you'll see enough to cover the principles involved. It will give you some experience of stream operations with templates, as well as classes that contain pointers to other class objects.

Stream Support for Template Classes

Let's first think about how output of a **Stack<T>** object to a stream is going to work. The only data member of a template instance is the pointer **pHead**, which will contain the address of the first node if there is one, and 0 otherwise. We will have to write the **Node** object to which **pHead** points to the file, and we could consider a friend function to the inner class **Node** for this, but this class is private to **Stack**, and it would be better to keep it so. An alternative approach would be to declare a helper function, **writeNodes()**, as a member of the **Stack** template that would write all the **Node** objects to the file. The principle of how this is going to work is illustrated below.

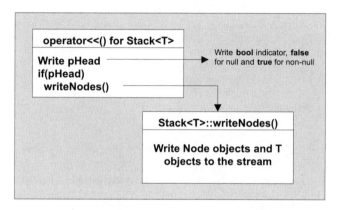

There is no point in writing addresses contained in pointers to a stream, as they will be invalid when they are read back. What's important about a pointer is whether or not it is null, since this will tell us whether there is an object in the file that the pointer used to point to. We can easily write this information about a pointer to the stream as a **bool** value.

The **writeNodes()** function will also need to take care of the object pointed to by the **Node** data member, **pItem**, since no one else is going to! The object pointed to is of type **T**, and since we have to write it to the stream, we will assume that there is an implementation of the insertion operator for objects of class **T**. Clearly, this has to be the case if our function is going to work.

We now have a clearer idea of how a **Stack<T>** object with an arbitrary number of nodes is going to get written to a stream:

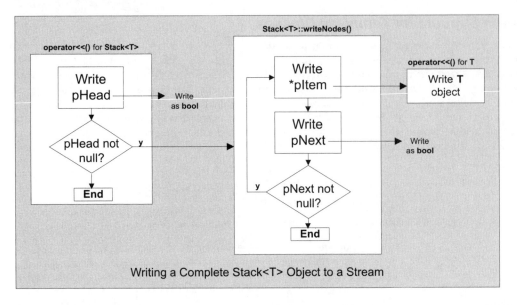

Writing a Complete Stack<T> Object to a Stream

The **Stack<T>** insertion operator will write the **pHead** pointer to the stream as **true** if it is not null, and **false** otherwise. Then it will call the **writeNodes()** member of **Stack<T>** to write the **Node** objects to the file. For each **Node** object, the **writeNodes()** function will also write the **T** object that the pointer **pItem** points to, using the **operator<<()** function for objects of type **T**. Note that we *don't* need to write information about the **pItem** member to the stream. If there is a **Node**, we just write the **T** object — the pointer is never null.

So: we understand roughly how writing a **Stack<T>** object to a stream is going to work, and we can itemize the things we will need to take care of in terms of our code:

▶ Each **Stack<T>** class instance will need a friend function that overloads the insertion operator.

▶ Each **Stack<T>** class instance will need a **private** member function, **writeNodes()** that writes all **Node** objects to the stream.

▶ The friend function for insertion of **Stack<T>** objects and the **writeNodes()**, member function will need to be defined by templates.

Implementing Insertion for the Stack Class Template

First of all, we can add the friend declaration for **operator<<()** and the declaration for the **writeNode()** member function to the **Stack** template:

```
template <typename T> class Stack
{
  public:
    Stack():pHead(0){}                              // Default constructor
    Stack(const Stack& aStack);                     // Copy constructor
    ~Stack();                                       // Destructor
    Stack& operator=(const Stack& aStack);          // Assignment operator
```

```
    void push(T& rItem);                     // Push an object onto the stack
    T& pop();                                // Pop an object off the stack
    bool isEmpty() {return pHead == 0;}   // Empty test

  friend ostream& operator<<(ostream& out, const Stack& rStack);

  private:
    class Node
    {
      public:
        T* pItem;                          // Pointer to object stored
        Node* pNext;                       // Pointer to next node

        Node(T& rItem) : pItem(&rItem), pNext(0) {}    // Construct a node from an
                                                       // object
        Node() : pItem(0), pNext(0) {}     // Construct an empty node
    };

    Node* pHead;                           // Points to the top of the stack
    void copy(const Stack& aStack);         // Helper to copy a stack
    void freeMemory();                     // Helper to release free store memory
    ostream& writeNodes(ostream& out, Node* pNode) const;  // Write Node objects
                                                           // to a stream
};
```

The form of the friend function is the same as previous non-member implementations we have seen. The first argument is a reference to the **ostream** object, and the second argument is a **const** reference to the object to be written. The return value must be a reference to the **ostream** object if we are to be able to use it in a succession of **<<** operations in a single statement. Note that this function is not a member function, and that the use of **Stack&** as the type of the second parameter implies **Stack<T>&**, so this is a function template that is a friend of the class template.

The **writeNodes()** function has two parameters. The first is a reference to a stream, and the second is a pointer to the **Node** object. A pointer will be easier to work with here, because a **Node** object is always referenced through a pointer. For convenience, the function returns a reference to the stream object.

We can add a function template for the **operator<<()** function to the **Stack.h** file:

```
template <typename T> ostream& operator<<(ostream& out, const Stack<T>& rStack)
{
  out << ' ' << (rStack.pHead != 0);
  return rStack.writeNodes(out, rStack.pHead);
}
```

This function writes a **bool** value to the stream that will be **true** if the **pHead** member of **rStack** is not null, and then passes the same pointer to the **writeNodes()** function, to write the **Node** objects to the stream. Not too difficult, is it?

We need to bear in mind that data items need whitespace separating them if they are to be read from a stream by an extraction operator. We can make sure that this is the case by always outputting a space before each item, as we have done here with the **bool** data.

The template defining the **writeNodes()** member function will also go in **Stack.h**:

```
template <typename T> ostream& Stack<T>::writeNodes(ostream& out, Node* pNode)
const
{
  while(pNode)
  {
    out << ' ' << *(pNode->pItem);
    out << ' ' << (pNode->pNext != 0);
    pNode = pNode->pNext;
  }
  return out;
}
```

The pointer **pNode** determines whether a **Node** object is written. We first write the **T** object pointed to by **pItem** to the stream, and then the **bool** indicator for the **pNext** pointer. We then store the **pNext** pointer for the current node in **pNode** for the next iteration.

It might have sounded difficult to begin with, but that's all we need to write **Stack<T>** objects to a stream. Let's see if we can figure out how to read them back.

Understanding Extraction for the Stack Class Template

A good place to start is to look at exactly what ends up in a stream when a **Stack** object is written to the stream by the functions we've just created. A **Stack<T>** object with four nodes is illustrated below.

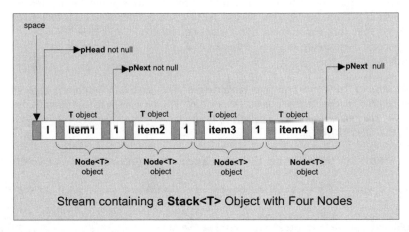

Stream containing a **Stack<T>** Object with Four Nodes

The first value in the stream is a space, followed by the **bool** value for **pHead**, which will be **true** if there is a following **Node** object. Each **Node<T>** object is just the **T** object to which its **pItem** member points, followed by a **bool** value that is **true** if there's a 'next' **Node** object. The last **Node** object will have the **bool** indicator for **pNext** set to **false**, because there is no next node in that case.

The friend **operator>>()** function in **Stack<T>** can read the **pHead** indicator, and then call a **private** helper function named **readNodes()** if the indicator is **true**, so the input process will be a mirror of the output process.

When we read a **Node** object from a stream, we will need to create the object that the data member **pItem** points to. This raises some serious complications that must be considered very carefully. Since *we* are now creating these objects of type **T**, we must take responsibility for deleting them. This implies we must use a different strategy for dealing with objects in the stack. If we provide the capability to write a **Stack** to a stream, we should always create objects in the free store, even when they are pushed on the stack. We can then return a copy rather than a reference, and delete the object from the free store when it is popped from the stack, or when a node is destroyed.

Managing Objects in the Stack

We must add the **Node** class destructor to the template, and modify the constructor to accept a pointer argument rather than a reference. We also need to alter the **pop()** member function to return an object rather than a reference:

```
template <typename T> class Stack
{
public:
    Stack():pHead(0){}                              // Default constructor
    Stack(const Stack& aStack);                     // Copy constructor
    ~Stack();                                        // Destructor
    Stack& operator=(const Stack& aStack);          // Assignment operator

    void push(T& rItem);                            // Push an object onto the stack
    T pop();                                        // Pop an object off the stack
    bool isEmpty() {return pHead == 0;}             // Empty test

    friend ostream& operator<<(ostream& out, const Stack& rStack);

    private:
      class Node
      {
        public:
          T* pItem;                                 // Pointer to object stored
          Node* pNext;                              // Pointer to next node

          Node(T* pNew) : pItem(pNew), pNext(0) {}  // Construct a node from an
                                                    //object
          Node() : pItem(0), pNext(0) {}            // Construct an empty node
          ~Node() {delete pItem;}
    };

      Node* pHead;                                  // Points to the top of the stack
      void copy(const Stack& aStack);               // Helper to copy a stack
      void freeMemory();                            // Helper to release free store memory
      ostream& writeNodes(ostream& out, Node* pNode) const;  // Write a Node object
                                                    // to a stream
    };
```

The destructor just deletes the object pointed to by **pItem**. We don't need to test **pItem** for null — it should never be so, and calling **delete** on a null pointer is always safe anyway. In the **Stack** template, we have changed the return type of the **pop()** member to **T**, so that we will return a copy of the object in the stack.

We have to alter the implementations of **push()** and **pop()** for the **Stack** template. Let's deal with **push()** first. We must modify the **Stack<T>::push()** template definition to create a **T** object in the free store that's a *copy* of the object passed as a reference, rather than just storing the address of the original object:

```
template <typename T> void Stack<T>::push(T& rItem)
{
   Node* pNode = new Node(new T(rItem));       // Create node from object copy
   pNode->pNext = pHead;                        // Point to the old top node
   pHead = pNode;                               // Make the new node the top
}
```

The `Stack<T>::pop()` template must now make a local copy of the free store object, and then delete the free store object:

```
template <typename T> T Stack<T>::pop()
{
   if(!pHead)                                   // If it is empty
      throw std::logic_error("Stack empty");    // Pop is not valid so throw exception

   T item(*pHead->pItem);                       // Local copy of top object
   Node* pTemp = pHead;                         // Save address of top node
   pHead = pHead->pNext;                        // Make next node the top
   delete pTemp;                                // Delete the previous top node
   return item;                                 // Return copy of top object
}
```

Of course, the return mechanism will also make a copy of the object, **item**, before the local object is destroyed. Our **Stack** template is now self-contained, since it creates and manages copies of all the objects in the stack in the free store, regardless of whether they were pushed onto the stack or created from a stream.

Implementing Extraction for the Stack Class Template

We can now add a friend declaration for the **operator>>()** function and the declaration of **readNodes()** to the **Stack<T>** template:

```
template <typename T> class Stack
{
  public:
    Stack():pHead(0){}                          // Default constructor
    Stack(const Stack& aStack);                 // Copy constructor
    ~Stack();                                   // Destructor
    Stack& operator=(const Stack& aStack);      // Assignment operator

    void push(T& rItem);                        // Push an object onto the stack
    T pop();                                    // Pop an object off the stack
    bool isEmpty() {return pHead == 0;}         // Empty test

    friend ostream& operator<<(ostream& out, const Stack& rStack);
    friend istream& operator>>(istream& in, Stack& rStack);

  private:
    class Node
    {
      public:
        T* pItem;                               // Pointer to object stored
        Node* pNext;                            // Pointer to next node

        Node(T* pNew) : pItem(pNew), pNext(0) {}    // Construct a node from an
                                                    // object
```

```
        Node() : pItem(0), pNext(0) {}          // Construct an empty node
        ~Node() {delete pItem;}
    };

    Node* pHead;                                 // Points to the top of the stack
    void copy(const Stack& aStack);              // Helper to copy a stack
    void freeMemory();                           // Helper to release free store memory

    ostream& writeNodes(ostream& out, Node* pNode) const;  // Write Node objects
  to a stream
    Node* readNodes(istream& in);                // Read Node objects from stream
  };
```

The **readNodes()** function returns a pointer to the first **Node** read, so that it can be stored in **pHead** in the **operator>>()** function. We can define the function template for the extraction operator for **Stack<T>** objects as follows:

```
template <typename T> istream& operator>>(istream& in, Stack<T>& rStack)
{
  bool notEmpty;
  in >> notEmpty;
  if(notEmpty)
    rStack.pHead = rStack.readNodes(in);
  else
    rStack.pHead = 0;
  return in;
}
```

The first **bool** value from the stream is stored in the variable **notEmpty**. It this is **true**, we know that a **Node** object follows, so we call **readNodes()** to read the **Node** objects from the stream. If it's **false**, we just set **pHead** to null.

We can implement the template for the **readNodes()** function like this:

```
template <typename T> Stack<T>::Node* Stack<T>::readNodes(istream& in)
{
  Node* pNode = new Node;                  // Create a Node object
  pNode->pItem = new T;                    // Create the T object and store its address
  in >> *pNode->pItem;                     // Read the T object from the stream

  bool isNext;
  in >> isNext;
  if(isNext)
    pNode->pNext = readNodes(in);
  else pNode->pNext = 0;
  return pNode;
}
```

As long as we make sure we read from the stream in the same sequence as we write to it, all the objects just fall into place. We create the new **Node** object and the new object of type **T**, and store the address of the **T** object in the **pItem** pointer of the **Node** that we have just created. We then read the **bool** indicator for the **pNext** pointer. If that is **true**, it indicates there is another **Node** object to be read, so we read that from the stream by calling **readNodes()** and storing the pointer returned in the **pNext** member of the **Node** object. This will continue until a **Node** object is read that has the **pNext** indicator as **false**, when the sequence of function calls will unwind.

Try It Out – Stream Operations with Template Class Instances

We can try out our modified template class with a set of **Box** objects. The version of the **Box** class we used earlier in this chapter has a default constructor. We also implemented the insertion and extraction operators for **Box** objects, and the default copy constructor will be fine, so the class is fully equipped for stream operations in a stack. Here's the code to test it:

```
// Program 19.9 Writing a stack to a stream
#include <fstream>
#include <iostream>
using namespace std;

#include "Stack.h"
#include "Box.h"

int main()
{
  Box Boxes[10];                                        // 10 default boxes

  for(int i = 0 ; i < 10 ; i++)                         // Create different objects
    Boxes[i] = Box(10 * (i + 1), 10 * (i + 2), 10 * (i + 3));

  Stack<Box> boxStack;                                  // A stack for Box objects

  // Push all Box objects onto the stack
  for(int i = 0 ; i < 10 ; i++)
    boxStack.push(Boxes[i]);

  const string boxFileName = "C:\\JunkData\\boxes.txt";   // Stack file
  ofstream outBoxFile(boxFileName.c_str());            // Output file stream for file

  outBoxFile << boxStack;                               // Write the stack
  outBoxFile.close();                                   // Close the stream

  // Display volumes for original set
  while(!boxStack.isEmpty())
    cout << endl << "Volume = " << boxStack.pop().volume();

  Stack<Box> copyBoxStack;                              // New stack for Box objects

  ifstream inBoxFile(boxFileName.c_str());             // Open input file stream
  inBoxFile >> copyBoxStack;                            // Read the stack

  // Output volumes of Box objects off the stack from the stream
  int i = 0;
  while(!copyBoxStack.isEmpty())
    cout << endl
         << "Volume of Box[" << (i++) << "] is "
         << copyBoxStack.pop().volume();

  cout << endl;
  return 0;
}
```

This should produce the following output:

```
Volume = 1.32e+006
Volume = 990000
Volume = 720000
Volume = 504000
Volume = 336000
Volume = 210000
Volume = 120000
Volume = 60000
Volume = 24000
Volume = 6000
Volume of Box[0] is 1.32e+006
Volume of Box[1] is 990000
Volume of Box[2] is 720000
Volume of Box[3] is 504000
Volume of Box[4] is 336000
Volume of Box[5] is 210000
Volume of Box[6] is 120000
Volume of Box[7] is 60000
Volume of Box[8] is 24000
Volume of Box[9] is 6000
```

How It Works

You can see from the output that the **Box** objects popped from the stack that's read from the file have exactly the same volumes as the original objects. In **main()**, we create an array of default **Box** objects:

```
Box Boxes[10];                                          // 10 default boxes
```

We set the array elements to different **Box** objects in a loop:

```
for(int i = 0 ; i < 10 ; i++)                    // Create different objects
  Boxes[i] = Box(10 * (i + 1), 10 * (i + 2), 10 * (i + 3));
```

The first object will have dimensions (10, 20, 30); the next will have (20, 30, 40), and so on. We then create an empty stack that can store **Box** objects with this statement:

```
Stack<Box> boxStack;                               // A stack for Box objects
```

Next, we push the elements of the **Boxes** array onto the stack in a **for** loop:

```
for(int i = 0 ; i < 10 ; i++)
  boxStack.push(Boxes[i]);
```

The **push()** member of **boxStack** will make a copy of the object passed as a reference argument and use that internally to the stack. The next step is to write **boxStack** to a file stream:

```
const string boxFileName = "C:\\JunkData\\boxes.txt";   // Stack file
ofstream outBoxFile(boxFileName.c_str());         // Output file stream for file

outBoxFile << boxStack;                                 // Write the stack
outBoxFile.close();                                     // Close the stream
```

This uses the `<<` operator that we implemented for the **Stack** template. After writing the **Stack<Box>** object, we close the file. For reference, we pop the **Box** objects off the original stack and display their volumes:

```
while(!boxStack.isEmpty())
  cout << endl << "Volume = " << boxStack.pop().volume();
```

Of course, we are working with copies of the **Box** objects that are internal to the stack here. The **pop()** member will delete the node corresponding to the popped **Box** object, and the destructor for **Node<Box>** will delete the **Box** object from the free store.

We now want to read the stack back from the stream, so we create another stack to store **Box** objects, and an input file stream for the file that we just wrote:

```
Stack<Box> copyBoxStack;                              // New stack for Box objects
ifstream inBoxFile(boxFileName.c_str());             // Open input file stream
```

To read the stack, we use the extraction operator:

```
inBoxFile >> copyBoxStack;                            // Read the stack
```

The last step is to pop the objects off the stack and display the volumes to show they are the same as the originals:

```
int i = 0;
while(!copyBoxStack.isEmpty())
  cout << endl
       << "Volume of Box["
       << (i++) << "] is " << copyBoxStack.pop().volume();
```

As I'm sure you've gathered, implementing stream operations is quite a tricky business on the whole, so if your C++ implementation provides its own support for this, it will save you a lot of work!

Summary

In this chapter, we have covered the basics of stream operations and how you can apply them to using files in your C++ programs. The important elements in this chapter include:

▶ The standard library supports input-output operations on character streams.

▶ The standard streams for input and output are **cin** and **cout**. There are also error streams called **cerr** and **clog**.

▶ The extraction and insertion operators provide formatted stream input-output operations.

▶ A file stream can be associated with a file on disk for input, for output, or for both.

▶ The file open mode determines whether you can read from a stream or write to a stream.

▶ If you create a file output stream and associate it with a file name for which no file exists, a file will be created.

▶ A file has a beginning, an end, and a current position.

▶ You can alter the current position in a file stream to a position that was recorded previously. This can be a position that is a positive offset from the beginning of the stream, a position that is a negative offset from the end of a stream, or a position that is a positive or negative offset from the current position.

▶ To support stream operations for your class objects, you can overload the insertion and extraction operators with operator functions that are friends of your class.

▶ The string stream classes provide stream input-output operations to or from **string** objects.

Exercises

Ex 19.1 Write a **Time** class that stores hours, minutes and seconds as integers. Provide an overloaded insertion operator (**<<**) that will print the time in the format *hh:mm:ss* to any output stream.

Ex 19.2 Provide a simple extraction operator (**operator>>()**) for the time class, which will read time values in the form *hh:mm:ss*. How are you going to cope with the **:** characters? (Hint: what sort of variable would you use to hold a **':'**?)

Ex 19.3 Write a program to log time values to a file. Write a matching program to read a file of time values and output them to the screen.

Ex 19.4 Write a program that reads lines of text from standard input and writes them to standard output, removing all leading whitespace, and converting multiple spaces to single spaces. Test it on input from the keyboard, and on characters read from a file. Write a second program that converts lower case characters to upper case, and test that too.

Introducing the Standard Template Library

As you already know, C++ provides an extensive standard library that simplifies many programming tasks. In addition to what you have seen up to now, this library also provides a range of templates that provide a much higher level of capability. You can use these templates to create standard **containers**, **algorithms**, and **functions** for your data types whenever you need such facilities in your programs. Collectively, these templates are known at the **Standard Template Library** (STL). This chapter will introduce the basic STL containers and the algorithms that work alongside these containers.

In this chapter you will learn:

▶ The basic architecture of the Standard Template Library

▶ How to create and use the sequence containers **vector<>** and **list<>**, and the associative containers **map<>** and **multimap<>**

▶ The special ways that **vector<>** and **list<>** manage storage

▶ How **iterators** bridge containers with plain, old-fashioned, standard C++ arrays

▶ How the STL uses specialization to achieve high performance

An Introduction to the STL Architecture

One important characteristic of the STL is that it provides you with a generic set of tools. Because all of the facilities provided by the STL are template based, they work with almost any type of data that you want. Using the STL, you can create a class that defines a linked list for any of your data types. If you need a linked list to store **Box** objects or **FootballPlayer** objects, it's no problem with the STL. When you need to process your objects in a standard way, the STL is there to help. If you need to sort your **Box** objects in ascending sequence, then the STL can generate a sort function that will work with any data type that that defines the overloaded comparison operators necessary to determine their sequence. Whatever the kinds of objects that your program uses, if you need a standard way of organizing or analyzing them, the chances are that the STL can help.

The STL provides you with three main categories of tools — containers, iterators and algorithms.

Containers provide ways of organizing objects of an arbitrary type — a linked list is one example of a container. There are two main categories of container provided by the STL:

▶ The sequence containers (**vector**, **deque** and **list**) that contain objects of a given type organized in a linear sequential fashion.

▶ The associative containers (**map**, **multimap**, **set** and **multiset**) that allow objects of a given type to be stored and retrieved using keys of a different type. A simple example might involve storing **Employee** objects using personnel numbers as the keys for the objects. An **Employee** object could be retrieved by supplying the personnel number.

Iterators are the glue that hold the STL together. No matter what kind of container you use, its elements will be accessed almost exclusively through iterators, and you use iterators to apply algorithms to the objects in a container. An iterator is a form of smart pointer. In Chapter 14, we defined a simple iterator class of our own — the **BoxPtr** class — for our **TruckLoad** container. There are also iterators in the STL that you can use to transfer objects to or from a stream.

Algorithms provide computational and analysis mechanisms for sets of objects accessed using iterators. Examples of algorithms include searching or sorting the objects in a container. All of the algorithms provided by the STL take iterators as arguments.

We can't possibly cover the whole of the STL in this chapter. To deal with the STL comprehensively would take a whole book, so what we will go into here is just a fraction of the potential. What we can do is explore a few of the basic tools and see how you can combine them to solve some simple problems. This should provide you with enough of a start to give you the confidence to try some of the other features of the STL for yourself.

The most important tools in the STL are the containers — you are likely to use these most frequently. However, you can't use containers without using iterators, so you really need to get a good understanding of those too.

The algorithms are the largest collection of tools in the STL. However, not many of them are relevant to a lot of applications, and some of them are quite specialized in their use. We will not cover the STL algorithms in detail in this chapter, but we will *apply* some of them. The following table will give you the general flavor of what is available.

Algorithm family	Based on	Examples
membership	`operator=`	`copy`, `remove`, `replace`
positioning	`operator=swap`	`random_shuffle`, `rotate`, `reverse`, `permute`
order	`operator<`	`sort`, `partition`, `merge`, `find`, `min`, `max`
matching and selecting	`operator==`	`unique`, `match`, `count`, `search`, `copy_if`, `remove_if`, `replace_if`
transform	function object	`for_each`, `transform`, `generate`, `fill`
numeric	function object	`inner_product`, `partial_sum`, `accumulate`, `adjacent_difference`

These are informal families, and I've only listed a small fraction of the total number of available algorithms here. The algorithms generally work with objects stored in containers, but they don't need to know anything about the particular container being used, because the objects are always accessed using iterators.

The first two groups — **membership** and **positioning** — deal with moving elements around. The primary operators used for this purpose are assignment and swap.

The **order** family of algorithms is the most important. Sorting is an immense discipline in its own right and using the right technique is critical to good performance. The algorithms provided by the STL for this are among the best known. Many of the STL algorithms are easy enough to replicate by hand, but the order algorithms are the big exception. If you only learn one family of algorithms, then learn the **order** algorithms.

The **matching and selecting** algorithms are simple yet very handy. These algorithms concern themselves with situations where elements are equal.

The **transform** family is less often seen in application programs. Unless the case is very simple, it often proves easier just to write out a **for** loop by hand. These algorithms serve as building blocks for extending the STL. The STL implementation is allowed to optimize these algorithms in ways that you can't gain access to when optimizing your own code. You should consider the use of these algorithms when performance is paramount.

The **function objects** on which the transform and numeric groups are based are class objects that overload the function call operator, **operator()**, and are specifically designed to pass a function as an argument more efficiently than using a raw function pointer.

> *The table above broadly classifies the algorithms according to the kind of object manipulation that dominates, but there are other ways of dividing them up. You will often see subsets of the algorithms being described as* mutating *and* non-mutating *algorithms. The former are the algorithms that change the contents of a container, and the latter are the algorithms that do not.*

STL Header Files

The facilities provided by the STL are declared in the following header files.

Header file	Purpose
<vector>	single-ended array container
<deque>	double-ended array container
<list>	bi-directional linked list container
<map>	associative array container

Table Continued on Following Page

Header file	Purpose
`<set>`	ordered set container
`<queue>`	double ended queue (container adaptor)
`<stack>`	stack (container adaptor)
`<iterator>`	iterators and container support
`<algorithm>`	general pupose algorithms
`<numeric>`	numeric algorithms
`<functional>`	function object support for algorithms
`<bitset>`	objects representing sequences of bits
`<valarray>`	arrays of numerical values
`<complex>`	complex number support
`<utility>`	support for function objects

There are also some STL components declared in the family of stream headers — `<iostream>`, `<istream>`, `<ostream>` and `<sstream>`. These work with STL to support input and output based on the fundamental STL algorithms.

Using the vector Container

The best place to begin a study of the STL is with the **vector** container. The vector container comes closest to mimicking a plain C++ array. In fact, the **vector** container can be used almost anywhere a C++ array might be used. The vector is much easier to use than a C++ array — with an array, you must take on the responsibility for managing the size and capacity of the array yourself, but with a **vector**, all of this administrative work is automated within the container.

Once you get used to **vector**, you may decide never to use a plain array again. The one task that still requires the use of a C++ array is in declaring static initializers:

```
string names[] = { "Alf", "Bjarne", "Zaphod" };
```

In a large program, you need to keep this kind of thing to a minimum. It is usually better to obtain fixed initializers from a program resource at runtime.

Try It Out – Comparing vector<> with the C++ Array

Let's take a quick look at an **int** array and a **vector** of **int**, and how they function in much the same way.

```cpp
// Program 20.1 A quick comparison of array and vector
#include <iostream>
#include <vector>
using namespace std;
```

```
int main()
{
  int a[10];                          // C++ array declaration
  vector<int> v(10);                  // Equivalent STL vector declaration

  cout << "size of 10 element array:  " << sizeof a << endl;
  cout << "size of 10 element vector: " << sizeof v << endl;

  for (int i = 0; i < 10; ++i)
    a[i] = v[i] = i;

  int a_sum = 0, v_sum = 0;
  for (int i = 0; i < 10; ++i)
  {
    a_sum += a[i];
    v_sum += v[i];
  }

  cout << "sum of 10 array  elements: " << a_sum << endl;
  cout << "sum of 10 vector elements: " << v_sum << endl;

  return 0;
}
```

When you run this program, it produces the output:

```
size of 10 element array:  40
size of 10 element vector: 16
sum of 10 array  elements: 45
sum of 10 vector elements: 45
```

How It Works

All STL objects are part of the standard library, and are therefore defined within the namespace **std**. Of course, you must include the appropriate header files for the STL facilities you need *before* you use them, and if you don't want to use names qualified with **std**, you can make the **std** namespace accessible with a **using** directive, as we have done here:

```
#include <vector>
using namespace std;
```

The only difference between using an array and a vector here is in the declarations:

```
int a[10];                          // C++ array declaration
vector<int> v(10);                  // Equivalent STL vector declaration
```

The C++ array is a built-in language type declared with **[]** syntax. On the other hand, **vector** is a standard library type implemented as a **class template**. The template parameter specifies the kind of object that the vector will contain. In this case we declare a vector to hold objects of type **int**.

In this example, the array **a** and the vector **v** are both automatic variables. For the array, this means that storage for 10 integers is created in automatic storage. On my machine, a variable of type **int** takes up 4 bytes of memory, so the array **a** will occupy 40 bytes, as you can see from the output.

The **vector** object **v** also lives in automatic scope, but (unlike the array) it doesn't store its contents in automatic storage. Instead, a vector internally allocates storage on the free store for the space to store the elements. Initially, it obtains at least enough storage for the elements stored — but you can add as many new elements as you wish. The vector's internal mechanism handles all the problems of storage allocation, and of obtaining enough free store memory to hold whatever you put into it (subject to the size of your free store!).

The size reported for the **vector** object does not include the space needed to store the elements. For this reason, this kind of object is often called a **handle**. It only contains enough memory to allow the vector to manage the storage of its elements. You can see that **sizeof** the **vector** object **v** occupies only 16 bytes. The *real* contents of **v** — the space needed to contain the values or objects that it stores — are allocated dynamically, and take up another 40 bytes in the free store.

Clearly, the array object does use less storage than the vector container. However, the overhead for each **vector** object is very low. One drawback of the array object is that it is allocated on the program stack, and the space and number of elements are fixed at compile time. The compensation for the small overhead of **vector** is twofold: first, your memory management is performed automatically, and second, you can add elements to the **vector** as and when you need.

Basic Operations on a vector Container

You can achieve enormous flexibility when working with a **vector**, far beyond that of a regular array. For example, you can add elements at the end of a **vector**, you can insert elements in the middle of the **vector** and you can delete elements. The space required is always managed automatically. At any time, you can find out how many elements there are in a **vector** object (by calling its **size()** member), and its **empty()** member will return **true** if the **vector** contains no elements.

The basic **vector** operations to add or remove elements are:

insert()	Insert one or more objects
push_back()	Add the object passed as an argument to the end of the vector
erase()	Erase one or more elements
clear()	Erase all elements

To understand how these operations work, let's try them out in an example. We'll need to jump right in with iterators here, but you've already seen them at work in Chapter 14, so you shouldn't find this too daunting. The **begin()** member of a **vector** object returns an iterator that points to the first element; and the **end()** member returns an iterator that points one beyond the last element of the vector. You can use these iterators to run through the elements of a vector if you wish — just increment the iterator returned by **begin()** until it equals the iterator returned by **end()**. Of course, you can also use the subscript operator, **[]**; it's entirely up to you.

Try It Out – A Quick Tour of the vector Container

This program runs through the simple **vector** operations that we've just introduced. We will try adding and removing some elements from a **vector** object, and various ways of inspecting the **vector**'s contents.

FYI

> Note that your implementation of the STL might not work with this example exactly as written, because at the present time there are considerable variations in the level of implementation of the STL. The ANSI/ISO standard should gradually put that right, as more and more C++ implementations are brought up to date. If the example doesn't work, you will need to check your library documentation to figure out what needs to be altered.

In this example, the function **show_sequence()** has been written to illustrate the equivalence of C++ pointers and **vector** iterators, as it existed in the original STL reference implementation. The **inspect_vector()** function, which we use to output the contents of a **vector** at various points, calls the **show_sequence()** function with iterator arguments.

```cpp
// Program 20.2 Manipulations of the vector<> container
#include <iostream>
#include <vector>                              // STL vector container
#include <algorithm>                           // For the copy() function

using namespace std;

// Display a sequence of elements
void show_sequence(const int* first, const int* last)
{
  cout << "{ ";
  copy(first, last, ostream_iterator<int>(cout, " "));
  cout << "}" << endl;
}

// Display the contents of a vector
void inspect_vector(const vector<int>& v)
{
  cout << "  vector has " << v.size() << " elements: ";
  show_sequence(v.begin(), v.end());
}

int main()
{
  vector<int> v;                               // Create empty vector
  cout << "new vector created" << endl;
  inspect_vector(v);

  cout << "filling vector from array" << endl;
  int values[] = {1, 3, 7, 5};
  v.insert(v.end(), values+1, values+3);       // Insert two elements
  inspect_vector(v);
```

```
    cout << "appending value 5" << endl;
    v.push_back(5);                                 // Add an element at the end
    inspect_vector(v);

    cout << "erasing element at offset 1" << endl;
    v.erase(&v[1]);                                 // Remove the second element
    inspect_vector(v);

    cout << "inserting element 4 at offset 1" << endl;
    v.insert (v.begin()+1, 4);                      // Insert an element
    inspect_vector(v);

    cout << "clearing all elements" << endl;
    v.clear();                                      // Delete all elements
    inspect_vector(v);

    return 0;
}
```

The output summarizes the contents of the **vector** object after each **vector** operation:

```
new vector created
  vector has 0 elements: { }
filling vector from array
  vector has 2 elements: { 3 7 }
appending value 5
  vector has 3 elements: { 3 7 5 }
erasing element at offset 1
  vector has 2 elements: { 3 5 }
inserting element 4 at offset 1
  vector has 3 elements: { 3 4 5 }
clearing all elements
  vector has 0 elements: { }
```

You can see that the **vector** container is good at keeping track of what it contains. With an array, you would have to shovel all these elements around the hard way.

How It Works

The code begins with **#include** directives for two of the STL header files:

```
#include <vector>                                  // STL vector container
#include <algorithm>                               // For the copy() function
```

The **vector** header file defines the **vector** container and all of its built-in operations. The STL allows you to do many things with a **vector** beyond what is provided directly by an instance of the **vector** template. The **algorithm** header file provides most of the extra goodies.

Next, we define the function **show_sequence()** to display a sequence of elements:

```
void show_sequence(const int* first, const int* last)
{
  cout << "{ ";
  copy(first, last, ostream_iterator<int>(cout, " "));
  cout << "}" << endl;
}
```

This function uses the STL algorithm, **copy()**, to output to **cout** an interval of values referenced through a pair of pointers. You can see from the program output that this works just fine. We'll come back to **ostream_iterator<>** later on, when we examine **output iterators** in more detail.

The **copy()** function is the only function in this example that is not internal to the **vector** template itself. The first two arguments of **copy()** define the source interval. Copying begins with **first** and proceeds up to, but not including, **last**. The **copy()** function will accept any iterators for its first two arguments — here we have used ordinary pointers.

The third argument to **copy()** is the destination position, which is also specified by an iterator. In this example, we supply an output iterator created by the expression **ostream_iterator<int>(cout, " ")** for the destination position. The STL is unique in allowing this much flexibility. The **copy()** algorithm assigns each source element into our destination object, without knowing exactly what kind of destination object it's dealing with. The **copy()** function just passes the objects to be copied to the iterator specified by the third argument, and assumes that the iterator knows where to put them. This makes the **copy()** function independent of the source and destination of the objects it is copying. In this case, the destination object echoes each value that is copied to the standard output stream, **cout**.

> *You can supply many different kinds of iterators to the STL algorithms, and they will act accordingly. An iterator can be like a pointer that reads and writes values into memory, or it can be a more sophisticated object that reads or writes values from a stream. The* copy() *function is as happy transferring objects from a vector to a stream as it is with transferring objects from one kind of container to another.*

The **inspect_vector()** function calls our **show_sequence()** function:

```
void inspect_vector(const vector<int>& v)
{
  cout << "  vector has " << v.size() << " elements: ";
  show_sequence(v.begin(), v.end());
}
```

This function definition demonstrates a rather nice feature of **vector** — notice that we're passing a **vector** object as a single argument. We don't need to pass a second argument, indicating how many elements the **vector** contains — or worse, how many elements the **vector** is *allowed* to contain. We output the number of elements in the **vector** object by calling its **size()** member. A **vector** always knows how many elements it stores.

Note that we obtain iterators to the first and last elements in our **vector** object by calling its **begin()** and **end()** members, and we pass these to the **show_sequence()** function. These iterators will be automatically converted to the type of the parameters for the **show_sequence()** function, **int***.

FYI

Vector iterators are almost identical to regular C++ pointers. In fact, many STL implementations define vector<T>::iterator to be a regular C++ pointer exactly, of type T*. This is what makes the vector such a good replacement for regular arrays. Pretty much anything you have learned to do with pointers can also be achieved with a vector container.

831

As we have already indicated, **v.begin()** points to the first element of the sequence. You can access the first element of the sequence by writing the expression ***v.begin()**, or **v[0]**, or **v.front()**. Which one to use depends on your purpose. Later in the chapter, we'll see situations in which each one of these might be considered the most natural method.

Note that you can't use the value pointed to by the pointer **end()** — it always points to the address one step *past* the last element in the container. The **end()** pointer is often referred to as a *past-the-end* value. Hence, ***v.begin()** is fair game, while the very similar expression ***v.end()** invites mayhem! Instead, ***(v.end()-1)** is a legal and useful way to gain access to the very last value of a sequence. You can also access the last element of a sequence by using the expression ***(v.begin()+v.size()-1)**, or **v[v.size()-1]**, or simply **v.back()**.

Before you attempt to access an element, you want to be sure that there *is* a last element. The quick way to check this is with the member function **v.empty()**, which returns **true** when the **vector v** contains no elements at all.

Our program uses the **vector** instance **vector<int>**, so we get a vector container that stores **int** values:

```
vector<int> v;                              // Create empty vector
```

Here we declare **v** as an instance of a class template **vector<int>** by calling the default constructor. You can see from the program output that our new vector starts life in the empty state. Of course, there are other constructors you can use. For example, if you wanted to accommodate 50 elements of type **double**, you could declare a vector **data** as:

```
vector<double> data(50);
```

There are many ways to put values into our new vector. One of the most powerful ways of adding elements is the **insert()** member function that copies an entire sequence into **v**, as in the following example:

```
cout << "filling vector from array" << endl;
int values[] = {1, 3, 7, 5};
v.insert(v.end(), values+1, values+3);      // Insert two elements
inspect_vector(v);
```

Here you can see again that the STL likes to define sequences as intervals, delimited between a pair of pointers. The first argument to the **insert()** function, **v.end()**, is a pointer to the location where we want the new elements to be inserted. Note that we are using the *past-the-end* value here — it's legitimate to use this address when you are concatenating.

> *Here's an easy way to remember what the* past-the-end *position signifies: it's where the next element will go when you append something new. Hence, you can use* **end()** *to add new elements to at the end of a* **vector** *— but don't try retrieving values by dereferencing* **end()**.

The second and third arguments to **insert()**, the expressions **values+1** and **values+3**, together specify the extent of the source sequence to be inserted. Our source sequence is the array **values**, and here we copy only the second and third elements — that is, beginning at **values+1**, and ending at the element *preceding* the position **values+3**. It's just like the iterators returned by **begin()** and **end()** for the contents of a **vector**.

FYI   Intervals are typically specified like this in the STL — an interval that includes the first position but excludes the last is referred to as a semi-open interval. You will see them written as [begin, end), where the brackets indicate that the interval is closed at the left end but open at the right end. Thus, the interval includes the position begin but not the position end.

> *When you specify [begin, end) intervals, such as with the expressions* `values+1` *and* `values+3`, *make certain that the end expression is larger than the begin expression — and that both pointers are associated with the same source object. These are common sources of costly mistakes.*

Let's return to the discussion of Program 20.2. We add an element using the **push_back()** member of the **vector**:

```
v.push_back(5);                              // Add an element at the end
```

This adds 5 as a new element, tacked on to the end of the vector **v**. Why isn't this function simply called **append()**? If *push* makes you think of stacks, then you are on the right track. In fact, the STL provides a **stack adaptor**, that can you can use to turn a **vector** into a stack. We won't go into the STL adaptors here, so will you need to consult your STL reference documentation for more details. Many of the STL names reflect the fact that the containers can be adapted to perform different functions, such as making **stacks** and **queues**.

Next, we exercise the **erase()** and **insert()** operations:

```
v.erase(&v[1]);                              // Remove the second element
```

The **erase()** and **insert()** operations involve 'sliding' elements around to open and close gaps where elements are added or removed. Internally, the **vector** container copies elements to keep things in the proper arrangement. This can be an expensive operation, as we shall see when we come to discuss vector storage management.

Since the **vector** container is a class template, it can also hold class objects, and in this case **erase()** must call the class destructor call for each object removed.

This statement removes the second element from the vector **v**. It uses the simplest form of **erase()**, which takes a single iterator argument that specifies a single element to be removed from **v**. A pointer argument is automatically converted to an iterator. Instead of using the **begin()** and **end()** members to generate iterators, we have used array notation to demonstrate how **v** pretends to be an array. The expression **&v[1]** refers to the address of the second element of **v**. As a result of this statement, the second element, whose value is 7, is eliminated from **v**.

Next, we insert a new element with the statement:

```
v.insert (v.begin()+1, 4);                   // Insert an element
```

We've already used **insert()** once, with two iterator arguments. In this form of **insert()**, the two arguments are an iterator and an integer. We specify an interior position using the expression **v.begin()+1**, and insert the new element — the value 4 — at this destination position. The element currently occupying the destination position, and all the elements following it must slide down to make a suitable gap for the new arrival. Once again, the **vector** object allocates new space and copies elements as necessary to keep things organized.

FYI

All this automatic copying is very convenient. However, your programs will certainly slow to a crawl if the vector is large and insertions and erasures near the front are frequent. STL offers another container, the list<>, that can do these same tricks without needing to slide anything around at all. We'll see the list in action very soon.

Our quick tour of the vector ends with a convenient way to clean things up:

```
v.clear();                                    // Delete all elements
```

We can use **clear()** to erase all the elements from the vector explicitly. However, this is not a necessity. When the vector instance **v** goes out of scope (at the end of the enclosing block), **v** and its contents are all cleaned up automatically by the destructor for **v**.

In fact, **v.clear()** is a short form of the expression **v.erase (v.begin(), v.end())**.

Using vector Containers with Array Operations

Let's look for a moment at an example that we first met with when discussing functions back in Chapter 8. This is the **average()** function, from Program 8.5, and it is interesting because it takes an **array[]** argument:

```
// Function to compute an average
double average(double array[], int count)
{
  double sum = 0.0;                           // Accumulate total in here
  for(int i = 0 ; i < count ; i++)
    sum += array[i];                          // Sum array elements

  return sum/count;                           // Return average
}
```

Before STL came on the scene, all C and C++ programs were written in this style. In spite of everything we've covered since Chapter 8, you can probably still recall that **double array[]** and **double* array** in this context mean exactly the same thing — so the first argument to **average()** is a pointer. Since an array does not know how many elements it contains, we always need to pass an extra argument indicating the **count** of the array. (In some cases, we'd also need to pass the **capacity**.)

Now let's look again at our **show_sequence()** function, from Program 20.2. This function *also* takes a pointer as its first argument, but uses a very different idiom. The second argument is also a pointer:

```
void show_sequence(const int* first, const int* last)
{
  cout << "{ ";
  copy(first, last, ostream_iterator<int>(cout, " "));
  cout << "}" << endl;
}
```

Remembering the equivalence between pointers and iterators, we can regard the parameters here as iterators. Again, the interval between **first** and **last** is a semi-open interval — **first** is contained in the interval, but **last** is not. However, this is significantly different from using a pair of index values, because the type of the objects in the interval is implicit in the iterators.

While using a vector and an interval is different from having an array and a variable **count**, it is still very easy to find out how many elements we are working with:

```
int count = last - first;
```

So why does the STL work with intervals rather than arrays and counts? There are several reasons. First, people doing a lot of work with arrays discovered that working with pointers is usually more convenient. Second, it can also be a lot more efficient. When you see a statement involving a multi-dimensional array, the compiler is doing a lot of work. For example, consider this code:

```
// what you write
double air_pressure[200][200][200];
double pressure_near_middle = air_pressure[99][100][101];
```

The compiler performs the task of finding the element **air_pressure[99][100][101]** by performing the following:

```
// what the compiler really does
double* temp =  air_pressure +
                99 * sizeof (air_pressure[0]) +
                100 * sizeof (air_pressure[0][0]) +
                101;
double pressure_near_middle = *temp;
```

As you can see, the compiler ends up doing all this arithmetic, simply to convert it all back to a pointer expression. A good compiler will also perform a lot of tricks to simplify this when it can — but even so, all those multiplications and additions don't come cheap.

The simple truth is that pointers are more basic than arrays, and remembering that an iterator is an object that acts like a pointer, this is one of the reasons why intervals specified by pairs of iterators are generally preferred in the STL.

Computing Averages using Iterators

We could define a template for the **average()** function that uses iterators instead of arrays. The code for the template in this case would be:

```
template <typename Iter>
double average (Iter a, Iter end)
{
  double sum = 0.0;
```

```
      int count = 0;
      for( ; a != end ; ++count)
        sum += *a++;
      return sum/count;                    // lets bad things happen if count==0
   }
```

Notice how few operations we perform on the parameter variable **a**:

a != end	check for last value
*a	obtain current value
a++	advance to next value

The last two were combined into the single expression ***a++**. You should recognize ***a++** by now as one of the most common C++ idioms. The way we have coded the template implies that the operations ***** and postfix **++** must work for the type **Iter**, and this will be the case for either pointer types or iterators. Using iterators has simplified the code quite a bit. Let's take it for a run.

Try It Out – Computing Averages with Template Iterators

Here's a program that calculates averages using our template:

```cpp
// Program 20.3 Computing the average function with template iterators
#include <iostream>
#include <vector>
using namespace std;

template <typename Iter>
double average(Iter a, Iter end)        // improves average(double*a,double*end)
{
  double sum = 0.0;
  int count = 0;
  for( ; a != end ; ++count)
    sum += *a++;
  return sum/count;                      // lets bad things happen if count==0
}

int main()
{
  double temperature[] = { 10.5, 20.0, 8.5 };
  cout << "array average = "
       << average(temperature, temperature +
                                     (sizeof temperature/sizeof temperature[0]))
       << endl;

  vector<int> sunny;
  sunny.push_back(7);
  sunny.push_back(12);
  sunny.push_back(15);
  cout << sunny.size() << " months on record" << endl;
  cout << "average number of sunny days: ";
  cout << average(sunny.begin(), sunny.end()) << endl;

  return 0;
}
```

The output from this program is:

```
array average = 13
3 months on record
average number of sunny days: 11.3333
```

How It Works

The great thing about templates is that you get as many versions as you want for the price of one. This example generates two instances of the function template **average**.

The first instantiation of **average** is for values stored in a regular C++ array:

```
double temperature[] = { 10.5, 20.0, 8.5 };
cout << "array average = "
    << average(temperature, temperature +
                        (sizeof temperature/sizeof temperature[0]))
    << endl;
```

The type for the template instance is determined implicitly from the function arguments. The second argument must be a pointer to the element *after* the last element we want to include — we calculate this by adding the number of elements in the array to the pointer **temperature**.

The second instantiation of **average** is for values stored in a **vector** of **int** values. First we declare the **vector<int>** object, **sunny**:

```
vector<int> sunny;
```

Then the instantiation is generated by the statement:

```
cout << average(sunny.begin(), sunny.end()) << endl;
```

The values returned by **sunny.begin()** and **sunny.end()** are of type **vector<int>::iterator** — this type is used to instantiate the second version of the template. Consequently, the two instantiations of the template function **average()** have the following signatures:

```
double average<double*>(double* a, double* end);
double average<vector<int>::iterator>(vector<int>::iterator a,
                                      vector<int>::iterator end);
```

As I've mentioned, some STL implementations of **vector** use pointers (such as **int***) as iterators. In this case, the second instance of **average()** would turn out to be:

```
double average<int*>(int* a, int* end);
```

However, not all STL implementations do this, and it's really not correct to assume that you can get away with the short declaration.

So that you can understand why we write the **::iterator** part in the type, here is a peek at what the class template vector might look like on the inside:

```
template <typename Value>
class vector
```

```
{
public:
  typedef Value* iterator;
  // lots more code ...
};
```

When we instantiate the **vector** template as **vector<int>**, it becomes equivalent to something along the lines of:

```
class vector<int>
{
public:
  typedef int* iterator;
};
```

Thus, **vector<int>::iterator** is just a way of referring to whatever type the vector has chosen to implement its iterators. The name **iterator** represents that type.

As you can see from the output, the calculation of the averages proceeds as we expected. Our function works just as well with elements in a **vector** container as it does with an ordinary array.

The Template Array Alternative

In Program 20.3, we used the interval convention for our template. Of course, we could have taken advantage of templates using the array idiom instead.

Try It Out – Computing Averages with Template Arrays

Here's an alternative version of Program 20.3:

```
// Program 20.4 Computing an average with template arrays
#include <iostream>
#include <vector>
using namespace std;

template <typename Array>
double average(Array a, long count)     // Array can be a pointer or an iterator
{
  double sum = 0.0;
  for (long i = 0; i < count; ++i)
    sum += a[i];
  return sum/count;                     // let bad things happen when count==0
}

int main()
{
  double temperature[] = { 10.5, 20.0, 8.5 };

  // second argument is now the count
  cout << "array average = "
       << average(temperature, (sizeof temperature/ sizeof temperature[0]))
          << endl;
```

```
    vector<int> sunny;
    sunny.push_back(7);
    sunny.push_back(12);
    sunny.push_back(15);
    cout << sunny.size() << " months on record" << endl;
    cout << "average number of sunny days: ";
    cout << average(sunny.begin(), sunny.end() - sunny.begin()) << endl;
    return 0;
  }
```

The output for this program is just the same as Program 20.3. The code looks even simpler! Note how we now only need one operation on the element **a**, namely **a.operator[](long)**. We can see from this notation that the subscript operator takes an argument of type **long** to represent the index value. In this version, we also have to declare our own loop variable **i** — with the previous version, that was unnecessary.

The istream_iterator Iterator

The next example shows how you can combine template algorithms with unusual kinds of iterators. We've seen **ostream_iterator** in action already — this time we use its complement, **istream_iterator**, to obtain data from an input stream.

Try It Out – The Magical istream_iterator<>

In the Programs 20.3 and 20.4, we used our **average()** function on values that already existed in an array or container. This time, the **average()** function will obtain values directly from an input stream, just by using another instance of the function template. We'll use the **average()** function template from Program 20.3 again:

```
// Program 20.5 Taking the average of values from a stream
#include <iostream>
#include <iterator>              // For the istream_iterator<> template
using namespace std;

template <typename Iter>
double average(Iter a, Iter end)
{
  double sum = 0.0;
  int count = 0;
  for( ; a != end ; ++count)
    sum += *a++;
  return sum/count;             // Lets bad things happen when count==0
}

int main()
{
  cout << "Enter some real numbers separated by whitespace - spaces, " << endl
       << "tabs or newline. Then press the special key sequence " << endl
       << "that marks the end-of-file (Ctrl-Z on a PC)" << endl;

  double av = average(istream_iterator<double>(cin), istream_iterator<double>());
  cout << "The average value is " << av << endl;
  return 0;
}
```

When you run the example, take care to use the right convention for closing the input stream. In the PC world, the magic keystroke for this purpose is *Ctrl-Z*. You may then need to press *Enter*. One popular programming environment comes from a company that needs to hear everything twice, so if at first you don't succeed in closing the stream, try pressing *Ctrl-Z* a few times on a separate lines.

Here's what the program output:

```
Enter some real numbers separated by whitespace - spaces,
tabs or newline. Then press the special key sequence
that marks the end-of-file (Ctrl-Z on a PC)
   3.6
   4.5
   5.7
   ^Z
The average value is 4.6
```

Your system may display something slightly different. Don't worry too much about running this example if it gives you difficulties. There's another example coming up that avoids the use of the console. We'll come back to the **istream_iterator** again soon.

How It Works

The following statement generates an instance of our template:

```
double av = average(istream_iterator<double>(cin), istream_iterator<double>());
```

We are now passing some really strange looking expressions into our average function! Let's write this another way, so that we can take a closer look at it:

```
istream_iterator<double> begin(cin);
istream_iterator<double> end;
double av = average(begin, end);
```

The object **begin** is an instance of the template class **istream_iterator<double>**. The stream object **cin** is passed in to the constructor, so that the iterator will read from the standard input stream.

The object **end** is also an instance of **istream_iterator<double>**. We create **end** using the default constructor for the **istream_iterator<double>** class. The variable **end**, when created in this way, behaves like a magic *past-the-end* value that corresponds to *end-of-file*.

Our new versions of **begin** and **end** definitely aren't pointers — they are class objects, so why does this work? The answer is that these class objects are iterators, which means that they can behave like pointers. They still provide the three operators that we are depending upon in our **average()** function, namely:

`bool Iter::operator!=(Iter end_value);`	Comparison
`double Iter::operator*();`	De-reference
`Iter Iter::operator++(int);`	Increment

This time, I've presented these as if they were class functions, because they really *are* class functions. They are overloaded operators functions in the class **istream_iterator<double>**. Remember that **operator++(int)** does not really take an **int** argument — that's just how we remind the compiler that we are specifying the postfix version of the increment operator. Any object of type **istream_iterator<double>** will allow us to perform these operations.

istream_iterator Iterators with Functionality

The **istream_iterator** objects above are pretending to be pointers, just as our **BoxPtr** class objects were in Program 14.6. However, these objects are capable of much more — they can provide you with the functionality of something as complex as stream I/O operators.

This is a fundamental concept, which helps to make the STL such a powerful library. Once we combine template functions and iterators, we can capture our intervals from *any* source. You can't do that using the old array notation.

Try It Out – More istream_iterator<> Magic

To emphasize the general nature of iterators, here's one final example. This time we'll exercise our semi-open interval around values contained in a string. If you had difficulty running Program 20.5, then try this one instead.

```
// Program 20.6 Taking the average of values from a string stream.
#include <iostream>
#include <iterator>
#include <sstream>                    // Source of the magic istringstream iterator
using namespace std;

template <typename Iter>
double average(Iter a, Iter end)
{
  double sum = 0.0;
  int count = 0;
  for( ; a != end ; ++count)
    sum += *a++;
  return sum/count;              // Lets bad things happen when count==0
}

int main()
{
  char* stock_ticker = "4.5 6.75 8.25";
  istringstream ticker(stock_ticker);
  istream_iterator<double> begin(ticker);
  istream_iterator<double> end;

  cout << "Readings: " << stock_ticker << ". Today's average is ";
  cout << average (begin, end) << endl;
  return 0;
}
```

The program produces the output:

```
Readings: 4.5 6.75 8.25. Today's average is 6.5
```

How It Works

If you look closely you will see that it is almost identical to Program 20.5, our example program that read from the stream **cin**. The difference is that, as a replacement for **cin**, we have created our own stream, **ticker**, using the class **istringstream**:

```
char* stock_ticker = "4.5 6.75 8.25";
istringstream ticker(stock_ticker);
```

We initialize our input stream, **ticker**, so that it takes its values directly from the program string **stock_ticker**. We then pass our stream object to the **istream_iterator<double>** constructor:

```
istream_iterator<double> begin(ticker);
```

The nice thing about our new stream **ticker** is that it can be used in most places where we might have put **cin** instead — **istream_iterator** is not too fussy. It's happy taking our **istringstream** object **ticker**, or taking a source of characters, in place of the file stream **cin**. Everything else remains the same, including our **average()** template!

The Iterator Plus

In Programs 20.3 – 20.6, we managed to get quite a lot of mileage out of our template version of the function **average()**. In fact, we only created three unique instances:

```
double average<double*>(double*, double*);
double average<int*>(int*, int*);
double average<istream_iterator<double> >
                    (istream_iterator<double>, istream_iterator<double>);
```

You can see clearly that the first two instances deal with simple pointers, while the third deals with **istream_iterator**, which is a class object. In Program 20.3, for example, we passed elements from a **vector<int>** container into the **average<int*>** version. We got extra mileage from the use of **istream_iterator** — in Programs 20.5 and 20.6, it allowed us to read numeric values from the console, and directly from a string.

The pointer versions cover both basic C++ arrays and vectors, while the **istream_iterator** version covers both files and strings. And we've still barely scratched the surface, where iterators are concerned.

The iterator class object still looks rather mysterious, so let's pause for a moment and dig a little deeper into how iterator class objects really work. You'll soon see that it's not that difficult to create iterator classes of your own.

Understanding Iterators

We have a little experience of a very simple iterator, from the **BoxPtr** class in Chapter 14; but there's a great deal more to it than that. We can understand how the STL iterators work by building one of our own, from the ground up. We'll start off with the simplest possible iterator, and extend it until we get to where we want to be — a full member of the STL iterator fraternity.

Try It Out – Creating your own Iterator

We'll start with the simplest of iterators, that iterates over the integers. Here's the code for our example:

```
// Program 20.7 Simple integer iterator class
#include <iostream>
using namespace std;

class Integer
{
  public:
    Integer (int arg = 0) : X(arg) {}

    bool operator!=(const Integer& arg) const     // Comparison !=
    {
      if (X == arg.X)                              // Debugging output
        cout << endl
              << "operator!= returns false" << endl; // Just to show that we are
                                                     // here
      return X != arg.X;
    }

    int operator*() const { return X; }            // De-reference operator

    Integer& operator++()                          // Prefix increment operator
    {
      ++X;
      return *this;
    }

  private:
    int X;
};

int main()
{
  Integer begin(3);
  Integer end(7);
  cout << "Today's integers are: ";
  for( ; begin != end ; ++begin)
    cout << *begin << " ";
  cout << endl;
  return 0;
}
```

When run, this program produces the exciting output:

```
Today's integers are: 3 4 5 6
operator!= returns false
```

How It Works

The program works as if we had declared **begin** and **end** to be plain integers and assigned them the same values, except that our **Integer**s create an output line when the overloaded **!=** operator returns **false**. We define the constructor for the **Integer** class as:

```
Integer (int arg = 0) : X(arg) {}
```

The **Integer** class has a data member **X** that stores the current value. If we fail to initialize an **Integer** object when we declare it, then the data member **X** will default to 0

The class defines an operator function for **!=**:

```
bool operator!=(const Integer& arg) const        // Comparison !=
{
  if (X == arg.X)                                 // Debugging output
    cout << endl
         << "operator!= returns false" << endl;   // Just to show that we are
                                                   // here
  return X != arg.X;
}
```

It takes an **Integer** object as the right argument and returns a Boolean value. You can see from the program output that as soon as **begin** is equal to **end**, the **!=** operator returns **false** and our loop terminates.

The de-reference operator is defined as:

```
int operator*() const { return X; }              // De-reference operator
```

This returns the data member **X** for the current **Integer** object, effectively 'de-referencing' the **Integer** object. This function, along with **operator!=()**, is declared **const** because it leaves the internal state of the object unchanged.

We have defined the prefix increment operator as:

```
Integer& operator++()                            // Prefix increment opertor
{
  ++X;
  return *this;
}
```

For the **average()** *algorithm of preceding examples, we used the expression* ***a++**, *which involved instead the* postfix **operator++(int)**.

Our **Integer** class now has four simple functions. In fact, that's all we need to make it behave sufficiently like a pointer to allow us to do some fancy things. In the function **main()**, we use the statement:

```
for( ; begin != end ; ++begin)
  cout << *begin << " ";
```

This sort of statement should look pretty familiar by now. We used something very similar in the like it in the **average()** algorithm, but there we used the expression ***a++**. In fact, replacing ***begin** with ***begin++** in the output statement won't work here, because we haven't defined the operator function **operator++(int)** that supports the postfix increment notation for the **Integer** class. Instead, we use ***begin** in the output line and **++begin** in the loop control. In fact, we could have written:

```
   for( ; begin != end ; )
     cout << *++begin << " ";
```

Here, the loop would output the values 4 through 7 instead. The return value from ***++begin** is the value of the data member **begin.X** *after* the increment has taken place.

Passing Iterators to an Algorithm

So what good is our **Integer** class? What can **Integer** do that a plain old **int** can't? Let's see.

Try It Out – Passing an Integer Object to average<>

```
// Program 20.8 Averaging values from Integer
#include <iostream>
using namespace std;

class Integer
{
  public:
    Integer (int arg = 0) : X(arg) {}              // Constructor

    bool operator!= (const Integer& arg) const    // != operator
    {
      return X != arg.X;
    }

    int operator*() const { return X; }           // * operator

    Integer& operator++()                          // Prefix ++ operator
    {
      ++X;
      return *this;
    }

    const Integer operator++(int)                  // Postfix ++ operator
    {
      Integer temp(*this);                         // save our current value
      ++X;                                          // change to new value
      return temp;                                 // return unchanged saved value
    }

  private:
    int X;
};

template <typename Iter>
double average(Iter a, Iter end)
{
  double sum = 0.0;
  int count = 0;
  for( ; a != end ; ++count)
    sum += *a++;
```

```
      return sum/count;              // Lets bad things happen when count==0
}
```

```
int main()
{
  Integer first(1);
  Integer last(11);
  cout << "The average of the integers from " << *first << " to " << -1+*last;
  cout << " is " << average(first, last) << endl;
  return 0;
}
```

This program produces the output:

```
The average of the integers from 1 to 10 is 5.5
```

How It Works

We didn't change much. We just added the postfix version of **operator++()**:

```
const Integer operator++(int)            // Postfix ++ operator
{
  Integer temp(*this);                   // save our current value
  ++X;                                   // change to new value
  return temp;                           // return unchanged saved value
}
```

We already know that to implement the postfix increment operator, we have to create a copy of the current object — something we don't have to do with the prefix form. Of course, this creates extra work because it calls the copy constructor. For this reason, most of the examples that follow will use the prefix form **++iter** wherever possible, because it's more efficient. It doesn't make much difference for our simple class, **Integer**, but when working through template algorithms you can't be sure just how expensive it might be to create the copy of the object that the expression **iter++** involves.

We apply our **Integer** class in the statements:

```
Integer first(1);
Integer last(11);
cout << "The average of the integers from " << *first << " to " << -1+*last;
cout << " is " << average(first, last) << endl;
```

Once again, **last** is a *past-the-end* value. We have to subtract one to get the inclusive range. Also, if **first** was a plain **int** instead of an iterator, then we wouldn't need to write the pointer expression ***first** in order to obtain its value.

If you stop to think about it, we've done something very different by calling **average()** with our new iterator **Integer**. In all the other examples, the values we averaged were associated with a source — they lived in arrays, they lived in vectors, or they lived in streams. In this example, the values don't exist anywhere. They are computed inside the **Integer** class as the **average()** algorithm invokes the fearsome **operator!=()**, **operator*()** and **operator++()** troika.

Imitating istream_operator and ostream_operator

It is not difficult to create class objects that behave like `istream_iterator` and `ostream_iterator`. Strangely, the STL does not provide any objects that work like our simple `Integer` iterator.

Try It Out – Calculating Averages Using partial_sum and accumulate

This program solves the same problem as Program 20.8, but uses only 'stock' STL components:

```cpp
// Program 20.9 Average of integer sequence using partial_sum and accumulate
#include <iostream>
#include <vector>
#include <algorithm>
#include <numeric>
using namespace std;

template <typename RndIter>
double average (RndIter first, RndIter last)
{
  return accumulate(first, last, 0.0)/(last-first);
}

int main()
{
  vector<int> v(10, 1);                    // Ten copies of value 1
  partial_sum(v.begin(), v.end(), v.begin());
  copy(v.begin(), v.end(), ostream_iterator<int>(cout, " "));

  cout << endl;
  cout << "The average is " << average (v.begin(), v.end()) << endl;
  return 0;
}
```

This program produces the output:

```
1 2 3 4 5 6 7 8 9 10
The average is 5.5
```

How It Works

Talk about doing things the hard way! However, the program works successfully, and it's actually more efficient than it looks. The **partial_sum** algorithm is one of the more exotic STL components. It behaves a lot like a sub-total function on an adding machine, replacing each term in a sequence with the sum of all terms up to and including the current element. Thus, the sequence 1, 2, 3, 4, 5 is replaced by 1, 3, 6, 10, 15.

In this example, we invoke **partial_sum** on a vector with 10 elements, each containing the value 1. The resulting values of the vector elements are shown in the output.

> *Thus, the **partial_sum** algorithm can be used to produce the integers from 1 to **N**. The moral of the story is that the STL doesn't always provide the most obvious routes to a simple goal. It has no direct equivalent of our **Integer** iterator.*

Iterator Requirements

So far our example class **Integer** has served adequately as an iterator for our simple purposes. However, the STL places a number of specific requirements on objects that purport to be iterators — this is to ensure that all the algorithms that accept iterators will work as expected.

One problem with template programming is that you don't always know all the types you need to use, before you use them. Consider the following example:

```
template <typename Iter>
void Swap(Iter& a, Iter& b)
{
  tmp = *a;  // error -- variable tmp undeclared
  *a = *b;
  *b = tmp;
}
```

What type should **tmp** be? We have no way of knowing — we know that it's the type pointed to by the iterator, but we have no idea what that might be. How do we declare a variable whose type we don't know?

The simple solution is to ensure that every iterator contains a **public** type definition for the **value_type** of the returned quantity:

```
template <typename Iter>
void Swap (Iter& a, Iter& b)
{
  typename Iter::value_type tmp = *a;        // better - but still not good enough
  *a = *b;
  *b = tmp;
}
```

In fact, this works fine with *most* of the STL iterators. However, if **Iter** is a pointer type such as **int*** — as is often the case — then this approach is not viable. The problem is that you can't simply write **int*::value_type** — pointers are built-in language types that do not contain internal type definitions.

The STL solves this problem, and other related problems, through the template **iterator_traits**, **iterator tags**, and a set of required **iterator types**:

```
template <typename Iter>
void Swap (Iter& a, Iter& b)
{
  // cumbersome, but always works
  typename iterator_traits<Iter>::value_type tmp = *a;
  *a = *b;
  *b = tmp;
}
```

The template **iterators_traits** determines whether or not the parameter **Iter** is a pointer. If **Iter** is a pointer, then we have something of the form **iterator_traits<T*>::value_type**, which is equivalent to the object type **T**. If **Iter** is a class object, then we have something of the form **iterator_traits<C>::value_type**, which is equivalent to **C::value_type**.

Therefore, to make our **Integer** iterator work with **iterator_traits**, it must contain an internal **public** type definition for **value_type**.

The following table lists all of the types that STL requires a custom iterator to define. For example, if you have an unknown template parameter **Iter**, you can write **Iter::pointer** when you need to declare a pointer to the type that the iterator provides when de-referenced.

Iterator types for Iter to T	Meaning
iterator_category	in, out, forward, bidirectional, or random
difference_type	iterator subtraction
value_type	T
reference	T&
pointer	T*

The values of **iterator_category** are taken from a fixed set of category tags. The iterator **category** determines what classes of algorithms the iterator is capable of working with.

Iterator type	Required category tag
input	**input_iterator_tag**
output	**output_iterator_tag**
forward	**forward_iterator_tag**
bidirectional	**Bidirectional_iterator_tag**
random	**random_access_iterator_tag**

A C++ pointer has the full functionality of a random access iterator. The other iterator categories are more restricted. As an example, we'll shortly look at a list container that provides **bidirectional** iterators. This kind of iterator can move forward or backward in single steps, but it can't be used with the subscript **operator[]** to perform random access.

FYI Once we've taken another look at **Integer** with all the new requirements, we'll come back and take a closer look at the stream iterators. You've already seen **ostream_iterator** in action. In fact, **ostream_iterator** is an example of an **output_iterator**. We'll look at the details of how this works shortly, but first let's press forward with our **Integer** iterator.

Integer Iterator Fortified

In Program 20.8, we were able to pass our **Integer** objects directly into the template function **average()**. That was something you couldn't have done with a plain old **int**. It turns out that you can do much more spectacular things with custom iterators and the STL, but there's a stiff price. Before your iterator will work with the facilities of the STL in general, you need to fill out your iterator class with a lot of boiler-plate declarations and member functions. Let's see how that pans out in practice.

Try It Out – A Fully Fledged Iterator

We'll now look at how class **Integer** looks with all the bells and whistles included that the STL requires of a full-blown random access iterator.

```
// Program 20.10 Full "random access" Integer iterator
#include <iostream>
#include <iterator>
#include <algorithm>
using namespace std;
#include <utility>
using namespace std::rel_ops;

class Integer : public iterator<random_access_iterator_tag, int, int, int*, int>
{
  public:
    Integer(int x=0) : X(x) {}                      // Default constructor

    Integer(const Integer& x) : X(x.X) {}           // Copy constructor

    ~Integer() {}                                   // Destructor

    Integer& operator=(const Integer& x)            // Assignment operator
    {
      X = x.X;
      return *this;
    }

    // Relational operators
    bool operator==(const Integer& x) const { return X == x.X; }
    bool operator!=(const Integer& x) const { return !(*this == x); }
                                                    // Delegate to operator==
    bool operator<(const Integer& x)  const { return X < x.X; }

    int operator*() const { return X; }
    int operator[](int n) const { return X+n; }

    // Bidirectional operators
    Integer& operator++()
    {
      ++X;
      return *this;
    }

    Integer& operator--()
    {
      --X;
      return *this;
    }

    Integer& operator++(int)
    {
      Integer temp(*this);
      ++X;
      return temp;
    }
```

```
      Integer& operator--(int)
      {
        Integer temp(*this);
        --X;
        return temp;
      }

      // Random access operators
      Integer operator+(int n) const { return Integer (X+n); }
      Integer operator-(int n) const { return Integer (X-n); }

  private:
    int X;
};

int main()
{
  Integer F1(-1);
  Integer L1(10);
  cout << "The values [-1..10) in forward order: " << endl;
  copy (F1, L1, ostream_iterator<int>(cout, " "));
  cout << endl;

  typedef reverse_iterator<Integer> CountDown;
  CountDown F2(10);
  CountDown L2(-1);
  cout << "the values (10..-1] in reverse order: " << endl;
  copy (F2, L2, ostream_iterator<int>(cout, " "));
  cout << endl;

  return 0;
}
```

Our tiny **Integer** class isn't so tiny any more. It now has everything a full-blown STL iterator requires. The interesting thing is our use of our fleshed out **Integer** with the fancy STL **adaptor**, **reverse_iterator**.

When run, the program produces this output:

```
The values [-1..10) in forward order:
-1 0 1 2 3 4 5 6 7 8 9
The values (10..-1] in reverse order:
9 8 7 6 5 4 3 2 1 0 -1
```

We shouldn't be too surprised to see that we get the same set of values viewed in either directions. Reversing a sequence leaves us with the same set of values, but in the opposite order. In forward order, the value 10 was *past-the-end*; in reverse order, it takes on the new a life as *before-the-beginning*.

This program may have difficulty compiling on some older compilers. While the C++ draft standard requires that the iterator template (which is used as a base class for Integer here) has 5 parameters, you may find that it has been implemented with only 4.

How It Works

This time, we'll start where the action is and work upwards. The magic here is the creation of the iterator class **CountDown**:

```
typedef reverse_iterator<Integer> CountDown;
CountDown F2(10), L2(-1);
cout << "the values (10..-1] in reverse order: " << endl;
copy (F2, L2, ostream_iterator<int>(cout, " "));
```

This is a class just like **Integer**, and yet it's different. The **reverse_iterator** type is known as an adaptor class. It is a template class that takes an iterator as its parameter and creates a new iterator as the result. The new iterator is exactly like the iterator we started with, but with a twist. Everything is now in reverse order.

We'll complete the discussion of Program 20.10 in a moment; but let's back up and take a look at two ways that we might use to call our old function **show_sequence()**, which we saw back in Program 20.2. Here's a very short program that has two calls to the function **show_sequence**. If you uncomment the second call, you'll get an error:

```
// Program 20.11 {rbegin} Problem with non-template algorithm
#include <iostream>
#include <algorithm>
#include <vector>
using namespace std;

// Display a sequence of elements
void show_sequence(const int* first, const int* last)
{
  cout << "{ ";
  copy(first, last, ostream_iterator<int>(cout, " "));
  cout << "}" << endl;
}
```

```
int main()
{
  int values[] = { 11, 88, 99 };
  vector<int> V(values, values+3);

  show_sequence(V.begin(), V.end());               // Might work, might not

//show_sequence(V.rbegin(), V.rend());             // Uncomment for an error
  copy(V.rbegin(), V.rend(), ostream_iterator<int>(cout, ".0 "));

  cout << endl;
  return 0;
}
```

This program produces the following output:

```
{ 11 88 99 }
99.0 88.0 11.0
```

As you can see, the **vector** container provides reverse iterators just for the asking. The member functions used are **rbegin()** and **rend()**. However, there are unanswered questions here: Why does **show_sequence()** work for the forward iterators and not the reverse iterators? Why does **copy()** work for both the forward iterators and for the reverse iterators?

852

The problem stems from the fact that we declared **show_sequence()** with the assumption that its arguments would be pointers — this is not a proper generic algorithm. A *true* generic algorithm should written as a template function:

```
template <typename FwdIter>
void show_sequence(FwdIter first, FwdIter last)
{
  cout << "{ ";
  copy (first, last, ostream_iterator<int>(cout, " "));
  cout << "}" << endl;
}
```

As we've already mentioned, some versions of STL (but not all) assume that **vector<int>::iterator** will be of type **int***. This generic algorithm covers all the bases without making any unnecessary assumptions.

What type does **rbegin()** return from the **vector** container? It is very probably an adaptation of the regular **iterator**, using the **reverse_iterator** adaptor:

```
reverse_iterator<vector<int>::iterator>
```

The adaptor **reverse_iterator** is a template class that adapts a regular **iterator** to life in reverse. Adaptors are an advanced STL concept, so we won't worry here about how this is accomplished. The important point is simply that there are many different iterator types and we shouldn't make too many assumptions.

Now we'll return to Program 20.10. The first line of the **Integer** class definition is the crucial statement that allows **reverse_iterator<>** to accept our **Integer** class:

```
class Integer : public iterator<random_access_iterator_tag, int, int, int*, int>
```

We are now hip deep in the syntactic briar patch. The base class, **iterator**, is an instance of a class template that is a helper class, to ensure that our **iterator** class declares all the required types (such as **iterator_category**, **value_type** and **pointer**).

Breiefly, here's how this works. The **Integer** class inherits from the **iterator** instance, and each argument passed to the **iterator** template defines one of the required iterator types. Since we inherit publicly from the **iterator** template, the types declared inside the **iterator** template end up as part of the **Integer** class's interface.

The first parameter is the iterator category. The **Integer** class has all the functions it needs to be included in the most powerful category **random_access_iterator**, so we base ourselves on that category tag.

The other four parameters define **value_type**, **difference_type**, **pointer** and **reference** respectively. The value type returned by **Integer** is an **int**, so we pass **int** as the argument for the **value_type** parameter position. Likewise, we pass **int*** for the argument position that defines the type **pointer**. The mechanics are not crucial. What's important is that our **Integer** class provides all the required type definitions and this is merely one way to get that job done.

The bulked out **Integer** class now has many more member functions, but they are all very simple. It helps if we collect them into groups.

The first group is the **constructors**. This includes some very important functions that all complex classes need to have: the **default constructor**, the **copy constructor** and the **assignment operator**. As a rule of thumb, if you write any of these functions for an iterator, then you should also write an explicit **destructor**. In this case we didn't need one; for **Integer** it does nothing. The prototypes for these functions are:

```
Integer(int x=0);                        // Default constructor
Integer(const Integer& x);               // Copy constructor
~Integer();                              // Destructor
Integer& operator=(const Integer& x);    // Assignment operator
```

We have cheated a little on our default constructor, since we get it through the default value for our constructor parameter. The STL uses the default constructor when it creates new elements for us in our containers, so it is essential that is defined.

The **equality** and **relational** operators defined in our class are:

```
bool operator==(const Integer& x) const;
bool operator!=(const Integer& x) const;
bool operator<(const Integer& x)  const;
```

The **#include** directive for the **utility** header file is relevant here:

```
#include <utility>
using namespace std::rel_ops;
```

If you provide **operator==()** and **operator<()** for your class type, then the **rel_ops** namespace contains function templates that will automatically generate operator functions for **!=**, **>**, **>=** and **<=**, for your class type. So activating **rel_ops** with the **using** declaration saves us the work of defining these four operators by hand.

In this example, we provided our own **operator!=**. Because of this, it takes precedence over the **operator!=()** that the **rel_ops** namespace creates on our behalf.

The operator **operator<()** is special. It is called the **ordering relation**. It will come up again when we look at searching and comparison algorithms. The STL makes enormous use of ordering relations. Given an **operator<()**, **rel_ops** automatically creates for us an **operator>()** with the following definition:

```
template<typename T> bool operator>(const T& x, const T& y) { return y<x; }
```

This one is accomplished just by reflecting the arguments **x** and **y**.

The operator **operator==()** is the **equality operator**, and is used to test for when two containers or objects have the exact same contents. There's an interesting consequence of how this works. You might think that for any pair of values **x** and **y**, the expression **(x<y || y<x || x==y)** must always return **true** — exactly one of the three component expressions must be true. In fact, it doesn't necessarily have to work that way. It's clear that if **(x==y)** is **true**, then neither **(x<y)** nor **(y<x)** can be **true**. One thing we can be certain about is that equal elements can't be different.

However, if **(x!=y)** we *must not* assume that one of **(x<y)** or **(y<x)** is **true** — when **(!(x<y)) && (!(y<x))** is **true**, the elements **x** and **y** are said to be *inequivalent*, which simply means we don't have a preference when sorting. A common example of this occurs when ordering strings, but ignoring case. On a case-insensitive basis, the strings **"A123"** and **"a123"** are inequivalent (neither belongs first), but they are not the same, nor are they equal.

Let's get back to the features of our **Integer** class. The following operators are known as the **access** operators:

```
int operator*() const;
int operator[](int) const;
```

They are used to return values from within the sequence. The operator **operator[]** is only found in iterators that belong to the powerful **random_access** category.

The group known as the bidirectional operators is as follows:

```
Integer& operator++();
Integer& operator--();
Integer& operator++(int);
Integer& operator--(int);
```

These allow you to step forwards or backwards one element at a time. Forward iterators don't go backwards, and so they don't provide either of the two decrement forms.

The operators that support **random access** are:

```
Integer operator+(int n) const;
Integer operator-(int n) const;
```

These are found whenever **operator[]** is present in a sequence container. They allow us to access any element in the sequence directly from any other, simply by subscripting with the appropriate offset. For example, consider the following code:

```
vector<int> V;
V.push_back(13);
V.push_back(42);
cout << V.end()[-1];    // Explicit use of operator[]()
cout << *(V.end()-2);   // Implies operator-()
```

The first output expression features legal use of **operator[]**. We can use negative subscripts if we start from a position beyond the front. In this case we refer to the element one spot before the *past-the-end* position, which is the value 42 (the last value in the sequence). It's up to us to ensure that the subscript used refers to a valid element within the sequence. The second output expression uses **operator-()** to directly access the first element of the **vector** from a base position at the end of the **vector**.

Input and Output Iterators

Input iterators are a category of iterators that can only be used to read values. Conversely, **output iterators** are iterators that can only be used to write values. These iterator categories do not support random access or stepping backwards. In fact, with these iterators you should be careful to read or write only once at each position.

The primary use of these iterators is to allow the STL algorithms such as **copy()** to act on streams. We've already made use of both **ostream_iterator** and **istream_iterator** along the way.

There is another very useful kind of **output_iterator**, that we can refer to as the **insert** iterator family. You can use these when you want to insert elements into a container using an algorithm such as **copy()**. For example, you can use the **back_inserter()** function to add elements to the end of a container:

```
template <typename Container, class Iter>
void append(Container& C, Iter src, Iter src_end)
{
  copy(src, src_end, back_inserter(C));
}
```

This defines a function template that will append elements to the container specified by the first parameter. The elements to be copied to the container are specified by the second and third parameters, which are iterators. The **back_inserter()** function takes a container as its argument and returns an **output_iterator** that appends each value received to the target container. If we copied to **C.end()** directly, the **copy** would function in *overwrite* mode, and we would violate the vector bounds by writing into areas of the vector that aren't available for writing. The output iterator functions in *insert mode*, so it grows the container as necessary.

The inserter **front_inserter()** is another useful one — it enables you to insert elements at the beginning of a container. Note that you can't use this with a **vector** container, because **front_inserter()** relies on a member of the container **push_front()** to insert elements at the beginning, and **vector** containers do not declare this member function.

Finally, the inserter **inserter()** inserts at any given position. For example:

```
copy(src, src_end, inserter(C, any_iterator_position_within_C));
```

This inserter inserts each element and then advances to the next position. The inserted elements occur as a group, in forward order, starting at the beginning insert position, so the container is expanded by the number of elements that are inserted.

Try It Out – Using an Inserter

We can try out **front_inserter()**. Since we can't use it with a **vector** container, we can try it out on a **list** container instead. We'll use a variation of the Program 20.11:

```
// Program 20.12 - Using an inserter
#include <iostream>
#include <iterator>
#include <algorithm>
#include <list>
using namespace std;

template <typename Container, class Iter>
void append(Container& C, Iter src, Iter src_end)
{
  copy(src, src_end, front_inserter(C));
}
```

```
int main()
{
  int A[] = { 1, 9, 7, 5, 15 };
  list<int> L;

  append (L, A, A+5);
  copy(L.begin(), L.end(), ostream_iterator<int>(cout," "));
  cout << endl;
  return 0;
}
```

The output of this program displays the inserted values in reverse order:

```
15 5 7 9 1
```

How It Works

The values from the array are reversed because we used **front_inserter()** in our **append()** function template. The values are inserted successively at the beginning of the **list<int>** container, **L**, starting with the first element in the array and ending with the last — so the last element of the array ends up as the first element in the container. As I said, you can't apply **front_inserter** to a **vector** container, but you can apply **back_inserter()** to both **vector** and **list** containers.

The Story So Far

So far we've taken a close look at the **vector** container, the template algorithm **average<>**, our roll-your-own iterator object **Integer** and the adaptor **reverse_iterator**; and we've witnessed in passing some uses of **input_iterator**, **output_iterator** and **stringstream**, as well as a few standard algorithms such as **copy()**.

You should be getting a feel by now for how the components of the STL fit together. The backbone of the STL is the melding together of **containers**, **iterators** and **algorithms**. **Containers** manage storage and provide us with iterators through which we can access the contents. **Iterators** define positions and intervals. **Algorithms** are template functions that are able to work with many different kinds of iterators using only a basic set of simple operations.

When we looked at our class **Integer**, we saw how most of this is accomplished through **emulation**. Our **Integer** class defined all the same operators that a normal pointer provides, so it can behave as if it were a pointer. This mimicry allows us to pass our custom **Integer** into any template function that might normally take a pointer.

We've now seen most of the crucial aspects of STL at work. The remainder of this chapter builds on this foundation. Now it's time to come back to **vector** and look more closely at how it manages storage.

Peeking at Storage Management

It's hard to peer inside the STL to figure out what is really going on. The STL specification is very concerned with performance (how often each kind of operator is invoked to satisfy an algorithm) and it devotes a lot of space to technicalities such as whether insertions and erasures invalidate other iterators that might be pointing at the same object.

It can be hard to get a feeling for what lies behind all this abstract discussion. The best way to get a feel for what is going on is to send in an advance scout.

We will define two simple classes — **Account** and **Bean** — that will define allow us to spy on all the element manipulations that are normally concealed. You can employ this technique whenever a you feel the need for the 'fundamental truth'.

The Account Helper Class

The class **Account** is used for counting events. It is implemented using the STL **map** container. This is one of the associative containers we will discuss later. For now, all you need to understand is the 'abstract interface' — how the class is required to behave.

```
// Account.h
#ifndef ACCOUNT_H
#define ACCOUNT_H
#include <iostream>
#include <iomanip>
#include <string>
#include <map>
using namespace std;

class Account
{
  typedef map<string, int> Ledger;

  public:
    Account(void) {}
    void clear(void) { L.clear(); }

    Account& operator<<(const string& item)
    {
      L[item]++;
      return *this;
    }

    void audit(void) const
    {
      Ledger::const_iterator iter;
      for(iter = L.begin(); iter != L.end(); ++iter)
        cout << setw(7) << iter->second << " " << iter->first << endl;
    }

  private:
    Ledger L;
};
#endif
```

The two main functions in class **Account** are **operator<<()** and **audit()**.

Try It Out – The Account Class

If you want to try the **Account** class out, you could use the following short program:

```cpp
// Program 20.13 A first run with the account class
#include <iostream>
#include "Account.h"
using namespace std;

int main()
{
  Account A;

  cout << "First audit" << endl;
  A << "event1";
  A << "event2";
  A << "event1";
  A.audit();

  cout << "Second audit" << endl;
  A << "torpedo";
  A << "event1";
  A.audit();

  return 0;
}
```

This program produces the output:

```
First audit
        2 event1
        1 event2
Second audit
        3 event1
        1 event2
        1 torpedo
```

FYI

Your compiler may produce a number of warnings when you try to compile this code. This is because the names of the objects involved are rather long — remember that the *full* names will include the names of all the templates from which your objects' classes were instantiated. Although this is unlikely to cause problems for the compiler itself, some debugging tools can't handle very long names, and the compiler is warning you on their behalf.

It's likely that you'll be able to get rid of the warnings by disabling them with a **#pragma** preprocessor directive placed at the top of your source files, but you'll need to consult your compiler's documentation for precise details on how to do so.

As you can see, calling **audit()** just outputs a summary of the insertion operations on the **Account** object up to the point when it was called. We will now use the **Account** class in the definition of another class.

STL Element Requirements and the Ideal Bean

The **Bean** class will define an object that we can use as a container element, to spy on what the container is doing. So, rather than having, say, **vector<int>**, we will use **vector<Bean>**. You can store **Bean** objects in the container, and at any time you can request a **usage_report**, which shows exactly how many times each **Bean** operator was invoked during the proceedings.

The **Bean** class will use an **Account** object, **log**, to keep track of how often a container invokes each **Bean** operation. To make it easy to use, the events counted are strings that describe the operators invoked. One crucial trick is involved here: the **Account** object **log** is declared as a **static** member variable in the **Bean** class. We are not trying to count the operations on individual **Bean** objects, but rather the total operation count for *all* the **Bean** objects that co-exist in a container at the same time. Declaring **log** as **static** makes all **Bean** objects share the same set of event counts.

Take a quick look at the operators defined by class **Bean**. They are a very important group.

```cpp
// File "Bean.h"
#ifndef BEAN_H
#define BEAN_H

#include <iostream>
#include <string>
#include "Account.h"
using namespace std;

class Bean
{
  public:
    Bean(void) { log << "default_constructor"; }        // Default constructor

    Bean(const Bean& x) { log << "copy_constructor"; }  // Copy constructor

    Bean& operator=(const Bean& x)                       // Assignment operator
    {
      log << ((this == &x) ? "self_assignment" : "assignment");
      return *this;
    }

    ~Bean() { log << "destructor"; }                     // Destructor

    bool operator==(const Bean& x) const                 // Equality
    {
      log << "equality_test";
      return true;
    }

    bool operator<(const Bean& x) const                  // Comparison
    {
      log << "operator_less";
      return false;
    }

    friend void clear_bean_log(void) { log.clear(); }
```

```
        friend void usage_report(const string& caption = "")
        {
          if (caption != "") cout << caption << endl;
          log.audit();
          cout << "-end-" << endl;
          log.clear();
        }

      private:
        static Account log;
    };
    #endif
```

The class **Bean** defines all of its member functions within the class declaration. However, there is one aspect of class **Bean** that is not suitable for placement in the **Bean.h** header file: we must declare the **static** variable **log** in a separate compilation unit, **Bean.cpp**, to ensure that it does not become multiply-defined:

```
// File "Bean.cpp"
#include "bean.h"

Account Bean::log;
```

This calls the default constructor for the **Account** class to create the **log** member of the **Bean** class.

> *Remember to include the object file produced by compiling* **bean.cpp** *as one of your link objects, or your linker will complain that the variable* **Bean::log** *is undefined.*

Required Features of Container Elements

Since the **Bean** class is intended to be a kind of 'ideal' container element, for the purposes of spying on what STL containers are really doing, it also serves as a good illustration of what all good container elements ought to be. The STL imposes a minimum set of requirements on what member functions should be provided by any element that is stored in a container. These are shown in the following chart:

Family	Required functions
constructors	`Element()` `Element(const Element& X)`
assignment	`Element& operator=(const Element& X)`
equality	`bool operator==(const Element& X) const`
order	`bool operator<(const Element& X) const`

This list is not too onerous — in fact, just about any interesting class will provide all of these operators.

You should note that **operator<()** is not *strictly* required. However, it is best to provide a definition for ordering your elements whenever it makes sense. If you don't, then your element class will be unusable in any of the associative containers (such as **map** and **set**) and your element sequences won't work with any of the ordering algorithms.

Once again, this table assumes that **std::rel_ops** is in effect to synthesize the variants **!=**, **<=**, **>** and **>=**. If you don't bring in the namespace **std::rel_ops**, you will also have to define these additional operators.

Don't forget to provide a **destructor** if your class is managing its own storage; and be certain to make that a **virtual** destructor if your object participates in an inheritance hierarchy.

Try It Out – A Bean in Action

Now let's take a quick look at our ideal **Bean** element in action.

```
// Program 20.14 A Bean in action
#include "bean.h"

int main()
{
  Bean A;
  Bean B;
  A = B;

  if(A==B)
    cout << "All Beans are created equal" << endl << endl;
  if(A<B)
    cout << "Big trouble" << endl;

  usage_report("assign, compare, and order");

  Bean* pB = new Bean[10];
  delete[] pB;

  usage_report("new and delete 10 elements");

  return 0;
}
```

When run, this short program produces the following results:

```
All Beans are created equal

assign, compare, and order
      1 assignment
      2 default_constructor
      1 equality_test
      1 operator_less
-end-
new and delete 10 elements
     10 default_constructor
     10 destructor
-end-
```

Note that after each report, the statistics are cleared. You can elaborate on that behavior if you wish with a few simple changes.

You should keep **Account** and **Bean** in your toolbox! They're always handy to have around if you need to understand the mechanics of what happens behind the scenes. This is especially true if you are working with polymorphic classes. Embedding a **Bean** in the right place can be a quick way to learn whether C++ is calling constructors, assignment operators and destructors as often as your design intends.

Measuring vector and vector Storage Management

This simple benchmark program uses **Bean** to put **vector** through its paces. You can get a good understanding of each vector function by comparing the source with the results.

Try It Out – vector Size, Capacity and Resize

Here's the code:

```
// Program 20.15 Vector size, capacity and resize
#include <vector>
#include "bean.h"              // Includes all the other standard headers needed
using namespace std;

void constructor_tests(void)
{
  clear_bean_log();
  vector<Bean> V;
  usage_report("vector<Bean> V");
  vector<Bean> W(3);
  usage_report("vector<Bean> W(3)");
  vector<Bean> X(5,Bean());
  usage_report("vector<Bean> X(5,Bean())");
  vector<Bean> Y(X.begin(),X.end());
  usage_report("vector<Bean> Y(X.begin(),X.end())");
}

void resize_tests(int reserve = 0)
{
  vector<Bean> V;
  if(reserve != 0)
  {
    cout << "resize_tests performed after reserving space for "
         << reserve << " elements" << endl;
    V.reserve(reserve);
  }
  clear_bean_log();
  int sizes[8] = { 1, 10, 100, 20, 50, 101, 0 };
  for(int i = 0; i < 7; ++i)
  {
    V.resize (sizes[i]);
    cout << "resizing V to " << sizes[i] << endl;
    usage_report();
  }
}
```

```
void insert_tests(void)
{
  Bean E;
  vector<Bean> W;
  vector<Bean> V;
  clear_bean_log();
  for(int j = 0; j < 1000; ++j)
    W.push_back(E);
  usage_report("1000 push_back() operations");
  for(int k = 0; k < 1000; ++k)
    V.insert(V.begin(), E);
  usage_report("1000 inserts at front");
}

void assign_and_compare_tests(void)
{
  vector<Bean> X(77);
  vector<Bean> Y(456);
  cout << "X has 77 members; Y has 456 members" << endl;
  clear_bean_log();
  X==Y;  usage_report("compare: X==Y");
  X=X;   usage_report("assign self: X=X");
  X<Y;   usage_report("order: X<Y");
  X=Y;   usage_report("assign: X=Y");
  X==Y;  usage_report("compare: X==Y");
}

int main()
{
  constructor_tests();
  resize_tests();
  resize_tests(100);
  insert_tests();
  assign_and_compare_tests();

  return 0;
}
```

If you don't want to get all the output in one go, you can comment out the statements in **main()** for bits you don't want. In the following discussion we'll break down the output into the relevant parts.

How It Works: Constructor tests

The output from the **constructor_tests()** function is:

```
vector<Bean> V
-end-
vector<Bean> W(3)
      3 copy_constructor
      1 default_constructor
      1 destructor
-end-
vector<Bean> X(5,Bean())
      5 copy_constructor
      1 default_constructor
      1 destructor
-end-
```

```
vector<Bean> Y(X.begin(),X.end())
       5 copy_constructor
-end-
```

There's nothing unexpected here. The first report shows that the **Bean** constructor isn't called when an empty vector is declared. The declaration of vector **W** will initially contain 3 **Bean** objects — the constructor **W(3)** invents a **Bean** object argument to serve as the default element, just as if we had written it ourselves. We can see the resulting calls in the second report.

The declaration of the vector **X** is very similar to the declaration of **W**. Again, the report shows that the **Bean** argument value is constructed and destroyed as part of the function call semantics. This adds to the work, beyond what takes place inside the vector constructor. Finally, the report on the declaration of vector **Y** shows that the copy constructor is called — it copies elements from **X** into **Y**. In this case, no default element is needed and so we don't see the **default_constructor** and **destructor** events.

Resize tests

The output for the **resize_tests()** function is as follows:

```
resizing V to 1
       1 copy_constructor
       1 default_constructor
       1 destructor
-end-
resizing V to 10
      10 copy_constructor
       1 default_constructor
       2 destructor
-end-
resizing V to 100
     100 copy_constructor
       1 default_constructor
      11 destructor
-end-
resizing V to 20
       1 default_constructor
      81 destructor
-end-
resizing V to 50
      30 copy_constructor
       1 default_constructor
       1 destructor
-end-
resizing V to 101
     101 copy_constructor
       1 default_constructor
      51 destructor
-end-
resizing V to 0
       1 default_constructor
     102 destructor
-end-
```

This output shows how **vector** storage management comes at a price — there's a lot of destroying and copying of objects happening behind the scenes, as **vector** ensures that it has a large enough block of memory to contain the entire sequence. Note what happens when **v** is resized to 100 — we can infer from the report that the STL implementation has obtained new storage for the entire sequence! It copies the ten existing elements into the new storage, creates the additional ninety elements requested using the copy constructor, and then cleans up by destroying the original ten elements in the storage they occupied before they were copied.

You should keep in mind that once a vector grows, it never shrinks back down unless you call a special function (such as **resize()**) to shrink it explicitly. After a **vector** reaches a sufficient size for the task at hand, the overhead of destroying and copying disappears. When you add it all together, the total overhead never greatly exceeds the maximum number of elements that the vector is asked to contain. You shouldn't worry much about this overhead.

Sometimes it pays to be aware that a vector retains *all* the storage it has used, even if you erase all-but-one of the elements. If such memory allocation becomes a problem — say, if you have a large, sparse vector taking up free store memory that you need for a new vector — you can take control by using vector assignment or **swap()**. For example, here's a function that trims the storage owned by a vector back to that required for the elements that are in use:

```
template <typename T>
void trim_vector(vector<T>& V)
{
  vector<T> tmp(V.begin(), V.end());
  V = tmp;        // Alternatively, use   V.swap(tmp);  ...
                  // ... swap() has the same effect, but is more efficient
}
```

Either way, the argument vector **v** ends up just owning the storage associated with **tmp**, and its original storage (which might have grown to be excessive) will be released because the original object, **v**, will have been destroyed.

More resize tests

Here's the output from the function call **resize_tests(100)**:

```
resize_tests performed after reserving space for 100 elements
resizing V to 1
        1 copy_constructor
        1 default_constructor
        1 destructor
-end-
resizing V to 10
        9 copy_constructor
        1 default_constructor
        1 destructor
-end-
resizing V to 100
       90 copy_constructor
        1 default_constructor
        1 destructor
-end-
resizing V to 20
        1 default_constructor
       81 destructor
-end-
```

```
resizing V to 50
     30 copy_constructor
      1 default_constructor
      1 destructor
-end-
resizing V to 101
    101 copy_constructor
      1 default_constructor
     51 destructor
-end-
resizing V to 0
      1 default_constructor
    102 destructor
-end-
```

Compare this with the output from the function call **resize_tests()**, with the default parameter. Here, we have avoided the overhead of reallocating the 100-element vector by specifying an adequate **reserve()** when the vector is declared. There is no overhead until you insert more elements than you reserved.

Insert tests at front and back

Here's the output generated from **insert_tests()**:

```
1000 push_back() operations
   2023 copy_constructor
   1023 destructor
-end-
1000 inserts at front
 498477 assignment
   2023 copy_constructor
   1023 destructor
-end-
```

From the numbers shown in this output, it's easy to see that inserting into a **vector** at positions other than **end()** can lead to a lot of grief. This is one aspect of the **vector** container that is far from ideal.

If inserting elements in the interior of a sequence is a dominant operation in your design, then you should seriously consider using the **list** container instead. In fact, if you tweak this test to use **list** instead of **vector**, you will see that both **push_back** and **insert** require just 1000 copy constructor calls — one for each element inserted. We'll see **list** in action shortly.

Assignment, comparison and order tests

Finally, here's the output when **assign_and_compare_tests()** is called:

```
X has 77 members; Y has 456 members
compare: X==Y
-end-
assign self: X=X
-end-
order: X<Y
    154 operator_less
-end-
assign: X=Y
```

```
    456 copy_constructor
     77 destructor
-end-
compare: X==Y
    456 equality_test
-end-
```

You can see from the first report that the first **X==Y;** statement generated no events — so how does the STL compare two vectors without comparing any elements? In fact, it's more efficient to check the **size()** of each vector first. If the two vectors are not the same size, then they can't be equal.

Likewise, the **vector** container is clever about self-assignment. It checks to see if the argument vector has the same address as its own vector. If the addresses match, **vector** can assume that all the copying of its own elements is unnecessary. Hence, there are no events ereported for the statement **X=X;**.

Why does **operator<()** take 154 comparisons rather than 77? It turns out you have to use **operator<()** *twice* to determine that two elements are equivalent under ordering:

```
    elements_are_equivalent = !(a<b) && !(b<a);   // operator<() used twice
```

This simply says that if neither element belongs first, you can assume that they are equivalent. As we already said, *equivalent* does not necessarily mean *equal*. If, for example, **operator<()** is a case-insensitive string comparison, then elements that differ only in case will be equivalent, but that doesn't make them equal. Consider the strings **"macnee"** and **"MacNee"** — these strings are not equal, but they might considered equivalent under a case-insensitive ordering.

The order of **X** and **Y** is determined by the first position where the compared elements are not equivalent. In this example, **X** and **Y** are exactly the same, so every position must tested twice with **operator<()** to establish equivalence.

The list Container

We've covered a lot of ground on the **vector** container: we've seen how it manages storage, how iterators function, and how iterators serve as generic arguments for template algorithms. That covers the basic concepts implicit in the STL architecture. The **list** container is a variation on a theme. It provides largely the same interface and functionality as **vector**, but it is optimized for different circumstances.

A paramount concern for the designers of the STL was to provide efficient mechanisms for any task that might arise. The **vector** serves well in any situation where a C++ array might be used — it is a very useful, general purpose container. However, there are situations, as we've seen, where the use of **vector** is not ideal. In Program 20.15 we observed that the **vector** container must perform hidden reallocations, and sometimes vast numbers of assignment operations to support the **insert** and **erase** functionality. It worked quite well when we inserted at the **back** position, and not at all well when we inserted and deleted elements near the **front** position.

Unlike **vector**, the **list** container is ideally suited to handle inserts and erasures at any position. Let's acquaint ourselves with **list** by returning to a familiar example program.

Try It Out – Using the list Container

We took a long look at the **list** data structure in Chapter 13, when we developed the **Package** class for storing boxes by the truckload. Now we are ready to look an implementation of **TruckLoad** with the full power of the STL list container at our disposal.

```
// Program 20.16 A TruckLoad container implemented using an STL list container
// Recapitulates Program 13.1
#include <iostream>
#include <algorithm>
#include <list>
using namespace std;

class Box
{
  public:
    Box(double l = 1.0, double w = 1.0, double h = 1.0) : L(l), W(w), H(h) {}

    double volume() const { return L*W*H; }
    bool operator<(const Box& x) const { return volume() < x.volume(); }

    friend ostream& operator<<(ostream& out, const Box& box)
    {
      out << "(" << box.L << "," << box.W << "," << box.H << ")";
      return out;
    }

  private:
    double L;
    double W;
    double H;
};

class TruckLoad
{
  typedef list<Box> Contents;

  public:
    TruckLoad() {}
    TruckLoad(const Box& one_box) : Load (1, one_box) {}

    template<typename FwdIter>
    TruckLoad(FwdIter first, FwdIter last) : Load (first, last) {}

    void add_box(const Box& new_box) { Load.push_back (new_box); }

    typedef Contents::const_iterator const_iterator;

    const_iterator begin() const { return Load.begin(); }
    const_iterator end() const { return Load.end(); }
```

```
  private:
     Contents Load;
};

inline int random(int count)
{
  return 1 + static_cast<int>((count*static_cast<long>(rand()))/(RAND_MAX+1));
}

inline Box random_box(int range)
{
  return Box(random(range),random(range),random(range));
}

int main()
{
  TruckLoad Rig(Box(30,30,30));
  for(int i = 0; i < 8; ++i)
    Rig.add_box(random_box(100));

  cout << "Contents of Rig1" << endl;
  copy(Rig.begin(), Rig.end(), ostream_iterator<Box> (cout, "\n"));
  cout << endl;

  typedef TruckLoad::const_iterator BoxIter;
  BoxIter big_one = max_element(Rig.begin(), Rig.end());

  cout << "The biggest box in Rig1 is " << *big_one
       << " with volume " << big_one->volume() << endl;
  cout << endl;

  cout << "Copying all boxes starting at big box to Rig2" << endl;
  TruckLoad Rig2(big_one, Rig.end());
  cout << "Contents of Rig2" << endl;
  copy(Rig2.begin(), Rig2.end(), ostream_iterator<Box> (cout, "\n"));
  cout << endl;

  return 0;
}
```

When you run this program, it produces the following output.

```
Contents of Rig1
(30,30,30)
(20,57,1)
(48,59,81)
(83,90,36)
(86,18,75)
(31,52,72)
(37,10,2)
(99,17,15)
(1,12,45)

The biggest box in Rig1 is (83,90,36) with volume 268920
```

```
Copying all boxes starting at big box to Rig2
Contents of Rig2
(83,90,36)
(86,18,75)
(31,52,72)
(37,10,2)
(99,17,15)
(1,12,45)
```

How It Works

Before we look at what happens in **main()**, let's cover the groundwork. We are already familiar with class **Box** and how it is used. This version of the **Box** class supplies two operator functions. The first is:

```
bool operator<(const Box& x) const { return volume() < x.volume(); }
```

By providing **operator<()** we can compare pairs of boxes — this is necessary when we use the **max_element()** function from the STL.

We also overload the insertion operator for a stream:

```
friend ostream& operator<<(ostream& out, const Box& box)
{
  out << "(" << box.L << "," << box.W << "," << box.H << ")";
  return out;
}
```

Defining **operator<<()** for use with an **ostream** object makes it easy to write a **Box** object to an output stream. Remember that a **friend** function of a class is *not* a member function, so it does not receive a **this** pointer. The **Box** object output by this function is passed to the **operator<<()** function explicitly as the second argument. The return type for the function is **ostream&**. This makes our function more convenient to use in compound statements, since it makes it possible to use the function in a series of successive writes to a stream.

Our definition of **TruckLoad** is very simple:

```
class TruckLoad
{
  typedef list<Box> Contents;

  // public members ...

  private:
    Contents Load;
};
```

This definition provides us with our own interface, on top of what the **list** container gives us for free. The contents of the **TruckLoad** are contained in a member variable called **Load**, which is a **list** of **Box**es. Almost every function we define is implemented by a single use of an equivalent function provided by **Load**. We use the **typedef** for **Contents** as a convenience for declaring other class functions. It's exactly the same as if we had written:

```
private:
  list<Box> Load;
```

We have three constructors in the **TruckLoad** class:

```
TruckLoad() {}
TruckLoad(const Box& one_box) : Load (1, one_box) {}

template<typename FwdIter>
TruckLoad(FwdIter first, FwdIter last) : Load (first, last) {}
```

The first constructor is a default constructor, and the second constructor initializes the **TruckLoad** object to contain a single **Box** element.

The third constructor is a template constructor. We can pass iterators to this constructor, to initialize our **TruckLoad** to contain a copy of any sequence of **Box** objects we have already created. The iterators are declared using a class template; so the type of the iterators is very flexible — they might be pointers to an array of boxes, iterators into a **vector<>**- or **list<>**- based collection of boxes, or even iterators into the contents of another **TruckLoad**.

This is easy for us to implement. The **Load** object is a **list**, so it already provides us with a template sequence constructor. All we have to do is pass along the **first** and **last** arguments just as we received them, and the **Load** constructor does the rest.

Adding a **Box** object to a **TruckLoad** object is done with the function **add_box()**:

```
void add_box(const Box& new_box) { Load.push_back (new_box); }
```

We could have used **push_front()** to put the new **Box** object at the front of the **Load** list. Trucks aren't usually loaded that way, so we use **push_back** and add our new **Box** to the end of the list.

Next we have another **typedef**:

```
typedef Contents::const_iterator const_iterator;
```

Here, **Contents** is a synonym for the type **list<Box>**, so **Contents::const_iterator** is a synonym for **list<Box>::const_iterator**. It's a useful shorthand if you can remember what all the synonyms mean!

We make it possible for clients of class **TruckLoad** to gain access to iterators to the truck's contents with the members following the **typedef**:

```
const_iterator begin() const { return Load.begin(); }
const_iterator end() const { return Load.end(); }
```

These are constant iterators. We don't want our clients changing the contents of our **TruckLoad** behind our backs, just before we attempt to clear customs!

Our two functions **begin()** and **end()** return the **Load** iterators directly. It's not a perfect design, since we expose part of our implementation — the fact that we are using a **list** internally to track our contents. However, it is very convenient, and if our clients are well behaved they won't take advantage of any special knowledge that these iterators point to a **list**, rather than some other kind of container we might have chosen.

Because we are returning iterators, our **TruckLoad** behaves a lot like a container. That's not a bad thing, since our **TruckLoad** is a lot like a container to begin with.

The program uses the global functions **random()** and **random_box()**, which provide an easy way to create random boxes for use in the example program:

```
inline int random(int count)
{
  return 1 + static_cast<int>((count*static_cast<long>(rand()))/(RAND_MAX+1));
}

inline Box random_box(int range)
{
  return Box(random(range),random(range),random(range));
}
```

We saw this same definition of **random()** in the previous **TruckLoad** example — the details of how it works are covered in Chapter 13.

Now we can look at some of the more interesting parts of the function **main()**. Consider the statements:

```
cout << "Contents of Rig1" << endl;
copy(Rig.begin(), Rig.end(), ostream_iterator<Box> (cout, "\n"));
cout << endl;
```

The third argument of the **copy()** call can be translated as follows:

```
ostream_iterator<Box> out(cout, "\n");
*out = random_box();
```

Here, **ostream_iterator** creates a temporary variable called **out**. The constructor takes two arguments: the output stream, to which the text is written, and an optional separator value that is written after each element. We set this up to write a **newline** (the **"\n"** character) after each **Box** is printed.

The variable **out** is an iterator of type **ostream_iterator<>**. That means that **out** can be used the same way as any other output iterator. When we assign into ***out**, a **Box** object is assigned, and written to the stream **cout**, and a newline is automatically appended. So essentially, we are creating an object that the **copy()** algorithm can use as a place to write the **Box** objects copied, and this causes each **Box** to appear formatted on **cout**.

The first two arguments to the **copy()** algorithm are the range of boxes to **copy()**, which in this example is the entire **TruckLoad** from **begin()** to **end()**.

This is very dense and typical of how STL objects work together. Note that **ostream_iterator** is making use of our **Box::operator<<(ostream,Box)** to control how the **Box** object is written to the stream **cout**. It all fits together into a very compact way of saying "print out all the boxes".

We have a **typedef** statement defining **BoxIter**, which is then used to declare a constant iterator, **big_one**:

```
typedef TruckLoad::const_iterator BoxIter;
BoxIter big_one = max_element(Rig.begin(), Rig.end());
```

Remember that **TruckLoad::const_iterator** is a synonym for **list<Box>::const_iterator**. This time there is an important difference: the client doesn't know this, and doesn't need to. As far as the client is concerned, **const_iterator** is an anonymous type provided by the **public** interface of **TruckLoad**, that is used for any iterators received from **TruckLoad::begin()** and **TruckLoad::end()**.

We've used another STL algorithm, **max_element()**, here. Its arguments define a range which it searches, returning an iterator to the largest value found within the range. If the range is empty, the return iterator will be at, or beyond, **Rig.end()**, where there are no elements.

> *A key feature of working with the STL is the ability to work with types that are defined by objects within your programs. We can see in this example that **BoxIter** is some kind of iterator provided by class **TruckLoad**, but we don't know at this level that this is actually an iterator from the STL list container. Only **TruckLoad** knows that kind of internal detail.*

To copy *part* of the **TruckLoad**, starting with the biggest box found, we use the statements:

```
cout << "Copying all boxes starting at big box to Rig2" << endl;
TruckLoad Rig2(big_one, Rig.end());
```

We use the copy constructor, which takes an iterator range to make this copy. This shows that the iterator returned from the algorithm **max_element()** functions just the same as any other iterator and can be used to refer to positions within the **TruckLoad** sequence of **Box** elements.

Comments on the list Container

The **list** container has several advantages over **vector**. The primary advantage of **list** is that all insertions and deletions take constant time. This means that inserting and erasing at any sequence position is more efficient with **list**. With the **vector** container, insertions and erasures at positions other than the **back** position can be particularly costly.

The **list** container also has the special function **splice()** — this function automatically removes elements from a given source, and grafts them into the specified destination. It saves you from having to combine separate **insert** and **erase** steps to accomplish the same thing.

One drawback of **list** is that you lose the ability to perform random access, using **operator[]**. If random access is important to your application, then you need a **vector** (or its near relative, the **deque**).

The iterators for **list** are called **bidirectional**. You can move forward and backward efficiently, but you can't make big jumps. Most algorithms can be performed efficiently on lists, even without the random access capability that **operator[]** provides.

The general purpose **sort()** algorithm is one that does not work with a **list**. However, **list** does provide a special **sort()** function which you can use in place of the general **sort()** algorithm:

```
vector<int> V;
list<int> L;

sort(V.begin(), V.end());   // OK
sort(L.begin(), L.end());   // Illegal!!! Can't use sort() on list
L.sort();                   // OK, list provides special sort() function of its own
```

The **list** and **vector** containers differ in many other small ways. You need to consult a full reference work on the STL containers if you wish to learn all the details.

The Associative map Containers

So far, we have only exercised the **vector** and **list** containers. We've seen how they keep track of a sequence of elements — the elements exist in an order which is established by whichever method you choose to insert the elements. They belong to a group of containers known as the **sequence containers** (the third container in this group is **deque**).

Sequence containers are less useful when you need to access the elements according to their *value*. The ordering term, by which we access these elements, is called the **key**. For example, we could attempt to find all the **Person** elements in a container whose family name is **"Smith"** — the family name is the key in this case. Of course, it's possible to access elements of sequence containers in this way. However, the STL also provides **associative containers**, that are more suitable to this kind of access problem.

Associative containers work by storing all the objects internally to the container in a sequence sorted by key. When you insert a new element, the key is automatically used to place the element in the container, in the position that maintains the sorted order. You also access elements in an associative container by key. If a data type is to be used as a key then it *must* provide an ordering relation, via **operator<()**. Elements for which **operator<()** is not defined cannot be used as keys in an associative container. There are no other restrictions on the data types used for keys — so your associated values can be of any convenient data type that has a well-defined order.

There are four varieties of associative containers: **map**, **set**, **multimap** and **multiset**. To see how these containers differ, we can look at them pairwise. The **map** and **set** containers are suitable when we are sure that keys are unique, while the **multimap** and **multiset** containers are used when duplicate keys are required. On the other hand, the keys of the **map** and **multimap** containers have associated values (which are typically objects); the **set** and **multiset** containers only have keys.

Let's illustrate what this means. For example, we might use a **map** or a **multimap** to store names and phone numbers. Each of these containers stores a collection of elements which associate a *key* with an *object* — in this case, the name is the key, and the phone number is the associated object. Which should we use? If we use a **map**, then the key must be unique: this means that each person can only have one phone number. Since many people have more than one phone number, we really need to be able to duplicate the 'person' key, with multiple associated 'phone number' objects. The **multimap** container allows this.

> *In some ways, the* **multimap** *is the most general of the associative containers. However, using the* **multimap** *is not a free lunch. When you opt for the more general* **multimap** *you give up the convenience of the very handy* **operator[]**, *which is used for accessing elements by key.*

The **set** containers have keys, but (unlike the **map** containers) do not associate objects with the keys. The key essentially becomes the value. This makes them simpler than **maps**, but less flexible. Let's look how each of these associative containers is used, and consider the trade-offs involved in selecting the variety of associative container that best suits a task.

Try It Out – Using Maps to Collect Collocations

A common form of collocation is to count how often each word occurs in a text.

```cpp
// Program 20.17 A simple word collocation
#include <iostream>
#include <iomanip>
#include <string>
#include <sstream>
#include <map>

using namespace std;

const char* twister =
  "How much wood would a woodchuck chuck if a woodchuck "
  "could chuck wood?  A woodchuck would chuck as much wood "
  "as a woodchuck could chuck if a woodchuck could chuck wood.";

int main()
{
  typedef map<string, int> Collocation;
  typedef Collocation::const_iterator WordIter;

  Collocation M;

  istringstream text(twister);
  istream_iterator<string> begin(text);
  istream_iterator<string> end;

  for( ; begin != end ; ++begin)
    M[*begin]++;

  for(WordIter m = M.begin() ; m != M.end() ; ++m)
    cout << setw(6) << m->second << " " << m->first << endl;

  return 0;
}
```

This program produces the following output:

```
     1 A
     1 How
     4 a
     2 as
```

```
5 chuck
3 could
2 if
2 much
2 wood
1 wood.
1 wood?
5 woodchuck
2 would
```

How It Works

We have an **#include** directive for the header file **map**:

```
#include <map>
```

Both the **map** and **multimap** containers are declared in the header **<map>**. We don't want to type out **map<string,int>::const_iterator** in full very often. It's better to take advantage of **typedef**:

```
typedef map<string, int> Collocation;
typedef Collocation::const_iterator WordIter;

Collocation M;
```

The **map<>** template takes two parameters. The first is the data type of the key, and the second is the data type of the associated object. In this program, our keys are **string**s, which represent words found in our sample text, and the associated value for each string is an **int**, which we use to count the number of occurrences of the key. We will use **WordIter** to display the contents of our collocation.

Next, we use a **string** stream object in combination with an iterator:

```
istringstream text(twister);
istream_iterator<string> begin(text);
istream_iterator<string> end;

for( ; begin != end ; ++begin)
  M[*begin]++;
```

We've made use of **istringstream** before. We attach our tongue twister to the iterator **begin**, and iterate over each lexeme in our text. I say *lexeme*, rather than *word*, because **istream_iterator** isn't very intelligent — it simply breaking out sequences of printable characters embedded between stretches of white space, as this section of the output shows:

```
2 wood
1 wood.
1 wood?
```

You can see that the word **wood** was found in three difference 'lexemes', namely '**wood**', '**wood.**' and '**wood?**'.

Inserting and counting within the collocation is so easy that you might have missed it. It's all performed within the single statement:

```
for( ; begin != end ; ++begin)
  M[*begin]++;
```

The expression ***begin** returns a string, that contains one of the lexemes peeled out of our tongue twister. The container **M** is subscripted with a key of type **string**. Elements in associative containers are accessed *associatively* — this means that when the map is given a key, it returns the associated value.

For a **map** container, **operator[]** is actually a shorthand for **insert()**. This means that you have to be a bit careful sometimes. Consider the statement:

```
if(M["brawn"] > 0)
    cout << "too much muscle" << endl;
```

This looks like a test to see if the string **"brawn"** has a positive count, but beware! Because of the way **operator[]** is defined for maps, this statement will insert **"brawn"** if it didn't already exist in the container. When elements are inserted in this way, the value part is initialized with the default constructor. For an integer value, this means that value is initialized by the expression **int()**. As with all initializers for built-in types, **int()** returns the default value for an **int**, which is zero. So any new keys inserted in this way start life with a count of zero.

If you want to check for the existence of a key, you can use the **count()** method:

```
if (M.count("brawn"))
    cout << "too much muscle" << endl;
```

The expression **M.count()** returns 1 if the key **"brawn"** is present, and 0 otherwise. Hence, this expression determines whether there is too much muscle *without* the side effect of creating new entries in the map that didn't already exist.

The expression **M[*begin]** returns a reference to the value associated with the key ***begin**, that is stored in the **map** container. This allows us to increment the count with the simple expression **M[*begin]++**.

Once we have the collocation, displaying it involves a simple loop using **map** iterators.

```
for(WordIter m = M.begin() ; m != M.end() ; ++m)
  cout << setw(6) << m->second << " " << m->first << endl;
```

Let's try getting the collocation in descending sequence using a **multimap**.

Try It Out – Inverting the Collocation with multimap

Let's extend Program 20.17 to use the **multimap** container.

```
// Program 20.18 An inverted word collocation
#include <iostream>
#include <iomanip>
#include <string>
#include <sstream>
#include <map>
```

```
using namespace std;

const char* twister =
  "How much wood would a woodchuck chuck if a woodchuck "
  "could chuck wood?  A woodchuck would chuck as much wood "
  "as a woodchuck could chuck if a woodchuck could chuck wood.";

int main()
{
  typedef map<string, int> Collocation;
  typedef Collocation::const_iterator WordIter;

  Collocation M;

  istringstream text(twister);
  istream_iterator<string> begin(text);
  istream_iterator<string> end;

  for( ; begin != end ; ++begin)
    M[*begin]++;

  typedef multimap<int,string,greater<int> > WordRank;
  typedef WordRank::const_iterator RankIter;

  WordRank R;

  for(WordIter m = M.begin() ; m != M.end() ; ++m)
    R.insert(make_pair(m->second,m->first));

  for(RankIter r = R.begin() ; r != R.end() ; ++r)
    cout << setw(6) << r->first << " " << r->second << endl;

  return 0;
}
```

This program produces the following output:

```
     5 chuck
     5 woodchuck
     4 a
     3 could
     2 as
     2 if
     2 much
     2 wood
     2 would
     1 A
     1 How
     1 wood.
     1 wood?
```

How It Works

We have added two more **typedef**s:

```
typedef multimap<int,string,greater<int> > WordRank;
typedef WordRank::const_iterator RankIter;

WordRank R;
```

879

This time we use a **multimap** rather than a **map**, and we specify our own comparison criteria. The function **greater()** is one of the standard STL comparison functions. By using **greater<int>**, rather than the default **less<>**, we will see our ranks printed in descending order. Of course, we could have iterated the **WordRank** table in reverse order just by using **rbegin()** and **rend()**, but we've already seen those.

Next we insert elements into **R**. When we used the **map** container in Program 20.17, we were able to insert elements using **operator[]()**. We can't do that now, because **multimap** doesn't even *have* an **operator[]()** — this is because in the context of **multimap**, the subscript operator doesn't make sense, since the keys are allowed to be non-unique. Instead, we use the method **R.insert()**:

```
for(WordIter m = M.begin() ; m != M.end() ; ++m)
  R.insert(make_pair(m->second,m->first));
```

The trick is in creating the right kind of argument to suit **R.insert()**. In this case, **R.insert()** expects an argument that is an associated pair, combining an **int** and a **string**. Fortunately, the STL has a special data type, **pair<>**, that is used in many contexts — defining elements from maps is one such application. The **pair<>** data type looks a little bit like this:

```
template <typename Key, class Value>
struct pair
{
  Pair(const Key& f, const Value& s) : first(f), second(s) {};
  Key first;
  Value second;
};
```

As you can see, it's just a template structure that associates two data elements of different types. By convention, the key element is called **first** and the value element is called **second**. Now, the **make_pair()** function is one of the few functions that does exactly what common sense dictates. It's defined as:

```
template <typename T1, class T2> pair<T1,T2>
make_pair(const T1& key, const T2& value)
{
  return pair<T1,T2>(key,value);
}
```

So **make_pair()** simply returns a pair that matches the types of the arguments we supply. Hence, in our program, we could replace the **make_pair()** call with the following statement:

```
for(WordIter m = M.begin() ; m != M.end() ; ++m)
  R.insert(pair<int, string>(m->second, m->first));
```

This illustrates what we are achieving with **make_pair()**. The first argument, **m->second**, has type **int**, and the second argument, **m->first**, has type **string** — so it's exactly the kind of pair we were expecting.

Take a closer look at the statements inside the two **for** loops:

```
for(WordIter m = M.begin() ; m != M.end() ; ++m)
  R.insert(make_pair(m->second,m->first));
```

```
for(RankIter r = R.begin() ; r != R.end() ; ++r)
  cout << setw(6) << r->first << " " << r->second << endl;
```

The first is from the **Collocation** iterator, and the second is from the **WordRank** iterator. Remember that the **WordRank** map is a *reversal* of the **Collocation** — so we have a very nasty and dangerous state of affairs here. In the first line, **m->first** is the lexeme, but in the second line **r->second** is the lexeme — there's plenty of scope for confusion! It seems easy enough to keep the two straight in this example, but in a big program with many interrelated maps, **first** and **second** can become tiresome in a big hurry. In such a case, you'd probably want to add a few careful comments to your code to indicate exactly what's going on.

Performance and Specialization

At the beginning of this chapter, when we first encountered iterators and algorithms, we saw many examples of how the function **average()** might be written. Here is a representative implementation of **average()**, using a pointer interface, which is simple and efficient.

```
// Simple average function written without using any STL algorithms
double average(float* first, float* last)
{
  double sum = 0.0;
  for ( ; first != last ; ++first)
    sum += *first;
  return sum / (last-first);
}
```

Alternatively, we can make use of the built-in STL template algorithm **accumulate()**:

```
// An average function based on the STL accumulate algorithm
template <typename RndIter>
double average(RndIter first, RndIter last)
{
  return accumulate(first, last, 0) / (last-first);
}
```

It's also reasonably simple, but what do we really gain by digging up a library function to replace three simple lines of code? To answer this, let's take a look at something that you might find in an aggressive implementation of the STL:

```
// Possible specialization of template accumulate<> for float* iterators
#include <numeric>

template<> float std::accumulate(float* first, float* last, float init)
{
  double s0 = 0.0;
  double s1 = 0.0;
  double s2 = 0.0
  double s3 = 0.0;
  int burst_blocks = (last - first) / 4;
  float* burst = first + 4 * burst_blocks;

  for( ; first < burst ; first+=4)
  {
```

```
      s0 += first[0];
      s1 += first[1];
      s2 += first[2];
      s3 += first[3];
   }

   for( ; burst < last ; ++burst)
   {
      s0 += *burst;        // Capture up to three tail elements
   }

   return init + (s0 + s1 + s2 + s3);
}
```

This technique is called **specialization**. This means that extra versions of routines are supplied that deal with common cases in better ways than a fully generic algorithm can achieve. This particular specialization is targeted at summing a sequence of **float** values referenced through pointers. It looks more complicated than our simple loop, yet it computes the same result:

```
template<> float accumulate<float*>(float* first, float* last, float init)
```

The key to this specialization is the block of four statements:

```
      s0 += first[0];
      s1 += first[1];
      s2 += first[2];
      s3 += first[3];
```

The idea is to create more parallelism. Instead of directing all the sums into a single variable, which can become a bottleneck, this version keeps four separate subtotals going in parallel. A fast machine might have all four of these additions going at the same time.

How does this specialization compare against the simple loop? Well, that depends on your compiler, your implementation of the STL, and the size of your vectors. The specialization might not be any faster at all, but it could be up to four times as fast.

It is interesting to note that the specialization also offers greater precision. When we first encountered the floating point data type, in Chapter 2, we observed that summing sequences of floating point values is an inherently risky operation. If you are unlucky, the result can have very poor accuracy due to rounding errors accumulated during the summation.

This specialization uses the more precise **double** type for internal calculations, so it is also more accurate than the simple loop, even running at the higher speed. A really good specialization — one that is more sophisticated than this example — can employ clever tricks to eliminate almost all of the rounding errors and still maintain high performance. It's very tricky to write such code yourself.

Even the simplest algorithms can be written in surprising and clever ways. Implementations of the STL are always improving. If performance is important, use STL algorithms whenever the opportunity arises. They are likely to be more sophisticated than anything you might write yourself.

Summary

This has been something of a short stroll through new territory, pointing out the interesting sights as we go. We have barely scratched the surface of the potential for the STL here, but you should have enough of an idea to be capable of and interested in a bit of exploration on your own.

Some of the fundamental points we have investigated are:

▶ The STL provides functionality through three broad classifications of templates — containers, iterators and algorithms.

▶ Containers provides various ways of storing and organizing objects of arbitrary types, provided the types of objects that are to be stored meet the basic requirement for an element.

▶ Iterators are objects that can behave like pointers. Iterators are examples of smart pointers.

▶ Iterators are used to access objects in a container, or to retrieve objects from a stream.

▶ Iterators are used in pairs to define a set of objects in a semi-open interval within a sequence. The first object is included in the interval, and the last object is not.

▶ Algorithms are generalized, standard functions that can be used with sets of objects specified by iterators.

▶ The algorithms are independent of the containers, but can be applied to objects in virtually any container through iterators.

Exercises

Ex 20.1 Write a program that uses a **vector** to store an arbitrary number of cities read from the keyboard as **string** objects, and then lists them.

Ex 20.2 Add code to the previous example to use the **sort()** algorithm to sort the cities in ascending sequence before listing them.

Ex 20.3 Write a program to read an arbitrary number of names and associated telephone numbers from the keyboard (in the form "Laurel, Stan" 5431234, for example) and store them in a **map** container so that given a name, the number can be retrieved. Provide for an arbitrary number of random retrievals from the **map** after a series of names and numbers has been entered.

Ex 20.4 Using your code from the previous exercise, use an iterator to list the contents of the **map**.

Ex 20.5 Add code to Program 20.17 to replace punctuation characters in the input with spaces, and to output the collocation with the words sorted in ascending sequence.

A

ASCII Codes

The first 32 ASCII (American Standard Code for Information Interchange) characters provide control functions. Many of these have not been referenced in this book but are included here for completeness. In the following table, only the first 128 characters have been included. The remaining 128 characters include further special symbols and letters for national character sets.

ASCII Characters 0 - 31

Decimal	Hexadecimal	Character	Control
000	00	null	NUL
001	01	☺	SOH
002	02	•	STX
003	03	♥	ETX
004	04	♦	EOT
005	05	♣	ENQ
006	06	♠	ACK
007	07	•	BEL (Audible bell)
008	08		Backspace
009	09		HT
010	0A		LF (Line feed)
011	0B		VT (Vertical feed)
012	0C		FF (Form feed)
013	0D		CR (Carriage return)
014	0E		SO
015	0F	¤	SI
016	10		DLE
017	11		DC1

Decimal	Hexadecimal	Character	Control
018	12		DC2
019	13		DC3
020	14		DC4
021	15		NAK
022	16		SYN
023	17		ETB
024	18		CAN
025	19		EM
026	1A	→	SUB
027	1B	←	ESC (Escape)
028	1C	L	FS
029	1D		GS
030	1E		RS
031	1F		US

ASCII Characters 32 - 127

Decimal	Hexadecimal	Character	Decimal	Hexadecimal	Character
032	20	space	060	3C	<
033	21	!	061	3D	=
034	22	"	062	3E	>
035	23	#	063	3F	?
036	24	$	064	40	@
037	25	%	065	41	A
038	26	&	066	42	B
039	27	'	067	43	C
040	28	(	068	44	D
041	29	)	069	45	E
042	2A	*	070	46	F
043	2B	+	071	47	G
044	2C	,	072	48	H
045	2D	-	073	49	I
046	2E	.	074	4A	J
047	2F	/	075	4B	K
048	30	0	076	4C	L
049	31	1	077	4D	M
050	32	2	078	4E	N
051	33	3	079	4F	O
052	34	4	080	50	P
053	35	5	081	51	Q
054	36	6	082	52	R
055	37	7	083	53	S
056	38	8	085	55	U
057	39	9	086	56	V
058	3A	:	087	57	W
059	3B	;	088	58	X

Decimal	Hexadecimal	Character	Decimal	Hexadecimal	Character
089	59	Y	109	6D	m
090	5A	Z	110	6E	n
091	5B	[	111	6F	o
092	5C	\	112	70	p
093	5D	]	113	71	q
094	5E	^	114	72	r
095	5F	_	115	73	s
096	60	´	116	74	t
097	61	a	117	75	u
098	62	b	118	76	v
099	63	c	119	77	w
100	64	d	120	78	x
101	65	e	121	79	y
102	66	f	122	7A	z
103	67	g	123	7B	{
104	68	h	124	7C	|
105	69	i	125	7D	}
106	6A	j	126	7E	~
107	6B	k	127	7F	delete
108	6C	l			

B

C++ Keywords

Keywords are words that have been assigned special significance within the C++ language, so you must not use them as names within your programs. The following keywords are defined:

asm	false	sizeof
auto	float	static
bool	for	static_cast
break	friend	struct
case	goto	switch
catch	if	template
char	inline	this
class	int	throw
const	long	true
const_cast	mutable	try
continue	namespace	typedef
default	new	typeid
delete	operator	typename
do	private	union
double	protected	unsigned
dynamic_cast	public	using
else	register	virtual
enum	reinterpret_cast	void
explicit	return	volatile
export	short	wchar_t
extern	signed	while

There are also words that are reserved for use as alternatives to the bitwise and logical operators in C++. These are:

and	compl	or_eq
and_eq	not	xor
bitand	not_eq	xor_eq
bitor	or	

Standard Library Header Files

All the header files for the standard library have names without an extension. There are a total of fifty standard header files, eighteen of which provide C library facilities. Standard header file names that begin with **c** (with the exception of **complex)** are equivalent to header files that are included with ISO-standard C.

The contents of the library can be subdivided into ten categories:

Language Support	**Input/Output**	**Diagnostics**	**General Utilities**
Strings	**Containers**	**Iterator Support**	**Algorithms**
Numerical Operations	**Localization**		

Each of these categories spans a substantial range of functionality with the necessary definitions and declaration spread over several header files in some instances.

Language Support

The header files that relate to standard library support for the language capability are:

Header File	Description
<cstddef>	Defines **NULL** and additional standard types **size_t** and **ptrdiff_t**.
<limits>	Provides definitions relating to the basic data types. For example, for each numeric data type, it defines the maximum and minimum values that can be represented and the number of binary digits. We use these library facilities in Chapter 2.
<climits>	Provides C style definitions relating to the basic integer data types. The same information is provided in C++ style in **<limits>**.
<cfloat>	Provides C style definitions relating to the basic floating point data types. The same information is provided in C++ style in **<limits>**.
<cstdlib>	Provides macros and functions supporting program start-up and termination. This header file also declares a number of other functions of a miscellaneous nature such as searching and sorting functions and conversions from string to numeric values for example. In this, it exactly matches the equivalent standard C header, **<stdlib.h>**.

Header File	Description
`<new>`	Support for dynamic memory allocation.
`<typeinfo>`	Support for runtime type identification of a variable.
`<exception>`	Supports exception handling — which is a way of handling error conditions that may arise in your program.
`<cstdarg>`	Supports functions that will accept a variable number of arguments — that is, functions to which you can transfer a variable number of data items when you call the function.
`<csetjmp>`	Provides functions for C style non-local jumps. These are not usually used in C++ programs.
`<csignal>`	Provides C style support for interrupt handling.

Input/Output

Header File	Description
`<iostream>`	Supports input and output for the standard streams, **cin**, **cout**, **cerr** and **clog**. It also supports the wide character standard streams, **wcin**, **wcout**, **wcerr** and **wclog**.
`<iomanip>`	Provides manipulators that enable you to modify the state of a stream — to alter the formatting of output, for example.
`<ios>`	Defines the base classes for **iostream**.
`<istream>`	Defines template classes for managing input from an input stream buffer.
`<ostream>`	Defines template classes for managing input from an output stream buffer.
`<sstream>`	Supports stream input and output for strings.
`<fstream>`	Supports file stream input and output
`<iosfwd>`	Provides for forward declarations for input and output objects.
`<streambuf>`	Supports buffering of stream input and output.
`<cstdio>`	Supports C style input and output for standard streams
`<cwchar>`	Supports C style input and output of wide characters.

Diagnostics

The C++ diagnostics capability is defined in three header files:

Header File	Description
`<stdexcept>`	Defines standard exceptions. Exceptions are the way error conditions are handled.
`<cassert>`	Defines the assert macro that you can use for checking runtime conditions.
`<cerrno>`	Supports C style error information.

General Utilities

Header File	Description
<utility>	Defines overloaded relational operators to simplify the writing of your own relational operators, and the **pair** type that is simply a templated type that holds a pair of values. These features are used elsewhere in the library.
<functional>	A function object is any object that supports **operator()**, the function call operator. This header defines a number of functional object types and features that support functional objects.
<memory>	Defines the standard memory allocator for containers, functions for managing memory and the **auto_ptr** template class.
<ctime>	Supports system clock functions.

Strings

Header File	Description
<string>	Provides support and definitions for string types, including **string** for narrow character strings (i.e. composed of **char**) and **wstring** for wide character strings (i.e. composed of **wchar_t**).
<cctype>	Classification for narrow characters.
<cwctype>	Classification for wide characters.
<cstring>	Provides functions for manipulating null-terminated byte sequences and blocks of memory.
<cwchar>	Provides functions for manipulating, performing I/O and converting wide character sequences.
<cstdlib>	Provides functions for converting narrow character strings to numerics and converting between wide characters and multibyte strings.

Containers

Header File	Description
<vector>	Defines the **vector** sequence template, which is a resizable array type that is safer and more flexible than plain arrays.
<list>	Defines the **list** sequence template, which is a linked list for sequences that often have elements inserted and removed from arbitrary positions.
<deque>	Defines the **deque** sequence template, which supports efficient insertion and removal at each end.
<queue>	Defines sequence adaptors, **queue** and **priority_queue**, for queue (*first in, first out*) data structures.

Header File	Description
`<stack>`	Defines a sequence adaptor, **stack**, for stack (*last in, first out*) data structures.
`<map>`	A **map** is an associative container type that allows values to be searched by a key value where the key values are unique and held in ascending order. A **multimap** is similar to a **map**, except that keys need not be unique.
`<set>`	A **set** is an associative container type for holding unique values in ascending order. A **multiset** is similar to a **set**, except that the values need not be unique.
`<bitset>`	Defines the **bitset** template for fixed length sequences of bits, which can be treated as a packed fixed-length array of **bool**.

Iterator Support

There is only one header file for iterators:

Header File	Description
`<iterator>`	Provides definitions and support for iterators.

General Purpose Algorithms

There are two header files for algorithms:

Header File	Description
`<algorithm>`	Provides a range of algorithm-based functions including permuting, sorting, merging and searching.
`<cstdlib>`	Declares C standard library functions **bsearch()** and **qsort()** for searching and sorting.
`<ciso646>`	Allows you to use **and** instead of **&&**, and so on, in your code.

Numerical Operations

This group includes capability for operations with complex numbers as well as mathematical functions. There are five header files:

Header File	Description
`<complex>`	Support for definition of, and operations on, complex numbers.
`<valarray>`	Supports operations on numerical vectors.
`<numeric>`	Defines a set of general mathematical operations on sequences of numbers, such as `accumulate` and `inner_product`.
`<cmath>`	Is the C math library with additional overloads to support C++ conventions.
`<cstdlib>`	Provides functions for taking the absolute value of an integer and performing remainder division on integers.

Localization

Localization provides facilities for dealing with things that vary regionally, such as currency symbols, date representation and sort sequences. The two header files are:

Header File	Description
`<locale>`	Provides for localization including character classification, sort sequences and monetary and date representation.
`<clocale>`	Provides C style support for localization.

D

Operator Precedence and Associativity

The sequence in which different operators in an expression are executed is determined by the precedence of the operators. Operators with a higher precedence are executed before operators with a lower precedence. In the following table, operators are in descending order of precedence, so those with the highest precedence are at the top. Operators within the same group in the table are of equal precedence.

Description	Operator
Scope resolution	`::`
Direct member selection	`.`
Indirect member selection	`->`
Subscript	`[]`
Function call	`()`
Postfix increment	`++`
Postfix decrement	`--`
Explicit static cast (checked at compile time)	`static_cast`
Dynamic cast	`dynamic_cast`
Cast away const	`const_cast`
Unchecked cast	`reinterpret_cast`
Type identification	`typeid`
Unary plus	`+`
Unary minus	`-`
Prefix increment	`++`
Prefix decrement	`--`
Logical negation – not	`!`
Bitwise complement	`~`
Address-of	`&`
Dereference	`*`
Explicit cast (old style)	`(type)`
Size of object or type	`sizeof`
Allocate memory	`new`
Deallocate memory	`delete`

Description	Operator
Direct pointer-to-member selection	.*
Indirect pointer-to-member selection	->*
Multiply	*
Divide	/
Modulus	%
Binary addition	+
Binary subtraction	–
Shift left	<<
Shift right	>>
Less than	<
Less than or equal to	<=
Greater than	>
Greater than or equal to	>=
Equal to	==
Not equal to	!=
Bitwise AND	&
Bitwise exclusive OR	^
Bitwise OR	|
Logical AND	&&
Logical OR	||
Conditional operator	? :
Assignment	=
Apply operator and then assign	*= /= %= += -= &= ^= |= <<= >>=
Throw exception	**Throw**
Comma	,

The associativity of an operator determines how it groups with its operands in an expression. All unary operators and all assignment operators are right associative. All other operators are left associative.

The right associativity of the assignment operator means that a statement such as:

```
x = y = z = t;
```

is evaluated as though it were written as:

```
x = ( y = ( z = t));
```

Thus the assignment **z = t** is performed first. The value of that assignment expression, which will be the same as the value of **t**, is assigned to **y**, and the value of that is assigned to **x**.

The left associativity of the binary addition operator implies that a statement such as:

```
result = x + y + z + t;
```

is evaluated as though it were written:

```
result = ((x + y) + z) + t;
```

Thus **x** and **y** are added, then that result is added to **z**, then that result is added to **t**.

Note that the precedence and associativity of an expression does not fully determine the order of evaluation in that expression. Where it is not determined, the order will depend on your compiler. For example, in the expression,

```
int x = 1;
int z = (++x * y) - (++x * t);
```

the order in which the parenthesized expressions are evaluated is unspecified. In consequence, the returned value of **x** may be either 2 or 3 in the first parenthesis, and vice versa in the second.

Example Project

You've read the book. You've digested the text. Now it's time to apply your newfound knowledge to a small, but perfectly formed, project. In this appendix we'll set the problem, and give some hints to its solution.

FYI   For the model answer source code, look on either of the Wrox web sites.

Outline

The aim of the example project is to create an object-oriented program that will keep track of information about teachers and students in an educational establishment. This information will be held as a series of 'Teacher' and 'Student' records, both of which will contain the following common attributes:

Attribute	Type	Max. Length	Restrictions/Comments
First Name	Alphabetic	20 chars	
Surname	Alphabetic	20 chars	
Address1	Mixed	30 chars	First line of street address
Address2	Mixed	30 chars	Second line
Address3	Mixed	30 chars	Last line
City	Alphabetic	20 chars	
State	Alphabetic	3 chars	
Zip Code	Numeric	6 chars	
Phone Number	Numeric	8 chars	Must be of the form ###-####

All Student records will have the following additional attributes:

Attribute	Type	Max. Length	Restrictions/Comments
Student ID	Mixed	6 chars	
Grade (or GPA)	Number	-	Must be between 0 and 100

All Teacher records will have the following additional attributes:

Attribute	Type	Max. Length	Restrictions/Comments
Teaching experience (in years)	Number	-	Must be positive integer
Salary	Number	-	Must be positive integer

The program should be menu driven, and the user should be allowed to perform the following operations:

▶ Add records

▶ Delete records

▶ Search the records

▶ Display the records

▶ Clear all records

▶ Save the records to a 'database' file

▶ Retrieve the set of records from a database file

When adding a record, all the attributes of the Student or Teacher record should be properly entered. The street address can consist of up to three lines; if it is less than three lines, input can be terminated by entering a '.' on a line by itself.

When deleting a record, the user should be prompted to enter the surname of the Teacher or Student record they wish to delete. Once deleted, a record cannot be searched for or displayed.

When searching for a record, the user should be prompted to enter the surname of the record they wish to find. The program should then display all the attributes of the record containing the desired surname (i.e. if the record refers to a Student, then the GPA and Student ID fields should be displayed). A deleted record cannot be searched for.

When displaying records, the user should be given the following options:

▶ Display all Student records, and display their attributes

▶ Display all Teacher records, and display their attributes

▶ Display all Teacher AND Student records, and display their attributes

Records should be saved to a plain text file in a suitable format. On saving, the user should be prompted for the name of a file, and it should be verified that this file can be created before proceeding.

When reading a file, the program should prompt the user for a file name and verify that it can be opened. Records should be read from the file, validated and added to the current record set.

Improving the Project Specification

Having stated the problem, you should be able to see some potential gray areas in the specification:

> We're searching the data by surname, so we're effectively using the surname field as the search key. You might like to think about how you'd handle duplicate names — if there are two Smith's in the database, how could you handle a search on Smith?

> Just about everyone is going to have an address, but how about if the person hasn't got a phone?

Developer's Notes

Having stated the problem, here are some suggestions on how we might implement the program.

The overall design of this project is based on these simple rules:

> Have the objects take care of themselves

> Implement a container class to organize the objects.

> Use the **main()** function as a simple "traffic cop". It directs program execution but has no effect on the individual objects, apart from adding and deleting objects in the container.

The Person class is at the heart of the project. It implements the very basic functionality of all objects in the project. It is the base class of the other classes found in this project, namely the Student class and the Teacher class. All objects within this program are of type Teacher or Student, and these derived classes implement only specific functionality according to their type. For example, the Teacher class includes a member variable unique to teachers denoting the "number of years experience".

Each class performs its own validation. The class member functions are designed to validate user input because, as a rule, objects need to be responsible for the integrity of their own data. If validation was to occur somewhere outside the class, then you are placing objects at the mercy of an external entity and code maintenance becomes very cumbersome, as well as violating one of the principles of OO design.

The container we'll use for our Student and Teacher objects is one from the Standard Template Library, namely a **deque**. In this program we'll not stretch its capabilities, as we are only adding, deleting and searching for objects. The deque container is chosen for its relative ease of use, but you could also use a map or a multi-set if you wished. We'll use the deque container to store objects of type Person*, since, with polymorphism, we are then able to store both Student and Teacher objects, both of which are derived from the Person class.

The **main()** function and the other functions contained in the **MainProg.cpp** file have few responsibilities. First and foremost, **main()** directs program execution. However it also validates user selection with the use of menus, and it utilizes the container class. The **main()** function contains no object specific code, but, rather, directs program execution.

The Person Class

The Person class contains the basic structure of both the Student and Teacher derived classes. It is the base class of the Student and Teacher classes, and it is here where most of the code associated with all the classes is found. It is structured to take full advantage of member variable data-hiding:

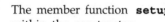   The member function **setup()** is declared **private** as it will only be called from within the constructor

   The virtual function **set_other_info()** is also **private** because it is called from public member functions of the derived classes

   All the member variables are **private**, again to take full advantage of data-hiding and the security that gives you

The Student and Teacher Derived Classes

The Student and Teacher classes are derived from the Person class. Each of these classes contain member variables and member functions specific to their type. Also, each class will implement a unique version of the virtual function **set_other_info()**.

The Container

The container class is created with a pointer to the Person class in order to take full advantage of polymorphism. Because of this implementation, the container can contain elements of both the Teacher and Student derived classes. Maintenance is easy, as there is only one container to worry about. Anytime a record is required within the container; a simple **for** loop will do the trick. The following functions are performed on this container:

   Adding elements
   Deleting elements
   Searching elements

Also, before the program exits, the container needs to be emptied, as we should always tidy up after ourselves.

Saving and Restoring Data

When we exit from the program we'll lose all the data we've entered, unless we take steps to save it to disk. Since we don't want to get too complicated, we'll adopt a very simple approach, and allow the user to save the records in text form to a standard disk file. Not only is this simple to implement using the **iostream** classes, it also aids debugging because you can see what is being written into the file.

You can make up the record format to suit yourself, but I'd suggest that you make the first line of the file contains some sort of special token, so that you can easily verify that you're trying to read a file of the right type.

Summary

There are a lot of ways in which this program can be improved, but it does form a basis on which to build and extend its functionality (so that, for example, you could add a Principal class). It also brings together many pieces of the C++ puzzle.

Above all, remember that C++ can be used in a clean and simple way, and this is very important for code maintenance. Always assume that the next developer looking over your code is a relative beginner — you'll be thanked in the long run!

Beginning

C++

The Complete Language

Symbols

!, logical NOT operator 127, 129

!=, relational operator 111, 207

#

operator overloading 534

preprocessor directives 383

string substitution,
preprocessor macros 391

##

multiple macro arguments
392

operator overloading 534

**#define, preprocessor
directive 386**

see also **macros**, preprocessor

advantages 387

const, #define advantages 386

string substitution 391

tokens 386

removing from program 387

#else, logical directive 397

see also **if-else statements**

**#error, preprocessor directive
399**

#if, logical directive 393

#endif 393

#ifdef 394

#ifndef 394, 396

environment support 396

code, preventing duplication
of 394

constant expression values,
testing for 396

environment support 396

symbols, testing for
predefinition 393, 394

example 394

**#include, preprocessor
directive 358, 15, 43, 509, 524**

<>, spaces between angled
brackets 11, 384, 385

classes, deriving 581

custom source files 385

"..." 385

header files 384

namespaces, extending 367

**#line, preprocessor directive
398**

**#pragma, preprocessor
directive 399**

#undef, preprocessor directive

identifiers, undefining 387

example 387

%, modulus operator 39

&

address-of operator 233

bitwise AND 84

pass-by-reference 297

reference declaration 300

&&, logical AND 127, 128

()

pointers to functions 338

relational operators 114

stream manipulator functions
764

*

indirection operator 234

pointer declaration 232

pointers to functions 338

+

addition operator 551

string concatenation 202

**++, increment operator
53, 566**

postfix form 53

prefix form 53

--, decrement operator 53, 566

postfix form 53

prefix form 53

->

pointer member access
operator 426, 467, 477

indirect member access
operator 732

**->*, indirect pointer to
member operator 659**

"..."

#include, custom source files
385

string literals 32

., member access operator 451

for structures 419

for unions 430

**.*, direct pointer to member
operator 659**

.cpp files 357, 507, 524

.exe, executable files 16, 358

.h, header files 357, 369

.hpp, header files 357

.obj, object files 358

/, integer division operator 39

\0, null character, strings 188

:, with access specifier 450

**::, scope resolution operator
104, 361**

E

early binding. *see* **static resolution**

EBCDIC. *see* **Extended Binary Coded Decimal Interchange Code (EBCDIC)**

element inspection, debugging 400

elements

arrays 180
  sizeof() 186
    example 187
containers 860
  example 862
  requirements 860, 861
lists 499

else 123

see also **if** *and* **if-else statements**

conditional operator (?:) vs. if-else 132

dangling else problem 125

empty() 828

emulation 857

encapsulation 444

data hiding 445

end() 828

endl, newline character 21, 22

enumeration 93

anonymous enumerations 95
casting
  see also **data types**, mixing in expressions
casting to int 96
classes vs. 414
enumerators 94
  explicit values, assigning to 95
example 96

eof() 768, 774, 783, 787

equality operator, operator==() 854

erase() 225, 828, 833

error handling 669

see also **debugging**

exceptions 670

abort() 698
base class handlers 687
catch blocks 670
  (...) 693
    example 671, 672
  handler-exception match 683
  object slicing 689
class hierarchies 683
  base class handlers 687
  example 684, 685
code source of exception
  try blocks 676
const 671
constructors, throwing exceptions in 698
  try blocks 699
destructors 699
  abort() 675
  exit() 676
  uncaught_exception() 699
exception object
  copy constructor 674
  class objects 681
  exception classes 682
exception, standard header file 675
  exception classes 701
exit() 698
functions, throwing exceptions with 695
handling process, detailed look at 674
new, bad_alloc 699
object slicing, rethrowing exceptions 692
pass-by-value 689
  object slicing 689
rethrowing exceptions 689, 690
  object slicing 692
scope 674
set_unexpected() 698
terminate() 675, 698
throwing 670, 671
try blocks 670, 676
  constructors, throwing exceptions in 699
    exception code source 676
    function try blocks 695
    nesting 678, 679
unhandled exceptions 675

exceptions functions
  throwing exceptions through, constructors 698

errors

see also **debugging** *and* **exceptions, error handling**

#error 399

class destructor 523

exceptions
  streams 784

function templates, errors through using 332

preprocessor macros, as source of errors 389

streams 782
  flags
    clear() 784
    functions to test flags, listing 783
    listing 782
    functions to test flags, listing 783
    stream state
      testing 783
      testing, operatorvoid*() 783

escape sequence 19

backslash, use of 19

example programs

abstract classes 647
  indirect inheritance 649
access control under inheritance 586
access specifiers
  virtual functions 634
algorithms
  iterators, passing to 845
arithmetic operators 39
arrays
  elements, getting number of 187
  initializing 185
  multidimensional character arrays 197
  objects of a class, arrays of 482
  strings, character arrays 189
  using 181
  vector container, computing averages with arrays 838
assert() Macro, debugging with 407

F

void 280, 284
volume()
452, 553, 555, 625, 629, 634, 636, 648
what() 721
write() 782, 788, 789
writeNodes() 811

G

gcount() 781
get() 760, 780, 785, 809
  int_type get() 780
  istream& get(char& ch) 780
  istream& get(char* pArray, streamsize n) 781
  istream& get(char* pArray, streamsize n, char delim) 781
getline() 191, 206, 748, 760
  istream& getline(char* pArray, streamsize n) 781
  istream& getline(char* pArray, streamsize n, char delim) 781
global namespace 362, 366
  see also **global scope**
  scope resolution operator, :: 362
    unary form of 362
global operator functions 539
  binary operators 543
  const 539
  unary operators 544
global scope 102, 359
  see also **scope**
  linkage 359
    external variables 360, 362, 363
  scope resolution operator, :: 104, 361
    example 104
good() 783
goto statements 139
  statement labels 139
greater() 880

H

handlers. *see* catch blocks
handles, objects 828
'has a' test 580
header files 11, 14
  see also **translation units**
  #include directive 384, 509, 524
  .h 369
  .hpp 357
  Box.h 506, 523
  cctype 119
    see also herein cwctype
    functions, listing 119
    tolower() 138
  cstring 260
    pointers 260
  cwctype 122
    see also cctype
    functions, listing 122
  iostream 524
  List.h 507, 518, 524
  source files 358
    #include 358, 384
  standard
    cstddef 77
    limits 79, 80
  standard header files 385
    .h 369
  Standard Template Library (STL) 825
    header file listing 825
    stream headers 826
  use of 358
header, functions 280
  function name 280
  general form of 280
  parameters list 280
    arguments, relationship with parameters 283
    default values 302
      example 302
      multiple default values 303, 306
  return value 280, 283
    new variables 311

  memory leaks 311
  pointers 306
    example 307
    variable scope 306
  references 311
    variable scope 311
  return statement 284
  void 284
heap. *see* free store
hexadecimal notation 20, 34, 35, 37
  hex 90
  pointers 237
hierarchies, class 578
  access specifiers in 592
  constructors and 599
  destructors and 602
horizontal tab, escape sequence for 20

I

identifiers
  #if 393, 394
    constant expression values, testing for 396
  #undef 387
    example 387
  __ and _X 44
  characters restrictions for 12
  linkage 359, 360
    external 359
    identifiers without linkage 360
    internal 359
  scope 359
    block scope 359
    global scope 359
  standard library 13
  variables 44
    unqualified scope, variables with 370
if statements 115
  example 115, 116
  if-else. *see* **if-else statements**
  indentation 115, 123